Peterson's American and Canadian Boarding Schools and Worldwide Enrichment Programs

Internados en los Estados Unidos y Canadá y Programas
Mundiales de Enriquecimiento

Internats Américains et Canadiens, et Programmes de
perfectionnement internationaux

米国、カナダの全寮制学校および世界各地での
強化プログラム

美國與加拿大寄宿學校及國際強化項目

THOMSON

PETERSON'S

MAR 1 5 2005

Australia • Canada • Mexico • Singapore • Spain • United Kingdom • United States

About Thomson Peterson's

Thomson Peterson's (www.petersons.com) is a leading provider of education information and advice, with books and online resources focusing on education search, test preparation, and financial aid. Its Web site offers searchable databases and interactive tools for contacting educational institutions, online practice tests and instruction, and planning tools for securing financial aid. Thomson Peterson's serves 110 million education consumers annually.

For more information, contact Thomson Peterson's, 2000 Lenox Drive, Lawrenceville, NJ 08648; 800-338-3282; or find us on the World Wide Web at www.petersons.com/about.

Editor: Joe Krasowski; Production Editor: Linda Seghers; Research Project Managers: Daniel Margolin, Jennifer Fishberg; Manufacturing Manager: Judy Coleman; Client Relations Representatives: Mimi Kaufman, Lois Regina Milton, Mary Ann Murphy, Jim Swinarski, Eric Wallace.

ISBN 0-7689-1548-1

Printed in the United States of America

10 9 8 7 6 5 4 3 2 1   06 05 04

Eleventh Edition

CONTENTS

CONTENIDO • TABLES DES MATIÈRES • 目次 • 目録

SECTION II

Section I

American and Canadian Boarding Schools

Internados en los Estados Unidos y Canadá

Internats américains et canadiens

米国とカナダの全寮制学校

美國與加拿大寄宿學校

INTRODUCTION

INTRODUCCIÓN • INTRODUCTION • はじめに • 導言

For international families interested in the best education for their sons and daughters, university-preparatory schools in the United States and Canada offer a wide variety of educational options. Families may choose from among schools that are single-sex or coeducational, have a religious affiliation or military structure, offer rigorous pre-university or even university-level course work, or provide special support for students with learning differences or for students wishing to learn English.

Peterson's American and Canadian Boarding Schools and Worldwide Enrichment Programs is the authoritative source of information for families interested in educational opportunities in the United States and Canada. Careful reading of the "Family Guide to University-Preparatory Bording Schools," "Understanding the Admissions Process," and the schools' presentations will provide much of the information needed to make decisions about boarding schools. Once families have narrowed the list of schools from which to seek additional information, the "Information Request Forms" at the back of this book can be photocopied and faxed to the appropriate schools to receive school brochures and admissions information.

Para las familias extranjeras interesadas en la mejor educación para sus hijos e hijas, los colegios con programa de preparación para la universidad en los Estados Unidos y Canadá ofrecen una amplia variedad de opciones de educación. Las familias pueden escoger entre colegios para estudiantes del mismo sexo o colegios mixtos, los que tienen afiliación religiosa o estructura militar, los que ofrecen un exigente programa preuniversitario o, incluso, cursos a nivel universitario, o los que dan apoyo especial para estudiantes con problemas de aprendizaje o para los que desean aprender inglés.

Internados en los Estados Unidos y Canadá y Programas Mundiales de Enriquecimiento es la fuente de información con más autoridad para las familias interesadas en oportunidades de estudios en los Estado Unidos y Canadá. Las secciones "Guía de Familia", "Familiarizándose con el proceso de admisión" y las presentaciones de los colegios, contienen mucha información necesaria para tomar decisiones sobre los internados. Una vez que las familias hayan elaborado una pequeña lista de colegios sobre los que desean obtener información adicional, pueden fotocopiar los Formularios de solicitud de información en la parte posterior de este libro y enviarlos por fax a los colegios seleccionados para recibir folletos e información sobre los requisitos de admisión.

Les établissements qui ont un programme de préparation aux universités américaines et canadiennes offrent une variété de choix pédagogiques aux familles étrangères qui veulent la meilleure éducation possible pour leurs enfants. Les familles peuvent choisir entre des établissements scolaires mixtes ou non-mixtes, religieux ou laïcs, et ceux ayant une structure militaire ou non-militaire. Certaines écoles offrent des programmes d'enseignement général ou même des cours de niveau universitaire, d'autres proposent des cours de rattrapage pour les élèves qui ont des difficultés scolaires ou pour les élèves qui désirent apprendre l'anglais.

Internats américains et canadiens, et programmes de perfectionnement internationaux est la source autorisée d'information aux familles intéressées par les différents programmes scolaires aux États-Unis et au Canada. Avant de prendre une décision sur le choix d'un internat, il est nécessaire de lire attentivement le "Guide familial", "Comprendre le processus d'admissions" et les présentations des écoles. Lorsque les familles ont sélectionné et préparé la liste des établissements qui les intéressent et dont elles aimeraient recevoir plus d'informations, il leur est conseillé de photocopier ou de faxer à ces établissements le formulaire qui se trouve à la dernière page de ce livre afin de recevoir les brochures et les informations concernant les admissions.

子女に最良の教育をと願う各国のご家庭にとって、大学進学に重点を置くアメリカ・カナダの全寮制私立学校は、幅広い教育の機会を提供する機関です。各ご家庭のニーズに合わせて、男子校、女子校、共学校、特定の宗派に属する学校、軍隊式教育を採用している学校、大学予備校、大学レベルの講義を行う学校、また特別な学習方法を必要とする生徒のための学校、英語を学びたい生徒のための学校など、さまざまな特徴を持つ私立学校が揃っています。

「ピーターソンの米国、カナダの全寮制学校および世界各地での強化プログラム」は、アメリカとカナダの教育機関に関する情報を網羅した、もっとも信頼できる案内書です。「ご家族へのご案内」、「入学手続きについて」、そして各校のご案内の内容は、各校を選択される際に必要な情報を満載したものです。ご志望校の数を絞られましたら、本書の最後に添え付けした「案内請求用紙」をコピーし、内容ご記入の上、各志望校にファックスで送って、各校の入学案内書及び便覧をお取り寄せください。

對於有意為自己的子女提供最佳教育的外國家庭來說，美國和加拿大的大學預科學校提供了多種就讀選擇。這些家庭可以選擇祇招收單一性別學生或男女同校的學校主辦的學校或軍校開設高難度大學預科甚或大學程度課程的學校，或者選擇專為具有不同學習作風或有意學習英文的學生開設的學校。

對那些打算了解美國和加拿大的教育機會的家庭來說，美國與加拿大寄宿學校及國際強化項目是具有權威性的資訊來原。通過認真查閱家庭指南的了解入學程序及各個的自我介紹，您可以了解有關選擇寄宿學校所需的大量資訊。這些家庭一旦確定自己打算向哪幾家學校索要詳細資訊，就可以複本手冊封底的資訊索要表並將其傳真給有關學校以獲得學校手冊和入學資訊。

American and Canadian Boarding Schools— HOW TO USE THIS SECTION

This section is divided into four main parts: introductory advice, one-page presentations of university-preparatory schools, an appendix of boarding schools, and information request forms. To make the most of all the information found in *Peterson's American and Canadian Boarding Schools and Worldwide Enrichment Programs*, follow the steps outlined below.

Step One

Before you begin to search through the book for the perfect school, read "Family Guide to University-Preparatory Boarding Schools" and "Understanding the Admissions Process" by Diane Rapp, which begin on page 6. The articles provide invaluable information about school programs, facilities, duration, enrollment, and costs as well as a description of campus life, rules and safety, application procedures, and transportation arrangements.

Step Two

Next, consult the "Explanation of the One-Page Presentations," which shows you where on each page you'll find the information you need to make a choice. Then turn to the "One-Page Presentations," which begin on page 35. Listings for schools located in the United States begin on page 37; listings for Canadian schools begin on page 115. (If you would like to search for schools by state or province, consult the "Geographical Index" on page 142.) For each school, you'll find location and contact information as well as an expanded description, photographs of the school's facilities, and in-depth information about international participant enrollment, English as a second language course availability, English language proficiency necessary for enrollment, session dates and application deadlines, costs, housing, rules, and much more. To help you use the "One-Page Presentations," a "Key to the Graphical Icons" can be found on page 34 as well as on the inside cover.

Step Three

This book also includes an "Appendix of University-Preparatory Schools," which begins on page 121. In this appendix you'll find names and contact information for more than 400 schools not highlighted in the "One-Page Presentations" section. Use the contact information found here to request additional information from the schools, who expressed an interest to Peterson's in enrolling international participants.

Step Four

When you've finished compiling a list of schools that have piqued your interest, use the "Information Request Forms" to receive additional information or request admission materials. These forms can be faxed or mailed to program contacts; use the fax numbers and addresses found in the Contact section of the "One-Page Presentations" or in the Appendix to ensure correct transmission of the form. Feel free to photocopy the forms and use them to contact as many programs as you like. Once the programs are contacted, they will send you additional detailed information about their program's offerings.

EXPLANATION OF ONE-PAGE PRESENTATIONS

The "One-Page Presentations" beginning on page 35 provide in-depth information about university-preparatory boarding schools. This information was provided to Thomson Peterson's in the spring and summer of 2004 by representatives from the schools, who completed a special questionnaire developed by Thomson Peterson's.

What You'll Find in the One-Page Presentations

1. Country indicator
2. School name and crest (if available)
3. Contact information
4. School accreditations
5. School photographs
6. Expanded description of school
7. Location of school
8. Seasonal temperature icons (showing average fall, winter, and spring temperature ranges)
9. National time zone map and distance from nearest international airport and large city

School Icons

10. Type of school
11. Enrollment: number of boys, number of girls
12. Percentage of boarding students
13. Percentage of international participants
14. Number of students who applied, number who were accepted
15. Tests required for admission and average level of proficiency attained by international students
16. Tests recommended for admission and average level of proficiency attained by international students
17. Countries most frequently represented and length of time school has served them
18. Application deadline
19. Entrance available during which months
20. Student-faculty ratio; percentage of faculty who reside on campus
21. Student-computer ratio
22. Tuition, room and board, and additional mandatory fees
23. Colleges and universities attended by the largest number of students in the last three years
24. Availability of English as a second language course
25. Secondary-level summer program
26. Dress code
27. Personal interview required
28. Telephone interview required

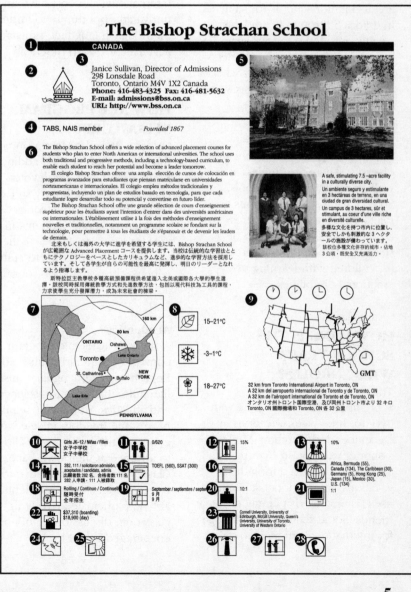

The Bishop Strachan School

CANADA

Janice Sullivan, Director of Admissions
298 Lonsdale Road
Toronto, Ontario M4V 1X2 Canada
Phone: 416-483-4325 Fax: 416-481-5632
E-mail: admissions@bss.on.ca
URL: http://www.bss.on.ca

TABS, NAIS member   *Founded 1867*

The Bishop Strachan School offers a wide selection of advanced placement courses for students who plan to enter North American or international universities. The school uses both traditional and progressive methods, including a technology-based curriculum, to enable each student to reach her potential and become a leader tomorrow.

El colegio Bishop Strachan ofrece una amplia elección de cursos de colocación en programas avanzados para estudiantes que piensan matricularse en universidades norteamericanas e internacionales. El colegio emplea métodos tradicionales y progresistas, incluyendo un plan de estudios basado en tecnología, para que cada estudiante logre desarrollar todo su potencial y convertirse en futuro líder.

The Bishop Strachan School offre une grande sélection de cours d'enseignement supérieur pour les étudiants ayant l'intention d'entrer dans des universités américaines ou internationales. L'établissement utilise à la fois des méthodes d'enseignement nouvelles et traditionnelles, notamment un programme scolaire se fondant sur la technologie, pour permettre à tous les étudiants de s'épanouir et de devenir les leaders de demain.

北米もしくは海外の大学に進学を希望する学生には、Bishop Strachan School が広範囲な Advanced Placement コースを提供します。当校は伝統的な学習法とともにテクノロジーをベースとしたカリキュラムなど、進歩的な学習方法を採用しています。そして各学生が自らの可能性を最高に発揮し、明日のリーダーとなれるよう指導します。

斯特拉臣主教學校多種高級預備課程供希望進入北美或國際各大學的學生選擇。該校同時採用傳統教學方式和先進教學方法，包括以現代科技為工具的課程，力求使學生充分發揮潛力，成為未來社會的棟梁。

A safe, stimulating 7.5-acre facility in a culturally diverse city.

Un ambiente seguro y estimulante en 3 hectáreas de terreno, en una ciudad de gran diversidad cultural.

Un campus de 3 hectares, sûr et stimulant, au coeur d'une ville riche en diversité culturelle.

多様な文化を持つ市内に位置し、安全でしかも刺激的な3ヘクタールの施設が備わっています。

該校位多種文化保存的城市，佔地3公頃，既安全又充滿活力。

160 km
80 km
ONTARIO   Oshawa
Toronto   Lake Ontario
St. Catharines   NEW YORK
Buffalo
Lake Erie
PENNSYLVANIA

15–21°C
-3–1°C
18–27°C

GMT

32 km from Toronto International Airport in Toronto, ON
A 32 km del aeropuerto internacional de Toronto y de Toronto, ON
A 32 km de l'aéroport international de Toronto et de Toronto, ON
オンタリオ州トロント国際空港、及び同州トロント市より32キロ
Toronto, ON 國際機場和Toronto, ON 各32公里

10. Girls JK–12 / Niñas / Filles 女子中学校 女子中學校
11. 0/620
12. 15%
13. 10%
14. 282, 111 / solicitaron admisión, aceptados / candidats, admis 出願者数282名，合格者数111名 282人申請，111人被錄取
15. TOEFL (560), SSAT (300)
16.
17. Africa, Bermuda (55), Canada (134), The Caribbean (30), Germany (5), Hong Kong (25), Japan (15), Mexico (30), U.S. (134)
18. Rolling / Continuo / Continuell 随時受付 全年招生
19. September / septiembre / septem 9月 9月
20. 10:1
21. 1:1
22. $37,310 (boarding) $18,900 (day)
23. Cornell University, University of Edinburgh, McGill University, Queen's University, University of Toronto, University of Western Ontario
24.
25.
26.
27.
28.

FAMILY GUIDE TO UNIVERSITY-PREPARATORY BOARDING SCHOOLS

American and Canadian boarding schools provide international students with a unique opportunity to obtain a pre-university education while living among young people and adults of many cultures. North American boarding schools first began to appear in the eighteenth century. Modeled on the English system, the schools sought to provide superior academic instruction and develop the moral character and physical strength of their students. Today's university-preparatory schools carry on much of this tradition by offering small classes and individual attention from dedicated and caring faculty members. Unlike the homogeneous institutions of the past, however, today's schools meet the needs of students with many interests and abilitites.

WHAT ARE THE OPTIONS?

Most boarding schools in this book provide a university-preparatory program for students in grades 9 through 12. Some offer a year of postgraduate (PG) studies. There are also junior schools for students in grades 5 through 8. Students usually enroll two to four years, but some schools permit shorter stays of a semester or year. Schools may also provide four- to six-week summer programs.

Institutions listed in the International Directory show great diversity. There are single-sex as well as coeducational schools. Some have a strong religious or military tradition. Others stress an academic area—such as art or science—or offer special programs for children with learning or emotional disabilities.

HOW LONG IS THE SCHOOL YEAR? WHO ENROLLS?

The school year begins in September and ends in June with two- to three-week vacations in December and March or April and a shorter vacation in November. Schools are closed during these vacations. International students use this time to visit family or friends. Some schools may arrange for international students to stay with local families during long vacations. Most schools enroll students from many parts of North America and from several other countries. Surrounded by native English speakers and living in an American or Canadian community, international students have an unrivaled opportunity to improve their English language skills and acclimate to North American academic life.

HOW ARE PROGRAMS STRUCTURED?

Students attend classes Monday through Friday. Several additional hours each week are devoted to class preparation, library study, and extracurricular activities. During weekends, students may take part in organized activities, sports events, and trips to cultural centers, shopping areas, or other attractions.

Academics

A school's academic program consists of required courses in English, another language, history, literature, mathematics, science, and athletics. Students generally have some freedom in selecting courses, and they may be allowed to advance at their own pace. Classes are small—with five to fifteen students—and students are able to participate actively in classroom discussions. Students are encouraged to work independently. Teachers often live on or near the campus and are available to help students outside of class. In the upper grades, classes require a considerable amount of reading and writing. International students will need a high level of English proficiency to be able to meet these demands.

College Counseling

Most graduates of boarding schools attend four-year colleges and universities. Counselors will help students identify appropriate colleges and prepare applications. To gain admission to highly competitive colleges, international students will need to show superior English language skills.

Activities

Outside the classroom, students may choose from a variety of organized activities ranging from choral groups, music lessons, and drama clubs to school newspapers, student government organizations, and chess clubs. These activities provide a balance to rigorous academic work and a chance to meet new friends and learn new skills.

Sports

Sports are an important part of boarding school life. Most schools have extensive athletic facilities and offer a variety of competitive and noncompetitive activities. Students may participate in team sports, such as American football, soccer, basketball, baseball, field hockey, and lacrosse, or individual sports such as track and field, swimming, gymnastics, and tennis.

Food

Meals are served in a school dining hall; attendance is usually required. In some schools, students may also be required to help serve meals and clean the kitchen or dining room. International students who find it difficult to adjust to school food often bring some nonperishable items from home. Schools will usually provide special meals for students who require a special diet.

Clothing

Dress at boarding schools is informal. Few schools require uniforms, but many have standards of dress (they may prohibit blue jeans, for example). Some schools require students to dress more formally for evening meals. Schools provide a list of what to bring as well as information about the local weather and climate.

Rules and Policies

In order for a school to run smoothly, it is important for all members of the community to cooperate and work together. Strict rules include prohibition of smoking, using or possessing alcohol and other illegal substances, leaving the grounds without permission, and cheating. Failure to obey these rules may result in expulsion.

Health and Safety

All schools require students to have a doctor's examination and basic immunizations before they arrive. Schools have health centers staffed by nurses, and doctors and hospital services are always available. Parents must give permission for emergency medical care. Students are required to have medical insurance.

Schools are carefully supervised. Students must take responsibility for their own safety, however, when traveling or leaving the campus. Parents should teach their children basic rules of safety before they leave for school. Although drugs and alcohol are prohibited on school campuses, your child should be warned that some students may possess them illegally and that such people should be avoided.

Housing

Dormitories usually house two students per room. Each student is provided with a bed, desk, and dresser. Students are responsible for keeping their rooms neat and doing their own laundry (using coin-operated washing machines located in the dormitory).

Transportation

This book will help families locate the international airports that are nearest schools. Schools will usually provide transportation to and from airports; there may be a fee for this service. Most schools do not allow boarding students to own cars.

Communication with Parents and Guardians

Parents follow their child's progress through written reports and visits to school. Parents who are not able to visit the school may want to have a relative or guardian handle these details.

WHAT TO EXPECT

The expectations of teachers in North American schools may differ from those at home. Students are expected to ask questions, raise their hands in class to volunteer answers, think for themselves, work independently, and seek out teachers for extra help when needed. Teachers expect that students will participate actively and they encourage lively discussion and differences of opinion.

Families should realize that their children will need to make adjustments during the school years. In the first few months of school, international students may have periods of unhappiness and loneliness as they adjust to a new language, people, customs, food, and climate. It is important for students to come to school with strong motivation and a willingness to work hard, make new friends, and try new things. International student advisers, counselors, teachers, and dormitory parents can help international students become more comfortable with the campus academic and social expectations.

Today's American and Canadian boarding schools are producing the leaders of the future by teaching students to think independently, work hard, and understand other peoples and cultures. The benefits of this education will last a lifetime.

Diane Rapp is president of Diane Rapp Associates, Educational Consultants, 85 River Road, Scarborough, New York 10510.

UNDERSTANDING THE ADMISSIONS PROCESS

Once you have decided to send your child overseas to school, you will need to become familiar with the admissions procedures usually required by university-preparatory schools. Because the requirements of individual institutions may vary, families are encouraged to contact schools directly for a list of application deadlines and instructions. The following guidelines will help you know what to expect during the admissions process.

Beginning Your Search

After reading the Family Guide and One-Page Presentations, choose three to five schools that you think match your child's educational goals. As you read the school descriptions, consider these questions. Is your child academically prepared to meet the demands of this institution? Is the school the right size for your child? If the student will need extensive English language support, does the school offer an English as a second language program? Does the school's location meet your needs?

Next, use the information request forms in the back of this book to obtain more information and application instructions for the schools on your list. Although some schools may be able to supply you with some information in your language, most will communicate in English. Parents must be able to understand some English or rely on someone with English language skills to review school materials and complete applications. Make a note of the application deadlines and test dates for those schools to which your child will apply.

Applying

Study the schools' information to decide whether your child meets the qualifications. If possible, arrange to visit several schools. To decide which school is best for your child, you will want to meet admissions officers and teachers

and tour the campus. If you cannot visit, you may want to meet with local representatives, who are usually graduates of the school under consideration. Occasionally, admissions officers travel overseas to meet candidates for admission. If a trip to your country is planned, an admission officer will contact you to arrange a meeting.

Completing Application Forms

Complete the application forms and return them to the schools with the appropriate fees in U.S. or Canadian dollars. The application deadline for most schools is February 1. Since many schools extend the application period for international students, however, you will want to check each school's admissions policies.

Next, ask the student's current teachers to complete the teacher recommendations forms required by most schools. Schools may require one recommendation from the child's English teacher and another from a mathematics teacher. Include an envelope, addressed to the school and with correct postage, so that the teacher can complete and mail the form directly to the school.

School records should be in English and should be as accurate as possible. Only students with accurate, honest records and recommendations are considered eligible for acceptance.

Students may also be asked to write one or more essays. It is important for applicants to write these essays by themselves and not ask someone with better English skills to complete them.

Keep in mind that the best boarding schools have highly competitive admissions. It is important for the school to know how prepared your child is and why he or she wants to study abroad. Admission is based on the student's grades, the quality of academic courses, teacher comments and recommendations, and scores on standardized tests.

Meeting Other Admissions Requirements

Many of the schools listed in this guide require students to take one or more standardized tests. Several of the schools you select may ask your child to take the Secondary School Admission Test or SSAT. This test measures a student's ability in mathematics and English. The international version of the SSAT, which is designed for students even with low levels of English proficiency, is given three times a year in many countries. Test dates may be obtained from the boarding schools or by contacting the Secondary School Admission Test, CN 5339, Princeton, NJ 08543 U.S.A., Phone: (609) 683-4440, Fax: (609) 683-4507.

Besides the SSAT, many schools will ask to see TOEFL, or Test of English as a Foreign Language, scores. Again, read the school's admissions information to verify specific testing requirements.

What Happens Next?

Most schools will let applicants know whether they have been accepted in March. Late applicants may find out a school's decision when the admissions staff has reviewed the application. If your child has been accepted and intends to enroll, you must return a signed contract and a deposit (payable in U.S. or Canadian dollars) to reserve a place. During the summer, the school will send the following information:

- An I-20 Immigration Form, signed by a school official. You must take this form to the nearest American Embassy to obtain an F-1 Student Visa, which is usually valid for four years.

- Medical Forms. Every school requires that entering students have a complete physical examination and submit a record of immunizations. These medical requirements are mandated by local health departments. If a student arrives at school without proper immunizations, he or she must receive them from the school's medical staff. Parents will be required to submit forms that grant the school permission to authorize medical treatment in the event of a medical emergency.

- Insurance Forms. These show who will pay for students' medical treatment while they are at school. Families may have their own insurance. Some schools will also provide insurance coverage for a fee.

- Financial Information. Parents will be asked to pay first-semester costs, which include tuition, housing, and meals. Books, students' school supplies, and travel expenses are additional. There may also be fees for laundry services, music lessons, laboratories, art, or athletics. You may be asked to deposit money in a school account for use by the student.

- Directions for New Students. Schools will send a list of clothing and other articles that students should bring. They will also provide information about transportation arrangements. Many schools will meet international students at the nearest major airport. Be sure to notify the school of your child's flight information well in advance.

You may want to accompany the new student to school. Although schools cannot provide accommodations for parents on campus, they will help make arrangements with nearby hotels. Schools also welcome parent visits several times a year.

For More Information

The procedures mentioned above may vary from school to school. If you have questions about the admissions process of a particular institution, contact the school admissions staff or international student adviser directly. To help you in your search, Peterson's *American and Canadian Boarding Schools and Worldwide Enrichment Programs* lists the telephone numbers, mailing addresses, and names of admissions officers of over 400 schools in the United States and Canada. We wish you and your child much success in finding a university-preparatory school that meets your needs.

Diane Rapp is president of Diane Rapp Associates, Educational Consultants, 85 River Road, Scarborough, New York 10510.

Internados de los Estados Unidos y Canadá— CÓMO USAR ESTA SECCIÓN

Esta guía se divide en cinco secciones principales: consejos iniciales, presentaciones de una página de colegios con programas de preparación para la universidad y un apéndice de internados, una lista de abreviaturas y los formularios de solicitud de información. Para aprovechar al máximo toda la información contenida en el *Internados en los Estados Unidos y Canadá y Programas Mundiales de Enriquecimiento*, siga los pasos que se indican a continuación.

Primer Paso

Antes de empezar a buscar el colegio perfecto en las páginas de este libro, lea las secciones, "Guía de familia sobre internados" y "Familiarizándose con el proceso de admisión" por Diane Rapp, que comienza en la página 12. Los artículos contienen valiosa información sobre los programas, las instalaciones, el período escolar, las matrículas y los precios de los colegios, así como una descripción de la vida en el colegio, los reglamentos y las normas de seguridad, los procedimientos de solicitud y los arreglos de transporte.

Segundo Paso

Consulte la "Explicación de las presentaciones de una página" que le muestra el lugar en cada página donde usted puede encontrar la información que necesita para tomar su decisión. Luego pase a las "Presentaciones de una página" que comienzan en la página 35; las descripciones de colegios en los Estados Unidos comienzan en la página 37, las de colegios canadienses comienzan en la página 115. (Si usted quiere revisar los colegios por estado o provincia, consulte el "Indice geográfico" en la página 142). Usted encontrará para cada colegio información sobre la ubicación y la forma de establecer los contactos, una descripción ampliada, fotografías de las instalaciones e información detallada sobre las matrículas para estudiantes extranjeros, la disponibilidad de cursos de inglés como segundo idioma, el nivel de conocimientos del inglés necesario para matricularse, las fechas de las sesiones y las fechas límites para presentar las solicitudes, costos, alojamiento, reglamentos y mucho más. Para ayudarlo a usar las "Presentaciones de una página", se incluye en la página 34 una "Leyenda para los íconos gráficos" así como en la parte interior de la contraportada.

Tercer Paso

Este libro incluye también un "Apéndice de colegios con programa de preparación para la universidad" que comienza en la página 121. En este apéndice usted encontrará nombres e información sobre los contactos con respecto a más de 400 colegios no destacados en las "Presentaciones de una página". Use la información sobre los contactos en esta sección para solicitar información adicional a colegios que manifestaron a Peterson interés en recibir estudiantes extranjeros.

Cuarto Paso

Cuando haya concluído su lista de colegios que han despertado su interés, use los "Formularios de solicitud de información" para recibir información adicional o solicitar materiales de admisión. Estos formularios pueden ser enviados por fax o por correo a los contactos en los colegios; use los números de fax y las direcciones incluídas en la sección de "Contactos" de las "Presentaciones de una página" o en el apéndice para asegurar que los formularios lleguen a su destino. Puede fotocopiar los formularios y usarlos para ponerse en contacto con todos los colegios que le interesen. Cuando los colegios reciben los formularios, envían a los interesados información detallada adicional sobre sus respectivos programas.

EXPLICACIÓN DE LAS PRESENTACIONES DE UNA PÁGINA

Las "Presentaciones de una página" que comienzan en la página 35, contienen información detallada sobre los internados con programa de preparación para la universidad. Esta información fue proporcionada a Thomson Peterson en la primavera y el verano de 2004, por representantes de los colegios, quienes llenaron un cuestionario especial diseñado por Thomson Peterson.

Qué encontrará en las "Presentaciones de una página"

1. Indicación del país
2. Nombre del colegio y emblema (si está disponible)
3. Información sobre los contactos
4. Acreditaciones del colegio
5. Fotografías del colegio
6. Descripción ampliada del colegio
7. Ubicación del colegio
8. Gráficos sobre temperatura en las distintas estaciones (con las variaciones promedios de temperatura en el otoño, invierno y primavera)
9. Mapa del huso horario nacional y las distancias desde el aeropuerto internacional y la ciudad importante más cercanos

Gráficos de cada colegio

10. Clase de colegio
11. Matrícula; número de estudiantes varones; número de estudiantes mujeres
12. Porcentaje de estudiantes internos
13. Porcentaje de estudiantes extranjeros
14. Número de estudiantes que solicitaron admisión; número de estudiantes aceptados
15. Exámenes exigidos para la admisión y el nivel promedio de conocimientos alcanzado por los estudiantes internacionales
16. Exámenes recomendados para la admisión y el nivel promedio de conocimientos alcanzado por los estudiantes internacionales
17. Países representados con más frecuencia y el tiempo en que el colegio les ha servido
18. Fechas límites para presentar solicitudes
19. Los meses en que está abierta la admisión
20. Proporción de profesores con respecto a estudiantes; porcentaje de profesores que residen en el colegio
21. Proporción de estudiantes con respecto a las computadoras
22. Derechos de matrícula, alojamiento y derechos obligatorios adicionales
23. Universidades a las que ha asistido el mayor número de estudiantes en los últimos tres años
24. Cursos de inglés como segundo idioma disponibles
25. Programa de verano para el nivel secundario
26. Normas de vestir
27. Entrevista personal
28. Entrevista por teléfono

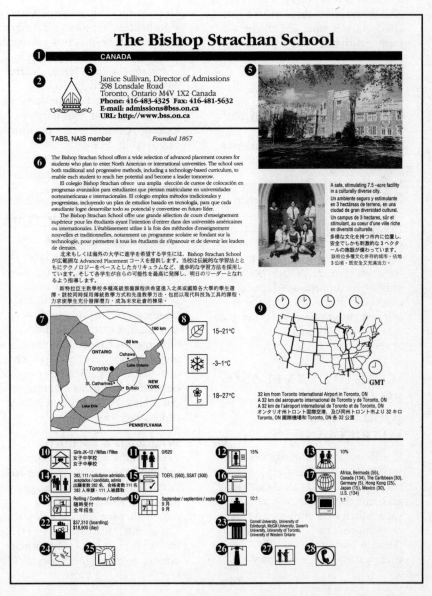

GUÍA FAMILIAR SOBRE INTERNADOS CON PROGRAMAS DE PREPARACIÓN PARA LA UNIVERSIDAD

Los internados de los Estados Unidos y el Canadá brindan a los estudiantes extranjeros una oportunidad única de obtener una educación preuniversitaria mientras viven con jóvenes y adultos de diferentes culturas. Los primeros internados de América del Norte surgieron en el siglo XVIII. Basados en el sistema inglés, los internados tenían como objetivo proporcionar instrucción académica superior y desarrollar el carácter moral y la fuerza física de sus alumnos. Actualmente, los colegios con planes de estudios preuniversitarios continúan gran parte de esta tradición al ofrecer clases con pocos alumnos y atención individual a cargo de profesores que se preocupan por sus alumnos. No obstante, a diferencia de las instituciones homogéneas del pasado, los colegios de la actualidad satisfacen las necesidades de estudiantes con diversidad de intereses y habilidades.

¿CUÁLES SON LAS OPCIONES?

La mayoría de los internados incluídos en este libro ofrecen un programa de preparación para la universidad a estudiantes del 9no al 12mo grado. Algunos ofrecen un año de estudios de postgrado (PG). Existen también colegios para estudiantes del 5to al 8vo grado. Los estudiantes usualmente se matriculan para estudiar de dos a cuatro años, pero algunos colegios permiten estancias más cortas, de un semestre a un año. Algunos colegios ofrecen programas de verano de cuatro a seis semanas.

Las instituciones incluídas en el Directorio Internacional tienen características muy diversas. Existen colegios para estudiantes del mismo sexo y colegios mixtos. Algunos tienen una sólida tradición religiosa o militar. Otros ponen énfasis en un área académica, como las artes o las ciencias, u ofrecen programas especiales para niños con problemas de aprendizaje o emocionales.

¿CUÁNTO DURA EL AÑO ESCOLAR? ¿QUIÉNES SE MATRICULAN?

El año escolar comienza en septiembre y termina en junio, con vacaciones de dos a tres semanas en diciembre y marzo o abril, y vacaciones más cortas en noviembre. Los colegios cierran durante estos períodos de vacaciones. Los estudiantes extranjeros aprovechan las vacaciones para visitar a familiares o amigos. Algunos colegios pueden hacer arreglos para que estudiantes extranjeros vivan con familias locales durante las vacaciones largas.

La mayoría de los colegios aceptan estudiantes de países de América del Norte y de muchos países de otras regiones. Rodeados por compañeros cuya lengua materna es el inglés y viviendo en comunidades estadounidenses o canadienses, los estudiantes extranjeros tienen una oportunidad inigualable de mejorar sus conocimientos del inglés y adaptarse a la vida académica de América del Norte.

¿CÓMO SE ESTRUCTURAN LOS PROGRAMAS?

Los alumnos asisten a clases de lunes a viernes. Dedican varias horas adicionales durante la semana a prepararse para las clases, estudiar en la biblioteca y a actividades extracurriculares. Durante los fines de semana, los alumnos pueden participar en actividades organizadas, eventos deportivos y visitas a centros culturales, zonas comerciales y otras atracciones.

Programas académicos

El programa académico de un colegio está compuesto por los cursos exigidos en inglés, otro idioma, historia, literatura, matemáticas, ciencias y deportes. Los estudiantes usualmente tienen cierta libertad para seleccionar cursos, y se les puede permitir que progresen según su propio ritmo. Las clases tienen pocos alumnos, entre cinco y quince estudiantes, y los alumnos pueden participar activamente en discusiones en las aulas. Se anima a los estudiantes a desarrollar trabajos en forma independiente. Los profesores con frecuencia viven cerca del colegio y pueden ayudar a los estudiantes fuera de las clases. En los grados avanzados, los cursos exigen mucha lectura y escritura. Los estudiantes extranjeros necesitarán un alto nivel de conocimientos del inglés para poder satisfacer tales requisitos.

Asesoramiento para las universidades

La mayoría de los estudiantes que se gradúan de los internados pasan a cursar carreras universitarias de cuatro años. Hay asesores que ayudan a los estudiantes a identificar las universidades que más les convengan y a preparar las solicitudes correspondientes. Para lograr ser admitidos en universidades con procesos de admisión muy competitivos, los estudiantes extranjeros necesitan conocimientos avanzados de inglés.

Actividades

Fuera de las aulas, los estudiantes pueden elegir entre una variedad de actividades organizadas que van desde grupos corales, lecciones de música y clubes teatrales, hasta periódicos escolares, organizaciones gubernamentales de estudiantes y clubes de ajedrez. Estas actividades son un contrapeso al riguroso trabajo académico y brindan la oportunidad de hacer nuevas amistades y aprender nuevas habilidades.

Deportes

Los deportes constituyen una parte importante de la vida en un internado. La mayoría de los colegios tienen amplias instalaciones deportivas y ofrecen una gran variedad de actividades competitivas y no competitivas. Los estudiantes pueden participar en deportes en equipos, tales como fútbol ("soccer"), baloncesto, béisbol, hockey sobre hierba y lacrosse, o deportes individuales, tales como atletismo, natación, gimnasia y tenis.

Alimentos

Las comidas se sirven en el salón comedor del colegio; las asistencia es usualmente exigida. En algunos colegios, puede exigirse a los estudiantes que sirvan la comida y limpien la cocina o el comerdor. Los estudiantes extranjeros que tienen dificultades para adaptarse a la comida del colegio con frecuencia llevan de sus hogares productos alimenticios no perecederos. Los colegios usualmente facilitan comidas especiales a los estudiantes que necesitan dietas especiales.

Ropa

En los internados los alumnos usan ropa informal. Muy pocos colegios exigen uniforme, pero pueden tener normas de vestir (por ejemplo, podrían estar prohibidos los pantalones de mezclilla). Algunos colegios exigen a sus alumnos que se vistan de una manera más formal para la cena. Los colegios facilitan una lista con los artículos que deben llevarse a la escuela e información sobre el clima local.

Reglamentos y normas

Para que un colegio pueda desarrollar sus programas sin problemas, es importante que todos los miembros de la comunidad cooperen y trabajen juntos. Las normas estrictas prohíben fumar, el uso o posesión de bebidas alcohólicas y otras substancias ilegales, ausentarse sin permiso y hacer trampas. No obedecer estas normas podría tener como resultado la expulsión del alumno.

Salud y seguridad

Todos los colegios exigen a sus alumnos someterse a un examen médico y a recibir las vacunas básicas antes de su llegada. Los colegios tienen clínicas con enfermeras, y siempre están disponibles servicios de médicos y hospitales. Los padres deben dar permiso para la atención médica en casos de urgencia. Es exigido que los estudiantes tengan seguro médico.

Los colegios son supervisados detenidamente. No obstante, los estudiantes deben hacerse responsables de su propia seguridad al viajar o abandonar el colegio. Los padres deben enseñar a sus hijos las normas básicas de seguridad antes de ir al colegio. Aunque las drogas y las bebidas alcohólicas están prohibidas en los recintos escolares, debe advertir a su hijo que algunos estudiantes podrían poseer estas substancias de manera ilegal y que deben evitar la compañía de tales personas.

Alojamiento

Usualmente, los dormitorios alojan dos estudiantes por habitación. Cada estudiante tiene una cama, un escritorio y un ropero. Los estudiantes son responsables de mantener sus habitaciones arregladas y de lavar su ropa (usando máquinas lavadoras activadas por monedas, ubicadas en el dormitorio).

Transporte

Este libro ayudará a las familias a localizar los aeropuertos internacionales que están más cerca de los colegios. Los colegios usualmente facilitan transporte de ida y regreso al aeropuerto; podría haber un cargo por este servicio. La mayoría de los colegios no permiten a los estudiantes tener automóviles.

Comunicación con los padres y tutores

Los padres se mantienen al tanto del progreso de sus hijos por medio de informes escritos y visitas al colegio. Los padres que no pueden visitar el colegio podrían encomendar a un pariente o tutor el hacerse cargo de estos detalles.

¿QUÉ ESPERAR?

Las expectativas de los profesores en los colegios de América del Norte pueden ser diferentes a las del país de donde proviene el estudiante. Se espera que los alumnos hagan preguntas, levanten la mano en clase para dar alguna respuesta, piensen por sí mismos, desarrollen trabajos de manera independiente y soliciten la ayuda de los profesores cuando la necesiten. Los profesores esperan que los estudiantes participen activamente y fomentan las discusiones y las diferencias de opinión.

Las familias deben tener en cuenta que sus hijos necesitarán hacer ajustes durante el año escolar. En los primeros meses de colegio, los estudiantes extranjeros pueden sentirse tristes y solos en algunos momentos mientras se adaptan a un nuevo idioma, a nuevas personas y costumbres, a comidas y climas diferentes. Es importante que los estudiantes ingresen en el colegio bien motivados y dispuestos a trabajar duro, hacer nuevas amistades y probar nuevas cosas. Los asesores, consejeros, profesores y supervisores de dormitorios pueden ayudar a los estudiantes extranjeros a sentirse más cómodos con las expectativas académicas y sociales del colegio.

Actualmente los internados de los Estados Unidos y Canadá están produciendo los líderes del futuro, enseñando a los estudiantes a pensar de manera independiente, trabajar duro y comprender otras culturas. Los beneficios de esta educación duran toda la vida.

Diane Rapp es presidenta de Diane Rapp Associates, Educational Consultants, 85 River Road, Scarborough, New York 10510.

FAMILIARIZÁNDOSE CON EL PROCESO DE ADMISIÓN

Una vez que ha decidido enviar a su hijo a estudiar en el exterior, usted necesitará familiarizarse con los procedimientos de admisión usualmente exigidos por los colegios con programas de preparación para la universidad. Debido a que los requisitos de las distintas instituciones pueden variar, se recomienda a las familias ponerse en contacto con los colegios directamente para solicitar una lista de requisitos y fechas límites de admisión. Las siguientes directrices lo ayudarán a conocer lo que puede esperar de un proceso de admisión.

Comience su búsqueda

Después de leer la "Guía de Familia" y las "Presentaciones de una página", seleccione de tres a cinco colegios que usted considere satisfacen los objetivos de educación de su hijo. Cuando esté leyendo las descripciones de los colegios, hágase estas preguntas: ¿Está su hijo académicamente preparado para satisfacer las exigencias del colegio? ¿Tiene el colegio las dimensiones adecuadas para su hijo? Si el alumno necesitará mucha ayuda con el inglés, ¿ofrece el colegio un programa de enseñanza del inglés como segundo idioma? ¿Le conviene la ubicación del colegio?

Posteriormente, use los formularios de solicitud de información en la parte posterior de este libro para obtener más información e instrucciones sobre cómo solicitar admisión en los colegios de su lista. Aunque algunos colegios están en capacidad de suministrarle información en su propio idioma, la mayoría se comunicará con usted en inglés. Los padres deberán entender algo de inglés o confiar en alguien con conocimientos del inglés para que revise los materiales y llene las solicitudes. Tome nota de las fechas límites de admisión y las fechas de los exámenes de los colegios en los que su hijo solicitará ser admitido.

Cómo solicitar admisión

Estudie la información sobre los colegios para decidir si su hijo llena los requisitos. Si es posible, haga los arreglos necesarios para visitar varios colegios. Para decidir qué colegio es mejor para su hijo, es conveniente que se entreviste con los funcionarios de admisión y con los profesores y que visite el recinto escolar. Si no puede hacerlo, podría reunirse con representantes locales que, generalmente, son graduados del colegio que usted está considerando. Ocasionalmente, los funcionarios de admisión viajan al exterior para reunirse con los candidatos. Si está planificado un viaje a su país, un funcionario de admisión se pondrá en contacto con usted para concertar una cita.

Cómo llenar los formularios de solicitud

Llene los formularios de solicitud y envíelos a los colegios con los derechos correspondientes en dólares de EE.UU. o Canadá. La fecha límite para presentar solicitudes en la mayoría de los colegios es el 1 de febrero. No obstante, debido a que muchos colegios amplían el período para presentar solicitudes para los estudiantes extranjeros, es necesario que revise las normas de admisión de cada colegio.

Pida a los actuales profesores de su hijo que llenen los formularios de recomendaciones de los profesores exigido por la mayoría de los colegios. Los colegios pueden exigir una recomendación del profesor de inglés y otra del profesor de matemáticas. Incluya un sobre, con la dirección del colegio y el porte correspondiente, para que el profesor pueda llenar el formulario y enviarlo por correo directamente al colegio.

Los documentos del colegio deben estar traducidos al inglés y ser lo más precisos posible. Sólo los estudiantes con historial preciso y veraz y con las debidas recomendaciones son tomados en cuenta para su admisión.

Puede pedirse a los estudiantes que escriban uno o más ensayos. Es importante para los solicitantes escribir estos ensayos por sí mismos y no pedir a alguien con más conocimientos del inglés que los escriba.

Tenga en cuenta que los mejores internados tienen procesos de admisión muy competitivos. Es importante que el colegio conozca el grado de preparación de su hijo y por qué desea estudiar en el extranjero. La admisión se basa en las notas del estudiante, la calidad de los cursos académicos, los comentarios y las recomendaciones de los profesores y los resultados de los exámenes estandarizados.

Cómo satisfacer otros requisitos de admisión

Muchos de los colegios incluídos en esta guía exigen a los estudiantes someterse a uno o más exámenes estandarizados. Muchos de los colegios que usted seleccione podrían pedir a su hijo que tome el Examen de Admisión en un Colegio Secundario (SSAT). Este examen evalúa la capacidad de un estudiante en matemáticas e inglés. La versión internacional del SSAT, que ha sido diseñada tomando en cuenta a los estudiantes con pocos conocimientos de inglés, se rinde tres veces al año en muchos países. Las fechas pueden obtenerse de los internados o escribiendo a The Secondary School Admission Test, CN 5339, Princeton, NJ 08543 U.S.A., Teléfono: (609) 683-4440, Fax: (609) 683-4507.

Además del SSAT, muchos colegios le pedirán los resultados del TOEFL o Examen de Inglés Como Segundo Idioma. Lea la información sobre los requisitos de admisión de cada colegio para verificar los exámenes de admisión específicos que se exigen.

¿Qué pasa a continuación?

La mayoría de los colegios informan a los solicitantes en marzo, si han sido aceptados. Los que han presentado solicitudes tardías podrán conocer la decisión de un colegio cuando el personal de admisión haya revisado la solicitud. Si su hijo ha sido aceptado y tiene intenciones de matricularse, usted debe devolver un contrato firmado con un depósito (pagadero en dólares de EE.UU. o Canadá) para reservar cupo. En el verano, el colegio le enviará la siguiente información.

• Un Formulario de Inmigración I-20 firmado por un funcionario del colegio. Usted debe llevar este formulario a la Embajada de los Estados Unidos más cercana para obtener una Visa de Estudiante F-1, que generalmente es válida por cuatro años.

• Formularios Médicos. Todos los colegios exigen que los estudiantes que ingresan se sometan a un examen físico completo y que presenten un historial de vacunas. Estos requisitos médicos son exigidos por los departamentos de salud locales. Si un estudiante llega a un colegio sin las debidas vacunas, deberá recibirlas por parte del personal médico del colegio. A los padres se les exigirá presentar formularios que permitan al colegio autorizar tratamientos médicos en casos de urgencia.

• Formularios de Seguros. Estos muestran quién pagará por los tratamientos médicos del estudiante mientras esté en el colegio. Las familias pueden tener sus propios seguros. Algunos colegios ofrecen seguros por una cuota determinada.

• Información Financiera. Se pedirá a los padres que paguen los costos del primer semestre que incluyen derecho de matrícula, alojamiento y comidas. Los libros y útiles escolares y los gastos de viaje son adicionales. Puede haber un cargo por servicios de lavado de ropa, lecciones de música, laboratorios, arte o deportes. Se le podrá pedir que deposite dinero en la cuenta del colegio para uso del estudiante.

• Instrucciones para los nuevos estudiantes. Los colegios enviarán una lista de ropa y otros artículos que los estudiantes deben llevar consigo. También le darán información sobre arreglos de transporte. Muchos colegios reciben a los estudiantes extranjeros en el aeropuerto importante más cercano. Asegúrese de notificar al colegio la información relacionada con el viaje de su hijo con mucha antelación.

Usted podría querer acompañar al nuevo alumno al colegio. Aunque los colegios no pueden proporcionar alojamiento a los padres en el colegio, lo ayudarán a hacer los arreglos necesarios en los hoteles vecinos. Los colegios también reciben con agrado las visitas de los padres varias veces durante el año.

Para más información

Los procedimientos mencionados arriba pueden variar de un colegio a otro. Si tiene preguntas sobre el proceso de admisión de una institución específica, póngase en contacto directamente con el personal de admisión o con el asesor de los estudiantes extranjeros. Para ayudarlo en su búsqueda, el *Internados en los Estados Unidos y Canadá y Programas Mundiales de Enriquecimiento*, incluye los números de teléfono, dirección para correspondencia y nombres de los funcionarios de admisión de más de 400 colegios en los Estados Unidos y Canadá. Deseamos éxito a usted y a su hijo en su búsqueda de un colegio con educación preuniversitaria que satisfaga sus necesidades.

Diane Rapp es presidenta de Diane Rapp Associates, Educational Consultants, 85 River Road, Scarborough, New York 10510.

Internats américains et canadiens—
COMMENT UTILISER CETTE SECTION

Ce guide est divisé en cinq parties principales : Conseils d'introduction, des présentations d'une page, des écoles préparatoires aux universités, un appendice sur les internats, une liste des abréviations, et un formulaire de demande d'information. Afin de profiter de toutes les informations contenues dans le *Internats américains et canadiens, et Programmes de perfectionnement internationaux*, il est nécessaire de suivre les étapes indiquées ci-dessous :

Première étape

Avant de commencer à rechercher l'école qui vous convient, lisez à la page 18, le « Guide familial des internats » et « Comprendre les processus d'admission » de Diane Rapp. Les articles vous donnent aussi bien des infomations importantes sur les programmes des écoles, leurs installations, la durée scolaire, l'inscription et le coût, que sur la vie au campus, les règlements, la sécurité, les procédures d'obtention d'un dossier d'inscription, ainsi que les moyens de transports disponibles.

Deuxième étape

Consultez ensuite, « l'Explication des présentations d'une page », qui vous montrera sur quelle page vous trouverez l'information dont vous avez besoin pour faire votre choix. Enfin, passez aux « Présentations d'une page » qui commencent à la page 35. La liste des établissements scolaires aux Etats-Unis commence à la page 37; la liste des établissements scolaires au Canada commence à la page 115. (Si vous désirez chercher les établissements scolaires par états ou provinces, consultez « l'index géographique » à la page 142.) Pour chaque établissement scolaire, vous trouverez aussi bien les informations sur l'emplacement et la personne à contacter, qu'une description complète, des photos des installations de l'école et des informations détaillées sur l'inscription des élèves étrangers, sur la disponiblitité des cours d'anglais comme langue étrangère, sur les dates des cours et les délais pour la réception des dossiers, sur les coûts, le logement, les règlements, et sur d'autres questions. Pour vous aider à utiliser les « Présentations d'une page », une « Clé des icônes graphiques » se trouve à la page 34 et au recto de la dernière couverture.

Troisième étape

Ce livre comprend aussi un « Appendice aux écoles préparatoires aux universités », lequel commence à la page 121. Dans cet appendice, vous trouverez les noms des personnes à contacter pour plus de 400 établissements. Ces derniers n'ont pas été mis en relief dans la partie « Présentations d'une page ». Utilisez le nom de la personne à contacter que vous trouverez dans cette section, pour demander de plus amples informations sur les établissements qui ont exprimé à Peterson leur intention d'inscrire des élèves étrangers.

Quatrième étape

Lorsque vous aurez terminé la liste des établissements scolaires qui vous intéressent le plus, utilisez les « Formulaires de demande d'information » pour recevoir de plus amples informations ou une demande de dossier d'inscription. Ces formulaires peuvent être faxés ou envoyés aux personnes en charge du programme ; utilisez les numéros de fax et les adresses que vous trouverez dans la partie « Personne à contacter », dans la « Présentation d'une page » ou dans l'Appendice pour vous assurer d'une transmission correcte du formulaire. N'hésitez pas à photocopier autant de programmes que vous le désirez. Une fois que les établissements sont contactés, ils vous enverront des renseignements plus détaillés sur les programmes qu'ils offrent.

EXPLICATION DES PRÉSENTATIONS D'UNE PAGE

Les « Présentations d'une page » se trouvent à partir de la page 35 et fournissent des informations détaillées sur les internats qui préparatoires aux universités. Ces informations ont été fournies à Thomson Peterson durant le printemps et l'été 2004 par des représentants des écoles qui ont dûment rempli le questionnaire développé par Thomson Peterson.

Vous trouverez dans les « Présentations d'une page » les indications suivantes :

1. Indicateur du pays
2. Nom et emblème de l'établissement scolaire (si disponible)
3. Personne à contacter pour les informations
4. Habilitation de l'établissement scolaire
5. Photos de l'établissement scolaire
6. Description complète de l'établissement
7. Emplacement de l'établissement scolaire
8. Icônes décrivant les températures saisonnières (moyennes de températures en automne, en hiver et au printemps)
9. Carte nationale des fuseaux horaires et distance de l'aéroport et de la grande ville les plus proches

Icônes des écoles

10. Type d'école
11. Effectif : nombre de garçons, nombre de filles
12. Pourcentage de pensionnaires
13. Pourcentage d'élèves étrangers
14. Nombre d'élèves étrangers qui ont fait une demande d'inscription, nombre de ceux qui ont été acceptés
15. Tests requis pour être admis et niveau moyen de compétence acquis par les élèves étrangers
16. Tests recommandés pour les admissions et niveau moyen de compétence acquis par les élèves étrangers
17. Pays les plus représentés et la durée de temps pendant laquelle les écoles ont servi ces pays
18. Délai d'inscription
19. Mois d'admission
20. Proportion élèves-professeurs : pourcentage des professeurs qui résident au campus
21. Proportion élèves-ordinateurs
22. Frais de scolarité, de pension et frais obligatoires supplémentaires
23. Liste des universités et des collèges fréquentés par le plus grand nombre d'étudiants les trois dernières années
24. Disponibilité de cours d'anglais en langue étrangère
25. Programme d'été au niveau secondaire
26. Code vestimentaire
27. Entrevue requise, en personn e
28. Entrevue requise, par téléphone

GUIDE FAMILIAL DES
INTERNATS PRÉPARATOIRES AUX UNIVERSITÉS

Les internats américains et canadiens offrent une chance unique aux élèves étrangers, celle d'obtenir une éducation pré-universitaire tout en vivant avec des personnes de cultures différentes. Les internats de l'Amérique du Nord ont été mis en place à partir du dix-huitième siècle. Conçus d'après le système anglais, ces établissements cherchaient à prodiguer une éducation scolaire supérieure et à développer le caractère moral et la santé physique de leurs élèves. Les écoles préparatoires aux universités d'aujourd'hui suivent la même tradition, en offrant de petites classes et une attention individuelle de la part des professeurs dédiés et attentionnés. Les écoles, de nos jours, répondent aux besoins des élèves de par leurs intérêts et leurs capacités, contrairement aux établissements homogènes d'autrefois.

QUELLES SONT LES OPTIONS?

La plupart des internats dans ce guide offrent un programme préparatoire aux universités pour les classes allant de la 3ème à la terminale (âges de 14 à 17 ans). D'autres offrent des études plus avancées. Il existe aussi des écoles primaires avec des classes du cm2 à la 4ème (âges de 10 à 13 ans). Les élèves s'inscrivent générale-ment pour deux à quatre ans, mais quelques écoles permettent des séjours plus courts, tels qu'un semestre ou un an. Certaines écoles offrent aussi des program-mes d'été de quatre à six semaines.

Les établissements figurant sur le Répertoire International montrent une grande diversité. Il existe des écoles mixtes aussi bien que non-mixtes. Certaines d'entre elles ont de fortes traditions religieuses ou militaires. D'autres mettent davantage l'accent sur certaines matières - comme les sciences - ou offrent des programmes pour les enfants qui ont des difficultés émotives ou scolaires.

COMBIEN DE TEMPS DURE L'ANNEE SCOLAIRE? QUI S'INSCRIT AU PROGRAMME?

L'année scolaire débute en septembre et se termine en juin, avec deux à trois semaines de vacances en décembre, en mars ou avril et de plus petites vacances en novembre. Les écoles sont fermées durant ces vacances. Les élèves étrangers peuvent profiter de ces vacances pour rendre visite à leurs amis ou à leur famille. Quelques écoles organiseront pour les élèves étrangers des séjours avec des familles d'accueil locales durant des périodes de longues vacances.

La plupart des élèves inscrits dans ces écoles viennent de différentes parties d'Amérique du Nord ou de divers pays. Les élèves étrangers ont une occasion unique d'améliorer leur anglais parlé et de s'intégrer à la vie scolaire américaine, puisqu'ils sont entourés de personnes originaires d'Amérique du Nord ou du Canada et qu'ils vivent dans leur communauté.

COMMENT SONT ORGANI-SES LES PROGRAMMES?

Les élèves suivent des cours du lundi au vendredi. Durant la semaine, ils consacrent plusieurs heures supplémentaires à la pré-paration des cours, aux études dans les bibliothèques, ou se consacrent à différentes activités périscolaires. Pendant les week-ends, les étudiants peuvent participer aux activités organisées, à des événements sportifs et à des excursions dans des centres culturels, des centres commerciaux ou à d'autres activités.

Programme académique

Le programme académique de l'école consiste en plusieurs cours obligatoires en anglais, une autre langue, des cours d'histoire, de littérature, de mathématiques, de sciences et de sports.
Généralement, les élèves peuvent choisir leurs matières, et il est possible qu'ils puissent progresser selon leur propre cadence. Les classes sont petites - avec de cinq à quinze étudiants - et les élèves peuvent ainsi participer de façon active aux discussions de classe. Les élèves sont encouragés à travailler indépendamment. Les professeurs habitent souvent sur le campus ou dans des endroits proches et sont ainsi à la disposition des élèves en dehors des cours. Dans les classes supérieures, les études exigent beaucoup de lectures et de rédactions. Les élèves étrangers devront avoir un haut niveau de compétence de l'anglaise pour répondre à ces exigences.

Service d'orientation et d'assistance universitaire

La plupart des élèves qui achèvent leurs études dans les internats poursuivent des cours universitaires de quatre ans. Les conseillers aideront les élèves à identifier les universités convenables et à rédiger les demandes d'inscription. Pour être reçu dans les meilleures universités, il faut avoir un niveau supérieur de l'anglaise.

Activités

En dehors des classes, les élèves peuvent choisir entre plusieurs acti-vités, telles que la chorale, des cours de musique, ou d'art dramatique. Ils peuvent aussi faire partie du journal de l'école, de l'organisation gouvernementale des étudiants ou des clubs d'échec. Ces activités font le contrepoids au travail scolaire rigoureux et donne la possibilité de se faire des amis ainsi que d'acquérir de nouvelles compétences.

Sports

Les sports font une partie importante dans la vie de l'internat. La plupart des établissements possèdent des complexes sportifs et offrent une sélection de sports de compétition ou individuels. Les élèves peuvent participer à des sports d'équipe, tels que le football américain, le football, le baseball, le hockey, le lacrosse ou des sports individuels tels que la course à pied sur une piste, la natation, la gymnastique et le tennis.

Nourriture

Les repas sont servis au réfectoire de l'école ; la présence aux repas est, en général, obligatoire. Dans certains établissements, il est possible que les élèves aident à servir le repas et à nettoyer la cuisine et la salle à manger. Les élèves étrangers qui ont du mal à s'habituer à la nourriture de l'école, apportent d'habitude des aliments non-périssables de chez eux. En général, les établissements essayent d'accommoder les élèves qui ont besoin d'un régime alimentaire particulier.

Code vestimentaire

La tenue vestimentaire aux internats est décontractée. Peu d'écoles exigent un uniforme, mais la plupart ont des codes vestimentaires à respecter (ils n'acceptent pas les jeans, par exemple). Quel-ques établissements demandent aux étudiants de s'habiller d'une façon plus élaborée pour le dîner. Les établissements vous donneront une liste de ce qu'il faut amener ainsi que des informations sur le climat.

Règles et règlements

Il est important pour tous les membres de la communauté de coopérer et de travailler ensemble, afin d'assurer le bon fonctionnement de l'école. Parmi les stricts règlements, on peut citer la défense de fumer, d'utiliser ou de posséder de l'alcool et toutes autres substances illégales, défense de quitter les lieux sans permission, et défense de tricher. Si ces règlements ne sont pas respectés par un élève, son expulsion peut en résulter.

Santé et sécurité

Toutes les écoles exigent que les élèves soient examinés par un médecin et vaccinés avant leur arrivée. Les établissements ont des infirmeries pourvues d'infirmières qualifiées ; de plus, les services de médecins et des hôpitaux sont toujours disponibles. Les parents doivent approuver les soins médicaux d'urgence. Les élèves doivent posséder une assurance médicale.

Les établissements sont très bien surveillés. Les élèves doivent se rendre responsables de leur propre sécurité lorsqu'ils voyagent ou lorsqu'ils quittent le campus. Les parents doivent enseigner à leurs enfants les règles de base de sécurité avant qu'ils n'arrivent à l'école. Bien que la drogue et l'alcool soient interdits sur le campus, votre enfant doit être averti qu'il est possible que certains élèves en possèdent de façon illégale, et qu'il faudrait éviter de fréquenter de tels individus.

Logement

Les dortoirs, en général, abritent deux élèves par chambre. Chaque élève a un lit, un bureau et une commode. Les élèves sont responsables de la propreté des chambres et de leurs lessives ; (des machines à laver et des séchoir sont à leur disposition dans le dortoir ; elles fonctionnent avec des pièces de monnaie.)

Transport

Ce guide aidera les familles à repérer les aéroports internationaux les plus proches des établissements scolaires. Les écoles, normalement, offrent un service de transport entre l'aéroport et l'école, dans les deux sens. Il est possible que ce moyen de transport soit payant. La plupart des internats défendent aux pensionnaires d'avoir leur propre voiture.

Communication avec les parents et les tuteurs

Les parents suivront les progrès de leurs enfants par le biais de rapports écrits et de visites à l'école. Les parents qui ne peuvent pas visiter l'école pourront déléguer à un membre de la famille ou à un tuteur le soin de s'occuper de ces détails.

A QUOI S'ATTENDRE?

Ce que les professeurs des écoles d'Amérique du Nord attendent de leurs élèves peut différer des écoles de leur pays d'origine. On s'attend à ce que les élèves posent des questions, lèvent la main pour répondre aux questions, pensent et travaillent indépendamment, et s'adressent aux professeurs lorsqu'ils ont besoin d'une aide supplémentaire. Les professeurs espèrent que les élèves participeront de façon active aux discussions de classe et encouragent les discussions animées et les différences d'opinion.

Les familles doivent être sensibles au fait que leurs enfants devront s'adapter aux changements durant l'année scolaire. Durant les premiers mois d'école, les élèves étrangers pourront passer par des moments de tristesse et de solitude, avant qu'ils ne s'adaptent à une nouvelle langue, de nouvelles personnes, coutumes, à la nourriture et au climat. Il est nécessaire que ces élèves soient motivés et prêts à travailler dur, à se faire de nouveaux amis et à découvrir de nouveaux horizons. Les conseillers pour les élèves étrangers, les professeurs et les parents de la résidence universitaire peuvent aider les élèves à s'intégrer plus facilement à la vie scolaire, académiquement et socialement.

Les internats américains et canadiens de nos jours produisent les leaders de demain, en enseignant aux élèves à penser de façon indépendante, à travailler dur et à comprendre d'autres peuples et cultures. Les fruits de cette éducation leur resteront pour la vie.

Diane Rapp est présidente de Diane Rapp Associates, Educational Consultants, 85 River Road, Scarborough, New York 10510.

COMPRENDRE LE PROCESSUS D'ADMISSION

Lorsque vous aurez décidé d'envoyer votre enfant dans un établissement à l'étranger, vous aurez besoin de connaître davantage les procédures d'admission normalement requises par les écoles préparatoires aux universités. Du fait que les exigences de chaque établissement peuvent varier, les familles sont encouragées à contacter les établissements directement afin d'obtenir une liste qui contiendrait les délais pour les demandes d'inscription et les instructions. Les directives suivantes vous aideront à travers le processus d'inscription.

Commencer votre recherche

Après avoir lu le « Guide familial » et « les Présentations d'une page », choisissez trois à cinq écoles que vous croyez correspondre aux buts pédagogiques de votre enfant. Lorsque vous lirez la description de l'école, essayez de vous poser les questions suivantes. Mon enfant est-il capable de satisfaire les demandes de cet établissement? La dimension de l'école conviendrait-elle à mon enfant? Au cas où votre enfant a besoin de cours de rattrapage en anglais, l'école offre-t-elle un programme d'anglais comme langue étrangère? Est-ce que cette école se situe dans une localité qui me convient?

Ensuite, utilisez le formulaire de demande d'information à la dernière page du guide afin d'obtenir de plus amples informations et explications pour s'inscrire aux écoles que vous aurez choisies. Bien qu'il soit possible à quelques écoles de vous communiquer des informations dans votre langue, la plupart communiqueront en anglais. Les parents doivent être capables de comprendre un rudiment d'anglais ou bien se référer à quelqu'un qui comprend suffisamment l'anglais pour examiner et remplir les dossiers d'inscription de l'école. Il vous faudra noter les délais d'inscription et les dates des tests des écoles qui intéressent votre enfant.

Faire une demande d'inscription

Étudiez les informations des écoles afin de voir lesquelles correspondent aux aptitudes de votre enfant. Si possible, essayez de visiter plusieurs écoles. Afin de décider de la meilleure école pour votre enfant, il vous faudra rencontrer les responsables d'admission, les professeurs et visiter le campus. Si vous ne pouvez pas visiter l'école, essayez alors de rencontrer des représentants locaux qui sont, en général, des anciens élèves de l'école. Quelquefois, les responsables d'admission voyagent pour rencontrer les candidats. Si un voyage était envisagé dans votre pays, un responsable d'admission vous contacterait pour établir un rendez-vous avec vous.

Remplir les formulaires d'inscription

Remplissez les formulaires d'inscription et adressez-les aux écoles avec les montants requis en dollars américains ou canadiens. Le délai d'inscription, pour la plupart des écoles, est le 1er février. Du fait que plusieurs écoles rallongent la période d'inscription pour les étudiants étrangers, il vous faudra vérifier les directives d'inscription pour chaque école.

Ensuite, demandez aux professeurs actuels de votre enfant de remplir les lettres de recommandation requises par la plupart des écoles. Il est possible que les écoles demandent une lettre de recommandation du professeur d'anglais, d'une part, et du professeur de mathématiques, d'autre part. Joignez-y une enveloppe, adressée à l'école, avec le tarif d'affranchissement nécessaire pour que le professeur puisse remplir et envoyer le formulaire directement à l'école.

Les rapports de l'école doivent être en anglais et aussi exacts que possible. Seuls les étudiants qui ont des dossiers avec des rapports exacts et honnêtes et des recommandations seront considérés comme admissibles.

Il est aussi possible que les écoles demandent aux élèves de rédiger une ou plusieurs dissertations. Il est nécessaire que les candidats eux-mêmes rédigent ces dissertations, sans qu'une personne qui a de meilleures connaissances d'anglais ne les aident.

Il convient de rappeler que les meilleurs internats ont des conditions d'admission très rigoureuses. Il est important pour l'école de savoir le niveau de préparation de votre enfant et les raisons pour lesquelles il ou elle veut étudier à l'étranger. L'admission est basée sur les notes de l'élève, la qualité des cours suivis, les remarques et les recommandations des professeurs, ainsi que les résultats des tests standardisés.

Autres demandes faisant partie du processus d'admission

Une grande partie des écoles mentionnées dans ce guide demandent aux élèves de passer un ou plusieurs tests standardisés. Certaines écoles que vous aurez sélectionnées pourront aussi demander à votre enfant de passer le Test d'admission aux études secondaires ou le SSAT. Ces examens permettent de mesurer l'habilité de l'élève en mathématiques et en anglais. La version internationale du SSAT, conçue même pour des élèves qui possèdent un bas niveau d'anglais, est présentée trois fois par an dans plusieurs pays. Les dates des tests peuvent être obtenues des internats ou en contactant la société suivante : Secondary School Admission Test, CN 5339, Princeton, NJ 08543 U.S.A., Téléphone: (609) 683-4440, Télécopieur: (609) 683-4507.

En plus du SSAT, plusieurs écoles demanderont à voir les résultats du TOEFL ou de l'Examen d'anglais comme langue etrangère. Encore une fois, lisez bien les informations concernant les admissions aux écoles qui vous intéressent pour vérifier quels tests spécifiques sont requis.

Qu'arrive-t-il ensuite?

La plupart des écoles feront savoir en mars aux candidats d'admission s'ils ont été acceptés. Les candidats retardataires recevront une réponse dès que le personnel d'admission aura examiné leurs dossiers. Si votre enfant a été accepté et veut s'inscrire, il vous faudra adresser à l'école le contrat signé et un acompte (en dollars américains ou canadiens) pour réserver sa place. Durant l'été, l'école enverra les informations suivantes :

• Un formulaire I-20 d'immigration signé par un responsable de l'école. Vous devez prendre ce formulaire à l'ambassade américaine la plus proche pour obtenir un visa d'étudiant F-1, valable d'habitude pour quatre ans.

• Formulaires médicaux. Chaque école exige que les élèves admis dans leur établissement subissent un examen médical complet et soumettent un carnet d'immunisations. Ces exigences médicales sont requises par les autorités sanitaires locales. Si un élève arrive à l'école sans les immunisations requises, il ou elle devra alors les obtenir par le biais du personnel médical de l'école. Les parents devront mandater par écrit l'école pour tout traitement médical dans le cas d'une urgence médicale.

• Formulaires d'assurance. Ces derniers indiquent qui paiera pour le traitement médical de l'élève pendant son séjour à l'école. Les familles peuvent avoir leur propre assurance. Quelques écoles ont une police d'assurance à votre diposition moyennant une certaine somme.

• Informations financières. Les parents doivent payer les coûts du premier semestre, lesquels incluent la scolarité, le logement et les repas. Les livres, les fournitures scolaires et les dépenses de déplacement exigent des coûts supplémentaires. Il est possible qu'il y ait des frais pour des services de blanchissage, de leçons de musique, de laboratoires, d'art, ou de sport. Quelques établissements scolaires demandent aux parents d'ouvrir un compte liquide à l'école pour subvenir aux besoins de leur enfant.

• Conseils aux nouveaux élèves. Les écoles vous enverront une liste indiquant les vêtements et autres objets pratiques que votre enfant devra amener. Elles fourniront aussi toutes les informations nécessaires concernant les modes de transport. Plusieurs écoles enverront un délégué pour accueillir les élèves étrangers à l'aéroport le plus proche. Assurez-vous d'informer l'école, bien à l'avance, sur les informations de vol de votre enfant.

Il est possible que vous vouliez accompagner votre enfant à l'école. Même si le campus n'offre pas de logement pour les parents, l'école vous aidera à trouver un hôtel dans les environs. Les écoles encouragent aussi les parents à rendre visite à leur enfant plusieurs fois par an.

Pour plus de renseignements

Les procédures mentionnées ci-dessus peuvent varier d'une école à l'autre. Si vous avez des questions sur le processus d'admission d'un établissement particulier, contactez directement les responsables d'admission de l'école ou le conseiller pour élèves étrangers. Pour vous aider dans vos recherches, *Internats américains et canadiens, et Programmes de perfectionnement internationaux* donne une liste des numéros de téléphone, des adresses postales et des noms des responsables d'admission de plus de 400 écoles à travers les États-Unis et le Canada. Nous vous souhaitons, à vous et à votre enfant, le plus grand succès dans vos recherches des écoles préparatoires aux universités qui correspondent le plus à vos besoins.

Diane Rapp est présidente de Diane Rapp Associates, Educational Consultants, 85 River Road, Scarborough, New York 10510.

米国とカナダの全寮制学校—
このセクションの使い方

「ピーターソンの米国、カナダの全寮制学校および世界各地での強化プログラム」は、概要、1ページずつの各校のご紹介、その他の全寮制私立学校一覧、省略記号一覧、そして案内請求用紙の5つの部分に分かれています。この案内書を最大限に活用するため、次のステップに従ってご利用下さい。

ステップ1

各校の案内をご覧になる前に、ダイアン・ラップの「全寮制私立学校に関するご家族へのご案内」と「入学手続について」（24ページから）をお読み下さい。全寮制学校のカリキュラム、施設、学期の期間、生徒数、費用等のほか、キャンパス・ライフ、安全と規則、入学手続、交通機関などについての説明があります。

ステップ2

「各校のご案内について」をお読み下さい。この章では、各ページの学校案内のどこにどのような情報が記されているかを説明します。次に、35ページからの「各校のご案内」をご覧下さい。アメリカの学校のご案内は37ページから、カナダの学校のご案内は115ページからです。（州別に学校を探す場合は、142ページの「地域別索引」をご利用下さい。）各校について、所在地、連絡先、詳しい内容紹介、施設の写真、留学生の入学手続の詳細、外国人のための英語講座の有無、入学時に必要な英語能力、学期開始月、願書提出の期限、費用、寮制度、校則、その他さまざまな情報が満載されています。「各校のご案内」をご利用になる際には、34ページと裏表紙内側の「記号凡例」をご参照下さい。

ステップ3

本書121ページの「その他の全寮制私立学校一覧」は、「各校のご案内」に記載されていない学校400校以上の名称と連絡先の一覧です。これらの学校も世界各国からの留学生を受け入れていく方針なので、詳しい案内をご希望の方は記載の連絡先までお申し込み下さい。

ステップ4

志望校の数を絞ったら、「案内請求用紙」を利用して詳しい案内や願書を取り寄せます。請求用紙に記入し、各志望校へファックスまたは郵送して下さい。請求用紙が確実に届くよう「各校のご案内」または「その他の全寮制私立学校一覧」に連絡先として記載されているファックス番号または住所へ送付して下さい。この用紙は、コピーして複数の志望校へ送ることができます。各校は請求用紙を受け取り次第、詳しい案内を直接皆様にお送りします。

「1ページ案内」について

35ページから始まる「各校のご案内」は、全寮制私立学校を、1ページに1校ずつ詳しくご紹介しています。このご案内は、2004年の春から夏にかけて、各校の代表者がトムソンピーターソンの特別なアンケートに答えた内容に基づくものです。

「各校のご案内」の内容

1. 国名
2. 学校名と校章
3. 連絡先
4. 学校の認定状況
5. 写真
6. 詳しい学校紹介
7. 所在地
8. 季節の平均気温を表す記号(秋・冬・春の平均気温の範囲を表す)
9. 国内の時間帯地図と、最も近い空港及び主要都市からの距離

学校案内の記号

10. 学校の種類
11. 生徒数--男子、女子
12. 寮生の割合
13. 留学生の割合
14. 留学生の出願者数及び合格者数
15. 入学試験の内容と合格した留学生の平均点数
16. 推奨される入学のための試験と留学生の平均点数
17. 生徒数の多い国と、その受入年数
18. 願書提出期限
19. 入学の可能な月
20. 学生と教師の比率及びキャンパスに住む教師の割合
21. 学生とコンピュータの比率
22. 授業料、寮費、食費、その他の必要経費
23. 過去3年間の卒業生の主な進学先
24. 留学生のための英語プログラム（ESL）あり
25. 中等レベルの夏期プログラムあり
26. 服装規定あり
27. 面接
28. 電話によるインタビュー

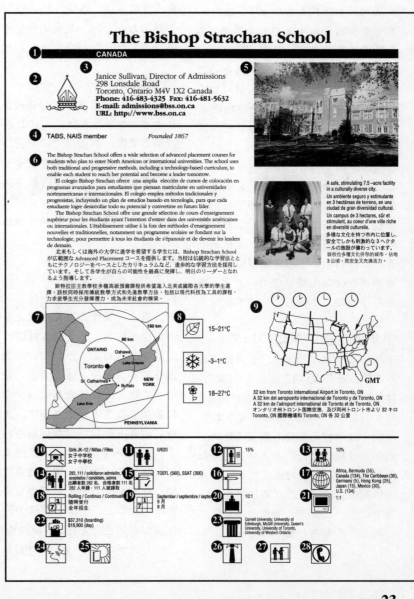

The Bishop Strachan School

❶ CANADA

❷
❸ Janice Sullivan, Director of Admissions
298 Lonsdale Road
Toronto, Ontario M4V 1X2 Canada
Phone: 416-483-4325 Fax: 416-481-5632
E-mail: admissions@bss.on.ca
URL: http://www.bss.on.ca

❹ TABS, NAIS member   *Founded 1867*

❻ The Bishop Strachan School offers a wide selection of advanced placement courses for students who plan to enter North American or international universities. The school uses both traditional and progressive methods, including a technology-based curriculum, to enable each student to reach her potential and become a leader tomorrow.

El colegio Bishop Strachan ofrece una amplia elección de cursos de colocación en programas avanzados para estudiantes que piensan matricularse en universidades norteamericanas e internacionales. El colegio emplea métodos tradicionales y progresistas, incluyendo un plan de estudios basado en tecnología, para que cada estudiante logre desarrollar todo su potencial y convertirse en futuro líder.

The Bishop Strachan School offre une grande sélection de cours d'enseignement supérieur pour les étudiants ayant l'intention d'entrer dans des universités américaines ou internationales. L'établissement utilise à la fois des méthodes d'enseignement nouvelles et traditionnelles, notamment un programme scolaire se fondant sur la technologie, pour permettre à tous les étudiants de s'épanouir et de devenir les leaders de demain.

北米もしくは海外の大学に進学を希望する学生には、Bishop Strachan School が広範囲な Advanced Placement コースを提供します。当校は伝統的な学習法とともにテクノロジーをベースとしたカリキュラムなど、進歩的な学習方法を採用しています。そして各学生が自らの可能性を最高に発揮し、明日のリーダーとなれるよう指導します。

斯特拉臣主教學校多種高級預備課程供希望進入北美或國際各大學的學生選擇。該校同時採用傳統教學方式和先進教學方法，包括以現代科技為工具的課程，力求使學生充分發揮潛力，成為未來社會的棟樑。

❺
A safe, stimulating 7.5 –acre facility in a culturally diverse city.

Un ambiente seguro y estimulante en 3 hectáreas de terreno, en una ciudad de gran diversidad cultural.

Un campus de 3 hectares, sûr et stimulant, au coeur d'une ville riche en diversité culturelle.

多様な文化を持つ市内に位置し、安全でしかも刺激的な3ヘクタールの施設が備わっています。
該校位多種文化併存的城市，佔地3公頃，既安全又充滿活力。

❼ [Map: 160 km, 80 km, ONTARIO, Oshawa, Lake Ontario, Toronto, St. Catharines, Buffalo, NEW YORK, Lake Erie, PENNSYLVANIA]

❽
🍃 15–21°C
❄ -3–1°C
🌸 18–27°C

❾ [U.S. map with time zones] GMT

32 km from Toronto International Airport in Toronto, ON
A 32 km del aeropuerto internacional de Toronto y de Toronto, ON
A 32 km de l'aéroport international de Toronto et de Toronto, ON
オンタリオ州トロント国際空港、及び同州トロント市より32キロ
Toronto, ON 國際機場和 Toronto, ON 各32公里

❿ Girls JK-12 / Niñas / Filles
女子中学校
女子中學校

⓫ 0/620

⓬ 15%

⓭ 10%

⓮ 282, 111 / solicitaron admisión, aceptados / candidats, admis
出願者数 282名、合格者数 111名
282人申請・111人被錄取

⓯ TOEFL (560), SSAT (300)

⓰

⓱ Africa, Bermuda (55), Canada (134), The Caribbean (30), Germany (5), Hong Kong (25), Japan (15), Mexico (30), U.S. (134)

⓲ Rolling / Continuo / Continuel
随時受付
全年招生

⓳ September / septiembre / septem
9月
9月

⓴ 10:1

㉑ 1:1

㉒ $37,310 (boarding)
$18,900 (day)

㉓ Cornell University, University of Edinburgh, McGill University, Queen's University, University of Toronto, University of Western Ontario

㉔ **㉕** **㉖** **㉗** **㉘**

全寮制私立学校に関する
ご家族へのご案内

アメリカとカナダの全寮制私立学校は、留学生が、さまざまな文化的背景を持つ若者や大人たちの中で生活しながら、大学進学のための教育を受けることのできる貴重な機会を提供しています。北米の全寮制私立学校の歴史は、18世紀に遡ります。これらの学校は英国の制度にならったもので、優れた勉学指導とともに、生徒の道徳と体力の養成を目指していました。今日の全寮制私立学校も、この伝統を受け継ぎ、少人数のクラスで熱心な教師陣が生徒ひとりひとりに行き届いた注意を配っています。しかし、単一的だった過去の学校と異なり、今日ではさまざまな興味対象や能力を持った生徒たちのニーズに合った教育を行っています。

幅広い選択肢

本書でご紹介する学校の大半は、9年生から12年生を対象としています。高校卒業後1年間の進学準備コースのある学校もあります。また、5年生から8年生までの中等部がある場合もあります。在学期間は通常2～4年間ですが、1年間あるいは1学期間だけの短期在学を許可している学校もあります。また学校によっては、4～6週間の夏季講座を開講しています。

ここでご紹介する各校は、さまざまな特徴を持っています。男子校、女子校、共学校があるほか、宗教や軍隊式規律を強調する学校、文化系あるいは理科系の学校、学習障害や情緒障害を持つ生徒のためのクラスのある学校などが揃っています。

学年度と在学生について

学年度は9月に始まり、6月に終わります。その間、12月と3月（または4月）に2～3週間の休暇があるほか、11月にも短い休暇が入ります。休暇中は学校の施設も閉まるため、留学生は帰省したり友人の家を訪ねたりします。学校によっては、長期の休暇中、留学生のために地元の家庭でのホームステイ制度を実施しているところもあります。

ほとんどの学校には、北米各地に加えて外国からも生徒が集まっています。アメリカやカナダの社会で、英語を母国語とする人たちに囲まれて暮らす環境は、留学生にとって、英会話の力をつけ、北米の学生生活に慣れるまたとない機会となります。

授業構成

月曜日から金曜日まで毎日授業があります。生徒たちは、そのほかにも授業の準備、図書館での学習、課外活動などに毎週数時間を費やします。週末には、クラブ活動、スポーツ大会、文化鑑賞、ショッピング、観光など各種行事に参加できます。

カリキュラム

英語、外国語、歴史、文学、数学、科学、体育が必修科目となっています。通常、講座の選択にはある程度の自由があり、生徒が各自のペースで勉強を進めることができる場合もあります。クラスは5人から15人の少人数で、生徒たちは活発な議論に参加することができます。また、各自の自主的な学習が奨励されます。キャンパス内あるいは近くに住む教師が多いため、課外時間にも質問や相談をすることができます。高学年になると、かなりの量の読書と作文が必須となるため、留学生にも、こうした要求についていける高度な

英語能力が必要となります。

大学進学相談

寮制私立高校の卒業生はほとんどが4年制大学に進学します。各校の大学進学カウンセラーが、志望校の選択や受験申込についてアドバイスをしています。競争率の高い大学に入るには、留学生は高度な英語能力を持っていなければなりません。

課外活動

コーラス、音楽のレッスン、演劇クラブから、校内紙、生徒会、チェスクラブまで、さまざまな課外活動の機会があります。こうした課外活動の場は、厳しい勉学の息抜きになると同時に、友人を作ったり、新しい技術を身につけるよい機会でもあります。

スポーツ

スポーツは学生生活の重要な部分を占めています。大半の学校には立派なスポーツ施設が揃っており、さまざまな競技スポーツ、非競技スポーツが楽しめます。アメリカン・フットボール、サッカー、バスケットボール、野球、陸上ホッケー、ラクロスなどのチーム・スポーツのほか、陸上競技、水泳、体操、テニスなどの個人スポーツもできます。

食事

通常、食事は校内の食堂で食べる規則になっています。給食係や、台所・食堂の後片付けを生徒がしなければならない場合もあります。学校の食事になじめない留学生は、保存のきく食料を持参することができます。通常、食餌制限の必要な生徒には、学校が特別な食事を用意してくれます。

服装

学校での服装はカジュアルが普通です。制服のある学校はあまりありませんが、服装規定(ジーンズ禁止など)のある学校はよく見られます。夕食時には多少きちんとした服装が要求される場合もあります。各校が、現地の気候や、どのような衣類を持参したらよいかなどの情報を提供しています。

規則・方針

学校の運営をスムーズに行うためには、関係者全員の協力が必要です。喫煙、アルコール類・麻薬などの使用または所持、無許可の外出、カンニングなどは厳しく禁止されており、違反者は退学処分となる場合もあります。

健康と安全

どの学校でも、新入生は入学前に、医師による健康診断と基本的な予防注射を済ませておかなければなりません。学校には看護士のいる保健センターがあり、医院や病院に行くこともできます。緊急時の医療にはご両親の許可が必要です。また、生徒は医療保険に入っていなければなりません。

学校内は慎重に監視されていますが、旅行時など学校外では生徒各自が安全に気をつけなければなりません。入学前にご両親から、安全上の基本的な注意事項を教えるようにし

て下さい。キャンパスでは麻薬やアルコール類は禁じられていますが、不法所持をする生徒がいるかもしれませんので、そのような生徒とは関わらないようにして下さい。

寮

寮は、通常2人部屋になっています。各人にベッド、机、たんすが与えられます。生徒は、自室の整理整頓と自分の服の洗濯は自分でしなければなりません(寮内にコイン式の洗濯機があります)。

交通

本書には、各校に最も近い国際空港が記載されています。多くの学校が空港からの交通手段を提供していますが、これは有料の場合もあります。寮生が車を持つことは、たいてい禁止されています。

ご両親あるいは保護者との連絡

ご両親は、成績表を受け取るほか、学校を訪問して子女の学習状況を知ることができます。ご両親が学校を訪問できない場合は、親戚や保護者の方が代理で訪問することもできます。

生徒に求められるもの

北米の学校で教師が生徒に求めるものは、他の国々の場合と違う場合もあります。生徒は、わからないことは質問し、授業中に手を上げて答え、自分の頭で考え、自分で学習し、必要ならば教師の援助を求めることを期待されます。教師は、生徒が積極的に授業に参加することを求め、活発な議論と多様な意見を奨励します。

生徒は、在学中はその環境に適応しなければなりません。留学生の場合、初めの何ヵ月間かは、新しい言葉、人々、習慣、食べ物、気候に慣れなければならず、憂鬱だったり孤独感

を感じることもあります。本人が強い意志を持つとともに、一生懸命勉強し、新しい友人を作り、新しい体験を受け入れる心構えがなければなりません。留学生担当のアドバイザーのほか、カウンセラー、教師、寮母・寮父などが、留学生がキャンパスでの学習・社交環境に適応するお手伝いをします。

アメリカ、カナダの全寮制私立学校は、生徒たちに自分の頭で考え、努力し、異文化の人々を理解することを教えることによって、将来の指導者を生み出しています。こうした教育から得られるものは、一生消えることのないものです。

Diane Rapp is president of Diane Rapp Associates, Educational Consultants, 85 River Road, Scarborough, New York 10510.

入学手続について

子女を海外に留学させる決心がついたら、こうした私立学校への入学手続について調査をしなければなりません。学校によって必要な手続が異なる場合もありますので、手続の期限や案内については、各校に直接お問い合わせ下さい。以下に、入学手続の過程を概説します。

志望校の選定

「全寮制私立学校に関するご家族へのご案内」と「各校のご案内」をお読みになり、子女の教育目標に最も合っていると思われる学校を3～5校選びます。各校の説明をお読みになる際は、次のような点を特にご検討下さい。その学校の学習レベルについていけるか、学校の規模は適当か、英語の補習が必要な場合、外国語としての英語の講座があるか、学校の所在地は適切かなどです。

次に、本書の最後に添付した案内請求用紙を使って、各志望校から案内を取り寄せます。外国語に翻訳した案内書を用意している学校もありますが、通常コミュニケーションは英語で行われます。従って、案内書を読んで願書を提出するには、ご両親がある程度英語を理解できるか、または英語のわかる人に手伝ってもらう必要があります。こうして、志望校の願書提出期限や試験日などを確認します。

願書提出

子女が志望校の入学資格を満たしているかどうかを調べて下さい。できれば、志望校を何校か実際に訪問してみます。入学担当官や教師に会い、キャンパスを見学してみると、どの学校が子女のニーズに最も合っているかがわかります。キャンパスを訪問できない場合には、各地でその学校の代表者(通常は卒業生)に面会することができます。時には入学担当官が外国へ出張して、入学希望者と会うこともあります。希望者の国で出張面接を行う場合は、入学担当者が希望者に連絡し、面接の日取りを決めます。

願書の記入

記入した願書に申請料を米ドルまたはカナダ・ドルで添えて、学校に返送します。願書受付の締切は、たいてい2月1日となっていますが、留学生に関しては締切日を延ばす学校も多いため、各校の受付期限を調べて下さい。

次に、現在通っている学校の先生の推薦状を用意します。例えば、英語の先生と数学の先生からの推薦状をそれぞれ提出しなければならない場合があります。志望校の宛て名を書き、切手を貼った返信用の封筒を用意し、推薦状を書いた先生が直接志望校宛に送れるようにします。

成績証明書は英文で、できる限り正確なものを提出します。正確かつ正直な内容の成績証明と推薦状を提出した生徒のみが、入学審査の対象となります。

作文をひとつまたはそれ以上書かされることもあります。こうした作文は必ず生徒自身によって書くことが重要であり、本人より英語力のある人に代筆させたりしてはなりません。

優秀な学校は入学審査の倍率も非常に高くなります。学校側は、入学志願者の学力レベルと、留学の動機を知る必要があります。成績のほか、授業の質、先生のコメント及び推薦、そして標準テストの点数が審査の基準となります。

その他の入学審査基準

本書に掲載されている学校の多くは、入学審査基準として、1種以上の標準テストを受けることを要求しています。中等学校入学試験(Secondary School Admission Test -- SSAT)を受けなければならない学校もあります。SSAT は数学と英語のテストです。外国人のためのSSAT は、英語力の低い生徒のためのテストで、年に3回、世界各国で実施されます。試験期日については、志望校または下記にお問い合わせ下さい。

Secondary School Admission Test
CN 5339, Princeton, NJ 08543 U.S.A.,
電話: (609) 683-4440,
ファックス: (609) 683-4507.

SSATに加えて、多くの学校では、外国語としての英語能力テスト(Test of English as a Foreign Language — TOEFL)の結果も必要としています。各校の入学案内を読んで、どのテストを受けなければならないかを確認して下さい。

次のステップ

合否の通知は通常3月に行われます。願書提出が遅い場合は、入学担当者が願書を審査した時点で結果を知らされる場合もがあります。入学が認められ、その学校に入学を決めたら、契約書に署名し保証金(米ドルまたはカナダ・ドル)を添えて返送しなければなりません。その結果、夏の間に学校から次のような書類が送られてきます。

● 学校関係者が署名した書式I-20。この用紙を最寄りのアメリカ大使館に持参し、F-1学生ビザを取得しなければなりません。学生ビザは通常4年間有効です。

● 健康診断用紙。どの学校でも、新入生は完全な健康診断を受けるとともに、予防接種の記録を提出しなければなりません。これは地元の衛生局によって義務づけられているもので、入学時に予防接種を正しく受けていない生徒は、学校の医療スタッフから接種を受けることになります。また、緊急時の医療処置を学校に委ねるという主旨の書類に両親が署名をしなければなりません。

● 保険用紙。これは、在学中の生徒の医療費を誰が支払うかを明らかにするものです。各家庭の保険を利用することができますが、有料の保険サービスを提供している学校もあります。

● 財政証明用紙。まず、第1学期分の経費(授業料、寮費、食費など)を支払わなければなりません。このほかに、教科書・教材費、交通費などがかかります。洗濯サービス、音楽のレッスン、ラボ施設使用料、芸術やスポーツ活動などに費用がかかる場合もあります。生徒が使えるよう、学校名義の口座に積立金を振り込む制度もあります。

● 新入生のための案内。新入生が持参するべき衣類その他のリストや、交通機関の案内が送られてきます。多くの学校では、最寄りの主要空港まで迎えの車を出してくれます。前もって到着便を学校にお知らせ下さい。

入学時にご両親が新入生に付き添うこともできます。学校が付添い者用の宿舎をキャンパスに用意することはありませんが、近くのホテルの予約をお手伝いします。学校では、年に何度かご両親がキャンパスを訪問されることを歓迎しています。

その他の情報

上記の手続内容は学校によって異なります。特定の学校の入学手続については、その学校の入学担当者や留学生担当のアドバイザーに直接おたずね下さい。「米国、カナダの全寮制学校および世界各地での強化プログラム」(*American and Canadian Boarding Schools and Worldwide Enrichment Programs*)には、400校を超えるアメリカとカナダの学校の住所、電話番号、入学担当者氏名が掲載されています。皆様のご希望に合った私立学校をお探し下さい。

Diane Rapp is president of Diane Rapp Associates, Educational Consultants, 85 River Road, Scarborough, New York 10510.

美國與加拿大寄宿學校—
如何使用本章

本指南分為五個主要章節：初步建議、大學預校單頁自我介紹、寄宿學校附錄、縮寫附錄以及諮詢索要表。您如欲盡量利用《彼得森美國與加拿大寄宿學校及國際強化項目》(Peterson's American and Canadian Boarding Schools and Worldwide Enrichment Programs)，請遵循下列步驟。

第一步

請您在查閱本手冊中的理想學校之前，閱讀 Diane Rapp 所著的《寄宿學校家庭指南》(Family Guide to Boarding Schools) 及《了解入學程序》(Understanding the Admission Process)，其正文始於第 30 頁。這兩篇文章就學校課程、設施、學制長度、招生及費用提供了寶貴的資訊，並說明校園生活、校規與安全問題、申請程序及交通安排。

第二步

然後，請查閱"學校單頁自我介紹"，該文說明您在每頁的何處可找到您做出選擇所需的資訊。接著您翻閱"學校單頁自我介紹"，該文史於第 35 頁。美國境內的學校名單始於第 37 頁；加拿大的學校名單始於第 115 頁。（如果您想按州或省查詢學校，請查閱第 142 頁的地理索引。）您會找到每家學校的地點、聯絡 資訊以及補充說明、學校設施照片，及有關外國留學生的詳細招生資訊、該校是否開設英語為第二語言課程、入學的英文程度要求、上課日期、申請期限、 費用、住房、校規及許多其他資料。為了協助您使用該單頁自我介紹，第 34 頁和本手冊封內上載有"地理圖示索引"(Key to the Graphical Icons)。

第三步

本手冊也包括《大學預校附錄》，該附錄始於第 121 頁。在這一附錄中，您將找到單頁自我介紹章節中未重點介紹的 400 多家學校的名稱及聯絡資訊。請利用該章節中的《資訊索要表》向學校索要補充資訊，因為這些學校表示願意招收外國留學生。

第四步

在您結束編寫使您感興趣的學校名單時，請利用《資訊索要表》索要補充資訊或入學資料。您可將這些資料郵寄或傳真給各項專業的聯絡人；為了確保表格的正確傳遞，請使用單頁介紹或附錄中的聯絡部份。歡迎您盡量多複印表格，並利用這些表格和您有興趣的科系聯絡。您一旦同這些科系取得 聯絡，有關人員將會寄給您有關其開設課程的補充資料。

夏令營單頁介紹解釋

始於第35頁單頁學校自我介紹的說明提供了有關大學預科寄宿學校的詳細資訊。各學校代表在2004年春季及夏季向《彼得森指南》提供這一資訊，並填寫由《彼得森指南》編製的一份問卷調查。

單頁學校自我介紹的內容

1. 國家索引
2. 學校名稱與校徽（如有）
3. 聯絡資訊
4. 學校認可
5. 學校照片
6. 學校補充說明
7. 學校地點
8. 季節溫度圖示（顯示秋季、冬季和春季溫度範圍）
9. 全國時區地圖及與最近的國際機場和大城市之間的距離

學校圖示

10. 學校類型
11. 招生：男生人數、女生人數
12. 寄宿學生百分比
13. 留學生百分比
14. 學生申請人數、錄取人數
15. 留學生入學考試成績要求及平均水平
16. 留學生入學考試建議成績要求及平均水平
17. 留學生人數最多的國家及最長留學時間
18. 申請期限
19. 上課日期
20. 師生比例：住校教員人數
21. 學生人均電腦比例
22. 學費、膳宿費及規定收取的其他費用
23. 學生過去三年中就讀比例最高的大學
24. 是否開設英語作為第二語言課程
25. 中學夏季班
26. 衣著規定
27. 要求面談
28. 要求電話約談

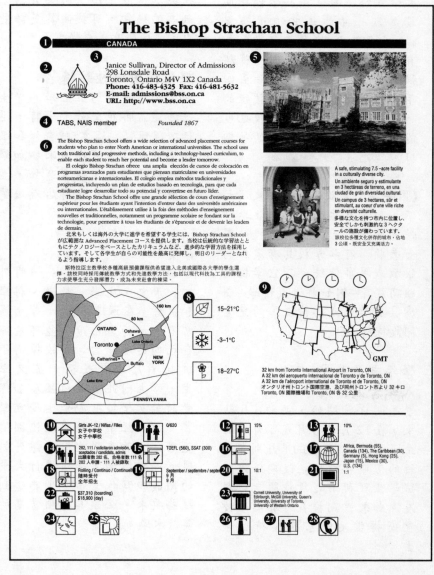

寄宿學校家庭指南

美加的預校爲留學生提供了獲得大學預科教育的獨特機會，同時學生亦可與來自多種文化的青少年及成人共同生活。北美洲的寄宿學校始於十八世紀。這些學校以英國系統爲原形，並尋求爲學生提供高品質的德育、智育和體育。今天的大學預校實行小班制，教員兢兢業業，對學生的關懷無微不至。然而，過去的學校課程單調，今天的學校卻有所不同；它們能夠滿足興趣和能力各不相同的學生的需求。

有何選擇？

本手冊中的大多數寄宿學校都爲9年級至12年級的學生開設大學預科課程。某些學校也開設爲期一年的畢業後進修課程。5年級至12年級的學生也有專設的初中部大學預科課程。學生通常就讀二年至四年，但是有些學校採取較短的一學期或學年學制。各校也可能會開設爲期四至六週的暑期班。

《國際指南》收錄的學校之間大不相同。有些學校只招收單一性別的學生，而有些學校卻男女兼收。有些學校具有濃厚的宗教或軍事傳統。其它學校則強調智育--例如藝術或科學--或爲具有學習或感情殘障的兒童開設特別課程。

學年有多長？
入學者爲何人？

學年從9月開始，並於6月結束，在12月及3月或4月有兩至三週的假期，在11月則有較短的假期。學校在假期停課。留學生可利用這段時間走訪親友。如果假期較長，有些學校會安排當地的家庭接待留學生。

大多數學校都從北美洲許多地區和若干國家招生。留學生由於身處英文爲母語人士中，並在美加社區生活，而具有獨一無二的機會，可提高其英語能力，並適應北美求學生涯。

課程採用何種結構？

學生於週一至週五上學。學生每週還需再花費若干小時，進行功課預習、圖書館自修和課外活動。學生可在週末參加學校組織的活動、體育運動，並參觀文化中心、逛商店或遊覽名勝。

學業

學校課程包括英語、一門外文、歷史、文學、數學、科學和體育。在選課方面，學生通常有一定的自由度，並可按照自己的進度學習。學校採用小班制，每班有五至十五名學生，學生因此能夠積極參加課堂討論。學校鼓勵學生獨立學習。教師經常在校園或校園附近居住，並爲學生提供課外輔導。高年級學生必須進行大量的閱讀和寫作。留學生要達到這些要求，必須具有相當高的英語水準。

大學諮詢

寄宿學校的大多數畢業生都就讀於四年制大學。學校顧問將協助學生確定適當的學校並填寫申請。大學的競爭非常激烈，爲了能夠入學，留學生必須具有相當高的英文能力。

活動

學生可在課堂外選擇學校組織的多種活動，其中有合唱隊、音樂課、戲劇俱樂部，也有學生報紙、學生會組織及象棋俱樂部。這些活動與要求嚴格的課業形成了平衡，並使學生有機會結交新有，學習新技能。

體育

體育是寄宿學校生活的一個重要部份。大多數學校都有許多體育設施，並提供多種競賽和非競賽項目。學校可參加團體體育運動，例如橄欖球、足球、籃球、棒球、曲棍球和長曲棍球，也可以參加個人體育運動，例如田徑、游泳、體操和網球。

飲食

學校餐廳供應三餐；學校通常要求學生在餐廳用餐。某些學校可能會要求學生協助餐廳服務，並打掃廚房餐廳。在適應學校食物方面有困難的留學生經常從家中攜帶某些容易保存的食物。有些學生在飲食方面有特殊要求，學校通常會滿足其要求。

衣服

寄宿學校不要求正式衣著。很少有學校要求學生穿制服，但是許多學校都有衣著標準（例如這些學校可能會禁止穿藍色牛仔褲）。有些學校要求學生在晚餐時衣著比較正式。有些學校列出須攜帶的衣服，並提供當地的氣候資訊。

校規和政策

為了便於學校管理，社區的所有成員都必須攜手合作。嚴格的校規包括禁煙、禁止持有酒和其它非法毒品、禁止不經請假擅自離校及禁止作弊。學生如不守校規，可能會遭開除。

保健與安全

所有學校都要求學生在入學前接受體檢和基本免疫注射。學校設有配備護士的保健中心，學生也可獲得醫生與醫院服務。提供急診必須經過家長允許。學生必須購買醫療保險。

學校在管理方面都非常嚴格。然而，學生在旅行或離校時必須為自己的安全負責。家長應在子女入學前教育他們了解基本的安全規則。

盡管學校禁毒禁酒，但您必須警告您的子女，有些學生可能會非法擁有毒品或酒，因此應該避開這些人。

住房

學生宿舍通常兩人住宿一間。學校為每名學生提供一張床、一張書桌和一張梳妝台。學生自己負責保持房間清潔和（利用宿舍中的投幣式洗衣機）洗衣。

交通工具

本手冊將幫助留學生家庭找到離學校最近的國際機場。學校通常提供往返機場的交通工具，並可能為這一服務收費。大多數學校不允許寄宿學生擁有自己的汽車。

同家長及監護人之間的溝通

家長通過書面報告和訪問學校了解子女的進展情況。家長如果無法親自到校，則不妨委託親屬或監護人處理這些細節。

應期待何事

北美洲學校的教師對學生的期待可能與在本國時不同。教師期待學生提問、在課堂上自願舉手發言、獨立思考、獨立完成功課，並僅在需要時向教師求助。教師期待學生積極參加活動，並鼓勵學生積極參加活動，並鼓勵學生熱烈討論，保留不同意見。

留學生家庭應當認識到，他們的子女在學校中需要調適。在開學最初幾個月中，留學生因為需要適應新的語言、人、習俗、食物和氣候，

可能會有一段時間的不快樂和寂寞。留學生在求學時必須具有強烈的學習動機，並必須願意刻苦學習、結交新友，並接受新事物。在學業和人際關係方面，留學生顧問、諮詢顧問、教師及舍監可幫助留學生更好地達到學校期望。

今天，美加的寄宿學校正在通過教育學生獨立思考、刻苦學習並了解其他民族和文化、培養未來的領袖。這種教育將使學生終生受益。

Diane Rapp 是聯合教育顧問諮詢公司的總裁,該公司的地址是 85 River Road, Scarborough, New York, 10510。

了解入學程序

您一旦決定送子女到海外留學，就必須了解大學預校通常要求的入學程序。由於各校的要求可能有所不同，我們鼓勵留學生家庭同學校直接聯繫，索要申請期限和說明材料。以下指南將幫助您了解應如何處理入學程序。

開始查詢

請您在閱讀《家庭指南》和學校單頁自我介紹後，選出三到五所您認爲同您的子女教育目標相符的學校。請您在查閱學校說明時考慮下列問題。您的子女在學業上是否能夠適應這所學校的要求？如留學生在英文方面需要大量協助，學校是否開設英語作爲第二語言課程？學校的地點是否符合您的需要？

然後，請您使用本手冊封底的《資訊索要表》，向您的學校名單上的學校索要補充資訊和申請說明。盡管某些學校可以您的母語向您提供一些資訊，大多數學校的函電採用英文。家長必須懂得一些英文，或依賴通曉英文者查閱學校資料並填寫申請。請注意您的子女既將申請的學校的申請期限及考試日期。

申請

請您仔細研究學校的資訊，以決定您的子女是否符合資格。在可能情況下，請安排訪問數所學校。爲了決定哪所學校最適合您的子女，您不妨同招生官員及教師見面，並考察校園。您如無法親自到訪，則不妨同學校在本地的代表團見

面，這些代表通常畢業於您考慮的學校。有時，招生官員也會到海外旅行，同申請人約談。招生官員如計劃到貴國旅行，則可能會同您聯絡，安排見面。

填寫申請表

請填寫申請表，將其寄回有關學校，並用美元或加元交付正確的手續費。大多數學校的申請期限是2月1日。然而，許多學校將留學生的申請期限延遲，因此您不妨了解每所學校的具體政策。

然後，您可請求申請學生的現任教師填寫大多數學校要求的推荐表。學校可能會要求學童的英文老師提供一封推荐信，並由數學老師提供另一封推荐信。請將材料放在信封中，在信封上寫明學校地址並貼足郵資，以便有關教師能夠填寫推荐表，並將其直接寄回學校。

學校記錄必須具有英文本，並儘可能保持準確。寄宿學校僅考慮錄取那些具有準備和誠實記錄及推荐信的學生。

學校可能會要求學生寫作一篇或多篇作文。申請人必須自己獨立完成這些作文，不得要求英文程度較佳者代筆。

請記住：最好的寄宿學校在入學方面競爭非常激烈。學校必須了解您的子女的準備程度以及其爲何願意出國求學。錄取的根據是學生的成績、課程品質、教師意見和推荐信及標準化考試成績。

達到其它錄取要求

本指南中所列的許多學校要求學生參加一項或多項標準化考試。您選擇的學校中，有若干所可能會要求您的子女參加中學入學考試(SSAT)。這一考試衡量學生的數學和英文能力。中學入學考試的國際版專爲英文程度較低的學生編寫，每年在許多國家舉行三次這類考試。您可向寄宿學校索要考試日期，也可向下列地址索要：Secondary School Admission Test, CN 5339, Princeton, NJ 08543. U.S.A., 電話: (609) 683-4440, 傳眞: (609) 683-4507.

中學入學考試外，許多學校還要求提供"托福"(Test of English as a Foreign Language)成績。請您再次查閱學校的招生資料，核對具體的考試要求。

下一步怎麼辦？

大多數學校在3月即向申請人發出錄取通知。申請誤期的學生在招生人員審閱申請材料後即可了解學校的決定。如果您的子女已被錄取，並打算入學，您必須寄回一份經過署名的合同及一筆（以美元或加元支付的）押金，以保留學籍。學校將在夏季寄來下列資料：

● 一份經過學校官員簽名的I-20移民局表格。您必須攜帶該表至最近的美國大使館，申請F-1學生簽證，通常該簽證有效期限爲四年。

● 體檢表。所有學校都要求入學學生接受全面體檢，並提供一份免疫記錄。這些醫療要求是當地的保健部門制定的。如果學生未經適當的免疫注射即入學，則必須接受學校醫療人員的免疫注射。學校將要求家長填表，允許學校爲學生提供急診。

● 保險表。這些表格顯示在學生就讀期間，應有何人支付其醫療費。留學生家庭可自己購買保險。某些學校也提供收費保險。

● 財物資訊。學校將要求家長支付第一學期費用，這一費用包括學費、住房和三餐。書籍費、學生文具品及旅費另記。學生可能還需要支付洗衣費、音樂課費、實驗費、繪畫費或體育運動費。學校可能會要求您向一個學校帳戶支付押金，供學生使用。

● 新生須知。學校將向學生郵寄一份物品單，上列學生應攜帶的衣物和其他物品。學校也將提供有關交通工具安排的資訊。許多學校將在最近的國際機場迎接學生。請務必提前將您的子女的航班資訊通知學校。

您可以陪伴新生入學。學校盡管無法在校園中爲家長提供膳宿，但可安排在附近的旅館中住宿。學校一年中也數次歡迎家長來訪。

欲知詳情

上述資訊因校而異。如您對某所學校的入學程序有疑問，請直接與招生人員或留學生顧問聯絡。爲了便于您查詢，《彼得森美國與加拿大寄宿學校及國際強化項目》收錄了美加400多所學校的電話號碼、通訊地址以及招生官員的姓名。預祝您的子女能夠找到一家如意的大學預科學校。

Diane Rapp 是聯合教育顧問諮詢公司的總裁, 該公司的地址是
85 River Road, Scarborough,
New York, 10510。

Type of school Grade range
Tipo de escuela Número de años escolares
Type d'école Niveaux offerts
学校の種類 学年範囲
學校類別 學歷等級範圍

Percentage of boarding students
Porcentaje de estudiantes internados
Pourcentage de pensionnaires
寄宿生の割合
住校學生的比例

Number of boys in upper school; number of girls in upper school
Número de estudiantes que solicitaron admisión, número de estudiantes
que fueron aceptados.
Nombre de garçons dans les cours supérieurs ; nombre de filles dans
les cours supérieurs
高等課の男子生徒数. 高等課の女子生徒数
上等學校的男生數目；上等學校的女生數目

Number of students who applied, number of students who were accepted
Número de estudiantes que solicitaron admisión;
múmero de estudiantes que fueron aceptados.
Nombre d'élèves ayant déposé une demande d'inscription, nombre d'élèves admis
願書提出者数，合格者数
申請學生的數目，被接受入學許可學生的數目

Percentage of international students
Porcentaje de estudiantes extranjeros
Pourcentage d'élèves étrangers
留学生の割合
外籍學生的比例

Tests required for admission and average level of proficiency attained
by international students accepted
Exámenes requeridos para la admisión y nivel promedio de capacitación
alcanzado por los estudiantes extranjeros aceptados.
Examens d'entrée requis et niveau moyen de compétence des élèves étrangers admis
願書提出前に受験が必要とされる試験と合格した留学生の平均成績
入學許可所需的測驗和外籍學生被接受的平均精通水準

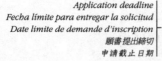

Tests recommended for admission and average level of proficiency
attained by international students accepted
Exámenes recomendados para la admisión y nivel promedio de capacitación
alcanzado por los estudiantes extranjeros aceptados.
Examens d'entrée recommandés et niveau moyen de compétence
des élèves étrangers admis
願書提出前に受験することが望ましい試験と合格した留学生の平均成績
入學許可所推薦的測驗和外籍學生被接受的平均精通水準

Application deadline
Fecha límite para entregar la solicitud
Date limite de demande d'inscription
願書提出締切
申請截止日期

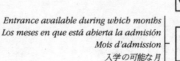

Countries from which the largest number of students come and length of time
school has served them
Los países de los cuales provienen la mayoría de los estudiantes y el tiempo
que éstos han asistido a la escuela
Pays d'où provient le plus grand nombre d'élèves et durée des relations avec l'école
最多数の学生の出身国、これらの学生を受け入れてきた年数
學生數目最多的國家及學生在學年數

Entrance available during which months
Los meses en que está abierta la admisión
Mois d'admission
入学の可能な月
可供入學的月分

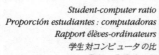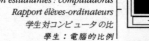

Student-faculty ratio; percentage of teachers living on campus
Proporción estudiantes-profesores; porcentaje de profesores que viven en el recinto
Rapport élèves-enseignants ; Pourcentage d'enseignants résidant sur le campus
学生対教師の比　　キャンパスに住込みの教師の割合
學生：教授的比例；住校教師的比例

Student-computer ratio
Proporción estudiantes : computadoras
Rapport élèves-ordinateurs
学生対コンピュータの比
學生：電腦的比例

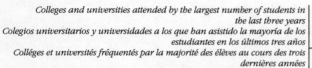

Tuition and room and board; additional mandatory fees
Matrícula y tarifas de alojamiento y comida; tarifas obligatorias adicionales
Frais de scolarité et pension ; autres frais obligatoires
学費と寄宿費・食費，それ以外の必要雑費
學費，住宿和夥食；其他應付費用

Colleges and universities attended by the largest number of students in
the last three years
Colegios universitarios y universidades a los que han asistido la mayoría de los
estudiantes en los últimos tres años
Collèges et universités fréquentés par la majorité des élèves au cours des trois
dernières années
過去3年間に卒業生の最大数が入学した大学
過去三年内學生數目最多的學院和大學

Availability of English as a second language (ESL) courses
Disponibilidad de los cursos de ingles como segundo idioma (ESL)
Disponibilité de cours d'anglais comme langue étrangère
学期開始前に英語プログラムおよび異文化教育プログラムあり
設有(ESL)課程

Secondary-level summer program
Programa de verano para nivel secundario
Programme d'été de niveau secondaire
中等レベルの夏期プログラムあり
第二階段暑期課程

Personal or telephone interview required
Se requiere entrevista personal o telefónica
Entrevue obligatoire par téléphone ou en personne
面接もしくは電話によるインタビューあり
必須當面或以電話面試

Dress code
Reglamento de vestimenta
Code vestimentaire
服装に関する規定あり
服飾慣例

ONE-PAGE PRESENTATIONS

LAS PRESENTACIONES DE UNA PÁGINA •
PRÉSENTATIONS D'UNE PAGE • 各校のご案内 • 單頁學校簡介

Schools in this section supplied additional information about themselves and supported the distribution of this directory to help international families understand the value of private schools and the spectrum of schools serving international students.

Los colegios en esta sección proporcionan información adicional sobre sus programas e instalaciones y apoyaron la distribución de este directorio para ayudar a las familias extranjeras a entender las ventajas de los colegios privados y la variedad de colegios que están a disposición de los estudiantes extranjeros.

Les écoles, dans ce paragraphe, donnent davantage de reseignements sur leurs établissements. Ces derniers ont contribué à la distribution de ce répertoire afin d'aider les familles étrangères à comprendre la valeur des écoles privées et de prendre connaissance de l'éventail d'écoles qui est à la disposition des élèves du monde entier.

ここに掲載されている各校には、詳しい学校案内を提供していただくとともに、本書の配布にご協力いただきました。外国に皆様に私立学校の長所をお伝えし、外国人生徒を受け入れている多くの学校を紹介することができれば幸いです。

本節中的學校提供補充資訊學並支持分發本指南學目的是幫助留學生了解私校的價值及各類招收留學生的學校。

Admiral Farragut Academy

UNITED STATES

David Graham, Admissions Director
501 Park Street North
St. Petersburg, Florida 33710
Phone: 727-384-5500 Fax: 727-384-5160
URL: http://www.farragut.org

NAIS member   *Founded 1933*

Admiral Farragut Academy is a coed, college-preparatory boarding and day school for grades 6–12 with military exposure. Located on a safe waterfront setting, international students come from about 15 different countries to prepare for America's best universities. A year-round ESOL program incorporates international students in all campus activities, including aviation, SCUBA, riflery, sailing, 17 sports, and various social activities.

Admiral Farragut Academy es una escuela diurna de preparación universitaria para estudiantes de ambos sexos en los grados de 6 a 12 con exposición militar. Localizada en un lugar seguro frente al agua, los estudiantes internacionales vienen de 15 países diferentes para prepararse para las mejores universidades estadounidenses. Durante todo el año el programa de Inglés para Estudiantes de otros Idiomas (siglas en inglés ESOL) incorpora estudiantes internacionales en todas sus actividades del recinto que incluyen aviación, SCUBA, tiro al blanco, vela, 17 deportes y varias actividades sociales.

Admiral Farragut Academy est un établissement mixte de préparation universitaire et une école militaire offrant internat et externat pour les étudiants des niveaux 6 à 12 (« 6 - 12 grades »). L'Academy offre un complexe situé en bord de mer dans un lieu garantissant de très bonnes conditions de sécurité. Les étudiants internationaux proviennent de 15 pays différents et s'inscrivent pour se préparer à l'entrée aux meilleures universités américaines. Un programme ESOL de cours d'anglais (English for speakers of other languages) est proposé aux étudiants internationaux et conjugué avec toutes les activités du campus comprenant notamment aviation, plongée, tir, voile, 17 sports et de nombreux activités sociales.

Admiral Farragut Academy は、男女共学の軍教育を基本にした、 大学進学のための寄宿校と全日制校で、6 年生から 12 年生までを対象にしています。安全な海岸に位置し、15 カ国からの留学生が、アメリカの最も優秀な大学入学を目指し準備しています。年間を通してのESOL プログラムが留学生に導入され、全キャンパスの活動には、スキューバ、ライフル、セーリング等、17 のスポーツと多彩な社会活動があります。

Admiral Farragut Academy 為男女生共校，提供住宿制和全天制的大學預科學校。6 至 12 年級的學生在此校將學到軍事知識。校址安全而臨水，來自 15 個不同的國家的國際學生選擇此校，在此為進入美國的頂尖大學做準備。學校全年開設 ESOL，以便國際學生積極融入所有的校園活動，包括飛行，潛水，步槍打靶，航海術，17 項體育運動以及各種社交活動。

A 55-acre waterfront on a safe boarding campus.

Un recinto de hospedaje seguro de 55 acres a orillas del agua.

Le campus de l'internat s'étend sur une zone au bord de l'eau de 22 hectares.

海岸沿い 22 ヘクタールの安全な寄宿学校。

位于 55 英畝安全的水景區的住宿校園。

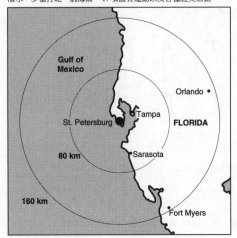

 15–30°C

 10–20°C

 15–25°C

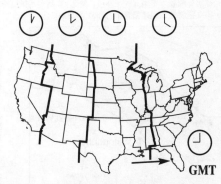

GMT

30 km from Tampa International Airport and Tampa, FL
A 30 km del aeropuerto internacional de Tampa y de Tampa, FL
A 30 km de l'aéroport international de Tampa et de Tampa, FL
フロリダ州タンパ国際空港及び同州タンパ市より 30 キロ
離 Tampa 國際機場和佛羅里達州 Tampa 市各 30 公里

 Coeducational / Mixto / Mixte
男女共学
男女合校

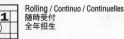 344/131

 38%

9%

 250, 175 / solicitaron admisión, fueron aceptados / candidats, admis
出願者数250 名，合格者数175 名
250 人申請，175 人被録取

 SLEP, SSAT, ISEE

Bahamas, Brazil, Cayman Islands, Czech Republic, Germany, Korea, Saudi Arabia

 Rolling / Continuo / Continuelles
随時受付
全年招生

 Rolling / Continuo / Continuelles
随時受付
全年招生

 10:1, 15%

1:1

 $28,100, $10,800; $4500

 Embry-Riddle Aeronautical University, Florida State University, United States Naval Academy, University of Florida, University of South Florida

The Andrews School

Rosanna S. Sprague, Director of Admission
38588 Mentor Avenue
Willoughby, Ohio 44094
Phone: 440-942-3606 or 800-753-4683
Fax: 440-954-5020

TABS, FAIS, NAFSA member *Founded 1910*

Andrews offers international students an outstanding college-preparatory program that fosters individual growth, intellectual achievement, and a desire to reach one's highest potential, resulting in 100 percent college placement. Activities on and off campus enhance formal study. Summer ESL Institute provides intensive academic training by experienced ESL teachers to prepare for classes and life in the U.S.

Andrews ofrece a los estudiantes extranjeros un programa de preparación para la universidad excepcional que estimula el crecimiento personal, el logro intelectual y el deseo de desarrollar al máximo las posibilidades individuales, lo que resulta en un 100% de ingresos universitarios. Las actividades dentro y fuera del recinto amplían los estudios formales. El Instituto de Verano de estudios del inglés como segundo idioma (ESL) ofrece un programa de capacitación académica intensivo, impartido por profesores de inglés con experiencia, que prepara a los alumnos para estudiar y vivir en los Estados Unidos.

Andrews propose aux étudiants étrangers un excellent programme préparant à l'entrée en université et favorisant le développement personnel, le succès intellectuel et le désir d'aller jusqu'au bout de ses possibilités. C'est pourquoi 100 % des étudiants sont admis dans les universités de leur choix. Les activités sur et en dehors du campus consolident les études académiques. L'institut chargé de l'enseignement de l'anglais comme langue étrangère à Andrews propose, l'été, une formation intensive dispensée par des professeurs d'anglais comme langue étrangère expérimentés afin de préparer les étudiants à la vie et à la scolarité aux États-Unis.

Andrews では、個々の成長、知的成就、一人一人が持つ最高の可能性に到達できるように願って、優れた大学準備プログラムを提供し、100% が大学に入学しています。キャンパス内外の活動は、正式な学習の手助けとなります。ESL の夏期講習は、アメリカでの授業と生活の準備をするため、経験豊かな ESL の教師による集中的なアカデミック・トレーニングを提供しています。

聖安德魯斯學校為小型、安全的住宿學校，提供要求嚴格的大學預科課程，其中包括中級和高級外國學生英語課程。該校花費 2,500 萬美元新建一座美術室和一個學生公共活動場，不久還將動工興建體育中心和表演藝術中心。

The 360-acre campus includes redecorated dormitories, equestrian center, a new field house, and a new observatory.
Las 146 hectáreas de terreno incluyen residencias estudiantiles redecoradas, un centro de equitación, una nueva casa de campo y un nuevo observatorio.
Le campus de 146 hectares comprend des dortoirs, un centre équestre, un complexe sportif et un observatoire.
146 ヘクタールのキャンパスには寮、乗馬センター、フィールド・ハウスの他、天文台が完備されています。
佔地 146 公頃的校園包括宿舍、騎馬中心，體育館和觀象臺。

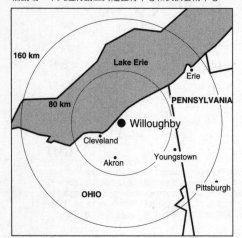

 1–23°C

 -8–3°C

 -2–21°C

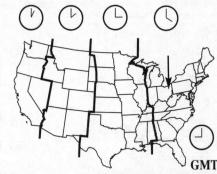

GMT

48 km from Cleveland Hopkins Airport; 29 km from Cleveland, OH
A 48 km del aeropuerto Hopkins de Cleveland; a 29 km de Cleveland, OH
A 48 km de l'aéroport Hopkins de Cleveland ; à 29 km de Cleveland, OH
クリーブランド・ホプキンズ空港より 48 キロ、オハイオ州クリーブランド市より 29 キロ
離 Cleveland 市 Hopkins 機場 48 公里；離 Cleveland, OH 29 公里

 Girls College Prep (6–12) / Niñas / Filles
女子中学校
女子中學校

 175, 112 / solicitaron admisión, fueron aceptadas / candidates, admises
出願者数 175 名、合格者数 112 名
175 人申請，112 人被錄取

 Rolling / Continuo / Continuelles
随時受付
全年招生

 $27,200; $1500

 ESL 1, 2, 3, 4 levels / ESL 1, 2, 3, 4 niveles / Anglais comme langue étrangère niveaux 1, 2, 3, 4
ESL レベル 1, 2, 3, 4
一、二、三、級水平

 0/175

 TOEFL, SLEP, SSAT, ISEE

 September, January, August / septiembre, enero, agosto / septembre, janvier, août
9 月、1 月、8 月
9 月，1 月，8 月

 ESL camp offered July/August
Campo de Inglés como segundo idioma (ESL) se ofrece en julio/agosto
Stage d'anglais comme langue étrangère juillet/août
ESL キャンプ 7/8 月
7 月/8 月開設 ESL 營校

 35%

 5:1, 40%

Boston University, Carnegie Mellon University, Case Western Reserve University, Purdue University

 19%

Africa, China, Dominican Republic, Germany, Jamaica, Japan, Korea, Mexico, Taiwan, Thailand, Venezuela

 3:1

Antelope Valley Christian School

UNITED STATES

3700 West Avenue L
Lancaster, California 93536
Phone: 661-943-0044 Fax: 661-943-6774
E-mail: iie@avcs.edu
URL: http://www.avcs.edu

RESIDENTIAL CENTER III

NAFSA member   *Founded 1988*

Students develop strong English and leadership skills in a caring community. A personalized ESL program and fully accredited college-prep academics are united with competitive athletics, fine arts, and Christian values. A variety of programs include a traditional school year, short-term home stays, and year-round academics.

Los estudiantes desarrollan excelentes aptitudes de liderazgo y dominio del inglés en una comunidad que se preocupa por el bienestar de sus integrantes. Un programa personalizado de inglés como segundo idioma (ESL) y un plan de estudios plenamente acreditado de preparación para la universidad, que se complementan con deportes competitivos, bellas artes y valores cristianos. Entre la variedad de programas se cuentan un año escolar tradicional, breves periodos de alojamiento con familias locales y un programa de estudios durante todo el año.

Les étudiants développent une solide maîtrise de l'anglais ainsi que des talents de leadership au sein d'une communauté humanitaire. Un programme d'anglais comme langue étrangère (ESL) personnalisé ainsi qu'un cursus scolaire agréé, préparant à l'entrée en université, sont complétés par des activités sportives de compétition, les beaux-arts et les valeurs chrétiennes. Une grande variété de programmes sont offerts tout au long de l'année, pendant l'année scolaire traditionnelle ou bien pendant des séjours à court terme.

学生は面倒見のよいコミュニティの中で英語と強固なリーダーシップスキルを身につけます。個別の ESL プログラムと完全に品質保証された大学準備コースは、競技スポーツや美術、キリスト教理念と一体化されています。プログラムは伝統的な学校年度、短期ホームステイ、および年間学科コースなど多様です。

學生們在富於愛心的集體環境中培養扎實的英語能力和領導技能。個人化的 ESL 課程及全面鑑定合格的大學預備課程，與競爭性體育活動、美術和基督教價值觀相結合。多種項目包括傳統學年，當地家庭短期寄宿，以及全年學習課程。

A 35-acre campus with a new technology center and gymnasium.
Un recinto escolar de 15 hectáreas de terreno con un nuevo centro de tecnología y un gimnasio.
Un campus de 14 hectares avec un nouveau centre technologique et un gymnase.
新テクノロジー・センターや体育館のある全 14 ヘクタールのキャンパス。
校園面積 14 公頃，擁有一座新的科技中心和體育館。

 8–32°C

 -2–16°C

 8–32°C

GMT

118 km from Los Angeles International Airport; 112 km from Los Angeles
A 118 km del Aeropuerto Internacional de Los Angeles; a 112 km de Los Angeles.
À 118 km de l'aéroport international de Los Angeles ; à 112 km de Los Angeles
ロサンゼルス国際空港から 118km、ロサンゼルス市から 112 km。
離洛杉磯國際機場 8 公里；離洛杉磯市 12 公里

 Coeducational pre-K–12 / Mixto / Mixte
男女共学
男女合校

 60/40

 15%

 15%

 40, 35 / solicitaron admisión, fueron aceptados / candidats, admis
出願者数 40 名、合格者数 35 名
40 人申請，35 人被錄取

 Taiwan (4), Korea (5), Hong Kong (4), Japan (4), Thailand (6)

 Rolling / Continuo / Continuelles
随時受付
全年招生

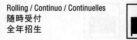 Rolling / Continuo / Continuelles
随時受付
全年招生

 14:1

 3:1

 $23,500; $100

 University of California–Riverside, California State University–Northridge, California State University–Long Beach, Pepperdine University, San Jose Christian College

Asheville School

Vicki Wright, Director of Admission
360 Asheville School Road
Asheville, North Carolina 28806
Phone: 828-254-6345 Fax: 828-210-6109
E-mail: admission@ashevilleschool.org
URL: http://www.ashevilleschool.org

TABS, FAIS member   *Founded 1900*

Academic excellence is the primary emphasis of Asheville School. Opportunities in afternoon athletics, mountaineering, horseback riding, art, music, and drama are available.

El logro de los objetivos académicos es el principal énfasis de Asheville School. Se encuentran disponibles actividades deportivas en las tardes, montañismo, equitación, arte, música y clases de actuación.

Pour Asheville School, la priorité est d'obtenir d'excellents résultats scolaires. Cependant, les élèves peuvent aussi faire du sport après les cours, ainsi que de l'alpinisme et de l'équitation, et participer à des programmes d'art, de musique et de théâtre.

Asheville School は卓越した教育・学問に最も重点を置いています。午後のスポーツ活動として、登山、乗馬、芸術、音楽、演劇などを提供しています。

Asheville 中學的教育著重學術的專精，同時學生也有機會參與午后運動、登山、騎馬、藝術、音樂及戲劇等活動。

Asheville School is set on 300 acres overlooking the Blue Ridge Mountains.

Asheville School está situado en 122 hectáreas con vista panorámica de las montañas Blue Ridge.

Asheville School est située dans un domaine de 122 hectares avec vue sur les monts Blue Ridge.

122 ヘクタールの当校キャンパスからは、ブルーリッジ山を見渡せます。

Asheville 中學佔地 122 公頃，校園俯瞰 Blue Ridge 。

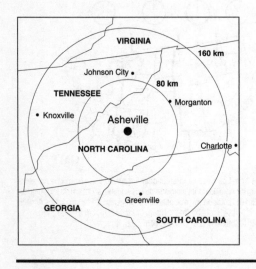

 22–24°C

 3–13°C

 28–33°C

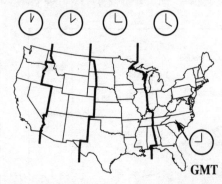

GMT

20 km from Asheville Airport / A 20 km del aeropuerto de Asheville / À 20 km de l'aéroport de Asheville
Asheville 空港より 20 キロ
離 Asheville 機場 20 公里

 Coeducational 9–12 / Mixto / Mixte
男女共学
男女合校

 259, 133 / solicitaron admisión, fueron aceptados / candidats, admis
出願者数 259 名、合格者数 133 名
259 人申請，133 人被録取

 February 1 / 1 de febrero / 1 février
2 月 1 日
2 月 1 日

 $30,675

 118/124

 TOEFL (500 Paper)
Computer (173)

 August / agosto / août
8 月
8 月

 Summer Academic Adventures

 83%

 5.1, 70%

 Appalachian State University, College of Charleston, Davidson College, Duke University, North Carolina State University, Rhodes College, The University of North Carolina at Chapel Hill, University of Virginia, Vanderbilt University

 15%

 1:1

 Bahamas, Bulgaria, Canada, Germany, Greece, Jamaica, Korea, Morocco, Philippines, Saudi Arabia, Scotland, Thailand, Zimbabwe

The Athenian School

Christopher Beeson, Director of Admission
2100 Mt. Diablo Scenic Boulevard
Danville, California 94526
Phone: 925-362-7223 Fax: 925-855-9342

TABS, NAIS, NAFSA member *Founded 1965*

Athenian's distinguished program options includes advanced and intermediate ESL, humanities seminars, required community service, outdoor education, and the Athenian Wilderness Experience. Virtually 100 percent of students attend university, and most gain admission to their first-choice four-year university.

Los prestigiosos programas de Atenían incluyen clases de inglés como segundo idioma (ESL), con niveles avanzado e intermedio, seminarios de humanidades, servicios requeridos a la comunidad, educación al aire libre y el programa de experimentación de la vida silvestre Athenian. Prácticamente el 100% de los estudiantes asisten a la universidad y la mayoría son aceptados en programas de estudios de cuatro años de las universidades que han seleccionado como primera opción.

Le programme réputé de l'établissement Athenian comprend des cours d'anglais comme langue étrangère (ESL) de niveaux « avancé » et « intermédiaire », des séminaires sur les sciences humaines, un bénévolat obligatoire, un programme pédagogique de plein air et la découverte de régions sauvages. Quasiment 100 % des étudiants entrent à l'université, la plupart d'entre eux étant admis à l'université de leur choix pour un programme de quatre ans.

Athenian の優れたプログラムには、上級および中級の ESL、人文科学セミナー、必修のコミュニティサービス、野外教育、および Athenian Wilderness Experience が含まれます。実質的に 100% の学生が総合大学に進学し、そのほとんどが第 1 志望の四年制大学から入学が許可されています。

Athenian 學校的有名課程包括高級和中級 ESL、人文學科研討會、必需的社區服務、戶外教育和 Athenian 野外生活體驗。參加此校的學生基本上百分之百升入大學，他們中絕大多數考入第一志願的大學。

75-acre campus, beautiful facilities, access to the San Francisco area.
El recinto de 30 hectáreas de terreno ofrece bellas instalaciones y acceso a la ciudad de San Francisco y sus alrededores.
Le campus de 30 hectares offre des installations magnifiques, ainsi qu'un accès vers San Francisco et ses alentours.
サンフランシスコを見渡す 30 ヘクタールのキャンパスと美しい施設が整っています。
佔地 30 公頃的校園，優雅的校舍，鄰近舊金山地區。

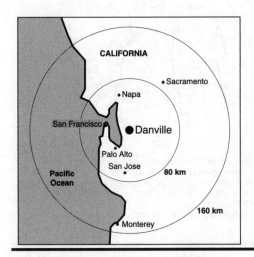

 4–26°C

 -2–21°C

 4–25°C

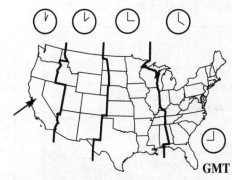

GMT

60 km from San Francisco Airport and San Francisco, CA
A 60 km del aeropuerto de San Francisco y de San Francisco, CA
A 60 km de l'aéroport de San Francisco et de San Francisco, CA
カリフォルニア州サンフランシスコ空港及びサンフランシスコ市より 60 キロ
離 San Francisco 機場和 San Francisco 市各 60 公里

 Coeducational 6–12 / Mixto / Mixte
男女共学
男女合校

 140/150

 14%

 11%

 300, 117 / solicitaron admisión, fueron aceptados / candidats, admis
出願者数 300 名，合格者数 117 名
300 人申請，117 人被録取

 TOEFL (CBT 110) or SLEP (47–50)

 Germany (6), Hong Kong (20), Japan (20), Korea (20), Taiwan (20), Thailand (11)

 Rolling / Continuo / Continuelles
随時受付
全年招生

 September / septiembre / septembre
9 月
9 月

 10:1, 50%

 10:1

 $34,500; $2775

 Boston University, Columbia University, New York University, University of California at Berkeley, University of California at Davis

Avon Old Farms School

UNITED STATES

Mr. Brendon Welker, Director of Admissions
500 Old Farms Road
Avon, Connecticut 06001
Phone: 860-673-3244 Fax: 860-675-6051
E-mail: admissions@avonoldfarms.com
URL: http://www.avonoldfarms.com

NAIS, TABS, FAIS, SSATB, CAIS member   *Founded 1927*

Avon is known for its close community, friendly boys, exuberant school spirit, and breathtaking architecture. The school's competitive academic program is supportive, with substantial individual help. Students participate in a strong athletic program with team and individual sports. There are excellent opportunities in visual arts, chorus, drama, and jazz band.

Avon es reconocido por su comunidad pequeña, sus estudiante amistosos, su exuberante espíritu académico y su asombrosa arquitectura. El excelente programa académico del colegio incluye considerable ayuda y apoyo individual. Los estudiantes participan en un exigente programa atlético que incluye actividades deportivas individuales y en equipo. Se ofrecen excelentes oportunidades en artes visuales, coro, teatro y bandas de jazz.

Avon est réputé pour sa communauté conviviale, ses étudiants chaleureux, son esprit communicatif et sa magnifique architecture. Le programme scolaire compétitif de l'école repose sur la coopération et sur l'aide individuelle substantielle. Les étudiants participent à un programme sportif solide composé de sports individuels et d'équipe. Avon propose également d'excellentes activités dans les arts visuels, le chant, le théâtre et le jazz.

Avon は親密なコミュニティ、親切な男子学生、熱気のある元気な校風と息をのむような美しい建造物で知られています。当校のすばらしい学業プログラムは、生徒一人一人へのサポートが充実しています。チームもしくは個人競技の強力な運動プログラムの他、視覚芸術、コーラス、演劇、そしてジャズ・バンドなどのすばらしい機会に恵まれています。

愛旺學校以社區親近、學生友好、學校精神昂揚、建築美觀而享有盛名。該校的學習課程既有競爭性，又注重幫助學生，提供大量的個人輔導。學生參加強盛的體育培訓課程，包括集體項目和個人項目。該校有絕佳的影視、合唱、戲劇及爵士樂隊等方面參與機會

A computer network provides campus-wide communication and Internet access.

Una red de computadoras proporciona al recinto escolar acceso a comunicaciones y a Internet.

Le réseau informatique de l'école permet d'avoir accès à Internet et de communiquer au sein du campus.

コンピュータネットワークにより、キャンパス内の通信およびインターネットにアクセスできます。

電腦網絡提供校園通訊手段和使用網際網路的能力。

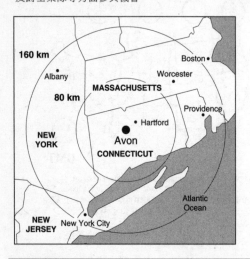

 11°C

 -3°C

 9°C

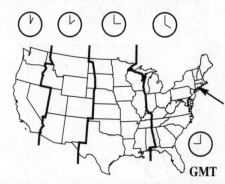

GMT

24 km from Bradley International Airport; 14 km from Hartford, CT
A 24 km del aeropuerto internacional de Bradley; a 14 km de Hartford, CT
A 24 km de l'aéroport international de Bradley ; à 14 km de Hartford, CT
ブラッドリー国際空港より 24 キロ、コネチカット州ハートフォード市より 14 キロ
離 Bradley 國際機場 24 公里；離 Hartford, CT 14 公里

 Boys 9–12 / Muchachos / Garçons
男子中學校
男子中學校

 433, 267 / solicitaron admisión, fueron aceptados / candidats, admis
出願者数 433 名、合格者数 267 名
433 人申請，267 人被錄取

 February 1, then rolling / 1 de febrero, continuo / 1 février, continuelles
2 月 1 日より随時受付
2 月 1 日起随時皆可

 $32,850; $2800

 385/0

 TOEFL (207)

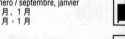 September, January / septiembre, enero / septembre, janvier
9 月、1 月
9 月、1 月

 80%

 6:1, 78%

 Boston College, Emory University, Trinity College, United States Naval Academy, Yale University

 10%

 Canada, Germany, Korea, Panama, Taiwan

 1:1

Baylor School

Bill Murdock, Director of Admission
Williams Island Ferry Road
Chattanooga, Tennessee 37405
Phone: 423-267-8505 Fax: 423-265-4276

TABS, FAIS, NAIS member   *Founded 1893*

Baylor offers rigorous college-preparatory academics, required study halls, 18 advanced placement courses, a range of honors courses, close student-faculty interaction, and a strong adviser system. Students participate in 40 extracurricular groups, 17 varsity sports, weekend social events, and a nationally known outdoor program. Each year, boarding students represent 10-15 foreign countries and 15-20 states in the U.S.

Baylor ofrece un riguroso programa académico de preparación para la universidad, salones de estudio obligatorio, 18 cursos avanzados, y una variedad de cursos de honor, una estrecha interacción entre alumnos y profesores y un sistema de asesoramiento bien estructurado. Los estudiantes participan en 40 grupos extracurriculares, 17 deportes universitarios, eventos sociales de fin de semana y un programa de actividades al aire libre de reconocido prestigio dentro del país. Cada año, los estudiantes internos representan de 10 a 15 países y de 15 a 20 estados de los EE.UU.

Baylor offre un programme scolaire rigoureux préparant à l'entrée dans les universités, avec des heures d'études obligatoires, 18 cours préparant à l'enseignement supérieur et un choix de cours de licence, une collaboration étroite entre élèves et professeurs et une solide structure de conseillers. Les étudiants ont à leur disposition 40 groupes d'activités périscolaires, 17 sports pratiqués entre équipes de différentes écoles, des animations le week-end, ainsi qu'un programme de plein air connu dans l'ensemble du pays. Chaque année, les étudiants internes représentent de 10 à 15 pays étrangers et de 15 à 20 États des États-Unis.

Baylor では、厳格な大学進学準備教育、必修の自習時間、18 の上級クラス進級コース、各優秀コース、教師と生徒の密接な関係、卓越した指導教師システムを提供しています。学生は 40 の課外グループ、17 のスポーツの代表チーム、週末の社会イベント、全国的に有名なアウトドア・プログラムに参加します。毎年、海外 10-15 ヶ国、また国内 15-20 州からの学生が寄宿します。

Baylor School 提供高強度的大學預科學術課程，必須使用的自學廳，18 種高級入學課以及一系列榮譽課程，密切的師生聯係，以及一個效力顯著的導師制。學生們參加 40 個課外團體，17 種校隊體育運動，各項周末活動，以及一項全國有名的戶外項目。每年有來自 10 至 15 個國家和美國 15 至 20 個州的學生住校就讀。

The beautiful 670-acre campus is on the Tennessee River

El bello recinto de 271 hectáreas se encuentra a la orilla del río Tennessee.

Le magnifique campus de 271 hectares est situé sur la rivière du Tennessee.

271 ヘクタールのキャンパスはテネシー川岸に位置しています。

校園佔地 271 公頃，位于田納西河畔。

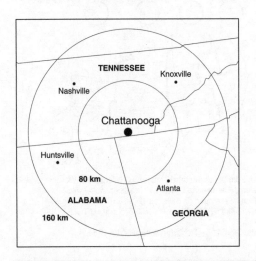

TENNESSEE
Knoxville
Nashville
Chattanooga
Huntsville
80 km
Atlanta
ALABAMA
160 km   **GEORGIA**

 9–22°C

 -3–8°C

 13–25°C

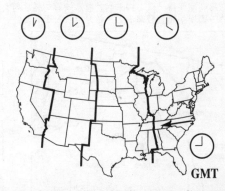

GMT

24 km from Chattanooga Airport; 8 km from downtown Chattanooga, TN
A 24 km del aeropuerto de Chattanooga; a 8 km del centro de Chattanooga, TN
A 24 km de l'aéroport de Chattanooga ; à 8 km du centre ville de Chattanooga, TN
チャタヌガ空港より 24 キロ、テネシー州チャタヌガ市のダウンタウンより 8 キロ
離 Chattanooga 機場 24 公里；離 Chattanooga, TN 8 公里

 Coeducational 9–12 / Mixto / Mixte
男女共学
男女合校

 325/290

 30%

 6%

 140, 80 / solicitaron admisión, fueron aceptados / candidats, admis
出願者数 140 名、合格者数 80 名
140 人申請，80 人被錄取

 ✓

 TOEFL, SSAT (480), SLEP (52), ISEE

 Germany (6), Japan (9), Korea (7), Saudi Arabia (18), Thailand (10)

 Rolling / Continuo / Continuelles
隨時受付
全年招生

 July / julio / juillet
7 月
7 月

 8:1, 30%

 3:1

 $25,028

 Vanderbilt University, University of Tennessee, University of Georgia, University of the South, Duke University

Blue Ridge School

David Hodgson, Director of Admissions
St. George, Virginia 22935
Phone: 434-985-2811 Fax: 434-985-7215
E-mail: admissions@blueridgeschool.com

TABS, NAIS member   *Founded 1909*

International students find small classes; a supportive ESL program; close interaction between students and faculty members; a consistent, daily routine; a wide variety of weekend activities; and frequent reports to parents, all of which help them to reach their full potential and prepare them for college admission.

Los estudiantes extranjeros encuentran clases con pocos alumnos; un programa de inglés como segundo idioma (ESL) con mucho apoyo; estrecha interacción entre alumnos y miembros del profesorado; una rutina diaria coherente; una amplia variedad de actividades de fin de semana y la información que se entrega frecuentemente a los padres, todo lo cual ayuda a los jóvenes a desarrollar al máximo su potencial y los prepara para ser admitidos en la universidad.

Les étudiants étrangers bénéficient de classes restreintes, d'un programme d'anglais comme langue étrangère (ESL) solide, d'une collaboration étroite entre étudiants et membres du corps enseignant, d'un emploi du temps quotidien homogène et d'une grande variété d'activités le week-end leur permettant de s'épanouir et de préparer leur entrée à l'université ; les parents reçoivent par ailleurs des compte-rendus bimensuels.

きめ細やかな ESL プログラム、学生と教授との親密な交流、一貫した毎日の日課、週末の多彩な催し、隔月の家庭への報告など、留学生は少人数クラスで自己の可能性を十分伸ばし、大学進学に備えることができます。

外國學生小班上課；外國學生英語課程提供週到的幫助；師生密切交流；每日作息時間保持一致；週末活動豐富多彩；經常向家長報告情況。這些均有助於外國學生充分發揮潛力，做好考入大學的準備。

Newly renovated academic building and dormitories on a 1,000-acre mountain campus with lakes, streams, and fields.

Edificio académico y residencias estudiantiles recién renovadas en un terreno montañoso de 400 hectáreas que contiene lagos, riachuelos y prados.

Avec ses installations scolaires nouvellement renovées et ses dortoirs, le campus est situé sur 400 hectares dans les montagnes et comprend des lacs, ruisseaux et des champs.

新たに修復された校舎と寄宿舎が、湖や小川、野原を含んだ山中の 400 ヘクタールのキャンパスにあります。

最新修善的教學樓和宿舍位於山區中占地 400 公頃的校園中，座落於湖泊、溪流和曠野之間。

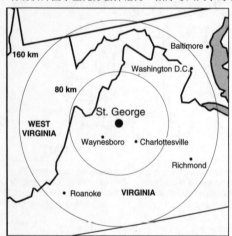

 4–24°C

 -3–14°C

 9–26°

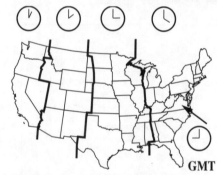
GMT

70 km from Dulles Airport; 12 km from Charlottesville, VA
A 70 km del aeropuerto Dulles; a 12 km de Charlottesville, VA
A 70 km de l'aéroport de Dulles ; à 12 km de Charlottesville, VA
ダラス空港より 70 キロ、バージニア州シャーロットビルより 12 キロ
離 Dulles 機場 70 公里；離 Charlottesville, VA 12 公里

 Boys 9–12 / Muchachos / Garçons
男子中学校
男子中學校

 194/0

 100%

 11%

 205, 140 / solicitaron admisión, fueron aceptados / candidats, admis
出願者数 205 名、合格者数 140 名
205 人申請，140 人被錄取

 TOEFL, SLEP

 China (1), Egypt (3), Georgia (1), Germany (6), Japan (3), Korea (14), Mauritania (2), Nigeria (2), Saudi Arabia (16), Spain (1), Taiwan (4)

 February 1, Rolling / 1 de febrero, Continuo / 1er février, Continuelles
2 月 1 日より随時受付
2 月 1 日起随時皆可

 Rolling / Continuo / Continuelles
随時受付
全年招生

 8:1, 95%

 6:1

 $29,358; $2000 ($2500 ESL)

 Hampden-Sydney College, James Madison University, Radford University, Roanoke College, Virginia Military Institute, Virginia Tech University, Western Maryland College, College of William & Mary

Brenau Academy

UNITED STATES

Leslie N. Miller, Director of Admissions
1 Centennial Circle
Gainesville, Georgia 30501
Phone: 770-534-6140 Fax: 770-534-6298
E-mail: enroll@lib.brenau.edu
URL: http://www.brenauacademy.org

TABS, NAIS member   *Founded 1928*

Brenau enrolls students from a variety of countries. We specialize in English mastery, performing arts, and chaperoned weekend activities. An hour from Atlanta's international airport, transportation from anyplace is easy.

Brenau admite estudiantes de una variedad de países. Nos especializamos en cursos para dominar el idioma inglés a la perfección, artes escénicas y actividades con acompañantes los fines de semana. A una hora del aeropuerto internacional de Atlanta, hay facilidad de transporte desde cualquier punto.

Brenau accueille des étudiants de différents pays. Nous sommes spécialisés dans la maîtrise de l'anglais, les arts du spectacle et les activités surveillées le week-end. À une heure de l'aéroport international d'Atlanta, la situation géographique de notre établissement facilite tous les déplacements.

Brenau には様々な国からの留学生が学んでいます。当校は英語修得、舞台芸術を専門とし、週末の諸活動にも付き添います。アトランタ国際空港から1時間など、どこからでも交通の便に優れています。

Brenau 招收很多國家的學生。本校專長提供英語精熟課程，表演藝術課程，以及由教師監護的週末活動。離亞特蘭大國際機場僅一小時路程，來往各處都很方便。

The 56-acre campus has fifty buildings.
Las 25 hectáreas de terreno tienen cincuenta edificios.
Le campus de 25 hectares est doté de cinquante bâtiments.
25 ヘクタールのキャンパスには 50 の建物が並んでいます。
校園面積 25公頃，有 50幢大樓。

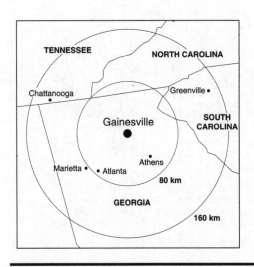

 15°–32° C

 7°–10° C

 16°–32° C

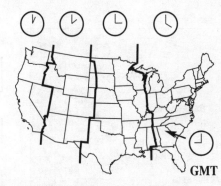

GMT

81 km from Atlanta Airport; 81 km from Atlanta, GA
A 81 km del aeropuerto de Atlanta; a 81 km del Atlanta, GA
A 81 km de l'aéroport d'Atlanta ; a 81 km de Atlanta, GA
ジョージア州アトランタ空港より 81 キロ、同州アトランタより 81 キロ
離 Atlanta 機場 81 公里；離喬治亞州 Atlanta 市 81 公里

 Girls 9–12 / Niñas / Filles
女子中学校
女子中學校

 0/80

 90%

 15%

 45, 30 / solicitaron admisión, fueron aceptadas / candidates, admises
出願者数 45 名、合格者数 30 名
45 人申請，30 人被錄取

 ✓

 Australia (1), Bermuda (2), China (1), Korea (3), Taiwan (1)

 Rolling / Continuo / Continuelles
随時受付
全年招生

 August / agosto / août
8月
8月

 8:1, 0%

 2:1

 $20,500; $500

 Boston College, Brenau University, Georgia Institute of Technology, University of Georgia, University of Mississippi, Savannah College of Art and Design, University of Texas at Austin

Brooks School

Judith S. Beams, Director of Admission
1160 Great Pond Road
North Andover, Massachusetts 01845-1298
Phone: 978-686-6101 Fax: 978-725-6298
E-mail: admission@brooksschool.org
URL: http://www.brooksschool.org

NAIS, TABS, NAFSA member   *Founded 1926*

Brooks has enrolled students from roughly 35 countries over the past five years and still enjoys exchange programs with schools in Hungary, Kenya, South Africa, and Scotland. Applicants must have a strong background in English.

En los últimos cinco años, se han matriculado en Brooks estudiantes provenientes de cerca de 35 países, y continúa ofreciendo programas de intercambio estudiantil con colegios en Hungría, Kenia, Sudáfrica y Escocia. Para ser admitidos en el colegio, los alumnos deben contar con buenas bases en el idioma inglés.

Depuis cinq ans, Brooks accueille des étudiants d'environ 35 pays différents et participe encore à des programmes d'échange avec des établissements scolaires de Hongrie, du Kenya, d'Afrique du Sud et d'Écosse. Les élèves qui désirent s'inscrire doivent avoir de très bonnes connaissances en anglais.

Brooks は過去5年間に、およそ35ヶ国の国々から学生を受け入れており、現在もハンガリー、ケニア、南アフリカ、及びスコットランドの学校との交換留学プログラムを実施しています。入学資格として、十分な英語力が要求されます。

過去五年，Brooks 招收的學生來自約三十五個國家，同時此校還與匈牙利、肯尼亞、南非和蘇格蘭的學校建立了交流項目。申請者必須有較強的英語背景。

The 251-acre waterfront campus with easy access to Boston has a new student center and will soon build a new athletic center.

Las 101 hectáreas de terreno costanero, con fácil acceso a Boston, tiene un nuevo centro estudiantil y contará en breve con un nuevo edifico de atletismo.

Brooks, qui est situé sur un campus de 101 hectares avec des espaces verts duquel il est facile de se rendre à Boston, dispose d'un nouveau centre pour étudiants et construira bientôt un tout nouveau gymnase.

ボストン市内へのアクセスが簡単なウォーターフロントの101ヘクタールのキャンパスには学生会館が完備されており、間もなく新体育館も設立されます。

校園濱水、佔地101公頃，前往波士頓交通便利並擁有新的學生中心。不久將建起一座新的體育館。

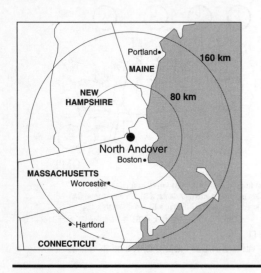

 0–30°C

 -7–4°C

 4–33°C

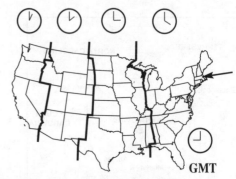

56 km from Logan International Airport, Boston, MA
A 56 km del aeropuerto internacional de Logan, Boston, MA
A 56 km de l'aéroport international de Logan, Boston, MA
マサチューセッツ州ボストン市のローガン国際空港から56キロ
離麻州波士頓 Logan 國際機場 56 公里

 Coeducational 9–12 / Mixto / Mixte
男女共学
男女合校

 191/158

 72%

 11%

 798, 272 / solicitaron admisión, fueron aceptados / candidats, admis
出願者数 798 名，合格者数 272 名
798 人申請，272 人被錄取

 SSAT (50%)

 TOEFL (550), SLEP (90%)

 Germany (22), Hong Kong (22), Japan (22), Korea (22), Thailand (10)

 February 1 / 1 de febrero / 1 février
2月1日
2月1日

 September / septiembre / septembre
9月
9月

 5:1

 5:1

 $32,640

 Bates College, George Washington University, Trinity College, University of Pennsylvania, Brown University

Buxton School

Margo Cardner, Senior Recruitment Officer
291 South Street
Williamstown, Massachusetts 01267
Phone: 413-458-5403 Fax: 413-458-9427
E-mail: admissions@buxtonschool.org
URL: http://www.buxtonschool.org

NAIS, NEASC, TABS member   *Founded 1928*

Buxton is a small, diverse community offering a challenging college-preparatory program that also includes art, music, drama, dance, and writing. ESL is individually arranged. Students help maintain the campus, and every year the entire school travels to a major city to study and perform. Close student-faculty interaction creates a supportive, family environment.

Buxton es una comunidad pequeña y variada que ofrece un estimulante programa de preparación para la universidad que también incluye arte, música, drama, danza y redacción. Las clases de inglés como segundo idioma (ESL) se programan individualmente. Los estudiantes colaboran con el mantenimiento del colegio y, todos los años, todos los alumnos viajan a una ciudad importante para estudiar y hacer representaciones. La estrecha interacción entre estudiantes y profesores crea un ambiente familiar con mucho apoyo.

Buxton est une petite communauté diversifiée qui propose un programme de préparation à l'université stimulant comportant également des cours d'art, de musique, de théâtre, de danse et d'écriture. Les cours d'anglais comme langue étrangère (ESL) sont organisés de façon individuelle. Les étudiants participent à l'entretien du campus et, tous les ans, tout l'établissement effectue un voyage vers une grande ville afin d'y étudier et d'y offrir un spectacle. L'étroite collaboration entre les étudiants et le corps enseignant permet de créer un environnement familial et coopératif.

Buxton は多様性に富んだ小さなコミュニティで、芸術、音楽、演劇、ダンス、および作文を含む挑戦的な大学進学準備コースを提供しています。ESL は個人にあわせてアレンジされます。学生はキャンパスの維持に助力し、毎年全学年が学習と実演のため主要都市に旅行します。学生と教員が一体となって、支援的で家族的な環境を創りだしています。

巴克斯頓學校規模不大但多樣化，所提供的挑戰的大學考試預備課程中包括美術、音樂、戲劇、舞蹈和寫作等內容。學校為外國學生單個安排外國學生英語課程。學生協助校方維護校園的整潔。每年整個學校均前往一座大城市學習和表演。師生密切交流，創造充滿相互支持的家庭氣氛。

The 150-acre campus is near Williams College and the Clark Art Institute.

Las 61 hectáreas de terreno están cerca de Williams College y del Clark Art Institute.

Le campus de 61 hectares est proche de Williams College et de Clark Art Institute.

61 ヘクタールのキャンパスは Williams College や Clark Art Institute に隣接しています。

校園佔地 61 公頃，靠近 Williams College 和 Clark Art Institute。

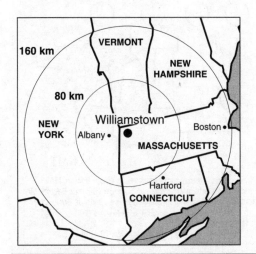

 4–21°C

 -15–4°C

 4–21°C

GMT

72 km from Albany Airport; 225 km from Boston, MA
A 72 km del aeropuerto de Albany; a 225 km de Boston, MA
A 72 km de l'aéroport d'Albany ; à 225 km de Boston, MA
アルバニー空港より 72 キロ、マサチューセッツ州ボストン市より 225 キロ
離 Albany 機場 72 公里；離 Boston, MA 225 公里

 Coeducational 9–12 / Mixto / Mixte
男女共学
男女合校

 46/44

 99%

 9%

 TOEFL

 China (18), Mexico (21), Spain (13)

 February 15 / 15 de febrero / 15 février
2 月 15 日
2 月 15 日

 September, January / septiembre, enero / septembre, janvier
9 月，1 月
9 月，1 月

 5:1, 75%

 4:1

 $32,500 plus books and all-school trip / $32,500 Incluye los libros y una excursión con toda la escuela / $32,500 Livres et excursions en plus
$32,500 と書籍代、諸旅行費
$32,500，外加書籍和所有學校組織的出遊

 Bennington College, Hampshire College, Mount Holyoke College, Oberlin College, Smith College

The Cambridge School of Weston

Trish Saunders, Director of Admissions
Georgian Road
Weston, Massachusetts 02493
Phone: 781-642-8650 Fax: 781-899-3870
E-mail: admissions@csw.org
URL: http://www.csw.org

TABS, NAIS member   *Founded 1886*

CSW welcomes students from 12 countries. It offers rigorous college preparation, with 3 intensive 90-minute classes per day, 300 courses, and challenging art, dance, drama, and music. The ESL curriculum is designed for students entering with intermediate or advanced English skills.

CSW recibe a estudiantes de 12 países. Ofrece un programa intensivo de preparación para la universidad, con 3 clases diarias intensivas de 90 minutos, 300 cursos y estimulantes clases de arte, danza, drama y música. El programa de estudios de inglés como segundo idioma (ESL) ha sido diseñado para estudiantes con conocimientos intermedios o avanzados del idioma inglés.

CSW accueille des étudiants de 12 pays différents. L'établissement offre un programme rigoureux de préparation à l'entrée dans les universités avec 3 sessions intensives de 90 minutes chacune par jour, 300 cours et d'excellents cours d'art, de danse, de théâtre et de musique. Le programme d'anglais comme langue étrangère (ESL) est conçu pour des étudiants possédant un niveau d'anglais "intermédiaire" ou "avancé".

CSW では、世界 12 カ国から生徒を受け入れています。一日に 1 クラス 90 分の集中クラスを 3 つ、300 種類のコース、刺激的な芸術、ダンス、演劇、音楽といった科目を含めて、本格的な大学進学準備クラスを提供しています。ESL のカリキュラムは入学時に中級から上級レベルの英語力を持った生徒に適用されます。

CSW 近來了 12 個國家的學生。該校提供嚴格的大學預備教育，每天有三門 90 分鍾的強化課程，共設有 300 種課程以及高難度的藝術、舞蹈、戲劇和英樂課目。為入血時具備中級或高級英語技能的學生設置英語作為第二語言（ESL）的課程。

The 65-acre suburban campus has 25 buildings and offers easy access to Boston and Cambridge.
Las 26 hectáreas de terreno se encuentran en un suburbio, tienen 25 edificios y ofrecen fácil acceso a las ciudades de Boston y Cambridge
Le campus de 26 hectares dans la banlieue comprend 25 immeubles et offre un accès facile vers les villes de Boston et Cambridge.
26 ヘクタールの郊外に広がるキャンパスには 25 の建物があり、ボストンやケンブリッジにも簡単にアクセスできます。
位於郊區的校園佔地 26 公頃，有 25 座建築，到 Boston 和 Cambridge 十分便利。

 7–21°C

 -4–10°C

 10–24°C

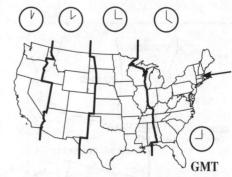

GMT

23 km from Logan International Airport; 19 km from Boston, MA
A 23 km del aeropuerto internacional de Logan; a 19 km de Boston, MA
A 23 km de l'aéroport international de Logan ; à 19 km de Boston, MA
マサチューセッツ州ローガン国際空港より 23 キロ、同州ボストン市より 19 キロ
離 Logan 國際機場 23 公里；離 Boston, MA 19 公里

 Coeducational 9–PG / Mixto / Mixte
男女共学
男女合校

 155/155

 30%

 10%

 500, 175 / solicitaron admisión, fueron aceptados / candidats, admis
出願者数 500 名、合格者数 175 名
500 人申請，175 人被錄取

 TOEFL (540+), SSAT, or ISEE

 Germany, Italy, Japan, Korea, Malaysia, Taiwan, Spain

 February 1, rolling / 1 de febrero, continuo / 1er février, continuelles
2 月 1 日より随時受付
2 月 1 日起隨時皆可

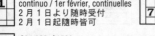 September, November, January, February / septiembre, noviembre, enero, febrero / septembre, novembre, janvier, février
9 月、11 月、1 月、2 月
9 月，11 月，1 月，2 月

 7:1, 30%

 8:1

 $34,230; $1500
($750 for returning students)

 Boston University, Brown University, Cornell University, Rensselaer Polytechnic Institute, Rhode Island School of Design, University of Southern California

Cranbrook Schools

Drew Miller, Dean of Admission
39221 Woodward Avenue, P.O. Box 801
Bloomfield Hills, Michigan 48304-0801
Phone: 248-645-3610 Fax: 248-645-3025
E-mail: admission@cranbrook.edu

TABS, NAIS, NAFSA member   *Founded 1922*

Cranbrook believes that in today's competitive environment, preparation for higher education should be comprehensive and challenging. Cranbrook offers a broad and challenging college-preparatory curriculum, outstanding programs in the arts and athletics, as well as ESL support at the high-intermediate level and above. All international students take a full schedule of mainstream classes.

Cranbrook considera que en el competitivo ambiente de hoy en día, la preparación para la educación superior tiene que ser exhaustiva y estimulante. Cranbrook ofrece un amplio y estimulante plan de estudios de preparación para la universidad, así como excepcionales programas de arte y deportes, y un programa de inglés como segundo idioma (ESL) que se ofrece desde el nivel intermedio-alto. Todos los estudiantes extranjeros reciben un programa completo de cursos regulares.

Cranbrook considère que, dans l'environnement concurrentiel d'aujourd'hui, la préparation aux études supérieures doit être intéressante et polyvalente. Cranbrook propose un cursus vaste et stimulant préparant à l'entrée en université, d'excellents programmes artistiques et sportifs, ainsi qu'un solide programme d'anglais comme langue étrangère (ESL) pour le niveau intermédiaire supérieur et au-delà. Tous les étudiants étrangers assistent aux cours réguliers.

Cranbrook は、競争の激しい今日の環境において高等教育への準備は包括的かつ挑戦的であるべきだと確信しています。Cranbrook は幅広く挑戦的な大学準備カリキュラムの他、芸術や運動における傑出したプログラム、そして高中級レベル以上の ESL サポートを提供します。海外からの留学生はすべてフルスケジュールで主流クラスを履修します。

Cranbook 學校堅信，在今天的競爭性環境中，為高等教育做準備應該全面，而且應該具有難度。本校提供種類廣泛的高難度大學預備課程，優秀的藝術、體育項目，以及高、中級以上水平的 ESL 幫助。所有國際學生都完整修習主要課程。

The 315-acre campus includes science and art museums.
Le campus de 128 hectares comprend un musée des sciences et un musée des arts.
Las 128 hectáreas de terreno incluyen museos de ciencias y ate.
128 ヘクタールのキャンパスには、科学と美術のミュージアムがあります。
校園佔地 128 公頃，擁有科學和藝術博物館。

 10–24°C

 -18–1°C

 10–24°C

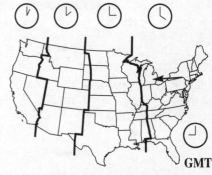

GMT

64 km from Detroit Metro Airport; 32 km from Detroit, MI
A 64 km del aeropuerto Metro de Detroit; a 32 km de Detroit, MI
A 64 km de l'aéroport Metro de Detroit ; à 32 km de Detroit, MI
デトロイト・メトロ空港より 64 キロ、ミシガン州デトロイト市より 32 キロ
離 Detroit Metro 機場 64 公里；離密西根州 Detroit 市 32 公里

 Coeducational 9–12 / Mixto / Mixte
男女共学
男女合校

 390/360

 34%

 12%

 390, 360 / solicitaron admisión, fueron aceptados / candidats, admis
出願者数 390 名、合格者数 360 名
390 人申請，360 人被錄取

 TOEFL (175 CBT)

Germany, Hong Kong, India, Japan, Korea, Mexico, Saudi Arabia, Taiwan, Thailand

 February 15, Rolling / 15 de febrero, Continuo / 15 février, Continuelles
2 月 1 日より随時受付
2 月 1 日起隨時皆可

 September / septiembre / septembre
9 月
9 月

 8:1, 75%

 8:1

 $29,290

 Brown University, Michigan State University, Northwestern University, Princeton University, University of Michigan, Washington University

 Intermediate and advanced levels

Culver Military Academy/Culver Girls Academy

UNITED STATES

Mr. Mike Turnbull
Director of Admissions
1300 Academy Road
Culver, Indiana 46511
Phone: 574-842-7100 Fax: 574-842-8066
E-mail: admissions@culver.org
URL: http://www.culver.org

NAIS, NAFSA member   *Founded 1894*

Culver Military Academy and Culver Girls Academy are college-preparatory boarding schools for grades 9–PG. About 15 percent of the enrollment comes from outside the U.S. The Academies offer challenging academics through an ESL program, small classes, and individual assistance in a nurturing, rural lakeside environment.

Culver Military Academy y Culver Girls Academy son internados de preparación para la universidad para grados del noveno a PG. Cerca del 15 por ciento de los estudiantes que se matriculan provienen de fuera de los Estados Unidos. Las academias ofrecen estimulantes programas académicos por medio de un programa de inglés como segundo idioma (ESL), clases con pocos alumnos y asistencia individual en un ambiente rural, a la orilla de un lago, que estimula el aprendizaje.

Culver Military Academy et Culver Girls Academy sont des internats préparant à l'entrée dans les universités pour les étudiants à partir de la troisième et pour les bacheliers. Quinze pour cent environ des étudiants sont étrangers. Ces établissements offrent un excellent programme scolaire grâce à des cours d'anglais comme langue étrangère (ESL), des classes restreintes et une assistance individuelle dans un environnement stimulant et rural au bord d'un lac.

Culver Military Academy と Culver Girls Academy は、中学3年生から高校卒業生までの全寮制大学進学準備校です。入学生のおよそ15パーセントは米国外からの生徒です。本アカデミーでは、ESLプログラム、少人数クラス、ゆとりある田舎の湖畔の環境で生徒一人一人を暖かく支えながら、チャレンジ精神溢れる学習の機会を提供しています。

Culver Military Academy 和 Culver Girls Academy 是為9年級以上和已畢業學生開辦的大學預備寄宿學校。注冊學生中約15%來自美國以外的國家。這兩所學校在有益身心的鄉村湖畔環境中，通過ESL課程、小型課堂和個別輔導提供高難度的學術教育。

The 1,800-acre campus has an airport, a library, and a golf course.

Las 729 hectáreas de terreno cuentan con un aeropuerto, una biblioteca y un campo de golf.

Le campus de 729 hectares comprend un aéroport, une bibliothèque et un terrain de golf.

729ヘクタールのキャンパスには空港、図書館、ゴルフコースがあります。

校園佔地729公頃，包括一座機場、圖書館和高爾夫球場。

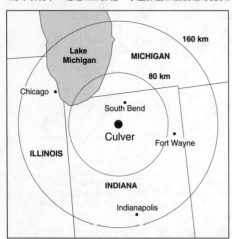

  5–18°C

  -3–7°C

  7–18°C

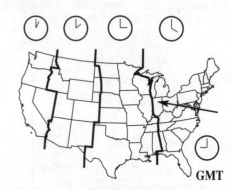

GMT

161 km from O'Hare International Airport and Chicago, IL
A 161 km del aeropuerto internacional de O'Hare y de Chicago, IL
A 161 km de l'aéroport international d'O'Hare et de Chicago, IL
オヘア国際空港とイリノイ州シカゴ市より161キロ
離 O'Hare 國際機場和 Chicago, IL 各 161 公里

 Coeducational 9–PG / Mixto / Mixte
男女共学
男女合校

 450/316

 90%

 15%

 801, 409 / solicitaron admisión, fueron aceptados / candidats, admis
出願者数801名、合格者数409名
801 人申請，409 人被錄取

 SSAT

 TOEFL

 China (20), Korea (20), Mexico (70), Saudi Arabia (20), Taiwan (20)

 Rolling / Continuo / Continuelles
随時受付
全年招生

September, January / septiembre, enero / septiembre, janvier
9月、1月
9月，1月

 7:1, 20%

 1:1

 $27,500; $950–$1500

 Boston College, University of Colorado-Boulder, Indiana University, Purdue University, Washington University-Missouri

 Enriched ESL / Programa enriquecido de inglés como segundo idioma (ESL) / Anglais comme langue étrangère renforcé
ESL 集中講座 / ESL 強化課程

Cushing Academy

Melanie J. Glines, Director of Admission
P.O. Box 8000
Ashburnham, Massachusetts 01430
Phone: 978-827-7300 Fax: 978-827-6253
E-mail: admission@cushing.org

THE ALFRED GAYLORD DREW '27 COMMON

TABS member   *Founded 1865*

Cushing offers a college-preparatory program with extensive athletic, artistic, and theatrical options. ESL, including an intensive 6-week summer session, and Advanced Placement courses are also provided.

Cushing ofrece un programa de preparación para la universidad que incluye una gran variedad de opciones deportivas, artísticas y teatrales. También se ofrecen cursos de inglés como segundo idioma (ESL), incluyendo una sesión de verano intensiva de 6 semanas y un programa para ingreso a cursos de niveles avanzados.

Cushing offre un programme préparatoire aux universités avec un programme complet dans le domaine du sport, de l'art et du théâtre. Une session d'été, d'une durée de 6 semaines, offre un programme intensif d'anglais comme langue étrangère (ESL) en plus de cours pour équivalences universitaires.

当校には、多様なスポーツ、芸術、演劇活動などを含んだ大学進学準備プログラムや、6週間集中夏期プログラムなどの ESL プログラム、また上級者向けプログラムなどがあります。

Cushing Academy 提供大學預備課程，並有各種體育、藝術、戲劇等選修課。也提供英語為第二語言的課程，包括為期六週的暑期密集班和高級大學入學前的課程。

The 152-acre campus has a new academic building for math, science, and the performing arts, along with a computer network with wireless access.

El recinto de 61 hectáreas tiene un nuevo edificio académico para las matemáticas, ciencias y artes escénicas, junto con una red de computadoras con acceso inalámbrico.

Le campus qui s'étale sur près de 61 hectares dispose d'un nouveau bâtiment pour les mathématiques, les sciences et le théâtre, ainsi que d'un réseau informatique équipé d'un accès sans fil.

61 ヘクタールのキャンパスには、ワイヤレスアクセスを備えたコンピュータ・ネットワークのある、数学、科学、芸術全般のための、近代的な新築のビルがあります。

佔地 61 公頃的校園設有嶄新的教學樓，為數學教學，科學研究，表演藝術，計算機聯網和無線交流等課程和活動提供場所。

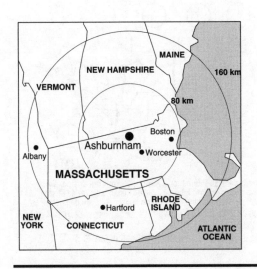

 12–18°C

 -6–2°C

 14–20°C

GMT

88 km from Logan International Airport and Boston, MA
A 88 km del aeropuerto internacional de Logan y de Boston, MA
A 88 km de l'aéroport international de Logan et de Boston, MA
ローガン国際空港とマサチューセッツ州のボストン市より88キロ
離 Logan 國際機場和 Boston, MA 88 公里

 Coeducational 9–PG / Mixto / Mixte
男女共学
男女合校

 252/168

 90%

24%

 663, 481 / solicitaron admisión, fueron aceptados / candidats, admis
出願者数 663 名、合格者数 481 名
663 人申請，481 人被錄取

 TOEFL (400–600), SSAT, SLEP

Brazil (14), Hong Kong (28), Japan (30), Korea (30), Taiwan (26)

 Rolling / Continuo / Continuelles
随時受付
全年招生

 September, January, / septiembre, enero, / septembre, janvier
9 月、1 月
9 月，1 月

 8:1, 85%

 7:1

 $34,415; $1300

 Bentley College, Boston University, Lynn University, Northeastern University, University of Colorado

---

Dana Hall School

Heather A. Cameron, Director of Admission
45 Dana Road
Wellesley, Massachusetts 02482
Phone: 781-235-3010 Fax: 781-235-0577
E-mail: admission@danahall.org
URL: www.danahall.org

NCGS, NAIS, TABS, NAFSA member *Founded 1881*

Founded in 1881 as a preparatory school for Wellesley College, Dana Hall is the only all-girls boarding school in the greater Boston area. Dana Hall is committed to fostering excellence in academics, the arts, and athletics as students prepare to enter college. Girls from 13 countries and 18 states represent a diversity of talents and interests. An International Student Advisor along with the International Student Association provides support for students from overseas. No ESL program is offered.

Fundada en 1881 como escuela preparatoria para el Wellesley College, Dana Hall es el único internado de señoritas en la zona del Gran Boston. Dana Hall tiene un profundo compromiso con la excelencia académica, artística y atlética de las estudiantes que se preparan para entrar a la universidad. Estudiantes de 13 países y 18 estados conforman una gran diversidad de talentos e intereses. Un Asesor de Estudiantes Internacionales, junto con una Asociación de Estudiantes Internacionales, brindan apoyo a las estudiantes que provienen del extranjero. No se ofrece ningún programa de inglés como segundo idioma (ESL).

Fondée en 1881 en tant qu'école préparant à l'entrée au Wellesley College, Dana Hall est le seul internat pour jeunes filles dans la région de Boston. L'établissement stimule l'excellence aussi bien au niveau du programme scolaire que des arts et des sports lors de la préparation à l'entrée à l'université. Les jeunes filles provenant de 13 pays et 18 états différents représentent une mosaïque de talents et d'intérêts divers. Un conseiller chargé des étudiants étrangers ainsi que l'association destinée à ces mêmes étudiants offrent un soutien aux élèves venant d'un pays étranger. Aucun programme d'anglais comme langue étrangère n'est offert.

1881 年に Wellesley College の進学予備校として設立された Dana Hall は、ボストン近郊では唯一の女子全寮制の学校です。Dana Hall は、大学入学に備え、学業、芸術、そして体育における卓越性を育むことに尽力しています。ここには、13 カ国、18 州から、様々な才能と興味を持った若い女性達が集まっています。また、留学生協会および留学生アドバイザーが、留学生のサポートをしています。ESL プログラムはありません。

Dana Hall 於 1881 年作為衛斯里大學的預科學校而創建，是大波士頓地區唯一全女生寄宿學校。Dana Hall 致力於幫助學生在大學準備過程中取得學術、藝術及體育運動方面的優異成績。來自 13 個國家及 18 個州的女生體現了多元化的人才和興趣。國際學生指導老師與國際學生協會共同為來自海外的學生提供幫助。不開設 ESL 課程。

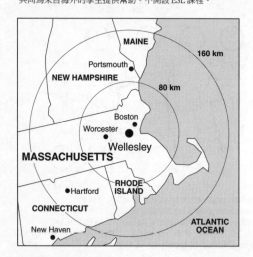

4–21°C

-18–10°C

4–27°C

The 50-acre campus is located in the suburban college town of Wellesley.

En el pueblo suburbano universitario de Wellesley se encuentra un recinto privado de 20 hectáreas.

Un campus privé de 20 hectares, situé dans la banlieue de la ville universitaire de Wellesley.

20 ヘクタールのキャンパスは、学園都市 Wellesley 郊外にあります。

佔地 20 公頃的私人校園位於郊區的 Wellesley 大學城內。

GMT

24 km from Logan International Airport; 21 km from Boston, MA
A 24 km del aeropuerto internacional de Logan; a 21km de Boston, MA
A 24 km de l'aéroport international de Logan ; à 21 km de Boston, MA
ローガン空港より 24 キロ、マサチューセッツ州ボストン市より 21 キロ
離 Logan 國際機場 24 公里；離 Boston, MA 21 公里

Girls 6–12 / Niñas / Filles
女子中学校
女子中學校

475, 100 / solicitaron admisión, fueron aceptadas / candidates, admises
出願者数 475 名、合格者数 100 名
475 人申請，100 人被錄取

February 1, rolling / 1 de febrero, continuo / 1er février, continuelles
2 月 1 日より随時受付
2 月 1 日起随時皆可

$34,425

0/450

TOEFL (500)

September 1 / 1 de septiembre / 1er septembre
9 月 1 日
9 月 1 日

50%

8:1, 50%

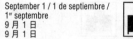
Boston University, Princeton University, Stanford University, Syracuse University, Wellesley College

14%

Canada, China, Ecuador, Hong Kong, Israel, Japan, Korea, Mexico, Philippines, Sweden, Taiwan, Thailand, West Indies

4:1

Darrow School

J. Kirk Russell III, Director of Admission
110 Darrow Road
New Lebanon, New York 12125
Phone: 518-794-6000 Fax: 518-794-7065
E-mail: jkr@darrowschool.org
URL: http://www.darrowschool.org

NAFSA, NAIS, TABS member   *Founded 1932*

Darrow believes in the formal and informal learning that takes place from living together. When students share language, music, or favorite ethnic foods, they are experiencing a vital extension of their education. Excellent ESL and college-preparatory academic programs with a friendly and caring faculty.

Darrow cree en el aprendizaje formal e informal que surge de la convivencia. Cuando los estudiantes comparten su idioma, su música o los alimentos favoritos de sus respectivos países, están experimentando una extensión importante de su educación. Excelentes programas académicos de inglés como segundo idioma (ESL) y de preparación para la universidad a cargo de un profesorado amable que se preocupa por los alumnos.

Au même titre que pour l'apprentissage formel, Darrow croît fermement à l'apprentissage informel qui émane de la vie en communauté. Lorsque des étudiants partagent une langue, un style de musique, ou un plat ethnique favori, ils élargissent considérablement l'étendue de leur formation. D'excellents programmes d'anglais comme langue étrangère (ESL) et de préparation à l'entrée dans les universités sont offerts grâce à des professeurs amicaux et dévoués.

Darrow は、共同生活の中から生まれる本格的な、または形式にこだわらない学習を信条とします。生徒は教育の最も重要な延長線上にある言語、音楽、好みのエスニック料理などを分かち合います。親切で思いやりのある教師による優れた ESL および大学準備学習プログラムもあります。

Darrow 學校信奉共同生活產生的正規的學習。當學生們分享語言、英樂和嗜好的民族食品時，他們正體驗其教育重要的延伸部分。優秀的 ESL 和大學預備學習科目，親好而關心的教員。

The 365-acre campus has 26 buildings, including science labs and our new Joline Arts Center.

El recinto de 148 hectáreas tiene 26 edificios, incluyendo laboratorios de ciencias y nuestro nuevo centro de arte Joline.

Le campus de 148 hectares comprend 26 bâtiments, notamment des laboratoires scientifiques et notre nouveau centre pour les arts, le centre Joline.

148 ヘクタールのキャンパスには、サイエンス・ラボや新築の Joline Arts Center を含む校舎が 26 棟あります。

校園佔地 148 公頃，擁有 26 所校舍，多個科學實驗室和嶄新的 Joline 藝術中心。

 0–24°C

 -17–-1°C

 4–29°C

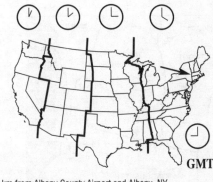

GMT

40 km from Albany County Airport and Albany, NY
A 40 km del aeropuerto Albany County y de Albany, NY
À 40 km de l'aéroport d'Albany County et d'Albany, NY
ニューヨーク州アルバニー郡空港およびニューヨーク州アルバニー市より 40 キロ
離紐約州 Albany 郡機場和紐約州 Albany 市均 40 公里

 Coeducational 9–12 / Mixto / Mixte
男女共学
男女合校

 60 / 60

 95%

 14%

 145, 71 / solicitaron admisión, fueron aceptados / candidats, admis
出願者数 145 名，合格者数 71 名
145 人申請，71 人被錄取

TOEFL

Chile, Indonesia, Japan, Korea, Nigeria, Netherlands, Singapore, Taiwan, Thailand

 Rolling / Continuo / Continuelles
随時受付
全年招生

 September, January / septiembre, enero / septembre, janvier
9 月、1 月
9 月，1 月

 4:1, 99%

 1:1

 $38,875 (ESL);
$31,975 (boarding non-ESL)

 Bennington College, Boston University, Carleton College, Clark University, Chicago School of Art, The Colorado College, Dickinson College, Guilford College, Hobart and William Smith College, Kenyon College, New York University, Oberlin College, Rensselaer Polytechnic Institute, Rhode Island School of Design, Syracuse University, Wesleyan College

---

Dublin School

Marylou T. Marcus, Director of Admission
18 Lehmann Way
P.O. Box 522
Dublin, New Hampshire 03444-0522
Phone: 603-563-8584 Fax: 603-563-8671

NAIS, TABS member   *Founded 1935*

A strong college-preparatory curriculum, individualized ESL and Learning Skills Programs, and committed faculty members create an environment where students continuously find success. The majority of graduates enroll at their first-choice college.

Un programa de preparación exigente para la universidad, clases individuales de inglés como segundo idioma (ESL), un curso de técnicas de aprendizaje y profesores dedicados a sus alumnos, crean un ambiente en el que los estudiantes se esfuerzan por sobresalir continuamente. La mayoría de los estudiantes se matriculan en la universidad de su primera selección.

Un solide programme de préparation universitaire, des cours individualisés d'anglais comme langue étrangère, des programmes sur les techniques d'assimilation et un corps enseignant attentif permettent de créer un environnement favorisant la réussite des étudiants. La majorité des diplômés s'inscrivent à l'université placée en tête de leurs préférences.

献身的な教師陣が、生徒が常に目標を達成できるような環境をつくりあげ、優秀な大学準備カリキュラム、個々の能力に合わせたESL、学習法プログラムを提供します。大多数の卒業生が第一志望の大学に進学しています。

高水平大學預備課程、個別輔導的ESL課程和學習技巧項目，以及盡心盡職的教員創造了讓學生在其中不斷進步的環境。大多數學生被他們理想的大學錄取。

Nurturing faculty members and community challenge students to reach their goals.

Los profesores y la comunidad estimulan el aprendizaje y ayudan a los estudiantes a lograr sus metas.

Le corps enseignant attentif et la communauté incitent les étudiants à atteindre leurs buts.

めんどうみのいい教師陣とコミュニティーの大学生が、生徒が目標を達成させる意欲を持つようにします。

關心備至的教師和集體促使學生實現其學習目標。

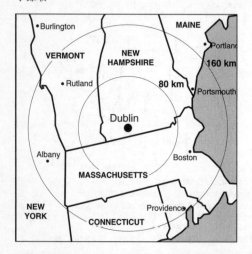

 15–21°C

 -7–6°C

 7–15°C

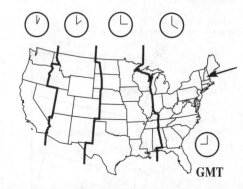
GMT

66 km from Manchester, NH airport; 115 km from Boston, MA
A 66 km del aeropuerto de Manchester, NH; a 115 km de Boston, MA
A 66 km de l'aéroport de Manchester, NH ; à 115 km de Boston, MA
ニューハンプシャー州マンチェスター空港より66キロ、マサチューセッツ州ボストン市より115キロ
離 Manchester, NH 機場66公里；離 Boston, MA 115公里

 Coeducational 9–12 / Mixto / Mixte
男女共学
男女合校

 78/54

 65%

16%

 181, 112 / solicitaron admisión, fueron aceptados / candidats, admis
出願者数181名、合格者数112名
181人申請，112人被錄取

TOEFL (410-420),
SLEP (40-46)

5:1, 50%

 Bermuda (13), Germany (13), Japan (13), Korea (13), Philippines (3), Saudi Arabia (13), Taiwan (8)

 March 10, then rolling / 1 de marzo, continuo / 1 mars, continuelles
3月10日より随時受付
3月10日起随時皆可

 September / septiembre / septembre
9月
9月

 5:1, 50%

5:1

 $35,400, $600;
$4200 (ESL)

 Colby College, Cornell University, Skidmore College, Tufts University, Wellesely College, Wesleyan College

The Fessenden School

Caleb W. Thomson '79,
Director of Admissions
250 Waltham Street
West Newton, Massachusetts 02465-1750
Phone: 617-630-2300 Fax: 617-630-2303
E-mail: admissions@fessenden.org
URL: http://www.fessenden.org

UBSA, NAIS, TABS member   *Founded 1903*

Fessenden offers a two-level ESL program and extensive athletic and weekend activities designed to help international students improve English language skills and become acquainted with American culture.

Fessenden ofrece un programa de enseñanza del inglés como segundo idioma (ESL) con dos niveles y una gran variedad de actividades deportivas y de fin de semana diseñadas para ayudar a los estudiantes internacionales a mejorar sus niveles de competencia con el idioma inglés y a conocer la cultura estadounidense.

Fessenden offre deux niveaux de programme d'anglais comme langue étrangère et des cours nombreux de sport, ainsi que des activités durant le weekend permettant aux étudiants étrangers d'améliorer leur anglais parlé et de s'adapter à la culture américaine.

当校では、2 レベルの ESL プログラムや幅広いスポーツ、週末の活動を行っており、留学生が英語の能力を伸ばしながらアメリカの文化に馴染めるように援助しています。

Fessenden 提供二種程度的英語為第二語言課程及各種體育和週末活動，以幫助國際學生提高語技能並增進對美國文化的了解。

The 41-acre campus has 2 swimming pools, a hockey rink, 13 tennis courts, 3 Gymnasiums and 9 athletic fields.

Las 17 hectáreas de terreno tienen 2 piscinas, una pista de hockey, 13 canchas de tenis, 3 gimnasios y 9 campos deportivos.

Le campus de 17 hectares comporte 2 piscines, une patinoire de hockey, 13 courts de tennis, 3 gymnases et 9 terrains sportifs.

17 ヘクタールのキャンパスにはプールが 2 つ、ホッケーリンク 9 面、テニスコート 13 面、体育館 3 つ、および 9 つの運動場があります。

校園佔地 17 公頃，有兩個游泳池、一個冰球場、十三個網球場、三個健身房、九個運動場。

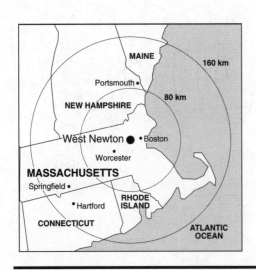

 13–26°C

 -18–10°C

 10–24°C

GMT

17 km from Logan International Airport and Boston, MA
A 17 km del aeropuerto internacional de Logan y de Boston, MA
A 17 km de l'aéropuert international de Logan et de Boston, MA
ローガン国際空港およびマサチューセッツ州、ボストン市より 17 キロ
離 Logan 國際機場和 Boston, MA 各 17 公里

 Boys 5–9 / Muchachos / Garçons
男子中学校
男子中學校

 210/0

 37%

 10%

 170, 42 / solicitaron admisión, fueron aceptados / candidats, admis
出願者数 170 名、合格者数 42 名
170 人申請，42 人被錄取

 ✓

Wechsler Intelligence Scale for Children

 Japan, Korea, Mexico, Thailand, Venezuela

 Rolling / Continuo / Continuelles
随時受付
全年招生

 September / septiembre / septembre
9 月
9 月

6:1, 70%

5:1

 $37,300; $2000

Phillips Exeter Academy, Brooks School, Middlesex School, Loomis Chafee, St. Mark's School

Fishburne Military School

Captain Carl V. Lambert, Director of Admissions
P.O. Box 988E
Waynesboro, Virginia 22980
Phone: 800-946-7773 Fax: 540-946-7738

Founded 1879

The Fishburne Military School program develops strong skills in English, communication, and leadership. Each student is assigned to a faculty member and a cadet mentor who work to ensure his adjustment to the college-preparatory curriculum and cadet life.

El programa de Fishburne Military School desarrolla los conocimientos del inglés, la habilidad de comunicación y las dotes de liderazgo. Cada estudiante es asignado a un miembro del profesorado y a un mentor cadete que trabajan para asegurar su ajuste al plan de estudios de preparación para la universidad y a la vida de los cadetes.

Le programme de Fishburne Military School développe des compétences solides en anglais et dans les domaines de la communication et du leadership. On attribue à chaque étudiant un membre du corps enseignant, ainsi qu'un élève officier qui joue le rôle de conseiller. Ces deux personnes attachées à l'étudiant garantissent sa bonne adaptation au programme scolaire préparant à l'entrée en université et à la vie des élèves officiers.

Fishburne Military School のプログラムでは、英語、コミュニケーション、リーダーシップにおける卓越した技能を築き上げます。各生徒を教員および士官候補生教員が担し、大学進学準備カリキュラムと兵学校生活への適応を助けます。

Fishburne Military 的課程培養英語、交流和領導方面的高能力。每位學員被分配給一名教師和一名輔導學友，他們努力保證該學員適應大學預備課程和軍校學員生活。

Rural Waynesboro surrounds the historic 10-acre campus.

La ciudad rural de Waynesboro rodea el histórico recinto situado en 4 hectáreas de terreno.

Le campus historique de 4 hectares est situé au coeur de la ville rurale de Waynesboro.

4ヘクタールの歴史的なキャンパスの周辺は、田舎町のウェイネスボロが取り囲んでいます。

校園佔地4公頃，為 Waynesboro 鄉鎮所環繞。

 16–24°C

 -4–5°C

 10–19°C

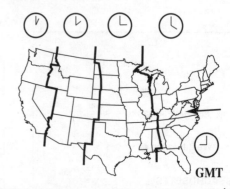

GMT

242 km from Washington, DC / A 242 km de Washington, DC / Á 242 km de Washington, DC
ワシントン D.C. より 242 キロ
離華盛頓特區 242 公里

 Boys 8–12 / Muchachos / Garçons
男子中学校
男子中學校

 144, 96 / solicitaron admisión, fueron aceptados / candidats, admis
出願者数 144 名、合格者数 96 名
144 人申請，96 人被錄取

 Rolling / Continuo / Continuelles
随時受付
全年招生

 $21,900; $1000-$2000

 200/0

 ✓

 September, January / septiembre, enero / septembre, janvier
9 月、1 月
9 月，1 月

 Virginia Military Institute, Virginia Tech, Marshall University, Embry-Riddle Aeronautical University, George Mason University

 90%

 8:1

 10%

 Aruba, Korea, Mexico, Thailand, Venezuela

 8:1

 June 27–July 31 / 27 julio–31 julio / 27 de juillet–31 de juillet
7 月 27 日～7 月 31 日
7 月 27 日～7 月 31 日

Fork Union Military Academy

UNITED STATES

Lt. Col. Jim Akers
Director of Admissions
P.O. Box 278
Fork Union, Virginia 23055
Phone: 434-842-4205 Fax: 434-842-4300
URL: http://www.forkunion.com

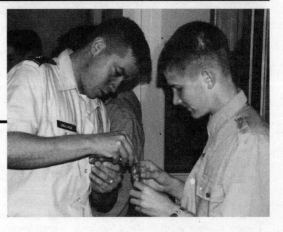

NAIS member   *Founded 1898*

Continuing its second century of service, Fork Union offers a one-subject plan of study (students focus on one subject for seven weeks), giving international students a chance to become fluent in English. Christian values and leadership training are emphasized; the Academy's technology and athletic programs are outstanding.

En su segundo siglo de servicio, Fork Union ofrece un plan de estudios de una materia (los estudiantes se concentran en una materia por siete semanas), dándole la oportunidad a estudiantes internacionales para que obtengan fluidez en inglés. Se recalcan los valores cristianos y la capacitación de líderes; la tecnología de la academia y sus programas atléticos son sobresalientes.

Saluant son deuxième siècle d'activité, Fork Union offre un programme d'études à matière unique (les étudiants se concentrent sur une matière pendant plusieurs semaines), ce qui donne aux étudiants internationaux la possibilité d'atteindre un niveau d'anglais courant. Les valeurs chrétiennes et la formation au leadership jouent un rôle très important ; les programmes de l'Academy relatif à la technologie et au sport sont exceptionnels.

開校から二世紀を誇る Fork Union では、生徒が7週間の間一教科のみに集中して学習するプランを提供することで、留学生が英会話を修得する機会を与えることが出来ます。キリスト教の価値とリーダーシップ・トレーニングの重要性を強調し、また科学技術、スポーツ競技のプログラムは顕著なものです。

Fork Union 具有過百年的歷史，為學生們提供單科計劃（學生們花七周時間集中攻讀一門課程），幫助國際學生掌握流利的英文。Fork Union 重視傳授基督教的價值觀，培養學生的領導才能，其科技和體育課程享有盛名。

The 500-acre campus includes a 19,000-volume library and technology center.

Las 202 hectáreas de terreno incluyen una biblioteca con 19.000 volúmenes y centro de tecnología.

Le campus de 202 hectares comprend une bibliothèque qui a près de 19 000 volumes et une centre de la technologie.

202 ヘクタールのキャンパスに、1万9千冊の草書を図書館と技術センターがあります。

校園占地面積202公頃，包括藏書一萬九千冊的圖書興天文館。

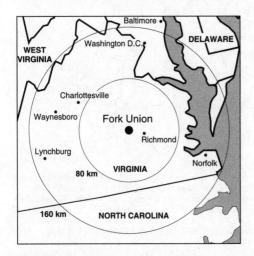

 2–18°C

 -6–7°C

 7–18°C

GMT

83 km from Richmond International Airport and Richmond, VA
A 83 kilómetros del aeropuerto internacional de Richmond y de Richmond, VA
A 83 kilomètres de l'aéroport international de Richmond et de Richmond, VA
リッチモンド国際空港及びバージニア州のリッチモンド市より83キロ
離列治文國際機場和弗吉尼亞列治市各83公里

 Boys, 6–PG / Muchachos / Garçons
男子中学校
男子中學校

 650/0

 99%

 9%

 500, 240 / solicitaron admisión, fueron aceptados / candidats, admis
出願者数 500名、合格者数 240名
500人申請、240人被錄取

 TOEFL(320)

 Japan (23), Korea (20), Mexico (23), Panama (23), Saudi Arabia (18), Venezuela (23)

 Rolling / Continuo / Continuelles
隨時受付
全年招生

 September, January / septiembre, enero / septembre, janvier
9月、1月
9月，1月

 15, 80%

4:1

 $19,990; $2990

Virginia Military Institute, College of William and Mary, The Citadel, Virginia Polytechnic Institute, University of Virginia

George School

Karen Hallowell, Director of Admissions
Route 413, P.O. Box 4460
Newtown, Pennsylvania 18940
Phone: 215-579-6547 Fax: 215-579-6549
E-mail: admissions@georgeschool.org
URL: http://www.georgeschool.org

TABS, FAIS member   *Founded 1893*

Founded as a Friends boarding and day school, George School provides a broad college-preparatory curriculum including the ESL and International Baccalaureate (IB) programs. Quaker values such as tolerance, equality, and social justice create a diverse community where academics, sports, arts, and service learning share emphasis.

El George School que fue fundado como un colegio para estudiantes cuáqueros internos y externos, ofrece un amplio plan de estudios de preparación para la universidad, que incluye el programa de inglés como segundo idioma (ESL) y el de Bachillerato Internacional (IB). Algunos de los valores de los cuáqueros como la tolerancia, la igualdad y la justicia social crean una comunidad diversa en la que se hace el mismo énfasis en los programas académicos, los deportes, las artes y el servicio.

George School, un externat/internat fondé par les Quakers, propose un vaste cursus scolaire préparant à l'entrée en université, y compris un programme d'anglais comme langue étrangère (ESL) et des cours préparant au baccalauréat international. Les valeurs des Quakers, comme par exemple la tolérance, l'égalité et la justice sociale, créent une communauté diversifiée, axée sur les études, le sport, l'art et l'enseignement du service communautaire.

フレンズ寄宿学校および全日スクールとして創設された George School は、ESL や International Baccalaureate (IB)などのプログラムを含む広範囲な大学準備カリキュラムを提供します。Quaker の価値観に基づき、忍耐や平等、社会正義を重視し、学科、スポーツ、芸術、および福祉などが同様に重きを置かれる多様性に富んだコミュニティを創出しています。。

George School 是作為一所教友會住宿及走讀學校而創立的。本校提供種類廣泛的大學預備課程，包括 ESL 和國際學士學位 (IB) 課程。寬容、平等、社會正義等教友會價值觀，造就了一個同等重視學業、運動、藝術和服務學習的多元化集體。

The campus is set on 265 park-like acres.

El colegio se encuentra en 107 hectáreas de terrenos estilo parque.

Le campus se trouve sur un parc de 107 hectares.

107 ヘクタールのキャンパスは公園さながらの美しい環境にあります。

校園佔地 107 公頃，如公園般美麗。

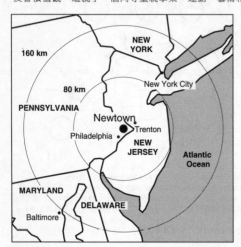

 7–29°C

 -6–7°C

 7–24°C

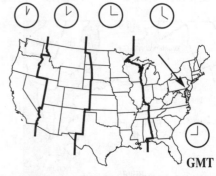

GMT

48 km from Philadelphia International Airport; 40 km from Philadelphia, PA
A 48 km del aeropuerto internacional de Filadelfia; a 40 km de Filadelfia, PA
A 48 km de l'aéroport international de Philadelphie ; à 40 km de Philadelphie, PA
ペンシルバニア州フィラデルフィア国際空港より 48 キロ、同州フィラデルフィア市より 40 キロ
離 Philadelphia 國際機場 48 公里；離 Philadelphia, PA 40 公里

 Coeducational 9-12 / Mixto / Mixte
男女共学
男女合校

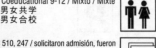 265/275

 55%

 16%

 510, 247 / solicitaron admisión, fueron aceptados / candidats, admis
出願者数 510 名、合格者数 247 名
510 人申請，247 人被錄取

SLEP or TOEFL

SSAT

Germany (58), Japan (73), Korea (13), Latin America (92), Southeast Asia (72), Taiwan (26)

 Rolling / Continuo / Continuelles
隨時受付
全年招生

September 4 / 4 de septiembre / 4 septembre
9 月 4 日
9 月 4 日

7:1, 70%

7:1

$32,000; $3800

Boston University, Brown University, George Washington University, Guilford College, New York University, Tufts University

Intermediate, advanced ESL / Cursos de inglés como segundo idioma (ESL) intermedios y avanzados / Anglais comme langue étrangère (ESL) niveaux intermédiaire et avancé.
中上級 ESL
中，高級 ESL

The Grand River Academy

UNITED STATES

Sam Corabi, Director of Admission
3042 College Street
Austinburg, Ohio 44010
Phone: 440-275-2811 Fax: 440-275-1825
E-mail: academy@grandriver.org

NAIS, TABS member   *Founded 1831*

Students develop English skills through ESL classes and through immersion in the culture and life of the academy. The school issues I-20s, coordinates TOEFL testing, and offers an ESL summer program.

Los estudiantes desarrollan destrezas de inglés mediante las clases de inglés como segundo idioma e inmersión de la cultura y vida de la academia. La escuela emite formas I-20, coordina exámenes de inglés (TOEFL) y ofrece un programa de verano de inglés como segundo idioma (ESL).

Les étudiants développent leurs connaissances en anglais grâce aux cours du programme ESL (anglais deuxième langue) et par l'immersion dans la culture et la vie de la faculté. L'établissement émet les visas pour étudiants I-20s et offre un programme ESL pour l'été.

生徒は、ESL クラスと当校に於ける生活や文化に没頭することで、英語の技能を発達させます。I-20 ビザの発行、TOEFL テストへの調整、夏期 ESL プログラムを提供しています。

學生們通過 ESL 課程，並在對校園文化的接觸中提高英語水平。學院簽發 I-20，組織有關 TOEFL 考試的安排，並開設 ESL 暑期課程。

The 200-acre campus has a new science center.

El recinto de 81 hectáreas tiene un nuevo centro de ciencias.

Le campus de 81 hectares abrite un nouveau centre pour les sciences.

81 ヘクタールのキャンパスには、新しい科学センターがあります。

佔地 81 公頃的校園設有新的科技中心。

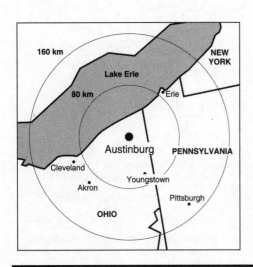

 16–27°C

 -18–5°C

 14–24°C

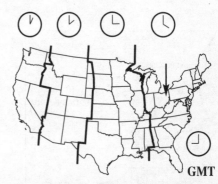

GMT

83 km from Cleveland Hopkins International Airport; 64 km from Cleveland, OH
A 83 km del aeropuerto internacional Hopkins de Cleveland; a 64 km de Cleveland, OH
A 83 km de l'aéroport international Hopkins de Cleveland; à 64 km de Cleveland, OH
クリーブランド・ホプキンス国際空港より 83 キロ、オハイオ州のクリーブランド市より 64 キロ
離 Cleveland Hopkins 國際機場和 83 公里；離 Cleveland 市 64 公里

 Boys 9–PG / Muchachos / Garçons
男子中学校
男子中學校

 118/0

 100%

 12%

 97, 88/ solicitaron admisión, fueron aceptados / candidats, admis
出願者数 97 名、合格者数 88 名
97 人申請，88 人被錄取

 6:1, 98%

 Mexico (3), Russia (5),
Saudi Arabia (5), South Korea (15),
Taiwan (10)

 Rolling / Continuo / Continuelles
隨時受付
全年招生

 Rolling / Continuo / Continuelles
隨時受付
全年招生

 2:1

 $25,100

 Ashland University, Eastern Michigan University,
The Pennsylvania State University at Erie—
The Behrend College, University of Cincinnati,
University of Toledo

Happy Valley School

UNITED STATES

Adrian Sweet, Director of Admissions
P.O. Box 850
Ojai, California 93024
Phone: 805-646-4343 Fax: 805-646-4371
E-mail: admin@hvalley.org
URL: http://www.hvalley.org

HAPPY VALLEY SCHOOL

TABS, NAIS, NAFSA member   *Founded 1946*

The Happy Valley School's ESL program prepares students for English-speaking classes while immersing them in American culture and activities. The School coordinates TOEFL testing and offers an ESL summer program.

El programa de inglés como segundo idioma (ESL) del Happy Valley School prepara a los estudiantes para las clases en inglés mientras se familiarizan con la cultura y las actividades de los Estados Unidos. El colegio coordina pruebas TOEFL y ofrece un programa de verano de aprendizaje del inglés como segundo idioma.

Le programme d'anglais comme langue étrangère (ESL) offert par Happy Valley School prépare les étudiants aux cours dispensés en anglais, tout en leur permettant de découvrir la culture et les activités américaines. L'école coordonne les évaluations pour le TOEFL et propose un programme d'anglais comme langue étrangère (ESL) pendant l'été.

Happy Valley School の ESL プログラムでは、アメリカ文化・活動に集中しながら英語での授業に参加するための準備を整えます。本校では、TOEFL の実施と ESL 夏期プログラムを提供しています。

Happy Valley School 提供的 ESL 課程，在使學生融入美國文化和活動的同時，為他們選修英語口語課程作準備。該校協調 TOEFL 測試，並提供一項 ESL 暑期課程。

Strong academics, sports, and fine arts on a 450-acre campus.

Énfasis en cursos académicos, deportes y bellas artes en un terreno de 182 hectáreas.

Le campus de 182 hectares comprend des champs de sport, un centre de beaux arts et un excellent programme académique.

182 ヘクタールのキャンパスでは、学術、スポーツ、美術が幅広く展開されています。

校園佔地 182 公頃，提供一流的學術、體育和美術課程。

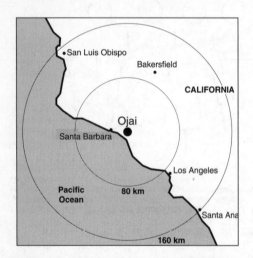

 8–18°C

 2–29°C

 4–15°C

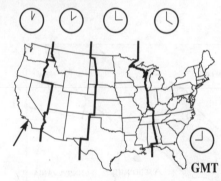

GMT

145 km from Los Angeles International Airport; 145 km from Los Angeles, CA
A 145 km del aeropuerto internacional de Los Angeles; a 145 km de Los Angeles, CA
A 145 km de l'aéroport international de Los Angeles ; à 145 km de Los Angeles, CA
ロスアンジェレス国際空個港より 145 キロ、ロスアンジェレス市より 145 キロ
離 Los Angeles 國際機場 145 公里；離 Los Angeles, CA 145 公里

 Coeducational 9–12 / Mixto / Mixte
男女共学
男女合校

 50/50

 80%

 25%

 64, 22 / solicitaron admisión, fueron aceptados / candidats, admis
出願者数 64 名、合格者数 22 名
64 人申請，22 人被錄取

 TOEFL, SLEP, SSAT, ISEE

 China, Germany, Hong Kong, India, Italy, Japan, Korea, Russia, Spain, Taiwan, Thailand

 Rolling / Continuo / Continuelles
隨時受付
全年招生

 Rolling / Continuo / Continuelles
隨時受付
全年招生

 5:1, 50%

 5:1

 $32,000 (res); $17,000 (day); $5500 (ESL)

 University of Southern California; University of California, Santa Cruz; University of California, Los Angeles; Occidental College; Bard College

Hebron Academy

Office of Admissions
P.O. Box 309
Hebron, Maine 04238-0309
Phone: 207-966-2100 Fax: 207-966-1111
E-mail: admissions@hebronacademy.org
URL: http://www.hebronacademy.org

NAIS, TABS member   *Founded 1804*

Hebron's academic program includes many honors and advanced placement options. ESL is available. Offerings in the arts and music are extensive, and the school has a full athletic program for girls and boys. The Academy offers excellent university placement.

El programa académico de Hebron incluye varias opciones de cursos avanzados y de honor. Se encuentra disponible inglés como segundo idioma (ESL). Los cursos en artes y música son extensos, y la escuela tiene un programa atlético completo para niños y niñas. La academia ofrece excelente colocación universitaria.

Hebron offre un programme de cours comprenant de nombreuses études spécialisées et une préparation à l'entrée dans les universités. Des cours d'anglais comme langue étrangère (ESL) sont proposés. Les cours relatifs aux arts et à la musique sont nombreux et l'école dispose d'un programme sportif complet, féminin et masculin. Hebron Academy assure par ailleurs un excellent soutien pour l'entrée à l'université.

Hebron の学科プログラムには、学力優秀者に対する多くの選択肢が含まれます。ESL も あり、提供される芸術・音楽は広範囲に渡ります。また、女子・男子各々のための運動競技 も充実しています。上級大学進学が可能です。

Hebron 的課程中包括多項榮譽和高級課程。ESL 可供選擇。學院開設豐富的藝術和音 樂課程並為男女生配備全套的健身設備。此學院為學生升入優秀大學做好準備。

Beautiful 1,500-acre campus with all facilities wired for Internet and e-mail.

Hermoso recinto escolar de 607 hectáreas de terreno. Todas las instalaciones cuentan con conexiones para Internet y correo electrónico.

Magnifique campus de 607 hectares. Tous les locaux sont équipés d'accès à Internet et aux messageries.

美しい 607 ヘクタールのキャンパス は、全施設がインターネットおよ び e メールに接続されています。

校園環境優美，面積 607 公頃。所 有建築為均備有網路，以供使用英

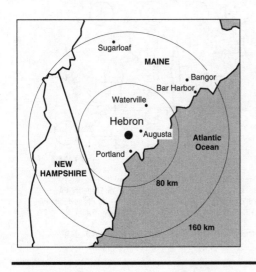

 10–24°C

 -1–7°C

 10–24°C

GMT

64 km from Portland Jetport; 64 km from Portland, Maine
A 64 km del Portland Jetport; a 64 km de Portland, Maine
À 64 km de Portland Jetport ; à 64 km de Portland, Maine
ポートランド・ジェットポートおよびメイン州ポートランドより各 64 km
離 Portland Jetport 機場 64 公里；離緬因州波特蘭市 64 公里

 Coeducational boarding 9–12 and postgraduate. / Mixto / Mixte
男女共学
男女合校

 209, 139 / solicitaron admisión, fueron aceptados / candidats, admis
出願者数 209 名、合格者数 139 名
209 人申請，139 人被錄取

 Rolling / Continuo / Continuelles
随時受付
全年招生

 $33,000; $100-$600

 128/92

 TOEFL, SLEP

 September, January / septiembre, enero / septembre, janvier
9 月、1 月
9 月，1 月

 60%

 TOEFL 231 (computer)

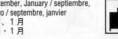 8:1, 80%

 Boston University, University of Maine, McGill University, Northeastern University, St. Anselm College

 22%

Brazil (2), Canada (10), Germany (10), Japan (10), Korea (10),

 5:1

The Hill School

Admission Office
717 East High Street
Pottstown, Pennsylvania 19464
Phone: 610-326-1000 Fax: 610-326-7471

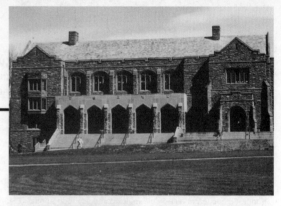

NAIS, TABS, FAIS member   *Founded 1851*

The Hill School offers small classes and extensive athletic and artistic activities to help prepare young men and women for college.

The Hill School ofrece clases con pocos alumnos y amplio programa de actividades deportivas y artísticas para ayudar a preparar a los jóvenes de ambos sexos para la universidad.

Hill School offre des classes restreintes ainsi qu'un grand nombre d'activités sportives et artistiques pour aider les jeunes gens à se préparer à la vie universitaire.

Hill School では大学に進学する若い皆さんに少人数クラス、様々な運動や芸術活動を提供します。

席爾學校提供小班教學以及內容廣泛的體育、藝術活動，幫助學生作好進入大學的準備。

The 300-acre campus has a new academic center and four new dormitories.
Las 121 hectáreas de terreno tienen un nuevo centro académico y cuatro nuevas residencias estudiantiles.
Le campus de 121 hectares dispose d'un nouveau centre éducatif et de quatre nouveaux dortoirs.
121 ヘクタールのキャンパスに新しいアカデミック・センターと4棟の新寄宿舎が増築されました。
校園面積 121 公頃，內有新建學習中心和四座新宿舍樓。

 10–27°C

 -7–4°C

 10–27°C

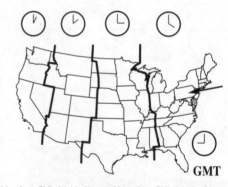

GMT

64 km from Philadelphia Airport; 62 km from Philadelphia, PA
A 64 km del aeropuerto de Filadelfia; a 62 km de Filadelfia, PA
A 64 km de l'aéroport de Philadelphie ; à 62 km de Philadelphie, PA
ペンシルバニア州フィラデルフィア国際空港より 64 キロ、同州フィラデルフィアより 62 キロ
離 Philadelphia 機場 64 公里；離 Philadelphia, PA 62 公里

 Coeducational 9-12PG/ Mixto / Mixte
男女共学
男女合校

 270/210

 80%

 13%

 310, 295 / solicitaron admisión, fueron aceptados / candidats, admis
出願者数 310 名、合格者数 295 名
310 人申請，295 人被錄取

 SSAT (72%)

ISEE, SSAT, PSAT, SAT

Canada, China, England, Korea, Thailand

 February 1 / 1 de febrero / 1 février
2 月 1 日
2 月 1 日

 September / septiembre / septembre
9 月
9 月

 7:1, 98%

1:1
Dell laptops are required for all students / Todos los estudiantes deben tener computadoras portátiles Dell / Chaque étudiant doit posséder un ordinateur portable Dell / 全ての学生は Dell のラップトップ・コンピュータが必要です。/ 所有學生均須備有戴爾筆記本電腦。

 $32,500

University of Pennsylvania, Boston College, Stanford University, Cornell University, Bucknell University

The Hockaday School

Jen Liggitt, Director of Admission
11600 Welch Road
Dallas, Texas 75229-2999
Phone: 214-363-6311 Fax: 214-265-1649
E-mail: admissions@mail.hockaday.org
URL: http://www.hockaday.org

TABS, FAIS member   *Founded 1913*

Intermediate and advanced English-speaking students are accepted into a challenging college-preparatory program. The first year includes a trip to Washington, D.C. 100% of graduates attend four-year colleges. Summer ESL is offered at all levels.

Los estudiantes que hablan inglés a nivel avanzado e intermedio se aceptan en un programa retador de preparación universitaria. El primer año incluye un viaje a Washington, D.C. El 100% de los egresados continúan sus estudios en la universidad. Se ofrecen cursos de inglés como segundo idioma (ESL) a todo nivel.

Les étudiants parlant l'anglais a niveau avancé ou intermédiaire sont acceptés dans un programme intense de préparation pour l'université. La première année comprend un voyage à Washington, D.C. 100% des diplômés de l'école poursuivent des études universitaires. Des cours d'anglais comme langue étrangère (ESL) sont offerts à touts les niveaux.

中級ならびに上級の英語力をもつ生徒は大学進学準備課程で学びます。入学1年目にワシントンD.C.への旅行があります。卒業生は100パーセント4年制大学へ進学します。夏のESL（留学生のための英語講座）はあらゆるレベルの生徒が受講できます。

本校富有挑戰性的大學預備課程接受具有中級和高級英語語言能力的學生。入學第一年的活動包括到美國首府華盛頓旅行。學校畢業生全都進入四年大學深造。夏季設有各級程度的英語為第二語言班。

The 100-acre residential, air-conditioned campus includes extensive science, arts, and sports facilities.

El terreno de 41 hectáreas con instalaciones residenciales y aire acondicionado incluye amplias instalaciones de ciencias, artes y atletismo.

Le campus de 41 hectares comprend des dortoirs et climatisation, ainsi que des amples établissements pour les sciences, les arts, et le sport.

41ヘクタールの住施設や空調設備が整ったキャンパスには、科学、芸術、スポーツの大きな施設があります。

佔地41公頃的住區校園擁有各類科學、藝術及體育設施，並配有空調設備。

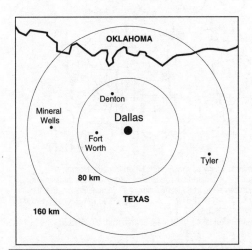

8–31°C

2–15°C

8–28°C

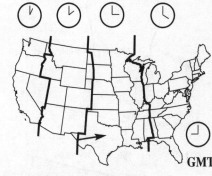

32 km from Dallas/Fort Worth Airport, TX
A 32 km del aeropuerto de Fort Worth y de Dallas, TX
A 32 km de l'aéroport de Fort Worth et de Dallas, TX
テキサス州ダラス・フォートワースから32キロ
離 Dallas/Fort Worth, TX 32 公里

 Girls PK–12 / Niñas / Filles
女子中学校
女子中學校

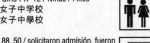 0/434

 16%

 3%

 88, 50 / solicitaron admisión, fueron aceptadas / candidates, admises
出願者数 88 名、合格者数 50 名
88 人申請，50 人被錄取

 TOEFL, SLEP or ISEE

 Korea (5), Mexico (14), Saudi Arabia (6), Taiwan (7), Thailand (4)

 Rolling / Continuo / Continuelles
随時受付
隨時皆可

 September, December / septiembre, diciembre / septembre, décembre
9 月、12 月
9 月，12 月

8:1, 0%

2:1

 $34,500; $1230–$3510

University of Texas, Stanford University, Duke University, Dartmouth College, Southern Methodist University

Hoosac School

Dean S. Foster
Director of Admissions
P.O. Box 9, Pine Valley Road
Hoosick, New York 12089
Phone: 518-686-7331 Fax: 518-686-3370
E-mail: info@hoosac.com
URL: http://www.hoosac.com

TABS member   *Founded 1889*

Hoosac School offers international students an opportunity to develop strong skills in English while being immersed in the culture of the school and region. Hoosac offers three levels of ESL and issues I-20s to enrolled students.

Hoosac School ofrece a los estudiantes internacionales la oportunidad de desarrollar altos niveles de conocimientos del inglés mientras viven inmersos en la cultura del colegio y la región. Hoosac ofrece tres niveles de Inglés como Segundo Idioma (ESL) y emite formularios I-20 para estudiantes matriculados.

Hoosac School offre aux élèves du monde entier l'occasion d'acquérir l'aisance de la langue anglaise tout en étant immergé dans la culture de l'école et de la région. L'école propose aussi trois niveaux de cours d'anglais comme langue étrangère (ESL) et procure des visas I-20 aux étudiants inscrits.

当校は留学生が学校や地域社会のなかで文化を体得しながら、英語力を高められるようカリキュラムを組んでいます。Hoosac では 3 段階別の ESL 講座を設け、入学した生徒には書式 I-20 を発行します。

Hoosac School 為國際學生提供在置身於學校和地區文化環境之中的同時，發展英文的幾會。學校舉辦三種級別的英語為第二語言暑期班，並簽發 I-20 表格。

The 350-acre wooded campus allows a variety of outdoor activities.

Las 142 hectáreas de terrenos boscosos permiten una gran variedad de actividades al aire libre.

Le campus boisé de 142 hectares permet une diversité de jeux en plein air.

142 ヘクタールの緑あふれるキャンパスではさまざまなスポーツができます。

校園佔地 142 公頃，樹木繁茂，可以從事各種戶外活動。

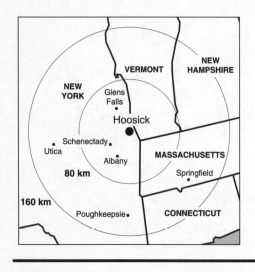

 0–18°C

 -12–4°C

 0–21°C

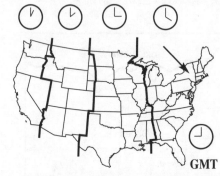

48 km from Albany County Airport; 17 km from Bennington, VT
A 48 km del aeropuerto del condado de Albany; a 17 km de Bennington, VT
A 48 km de l'aéroport d'Albany County ; à 17 km de Bennington, VT
アルバニー・カウンティ空港より 48 キロ、バーモント州のベニングトン市より 17 キロ
離 Albany 郡機場 48 公里；離 Bennington, VT 17 公里

  Coeducational 8–12, PG / Mixto / Mixte
男女共学
男女合校

 80/40

 90%

 20%

 90, 67 / solicitaron admisión, fueron aceptados / candidats, admis
出願者数 90 名、合格者数 67 名
90 人申請、67 人被錄取

 TOEFL

  Canada (10), China (3), Croatia (1), India (2), Japan (2), Korea (15), Romania (1)

 Rolling / Continuo / Continuelles
随時受付
全年招生

 5:1, 95%

 5:1

 $25,200; $3500

 Boston College, Northwestern University, Penn State University, Syracuse University, University of Southern California, Vanderbilt University, Wheaton College

The Hotchkiss School

William D. Leahy, Dean of Admission and
Financial Aid
P.O. Box 800
Lakeville, Connecticut 06039
Phone: 860-435-3102 Fax: 860-435-0042

TABS, NAIS member   *Founded 1891*

Hotchkiss, a school of 550 students, offers rigorous academics within a supportive environment, varied extracurricular activities, diverse student body, and international study/travel options.

Hotchkiss, una escuela de 550 estudiantes, ofrece cursos rigurosos en un ambiente con mucho apoyo, una gran variedad de actividades extracurriculares, estudiantado variado y opciones para estudios y viajes internacionales.

Hotchkiss, un établissement de 550 étudiants, offre un programme scolaire rigoureux, un climat d'entraide, une variété d'activités extra-scolaires, des élèves de divers pays et des possibilités d'études et de séjours à l'étranger.

生徒数 550 人の Hotchkiss は支援的な環境の下に厳格な学科教育を行っています。また生徒の幅も広く、様々な課外活動、留学や旅行の機会も提供しています。

Hotchkiss 有 550 名學生，該校提供有利的學習環境，包括嚴格的學術課程、多樣化的課外活動、多元化的學生團體以及國際遊學的機會。

The 525-acre rural campus includes fiber-optic classrooms.

Las 213 hectáreas de terreno en un ambiente rural incluyen aulas de fibra óptica.

Le campus rural de 213 hectares comprend des salles de classes de fibre-optiques.

郊外に広がる 213 ヘクタールキャンパスには繊維光学の教室もあります。

校園佔地 213 公頃，位於鄉村，包括織維光學玻璃教室。

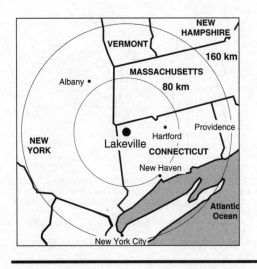

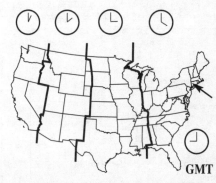

GMT

96 km from Bradley International Airport and Hartford, CT
A 96 km del aeropuerto internacional de Bradley y de Hartford, CT
A 96 km de l'aéroport international de Bradley et de Hartford, CT
ブラッドリー国際空港より 96 キロ、コネチカット州ハートフォードより 96 キロ
離 Bradley 國際機場和 Hartford, CT 96 公里

 Coeducational 9–PG / Mixto / Mixte
男女共学
男女合校

 1316, 356 / solicitaron admisión, fueron aceptados / candidats, admis
出願者数 1316 名、合格者数 356 名
1316 人申請，356 人被錄取

 January 15 / 15 de enero / 15 janvier
1 月 15 日
1 月 15 日

 $31,925; $850

 290/270

 TOEFL (600), SSAT

 September / septiembre / septembre
9 月
9 月

 $31,925; $850

 92%

SLEP, ISEE

5:1, 100%

Princeton University, Harvard University, Yale University, Georgetown University, Brown University, Cornell University

 10%

 Canada, Hong Kong, Jamaica, Saudi Arabia, South Korea

 2:1

Idyllwild Arts Academy

UNITED STATES

Karen Porter, Dean of Admission
P.O. Box 38, 52500 Temecula Road
Idyllwild, California 92549
Phone: 909-659-2171 Ext. 223
Fax: 909-659-2058
E-mail: kporter@idyllwildarts.org
URL: http://www.idyllwildarts.org

NAIS, TABS, NAFSA member   *Founded 1981*

In ESL classes, students learn reading, composition, speaking, and listening skills as well as grammar, vocabulary, and study skills needed to succeed in non-ESL courses at the Academy and later in college. An introduction to the Writing Center, Internet technology, and the College Counseling Center early in their education familiarize them with new ways to create opportunities for themselves in their educational and life goals.

En las clases de inglés como segundo idioma (ESL), los estudiantes aprenden lectura, composición, conversación, técnicas de comprensión, así como gramática, vocabulario y las técnicas de aprendizaje necesarias para tener éxito en los cursos regulares de la Academia y posteriormente en la universidad. La introducción al Centro de Redacción, la tecnología de Internet y el Centro de Asesoramiento para la Universidad, en los comienzos de su educación, los familiariza con los nuevos medios para crear oportunidades para sí mismos en sus objetivos académicos y personales.

Pendant les cours d'anglais comme langue étrangère (ESL), les étudiants apprennent la lecture, la composition, l'expression orale et les techniques d'écoute, ainsi que la grammaire, le vocabulaire et les techniques d'étude nécessaires aux autres cours aussi bien à l'Academy que plus tard à l'université. Une introduction au Centre de lettres, à la technologie Internet et au Centre d'orientation universitaire en début de scolarité permet aux étudiants de découvrir de nouvelles façons de créer leurs propres opportunités aussi bien sur le plan scolaire que personnel.

ESL クラスでは、学生は文法や語彙のほか、読解、作文、スペリング、および聴解スキルおよび Academy の ESL 以外のコースや後に大学に進むために必要な学習スキルを学びます。初期の段階でライティング・センターやインターネット技術、大学カウンセリングセンターを知ることにより、学生達は教育および人生の目標に向かって、自ら可能性を創造できる新しい方法に慣れ親しむことができます。

在外國學生英語課堂上，學生學習閱讀、作文、說話、聽力、語法、詞匯以及學習技能，從而今後在該校和大學的非外國學生英語課程中獲得成功。開學後不久，即向學生介紹寫作中心、網際網路技術、學校咨詢中心，幫助其以新途徑為實現自己的教育目標及人生目標創造機會。

A state-of-the-art library opened in August of 2000 on the 206-acre campus.

En agosto del año 2000 se inauguró una moderna biblioteca en el recinto escolar de 83 hectáreas de terreno.

Une bibliothèque ultra-moderne a ouvert ses portes en août 2000 sur le campus de 83 hectares.

2000 年 8 月には 83 ヘクタールのキャンパスに時代の先端を行く図書館がオープンしました。

校園佔地 83 公頃，內有一座極為現代化的圖書館，已於 2000 年 8 月啟用。

 13–21°C

 2–16°C

 9–27°C

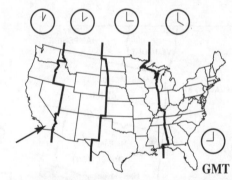

156 km from Los Angeles International Airport; 84 km from Palm Springs, CA / A 156 km del aeropuerto internacional de Los Angeles; a 84 km de Palm Springs, CA / A 156 km de l'aéroport international de Los Angeles ; à 84 km de Palm Springs, CA
カリフォルニア州ロサンゼルス国際空港から 156 キロ、同州パームスプリングスより 84 キロ
離 Los Angeles 國際機場 156 公里；離加州 Palm Springs 市 84 公里

 Coeducational 9–PG / Mixto / Mixte
男女共学
男女合校

 95/160

 95%

 28%

 270, 192 / solicitaron admisión, fueron aceptados / candidats, admis
出願者数 270 名、合格者数 192 名
270 人申請，192 人被錄取

 TOEFL, SLEP, SSAT

 Bulgaria (11), China (11), Germany (8), Japan (13), Korea (11)

 Rolling / Continuo / Continuelles
隨時受付
全年招生

 September, January / septiembre, enero / septembre, janvier
9 月，1 月
9 月，1 月

 9:1, 7%

15:1

 $35,800, $19,600

University of Southern California, New York University, University of Michigan, The Curtis Institute, The Juilliard School

Interlochen Arts Academy

Thomas Bewley, Director of Admissions
P.O. Box 199
Interlochen, Michigan 49643
Phone: 231-276-7200 Fax: 231-276-7464
E-mail: admissions@interlochen.org

TABS, NAIS member   *Founded 1963*

Interlochen Arts Academy is the premier fine arts high school in the United States, recognized as a model teaching center and outstanding presenter of artistic talent and achievement. The Academy offers instruction in music, theatre arts, dance, visual arts, creative writing, and college-preparatory academics. An English as a second language program is offered.

Interlochen Arts Academy es la principal escuela secundaria de bellas artes en los Estados Unidos, reconocida como un centro de enseñanza modelo y un excepcional presentador de talentos y logros artísticos. La Academia ofrece cursos de música, artes teatrales, danza, artes visuales, composición creativa y un programa académico de preparación para la universidad. Se ofrece un programa de inglés como segundo idioma (ESL).

En ce qui concerne les beaux-arts, Interlochen Arts Academy est le meilleur établissement secondaire des États-Unis. Considérée comme un centre d'enseignement modèle, l'école est prodigue en talents et réalisations artistiques. La musique, les arts de la scène, la danse, les arts plastiques, la création littéraire et un programme scolaire préparant à l'entrée en université y sont enseignés. Des cours d'anglais comme langue étrangère sont également proposés.

Interlochen Arts Academy はアメリカでトップレベルの芸術系高等学校です。模範教育センター、芸術の才能と業績において優れた贈与者として認定されています。当校では、音楽、舞台芸術、ダンス、ビジュアル・アート、クリエイティブ・ライティング入門と、大学準備講座の一般教養を提供しています。ESLプログラムも提供しています。

Interlochen 藝術學院是美國一流的美術高中學校，被譽為模範教學中心和藝術才能和成就的杰出展出者。該學院提供音樂、戲劇藝術、舞蹈、視覺藝術、創作以及大學預科教學。設有英語作為第二外語課程。

1200-acre campus includes newly renovated dorms and new piano/percussion facility.

Las 486 hectáreas de terreno incluye residencias estudiantiles renovadas recientemente y un nuevo centro de piano e instrumentos de percusión.

Le campus de 486 hectares comprend des dortoirs récemment rénovés, ainsi qu'un nouveau studio pour piano et percussions.

486 ヘクタールのキャンパスには、新しく改装された寮、新しいピアノ／打楽器の設備が完備されています。

佔地 486 公頃的校園其中有新改建的宿舍和新的鋼琴／打擊樂練習室。

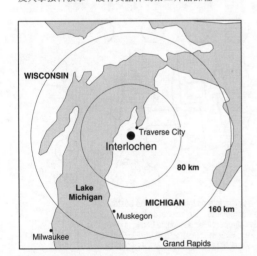

 5–28° C

 -10–5° C

 5–28° C

GMT

25 km from Traverse City Airport; 25 km from Traverse City, MI
A 25 km del aeropuerto Traverse; a 25 km de Traverse City, MI
A 25 km de l'aéroport Traverse City ; à 25 km de Traverese City, MI
トラバースシティー空港から 25 キロ、ミシガン州トラバースシティー市から 25 キロ
離 Traverse City 機場 25 公里；離 Traverse City 25 公里

  Coeducational 9–PG / Mixto / Mixte
男女共学
男女合校

  175/280

94%

  14%

 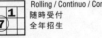 350, 275 / solicitaron admisión, fueron aceptados / candidats, admis
出願者数 350 名、合格者数 275 名
350 人申請，275 人被録取

TOEFL, SSAT

 China, Japan, Korea, Soviet Republics, Taiwan

 Rolling / Continuo / Continuelles
随時受付
全年招生

September, January / septiembre, enero / septembre, janvier
9月、1月
9月，1月

6:1

7:1

 $30,350, $5460, $1300

 Eastman School of Music, Indiana University, Oberlin Conservatory, The Juilliard School, University of Michigan, Carnegie Mellon University

 Beginning through Advanced ESL, ESL Multicultural Perspectives, ESL Government, ESL American Experience

Uniform required

Lawrence Academy

Andrea O'Hearn
Director of Admissions
Powderhouse Road, P.O. Box 992
Groton, Massachusetts 01450
Phone: 978-448-6535 Fax: 978-448-9208

NAIS, FAIS, NAFSA member   *Founded 1793*

A full-time English as a second language (ESL) director works closely with faculty. LA also arranges TOEFL testing, issues I-20s, sponsors an International Student Association and a host family program.

Un director a tiempo completo del programa de enseñanza del inglés como segundo idioma (ESL) trabaja de cerca con los profesores. L.A. ayuda con las pruebas TOEFL, emite formularios I-20, patrocina una asociación de estudiantes extranjeros y programas de familias anfitrionas.

Un directeur à plein temps travaille en étroite liaison avec les professeurs. LA organise aussi l'examen TOEFL, fournit les documents nécessaires à l'obtention d'un visa, parraine l'association internationale des étudiants aussi bien qu'un programme d'accueil en famille.

専任の ESL（第二外国語としての英語）プログラムのディレクターは、教師陣と密に連絡をとりながら指導を進めています。当校はまた、構内 TOEFL の実施、書式 I-20 の発行、留学生協会の後援、ホームステイプログラムを実施しています。

本校聘有一位全職的英語為第二語言指導主任與學校教師密切合作。LA同時也安排托福測試、發給 I-20表格、贊助國際學生協會和提供寄住家庭。

The 99-acre campus includes a Sony language lab, an athletic complex, an arts center, a new dormitory, and a new academic building.

El recinto de 99 acres incluye un laboratorio de idiomas Sony, un complejo atlético, un centro de arte, un nuevo dormitorio y un nuevo edificio académico.

Le campus de près de 40 hectares propose un laboratoire de langues Sony, un complexe sportif, un centre pour les arts, un nouveau dortoir et un nouveau bâtiment de salles de classe.

40 ヘクタールのキャンパスには。ソニーのランゲージ・ラボ、体育施設、芸術センター、そして新設の寄宿舎と校舎が在ります。

佔地 40 公頃的校園設有 Sony 語言教室，體育運動房，藝術中心，新建的宿舍和教學樓。

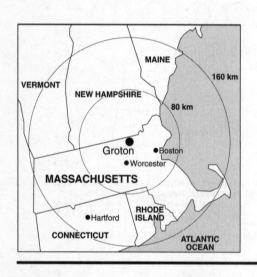

 10–24°C

 -12–10°C

 10–24°C

56 km from Logan International Airport and Boston, MA
A 56 km del aeropuerto internacional de Logan y de Boston, MA
A 56 km de l'aéroport international de Logan et de Boston, MA
マサチューセッツ州ローガン国際空港及びボストン市より 56 キロ
離 Logan, MA 國際機場和 Boston, MA 各 56 公里

 Coeducational 9–12 / Mixto / Mixte
男女共学
男女合校

  211/153

  50%

 14%

 532, 240 / solicitaron admisión, fueron aceptados / candidats, admis
出願者数 532 名、合格者数 240 名
532 人申請，240 人被録取

 TOEFL (480)

 SLEP (50)

 Germany, Japan, Korea, Mexico, Thailand

 February 1 / 1 de febero / 1er février
2 月 1 日
2 月 1 日

 September, / septiembre, / septembre,
9 月
9 月

 8:1, 70%

 4:1

 $34,800; $600

 Boston College, Northeastern University, Bowdoin College, University of Vermont, Boston University

Linden Hall School for Girls

UNITED STATES

Madelyn P. Nix, Director of Admissions
212 East Main Street
Lititz, Pennsylvania 17543
Phone: 717-626-8512 Fax: 717-627-1384
E-mail: admissions@lindenhall.org

NAIS, TABS, FAIS member   *Founded 1746*

Linden Hall offers a college-preparatory curriculum for international students. It offers beginning through advanced ESL, performing arts, athletics, equestrian studies, homestays, and coordination of travel. Chaperoned day, weekend, and optional international trips are available to all. Linden Hall is located in the small, safe town of Lititz, Pennsylvania.

Linden Hall ofrece un plan de estudios de preparación para la universidad para los estudiantes extranjeros. Ofrece un programa de inglés como segundo idioma (ESL) desde nivel de principiante hasta avanzado, artes escénicas, atletismo, estudios de equitación, alojamiento con familias locales y coordinación de viajes. También se ofrecen viajes con chaperón de día, fin de semana y opcionales al extranjero. Linden Hall está ubicado en la pequeña y segura ciudad de Lititz, en Pennsylvania.

Linden Halloffre aux étudiants étrangers un programme scolaire préparant à l'entrée à l'université. L'établissement propose également des cours d'anglais comme langue étrangère de niveau débutant à avancé, l'enseignement des arts du spectacle, des activités sportives, des cours d'équitation, des séjours en famille et l'organisation de voyages. Des excursions d'une journée ou sur un week-end ainsi que des voyages à l'étranger, surveillés par des adultes, sont disponibles à tous. Linden Hall est situé dans la petite ville calme de Lititz en Pennsylvanie.

Linden Hall では、留学生に大学準備講座のカリキュラムを提供しています。初級から上級までの ESL クラス、舞台芸術、体育、乗馬、ホームステイがあり、旅行のコーディネートもしています。誰でも 1 日あるいは週末単位の付添いサービスや、世界旅行がオプションで利用できます。Linden Hall は、PennsylvanIa 州の安全で小さな Lititz という町にあります。

Linden Hall為國際學生提供大學預備課程。本校提供從初級到高級的ESL課程、表演藝術、體育、馬術、家庭寄宿和旅行安排。所有學生均可參加由年長女伴監督的白天、週末及選擇性國際旅行。Linden Hall位於環境安全的賓州 Lititz 小鎮。

Small class sizes offer individualized attention.
Clases con pocos alumnos ofrecen atención individualizada.
Les classes, de taille restreinte, permettent une attention individualisée.
少人数クラスなので一人一人に注意が行き届きます。
小型課堂可提供個別關心。

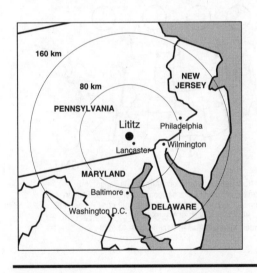

  4–24°C

  -12–4°C

  4–26°C

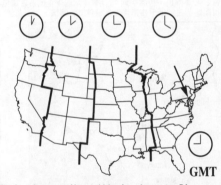

GMT

8 km from Lancaster Airport; 11 km from Lancaster, PA
A 8 km del aeropuerto de Lancaster; a 11 km de Lancaster, PA
A 8 km de l'aéroport de Lancaster ; à 11 km de Lancaster, PA
ランカスター空港から 8 キロ、ペンシルバニア州
ランカスター市から 11 キロ
離 Lancaster 機場 8 公里；離 Lancaster, PA 11 公里

 Girls 6–PG / Niñas / Filles
女子中学校
女子中學校

 0/90

 75%

 25%

 101, 52 / solicitaron admisión, fueron aceptadas / candidates, admises
出願者数 101 名、合格者数 52 名
101 人申請，52 人被錄取

TOEFL (475)

 China (4), Japan (25), Korea (18), Mexico (18), Saudi Arabia (25), Taiwan (4)

 Rolling / Continuo / Continuelles
隨時受付
全年招生

 Rolling / Continuo / Continuelles
隨時受付
全年招生

4:1, 30%

 2:1

 $32,450

American University, University of Chicago, George Washington University, Mount Holyoke College, Pratt Institute, Sweet Briar College

 Beginning, intermediate and advanced English, health, science and ESL American studies
Estudios de inglés, salud, ciencias e inglés americano como segundo idioma (ESL) a niveles de principiante, intermedio y avanzado.
Anglais débutant, intermédiaire et avancé, santé, sciences et anglais comme langue étrangère (civilisation américaine).
初級、中級、上級の英語、保健、科学、および ESL アメリカ研究。
初級、中級和高級英語、健康、科學以及 ESL 美國文化學習。

 Uniforms / Uniforme / Uniforme
制服あり
制服

Maine Central Institute

Director of Admission
125 South Main Street
Pittsfield, Maine 04967
Phone: 207-487-2282 Fax: 207-487-3512
E-mail: cwilliams@mci-school.org
URL: http://www.mci-school.org

TABS, NAFSA member   *Founded 1866*

MCI offers a rigorous, comprehensive college-preparatory curriculum, small classes, supportive residence hall supervision to foster individual growth and achievement, and an extensive ESL program, including a four-week intensive Summer ESL Program. The campus is located in a safe, rural environment on 23 acres and includes 14 buildings and lighted athletic fields. Boarding students are housed in single-sex residence halls on campus, supervised by resident faculty and staff members.

MCI ofrece un riguroso y completo plan de estudios de preparación universitaria, clases con pocos alumnos, supervisión y apoyo en las residencias para fomentar el desarrollo y los logros individuales, y un amplio programa de enseñanza del inglés como segundo idioma (ESL), incluyendo un programa intensivo de inglés como segundo idioma en el verano. El recinto se encuentra localizado en un ambiente rural y seguro e incluye14 edificios y campos de atletismo iluminados. Los estudiantes que se hospedan se alojan en residencias para un solo sexo, supervisados por el cuerpo docente residente y miembros del personal.

MCI offre un programme rigoureux et complet de préparation aux universités. La petite taille des classes alliée au soutien apporté aux élèves par le personnel d'encadrement des résidences leur permet de s'épanouir et d'obtenir de bons résultats. Un programme très complet d'anglais comme langue étrangère (ESL) est offert qui inclut un programme d'été intensif de 4 semaines. Le campus est situé sur un terrain protégé de 9.5 hectares, comprenant 14 bâtiments et un terrain de sport illuminé. Les étudiants internes sont logés dans des maisons pour filles ou garçons sur le campus, supervisées par des membres du corps enseignant et par le personnel d'encadrement.

当校は厳格で統合的な大学進学準備プログラムの他、小人数クラス制、個人の成長を促す支援的な寮制度、また4週間の夏期ESLプログラムを含む幅広いESLプログラムを提供しています。キャンパスは10ヘクタールの自然豊かで安全な田園地域にあり、14の建物とナイター設備のあるグランドがあります。キャンパス内には男子、女子各々の寮設備があり、住み込みの優秀なスタッフが指導にあたります。

MCI的大學嚴格的預備課程涉及面廣泛，旨再發展優異的學術能力；採用小班制教血，並配合宿舍督導來鼓勵學生學習成長。提供密集的英語為第二語言課程，包括為期四周的夏日ESL集訓班。校園佔地23英畝，地處安全的農莊環境之中。本校設施包括14座建築和夜間照明運動場。住宿生受在校員工的關懷，住宿在男女分開的宿舍中。

Our new Math and Science Center is a 2,300 square foot state-of-the-art building, providing 14 instructional spaces, 2 computer classrooms, and a botany area.

Nuestro nuevo Centro de Matemáticas y Ciencias es un moderno edificio de 2,300 pies cuadrados que provee 14 espacios de instrucción, 2 aulas de computadoras y un área de botánica.

Notre nouveau Centre de Mathématiques et de Sciences est un situé dans un immeuble ultra moderne de 230 m carré avec 14 salles de cours, 2 salles d'ordinateurs et un espace vert.

新しい数学・科学センターは2,300平方フィートの芸術の集合ビルで、14の教授用スペースを提供し、2つのコンピュータ教室と植物学教室があります。

我們新建的數學和科學中心面積2,300平方英尺，設備先進，具有14個學術空間，兩間計算機教室和一個植物園。

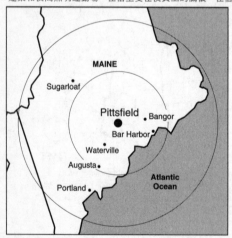

 2–24°C

 -6–7°C

 4–29°C

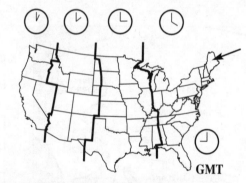

GMT

40 km from Bangor International Airport and Bangor, ME
A 40 km del aeropuerto internacional de Bangor y de Bangor, ME
A 40 km de l'aéroport international de Bangor et de Bangor, ME
メイン州バンガー国際空港及び同州バンガー市より40キロ
離 Bangor, ME 國際機場和 Bangor 市各40公里

 Coeducational 9–PG / Mixto / Mixte
男女共学
男女合校

 293/220

 20%

 11%

 80, 70 / solicitaron admisión, fueron aceptados / candidats, admis
出願者数80名，合格者数70名
80人申請，70人被錄取

 ✓

 TOEFL, SLEP, SSAT

 3.66:1

 Rolling / Continuo / Continuelles
随時受付
全年招生

Rolling / Continuo / Continuelles
随時受付
全年招生

 12:1, 20%

 Bahamas, Bermuda, Canada, China, Ecuador, Germany, Hong Kong, Japan, Kazakhstan, Korea, Mexico, Puerto Rico, Russia, Saudi Arabia, Spain, Taiwan, Vietnam, Yugoslavia

 $29,000; $2000

 University of Maine, Boston College, Fairleigh Dickinson University, Harvard University, Cornell University, Georgetown University, Rochester Institute of Technology

 $2500 (ESL support)

The Masters School

Susan D. Hendricks
Director of Admission
49 Clinton Avenue
Dobbs Ferry, NY 10522
Phone: 914-479-6920 Fax: 914-693-7295

TABS, NAIS member   *Founded 1877*

Masters has served international students exceptionally well for many years. The close school community and supportive faculty provide a secure and pleasant atmosphere. ESL classes are offered in several subject areas. International students are expected to have achieved an intermediate level of English proficiency before entering the school and to have reached mainstream proficiency by junior or senior year. Applicants should plan to take the TOEFL or SLEP test as part of the application process.

Masters ha atendido a estudiantes extranjeros excepcionalmente bien por muchos años. La comunidad escolar unida y el profesorado comprensivo provee una atmósfera agradable y segura. Las clases de inglés como segundo (ESL) se ofrecen en varias áreas. Los estudiantes internacionales deben haber obtenido un nivel intermedio de inglés antes de ingresar a la escuela y alcanzar un dominio del inglés en el 3er y 4to año de estudio. Los solicitantes deben pensar en tomar el examen TOEFL o SLEF como parte de la solicitud.

Depuis de nombreuses années, Masters propose un excellent programme aux étudiants étrangers. La communauté de l'établissement ainsi que le corps enseignant, dévoué et coopératif, s'associent pour créer une atmosphère agréable et rassurante. Les cours d'anglais comme langue étrangère (ESL) sont dispensés dans de nombreux domaines. Les étudiants étrangers doivent avoir un niveau moyen d'anglais avant de commencer les cours pour pouvoir intégrer les cours d'anglais réguliers pour la Première ou la Terminale. Les étudiants doivent se préparer à passer les examens TOEFL ou SLEF pour leur dossier d'admission.

Masters は長年に渡り留学生への抜群のサービスを誇っています。親密な学校地域社会と支援的で親切な教授陣が快適な雰囲気を作り出しています。多数の科目において ESL クラスが整っています。留学生は入学に際し上級レベルの英語力が必要ですが、入学後は更に各学年ごと英語力が熟達して行きます。入学希望者は TOEFL または SLEF テストを手続きの一貫として受験する必要があります。

斯斯特斯學校為外國學生提供出色服務已有多年。該校學生少，教師對學生關愛支持，提供令人愉快的環境。ESL英語課程涵蓋許多學科領域。外國學生在入學前應具有中等英語水平，並在高年級時修讀主流英語課程。申請入學的外國學生應提供TOEFL 和 SLEF的考試成績。

96-acre campus, 20 miles from Manhattan. Comfortable dormitories. Faculty members live in dorms and act as house parents.

39 hectáreas de terreno, a 32 kilómetros de Manhattan. Cómodas residencias estudiantiles. Miembros del profesorado viven en las residencias estudiantiles y actúan como padres en la casa.

Campus de 39 hectares, à 32 km de Manhattan. Dortoirs confortables. Les membres du corps enseignant résident dans les dortoirs et jouent le rôle de parent pour le groupe.

39 ヘクタールのキャンパスは Manhattan から 32 km。快適な寄宿舎。教授陣も house parent として寄宿舎に住んでいます。

校園面積39公頃，距曼哈頓32公里。校園有舒適的宿舍。教師住在宿舍，擔當在校父母的角色。

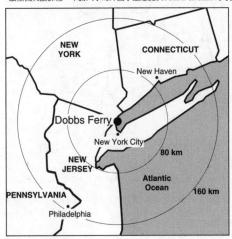

 10–27°C

 -3–4°C

 10–27°C

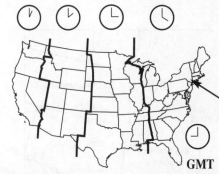

GMT

32 km from Kennedy Airport; 32 km from New York City, NY
A 32 km del aeropuerto Kennedy; a 32 km de la ciudad de Nueva York, NY
A 32 km de l'aéroport Kennedy ; à 32 km de New York City, NY
ケネディ空港より 32 キロ、ニューヨーク州のニューヨーク市より 32 キロ
離 Kennedy 機場 32 公里；離紐約州紐約市 32 公里

 Coed boarding 9–12 / Mixto / Mixte
男女共学
男女合校

 175/200

 40%

 13%

 500, 100 / solicitaron admisión, fueron aceptadas / candidats, admis
出願者数 500 名、合格者数 100 名
500 人申請，100 人被錄取

 TOEFL, SLEP

 Bulgaria, Colombia, Germany, Hong Kong, Japan, Korea, Romania, Russia, Taiwan, Thailand, United Arab Republic

 February 5 / 5 de febrero / 5 février
2 月 5 日
2 月 5 日

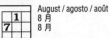 August / agosto / août
8 月
8 月

 7:1, 70%

 2:1

 $32,300; $3000 (first year); $1000 (subsequent years)

 Boston University, Harvard University, New York University, Yale University

Millbrook School

Cynthia McWilliams, Director of Admission
Millbrook School
School Road
Millbrook, New York 12545
Phone: 845-677-8261 Fax: 845-677-1265
E-mail: admissions@millbrook.org
URL: http://www.millbrook.org

Millbrook School

TABS, FAIS, NAFSA member   *Founded 1931*

International student advisor oversees individual academic and extracurricular experience. Millbrook School offers a rigorous curriculum and extraordinary opportunities in arts, community service, and athletics. Tutoring available in intermediate and advanced ESL.

Un asesor para los estudiantes internacionales supervisa la experiencia académica y extraescolar individual. Millbrook School ofrece un plan de estudio riguroso y oportunidades extraordinarias en las artes, servicio a la comunidad y atletismo. Se ofrecen clases particulares para los cursos intermedios y avanzados de inglés como segundo idioma.

Un conseiller pour les élèves étrangers supervise l'expérience individuelle académique et en dehors du plan d'études. Millbrook School offre un plan d'études rigoureux et des opportunités extraordinaires dans les arts, le service communautaire et les sports. Des cours particuliers d'anglais comme langue étrangère sont disponibles pour les niveaux "intermédiaire" et "avancé".

留学生アドバイザーは個人別に学科や他の各種活動を指導します。本校は厳しいカリキュラムを初め、芸術、コミュニティーサービスやスポーツなどの機会を提供します。 中級および上級の ESL では、個人指導も選択できます。

國際學生補導老師堅管個別學生的學習及課外活動。本校設有嚴格的課程以及藝術、社區服務和體育方面的課外活動，中級和高級 ESL 課程有專門補導。

Beautiful 500-acre campus with athletic center, arts center, and nationally accredited zoo.

El bello terreno de 202 hectáreas con centro deportivo, centro de artes y un zoológico acreditado a nivel nacional.

Un beau campus de 202 hectares avec un centre d'athlétisme, un centre artistique et un jardin zoologique reconnu nationalement.

美しい 202 ヘクタールのキャンパスには体育センターやアートセンター、全米でも知られている動物園などがあります。

校園佔地 202 公頃，設有運動中心、藝術中心和全國機構認可的動物園。

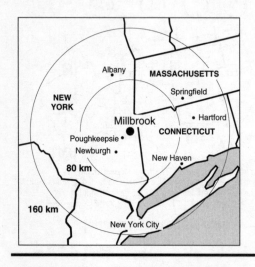

 13–24°C

 -18–4°C

 10–27°C

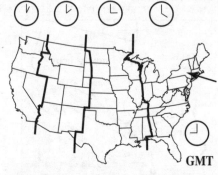

GMT

64 km from Stewart Airport, Newburgh, NY; 145 km from New York City, NY
A 64 km del Aeropuerto de Stewart, Newburgh, NY; a 145 km de la ciudad de Noueva York, NY
A 64 km de l'aéroport Stewart, Newburgh, NY ; à 145 km de New York City, NY
スチュアート空港より 64 キロ、ニューヨーク市より 145 キロ
離紐約州 Newburgh 市 Stewart 機場 64 公里；
離紐約州紐約市 145 公里

 Coeducational 9–12 / Mixto / Mixte
男女共学
男女合校

 133/115

 80%

 10%

 350, 150 / solicitaron admisión, fueron aceptados / candidats, admis
出願者数 350 名、合格者数 150 名
350 人申請，150 人被録取

 TOEFL (500)

 SSAT

 Bermuda, Canada, Germany, Hong Kong, Japan, Korea

 January 31 / 31 de enero/ 31 janvier
1 月 31 日
1 月 31 日

 September / septiembre / septembre
9 月
9 月

 5:1, 90%

 1.5:1

 $32,725; $425, $300

 Bates College, Middlebury College, St. Lawrence University, Skidmore, Union, Yale University

Miss Hall's School

Kimberly B. Boland, Director of Admission
492 Holmes Road, P.O. Box 1166
Pittsfield, Massachusetts 01201
Phone: 413-499-1300 Fax: 413-448-2994

NAIS member *Founded 1898*

Full-time Director of International Program coordinates an integrated ESL program, which includes a TOEFL preparation class. The school sponsors an International Student Alliance and issues I-20s. International students are encouraged to strengthen their English skills by joining clubs and committees and running for leadership positions.

El Director de tiempo completo del Programa Internacional, coordina un programa integrado de inglés como segundo idioma (ESL) que incluye una clase de preparación para el examen de inglés como idioma extranjero (TOEFL). El colegio patrocina una Alianza Internacional de Estudiantes y emite visas I-20. Se estimula a las estudiantes extranjeras a fortalecer sus conocimientos de inglés incorporándose a clubes y comités y postulándose para posiciones de liderazgo.

Le directeur du programme international coordonne à temps complet un programme d'anglais comme langue étrangère (ESL) intégré qui comporte des cours de préparation au TOEFL. L'établissement parraine une Alliance internationale d'étudiants et émet des formulaires I-20. Les étudiants étrangers sont encouragés à renforcer leur maîtrise de l'anglais en devenant membres de clubs et de comités, et en se présentant à des postes de leader.

インターナショナル・プログラムの専任ディレクターが、TOEFL 準備クラスを含めて ESL の統合プログラムをコーディネートします。当校は International Student Alliance を後援し、I-20 を発行します。留学生はクラブや委員会への参加やリーダーに立候補するなど、英語力上達を測ることが奨励されます。

該校有一位全職的外國學生計劃主任，協調綜合性的外國學生英語課程，其中包括托福預備班。該校建有外國學生聯盟並頒發 I-20 學生簽證表。該校鼓勵外國學生加入俱樂部、委員會，競選學校團體領導職位，從而提高英語技能。

Three new buildings complement this lovely 80-acre campus.

Tres nuevos edificios complementarán este hermoso recinto de 32 hectáreas de terreno.

Trois nouveaux bâtiments complémenteront bientôt cet agréable campus de 32 hectares.

3 つの新校舎が 32 ヘクタールの美しいキャンパスに建設予定。

校園美麗如畫，面積 32 公頃，即將建成 3 座新樓。

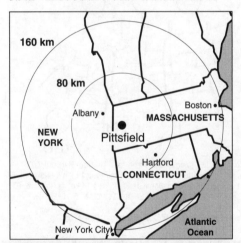

 7–21°C

 -18–4°C

 4–21°C

102 km from an airport in Albany, NY; 210 km from Boston
A 102 km de un aeropuerto de Albany, NY; a 210 km de Boston
À 102 km d'un aéroport d'Albany, NY; à 210 km de Boston
ニューヨーク州 Albany 市の空港より 102 キロ、ボストン市より 210 キロ
距紐約州奧爾巴尼的一個飛機場 102 公里；　距波士頓 210 公里

 Girls 9–12 / Niñas / Filles
女子中学校
女子中學校

 150, 100 / solicitaron admisión, fueron aceptadas / candidats, admis
出願者数 150 名、合格者数 100 名
150 人申請，100 人被錄取

 February 15 / 15 de febrero / 15 février
2 月 15 日
2 月 15 日

 $33,800; $3000–$5000

 Three levels / Tres niveles / Trois niveaux
3 レベル
三種程度

 0/175

 TOEFL; SLEP

September, January / septiembre, enero / septembre, janvier
9 月、1 月
9 月，1 月

75%

 5:1, 45%

 Cornell University, Yale University, Wheaton College, Middlebury College, Smith College

18%

 Bermuda, The Caribbean, Ecuador, Hong Kong, Japan, Korea, Mexico, Nigeria, Taiwan, Ukraine, Venezuela

4:1

Miss Porter's School

Deborah Haskins, Director of Admission
60 Main Street
Farmington, Connecticut 06032
Phone: 860-409-3530 Fax: 860-409-3531
URL: http://www.missporters.org

CAIS, NAIS, TABS, FAIS, NAFSA member   *Founded 1843*

A respected leader in preparing young women for competitive colleges since 1843. Miss Porter's offers a demanding curriculum, a collaborative environment, and a supportive community, which distinguish it as one of the best boarding schools in the nation.

Un respetado líder en la preparación de las jóvenes para las universidades competitivas desde 1843. Miss Porter's ofrece un plan de estudios exigente, un ambiente colaborador y una comunidad que brinda apoyo, lo que lo distingue como uno de los mejores internados del país.

Lieu hautement respecté pour la préparation des jeunes filles aux meilleures universités depuis 1843, l'école Miss Porter offre un programme exigeant, un environnement de collaboration et une communauté d'un grand soutien et se distingue comme l'une des meilleures écoles préparatoires du pays.

1843 年以来若い女性向けに一流大学進学を準備するリーダー的立場として定評があります。Miss Porter's は確かなカリキュラムと協力的な環境、サポーティブなコミュニティを提供し、それらが当校を全国でも最高の寄宿学校の１つとして傑出させています。

自 1843 年以來，本校為青年女生進入優質大學提供學習準備，是深受讚譽的優秀名校。要求嚴格的課程，協調合作的環境，相互扶助的集體，使本校成為

The campus includes a state-of-the-art library, science, math, and technology building.

Los terrenos del colegio incluye un moderno edificio de ciencias, matemáticas y tecnología, con una biblioteca.

Le campus comprend un bâtiment ultra-moderne pour les sciences, les mathématiques et la technologie, avec une bibliothèque.

キャンパスには最新設備の図書館、科学、数学、技術ビルがあります。

校內設有一座最新型的圖書館、科學、數學和技術中心。

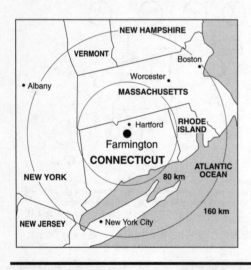

 2–18°C

 -21–4°C

 2–27°C

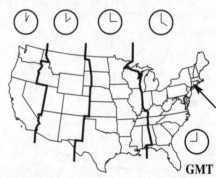

GMT

14 km from Bradley International Airport; 14 km from Hartford, CT
A 14 km del aeropuerto internacional de Bradley; a 14 km de Hartford, CT
A 14 km de l'aéroport international de Bradley ; à 14 km de Hartford, CT
ブラッドリー国際空港より 14 キロ、コネチカット州ハートフォードより 14 キロ
離 Bradley 國際機場 14 公里；離 Hartford, CT 14 公里

 Girls 9–12 / Niñas / Filles
女子中学校
女子中學校

 0/360

 66%

 12%

 415, 194 / solicitaron admisión, fueron aceptadas / candidats, admis
出願者数 415 名、合格者数 194 名
415 人申請，194 人被錄取

 TOEFL (550), SLEP, ISEE, SSAT (67)

 Canada, Hong Kong, Korea, Thailand, United Kingdom

 February 1, rolling / 1 de febrero, continuo / 1 février, continuelles
2 月 1 日より随時受付
2 月 1 日起随時皆可

 September / septiembre / septembre
9 月
9 月

 8:1, 60%

 2:1

 $31,500; $1100

 Connecticut University, Cornell University, New York University, Trinity College, Union College

Monte Vista Christian School

Susan S. Bernal, Director, Resident Admissions
International Admissions Coordinator
Two School Way
Watsonville, California 95076
Phone: 831-722-8178 Ext. 128 Fax: 831-722-6003
E-mail: sbernal@mvcs.org
URL: http://www.mvcs.org

Founded 1926

The school makes international students feel at home in their comfortable dorms, increases their English language proficiency, helps them adapt to life in the U.S., obtain a high school diploma and gain admission to a U.S. college or university.

El colegio hace a los estudiantes extranjeros sentirse en casa en las cómodas residencias, aumenta sus niveles de competencia en el idioma inglés, los ayuda a adaptarse a la vida en los Estados Unidos, a obtener un diploma de la escuela secundaria, y ser admitido en un colegio o universidad de los EE.UU.

L'école fait que les élèves de tous les pays se sentent chez eux dans des dortoirs confortables, les aide à améliorer leur niveau d'anglais, leur permet de s'adapter à la vie aux États-Unis, d'obtenir un diplome de fin de lycée et leur permettre l'entrée dans des universités américaines.

本校は、快適な寮を完備し、参加留学生の英語力の向上を図り、アメリカ生活に適応できるよう指導し、学生は高校卒業証書とアメリカ国内の大学入学資格を取得します。

學校提供國際學生舒適的住宿環境，使學生有賓至如歸之感，並協助學生增強英語能力和適應美國生活，獲得高中文憑，並且晉升美國大學。

The 100-acre campus is set in the foothills of the Santa Cruz Mountains.
Las 40 hectáreas de terreno se encuentran en las colinas al pie de las montañas de Santa Cruz.
Le campus de 40 hectares est niché au pied des collines de Santa Cruz.
40ヘクタールのキャンパスは、サンタクルーズ山脈の裾野にあります。
校園佔地 40 公頃，依傍在 Santa Cruz 的山丘上。

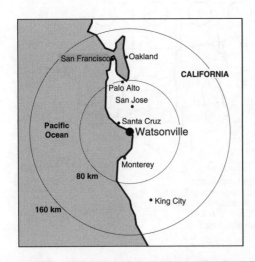

 4–26°C

 -1–15°C

 4–26°C

GMT

80 km from San Jose International Airport; 150 km from San Francisco, CA / A 80 km del aeropuerto internacional de San José; a 150 km de San Francisco, CA / A 80 km de l'aéroport international de San Jose ; à 150 km de San Francisco, CA
サンホゼ国際空港から 80 km、カリフォルニア州サンフランシスコ市から 150 km
離 San Jose 國際機場 80 公里；離加州 San Francisco 市 150 公里

 Coeducational 9–12 / Mixto / Mixte
男女共学
男女合校

 350/350

 14%

 15%

 130, 110 / solicitaron admisión, fueron aceptados / candidats, admis
出願者数 130 名、合格者数 110 名
130 人申請，110 人被錄取

 SLEP (40+), TOEFL (400+)

 China, Japan, Korea, Taiwan

 Rolling / Continuo / Continuelles
随時受付
全年招生

 September, January / septiembre, enero / septembre, janvier
9 月、1 月
9 月、1 月

 20:1, 25%

 $27,600

University of California, California State University, Westmont College, Mount Saint Mary's College, Boston College, New York University

 ESL, American Government, U.S. History, Mathematics

The Newman School

Karen Briggs, Director of Admission
247 Marlborough Street
Boston, MA 02116
Phone: 617-267-4530 Fax: 617-267-7070

Founded 1945

For more than fifty years the Newman School has provided a diverse community of American and international students a serious and values-oriented community in which they prepare together for college admission. Students and teachers enjoy the advantages of Newman's location in the cultural environment of Boston's Back Bay, which places opportunities for artistic, literary, and scientific enrichment within easy reach. Newman students participate in a program of athletic and extra-curricular programs that enhance their opportunities for forming friendships, while assisting their preparation for college admission.

Durante más de cincuenta años, Newman School ha proporcionado a estudiantes estadounidenses y extranjeros una comunidad seria y orientada hacia los valores fundamentales, en la que juntos se preparan para ser admitidos en la universidad. Estudiantes y maestros disfrutan de las ventajas de la ubicación de Newman en el ambiente cultural de la Bahía Back de Boston, que proporciona oportunidades fácilmente accesibles para el enriquecimiento artístico, literario y científico. Los estudiantes de Newman participan en programas de actividades deportivas y extracurriculares que amplían las oportunidades de entablar amistades y ayudan en su preparación para ser admitidos en la universidad.

Depuis plus de cinquante ans, Newman School propose à une communauté diverse d'étudiants américains et étrangers un environnement sérieux axé sur de solides valeurs au sein duquel les élèves préparent leur entrée à l'université. Les étudiants, tout comme le corps enseignant, profitent des avantages de la situation géographique de Newman au sein du quartier de Back Bay à Boston : un environnement culturel, artistique, littéraire et scientifique facilement accessible. À Newman, les étudiants participent à des programmes sportifs et parascolaires qui leur permettent de forger de nouvelles amitiés, tout en les aidant à préparer leur entrée à l'université.

過去 50 年以上にわたり、Newman School は米国人学生および海外からの多様な留学生達に、大学入学に共に備える真剣で目的指向の高いコミュニティを提供してきました。学生と先生は、芸術や文芸、科学的な諸機会が容易に得られるボストンのバックベイという文化的環境にある Newman の地の利を満喫できます。Newman の学生は、大学入学準備をアシストすると共に、友情を培うすばらしい機会であるアスレチックプログラムや課外プログラムに参加します。

五十多年来、Newman 學校為美國和其他國家各種文化背景的學生創造了一個誠懇認真、注重價值的集體，學生們在這個集體中共同為進入大學作準備。學生和教師享有校園位處波士頓後灣文化環境的優勢，易於得到擴展藝術、文學和科學眼界的機會。學生參加體育運動和課外活動項目，以此增加結交朋友的機會，有助大學入學準備。

Newman is located in two brownstone buildings in Boston's historic Back Bay.

Newman está ubicado en dos edificios de piedra rojiza en la histórica Bahía Back de Boston.

Newman occupe deux bâtiments élégants situés dans le quartier historique de Back Bay à Boston.

Newman は、歴史に名高いボストンバックベイの 2 棟のブラウンストーンビルに位置しています。

Newman 學校位處波士頓歷史悠久的後灣地區，建于兩幢褐砂石建築中。

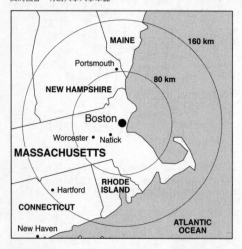

 9–19°C

 -3–4°C

 7–14°C

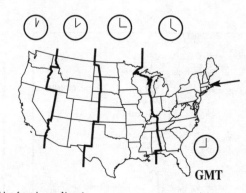

GMT

5 km from Logan Airport
A 5 km del aeropuerto de Logan
A 5 km de l'aéroport de Logan
Logan 空港より 5 キロ
離 Logan 機場 5 公里

 Coeducational 9–PG / Mixto / Mixte
男女共学
男女合校

 105/115

20% with Homestay Families

 20%

 137, 85 / solicitaron admisión, fueron aceptados / candidats, admis
出願者数 137 名、合格者数 85 名
137 人申請，85 人被録取

 China (10), Japan (10), Morocco (10), Russia (10), Spain (10)

 Rolling / Continuo / Continuelles
随時受付
全年招生

 September, January, June (for Summer session) / septiembre, enero, junio / septembre, janvier, juin
9 月、1 月、6 月
9 月，1 月，6 月

14:1

8:1

 $17,500

 14:1

 Boston University, Northeastern University, Suffolk University, University of Massachusetts, Clark University

Northfield Mount Hermon School

Ms. Deborah J. Wright,
Director of Admission
The Homestead, 206 Main Street
Northfield, Massachusetts 01360-1089
Phone: 413-498-3227 Fax: 413-498-3152
E-mail: admission@nmhschool.org
URL: http://www.nmhschool.org

TABS, FAIS, NAFSA member   *Founded 1879*

NMH attracts students from over 40 countries and offers an advanced ESL program, an office of international education, immigration and college counseling.

NMH atrae a estudiantes de más de 40 países y ofrece un programa avanzado de inglés como segundo idioma (ESL), una oficina de educación internacional, consejería para temas relativos a inmigración y a la universidad.

NMH attire des étudiants de plus de 40 pays différents et offre un programme d'anglais comme langue étrangère (ESL) supérieur, un bureau d'éducation internationale, des facilités d'immigration et des conseils pour aller à l'université.

NMH では世界 40 ヶ国以上から生徒を受け入れ、上級英語集中（ESL）プログラム、国際教育事務所、入国審査、大学進学のためのカウンセリング、大学進学へのアドバイスなどを提供しています。

NMH 吸引來自 40 多個國家的學生，提供高級 ESL 課程，設有國際教育處，並提供移民和大學咨詢。

The 3,500-acre campus includes 14 academic buildings, 21 dormitories, 2 libraries, and 27 athletic fields.

Las 1.417 hectáreas de terreno incluyen 14 edificios académicos, 21 residencias estudiantiles, 2 bibliotecas y 27 campos de atletismo.

Le campus de 1 417 hectares comprend 14 bâtiments scolaires, 21 dortoirs, 2 bibliothèques et 27 terrains de sports.

1,417 ヘクタールのキャンパスには学科棟が 14 棟、寮 21 舎、図書館が 2 つ、運動場が 27 あります。

校園佔地 1417 公頃，包括 14 座教學樓、21 座宿舍、2 座圖書館和 27 處體育場。

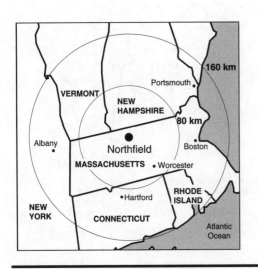

 4–21°C

 -9–13°C

 1–24°C

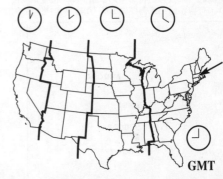

GMT

89 km from Bradley International Airport; 120 km from Boston, MA
A 89 km del aeropuerto internacional de Bradley; a 120 km de Boston, MA
A 89 km de l'aéroport international de Bradley ; à 120 km de Boston, MA
ブラッドリー国際空港より 89 キロ、マサチューセッツ州ボストン市より 120 キロ
離 Bradley 國際機場 89 公里；離 Boston, MA 120 公里

 Coeducational 9–PG / Mixto / Mixte
男女共学
男女合校

 467/409

 80%

 25%

 1159, 559 / solicitaron admisión, fueron aceptados / candidats, admis
出願者数 1159 名、合格者数 559 名
1159 人申請，559 人被錄取

 SSAT, ISEE, TOEFL, SAT

 TOEFL (550)

 Germany (8),Hong Kong (40), Japan (13), Korea (55), Taiwan (38), South & Central America (20)

 Rolling / Continuo / Continuelles
随時受付
全年招生

 September, November / septiembre, noviembre / septembre, novembre
9 月、11 月
9 月、11 月

 6:1, 97%

 1:1

 $33,000; $24,400

Cornell University, New York University, Carnegie Mellon University, Brown University, Tufts University, Johns Hopkins University, Wesleyan University, Boston University

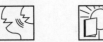

Peterson's American and Canadian Boarding Schools and Worldwide Enrichment Programs   *www.petersons.com*   **77**

Oak Creek Ranch School

David Wick, Jr., Headmaster
P.O. Box 4329
West Sedona, Arizona 86340-3577
Phone: 928-634-5571 Fax: 928-634-4915
E-mail: admissions@ocrs.com
URL: http://www.ocrs.com

NIPSIA, NAFSA member   NCA accredited   *Founded 1972*

The school offers small classes, a structured environment, and individualized programs for ages 11–19 (grades 6–12). It specializes in underachievers, slow learners, and students who are under-motivated or have ADD, ADHD, or low self-esteem as well as in leadership and character development. Continuous enrollment.

La escuela ofrece clases pequeñas, un ambiente estructurado, y programas personalizados para estudiantes entres las edades de 11 hasta 19 años (grados 6 hasta 12). Se especializa en estudiantes que no han tenido éxito en sus estudios, estudiantes rezagados y estudiantes sin motivación o que tienen Desorden de Déficit de Atención (siglas en inglés ADD) o Desorden de Déficit de Atención con Hiperactividad, o poca estima propia así como en el desarrollo del carácter o liderazgo.

L'école propose des cours en petits groupes et encadrés ainsi que des programmes personnalisés pour les étudiants entre 11 et 19 ans des classes de niveau 6 à 12 (« grades 6–12 »). Les programmes sont orientés tout particulièrement à l'attention des élèves qui n'exploitent pas leur potentiel, apprennent lentement, sont peu motivés, font preuve de troubles de l'attention, de déficit d'attention avec hyperactivité ou de manque de confiance en soi. Les cours encouragent le leadership et le développement personnel. Les inscriptions se font tout au long de l'année.

当校は6年生から12年生までの11歳から19歳の学生を対象に、少人数で個別化されたクラスを提供します。特に、成績不振、不十分な学習力、気力不足、ADD或はADHD所持者、自己不信による性格やリーダーシップの発達不足などの学生を専門にしています。継続入学制度です。

學校提供小型課堂以及富有建設性的環境，對11至19歲（6至12年級）的學生因材施教。學校特別善于幫助學績不良，接受速度慢，動力不足，患有ADD或ADHD，有自悲感，或需要領導能力培訓和性格塑造的學生。持續招生。

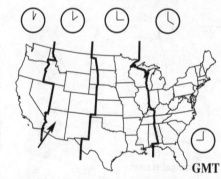

Activities include mountain biking, rock climbing, equestrian, competitive sports, skateboarding, snowboarding, trips to the Grand Canyon, and more.
Las actividades incluidas son ciclismo de montaña, escalada, ecuestres, deportes competitivos, "skateboarding", "snowboarding", viajes al Gran Canyón y más.
Les programmes d'activités comprennent vélo tout-terrain, escalade, équitation, sports de compétition, skate-board, snowboard, excursions au Grand Canyon et bien d'autres.
マウンテン・バイク、ロック・クライミング、乗馬、競技スポーツ、スケート・ボード、スノー・ボード、グランド・キャニオンへの旅行等の活動があります。
活動包括登山腳踏車，攀岩，馬術，競爭性體育運動，滑板，滑雪板，以及旅行去大峽谷等等。

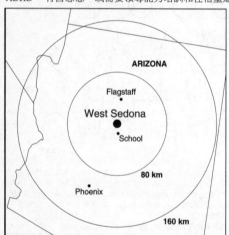

ARIZONA
Flagstaff
West Sedona
School
80 km
Phoenix
160 km

 7–29°C

 -5–15°C

 10–31°C

GMT

160 km from Phoenix Airport; 72 km from Flagstaff, AZ
A 160 km del aeropuerto de Phoenix; a 72 km de Flagstaff, AZ
A 160 km de l'aéroport de Phoenix ; à 72 km de Flagstaff, AZ
フェニックス空港より160キロ、アリゾナ州フラッグスタッフ市より72キロ
離鳳凰城機場160公里；離亞利桑那州Flagstaff市72公里

 Coeducational 7–12 / Mixto / Mixte
男女共学
男女合校

 64/22

 15, 12 / solicitaron admisión, fueron aceptados / candidats, admis
出願者数15名，合格者数12名
15人申請，12人被錄取

 Rolling / Continuo / Continuelles
随時受付
随時皆可

$29,500; $3950

 100%

 TOEFL, SSAT

 8:1, 0%

 Northern Arizona University, Arizona State University, Fort Lewis College, Phoenix Community College, University of Arizona

 15%

 China (3), Italy (3), Japan (10), Mexico (5), South Korea (7)

 2:1

Ojai Valley School

John H. Williamson, Director of Admission
723 El Paseo Road
Ojai, California 93023
Phone: 805-646-1423 Fax: 805-646-0362
URL: http://www.ovs.org
E-mail: jhw@ovs.org

NAIS, TABS, FAIS member   *Founded 1911*

English as a Second Language (ESL) for students ages 8–18 for any level of proficiency. The traditional secondary-preparatory and university-preparatory school is in a safe area close to mountains, beaches, and Santa Barbara. Summer programs and group study tours are available.

Se ofrece un curso de inglés como segundo idioma (ESL) para estudiantes entre las edades de 8 y 18 años con cualquier nivel de conocimiento. El tradicional colegio de preparación para la secundaria y para la universidad está localizado en un área segura cerca de las montañas, la playa y Santa Barbara. Se dispone de programas de verano y excursiones de estudio por grupos.

L'anglais comme langue étrangère (ESL) pour les étudiants âgés de 8 à 18 ans pour tous les niveaux de compétence. Cette école traditionnelle, préparant à l'enseignement secondaire et universitaire, offre un environnement sûr à proximité des montagnes, des plages et de Santa Barbara. Des programmes durant l'été, ainsi que des voyages d'études en groupe sont disponibles.

8–18才までのあらゆるレベルの留学生のために英語講座 (ESL) が用意されています。伝統的で保守的な本校の高校及び大学進学校は、山やビーチ、サンタ・バーバラ市に近い、安全な地域にあります。サマー・プログラム及びグループ・スタディ・ツアーもあります。

本校為 8-18 歲各種英語程度的學生開辦英語作為第二語言 (ESL) 的課程。這所較傳統的中學預備和大學預備學校，環境安全，緊靠群山、海灘和 Santa Barbara 。本校也設有暑期項目和團體外出實習。

195 hilltop acres with dormitories, swimming pool, art studio, ceramic studio, library, amphitheater, and student center.

79 hectáreas de terreno en la cumbre de una colina con residencias estudiantiles, piscina, estudio de arte, estudio de cerámica, biblioteca, anfiteatro y centro para estudiantes.

79 hectares au sommet d'une colline avec dortoirs, piscine, studio d'art, atelier de céramique, bibliothèque, amphithéâtre et centre pour les étudiants.

丘の上にある 79 ヘクタールのキャンパスには、寮、プール、アート・スタジオ、セラミック・スタジオ、図書館、円形競技場、学生センターが完備されています。

佔地 79 公頃，位居山頂，擁有宿舍、游泳池、藝術工作間、陶瓷製作間、圖書館、圓形劇場和學生中心。

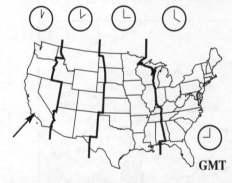

 4–29°C

 3–20°C

 4–29°C

145 km from Los Angeles International Airport; 38 km from Ventura, CA
A 145 km del aeropuerto internacional de Los Angeles; a 38 km de Ventura, CA
A 145 km de l'aéroport international de Los Angeles ; à 38 km de Ventura, CA
カリフォルニア州ロサンゼルス国際空港より 145 キロ、同州ベンチュラ市より 38 キロ
離 Los Angeles 國際機場 145 公里；離加州 Ventura 市 38 公里

 Coeducational PK–12 / Mixto / Mixte
男女共学
男女合校

 56/51

 80%

 20%

 195, 135 / solicitaron admisión, fueron aceptados / candidats, admis
出願者数 195 名、合格者数 135 名
195 人申請，135 人被錄取

 SSAT, TOEFL, SLEP, ISEE

 10:1

 Rolling / Continuo / Continuelles
隨時受付
全年招生

 September, January, rolling / septiembre, enero, continuo/ septembre, janvier, continuelles
9月、1月、随時受付
9月，1月，全年招生

 5:1, 50%

 Aruba (2), Belgium (2), Brazil (5), Canada (3), China (10), Germany (14), Hong Kong (12), Japan (40), Korea (40), Mexico (15), Russia (10), Taiwan (14), Thailand (10)

 $34,070; $1675

 University of California at Berkeley, University of California—Santa Barbara, University of Southern California, University of California at Davis, Cornell University, Mount Holyoke College

---

Oldfields School

1500 Glencoe Road
Glencoe, Maryland 21152
Phone: 410-472-4800 Fax: 410-472-3141

TABS, NAIS, NAFSA member   *Founded 1867*

Oldfields is known for its personalized, college-preparatory curriculum and nurturing, family-like environment. Fine and performing arts, athletics, dance, and horseback riding are available, as are extensive weekend activities. One hundred percent of faculty and students have laptop computers and the Internet is widely accessible. Overseas and off-campus programs are offered in May.

Oldfields es conocido por ofrecer un currículo individualizado y por su ambiente familiar que estimula el aprendizaje. También es conocido por su ambiente familiar que estimula el aprendizaje. Ofrece clases de bellas artes y artes escénicas, deportes, danza y equitación, así como muchas actividades durante los fines de semana. El cien por cien de profesores y estudiantes tienen computadoras personales y hay amplio acceso al Internet. En mayo ofrece programas en el exterior y fuera del recinto escolar.

Oldfields est renommé pour son programme scolaire personnalisé à deux niveaux, préparant à l'entrée en université, ainsi que pour son environnement familial et coopératif. Les beaux-arts, les arts du spectacle, le sport, la danse et l'équitation sont disponibles ainsi que de nombreuses activités le week-end. Tous les professeurs et étudiants possèdent un ordinateur portable, et le Web est largement accessible. Des programmes à l'étranger et hors campus sont offerts au mois de mai.

Oldfields は個別化された複式の大学進学準備カリキュラムと、家庭的なあたたかい環境で知られています。広範囲な週末活動には美術、舞台芸術、運動、ダンス、乗馬などが含まれます。全ての教授陣と学生はラップトップコンピュータを所持し、インターネットは広くアクセスが可能です。5月には海外および校外プログラムがあります。

Oldfields 學校以其因材施教的大學預科課程以及家庭式的培養環境而著稱。設有美術和表演藝術、體育、舞蹈、騎馬等項目，以及多種週末活動。教師和學生百分之百擁有筆記本電腦，校園多處可使用英特網。五月份提供海外及校外項目。

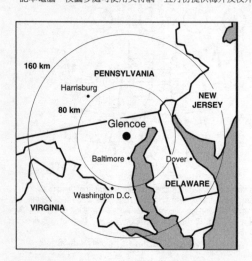

The 225-acre campus includes a state-of-the-art academic center, opened in 2001.

Las 91 hectáreas de terreno incluyen un moderno centro académico, que fue inaugurado en el 2001.

Le campus de 91 hectares comprend un centre scolaire ultra-moderne qui s'est ouvert en 2001.

91 ヘクタールのキャンパスには、2001 年にオープンした時代の最先端を行くアカデミックセンターがあります。

校園佔地 91 公頃，擁有一座於 2001 年開用的最先進的教學中心。

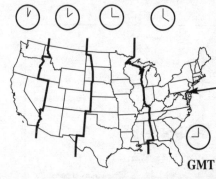

 6–18°C

 -6–5°C

 9–21°C

62 km from Baltimore Washington International Airport; 41 km from Baltimore
A 62 km del aeropuerto internacional de Baltimore Washington; a 41 km de Baltimore
A 62 km de l'aéroport international de Baltimore Washington; à 41 km de Baltimore
ボルチモアワシントン国際空港から 62 km、ボルチモア市から 41 km
離 Baltimore / Washington 國際機場 62 公里；Baltimore 市 41 公里

 Girls 8–12 / Niñas / Filles
女子中学校
女子中學校

 219, 172 / solicitaron admisión, fueron aceptados / candidats, admis
出願者数 219 名、合格者数 172 名
219 人申請、172 人被錄取

 February 1, rolling / 1 de febrero, continuo / 1ᵉʳ février, continuelles
2 月 1 日より随時受付
2 月 1 日起随時皆可

 $33,700; $21,400 (comprehensive fee)

 0/185

 TOEFL or SLEP

 September / septiembre / septembre
9 月
9 月

 80%

 TOEFL (450 for Grade 8-10; 520 for Grade 11-12)

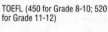 4:1, 74%

 American University, College of Charleston, Denison University, Muhlenberg College, University of Maryland

 16%

 Germany (50), Japan (10), Korea (9), Mexico (26), Saudi Arabia (9)

 1:1

 Optional / Opcional / Facultatif
自由選擇
供選擇

The Orme School

Alex Spence, Director of Admission
H.C. 63, Box 3040
Mayer, Arizona 86333
Phone: 928-632-7601 Fax: 928-632-7605
E-mail: admissions@ormeschool.org
URL: http://www.ormeschool.org

NAIS member   *Founded 1929*

The Orme School offers a traditional college preparatory program set in a wholesome, pristine learning environment. A tree-lined campus, surrounded by a carefully tended working cattle ranch, provides a comfortable, yet stimulating learning environment. Extra curricular activities include competitive sports, horsemanship, and outdoor leadership. One of The Orme School's greatest strengths is its ESL Program. International students are integrated into the larger culture of the school while receiving in-depth personalized attention from experienced and dedicated faculty. The International Club provides opportunities for students to share their culture and learn more about their peers.

La Orme School ofrece un programa tradicional de preparación para la universidad en un ambiente de enseñanza sano e impoluto. Un recinto escolar flanqueado de árboles, rodeado por una hacienda ganadera bien atendida, ofrece un ambiente escolar cómodo y estimulante a la vez. Las actividades extracurriculares incluyen deportes competitivos, equitación y liderazgo al aire libre. Uno de los puntos más sobresalientes de Orme School es el Programa de Inglés como Segundo Idioma (ESL). Los estudiantes extranjeros se integran completamente a la vida del colegio, mientras reciben atención personalizada y en profundidad de parte de un cuerpo docente experto y dedicado. El International Club proporciona a los estudiantes la oportunidad de compartir su cultura y aprender más acerca de sus compañeros.

Orme School propose un programme traditionnel préparant à l'entrée en université dans un cadre sain et naturel. Le campus bordé d'arbres, entouré par une exploitation bovine soigneusement entretenue, offre un environnement d'apprentissage simple et stimulant. Les activités périscolaires comprennent des sports de compétition, l'équitation et l'étude du leadership en pleine nature. Le programme d'anglais comme langue étrangère (ESL) est l'un des points les plus forts de l'Orme School. Les étudiants étrangers sont intégrés à la culture de l'établissement et reçoivent toute l'attention dont ils ont besoin des membres dévoués et chevronnés du corps enseignant. Le Club international permet aux élèves de partager leur culture et d'en apprendre plus sur les autres étudiants.

The Orme School では健全で素朴な学習環境の中で、伝統的な大学準備講座を提供します。入念に手入れされた家畜がいる牧場に囲まれた並木道のキャンパスが、快適で、しかも刺激的な学習環境を提供します。課外活動には、競技スポーツ、乗馬、野外リーダーシップが含まれます。The Orme School の最も強い分野のひとつは、その第二国語としての英語教育（ESL）です。経験豊かで熱意ある教師陣による、徹底して細やかな個別配慮を受けながら、留学生たちは当校において幅広い文化に溶け込んでいきます。また当校のインターナショナル・クラブでは、生徒たちは自分たちの文化背景をシェアすることで、学友たちへの理解をさらに深めることができます。

Orme 學校在健康、天然的學習環境中開設傳統的大學預科專業。樹木成行的校園，四周環繞著精心管理的生產牛飼養場，它提供了一個舒適但又刺激的學習環境。課外活動包括各種競賽性運動、騎馬術、以及野外領導能力。Orme School 的強項之一是 ESL 課程。資深並敬業的教師對外國學生應予施教，使他們融入校園多元文化環境。國際俱樂部為學生們提供體驗別國文化和互相了解的機會。

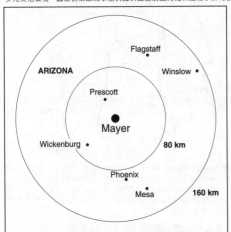

 -1–15°C

 -6–10°C

 4–26°C

The 260-acre campus is set on 40,000 acres of the Orme Ranch.

Las 105 hectáreas del colegio se encuentran en una superficie de 16.000 hectáreas del Rancho Orme.

Le campus de 105 hectares se situe sur 16 000 hectares du ranch d'Orme.

当校の 105 ヘクタールのキャンパスは 16,000 ヘクタールのオーム農場の中にあります。

佔地 105 公頃的校園座落在面積為 16,000 公頃的 Orme 牧場上。

GMT

104 km from Sky Harbor Airport; 96 km from Phoenix, AZ
A 104 km del aeropuerto de Sky Harbor; a 96 km de Phoenix, AZ
A 104 km de l'aéroport de Sky Harbor ; à 96 km de Phoenix, AZ
スカイハーバー空港より 104 キロ、アリゾナ州フェニックス市より 96 キロ
離 Sky Harbor 機場 104 公里；離亞歷桑那州 Phoenix 市 96 公里

 Coeducational 7–PG / Mixto / Mixte
男女共学
男女合校

 80/74

 80%

 18%

 140, 85 / solicitaron admisión, fueron aceptados / candidats, admis
出願者数 140 名、合格者数 85 名
140 人申請，85 人被錄取

 SLEP

 TOEFL (350), SLEP

 Germany (4), Hong Kong (3), Japan (9), Korea (6), Taiwan (6)

 February 15/ 15 de febrero / 15 février
2 月 15 日
2 月 15 日

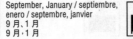 September, January / septiembre, enero / septembre, janvier
9 月，1 月
9 月，1 月

 7:1, 95%

 3:1

 $29,190 (boarding); $14,910 (day)

 University of Arizona, Arizona State University, University of California at Berkeley, California State University, Northern Arizona University

---

The Peddie School

Edward de Villafranca, Dean of Admission
and College Counseling
South Main Street
Hightstown, New Jersey 08520
Phone: 609-490-7501 Fax: 609-944-7901
URL: http://www.peddie.org

TABS member   *Founded 1864*

Peddie School offers a demanding curriculum, small classes, and a two-level
English program, within a safe setting, close to the cultural centers of
Philadelphia and New York.

Peddie School ofrece un plan de estudios exigente, clases con pocos
alumnos y un programa de enseñanza del inglés de dos niveles, en un
ambiente seguro, cerca de los centros culturales de Filadelfia y Nueva York.

Peddie School offre un programme rigoureux, dans de petites classes, et
un programme d'anglais à deux niveaux, dans un cadre tranquille qui se situe
près des centres culturels de Philadelphie et de New York.

当校は厳しいカリキュラム、小人数クラス制、2段階の英語プログラムを実施
しています。治安がよく、フィラデルフィアとニューヨークの文化センターが近
くにあります。

本校設有必修課、小班制教學以及兩種程度的英語課程，環境安全，靠近文化
中心費城和紐約。

Every student is equipped with a
multimedia laptop computer.

Cada estudiante cuenta con una
computadora portátil (laptop) de
multimedia.

Chaque étudiant dispose d'un
ordinateur multimédia portatif.

生徒全員に、マルチメディアのノ
ートブック・コンピュータが完備
されています。

每個學生都配備有一台多媒體攜
帶式電腦。

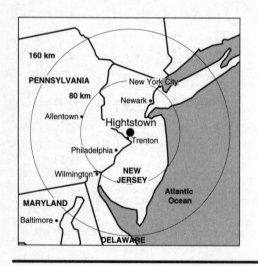

 15–30°C

 -6–10°C

 15–30°C

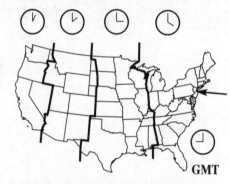

72 km from Newark Airport; 80 km from New York, NY
A 72 km del aeropuerto de Newark; a 80 km de Nueva York, NY
A 72 km de l'aéroport de Newark ; à 80 km de New York, NY
ニューアーク空港より72キロ、ニューヨーク州ニューヨーク市
より80キロ

離 Newark 機場 72 公里；離紐約州紐約市 89 公里

 Coeducational 8–12 / Mixto / Mixte
男女共学
男女合校

 280/236

 1,000, 301 / solicitaron admisión,
fueron aceptados / candidats, admis
出願者数 1,000 名、合格者数 301 名
1000 人申請，301 人被錄取

SSAT (62%), ISEE, SAT, or
PSAT

TOEFL (550)

62%

11%

Canada, China, Hong Kong,
Korea, Saudi Arabia, Thailand

January 15 / 15 de enero / 15 janvier
1 月 15 日
1 月 15 日

Septembe 11r / 11 de septiembre /
11 septembre
9 月 11 日
9 月 11 日

6:1, 80%

1:1

$32,100

Carnegie Mellon University,
Columbia University, Cornell
University, Georgetown University,
University of Pennsylvania

Pennington School

Diane P. Monteleone, Director of Admission
112 West Delaware Avenue
Pennington, New Jersey 08534
Phone: 609-737-6128 Fax: 609-730-1405
E-mail: admiss@pennington.org
URL: http://www.pennington.org

TABS, NAFSA, NAIS member   *Founded 1838*

Beginning to advanced ESL classes; evening tutoring; a broad offering of academic courses, including AP and honors levels; and diverse off-campus experiences prepare students for placement and life in competitive American universities.

Clases de inglés como segundo idioma (ESL) para principiantes y avanzadas, tutoría por la noche, una amplia gama de cursos académicos, incluyendo niveles de AP y de honor, y diversas experiencias fuera del recinto escolar, preparan a los estudiantes para matricularse y vivir en las universidades competitivas de los Estados Unidos.

Les cours d'anglais comme langue étrangère de niveau débutant à avancé, les cours particuliers le soir, la grande variété de cours d'enseignement général, y compris les tests d'équivalence et les cours de niveau avancé, ainsi que les différentes expériences en dehors du campus, préparent les étudiants à l'entrée et à la vie dans l'univers compétitif des universités américaines.

初級から上級の ESL クラス、夕方の学習指導、大学および優等レベルを含んだ豊富なアカデミック・コース、多様なキャンパス外の経験を経て、生徒は進学校の選定と競争の激しいアメリカの大学に備えることができます。

各種初級到高級的 ESL 課程，晚間輔導，廣泛的課程設置，包括優先錄取生和優等生級別的課程，以及各種校外體驗，幫助學生們進入並生活在競爭力強的美國大學作好準備。

A new Campus Center for the Arts opened on the school's 54-acre campus in fall 2004

En el otoño de 2004 se abrió un nuevo Centro para las Artes en el recinto de 22 hectáreas.

Un nouveau Centre pour les Arts a ouvert sur le campus de 22 hectares de l'école à l'automne 2004.

新しい芸術センター・キャンパスが 2004 年秋、22 ヘクタールの学校敷地内にオープンしました。

新的藝術校園中心于 2004 年秋季開放在 22 公頃的校址上。

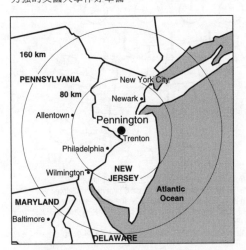

 10–23°C

 0–10°C

 20–24°C

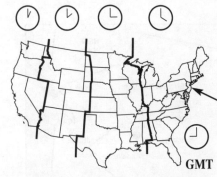

65 km from Newark Airport; 60 km from Philadelphia, PA
A 65 km del aeropuerto de Newark; a 60 km de Filadelfia, PA
A 65 km de l'aéroport de Newark ; à 60 km de Philadelphie, PA
ニューアーク空港より 65 キロ、ペンシルバニア州フィラデルフィア市より 60 キロ
離 Newark 機場 65 公里；離 Philadelphia, PA 60 公里

 Coeducational 6–12 / Mixto / Mixte
男女共学
男女合校

 191/169

 27%

 12%

 600, 145 / solicitaron admisión, fueron aceptados / candidats, admis
出願者数 600 名、合格者数 145 名
600 人申請，145 人被錄取

 SLEP, SSAT

 Germany, Japan, Korea, Nigeria, Russia, Taiwan

 February 10, then rolling / 10 de febrero, continuo / 10 février, continuelles
2 月 10 日より随時受付
2 月 10 日起隨時皆可

 September / septiembre / septembre
9 月
9 月

 9:1, 40%

 3:1

 $32,500; $1625

 Carnegie Mellon, University of Michigan, New York University, Penn State University

Perkiomen School

Carol Dougherty, Director of Admission
P.O. Box 130
Pennsburg, Pennsylvania 18073
Phone: 215-679-9511 Fax: 215-679-1146
E-mail: cdougherty@perkiomen.org
URL: http://www.perkiomen.org

TABS, SSATB, NAFSA member   *Founded 1875*

A safe and friendly school, Perkiomen has a three-level ESL program that helps international students master the English language quickly. All classrooms and dorm rooms feature fiber optics and Internet connections.

Perkiomen, un colegio seguro y amistoso, cuenta con un programa de inglés como segundo idioma (ESL) de tres niveles que ayuda a los estudiantes extranjeros a dominar el idioma con rapidez. Todas las aulas y las residencias estudiantiles proporcionan cableado de fibras ópticas y conexiones con la Internet.

Perkiomen, un établissement sûr et chaleureux, offre des cours d'anglais comme langue étrangère (ESL) de trois niveaux différents qui permettent aux étudiants étrangers de maîtriser rapidement la langue anglaise. Toutes les salles de classe et les dortoirs sont équipés de fibres optiques et de connexions à Internet.

安全でフレンドリーな Perkiomen School には３レベルの ESL プログラムがあり、留学生の迅速な英語習得を助けます。全ての教室および寮室は光ファイバとインターネット接続が整備されています。

Perkiomen 是一所環境安全、氣氛友好的學校，開設三種水平的 ESL 課程，幫助國際學生迅速掌握英語。所有教室和宿舍都設有光纖電話和互聯網線路。

The 165-acre campus includes a new dormitory, a fine arts center, and a gym.
Las 66 hectáreas de terreno tienen nuevas residencias estudiantiles, un centro de bellas artes y un gimnasio.
Le campus de 66 hectares comprend un nouveau dortoir, un centre de beaux-arts et un gymnase.
66 ヘクタールのキャンパスには、新築の寮、芸術センター、体育館が完備されています。

校園佔地 66 公頃，包括一座新的宿舍、藝術中心及體育館。

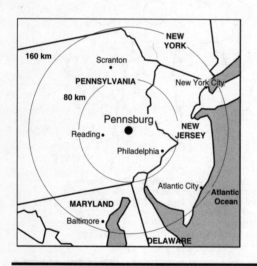

 7–24°C

 -1–7°C

 16–29°C

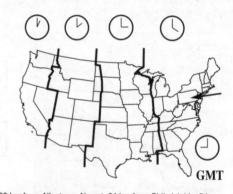

GMT

32 km from Allentown Airport; 64 km from Philadelphia, PA
A 32 km del aeropuerto de Allentown; a 64 km de Philadelphia, PA
A 32 km de l'aéroport d'Allentown ; à 64 km de Philadelphie, PA
アレントン空港から 32 km、ペンシルバニア州フィラデルフィア市から 64 km
離 Allentown 機場 32 公里；離 Philadelphia, PA 64 公里

 Coeducational 7–12 / Mixto / Mixte
男女共学
男女合校

 138/77

 60%

 20%

 74, 42 / solicitaron admisión, fueron aceptados / candidats, admis
出願者数 74 名、合格者数 42 名
74 人申請，42 人被錄取

  SLEP

China, Japan, Korea, Spain, Taiwan

 Rolling / Continuo / Continuelles
隨時受付
全年招生

 September / septiembre / septembre
9 月
9 月

 7:1,85%

 2:1

  U.S. Naval Academy, New York University, Boston University, Vanderbilt University, University of Michigan

 $31,200, $2500

Phillips Academy

Mrs. Jane F. Fried, Dean of Admission
180 Main Street
Andover, Massachusetts 01810
Phone: 978-749-4050 Fax: 978-749-4068
E-mail: admissions@andover.edu
URL: http://www.andover.edu

TABS, FAIS, NAFSA, NAIS member   *Founded 1778*

Andover's historical commitment to a diverse community annually brings students from more than thirty countries to the campus. With access to outstanding resources and the support of international advisers and local host families, Andover's international students are being prepared to meet the challenges of the global community in the twenty-first century.

El compromiso histórico de Andover con una comunidad diversa atrae anualmente a estudiantes de más de treinta países a la academia. Con acceso a recursos extraordinarios y el apoyo de asesores internacionales y familias locales que alojan a los estudiantes. A los estudiantes extranjeros de Andover se les prepara para enfrentar los desafíos de una comunidad global en el siglo XXI.

Chaque année, des étudiants de plus de trente pays différents viennent étudier à Phillips Academy, perpétuant ainsi la longue tradition de l'école pour la diversité. Grâce à d'excellentes ressources et au soutien des conseillers internationaux et des familles d'accueil locales, les étudiants étrangers de Andover sont préparés à répondre aux enjeux de la communauté internationale au siècle prochain.

Andover の多様性への伝統的なコミットメントが、毎年 30 ヶ国以上からの留学生を惹きつけています。情報源への卓越したアクセスやインターナショナル・アドバイザー、地元ホストファミリーの支援を得て、Andover の留学生は 21 世紀のグローバル社会での挑戦に適応するための準備を整えています。

安多瓦學校歷來重視學生多樣化，每年招收來自全世界 30 多國的學生。該校擁有豐富的資源，加上外國學生顧問和東道主家庭的支持，能培養外國學生應對 21 世紀國際社會面臨的各種挑戰。

The 500-acre campus includes fourteen academic buildings and eighteen playing fields.
Las 202 hectáreas de terreno incluyen catorce edificios académicos y dieciocho campos de juego.
Le campus de 202 hectares comporte quatorze bâtiments scolaires et dix-huit terrains de jeux.
202 ヘクタールのキャンパスには 14 の校舎と 18 の運動場があります。
校園面積 202 公頃，內有十四座教學樓和十八個操場。

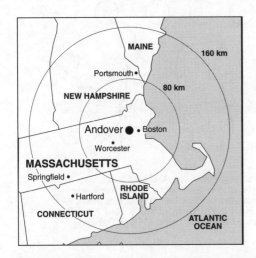

 13–22°C

 -6–3°C

 9–19°C

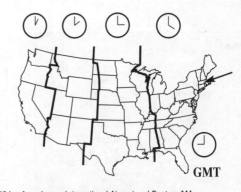
GMT

40 km from Logan International Airport and Boston, MA
A 40 km del aeropuerto internacional de Logan y de Boston, MA
A 40 km de l'aéroport international Logan et de Boston, MA
ローガン空港及びマサチューセッツ州ボストン市から 40 km
離麻州 Logan 國際機場和波士頓 40 公里

 Coeducational 9–PG / Mixto / Mixte
男女共学
男女合校

 534/549

 75%

 10%

 2658, 454 solicitaron admisión, fueron aceptados / candidats, admis
出願者数 2658 名，合格者数 454 名
2658 人申請，454 人被錄取

 SSAT, ISEE

 TOEFL (600)

 Canada, China, Japan, Korea, Saudi Arabia, Taiwan

 February 1 / 1 de febero / 1 février
2 月 1 日
2 月 1 日

 September / septiembre / septembre
9 月
9 月

 6:1, 98%

 5:1

 $31,160; $2000

 Harvard University, Brown University, Cornell University, University of Pennsylvania, Georgetown University, Princeton University

Phillips Exeter Academy

Michael Gary, Admissions Director
20 Main Street
Exeter, New Hampshire 03833-2460
Phone: 603-777-3437 Fax: 603-777-4399
E-mail: admit@exeter.edu
URL: http://www.exeter.edu

NAIS, TABS member   *Founded 1781*

With students and faculty from around the world, Exeter embraces diversity. In a safe environment, international students receive academic and emotional support from dormitory parents and teachers, as well as from student organizations like the Eastern European Exonians, Indian Society, Asian Student Collective, La Alianza Latina, and the Islamic Society.

Con estudiantes y una facultad de alrededor del mundo, Exeter es diversa. En un ambiente seguro, estudiantes internacionales reciben apoyo académico y emocional de padres y maestros de dormitorios, así como estudiantes de organizaciones como Eastern European Exonians, la Sociedad India, el Colectivo de Estudiantes Asiáticos, La Alianza Latina y la Sociedad Islámica.

Exeter privilégie le brassage des cultures en regroupant des étudiants et des professeurs des quatre coins du monde. Dans un environnement de toute sécurité, les étudiants de différentes nationalités reçoivent une assistante scolaire et morale de la part des responsables de l'internat et des professeurs ainsi que de la part des diverses organisations étudiantes telles que Eastern European Exonians, Indian Society, Asian Student Collective, La Alianza Latina et l'Islamic Society.

世界中からの才能ある学生と多様性を含め、安全な環境下、海外留学生は学問と精神面において、Eastern European Exonians、Indian Society、Asian Student Collective、La Alianza Latina、Islamic Society と同様、寄宿先の両親や教師からもサポートを受けます。

Exeter 學院的學生和教師來自世界各地。校區環境安全，學生們受到住宿家長和教師們在學術上和感情上的關懷，並受益于團體的支持。這些團體包括Eastern European Exonians, Indian Society, Asian Student Collective, La Alianza Latina, and the Islamic Society。

The 471-acre campus is home to the award-winning Phelps Science Center.

EL recinto de 191 hectáreas es el recipiente ganador del Centro de Ciencias Phelps.

Le campus de près de 191 hectares abrite le Centre scientifique Phelps Science Center qui a été récompensé.

191 ヘクタールのキャンパスには表彰された Phelps Science Center があります。

這所佔地 191 公頃的校園便是獲獎的 Phelps 科學中心所在地。

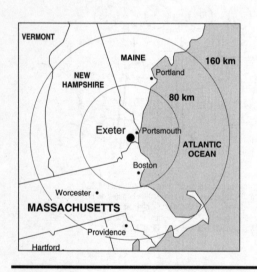

 4–21°C

 -2–4°C

 4–21°C

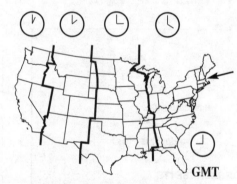

GMT

80 km from Logan International Airport and Boston, MA
A 80 km del aeropuerto internacional de Logan y de Boston, MA
A 80 km de l'aéroport international de Logan et de Boston, MA
マサチューセッツ州ローガン国際空港及びボストン市より80キロ
離 Logan, MA 國際機場和 Boston, MA 各 80 公里

 Coeducational 9–PG/ Mixto / Mixte
男女共学
男女合校

 520 / 525

 81%

 10%

 2128, 530 / solicitaron admisión, fueron aceptados / candidats, admis
出願者数 2128 名、合格者数 530 名
2128 人申請，530 人被錄取

 TOEFL (600) (268 CBT), SSAT

Canada, China, Korea,
Saudi Arabia, Singapore

 January 15 / 15 de enero / 15 janvier
1 月 15 日
1 月 15 日

 September / septiembre / septembre
9 月
9 月

5:1, 75%

3:1

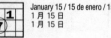 $31,600; $370

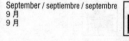
Brown University, Georgetown University,
Harverd Univrsity, University of Pennsylvania,
Yale University

Pomfret School

Erik C. Bertelsen, Jr.,
Assistant Head for Enrollment
398 Pomfret Street, P. O. Box 128
Pomfret, Connecticut 06258-0128
Phone: 860-963-6120   Fax: 860-963-2042
E-mail: admission@pomfretschool.org
URL: http://www.pomfretschool.org

NAIS member   *Founded 1894*

Challenging academics (AP courses in all disciplines), competitive athletics (fourteen varsity teams), and creative arts (recent chorus tour of Spain) continue the school's 110-year tradition of excellence. The academic experience is enhanced by the school's International Student Club and adviser, who assigns host families, organizes events, and assists with travel planning.

Plan de estudios estimulante (cursos avanzados en todas las disciplinas), atletismo competitivo (catorce equipos universitarios) y artes creativas (una reciente gira del coro a España) continúan la tradición de 110 años de excelencia del colegio. La experiencia académica se incrementa con el Club de Estudiantes Internacionales del colegio y un asesor que asigna a los estudiantes a familias dispuestas a alojarlos, organiza eventos y ayuda en los planes de viaje.

Un programme stimulant (cours de niveau supérieur dans toutes les disciplines), des sports de compétition (quatorze équipes sportives de première catégorie) et des activités créatives (la chorale a récemment fait un tour d'Espagne) perpétuent depuis 110 ans la tradition de l'excellence à Pomfret School. Outre la qualité du programme scolaire, les jeunes gens ont à leur disposition le Club international des étudiants de Pomfret ainsi qu'un conseiller chargé de l'assignation des familles d'accueil, de l'organisation des manifestations et des programmes de voyage.

意欲をそそる授業内容（全学科に AP コース）、優れた運動競技（14 の代表チーム）、創造的アート（最近スペインへのコーラスツアー実施）等、当校の 110 年の優れた伝統を継承しています。留学生クラブや、ホストファミリーの割り当て、イベント組織、旅行計画等をアシストするアドバイザーが、学園での経験を一層充実したものにします。

富有挑戰的學術課程（所有科目均採用 AP 課程）、深具競爭力的體育項目（14 個學校代表隊）以及極有創意的藝術（最近去西班牙表演合唱）傳承著該校 110 年的優良傳統。該校的外國學生俱樂部及顧問負責指定東道主家庭、安排活動、協助計劃旅行事宜，使學生的生活更加豐富。

The 500-acre campus has 26 buildings, including the Centennial Academic and Arts Center and science and music facilities.

Las 202 hectáreas de terreno contienen 26 edificios, incluyendo el Centro Académico y de Artes del Centenario ("Centennial") e instalaciones para ciencias y música.

Le campus de 202 hectares possède 26 bâtiments, y compris le Centennial Academic and Arts Center et des installations réservées aux sciences et à la musique.

202 ヘクタールのキャンパスには、26 棟の建物があり、センテニアル アカデミック アンド アーツ センターおよび科学、音楽用の施設が含まれています。

佔地 202 公頃的校園有 26 幢校舍，包括百年學術和藝術中心以及科學和音樂樓。

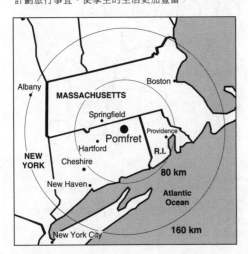

 13–24° C

 -6–4° C

 13–24° C

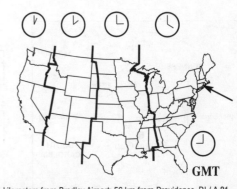

81 kilometers from Bradley Airport; 56 km from Providence, RI / A 81 kilómetros del aeropuerto de Bradley; 56 km de Providence, RI / À 81 km de l'aéroport Bradley ; á 56 km de Providence, RI
Bradley 空港から 81km、ロードアイランド州プロビデンス市より 56 キロ

 Coeducational, 9–PG / Mixto 9–PG / Mixte 9–PG
男女共学
男女合校

 172/168

 80%

10%

 600, 300 / solicitaron admisión, fueron aceptados / candidats, admis
出願者数 600 名、合格者数 300 名
600 申請，300 人被錄取

 TOEFL (525)

 SSAT (70)

Bermuda, Germany, Korea, Venezuela

 January 15 / 15 de enero / 15 janvier
1 月 15 日
1 月 15 日

 September / septiembre / septiembre
9 月
9 月

 5:1, 100%

1:1

 $34,550; $750, $1000

 Columbia University, Cornell University, Duke University, Hamilton College, Middlebury College

Rabun Gap – Nacoochee School

J. Timothy Martin
Director of Admission
339 Nacoochee Drive
Rabun Gap, Georgia 30568
Phone: 706-746-7467 Fax: 706-746-2594
E-mail: admission@rabungap.org
URL: http://www.rabungap.org

TABS, NAIS member   *Founded 1903*

RGNS seeks to enroll a geographically diverse population of international students of outstanding quality, superior motivation, and strong character. The ESL program at RGNS is comprehensive, includes both middle and upper shool courses, and is designed to serve students of all levels of English study and background.

RGNS tiene el propósito de matrícular una población geográficamente variada de estudiantes internacionales de calidad sobresaliente, motivación superior y carácter firme. El programa de inglés como segundo idioma (ESL) es completo; incluye cursos académicos superiores e intermedios, y ha sido concebido para servir a estudiantes de distintos niveles en el estudio del inglés y experiencias.

RGNS recherche a inscrire des étudiants d'origine internationale de qualité exceptionnelle, extrement motivée, avec une forte personnalité. Le programme d'anglais comme langue étrangère de RGNS est détaillé, comprend des cours pour les premier et second cycles du secondaire,et est concu pour des étudiants de tous niveaux d'anglais et de formation.

RGNS は世界各国からの顕著で優秀、かつ意欲的な学生を募集しています。当校の ESL プログラムは、中級、上級学校コースを含む包括的なもので、全ての英語レベルの学生に対応出来ます。

RGNS 在世界各地的優才生中選招具有杰出才能，有學習動力，性格頑強的學生。RGNS 所設的 ESL 課程完整，包括中等和高等課程，為來自不同背景的學生因才施教。

Rabun Gap classrooms have mountain views and advanced computer technology.

Las aulas de Rabun Gap tienen vistas a las montañas y tecnología avanzada de computación.

Les salles de classe de Rabun Gap ont vue sur les montagnes et disposent d'une technologie informatique de pointe.

Rabun Gap の教室からは、山の景色が見え、最新のコンピューター技術が完備されています。

Rabun Gap 的教室擁有山野景色和先進的電腦設備。

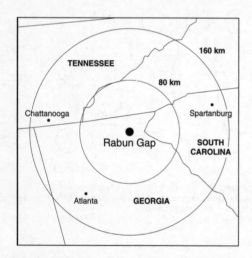

 4–24°C

 -4–18°C

 7–27°C

161 km from Atlanta Airport; 161 km from Atlanta, GA
A 161 km del aeropuerto de Atlanta; a 161 km de Atlanta, GA
A 161 km de l'aéroport d'Atlanta ; à 161 km d'Atlanta, GA
ジョージア州アトランタ空港より 161 キロ、同州アトランタ市より 161 キロ
離 Atlanta 機場 161 公里；離喬治亞州 Atlanta 市 161 公里

 Coeducational 6–12 / Mixto / Mixte
男女共学
男女合校

 90/120

50%

14%

 140, 91 / solicitaron admisión, fueron aceptados / candidats, admis
出願者数 140 名、合格者数 91 名
140 人申請，91 人被錄取

TOEFL, SLEP, SSAT, ISEE, SAT

3:1

Rolling / Continuo / Continuelles
隨時受付
全年招生

August / agosto / août
8 月
8 月

12:1, 65%

African continent, Germany, Korea, Spain, Turks & Caicos, Vietnam

$22,600; $3000

Berea College, Georgia College and State University, Oxford College at Emory, Savannah College of Art and Design, Western Carolina University

Intensive ESL only

Randolph-Macon Academy

Pia Crandell
Director of Admissions
200 Academy Drive
Front Royal, Virginia 22630
Phone: 540-636-5200 Fax: 540-636-5419

SACS, VAIS member   *Founded 1892*

Randolph-Macon Academy features America's only co-ed college prep school with Air Force JROTC and a flight program. Randolph-Macon offers an extensive ESL program with three distinct levels; trips to Washington, D.C. complement the program. The entire campus, including dorm rooms, is wired for Internet use. Ninety-nine percent of Randolph-Macon graduates attend college.

Randolph-Macon Academy tiene el único colegio mixto de preparación para la universidad con JROTC de la Fuerza Aérea y un programa de vuelo. Randolph-Macon ofrece un amplio programa de inglés como segundo idioma (ESL) con tres niveles; excursiones a Washington, D.C. complementan el programa Todo el recinto escolar, incluyendo las residencias estudiantiles, tiene conexiones para Internet. El noventa y nueve por ciento de los graduados de Randolph-Macon asisten a la universidad.

Randolph-Macon Academy est le seul établissement mixte préparant à l'entrée à l'université, qui propose également le programme de l'École des officiers de réserve (JROTC) de l'armée de l'air américaine, ainsi qu'un programme de vol. Randolph-Macon offre de nombreux cours d'anglais comme langue étrangère (ESL) de trois niveaux différents, ainsi que des excursions à Washington, D.C. L'ensemble du campus, y compris les dortoirs, est équipé de connexions à Internet. Quatre-vingt-dix-neuf pour cent des étudiants de Randolf-Macon sont admis à l'université.

Randolph-Macon Academy は、空軍予備将校訓練隊（Air Force JROTC）と航空プログラムのある米国唯一の男女共学大学予備校を特徴としています。Randolph-Macon には3レベルの広範囲な ESL プログラムがあり、ワシントン DC への旅行がプログラムを締めくくります。寮室を含めて全キャンパスはインターネットに接続されています。Randolph-Macon 卒業生の 99 ％は大学に進学します。

Randolph-Macon Academy 為美國唯一擁有空軍後備軍官訓練隊并提供飛行課程的男女生大學預科學校。分三級水平開設豐富的 ESL 課程，前往哥倫比亞特區華盛頓的旅遊活動為課程增添色彩。整個校園，包括宿舍房間，都設有互聯網線路。本校百分之九十九的畢業生昇入大學。

Randolph-Macon Academy's air-conditioned modern facilities are situated on 135 acres.

Las modernas instalaciones con aire acondicionado de Randolph-Macon están situadas en 55 hectáreas de terreno.

Les bâtiments modernes et climatisés de Randolph-Macon Academy sont situés sur un campus de 55 hectares.

モダンな空調付施設を含めた Randolph-Macon Academy は 55 ヘクタールの敷地にあります。

Randolph-Macon Academy 校園面積 55 公頃，擁有配備冷氣的現代化設施。

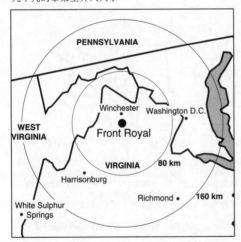

 9–25°C

 -6.6–6.3°C

 0–23°C

GMT

80 km from Dulles International Airport; 112 km from Washington D.C.
A 80 km del aeropuerto internacional de Dulles; a 112 km del Washington D.C. / A 80 km de l'aéroport international de Dulles; à 112 km de Washington D.C.
ダラス国際空港より 80 キロ、ワシントン D.C. より 112 キロ
離 Dulles 國際機場 80 公里；離 華盛頓特區 112 公里

 Coeducational 6–PG / Mixto / Mixte
男女共学
男女合校

 241/86

 82%

 17%

 212, 197 / solicitaron admisión, fueron aceptados / candidats, admis
出願者数 212 名、合格者数 197 名
212 人申請，197 人被錄取

 SLEP

 TOEFL, SSAT

 China (36), Egypt (36), Korea (36), Taiwan

 April 15 / 15 de avril / 15 Abril
4 月 15 日
4 月 15 日

 September, January, June (for Summer session) / septiembre, enero, junio / septembre, janvier, juin
9 月、1 月、6 月
9 月，1 月，6 月

 10:1

 2:1

 $21,370; $5135

 George Mason University, Christopher Newport University, The Citadel, Virginia Commonwealth University, Virginia Military Institute, Virginia Tech

 Air Force JROTC uniform / Uniforme del JROTC de la Fuerza Aérea / Uniforme Air force JROTC / 空軍 JROTC ユニフォーム / 空軍少年後備軍官訓練隊征服

 ESL levels 1, 2, and 3, and TOEFL Prep / Preparación de Inglés como segundo idioma (ESL) niveles 1, 2 y 3, y TOEFL / Anglais comme langue étrangère niveaux 1, 2, et 3 et préparation au TOEFL / ESL レベル 1, 2, 3 と TOEFL 準備 / 一、二、三級水平 ESL、以及 TOEFL 預備課程

 ESL summer program lasts 4 weeks. Starts the end of June. / El programa de verano de Inglés como segundo idioma (ESL) dura 4 semanas. Comienza a finales de junio / Le programme d'Anglais comme langue étrangère d'été dure 4 semaines et commence à la fin juin / 4 週間の ESL サマー・プログラムは 6 月末開始 / ESL 暑期課程為期四週，從 6 月底開始

Saint Andrew's School

Mr. Bradford L. Reed, Director of Admission
3900 Jog Road
Boca Raton, Florida 33434
Phone: 561-210-2020 Fax: 561-210-2027
E-mail: admission@saintandrewsschool.net
URL: http://www.saintandrewsschool.net

NAIS, TABS, SSATB member   *Founded 1962*

Saint Andrew's combines a small, safe boarding community with a demanding college-preparatory program, including intermediate and advanced English as a second language (ESL) courses. In a $25-million building campaign, Saint Andrew's opened a fine arts studio and a student commons. A new athletic center was completed in 2003 and the construction of a new performing arts center began in fall 2004.

Saint Andrew's School combina una comunidad de internado, pequeña y segura, con un exigente programa de preparación para la universidad que incluye cursos intermedios y avanzados de inglés como segundo idioma (ESL). En una campaña de construcción de $25 millones, Saint Andrew's inauguró un estudio de bellas artes y un comedor para estudiantes. En el 2003 se completó un nuevo centro atlético y en el otoño del 2004 se comenzó la construcción de un nuevo centro de bellas artes.

Saint Andrew's, un petit pensionnat situé dans un environnement sûr, propose un programme poussé préparant à l'entrée à l'université ainsi que des cours d'anglais comme langue étrangère (ESL) de niveaux « intermédiaire » et « avancé ». Après des travaux de rénovation de près de 25 millions de dollars, Saint Andrew's a ouvert un studio pour les beaux-arts et une salle commune pour les étudiants. Un nouveau complexe sportif a été construit en 2003 et à l'automne 2004, les travaux d'un nouveau centre de théâtre ont commencé.

Saint Andrew's School はこぢんまりとした安全な寄宿舎コミュニティと、中級および上級英語 ESL コースを含めて厳しい大学進学準備プログラムが一体となっています。2500 万ドルをかけた増築キャンペーンにより、Saint Andrew's は美術スタジオおよび学生会館をオープンしました。新設の運動競技センターは 2003 年に完成し、更に、新しい舞台芸術センターの建設が 2004 年秋に始まります。

聖安德魯斯學校為小型、安全的住宿學校，提供要求嚴格的大學預科課程，其中包括中級和高級外國學生英語課程。新型的健身中心已于 2003 年竣工。一座嶄新的表演藝術中心將在 2004 年秋季完工。

87-acre campus; newly renovated dormitories five miles from Atlantic Ocean.

35 hectáreas de terreno, residencias estudiantiles renovadas recientemente. A ocho kilómetros del Océano Atlántico.

Un campus de 35 hectares, des dortoirs récemment rénovés. À 8 km de l'océan atlantique.

35 ヘクタールのキャンパス。改築された寄宿舎、大西洋から 8km。

校園面積 35 公頃。宿舍樓最近翻修一新。距大西洋僅 8 公里之遙。

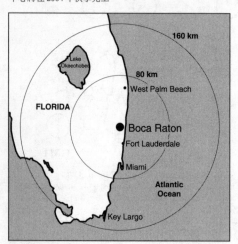

 20–26°C

 18–24°C

 20–26°C

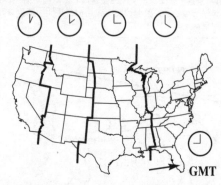

GMT

40 km from West Palm Beach International Airport, FL; 40 km from West Palm Beach / A 40 km del aeropuerto internacional de West Palm Beach; a 40 km de West Palm Beach, FL / À 40 km de l'aéroport international de West Palm Beach, FL ; à 40 km de West Palm Beach
フロリダ州西パームビーチ国際空港より 40 キロ、フロリダ州西パームビーチより 40 キロ
離 West Palm Beach 國際機場 40 公里；離佛羅里達州 West Palm Beach 市 40 公里

 Coeducational K–12 / Mixto / Mixte
男女共学
男女合校

 275/265

 20%

 20%

 250, 125 / solicitaron admisión, fueron aceptados / candidats admis
出願者数 250 名、合格者数 125 名
250 人申請，125 人被錄取

 SSAT

 SLEP (54)

 Austria, Bahamas, Brazil, Germany, Jamaica, South Korea

 February 10 / 10 de febrero / 10 fevrier
2 月 10 日
2 月 10 日

 August / agosto / août
8 月
8 月

 10:1, 37%

 2:1

 $31,500; $350

 Boston University, Brown University, University of Florida, Georgetown University, Harvard University, University of Miami, University of Pennsylvania, University of Virginia, Yale University

St. Catherine's School

Katherine S. Wallmeyer, Director of Admissions
6001 Grove Avenue
Richmond, Virginia 23226
Phone: 800-648-4982 Fax: 804-285-8169
E-mail: admissions@st.catherines.org
URL: http://www.st.catherines.org

TABS, FAIS member   *Founded 1890*

St. Catherine's School is an Episcopal diocesan day and boarding school for girls that provides a rigorous college-preparatory curriculum in grades junior-kindergarten through 12th grade. The school aims to develop in its students the desire and means to attain knowledge, a sense of personal worth and integrity, and an acceptance of responsibility in society.

St. Catherine's School es un colegio internado y externado Episcopal diocesano para niñas que provee un programa riguroso de preparación universitaria para grados desde el jardín de niños hasta el último año de colegio secundario. El colegio tiene como meta fomentar en sus estudiantes el deseo y la metodología para la obtención de conocimientos, el auto-aprecio, integridad y la responsabilidad social.

St. Catherine's School est une école de pension et externe de diocèse Episcopalienne pour les filles qui offre un programme rigoureux de préparation universitaire pour les classes de maternelle jusqu'à la dernière année de lycée. L'école a comme but le développement chez ses élèves du désir d'obtenir des connaissances et les moyens pour le faire, l'amour propre, l'honnêteté et la responsabilité sociale.

当校は幼稚園から12年生までの監督教会派の女子寄宿学校であり、大学準備のための厳しいカリキュラムで教育を行っています。知識欲を高め、知識を得る方法を学び、自己価値と高潔さ、社会における責任感を養うことを目的としています。

St. Catherine's School 是一所聖公會和住宿教會女子學校，設有從幼稚園到12年級的嚴格大學預備課程。學校宗旨是培養學生求知的能力，個人價值和正直感，以及在社會上承擔責任的能力。

The 16-acre campus includes a state-of-the-art Library Technology Center, chapel, photography lab, and ceramics studio.

Las 6 hectáreas de terreno incluyen una moderna Biblioteca y Centro de Tecnología, capilla, laboratorio fotográfico y estudio de cerámica.

Le campus de 6 hectares comprend une bibliothèque dotée des toutes dernières technologies, une chapelle, un laboratoire photo et un atelier de céramique.

6ヘクタールのキャンパスには礼拝堂、暗室、陶芸スタジオなどがあります。

校園佔地6公頃，包括一座最先進的圖書館科技中心、小教堂、攝影實驗室和制陶工作室。

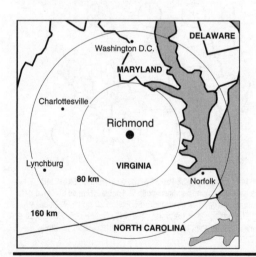

 24–29°C

 4–15°C

 24–26°C

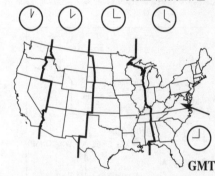

GMT

32 km from Richmond International Airport, VA / A 32 km del aeropuerto internacional de Richmond, VA / A 32 km de l'aéroport international de Richmond, VA
リッチモンド国際空港より32キロ
離維吉尼亞州 Richmond 國際機場 32 公里

 Girls 9–12 / Niñas / Filles
女子中学校
女子中學校

 $29,750; $85–$150

 Rolling / Continuo / Continuelles
随時受付
全年招生

 0/306

TOEFL (500), SSAT, SLEP

 September, January / septiembre, enero / septembre, janvier
9月、1月
9月，1月

 26%

 7:1, 35%

 University of North Carolina-Chapel Hill, Washington and Lee University, University of Virginia, Davidson College

 15%

 Australia, Korea

 6:1

Saint John's Preparatory School

UNITED STATES

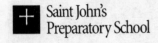

Bryan Backes, Director of Admission
1857 Watertower Road, Box 4000
Collegeville, Minnesota 56321
Phone: 320-363-3321 Fax: 320-363-3322
URL: http://www.sjprep.net

TABS member   *Founded 1857*

Located on 2,600 acres of woods and lakes, Saint John's Preparatory School attracts top students of many cultures, languages, and faiths. The college-preparatory, liberal arts program, ESL classes, travel opportunities, music/ art/theater classes, and sports teams are some of the many resources available.

Ubicado entre 1052 hectáreas de bosques y lagos, la Escuela Preparatoria Saint John atrae a estudiantes sobresalientes de muchas culturas, lenguas y religiones. Entre un sinnúmero de recursos disponibles, ofrece preparación universitaria, un programa de humanidades, clases de inglés como segundo idioma, oportunidades de viaje, clases de música, arte y teatro, y equipos deportivos.

Située sur 1052 hectares composés de bois et de lacs, Saint John's Preparatory School attire d'excellents étudiants issus de cultures, de langues et de religions diverses. De nombreuses ressources sont disponibles, comme par exemple un programme de formation générale préparant à l'entrée à l'université, des cours d'anglais comme langue étrangère, des excursions, des cours de musique, d'art et de théâtre, ainsi que des équipes sportives.

1052 ヘクタールの森林湖沼地帯に位置する、Saint John's Preparatory School は、あらゆる文化、言語、および宗教の背景を持つトップ・レベルの学生が集まってきます。大学準備、教養学科プログラム、ESL クラス、旅行のチャンス、音楽・芸術・演劇クラス、更にスポーツチーム等、多くのコースや活動があります。

Saint John's Preparatory School 校園坐落于湖泊和樹林環境之中，佔地 1052 公頃，吸引許多不同文化、語言和信仰背景的最優秀的學生來此就讀。提供大學預備課程，文科課程，ESL 課程，旅行機會，音樂／藝術／戲劇課程以及運動隊等。

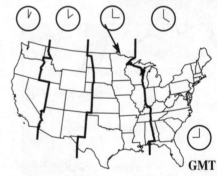

Students share the 2,500 acre campus with Saint John's University, using the university's computer technology, the libraries, athletic facilities, dining halls, and the possibility of enrolling in university courses.

Los estudiantes comparten el terreno de 1.012 hectáreas con Saint John's University y utilizan la tecnología informática, las bibliotecas, las instalaciones deportivas y los comedores de la universidad, y tienen la posibilidad de matricularse en los cursos de la universidad.

Les étudiants, qui partagent le campus de 1.012 hectares avec Saint John's University, utilisent les ordinateurs, bibliothèques, complexes sportifs et cafétérias de l'université. Ils ont également la possibilité de s'inscrire aux cours offerts par celle-ci.

学生たちは 1,012 ヘクタールのキャンパスを Saint John's University と共有し、大学のコンピュータ技術や図書館、食堂を使用できるほか、大学コース登録の可能性もあります。

本校學生與聖約翰大學合用 1,012 公頃的大學校園，可以使用大學的電腦技術設備、圖書館、體育設施、餐廳，而且還可以修習大學課程。

 7–25°C

 -30–5°C

 7–25°C

GMT

150 km from Minneapolis-St. Paul Airport; 20 km from St. Cloud, MN
A 150 km del aeropuerto de Minneapolis-St. Paul; a 20 km de St. Cloud, MN
A 150 km de l'aéroport de Minneapolis-St. Paul ; à 20 km de St. Cloud, MN
ミネアポリス・セントポール空港より 150 キロ、セントクラウドより 20 キロ
離 Minneapolis-St. Paul 機場 150 公里；離明尼蘇達州 St. Cloud 市 20 公里

 Coeducational 9–PG / Mixto / Mixte
男女共学
男女合校

 140/120

 35%

 14%

 133, 120 / solicitaron admisión, fueron aceptados / candidats, admis
出願者数 133 名，合格者数 120 名
133 人申請，120 人被錄取

 TOEFL (400), SLEP

 Austria, Brazil, Japan, Korea, Mexico, Taiwan

 Rolling / Continuo / Continuelles
随時受付
全年招生

 August, January, / agosto, enero / août, janvier,
8 月、1 月
8 月，1 月

 10:1, 10%

 7:1

 $23,407; $3306

 Carleton College, College of Saint Benedict, Harvard University, St. John's University, Notre Dame University, Stanford University, University of Minnesota

 ESL: Reading, Listening, Speaking, Composition, United States History, Advanced ESL

St. Johnsbury Academy

John J. Cummings, Director of Admissions
1000 Main Street
St. Johnsbury, Vermont 05819
Phone: 802-751-2130 Fax: 802-748-5463
E-mail: admissions@stjacademy.org
URL: http://www.stjohnsburyacademy.org

TABS, NAIS, NAFSA member   *Founded 1842*

Live and learn in this beautiful and safe Vermont community. Named an Exemplary School by the U.S. Department of Education, St. Johnsbury offers demanding academic, ESL, and pre-engineering programs as well as pre-professional programs in the arts.

Viva y aprenda en esta bella y segura comunidad en el Vermont. Designado como un colegio ejemplar por el Departamento de Educación de los EE.UU., St. Johnsbury ofrece una preparación académica exigente, cursos de inglés como segundo idioma (ESL) y programas de preingeniería y de arte a nivel pre-profesional.

Venez vivre et apprendre dans cette belle et sûre communauté située dans le Vermont. Nommée par le ministère de l'éducation des E.U. comme étant une école exemplaire, St. Johnsbury offre des programmes poussés de formation générale, d'anglais comme langue étrangère (ESL) et de préparation aux études d'ingénieur, ainsi que des programmes d'art préprofessionnels.

この美しく治安の良いバーモントの町で生活し学びます。米国教育省からモデル校に指定された当校は、高度な一般プログラムの他にも、ESL、工学課程進学準備プログラム、またアートでは職業訓練プログラムを実施しています。

在幽美安全的佛蒙特區生活和學習。作為被美國教育部命名的模範學校。本校提供優秀的學術、ESL 和工程先修課程，以及藝術專業先修課程。

The 42-acre campus provides outstanding facilities for science, art, music, and athletics.

El terreno de 16 hectáreas provee instalaciones de ciencias, arte, música y deportes.

Le campus de 16 hectares, comprend des installations de sciences, d'art, de musique et de sport.

16 ヘクタールのキャンパスには科学、芸術、音楽、スポーツなどの優れた施設があります。

校園佔地 16 公頃，提供一流的科學、藝術、音樂和體育設施。

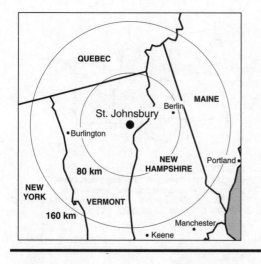

 3–18°C

 -15–24°C

 1–15°C

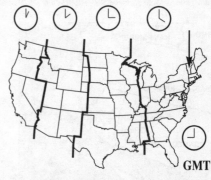

GMT

120 km from Burlington International Airport; 290 km from Boston, MA
A 120 km del aeropuerto internacional de Burlington; a 290 km de Boston, MA
A 120 km de l'aéroport international de Burlington; à 290 km de Boston, MA
バーリントン国際空港より 120 キロ、マサチューセッツ州ボストン市より 290 キロ
離 Burlington 國際機場 120 公里；離 Boston, MA 290 公里

 Coeducational 9–PG / Mixto / Mixte
男女共学
男女合校

 521/454

 20%

 8%

 473, 390 / solicitaron admisión, fueron aceptados / candidats, admis
出願者数 473 名、合格者数 390 名
473 人申請，390 人被錄取

 TOEFL, SLEP

Germany (25), Hong Kong (20), Japan, Korea, Mexico, Spain (20)

 Rolling / Continuo / Continuelles
隨時受付
全年招生

 August, January / agosto, enero / août, janvier
8 月、1 月
8 月、1 月

 9:1, 30%

 3:1

 $27,860
$3400 (ESL)

Boston College, Carnegie Mellon University, Cornell University, New York University, Rhode Island Institute of Design, University of Michigan

    ESL

Saint Thomas More School

Admissions Office
45 Cottage Road
Oakdale, Connecticut 06370
Phone: 860-823-3861 Fax: 860-823-3863
E-mail: stmadmit@stthomasmoreschool.com
URL: http://www.stthomasmoreschool.com

NAIS, TABS, NAFSA member   *Founded 1962*

Saint Thomas More School offers a structured environment with mandatory, monitored evening study halls to help students become successful. ESL is offered at three levels to help the non-English speaking student to be successful in an American school. Saint Thomas More is a Catholic school where boys of all faiths are enrolled.

Saint Thomas More School ofrece un ambiente estructurado con salas de estudio obligatorio y supervisado por las noches, para ayudar a los estudiantes a tener éxito en sus estudios. Los programas de inglés como segundo idioma (ESL) se ofrecen en tres niveles para ayudar a los estudiantes que no hablan inglés a estudiar con éxito en un colegio de los Estados Unidos. Saint Thomas More es un colegio católico en el que se aceptan estudiantes de diferentes credos.

Saint Thomas More School offre un environnement structuré. L'étude est obligatoire le soir dans des salles surveillées afin de permettre aux étudiants de se perfectionner. Des cours d'anglais comme langue étrangère sont proposés à trois niveaux différents pour aider les étudiants étrangers à réussir dans une école américaine. Saint Thomas More est une école catholique où les garçons de toutes les confessions peuvent s'inscrire.

Saint Thomas More School では、組織立った環境と生徒が学習をうまく進められるように、必須の管理付き学習ホールを提供しています。英語を話せない生徒がアメリカの学校で成功できるように、3レベルのESLクラスを提供しています。Saint Thomas More はカトリック系の学校ですが、全ての宗教の男子生徒が入学できます。

Saint Thomas More 學校提供井然有序的環境，必到的、受監督的晚自習室幫助學生取得好成績，有三種程度的 ESL 課程，幫助非英語學生在美國學校裡順利發展。Saint Thomas More 是一所招收各種信仰的男生天主學校。

Saint Thomas More School is situated on 100 acres of land with 1,000 feet of waterfront on Gardner Lake. The school offers small classes, structure, and study discipline.

Saint Thomas More School está situado en 40 hectáreas de terreno con 300 metros de terreno frente a Gardner Lake. El colegio ofrece clases con pocos alumnos, estructura y disciplina en los estudios.

Saint Thomas More School est située sur 40 hectares de terrain bordés sur un peu plus de 300 mètres par le Lac Gardner. L'école offre structure, discipline d'étude et classes restreintes.

Saint Thomas More School は、Gardner Lake に沿った 300m の湖岸がある 40 ヘクタールの敷地内にあります。学校では、小人数のクラス、規律、学習訓練を提供しています。

Saint Thomas More 學校座落在 40 公頃的土地上，濱臨 300 米英尺的 Gardner 湖岸線。本校提供小型課堂、優良秩序和學習紀律。

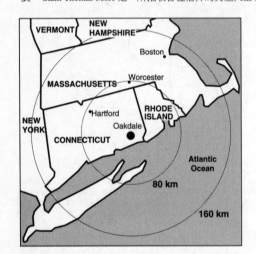

 4–18°C

 -7–2°C

 4–18°C

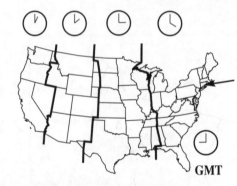

GMT

80 km from Bradley International Airport and Hartford, CT
A 80 km del aeropuerto internacional de Bradley y de Hartford, CT
A 80 km de l'aéroport international Bradley et de Hartford, CT
ブラッドリー国際空港及びコネチカット州ハートフォード市より 80 キロ
離 Bradley 國際機場和 Hartford, CT 80 公里

 Boys 8–PG / Muchachos / Garçons
男子中学校
男子中學校

 220, 170 / solicitaron admisión, fueron aceptados / candidats, admis
出願者数 220 名，合格者数 170 名
220 人申請，170 人被錄取

 Rolling / Continuo / Continuelles
随時受付
全年招生

 $30,325

 200/0

 ✓

 September, January / septiembre, enero / septembre, janvier
9 月、1 月
9 月，1 月

 100%

TOEFL, SLEP

 8:1, 100%

 University of Connecticut, Fairfield University, University of Massachusetts, Assumption College, Boston College

25%

Dominican Republic, Haiti, Hong Kong, Japan, Korea, Taiwan

10:1

St. Timothy's School

Office of Admission
8400 Greenspring Avenue
Stevenson, Maryland 21153
Phone: 410-486-7401 Fax: 410-486-1167

NAIS, TABS, FAIS member   *Founded 1882*

The school's small ESL program, for 6 students each year, enables international students to develop advanced proficiency in English and excel on the TOEFL. A challenging college-preparatory curriculum is enhanced by a large equestrian center, tennis courts, three computer labs, a fine arts center, and hiking trails.

El programa de inglés como segundo idioma (ESL) del colegio, para 6 estudiantes por año, permite a los estudiantes extranjeros adquirir conocimientos avanzados de inglés y sobresalir en el examen de inglés como idioma extranjero (TOEFL). El estimulante plan de estudios de preparación para la universidad, se complementa con un centro de equitación de grandes dimensiones, canchas de tenis, tres laboratorios de computación, un centro de bellas artes y senderos para practicar montañismo.

Chaque année, six étudiants peuvent participer au programme d'anglais comme langue étrangère (ESL) proposé par l'école. Ce programme permet aux étudiants étrangers de développer une excellente maîtrise de l'anglais et d'exceller à l'examen du TOEFL. L'établissement propose également un cursus intéressant préparant à l'entrée à l'université, un grand centre équestre, des courts de tennis, trois laboratoires informatiques, un centre pour les beaux-arts et des sentiers de randonnée pédestre.

当校の6人制 ESL プログラムで学ぶ留学生は上級英語能力を身につけ、TOEFL スコアで優秀な成績を残しています。難関大学進学予備カリキュラムには、大きな乗馬センター、テニスコート、3つのコンピューター・ラボ、ファインアートセンター、ハイキング・トレイルなども用意され、大変充実しています。

該校外國學生英語教學課程每年僅收6名學生，有利於外國學生提高英語能力，在托福考試中取得成績優異。該校除提供富於挑戰的大學預科課程外，還有大型馬術中心、網球場、三個電腦實驗室、藝術中心、遠足小徑。

145 acres, three computer labs, performing and visual arts center, equestrian center.

59 hectáreas de terreno, laboratorios de computación, un centro de artes interpretativas y visuales, un centro de equitación.

Un campus de 59 hectares, trois laboratoires informatiques, un centre pour les arts visuels et du spectacle et un centre équestre.

敷地面積 59 ヘクタール。3つのコンピューター・ラボ。演劇およびビジュアルアート・センター、乗馬センターがあります。

校園面積 59 公頃，有三個電腦實驗室、表演和影視中心、馬術中心。

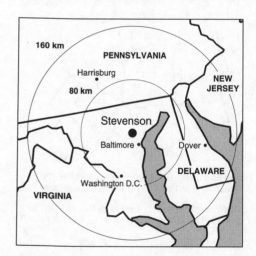

 10–27°C

 -2–10°C

 7–29°C

GMT

30 km from Baltimore-Washington International Airport; 16 km from Baltimore, MD
A 30 km del aeropuerto internacional de Baltimore-Washington; a 16 km de Baltimore, MD / A 30 km de l'aéroport international de Baltimore-Washington ; à 16 km de Baltimore, MD
バルチモア・ワシントン国際空港より 30 キロ、メリーランド州バルチモア市より 16 キロ
離 Baltimore-Washington 國際機場 30 公里；離馬里蘭州 Baltimore 市 16 公里

 Girls 9–12, PG/ Niñas / Filles
女子中学校
女子中學校

 0/125

 60%

 12%

 125, 75 / solicitaron admisión, fueron aceptadas / candidats, admis
出願者数 125 名、合格者数 75 名
125 人申請，75 人被録取

 TOEFL (450) or
SLEP (intermediate)

 Bahamas (17), Ecuador (15), Hong Kong (6), Japan (17), Korea (8), Mexico (5), Thailand (6), Venezuela (20)

 Rolling / Continuo / Continuelles
随時受付
全年招生

 September, January / septiembre, enero / septembre, janvier
9 月、1 月
9 月，1 月

 5:1, 60%

 2:1

 $32,875; $1000

 Columbia College, Swarthmore College, Tufts University, Wake Forest University, Washington and Lee University, Wesleyan University

Salisbury School

Peter B. Gilbert
Director of Admissions and Financial Aid
251 Canaan Road
Salisbury, Connecticut 06068-1623
Phone: 860-435-5700   Fax: 860-435-5750

TABS, NAIS, NAFSA member   *Founded 1901*

Salisbury School values the diversity that talented students from other nations can bring to the community. Ample support is provided so that international students can meet rigorous academic challenges and participate fully in athletics and extracurricular activities.

Salisbury School aprecia la diversidad que los estudiantes talentosos de otros países contribuyen a la comunidad. Se provee mucho apoyo para que los estudiantes internacionales puedan lograr los retos académicos y participar plenamente en los deportes y las actividades extraescolares.

Salisbury School apprécie la diversité que les étudiants doués des pays étrangers apportent à la communauté. Beaucoup de soutien est offert pour que les étudiants étrangers puissent faire face au programme scolaire rigoureux et participer dans les sports et les activités en dehors des cours.

当校は世界各国からの優秀な生徒達によってコミュニティが多様性に富むことを非常に大切にしており、留学生が厳しい授業に挑戦し、スポーツや課外活動に積極的に参加できるように、充実したサポート体制を備えています。

本校珍視有才華的學生從其他國家帶來的多樣化。學校全力協助國際學生完成嚴格學業並充分參與體育和課外活動。

The 700-acre campus is set in the Berkshires of southern New England.

El terreno de 283 hectáreas se encuentra en la región de los Berkshires en el sur de Nueva Inglaterra.

Le campus de 283 hectares est situé dans les montagnes de Berkshire au sud de la Nouvelle Anglaterre.

283 ヘクタールのキャンパスはニューイングランド南部のBerkshires にあります。

校園佔地 283 公頃，位於新英格蘭南部的 Berkshires 山區。

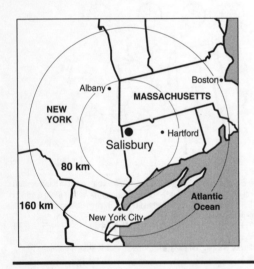

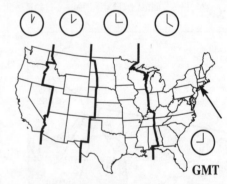

 4–21°C

 -17–10°C

 4–26°C

80 km from Hartford Airport, CT; 161 km from New York City, NY
A 80 km del aeropuerto de Hartford, CT; a 161 km de la ciudad de Nueva York, NY
A 80 km de l'aéroport d'Hartford, CT ; à 161 km de New York City, NY
コネチカット州、ハートフォード空港より 80 キロ、ニューヨーク市より 161 キロ
離 Hartford 機場 80 公里；離紐約州紐約市 161 公里

 Boys 9–PG / Muchachos / Garçons
男子中学校
男子中學校

 20, 10 / solicitaron admisión, fueron aceptados / candidats, admis
出願者数 20 名、合格者数 10 名
20 人申請，10 人被錄取

February 1 / 1 de febrero / 1er février
2 月 1 日
2 月 1 日

 $33,500; $600; $900

 285/0

July / julio / juillet
7 月
7 月

 Boston University, Carnegie Mellon University, Dickinson College, Duke University, Trinity College

 90%

 TOEFL (550), SLEP (26), SSAT (50), ISEE

 10:1, 65%

 10%

 Germany (31), Korea (11), Mexico (30), Spain (31), Thailand (11)

 8:1

Sandy Spring Friends School

Mecha Inman, Director of Admissions
16923 Norwood Road
Sandy Spring, Maryland 20860
Phone: 301-774-7455 Fax: 301-924-1115

TABS, FAIS, NAIS member   *Founded 1961*

Sandy Spring Friends School provides an excellent education in a safe and nurturing environment. The School offers intermediate and advanced ESL courses through the guidance of a full-time ESL director. All dorm rooms are networked for access to the Internet.

Sandy Spring Friends School ofrece una excelente educación en un entorno seguro y enriquecedor. La escuela ofrece cursos de inglés como segundo idioma (ESL) intermedios y avanzados bajo la supervisión de un director de ESL de dedicación exclusiva. Todas las habitaciones de las residencias estudiantiles tienen acceso a Internet.

Sandy Spring Friends School offre une excellente éducation dans un environnement sûr et stimulant. L'établissement propose des cours d'anglais comme langue étrangère (ESL) de niveaux intermédiaire et avancé sous la direction à temps complet du directeur chargé du programme d'ESL. Tous les dortoirs disposent d'un accès à Internet.

Sandy Spring Friends では、安全で快適な環境の中、卓越した教育を提供しています。また、常勤の ESL 部長の指導のもと、中級から上級までの ESL コースがあります。学生寮は、全室インターネットのアクセスが可能です。

Sandy Spring Friends School 在安全的培養環境中提供優秀的教育。該校提供在一名全時 ESL 主管老師指導下的中級和高級 ESL 課程。所有宿舍房間都備有英特網可供使用。

The 140-acre woodland campus has a historic Quaker Meeting House and a state-of-the-art science center.

Las 57 hectáreas de terrenos boscosos del recinto tienen una histórica casa de reunión de los Cuáqueros y un centro de ciencias con los últimos adelantos.

Le campus boisé de 57 hectares possède un bâtiment historique qui servait de lieu de réunion aux Quakers et un centre scientifique ultra-moderne.

57 ヘクタールの緑ゆたかなキャンパスには由緒ある Quaker Meeting House や芸術科学センターがあります。

林木覆蓋的校園佔地 57 公頃，包括歷史建築奎克會議廳和世界一流的科學中心。

 4–21°C

 4–10°C

 18–24°C

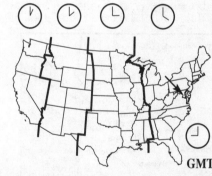

GMT

18 km from the Baltimore-Washington International Airport; 24 km from Washington, D.C. • A 18 km del aeropuerto internacional de Baltimore-Washington; a 24 km de Washington, D.C. • A 18 km de l'aéroport international de Baltimore-Washington ; à 24 km de Washington, D.C.

ボルチモア・ワシントン国際空港より 18 キロ、ワシントン D.C.より 24 キロ

離 Baltiimore-Washington 國際機場 18 公里；離華盛頓特區 24 公里

  Coeducational 9–12 / Mixto / Mixte
男女共学
男女合校

 52, 21 / solicitaron admisión, fueron aceptados / candidats, admis
出願者数 52 名，合格者数 21 名
52 人申請，21 人被錄取

 January 15 / 15 de enero / 15 janvier
1 月 15 日
1 月 15 日

 $32,150–$32,650; $1000

 102/116

 SLEP 75%

 September / septiembre / septembre
9 月
9 月

20%

SSAT, TOEFL, SLEP

7:1, 35%

Colgate University, Duke University, Guilford College, Haverford College, University of Maryland

12%

China, Korea, Nigeria, Russia, Taiwan, Thailand

4:1

Solebury School

Denise DiFiglia, Director of Admission
P.O. Box 429, Phillips Mill Road
New Hope, Pennsylvania 18940-0429
Phone: 215-862-5261 Fax: 215-862-3366
E-mail: admissions@solebury.com
URL: http://www.solebury.org

NAIS, TABS, NAFSA member   *Founded 1925*

Academic preparation for TOEFL, small classes, individual attention, excellent college-preparatory curriculum, competitive sports, art and theater, a safe friendly campus, integration with American students, homestays, conversation partners, community projects and field trips, three levels of ESL, full-time ESL director, and limited enrollment from various countries increase diversity. ESL spring and summer programs are also offered.

Preparación académica para el TOEFL, clases reducidas, atención individual, excelente currículo de preparación universitaria, deportes de competición, arte y teatro, recinto seguro y amigable, integración con estudiantes estadounidenses, alojamiento con familias locales, compañeros para práctica de conversación, proyectos comunitarios y viajes de campo, tres niveles de inglés como segundo idioma (ESL), y una matrícula limitada de varios países aumenta la diversidad. También se ofrecen programas de inglés como segundo idioma (ESL) durante la primavera y el verano.

Préparation au TOEFL, nombre d'élèves restreint par classe, attention individuelle, excellent programme scolaire préparant à l'entrée à l'université, sports de compétition, art et théâtre, campus sûr et amical, intégration au groupe d'étudiants américains, séjours en famille, partenaires pour conversation, projets communautaires et excursions, trois niveaux d'anglais comme langue étrangère (ESL), directeur chargé à temps complet du programme d'ESL, sans oublier le nombre d'inscription limité pour chaque pays qui permet d'accroître la diversité. Les cours d'ESL sont également proposés pendant le printemps et l'été.

TOEFL準備、小人数のクラス、個々の生徒に対する行き届いた気配り、卓越した大学準備カリキュラム、優れたスポーツ、芸術および演劇、安全で親しみやすいキャンパス、アメリカ人学生との融和、ホーム・ステイ、会話パートナー、地域社会参加プロジェクト、校外見学旅行、三段階に分れたESL、常勤のESL部長、国別在籍者数制限による高い多様性を提供します。ESL春期、夏期のプログラムもあります。

TOEFL 學習備考，小型課堂，個別指導，優秀的大學預備課程，競賽運動，藝術與戲劇，安全、友好的校園，與美國學生融為一體，當地家庭住宿，交談夥伴，社區項目以及實地旅行，三種水平的 ESL 課程，全時 ESL 主管老師。從每個國家招生名額有限，以此增加多元化特色。還開設春夏兩季的 ESL 課程。

The 90-acre campus is home to a new multimedia center, new math/science building, and a new International Student Center for the ESL program.

El recinto de 37 hectáreas es el nuevo hogar del nuevo centro de multimedios, el nuevo edificio de ciencia y matemática, y un nuevo centro internacional para estudiantes para el programa de inglés como segundo idioma (ESL).

Le campus de près de 37 hectares abrite les tout nouveaux centre multimédia, bâtiment pour les mathématiques et les sciences et centre pour les étudiants internationaux suivant le programme ESL.

37ヘクタールのキャンパスには、新メディア・センター、新数学・科学棟、ESLプログラムのための新しい国際学生センターがあります。

校園佔地約 37 公頃的校園擁有新多媒體中心、新數學／科學樓和開設 ESL 課程的國際學生中心。

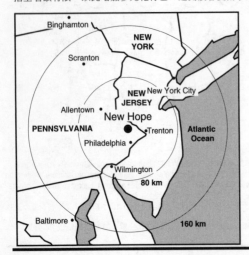

 4–21°C

 -4–7°C

 13–27°C

GMT

42 km from Philadelphia Airport and Philadelphia, PA
A 42 km del aeropuerto de Filadelfia y de Filadelfia, PA
A 42 km de l'aéroport de Philadelphie et de Philadelphie, PA
ペンシルバニア州フィラデルフィア空港及びフィラデルフィア市より 42 キロ
離 Philadelphia, PA 機場和 Philadelphia 市各 42 公里

 Coeducational 9–12 & PG / Mixto / Mixte
男女共学
男女合校

 218, 103 / solicitaron admisión, fueron aceptados / candidats, admis
出願者数 218 名、合格者 103 名
218 人申請，103 人被録取

 January 15, rolling / 15 de enero, continuo / 15 janvier, continuelles
1 月 15 日より随時受付
1 月 15 日起随時皆可

 $30,000, including $7700 ESL program fee; $1600 book deposit

  Full year, Spring, Summer

 112/108

 SLEP (44% or higher), or TOEFL

 September, (March–Spring ESL program) / septiembre, (marzo–programa ESL de primavera) / septembre, (mars– programme d'ESL de printemps)
9 月、(3 月～春期 ESL プログラム)
9 月、(3 月 ESL 春季學期)

 30%

 SSAT

 6:1, 58%

 Boston College, Boston University, Carnegie Mellon University, Cornell University, Drexel University, Duke University, The George Washington University, The Johns Hopkins University, Lehigh University, The Pennsylvania State University, Pratt Institute, Purdue University, Rochester Institute of Technology, Rutgers University, Tulane University, University of Chicago, University of Southern California, Vanderbilt University

 10%

Brazil (1), Bulgaria (3), Burkina-Faso (1), China (1), Germany (18), Hong Kong (5), India (1), Japan (38), Korea (18), Lithuania (1), Malaysia (3), Puerto Rico (3), Santo Domingo (1), Senegal (1), Singapore (1), Spain (1), Switzerland (1), Taiwan (18), Thailand (14), Venezuela (1), Zaire (1)

  2:1

Southwestern Academy

Jane Whitmire, Director of Admissions
2800 Monterey Road
San Marino, California 91108
Phone: 626-799-5010 Fax: 626-799-0407
E-mail: admissions@southwesternacademy.edu
URL: http://www.southwesternacademy.edu

TABS, FAIS, NAFSA, SSATB member   *Founded 1924*

Southwestern offers two distinctly beautiful and safe campuses: one next to Pasadena a in Southern California and one near the resort community of Sedona in Northern Arizona. Both offer a complete ESL program. Graduation requires completion of a college-preparatory high school curriculum.

Southwestern ofrece dos bellos recintos seguros y bellos: uno cerca de Pasadena en la parte sur de California y otro cerca de la comunidad vacacional de Sedona en la parte norte de Arizona. Ambos ofrecen un programa completo de inglés como segundo idioma (ESL). Los requisitos de graduación exigen que se complete un currículo preparatorio de la escuela secundaria para entrar a la universidad.

Southwestern propose deux superbes campus garantissant de très bonnes conditions de sécurité : l'un se situe près de Pasadena, dans la région sud de la Californie, et l'autre près de Sedona, un lieu de villégiature dans la région nord de l'Arizona. Les deux campus offrent un programme ESL (anglais deuxième langue) complet. Pour obtenir un diplôme de ces établissements, il est nécessaire d'avoir effectué et complété un programme d'études de préparation universitaire au lycée.

Southwestern は、カルフォルニア南部 Pasadena 近郊とアリゾナ北部のリゾート地 Sedona 近郊に、安全で美しい二つのキャンパスがあります。両キャンパス共 ESL プログラムがあり、また卒業には、大学進学のための高校全課程を修了する必要があります。

Southwestern 學院分別在南加州的 Pasadena 和亞利桑那州北部 Sedona 休養社區附近擁有兩座美麗的校園。兩處校園均開設 ESL 課程。畢業生均須完成大學預科高中課程。

The San Marino campus has 140 students in grades 6-12. The Beaver Creek campus in Arizona has 40 students in grades 9-12.

El recinto de San Marino tiene 140 estudiantes en los grados del 6 al 12. El recinto de Beaver Creek en Arizona tiene 40 estudiantes en los grados del 9 al 12.

Le campus de San Marino a 140 étudiants de la 6ème à la terminale. Le campus Beaver Creek en Arizona a 40 étudiants qui vont de la 3ème à la terminale.

San Marino キャンパスには、6 年生から 12 年生までの 140 名の生徒が、またアリゾナ州の Beaver Creek キャンパスには、9 年生から 12 年生までの 40 名の生徒が在籍しています。

在 San Marino 的校園中有 140 名 6 年級至 12 年級的學生。在亞利桑那州的 Beaver Creek 校園中有 40 名 9 年級至 12 年級的學生。

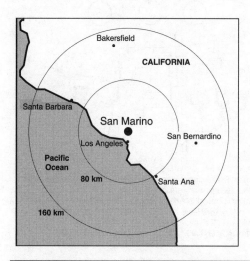

  24–35°C

  10–24°C

  15–24°C

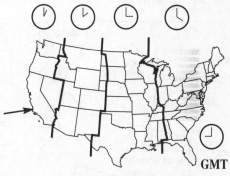

48 km from Los Angeles Airport; 3 km from Pasadena, CA
A 48 km del aeropuerto de Los Angeles; a 3 km de Pasadena, CA
A 48 km de l'aéroport de Los Angeles; à 3 km de Pasadena, CA
ロサンゼルス空港より 48 キロ、カリフォルニアパサディナ市より 3 キロ
離 Los Angeles 機場 48 公里；離加州 Pasadena 市 3 公里

 Coeducational 6–12 / Mixto / Mixte
男女共学
男女合校

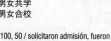 90/50

 75%

 60%

 100, 50 / solicitaron admisión, fueron aceptados / candidats, admis
出願者数 100 名、合格者数 50 名
100 人申請，50 人被錄取

China, Hong Kong, Indonesia, Japan, Kosovo, Korea, Mexico, Russia, Slovak Republic, Taiwan, Thailand

 Rolling / Continuo / Continuelles
随時受付
全年招生

 September, February, June / septiembre, febero, junio / septembre, février, juin
9 月、2 月、6 月
9 月，2 月，6 月

 6:1

 3:1

 $28,800; $2000

 University of California, Cal Poly Pomona, California State University, Loyola Marymount University, Occidental College, Pitzer College, Pasadena City College

 Full ESL Program offered at both campuses / Se ofrece un programa completo de ESL en ambos recintos / Le programme complet d'Anglais comme Langue Etrangère est offert dans les deux campus / 両キャンパスに ESL プログラム全課程 設置 / 兩個校園均開設全套 ESL 課程

Summer ESL Program on California campus / Se ofrece ESL en el recinto de California / Le programme d'été d'Anglais comme Langue Etrangère est offert sur le campus de Californie / カリフォルニアキャンパスでの夏期 ESL プログラム / 加州的校園開設 ESL 課程

Stoneleigh-Burnham School

Sharon Pleasant, Director of Admission
574 Bernardston Road
Greenfield, Massachusetts 01301
Phone: 413-774-2711 Fax: 413-772-2602
E-mail: admissions@sbschool.org
URL: http://www.sbschool.org

NAIS, TABS, NEASC member   *Founded 1869*

Stoneleigh-Burnham School provides girls with excellent college preparation in a supportive family environment. The international program is well established and includes a special orientation program for new international students and a three-level ESL program. The state-of-the-art Jesser Science Center enhances the already extensive science program, and the Geissler Galery offers extensive fine and performing arts opportunities.

Stoneleigh-Burnham School ofrece a las niñas una excelente preparación para la universidad, en un ambiente familiar con mucho apoyo. El programa internacional está bien establecido e incluye un programa de orientación especial, para las nuevas estudiantes extranjeras y un programa de inglés como segundo idioma (ESL) con tres niveles. El más moderno centro de ciencias Jesser realza el programa extensivo de ciencias y el Galery Geissler ofrece oportunidades extensivas de bellas artes.

Stoneleigh-Burnham School offre aux jeunes filles une excellente préparation universitaire dans un environnement familial et coopératif. Le programme international, établi depuis longtemps, est composé d'un programme spécial d'orientationpour les nouveaux(elles) étudiants(es) étrangers(ères), ainsi que decours d'anglais comme langue étrangère (ESL) de trois niveaux différents. Le Centre des sciences Jesser, ultra-moderne, souligne la part importante attribuée aux sciences dans le programme des cours qui est très complet. La Galerie Geissler rend hommage quant à elle aux talents artistiques en proposant de nombreux programmes consacrés aux beaux-arts et au théâtre.

Stoneleigh-Burnham School は、サポート体制の整った家族的な雰囲気で女子学生に優れた大学進学準備コースを提供します。当校の国際プログラムは堅固で、新しい留学生を対象とした特別オリエンテーションや3レベルの ESL プログラムが含まれます。最先端をゆく Jesser Science Center は、既に大規模な科学プログラムをますます増進し、また Geissler Galery は広範囲に渡る美術・舞台芸術の機会を提供します。

斯通雷－伯恩漢姆學校以家庭支持環境為女生提供絕好的大學預科課程。本校接收國際學生已有多年，為國際新生專設適應項目，並提供三種水平的 ESL 課程。設備一流的 Jesser 科學中心使得已經廣泛的科學課程更豐富，Geissler 畫廊為美術創造和表演藝術的發展提供更多的機會場所。

The 100-acre campus includes extraordinary art, dance, athletic, and equestrian facilities.

Las 41 hectáreas de terreno incluyen instalaciones extraordinarias para arte, danza, atletismo y equitación.

Le campus de 41 hectares comprend d'excellentes installations destinées à l'art, à la danse, au sport et à l'équitation.

41 ヘクタールのキャンパスには、芸術、ダンス、運動および乗馬のすばらしい施設があります。

校園面積 41 公頃，內有出色的藝術、舞蹈、體育、馬術設施。

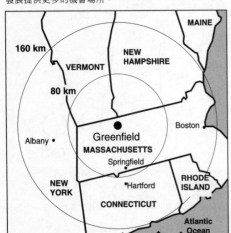

 10–21°C

 -6–4°C

 15–26°C

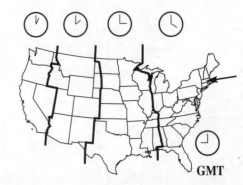

GMT

96 km from Bradley International Airport; 60 km from Springfield, MA
A 96 km del aeropuerto internacional de Bradley; a 60 km de Springfield, MA
A 96 km de l'aéroport international de Bradley ; à 60 km de Springfield, MA
ブラッドリー国際空港より 96 キロ、マサチューセッツ州、スプリングフィールドより 60 キロ
離 Bradley 國際機場 96 公里；離 Springfield, MA 60 公里

 Boarding and day school for Girls 7-PG / Niñas / Filles
女子中学校
女子中學校

 122, 90 / solicitaron admisión, fueron aceptadas / candidates, admises
出願者数 122 名、合格者数 90 名
122 人申請，90 人被錄取

Rolling for international students / Continuo para estudiantes internacionales / Continuelles pour les étudiants internationaux
海外留学受付 / 招收外國學生

$32,100; $1500

Extensive courses for beginners and advanced ESL students / Cursos extensivos para estudiantes principiantes y avanzados de ESL. / Cours d'approfondissement pour débutants et pour niveau supérieur pour l'Anglais comme Langue Etrangère / 広範囲にわたる ESL 初級、上級者用コース / 設有初級和高級的 ESL 課程。

 0/160

 TOEFL, SLEP, or SSAT

September, January / septiembre, enero/ septembre, janvier
9 月、1 月
9 月、1 月

70%

4:1, 40%

Bates College, Boston University, Skidmore College, Williams College

15%

Bangladesh, Bermuda (10), Eastern Europe (9), Germany (18), Hong Kong (7), Japan (11), Korea (11), Mexico (7), Middle East (5), Taiwan (5), Thailand (4)

3:1

Stuart Hall

Stephanie Shafer, Dean of Admissions
P.O. Box 210
Staunton, Virginia 24402
Phone: 540-885-0356 or 888-306-8926 (toll-free)
Fax: 540-886-2275

TABS, NAIS member   *Founded 1844*

The school has a full-time international ESL adviser/instructor as well as a coordinator for dorm life. It has a three-level ESL program and a learning resources center to assist with study skills, time management, and extra help in classes. Special trips are taken to Washington, D.C., Richmond, VA, and Charlottesville, VA.

El colegio tiene un asesor/instructor internacional de inglés como segundo idioma (ESL) de tiempo completo, así como un coordinador de las residencias estudiantiles. Tiene un programa de ESL de tres niveles, y un centro de recursos de aprendizaje para ayuda en técnicas de estudio, administración del tiempo y ayuda adicional en las clases. Se hacen excursiones especiales a Washington, D.C., Richmond, VA, y Charlottesville, VA.

L'établissement possède un conseiller/enseignant chargé, à temps complet, du programme d'anglais comme langue étrangère (ESL), ainsi qu'un coordinateur responsable des dortoirs. Stuart Hall propose un programme d'anglais comme langue étrangère (ESL) de trois niveaux différents, ainsi qu'un centre de ressources éducatives offrant une assistance sur les techniques d'étude, la gestion du temps et les cours en général. Des voyages sont également organisés à Washington, D.C., Richmond, VA, et Charlottesville, VA.

当校には寄宿舎での生活コーディネータの他、インターナショナル ESL アドバイザー/インストラクターが常勤しています。ESL プログラムは３レベルから成り、学習リソース・センターが学習スキル、時間の使い方を指導し、授業への特別サポートを行います。ワシントン D.C.、バージニア州リッチモンド、シャーロッツビルへの特別研修旅行が含まれています。

該校配備全職外國學生英語顧問和輔導員以及關照學生宿舍生活的協調員。該校還設有分為三個等級的外國學生英語課程和一個學習資源中心，幫助學生培養學習技巧，學會籌劃時間的本領，並向其提供額外的課程輔導。該校還特別安排學生去華盛頓，維吉尼亞州 Richmond 和 Charlottesville 參觀游覽。

The school has an outstanding Visual and Performing Arts Program.

El colegio tiene un programa excepcional de artes visuals y escénicas.

L'établissement propose un excellent programme d'arts visuels et du spectacle.

当校には特に優れたビジュアルアートと舞台芸術プログラムが揃っています。

該校設有一個優秀的觀賞與表演藝術項目。

 4–24°C

 -4–10°C

 4–29°C

GMT

193 km from Richmond Airport, VA; 241 km from Washington, DC
A 193 km del aeropuerto de Richmond, VA; a 241 km de Washington, DC
A 193 km de l'aéroport de Richmond, VA ; à 241 km de Washington DC
バージニア州、リッチモンド空港より 193 キロ、ワシントン DC より 241 キロ
離維吉尼亞州 Richmond 機場 193 公里；離 Washington DC 241 公里

 Coeducational 6-12 (girls boarding 8-12) / Mixto 6-12 / Mixte 6-12
男女共学
男女合校

 5/70

 70%

 12%

 7, 5 / solicitaron admisión, fueron aceptadas / candidates, admises
出願者数 7 名、合格者数 5 名
7 人申請，5 人被錄取

 SLEP, SSAT, TOEFL

 Germany, Japan, Korea, Mexico

 Rolling / Continuo / Continuelles
随時受付
全年招生

 September, March / septiembre, marzo / septembre, mars
9 月、3 月
9 月、3 月

7:1, 50%

 6:1

 $27,700; $2500 (ESL), $350

University of Virginia, Virginia Tech University, James Madison University, Hollins University

Suffield Academy

Terry Breault, Director of Admissions
P.O. Box 999, 185 N. Main Street
Suffield, Connecticut 06078
Phone: 860-386-4440 Fax: 860-668-2966
E-mail: saadmit@suffieldacademy.org

TABS, NAFSA member   *Founded 1833*

Suffield offers intermediate and advanced ESL assistance, secondary level summer school, and an International Student Adviser and Association to help students integrate into the school community.

Suffield ofrece asistencia en la enseñanza del inglés como segundo idioma (ESL) a nivel intermedio y avanzado, y un curso de verano a nivel secundario. Un asesor de estudiantes internacionales junto con una Asociación para Estudiantes Internacionales ayudan a los estudiantes a integrarse en la comunidad del colegio.

Suffield assiste les élèves dans le programme d'anglais comme langue étrangère (ESL) de niveau intermédiaire et avancé, et offre un programme d'été pour les cours du secondaire, un conseiller d'élèves étrangers et une association pour aider les étudiants à s'intégrer dans la communauté scolaire.

Suffield には、中級および上級の ESL プログラム、中等レベルの夏季スクールがあり、、留学生アドバイザーまたは協会が、参加学生が学校生活に馴れ親しみ、適応できるよう援助を行っています。

Suffield 提供中級與高級程度的 ESL（英語為第二語言）補導中學夏季學校課程，並有國際學生指導老師及協會幫助學生融入學校生活。

The 350-acre campus is set in the center of historic Suffield.

Las 141 hectáreas de terreno están situadas en el centro de la histórica Suffield.

Le campus de 141 hectares est situé au centre de la ville historique de Suffield.

キャンパスは 141 ヘクタールで、歴史的なサフィールドの中心部に位置しています。

校園佔地 141 公頃，位於歷史名城 Suffield 市中心。

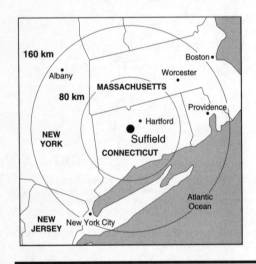

 5–17°C

 -7–2°C

 3–15°C

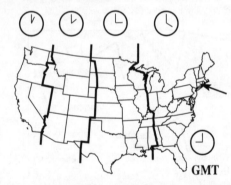

8 km from Bradley International Airport; 19 km from Springfield, MA
A 8 km del aeropuerto internacional de Bradley; a 19 km de Springfield, MA A 8 km de l'aéroport international de Bradley; à 19 km de Springfield, MA
ブラッドリー国際空港から 8 km、マサチューセッツ州スプリングフィールド市から 19 km
離 Bradley 國際機場 8 公里；離麻州 Springfield 市 19 公里

 Coeducational 9–PG / Mixto / Mixte
男女共学
男女合校

 220/185

 70%

 15%

 750, 280, / solicitaron admisión, fueron aceptados / candidats, admis
出願者数 750 名、合格者数 280 名
750 人申請，280 人被錄取

 TOEFL (550), SSAT (305)

 TOEFL, SSAT

 Bermuda, Canada, Germany, Hong Kong, Japan, Korea, Saudi Arabia, Taiwan, Thailand

 February 1, rolling / 1 de febrero, continuo / 1 février, continuelles
2 月 1 日より随時受付
2 月 1 日起隨時皆可

 September, December, January / septiembre, diciembre, enero / septembre, décembre, janvier
9 月、12 月、1 月
9 月，12 月，1 月

 8:1, 89%

1:1

 $31,500; $1000–$1500

 Boston University, Dartmouth College, Hamilton College, Hobart and William Smith College, Johns Hopkins University, Suffolk University, University of Colorado, University of Wisconsin, Williams College

The Taft School

Frederick H. Wandelt III
Director of Admissions
110 Woodbury Road
Watertown, Connecticut 06795
Phone: 860-945-7777 Fax: 860-945-7808
E-mail: admissions@taftschool.org
URL: http://www.taftschool.org

TABS, FAIS, NAFSA member   *Founded 1890*

Taft offers close student-faculty interaction and a rigorous academic program designed to foster intellectual growth and personal responsibility. About 400 Advanced Placement examinations are written each year.

Taft ofrece una estrecha interacción entre los alumnos y los profesores, y un riguroso programa académico diseñado para desarrollar la capacidad intelectual y la responsabilidad personal. Todos los años se ofrecen cerca de 400 exámenes para colocación en programas avanzados.

Taft offre une intéraction très étroite entre les élèves et les professeurs ainsi qu'un programme scolaire très rigoureux, pour promouvoir la responsabilité intellectuelle et personnelle de chacun. Environ 400 examens permettant l'entrée dans des établissements d'enseignement supérieur sont offerts chaque année.

Taft では、生徒と講師の間のコミュニケーションを密接にし、知性の発達及び責任感の育成を目的とした厳格な学科プログラムを提供しています。毎年およそ 400 種類の上級コース進級試験が用意されています。

Taft 擁有融洽的師生關係和優秀的學術課程，培養智力及個人責任感。每年約有 400 人參加大學入學測試。

The 220-acre campus includes an 18-hole golf course, a 56,000-volume library, and 4 computer labs.
Las 89 hectáreas de terreno incluyen un campo de golf de 18 hoyos, una biblioteca con 56,000 volúmenes y 4 laboratorios de computación.
Le campus de 89 hectares comprend un terrain de golf à 18 trous, une bibliothèque de 56 000 volumes et 4 laboratoires informatiques.
89 ヘクタールのキャンパスには 18 ホールのゴルフコース、蔵書 56,000 冊の図書館、コンピュータ・ラボが 4 つ完備されています。
校園佔地 89 公頃，擁有一座 18 洞的高爾夫球場、一座藏書 56,000 冊的圖書館以及 4 個電腦操作室。

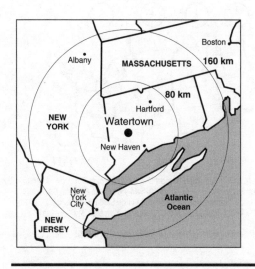

 7–26°C

 -6–4°C

 10–26°C

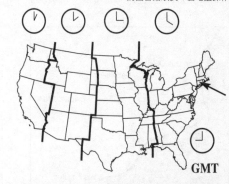

GMT

81 km from Hartford's Bradley Airport; 16 km from Waterbury, CT
A 81 km del aeropuerto Bradley de Hartford; a 16 km de Waterbury, CT
A 81 km de l'aéroport Bradley de Hartford ; à 16 km de Waterbury, CT
ハートフォード・ブラッドリー空港から 81 km、コネチカット州ウォーターベリー市から 16 km
離 Hartford 市 Bradley 機場 81 公里；離康州 Waterbury 市 16 公里

 Coeducational 9–12 / Mixto / Mixte
男女共学
男女合校

 291/275

 85%

 12%

 1400 / solicitaron admisión, fueron aceptados / candidats, admis
出願者数 1400 名
1400 人申請

 TOEFL (550), SSAT (80)

 Canada, Hong Kong, Japan, Taiwan, Thailand

 January 31 / 31 de enero / 31 janvier
1 月 31 日
1 月 31 日

 September / septiembre / septembre
9 月
9 月

 6:1, 90%

 6:1

 $32,900; $525

 Princeton University, Yale University, Brown University, Cornell University, Harvard University, Georgetown University

---

The Thacher School

William P. McMahon, Director of Admissions
5025 Thacher Road
Ojai, California 93023
Phone: 805-640-3210 Fax: 805-640-9377
E-mail: admission@thacher.org
URL: http://www.thacher.org

TABS member   *Founded 1889*

Cited as an Outstanding Boarding School by *U.S. News & World Report*, Thacher offers challenging academics, caring faculty, competitive athletics, performing arts, and outdoor programs. 92% enroll at one of top 3 college choices.

Destacado por la revista *U.S. News & World Report* como un internado excepcional, Thacher ofrece un estimulante programa académico, profesores que se preocupan por sus alumnos, deportes competitivos, música y teatro, y programas al aire libre. El 92% de sus egresados entran en una de las 3 universidades de su elección.

Citée comme une école préparatoire exceptionnelle par le magazine *U.S. News & World Report*, Thacher School offre un programme d'enseignement rigoureux, un corps enseignant attentionné ainsi que des sports de compétition, de la musique, de théâtre, et des activités de plein air. 92% des élèves entrent une des trois premières universités de leur choix.

U.S. News & World Report 誌上で「卓越した寄宿学校」と推賞された当校は、チャレンジングな学科クラス、配慮の行き届いた教師陣、スポーツ、舞台芸術、課外プログラムを持ち、92％の学生が志望校3位までの大学に進学しています。

Thacher School 被《美國新聞與世界報道》稱為"傑出的寄宿學校",擁有高難度的學術課程,關懷備至的教師,極具水準的體育運動、表演藝術和戶外活動。本校92%的學生進入前三志願大學就讀。

Direct T-1 Internet connections in every dorm room.

Conexión T-1 directa a la Internet en cada habitación.

Accès direct T-1 à l'Internet dans chaqu'une des chambres.

寮の全ての部屋からT-1インターネットに直接接続できます。

每個宿舍房間都有萬維網T-1直通線路。

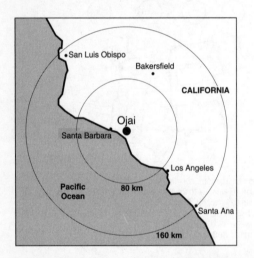

 21–35°C

 7–24°C

 15–26°C

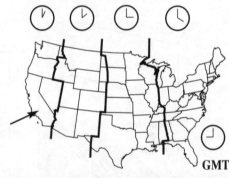

GMT

73 km from Santa Barbara Airport and Santa Barbara, CA
A 73 km del aeropuerto de Santa Bárbara y de Santa Bárbara, CA
A 73 km de l'aéroport de Santa Barbara et de Santa Barbara, CA
サンタバーバラ空港及びカリフォルニア州サンタバーバラ市より73キロ
離加州 Santa Barbara 機場和 Santa Barbara 市 73 公里

 Coeducational 9–12 / Mixto / Mixte
男女共学
男女合校

 115/120

 90%

 8%

 400, 90 / solicitaron admisión, fueron aceptados / candidats, admis
出願者数 400 名、合格者数 90 名
400 人申請、90 人被錄取

 SSAT

 TOEFL (570)

 Australia (2), Hong Kong (2), Japan (2), Kenya (1), Korea (5), Saudi Arabia (2)

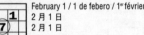 February 1 / 1 de febero / 1er février
2月1日
2月1日

 September / septiembre / septembre
9月
9月

6:1, 95%

3:1

 $32,750

 Brown University, Colombia College, University of California at Berkeley, Princeton University, Stanford University

Vermont Academy

William J. Newman, Director of Admissions
Pleasant Street, Box 500
Saxtons River, Vermont 05154
Phone: 802-869-6229, 800-560-1876
Fax: 802-869-6242
E-mail: epike@vermontacademy.org
URL: http://www.vermontacademy.org

Founded 1876

ESL classes and TOEFL preparation are included in the Academy's outstanding academic curriculum. Reading, writing, speaking, and listening skills, as well as vocabulary and grammar, are emphasized. The Academy offers small classes, supportive faculty members, friendly students, and a beautiful, safe campus. Many sports and creative arts classes are available.

Clases de inglés como segundo idioma (ESL) y preparación para la prueba TOEFL se incluyen en el excepcional plan de estudios de la Academia. Se hace énfasis en lectura, redacción, técnicas de conversación y comprensión, vocabulario y gramática. La Academia ofrece clases con pocos alumnos, profesores que brindan apoyo, estudiantes amistosos y un recinto escolar hermoso y seguro. Se ofrecen muchos deportes y clases de artes creativas.

Des cours d'anglais comme langue étrangère (ESL) et de préparation à l'examen du TOEFL sont inclus dans l'excellent programme scolaire de l'Academy. L'accent est mis sur la lecture, la rédaction, la production orale et les techniques d'écoute, aussi bien que sur le vocabulaire et la grammaire. L'Academy offre des classes restreintes, des professeurs coopératifs, des étudiants sympathiques ainsi qu'un campus sûr et agréable. De nombreux sports et des cours d'activités créatives sont également disponibles.

Academy の傑出した学科カリキュラムには ESL クラスと TOEFL 準備が含まれます。語彙および文法のほか、読解、会話、聞き取りスキルに重点が置かれます。少人数制クラス、支援的な教官、フレンドリーな学生、そして美しく安全なキャンパス。多種のスポーツや創造的な芸術クラスも受講できます。

該校出色的學術課程中包括ESL課程和TOEFL備考。特別著重閱讀、寫作、說話、聽力、詞匯、語法等項目。該校小班上課，教師輔導耐心，學生相互友愛，校園美觀而安全。學生可選擇各種體育課程和藝術創作課程。

Vermont academy is situated on a 500-acre campus in southeastern Vermont.
Vermont Academy está situada en 202 hectáreas de terreno en la región sureste de Vermont.
Vermont Academy est située sur un campus de 202 hectares dans le sud-est du Vermont.
Vermont Academy は、ベルモント南部の 202 ヘクトールのキャンパスにあります。
Vermont Academy 座落在佛蒙特州東南部，校園佔地 202 公頃。

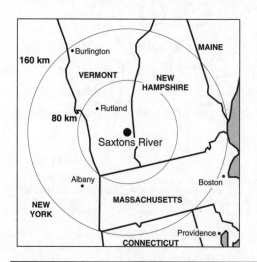

 10–21°C

 -6–9°C

 7–18°C

GMT

150 km from Hartford, CT Airport; 160 km from Boston, MA / A 150 km del aeropuerto de Hartford, CT; a 160 km de Boston, MA / A 150 km de l'aéroport Hartford, CT ; à 160 km de Boston, MA
コネチカット州ハートフォード空港より 150 キロ、マサチューセッツ州ボストンより 160 キロ
離 Hartford, CT 機場 150 公里；離麻州 Boston 市 160 公里

 Coeducational 9–PG / Mixto / Mixte
男女共学
男女合校

165/85

 75%

 9%

 300, 210 / solicitaron admisión, fueron aceptados / candidats, admis
出願者数 300 名、合格者数 210 名
300 人申請，210 人被錄取

SLEP

TOEFL, SSAT

Brazil (1), Germany (1), Japan (7), Korea (7), Mexico (5), Venezuela (1)

February 1, rolling / 1 de febrero, continuo / 1er février, continuelles
2 月 1 日より随時受付
2 月 1 日起随時皆可

September, January / septiembre, enero / septembre, janvier
9月、1月
9月，1月

 7:1

5:1

$33,560
+ ESL Fees

 Boston University, Brown University, University of Colorado, Rhode Island School of Design, Skidmore College, St. Lawrence University, University of Vermont

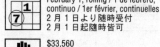

Walnut Hill School

UNITED STATES

Matthew A. Derr, Dean
Admission and Placement
12 Highland Street
Natick, Massachusetts 01760
Phone: 508-650-5020
URL: http://www.walnuthillarts.org

AISNE, NAIS membership   *Founded 1893*

Walnut Hill School, an independent conservatory–style school for the arts in the U.S., provides intensive, focused high school level study in ballet, creative writing, music, theater, and visual arts. The arts and academic curriculum prepare students for admission to top-ranked colleges, universities, conservatories, and art schools throughout the United States.

Walnut Hill School, una escuela independiente para las artes con un estilo de conservatorio en los EE.UU. ofrece estudios intensivos a nivel de enseñanza secundaria en estudios de ballet, redacción creativa, música, teatro, y artes visuales. El currículo académico y de las artes prepara a los estudiantes, para la admisión a colegios, universidades, conservatorios y escuelas para las artes en los Estados Unidos.

Walnut Hill School, une école conservatoire indépendante pour l'enseignement de l'art aux États-Unis, propose une formation intensive de niveau lycée et orientée dans le domaine de la danse, de la création littéraire, de la musique, du théâtre et des arts cinématographiques. Le programme académique des arts préparent les étudiants pour leur admission dans les meilleures universités, conservatoires et écoles d'arts a travers les États-Unis.

当校は米国で唯一の独立した芸術高校であり、バレエ、創作文、音楽、演劇、ビジュアルアートなど、 高校レベルの徹底したトレーニングを提供しています。芸術／学科の教科課程を土台に、学生は米国内中の一流大学、音楽（美術）学校に入学しています。

Walnut Hill School 是一家美國的獨立藝術高中，提供嚴格的高中水平的芭蕾、創造性寫作、音樂、戲劇、觀賞藝術的基礎訓練，為學生進入一流大學、音樂學院和專業藝術院校做準備。

The beautiful 45-acre campus contains 3 small recital halls, a 350-seat theater, and full-dance and visual art facilities.

Este hermoso recinto de 45 acres cuenta con 3 pequeñas salas de recitales, un teatro con 350 asientos, e instalaciones para las artes visuales y el baile completo.

Ce magnifique campus de 45 acres contient 3 petits ampithéatres, un théatre de 350 places et un équipement pour la danse et l'art cinématographique.

美しい１９ヘクタールのキャンパスには、３つの小ホール、３５０席収容の劇場があり、ダンスやビジュアルアートに対応出来ます。

美麗的校園佔地 45 公頃，有 3 所小型音樂廳和一座容 350 人的劇院以及全功能舞蹈和視覺藝術場所。

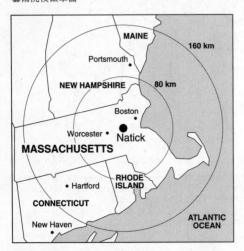

 7–21°C

 -9–7°C

 4–24°C

GMT

32 km from Logan International Airport; 22 km from Boston, MA
A 32 km del aeropuerto internacional de Logan; a 22 km de Boston, MA
A 32 km de l'aéroport international de Logan ; à 22 km de Boston, MA
マサチューセッツ州ローガン国際空港より 32 キロ、同州ボストン市より 22 キロ
離 Logan 國際機場 32 公里；離 Boston, MA 22 公里

 Coeducational 9–12 / Mixto / Mixte
男女共学
男女合校

 80/190

 76%

 30%

 141, 224 / solicitaron admisión, fueron aceptados / candidats, admis
出願者数 141 名、合格者数 224 名
141 人申請，224 人被錄取

 SLEP

 SLEP

 Canada, Germany, Japan, Korea, Taiwan

 Rolling / Continuo / Continuelles
隨時受付
全年招生

 September, January / septiembre, enero / septembre, janvier
9月、1月
9 月，1 月

 7:1, 50%

 5:1

 $31,700 (for boarding), $24,625 (for day)

 Art Institute of Chicago, Barnard College, Bennington College, Carnegie Mellon University, The Curtis Institute, Harvard University, The Juilliard School, Northwestern University, Oberlin Conservatory, Pratt Institute, Rhode Island School of Design, University of Michigan, Yale University

Washington Academy

Samra Kuseybi, Director of Admissions
High Street
P.O. Box 190
East Machias, Maine 04630
Phone: 207-255-8301 Fax: 207-255-8303
URL: http://www.washingtonacademy.org

TABS member   *Founded 1792*

A full-time ESL director works closely with faculty. Washington Academy has separate boys and girls dorms and a host family program. Washington Academy arranges TOEFL testing, issues I-20s, sponsors an International Student Association, provides weekend activities as well as trips during school vacations to New York, Boston, and Washington D.C.

Un director a tiempo completo de inglés como segundo idioma (ESL) trabaja directamente con la facultad. Washington Academy tiene dormitorios separados para niños y niñas y auspicia un programa familiar. Washington Academy ofrece los exámenes de ruso como lengua extranjera (TOEFL), emite formularios I-20, auspicia una asociación internacional para estudiantes, provee actividades de fin de semana así como giras durante las vacaciones a Nueva York, Boston, y Washington D.C.

Un directeur, chargé à plein temps du programme ESL (anglais deuxième langue), travaille étroitement avec les professeurs. Washington Academy dispose de dortoirs séparés pour les filles et les garçons et propose un programme d'accueil en famille. Washington Academy se charge d'organiser les examens du TOEFL, d'émettre les visas pour étudiants I-20s, de soutenir une association internationale des étudiants et d'organiser des activités pour le week-end et des voyages pendant les vacances scolaires vers New York, Boston et Washington D.C.

専任の ESL 指導者が細心の指導にあたります。Washington Academy には、男女別の寄宿舎とホスト・ファミリー制度があります。また、TOEFL テスト、I-20 学生ビザ、国際留学生協会主催による週末の活動と長期休暇中のニューヨーク、ボストン、ワシントン DC への旅行も提供します。

Washington Academy有和員工們密切合作的全職ESL導師。學校為男女學生分別安排宿舍和家庭住宿。Washington Academy開設 TOFEL 測試，簽發I-20，贊助國際學生協會，並為學生們安排周末活動，利用學校假期帶領學生們旅遊觀光紐約，波士頓和華盛頓首府。

The 45-acre campus has 8 buildings, including 2 newly renovated dormitories.

El recinto de 45 acres comprende 8 edificios incluyendo 2 dormitorios recientemente renovados.

Le campus de 18 hectares se compose de 8 bâtiments dont 2 dortoirs récemment rénovés.

18 ヘクタールのキャンパスには、最近改築した 2 つの寄宿舎を含む 8 つのビルがあります。

45 英畝的校園上有八座建築，包括兩座新裝修的宿舍樓。

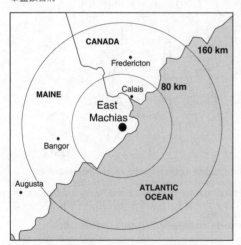

 10–24°C

 -8--2°C

 10–18°C

151 km from Bangor Airport; 107 km from Ellsworth, ME
A 151 km del aeropuerto de Bangor; a 107 km de Ellsworth, ME
A 151 km de l'aéroport de Bangor ; à 107 km de Ellsworth, ME
Bangor 空港より 151 キロ、メイン州 Ellsworth 市より 107 キロ
離 Bangor 機場 151 公里；離 Ellsworth, ME 107 公里

 Coeducational 9–12 / Mixto / Mixte
男女共学
男女合校

 47, 43 / solicitaron admisión, fueron aceptados / candidats, admis
出願者数 47 名、合格者数 43 名
47 人申請，43 人被錄取

 Rolling / Continuo / Continuelles
随時受付
全年招生

 $20,500; $1200

 167/155

 Rolling, September, January / Continuo, septiembre, enero / Continuelles, septembre, janvier
随時受付、9 月、1 月
全年招生，9 月，1 月

 8%

 TOEFL, SLEP, SSAT

 11:1

 Boston University, Bowdoin College, Maine Maritime Academy, Middlebury College, University of Maine

 10%

 Germany, Korea, Russia, Taiwan, Yugoslavia

 3:1

Western Reserve Academy

Gail Kish
Admission Office
115 College Street
Hudson, Ohio 44236
Phone: 330-650-9717 Fax: 330-650-5858
URL: http://www.wra.net

TABS, FAIS, NAIS, NAFSA member   *Founded 1826*

Reserve offers a rigorous academic program with one of the highest percentages per capita of National Merit Semifinalists and commendation winners of any U.S. boarding school. Strong English skills required.

Reserve ofrece un riguroso programa académico con uno de los más altos porcentajes per capita de semifinalistas al premio National Merit y más ganadores de menciones honoríficas que cualquier otro internado en los EE.UU. Es obligatorio que dominen muy bien el inglés.

Parmi tous les internats américains, le programme d'enseignement de Reserve produit un des taux les plus élevés de demi-finalistes et de lauréats du "National Merit". Un très bon niveau d'anglais est requis.

当校は National Merit 賞の準決勝出場者を最も多く輩出した学校の一つです。また、全米の全寮制学校の推奨校にもなりました。かなりの英語力が必要です。

Reserve 中學在全美住宿學校中，是擁有最高比例的學生進入全國優良學生決賽，以及獲得優勝者的學校之一。本校學術嚴謹，但學生必須具備良好的英語能力。

Reserve's 200-acre campus has a new library, dorm, and student center.

El terreno de 81 hectáreas tiene una nueva biblioteca, residencias para estudiantes y un centro estudiantil.

Le campus de 81 hectares de Reserve possède une nouvelle bibliothèque, un nouveau dortoir et un nouveau centre pour étudiants.

当校の 81 ヘクタールにおよぶキャンパスには、新図書館、寮および学生センターが含まれています。

校園佔地 81 公頃，擁有新建圖書館、宿舍和學生中心。

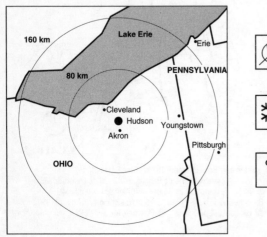

7–13°C

-3–4°C

8–11°C

GMT

40 km from Cleveland-Hopkins International Airport and Cleveland, OH
A 40 km del aeropuerto internacional de Cleveland-Hopkins y de Cleveland, OH
A 40 km de l'aéroport international de Cleveland-Hopkins et de Cleveland, OH
クリーブランド・ホプキンズ国際空港及びオハイオ州クリーブランド市より 40 キロ
離 Cleveland-Hopkins 國際機場和 Cleveland, OH 各 40 公里

Coeducational 9-12 / Mixto / Mixte
男女共学
男女合校

225/150

68%

10%

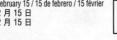
364, 229 / solicitaron admisión, fueron aceptados / candidats, admis
出願者数364 名、合格者数229 名
364 人申請，229 人被錄取

TOEFL (550), SSAT

Argentina, Canada, England, Germany, Korea, Thailand

February 15 / 15 de febrero / 15 février
2 月 15 日
2 月 15 日

September, January / septiembre, enero / septembre, janvier
9 月、1 月
9 月、1 月

12:1, 96%

2.5:1

$29,500; $800

Amherst College, Carnegie Mellon University, Cornell University, Case Western Reserve University, Denison University, Harvard University, University of Michigan, United States Naval Academy, Washington University

Westtown School

P.O. Box 1799
Westtown, Pennsylvania 19395
Phone: 610-399-7900 Fax: 610-399-7909

TABS, NAIS member   *Founded 1799*

Westtown School is a coeducational college preparatory school offering a challenging academic program. Founded in 1799 by Quakers, Westtown offers international students from over 20 countries the opportunity to develop strong English skills while becoming an integral part of a friendly community. A full-time International Student Coordinator works closely with the ESL teacher, students, and their advisors.

Westtown School es un colegio mixto de preparación para la universidad que ofrece un programa académico estimulante. Fundado en 1799 por los cuáqueros, Westtown ofrece a estudiantes extranjeros de más de 20 países la oportunidad de adquirir conocimientos avanzados de inglés mientras que ellos se integran a una comunidad acogedora. Un Coordinador de Estudiantes Extranjeros de tiempo completo trabaja estrechamente con los profesores de ESL, con los estudiantes y con sus asesores.

Westtown School, un établissement mixte préparant à l'entrée en université, propose un programme scolaire stimulant. Fondé en 1799 par les Quakers, Westtown donne aux étudiants venant de plus de 20 pays différents l'occasion de développer une solide maîtrise de l'anglais tout en devenant partie intégrante d'une communauté amicale. Un coordinateur chargé à temps complet des étudiants étrangers travaille en étroite collaboration avec le professeur d'ESL, les étudiants et leurs conseillers.

Westtown School は男女共学の大学進学準備校で、挑戦的な学科プログラムを提供しています。1799 年にクエーカー教徒によって創立された Westtown において、海外 20 カ国以上からの留学生たちは友好的コミュニティの一員となると共に、強靭な英語能力を発達させる機会が得られます。常勤留学生コーディネーター、ESL 担当教師、学生およびアドバイザーの全面サポートをいたします。

Westtown School 於 1799 年由教友會創辦，是一所男女同校的大學預科學校，提供高難度的學習課程。本校使來自二十多個國家的學生有機會融入一個友好的集體，成為其中的一分子，同時培養扎實的英語技能。一名全職國際學生協作人與 ESL 教師、學生及其導師密切合作。

The 600-acre campus includes newly renovated boys' and girls' dormitories.
Las 243 hectáreas de terreno incluyen residencias estudiantiles recién renovadas para jóvenes de ambos sexos.
Le campus de 243 hectares comprend des dortoirs pour garçons et des dortoirs pour filles nouvellement rénovés.
243 ヘクタールのキャンパスには新築された男子用および女子用寮が含まれます。
校園佔地 243 公頃，擁有新裝修的男女生宿舍。

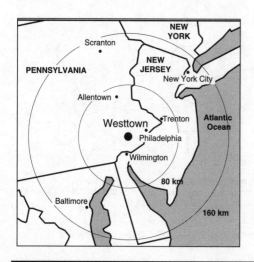

 8–32°C

 6–8°C

 16–32°C

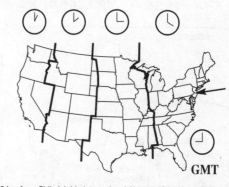

GMT

40 km from Philadelphia International Airport; 40 km from Philadelphia
A 40 km del aeropuerto Internacional de Filadelfia; a 40 km de Filadelfia
À 40 km de l'aéroport international de Philadelphie ; à 40 km de Philadelphie
フィラデルフィア国際空港およびフィラデルフィア市から 40 km
離 Philadelphia 國際機場 40 公里；離 Philadelphia 市 40 公里

 Coeducational boarding
Pre–K–12 / Mixto / Mixte
男女共学
男女合校

 200/200

 75%

 15%

 300, 127 / solicitaron admisión, fueron aceptados / candidats, admis
出願者数 300 名、合格者数 127 名
300 人申請，127 人被錄取

 TOEFL

 SSAT

 England, Germany, Japan, Kenya, Korea, Nigeria, Taiwan

 February 1, rolling / 1 de febrero, continuo / 1ᵉʳ février, continuelles
2 月 1 日より随時受付
2 月 1 日起随時皆可

 September / septiembre / septembre
9 月
9 月

 15:1, 85%

 3:1

 $30,730; $3000

 American University, Brown University, Haverford College, Swarthmore College, University of Pennsylvania

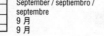

The White Mountain School

UNITED STATES

Laurie C. Zeizer, Director of Admission
371 West Farm Road
Bethlehem, New Hampshire 03574
Phone: 603-444-2928 Fax: 603-444-5568

Founded 1886

"Small School. Big Outdoors" is the phrase that best characterizes our traditional academic program alongside such nontraditional sports as mountaineering, flat & whitewater paddling, rock & ice climbing, and road & mountain biking. Winter sports include snowboarding, recreational and backcountry skiing, and cross-country. Program includes ESL, arts, and international community service.

"Colegio pequeño. Gran ambiente natural" dice la frase que mejor caracteriza nuestro programa académico tradicional junto con deportes no tradicionales como alpinismo, remo plano y en aguas rápidas, escalamiento de rocas y hielo y ciclismo en caminos y de montaña. Los deportes de invierno incluyen snowboarding, esquí backcountry, y cross country. El programa incluye cursos de inglés como segundo idioma (ESL), artes y servicio comunitario internacional.

« Petite école. Grands espaces. » Cette phrase symbolise le mieux notre programme scolaire traditionnel accompagné d'activités sportives originales, comme l'alpinisme, le canoe en rivière et sur lac, la varappe et l'escalade sur glace, le cyclisme et le VTT. Parmi les sports divers sont pratiqués le snowboard, le ski alpin et de randonnée et le ski de fond. Le programme comprend des cours d'anglais comme langue étrangère (ESL), des cours d'art et de service communautaire international.

「小さな学校、大きなアウトドア」。これが登山やフラットパドリング、急流下り、ロック＆アイスクライミング、路上バイク、マウンテンバイクといった非伝統的なスポーツと共に、当校の伝統的な学習プログラムをよく特徴づけています。冬季スポーツには、スノーボード、スキー競技とレクリエーション・スキー、クロスカントリーが含まれます。プログラムには ESL、アート、国際コミュニティサービスがあります。

"小學校，大環境" 用于描述本校特色恰如其分。本校擁有傳統的學科課程，另具非傳統的體育運動，例如登山，靜水和急流划槳，冰岩攀登以及平地和山地自行車。冬季體育運動包滑雪板，娛樂性野外滑雪和越鄉滑雪。課程包括 ESL、藝術和國際社區服務。

250-acre campus includes new library and student center.

Las 101 hectáreas de terreno cuentan con una nueva biblioteca y un centro estudiantil.

Le campus de 101 hectares possède une nouvelle bibliothèque et un nouveau centre pour étudiants.

101 ヘクタールのキャンパスには新図書館や学生センターもあります。

校園面積 101 公頃，擁有新建圖書館和學生宿舍。

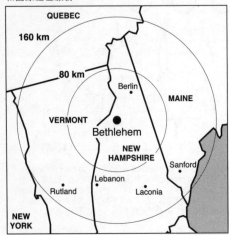

 15–23°C

 -12– -1°C

 10–21°C

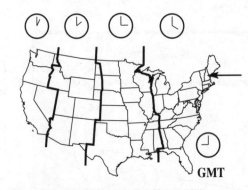

GMT

140 km from Manchester, NH; 120 km from Concord, NH
A 140 km del Manchester, NH; a 120 km del Concord, NH / A 140 km de Manchester, NH; à 120 km de Concord, NH
ニューハンプシャー州マンチェスター市より 140 キロ、
ニューハンプシャー州コンコード市より 120 キロ
離 Manchester, NH 機場 140 公里；離 Concord, NH 120 公里

 Coeducational 9–12 and PG / Mixto / Mixte
男女共学
男女合校

 60/50

 80%

 10%

 200, 40 / solicitaron admisión, fueron aceptados / candidats, admis
出願者数 200 名、合格者数 40 名
200 人申請，40 人被録取

 ✓

SSAT

Bermuda (1), Chile (1), Ethiopia (2), Germany (10), Japan (1), Korea (1), Russia (2), St. Lucia (1)

 Rolling / Continuo / Continuelles
隨時受付
全年招生

 September, January / septiembre, enero / septembre, janvier
9月、1月
9月，1月

4:1

5:1

 $33,900; $1500

American University, Boston University, Bryn Mawr College, Lewis & Clark College, Mount Holyoke College

The Winchendon School

J. William La Belle, Headmaster
172 Ash Street
Winchendon, Massachusetts 01475
Phone: 978-297-4476 Fax: 978-297-0911
E-mail: admissions@winchendon.org
URL: http://www.winchendon.org

NAIS, TABS, FAIS, AISNE member   *Founded 1926*

Winchendon offers an extensive ESL program, TOEFL preparation, and college placement. The campus' rural location is safe and scenic, yet near the cultural and recreational opportunities of Boston. The faculty is dedicated to helping students who have not yet performed up to their potential.

Winchendon ofrece un completo programa de inglés como segundo idioma (ESL), preparación para la prueba TOEFL y ayuda en la selección de universidades. El recinto está ubicado en un entorno rural panorámico y seguro, cerca de centros culturales y recreativos de la ciudad de Boston. La facultad se dedica a ayudar a aquellos estudiantes que no han logrado desempeñarse de acuerdo con su potencial.

Winchendon offre un programme d'anglais comme langue étrangère (ESL) intensif, les cours de préparation pour l'examen TOEFL et aide les étudiants dans la préparation de leurs dossiers d'inscription aux universités. Le campus rural offre une ambiance sûre et pittoresque et se situe près des centres culturels et de loisir de Boston. Les professeurs ont pour mission d'aider les étudiants qui ont connu jusqu'alors des difficultés pour développer leurs talents et tirer le meilleur d'eux-mêmes.

本校は生徒ひとりひとりに注目して教授するための少人数制クラス、3 レベルからなる ESL の会話、ライティングプログラム、充実したスポーツプログラム、素晴しい寮、スポーツ・教育施設や安全で美しいキャンパスを提供します。教師陣は、各々の能力を存分に発揮しきれていない生徒に対し、献身的にサポートします。

Winchendon 提供廣泛的英語為第二語言 (ESL) 課程、托福輔導和大學入學考試。安全幽美的校園雖位在鄉野，但靠近充滿文化和娛樂活動的波士頓市。校方致力于開發學生的潛力，幫助學生提高學業表現。

Modern and attractive dormitories and academic, arts, and athletic facilities on 350 acres.
Modernas y atractivas residencias estudiantiles e instalaciones académicas, así como para artes y atletismo, en 142 hectáreas de terreno.
Des dortoirs modernes et attrayants, et des installations scolaires, artistiques et sportives sur 142 hectares.
142 ヘクターのキャンパスには、近代的で素敵な寮、学術、芸術、スポーツの施設が完備されています。
校園佔地 142 公頃，擁有現代化引人注目的宿舍，以及學術、藝術和體育設施。

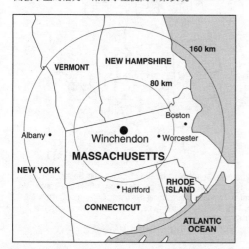

160 km

VERMONT   **NEW HAMPSHIRE**

80 km

Boston

Albany •   Winchendon   • Worcester

MASSACHUSETTS

NEW YORK

RHODE ISLAND

• Hartford

CONNECTICUT

ATLANTIC OCEAN

 10–24°C

 -12– -7°C

 10–27°C

GMT

105 km from Logan International Airport and from Boston, MA
A 105 km del aeropuerto internacional de Logan y de Boston, MA
A 105 km de l'aéroport international de Logan et de Boston, MA
ローガン国際空港、マサチューセッツ州ボストン市より 105 キロ
離 Logan 國際機場和 Boston, MA 各 105 公里

 Coeducational 8–PG / Mixto / Mixte
男女共学
男女合校

140/60

 99%

 20%

 70, 60 / solicitaron admisión, fueron aceptados / candidats, admis
出願者数 70 名、合格者数 60 名
70 人申請、60 人被錄取

 Croatia (2), France (3), Japan (10), Korea (10), Mexico (10), Poland (5), Taiwan (10), Thailand (4)

 Rolling / Continuo / Continuelles
隨時受付
全年招生

 Any month / cualquier mes / à tout moment
隨時受付
全年招生

 6:1, 100%

 10:1

 $32,250; $3400

American University, Boston University, Hamilton College, Northeastern University, University of Massachusetts

Worcester Academy

Marsha Bernstein
International Student Advisor
81 Providence Street
Worcester, Massachusetts 01604
508-754-5302 Fax: 508-752-2382
E-mail: admission@worcesteracademy.org
URL: http://www.worcesteracademy.org

TABS, FAIS, NAFSA member   *Founded 1834*

Located in a city of 170,000, the Academy is distinctive for its urban location. Within a traditional college-preparatory program, the Academy offers two levels of ESL and a daily extra help period. Sports, music, art, and drama programs are available.

Ubicada en una ciudad de 170.000 habitantes, la Academia se distingue por su ambiente urbano. Dentro de un programa tradicional de preparación para la universidad, la Academia ofrece dos niveles de inglés como segundo idioma (ESL) y un período de clase diario para asistencia adicional. Se ofrecen programas de deportes, música, arte y drama.

Située dans une ville de 170,000 habitants, l'Académie est caractérisée par son milieu urbain. Elle offre un programme de préparation traditionnel aux universités, deux niveaux d'anglais comme langue étrangère (ESL) et une période d'aide scolaire journalière. Des programmes consacrés aux sports, à la musique, à l'art et au théâtre sont également disponibles.

人口 17 万人の都市に所在する本アカデミーは都会の学校として有名です。本アカデミーの伝統ある大学進学プログラムでは、 2 レベルの ESL、毎日の補習時間を提供しています。スポーツ、音楽、芸術、演劇のプログラムもあります。

本校設在170,000人口的小城中，以其都市化的地點著稱。在傳統性的大學預科專業中，本校設有兩種程度的ESL課程，以及每日業余輔導時間。同時也有體育，音樂，美術和戲劇專業。

The 22-acre campus includes a student center, a theater, and a swimming pool.

El terreno de 9 hectáreas tiene un centro estudiantil, un teatro y una piscina.

Le campus de 9 hectares comprend un foyer d'élèves, un théâtre et une piscine.

9 ヘクタールのキャンパスには学生センター、劇場、プールなどがあります。

校園佔地 9 公頃，有學生中心、劇場和游泳池。

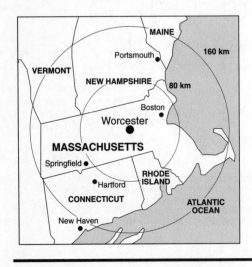

 15–26°C

 -6–10°C

 10–21°C

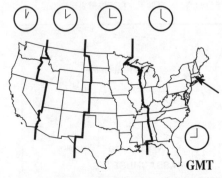

70 km from Logan International Airport; 65 km from Boston, MA
A 70 km del aeropuerto internacional de Logan; a 65 km de Boston, MA
A 70 km de l'aéroport international de Logan ; à 65 km de Boston, MA
ローガン国際空港より 70 キロ、マサチューセッツ州、ボストン市より 65 キロ
離 Logan 國際機場 70 公里；Boston, MA 65 公里

  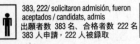 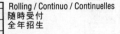 Coeducational 9–PG / Mixto / Mixte
男女共学
男女合校

247/211

 30%

 15%

Hong Kong (62), Japan (23), Korea (44), Taiwan (33), Thailand (49)

383, 222/ solicitaron admisión, fueron aceptados / candidats, admis
出願者数 383 名、合格者数 222 名
383 人申請，222 人被錄取

TOEFL, SSAT

Rolling / Continuo / Continuelles
隨時受付
全年招生

September / septiembre / septembre
9 月
9 月

 12:1, 34%

 6:1

 $33,200; $4200

 Boston College, Brandeis University, Carnegie Mellon University, Case Western Reserve University, The Ohio State University, University of Wisconsin

Wyoming Seminary

John R. Eidam, Dean of Admissions
201 North Sprague Avenue
Kingston, Pennsylvania 18704–3593
Phone: 570-270-2166 Fax: 570-270-2198
E-mail: jreidam@wyomingseminary.org

TABS, NAFSA, SSATB member   *Founded 1844*

Wyoming Seminary College Preparatory School blends a rigorous academic program with warm and caring teachers and is set in a suburb of a small, safe city.

Wyoming Seminary, un colegio preparatorio, combina un riguroso programa académico con profesores amables que se preocupan por sus alumnos, y está situado en uno de los suburbios de una pequeña y segura ciudad.

Le Wyoming Seminary, une école secondaire préparatoire (college prep), située dans une petite banlieue, offre un programme rigoureux scolaire avec des professeurs chaleureux et attentifs.

Wyoming Seminary は厳格な教育プログラムと暖かく親切な教師陣を併せもっており、小さな治安の良い都市の郊外に在る、大学進学予備校です。

Wyoming Seminary 大學預科學校提供優秀的學術課程，同時有熱情和關懷備至的教師。地處安全的小城市郊區。

The 18-acre campus enjoys access to shopping centers and ethnic restaurants.

Las 7 hectáreas de terreno tienen acceso a centros comerciales y restaurantes étnicos.

Le campus de 7 hectares se situe non loin des centres commerciaux et des restaurants avec différentes spécialités culinaires.

7 ヘクタールのキャンパスはショッピングセンターやエスニッククレストランにも近く便利です。

校園佔地 7 公頃，去購物中心和風味餐館十分方便。

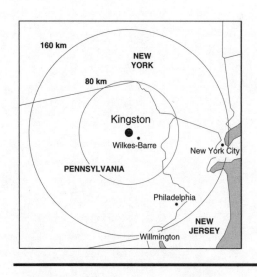

 10–26°C

 -6–4°C

 10–24°C

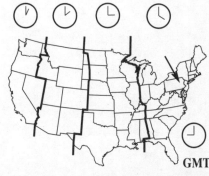

GMT

24 km from Wilkes-Barre/Scranton International Airport; 145 km from Philadelphia, PA / A 24 km del aeropuerto internacional de Wilkes-Barre/Scranton; a 145 km de Filadelfia, PA / A 24 km de l'aéroport international de Wilkes-Barre/Scranton ; à 145 km de Philadelphie, PA
ウィルケスバレ・スクラントン国際空港より 24 キロ、ペンシルバニア州フィラデルフィア市より 145 キロ
離 Wilkes-Barre / Scraton 國際機場 24 公里；離 Piladelphia, PA 145 公里

 Coeducational 9–PG / Mixto / Mixte
男女共学
男女合校

 250/215

 35%

 17%

 125, 50 / solicitaron admisión, fueron aceptados / candidats, admis
出願者数 125 名，合格者数 50 名
125 人申請，50 人被錄取

 ✓

 SLEP, SSAT

 Germany (21), Japan (33), Korea (103), Saudi Arabia (18), Thailand (11)

 Rolling / Continuo / Continuelles
随時受付
全年招生

 September / septiembre / septembre
9月
9月

 9:1, 70%

 8:1

 $31,000

 Boston University, Cornell University, Carnegie Mellon University, Lehigh University, University of Pennsylvania

 4, 5 or 9 weeks / 4, 5 o 9 semanas / 4, 5 ou 9 semaines
4 週間、5 週間及び 9 週間
四五或九星期

Canadian Schools

Colegios canadienses

Écoles canadiennes

カナダの学校

單頁學校簡介

The Bishop Strachan School

Janice Sullivan, Director of Admissions
298 Lonsdale Road
Toronto, Ontario M4V 1X2 Canada
Phone: 416-483-4325 Fax: 416-481-5632
E-mail: admissions@bss.on.ca
URL: http://www.bss.on.ca

TABS, NAIS member   *Founded 1867*

The Bishop Strachan School offers a wide selection of advanced placement courses for students who plan to enter North American or international universities. The school uses both traditional and progressive methods, including a technology-based curriculum, to enable each student to reach her potential and become a leader tomorrow.

El colegio Bishop Strachan ofrece una amplia elección de cursos de colocación en programas avanzados para estudiantes que piensan matricularse en universidades norteamericanas e internacionales. El colegio emplea métodos tradicionales y progresistas, incluyendo un plan de estudios basado en tecnología, para que cada estudiante logre desarrollar todo su potencial y convertirse en futuro líder.

The Bishop Strachan School offre une grande sélection de cours d'enseignement supérieur pour les étudiants ayant l'intention d'entrer dans des universités américaines ou internationales. L'établissement utilise à la fois des méthodes d'enseignement nouvelles et traditionnelles, notamment un programme scolaire se fondant sur la technologie, pour permettre à tous les étudiants de s'épanouir et de devenir les leaders de demain.

北米もしくは海外の大学に進学を希望する学生には、Bishop Strachan School が広範囲な Advanced Placement コースを提供します。当校は伝統的な学習法とともにテクノロジーをベースとしたカリキュラムなど、進歩的な学習方法を採用しています。そして各学生が自らの可能性を最高に発揮し、明日のリーダーとなれるよう指導します。

斯特拉臣主教學校多種高級預備課程供希望進入北美或國際各大學的學生選擇。該校同時採用傳統教學方式和先進教學方法，包括以現代科技為工具的課程，力求使學生充分發揮潛力，成為未來社會的棟梁。

A safe, stimulating 7.5 –acre facility in a culturally diverse city.

Un ambiente seguro y estimulante en 3 hectáreas de terreno, en una ciudad de gran diversidad cultural.

Un campus de 3 hectares, sûr et stimulant, au coeur d'une ville riche en diversité culturelle.

多様な文化を持つ市内に位置し、安全でしかも刺激的な3ヘクタールの施設が備わっています。

該校位多種文化併存的城市，佔地3公頃，既安全又充滿活力。

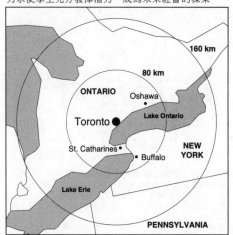

 15–21°C

 -3–1°C

 18–27°C

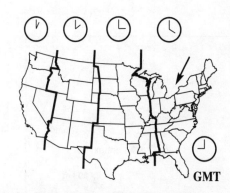

32 km from Toronto International Airport in Toronto, ON
A 32 km del aeropuerto internacional de Toronto y de Toronto, ON
A 32 km de l'aéroport international de Toronto et de Toronto, ON
オンタリオ州トロント国際空港、及び同州トロント市より32キロ
Toronto, ON 國際機場和 Toronto, ON 各32公里

 Girls JK–12 / Niñas / Filles
女子中学校
女子中學校

 0/620

 15%

 10%

 282, 111 / solicitaron admisión, fueron aceptados / candidats, admis
出願者数282名、合格者数111名
282人申請，111人被錄取

 TOEFL (560), SSAT (300)

 Africa, Bermuda (55), Canada (134), The Caribbean (30), Germany (5), Hong Kong (25), Japan (15), Mexico (30), U.S. (134)

 Rolling / Continuo / Continuelles
随時受付
全年招生

 September / septiembre / septembre
9月
9月

 10:1

 1:1

 $37,310 (boarding)
$18,900 (day)

 Cornell University, University of Edinburgh, McGill University, Queen's University, University of Toronto, University of Western Ontario

Bishop's College School

Theo Brinckman, Director of Advancement
P.O. Box 5001
Lennoxville, Quebec J1M 1Z8
Canada
Phone: 819-566-0227 Fax: 819-822-8917
URL: http://www.bishopscollegeschool.com

CAIS, TABS member   *Founded 1836*

BCS is dedicated to providing students with an exceptional academic experience in an environment fostering personal growth and development. Multiculturalism and international understanding are hallmarks of the campus community at BCS.

BCS se dedica a proveer a los estudiantes con una experiencia académica extensiva y un ambiente que fomenta el desarrollo y crecimiento personal. El multiculturalismo y la comprensión internacional son distintivos de la comunidad del recinto de BCS.

BCS a pour mission d'apporter à ses étudiants un enseignement exceptionnel dans un environnement mettant en avant la croissance et le développement personnels. Le multiculturalisme et l'ouverture internationale jouent un rôle clé dans la vie communautaire sur le campus de BCS.

BCS は自然な環境の中で、個々の成長と発育を促進させる、優れた学園体験を提供します。多彩な文化と国際的な相互理解は BCS における学生生活の特徴です。

BCS 致力于為學生們提供獨特的學術環境，以注重個人成長，開發多文化意識，促進國際了解而著名。

The 350-acre campus includes a fitness center, climbing wall, indoor skating rink, ski trails, tennis/squash courts, and numerous sports fields, as well as a brand-new student center with a state-of-the-art music facility, a new Black Box theatre with a digital filmmaking studio, a 22,000 volume library, and a spacious student lounge.

El recinto de 140 hectáreas incluye un centro de ejercicios, pared para escalar, una pista para patinar bajo techo, caminos de esquí, canchas de tenis y numerosos campos de deportes, así como un nuevo centro de estudiantes con las facilidades más modernas de música, y un nuevo teatro Black Box con un estudio de filmación digital, y una biblioteca que alberga 22,000 volúmenes y una espaciosa sala estudiantil.

Le campus de 140 hectares comprend un club de fitness, un mur d'escalade, une patinoire couverte, des pistes de ski de fond, des terrains de tennis et de squash et de nombreux terrains de sport. Le campus abrite également un centre pour étudiants tout nouveau comprenant des installations audio ultra-modernes pour la musique, une nouvelle salle de projection Black Box avec un studio de production numérique, une bibliothèque contenant 22 000 ouvrages et un salon pour les étudiants très spacieux.

142 ヘクタールのキャンパスには、フィットネスセンター、クライミングウォール、室内スケートリンク、スキートラック、テニス／スクワッシュのコート、沢山のスポーツ・フィールドがあり、また、舞台芸術や音楽の施設が整った真新しい学生センター、デジタル・フィルム製作スタジオのある新設の Black Box 劇場、22000 書籍を具備した図書館、ゆったりとした学生ラウンジがあります。

佔地 140 公頃的校園設有一座健身中心、攀登牆、室內溜冰場、滑雪雪道、網球／壁球場和眾多的運動場地。嶄新的學生中心設有一流的音樂設備，全新的黑箱劇場，數碼編劇製作室，以及一座帶 22,000 冊藏書的圖書館和寬敞的學生大廳。

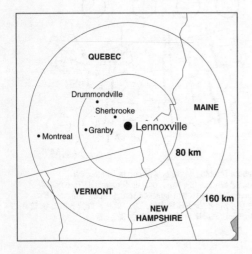

  -5–20°C

  -10–5°C

  10–25°C

GMT

150 km from Dorval Airport; 8 km from Sherbrooke, PQ
A 150 km del aeropuerto de Dorval; a 8 km de Sherbrooke, PQ
A 150 km de l'aéroport de Dorval ; à 8 km de Sherbrooke, PQ
ドーバル空港より 150 キロ、ケベック州シャーブルック市より 8 キロ
離 Dorval 機場 150 公里；離魁北克省 Sherbrooke 市 8 公里

 Coeducational 7–12 / Mixto / Mixte
男女共学
男女合校

 140/110

 80%

 42%

 TOEFL (460)

 Bermuda, Congo, France, Germany, Japan, Korea, Mexico, Taiwan, United Kingdom, United States

 Rolling / Continuo / Continuelles
随時受付
全年招生

 Rolling / Continuo / Continuelles
随時受付
全年招生

 8:1, 40%

 1:1

 $23,000 (USD) (Canadian students)
$26,200 (USD) (International students)

 Brown University, Dalhousie University, Princeton University, Queen's University, University of Toronto, University of Waterloo, University of Ottawa,

Stanstead College

Andrew N. Elliot, Director of Admissions
450 Dufferin, Stanstead, QC
Canada J0B 3E0
Phone: 819-876-2223 Fax: 819-876-5891
E-mail: admissions@stansteadcollege.com

TABS, CAIS member   *Founded 1872*

Stanstead provides a secure environment for its multicultural, international student body. The school's personalized approach to education features small class sizes and individual counselling provided by a well-qualified and caring faculty.

Stanstead ofrece un ambiente seguro para su estudiantado multicultural e internacional. El aborde personalizado hacia la educación del colegio se manifiesta por sus clases con pocos alumnos y asesoramiento individual provisto por profesores con excelente preparació y dedicación.

Stanstead offre une ambiance sûre à ses étudiants multiculturels internationaux. L'approche individualisé de l'école est illustrée par ses classes de petite taille, et les conseils individuels d'orientation donnés par des enseignants attentifs et hautement qualifiés.

Stanstead は文化交流が多い留学生達に安全な環境を提供します。本校の資格を持った思いやりのある講師陣による少人数制クラス授業、個人カウンセリングは個人別に合わせた教育を与えます。

本效為來自不同文化背景的國際學生提供全環境。學效個人化教育方針體現在小班制教學以及由合格而親切的教師所提供個人咨詢。

The school is set on a scenic landscaped campus within 720 acres of rural property.

El colegio se encuentra sobre un recinto ajardinado con 291 hectáreas de terreno rural.

L'école se trouve sur un campus jardiné dans un grand espace vert d'une zone rurale de 291 hectares.

本校の291ヘクタールのキャンパスは美しい風景の地方に位置します。

在近291公頃鄉間田野襯托下，效園景致十分優美。

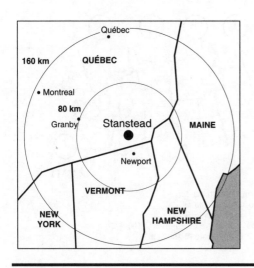

 4–21°C

 -12–5°C

 10–27°C

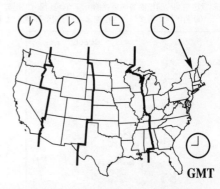

GMT

175 km from Dorval International Airport, Montreal
A 175 kilómetros del aeropuerto internacional de Dorval, Montreal
À 175 kilomètres de l'aéroport international de Dorval, Montréal
モントリオール市ドーバル国際空港より175キロ
離蒙特利爾多維奧機場175公里

 Coeducational 7–12 / Mixto / Mixte
男女共学
男女合校

130/95

 75%

 38%

   120, 75 / solicitaron admisión, fueron aceptados / candidats, admis
出願者数 120名、合格者数 75名
120人申請，75人被録取

TOEFL, SSAT

Germany (10), Japan (5), Korea (16), Mexico (29), Taiwan (16)

 July 31 / 31 de julio / 31 juillet
7月31日
7月31日

September / septiembre / septembre
9月
9月

8:1, 80%

1:1

 $33,990; $2000 (Canadian)

 Queen's University, Waterloo University, Guelph University, Dalhousie University, University of Western Ontario

Trinity College School

CANADA

Mrs. Kathryn A. LaBranche, Director of Admissions
Trinity College School
55 Deblaquire Street
Ontario L1A 4K7 Canada
Phone: 905-885-3209 Fax: 905-885-7444
E-mail: admissions@tcs.on.ca
URL: http://www.tcs.on.ca

Founded 1865

Trinity College School is one of Canada's finest coeducational independent schools. A day/boarding institution for grades 5 to 12, the School provides an extensive and challenging University preparation programme committed to students in their pursuit of academic excellence. Trinity School has a student body of more than 500 made up of young men and women representing Canada and 30 other countries.

La escuela Trinity College es una de las mejores escuelas independientes de enseñanza mixta. Una institución diurna y con pensión para los grados de 5 a 12, la escuela provee un programa de preparación universitaria extensiva e interesante dirigido a estudiantes que buscan la excelencia académica. La escuela Trinity tiene un estudiantado de más de 500 hombres y mujeres jóvenes que representan a Canadá y 30 otros países.

Trinity College School est l'un des meilleurs établissements privés mixtes du Canada. Pour les classes de niveau 5 à 12 « 5 to 12 Grades », en formule d'internat ou d'externat, l'École offre un programme complet et rigoureux de préparation universitaire pour des étudiants désireux de poursuivre leurs études sous le signe de l'excellence. Trinity School regroupe plus de 500 étudiants, jeunes garçons et jeunes filles du Canada et de 30 autres nationalités.

Trinity College School は、カナダ国内でも独立した男女共学校です。5 年生から 12 年生までの学年設定で、各生徒の学問的長所を追求する、広範囲で挑戦的な大学入学準備プログラムを提供します。当校には、カナダと 30 の他国から、500 人以上の若者が集まっています。

Trinity College 是加拿大最優秀的獨立的男女合校的學府之一，為 5 至 12 年級的學生提供白天制或住宿制的廣泛而有挑戰性的大學預科課程，以提高學生的學術表現。Trinity College 的 500 名年輕的男女學生來自加拿大和三十個其他的國家和地區。

The campus has an ice hockey arena, a pool, and tennis and squash courts in a rural setting.

El colegio tiene una pista de hockey sobre hielo, una piscina, y canchas de tenis y squash en un ambiente rural.

Le campus rural comprend une patinoire de hockey, une piscine et des courts de tennis et squash.

キャンパスは田舎にあり、アイスホッケー場、プール、テニス及びスカッシュのコートなどの設備があります。

位於鄉村的校園擁有曲棍球場、遊泳池、網球和回力球場。

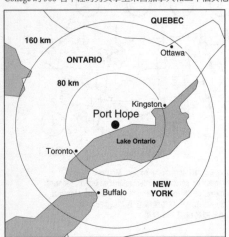

QUEBEC
160 km
ONTARIO
Ottawa
80 km
Kingston
Port Hope
Lake Ontario
Toronto
Buffalo
NEW YORK

 10–27°C

 -8–10°C

 0–27°C

GMT

100 km from Toronto, ON
A 100 km de Toronto, ON
A 100 km de Toronto, ON
オンタリオ州、トロント市より 100 キロ
離安大略省 Toronto 市 100 公里

 Coeducational 5–PG / Mixto / Mixte
男女共学
男女合校

 283/249

 65%

 30%

 470, 300 / solicitaron admisión, fueron aceptados / candidats admis
出願者数 470 名、合格者数 300 名
470 人申請，300 人被錄取

 TOEFL (grades 11–PG), SSAT (grades 9, 10)

Bahamas, Barbados, Bermuda, China, Mexico, Trinidad, United States

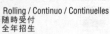 Rolling / Continuo / Continuelles
随時受付
全年招生

 September / septiembre / septembre
9 月
9 月

 8:1, 40%

 1:1

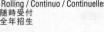 $31,750 (Canadian)

 Queen's University at Kingston, McGill University, Princeton University, Universities of Toronto and Western Ontario

APPENDIX OF UNIVERSITY-PREPARATORY SCHOOLS
APÉNDICE DE COLEGIOS CON PROGRAMAS DE PREPARACION PARA LA UNIVERSIDAD • APPENDICE AUX ÉCOLES PRÉPARATOIRES AUX UNIVERSITÉS • その他の全寮制私立学校一覧 • 大學預校附録

Schools in this list are accredited and offer full-week or five-day boarding programs.

Los colegios en esta lista están acreitados y ofrecen programas de internado durante toda la semana o de cinco días.

Les écoles sur cette liste offrent des diplômes reconnus par l'État et des programmes en internat d'une semaine ou de cinq jours.

ここに紹介する学校はすべて認定校であり、週7日または5日の寮制度を有しています。

本表中的學校獲得有關方面認可，並開設為期四週或五週的住宿就讀課程。

Academie Sainte Cecile International School
Miss Jacqueline P. Pigeon, Admissions Clerk
925 Cousineau Road
Windsor, ON N9G 1V8 Canada
Phone: 519-969-1291 Fax: 519-969-7953
E-mail: info@stececile.ca

The Academy at Cedar Mountain
Ms. Jodi Tuttle, Head of School
1441 South Campus Drive
Cedar City, UT 84720
Phone: 435-867-5555 Fax: 435-867-0005
E-mail: jtuttle@cedar-mountain.com

The Academy at Charlemont
Brett A. Carey, Director of Admissions
The Mohawk Trail, 1359 Route 2
Charlemont, MA 01339
Phone: 413-339-4912 Fax: 413-339-4324
E-mail: bcarey@charlemont.org

Academy at Swift River
Mrs. Ann M. Favre, EdD, Director of Admissions
151 South Street
Cummington, MA 01026
Phone: 800-258-1770 Ext. 102 Fax: 413-634-5090
E-mail: afavre@swiftriver.com

The Academy for Global Exploration
Greg Guevara, Director
P.O. Box 1602
Eugene, OR 97440
Phone: 541-913-0660 Fax:
E-mail: admissions@agexplore.org

Academy of the Holy Family
Sr. Mary Patrick, SCMC, Principal
54 West Main Street, P.O. Box 691
Baltic, CT 06330-0691
Phone: 860-822-9272 Ext. 23 Fax: 860-822-1318
E-mail: academy.holy.family@snet.net

Academy of the New Church Boys' School
R. Scott Daum, Principal
2805 Benade Circle
Bryn Athyn, PA 19009
Phone: 215-947-4200 Fax:

Academy of the New Church Girls' School
Margaret Y. Gladish, Principal
2815 Benade Circle
Bryn Athyn, PA 19009
Phone: 215-947-4200 Fax: 215-938-2617

The Academy of the Performing Arts
Elizabeth Durbin, Director of Admission
1165 West Broadway
Winona, MN 55987
Phone: 507-453-5400 Fax: 507-453-5406
E-mail: academy@mps.org

Academy of the Sacred Heart
Mrs. Carrie Foard, Director of Admission
1821 Academy Road
Grand Coteau, LA 70541
Phone: 337-662-5275 Ext. 3036 Fax: 337-662-3011
E-mail: admission@ashcoteau.org

Accelerated Schools
Jane T. Queen, Associate Director
2160 South Cook Street
Denver, CO 80210
Phone: 303-758-2003 Fax: 303-757-4336
E-mail: queenjbqueen@aol.com

Aiglon College
Mary Sidebottom, Head of Admissions
rue Centrale
1885 Chesieres-Villars, Switzerland
Phone: 41-24-4966126 Fax: 41-24-4966162
E-mail: info@aiglon.ch

The Albany Academy
Mrs. Barbara McBride,
Associate Director of Admission/Director of Financial Aid
135 Academy Road
Albany, NY 12208-3196
Phone: 518-465-1461 Ext. 116 Fax: 518-427-7016
E-mail: mcbrideb@albany-academy.org

Albert College
Heather Kidd, Director of Admission
160 Dundas Street West
Belleville, ON K8P 1A6 Canada
Phone: 800-952-5237 Fax: 613-968-9651
E-mail: hkidd@albertc.on.ca

Allen Academy
Camilla Viator, Director of Admissions
3201 Boonville Road
Bryan, TX 77802
Phone: 979-776-0731 Fax: 979-774-7769
E-mail: cviator@allenacademy.org

Alliance Academy
Mrs. Mary DeGolyer, Admissions Secretary
Casilla 17-11-06186
Quito, Ecuador
Phone: 593-2-226-6985 Fax: 593-2226-4350
E-mail: aa-admin@alliance.k12.ec

All Saints' Episcopal School
Mrs. Carole W. Martin, Admissions Coordinator
2717 Confederate Avenue
Vicksburg, MS 39180-5173
Phone: 601-636-5266 Ext. 127 Fax: 601-636-8987
E-mail: admissions@allsaintsweb.com

The American Boychoir School
Susan P. Houle, Director of Admissions
19 Lambert Drive
Princeton, NJ 08540
Phone: 609-924-5858 Ext. 34 Fax: 609-924-5812
E-mail: shoule@americanboychoir.org

The American Community School—Surrey Campus
Heather Mulkey, Dean of Admissions
Heywood, Portsmouth Road
Cobham, Surrey KT11 1BL United Kingdom
Phone: 44-1932 867 251 Fax: 44-1932-869-789
E-mail: hmulkey@acs-england.co.uk

American International School of Johannesburg
Dr. Leo Ruberto, Director
Private Bag X4
Bryanston 2021, South Africa
Phone: 27-11-464-1505 Fax: 27-11-464-1327
E-mail: info@aisj.jhb.school.za

American International School Salzburg
Ms. Felicia Gundringer, Office Manager
Moosstrasse 106
A-5020 Salzburg, Austria
Phone: 43-662-824617 Ext. 12 Fax: 43-662-824555
E-mail: office@ais-salzburg.at

American Overseas School of Rome
Mr. Don Levine, Admissions
Via Cassia 811
Rome 00189 Italy
Phone: 39-06-334381 Fax: 39-06-3326-0397
E-mail: admissions@aosr.org

American School of Institut Montana
Kevin O'Brien, Dean
Zugerberg
Zug CH6300 Switzerland
Phone: 41-417111722 Fax: 41-41-711-5465
E-mail: kob@montana.ch

Annie Wright School
Ms. Melinda Kinney, Director of Admission
827 North Tacoma Avenue
Tacoma, WA 98403
Phone: 253-272-2216 Fax: 253-572-3616
E-mail: admission@aw.org

Appleby College
Suzy Rebelo, Admissions Coordinator
540 Lakeshore Road, West
Oakville, ON L6K 3P1 Canada
Phone: 905-845-4681 Ext. 252 Fax: 905-845-9505
E-mail: srebelo@appleby.on.ca

Argo Academy
James Stoll, Director
P.O. Box 5477
Sarasota, FL 34277
Phone: 941-924-6789 Fax: 941-924-6075
E-mail: info@seamester.com

Arizona's Children Association Zemsky-Covert School
Mrs. Shelly A. Kilmer, Director of Education
P.O. Box 7277
Tucson, AZ 85725-7277
Phone: 520-622-7611 Ext. 1307 Fax: 520-624-7042
E-mail: skilmer@arizonachildren.org

Army and Navy Academy
Ms. Elizabeth Kalivas,
Acting Director of Admissions
2605 Carlsbad Boulevard, P.O. Box 3000
Carlsbad, CA 92018-3000
Phone: 760-729-2385 Ext. 261 Fax: 760-434-5948
E-mail: ekalivas@armyandnavyacademy.org

Ashbury College
Lisa E. Lewicki, Director of Admissions
362 Mariposa Avenue
Ottawa, ON K1M 0T3 Canada
Phone: 613-749-5954 Ext. 211 Fax: 613-749-9724
E-mail: admissions@ashbury.on.ca

Aspen Ranch
Aspen Ranch Admissions
2000 West Dry Valley, P.O. Box 369
Loa, UT 84747
Phone: 877-231-0734 Fax: 435-836-2277

Auburn Adventist Academy
Amber Serns, Director of Public Relations
5000 Auburn Way South
Auburn, WA 98092-7297
Phone: 253-939-5000 Ext. 279 Fax: 253-351-9806
E-mail: amberserns@hotmail.com

Auldern Academy
Ms. Diana Boyer, Director of Admissions
990 Glovers Grove Church Road
Siler City, NC 27344
Phone: 919-837-2336 Ext. 200 Fax: 919-837-5284
E-mail: dboyer@threesprings.com

Averill High School
Mr. Luke Irza, Admissions Coordinator
P.O. Box 159
Hinckley, ME 04944
Phone: 207-238-4033 Fax: 207-238-4007
E-mail: admissions@mint.net

Balmoral Hall School
Pamela K. McGhie, Director of Admissions
630 Westminster Avenue
Winnipeg, MB R3C 3S1 Canada
Phone: 204-784-1621 Fax: 204-774-5534
E-mail: admission@balmoralhall.com

Banff Mountain Academy
Ms. Doris Yi, Business Manager
1 Mount Norquay, P.O. Box 369
Banff, AB T1L 1A5 Canada
Phone: 403-762-4101 Ext. 221 Fax: 403-762-8585
E-mail: doris@banffacademy.org

Bass Memorial Academy
Vicki Moore, Registrar
6433 US Highway 11
Lumberton, MS 39455
Phone: 601-794-8561 Ext. 222 Fax: 601-794-8881
E-mail: vmoore@bassacademy.org

Belair School
Pauline Raynor, Receptionist/Registrar
43 DeCarteret Road
Mandeville, Jamaica
Phone: 876-962-2168 Fax: 876-962-3396

Belmont Hill School
Mr. Robert L. Greene, Jr., Director of Admission
350 Prospect Street
Belmont, MA 02478-2662
Phone: 617-484-4410 Fax: 617-484-4829
E-mail: rgreene@belmont-hill.org

The Bement School
Matt Evans, Director of Admission
Main Street
Deerfield, MA 01342
Phone: 413-774-7061 Fax: 413-774-7863
E-mail: admit@bement.org

Ben Lippen Schools
Mrs. Tina G. Catchings, Admissions Secretary
7401 Monticello Road
Columbia, SC 29203
Phone: 803-786-7200 Ext. 4110 Fax: 803-744-1387
E-mail: blsadmissions@benlippen.com

Berkshire School
Dr. Phillip J. Jarvis, Assistant Head of School for Enrollment
245 North Undermountain Road
Sheffield, MA 01257
Phone: 413-229-1003 Fax: 413-229-1016
E-mail: enrollment@berkshireschool.org

The Bethany Hills School
Mrs. Anne E. Scott, Executive Assistant, Admissions
P.O. Box 10, 727 Bethany Hills Road
Bethany, ON L0A 1A0 Canada
Phone: 705-277-2866 Fax: 705-277-1279
E-mail: ascott@bethanyhills.on.ca

Black Forest Academy
Mrs. Judy Thompson, Executive Secretary
Postfach 1109
79396 Kandern, Germany
Phone: 49-7626-91610 Fax: 49-7626-8821
E-mail: jthompson@bfacademy.com

Blair Academy
Barbara Haase, Dean of Admissions
2 Park Street
Blairstown, NJ 07825
Phone: 800-462-5247 Fax: 908-362-7975
E-mail: admissions@blair.edu

The Bolles School
Mr. Mark I. Frampton, Associate Director of Admission/San Jose Campus
7400 San Jose Boulevard
Jacksonville, FL 32217-3499
Phone: 904-256-5032 Fax: 904-739-9929
E-mail: framptonm@bolles.org

Boulder Creek Academy
Fred Lange, Director of Admissions
Route 1, Box 3400
Bonners Ferry, ID 83805
Phone: 877-457-6170 Fax: 208-267-5715
E-mail: bca@cedu.com

Brandon Hall School
Mr. Stephen F. Boyce, Director of Admissions
1701 Brandon Hall Drive
Atlanta, GA 30350-3706
Phone: 770-394-8177 Ext. 215 Fax: 770-804-8821
E-mail: pstockhammer@brandonhall.org

Branksome Hall
Karrie Weinstock, Vice Principal, Admissions
10 Elm Avenue
Toronto, ON M4W 1N4 Canada
Phone: 416-920-9741 Fax: 416-920-5390

Brehm Preparatory School
Erica Hunter, Executive Assistant
1245 East Grand Avenue
Carbondale, IL 62901
Phone: 618-457-0371 Ext. 309 Fax: 618-529-1248
E-mail: admissionsinfo@brehm.org

Brent School-Baguio
Mrs. Lourdes C. Balanza, Registrar
P.O. Box 35
Baguio City 2600 Philippines
Phone: 63-74-442-2260 Ext. 105
Fax: 63-74-442-3638
E-mail: brentreg@bgo.csi.com.ph

Brentwood College School
Mr. Andy D. Rodford, Director of Admissions
2735 Mount Baker Road
Mill Bay, BC V0R 2P1 Canada
Phone: 250-743-5521 Fax: 250-743-2911
E-mail: andy.rodford@brentwood.bc.ca

Brewster Academy
Peg Radley, Admission Coordinator
80 Academy Drive
Wolfeboro, NH 03894
Phone: 603-569-7200 Fax: 603-569-7272
E-mail: peg_radley@brewsteracademy.org

Bridgton Academy
Ms. Lisa M. Antell, Director of Admission and Financial Aid
P.O. Box 292
North Bridgton, ME 04057
Phone: 207-647-3322 Ext. 208 Fax: 207-647-8513
E-mail: admit@bridgtonacademy.org

British International School
Mrs. Louise Hoggins, Registrar
P.O. Box 4120 CPA P.O.E, Ciputat 15224
Jakarta 15224 Indonesia
Phone: 62-21-745 1670 Fax: 62-21-7451671
E-mail: enquiries@bis.or.id

Broadview Academy
David E. Loveland, Registrar
P.O. Box 307
La Fox, IL 60147
Phone: 630-232-7441 Ext. 1239 Fax: 630-232-7443
E-mail: davidloveland@broadview.org

Brockwood Park School
Ms. Claire Little, Admissions
Brockwood Park
Bramdean, Hampshire SO24 0LQ United Kingdom
Phone: 44-1962 771744 Fax: 44-1962-771875
E-mail: enquiry@brockwood.org.uk

Bronte College of Canada
Barbara de Serres, Administration
88 Bronte College Court
Mississauga, ON L5B 1M9 Canada
Phone: 905-270-7788 Ext. 2025 Fax: 905-270-7828
E-mail: bdeserres@brontecollege.ca

The Brook Hill School
Mrs. Terry Ellis, Assistant to Admissions and Marketing
P.O. Box 668
Bullard, TX 75757
Phone: 903-894-5000 Ext. 42 Fax: 903-894-6332
E-mail: admissions@brookhill.org

Brush Ranch School
Suzanne Weisman, Director of Admissions
HC 73, Box 33, North Highway 63
Terrero, NM 87573
Phone: 505-757-6114 Fax: 505-757-6118
E-mail: sweisman@cybermesa.com

Burke Mountain Academy
Marcia Berry, Administrative Coordinator
P.O. Box 78
East Burke, VT 05832
Phone: 802-626-5607 Fax: 802-626-3784
E-mail: info@burkemtnacademy.org

Burr and Burton Academy
Philip G. Anton, Director of Guidance and Admission
57 Seminary Avenue
Manchester, VT 05254
Phone: 802-362-1775 Ext. 125 Fax: 802-362-0574
E-mail: panton@burrburton.org

Camden Military Academy
Mr. Casey Robinson, Director of Admissions
520 Highway 1, North
Camden, SC 29020
Phone: 803-432-6001 Fax: 803-425-1020
E-mail: admissions@camdenmilitary.com

Canadian Academy
Dr. Charles A. Kite, Assistant Headmaster
4-1 Koyo-cho Naka, Higashinada-ku
Kobe 658-0032 Japan
Phone: 81-78-857-0100 Fax: 81-78-857-4095
E-mail: ckite@mail.canacad.ac.jp

Canterbury School
Keith R. Holton, Director of Admission
Caller Box 5000
New Milford, CT 06776
Phone: 860-210-3832 Fax: 860-350-1120
E-mail: admissions@cbury.org

Canyonville Christian Academy
Mrs. Pam Shepherd, Superintendent
P.O. Box 1100
Canyonville, OR 97417-1100
Phone: 541-839-4401 Fax: 541-839-6228
E-mail: cca@canyonville.net

Cardigan Mountain School
Shirley Lester, Admissions Administrative Assistant
62 Alumni Drive
Canaan, NH 03741-9307
Phone: 603-523-3548 Ext. 3548 Fax: 603-523-3565
E-mail: rryerson@cardigan.org

Carrabassett Valley Academy
Mrs. Dawn Smith, Director of Admissions
3197 Carrabassett Drive
Carrabassett Valley, ME 04947
Phone: 207-237-2250 Fax: 207-237-2213
E-mail: dsmith@cva.pvt.k12.me.us

Carson Long Military Institute
Lt. Col. David M. Comolli, Academic Dean
200 North Carlisle Street, P.O. BOX 98
New Bloomfield, PA 17068-0098
Phone: 717-582-2121 Fax: 717-582-8763
E-mail: clmiacademy@mmax.net

Cascadilla School
Patricia T. Kendall, Headmistress
116 Summit Street
Ithaca, NY 14850
Phone: 607-272-3110 Fax: 607-272-0747
E-mail: admissions@cascadillaschool.org

Cate School
Peter J. Mack, Director of Admission
1960 Cate Mesa Road
Carpinteria, CA 93013
Phone: 805-684-4127 Ext. 216 Fax: 805-684-2279
E-mail: peter_mack@cate.org

CCI The Renaissance School
Jocelyn Manchee, Admissions Officer
Via Cavour 13
Lanciano 66034 Italy
Phone: 905-508-7108 Fax: 905-508-5480
E-mail: cciren@rogers.com

The Cedars Academy
Robin Abel, Assistant Headmaster
P.O. Box 103
Bridgeville, DE 19933
Phone: 302-337-3200 Fax: 302-337-8496

CEDU Schools
Paula Riggs, Admissions Director
P.O. Box 1176
Running Springs, CA 92382
Phone: 800-884-2338 Fax: 909-867-7084
E-mail: admissions@cedu.com

CFS, The School at Church Farm
Rich Lunardi, Admissions Director
P.O. Box 2000
Paoli, PA 19301
Phone: 610-363-5346 Fax: 610-280-6746
E-mail: rlunardi@gocfs.net

Chaminade College Preparatory School
Roger L. Hill, Director of Admissions
425 South Lindbergh Boulevard
St. Louis, MO 63131-2799
Phone: 314-993-4400 Ext. 150 Fax: 314-993-4403
E-mail: rhill@chaminade-stl.com

Chapel Hill—Chauncy Hall School
Mrs. Julia T. Jones, Director of Admissions
785 Beaver Street
Waltham, MA 02452
Phone: 781-894-2644 Ext. 105 Fax: 781-894-5205
E-mail: juliajones@chch.org

Chatham Hall
Karen Stewart, Director of College Counseling
800 Chatham Hall Circle
Chatham, VA 24531
Phone: 434-432-2941 Fax: 434-432-2405
E-mail: kstewart@chathamhall.org

Cheshire Academy
Michael McCleery, Dean of Admission
10 Main Street
Cheshire, CT 06410
Phone: 203-272-5396 Ext. 250 Fax: 203-250-7209
E-mail: michael.mccleery@cheshireacademy.org

Choate Rosemary Hall
William W. Dennett, Director of Admission
333 Christian Street
Wallingford, CT 06492-3800
Phone: 203-697-2239 Fax: 203-697-2629
E-mail: admissions@choate.edu

Christchurch School
Mrs. Nancy M. Nolan, Director of Admission
49 Seahorse Lane
Christchurch, VA 23031
Phone: 800-296-2306 Fax: 804-758-0721
E-mail: admission@christchurchschool.org

Christ School
Mr. Colin Dunnigan, Director of Admission
500 Christ School Road
Arden, NC 28704
Phone: 828-684-6232 Ext. 118 Fax: 828-684-2745
E-mail: cdunnigan@christschool.org

The City International School
Mr. F. X. Nieberding, Vice President
Jacob Jordaensstraat 85-87
2018 Antwerp, Belgium
Phone: 32-3-218-54-31 Fax: 32-3-218-58-68
E-mail: info@euruni.be

CIV International School of Sophia Antipolis
Mme. Celine Livingstone, Admissions Secretary
BP 097, 190 Rue Frederic Mistral
06902 Sophia Antipolis Cedex, France
Phone: 33-4-92-96-52-24 Fax: 33-4-93-65-22-15
E-mail: admissions@civissa.org

College du Leman International School
Francis A. Clivaz, Director General
74 route de Sauverny
Versoix CH-1290 Switzerland
Phone: 41-22-775-5555 Fax: 41-22-775-5559
E-mail: info@cdl.ch

The Colorado Rocky Mountain School
Molly Hall, Associate Director of Admissions
1493 County Road 106
Carbondale, CO 81623
Phone: 970-963-2562 Fax: 970-963-9865
E-mail: mhall@crms.org

Colorado Timberline Academy
Alexander Schuhl, Admissions Director
35554 US Highway 550
Durango, CO 81301
Phone: 970-247-5898 Fax: 970-259-8067
E-mail: adm@ctaedu.org

Columbia International College of Canada
Mr. Evan Harris, Admissions Officer
Ainsliewood Building, 1003 Main Street West
Hamilton, ON L8S 4P3 Canada
Phone: 905-572-7883 Ext. 2835 Fax: 905-572-9332
E-mail: admissions02@cic-totalcare.com

Columbia International School
Mr. Yoshitaka Matsumura, Coordinator
153 Matsugo
Tokorozawa, Saitama 359-0027 Japan
Phone: 81-42-946-1911 Fax: 81-42-946-1955
E-mail: office@columbia-ca.co.jp

Community School
Valerie Behrens, Administrative Assistant
79 Washington Street
Camden, ME 04843
Phone: 207-236-3000 Fax: 207-236-2505
E-mail: cschool@cschool.acadia.net

Concord Academy
Pamela J. Safford, Associate Head for Enrollment and Planning
166 Main Street
Concord, MA 01742
Phone: 978-402-2250 Fax: 978-287-4302
E-mail: admissions@concordacademy.org

Concordia High School
Mr. Keith Kruse, Assistant Principal
7128 Ada Boulevard
Edmonton, AB T5B 4E4 Canada
Phone: 780-479-9390 Fax: 780-479-5050
E-mail: highschool@concordia.ab.ca

Conserve School
Admissions Office
5400 North Black Oak Lake Road
Land O' Lakes, WI 54540
Phone: 715-547-1321 Fax: 715-547-1390
E-mail: admissions@conserveschool.org

Cotter High School
Ms. Karen R. Sullivan, Director of Admission
1115 West Broadway
Winona, MN 55987-1399
Phone: 507-453-5403 Fax: 507-453-5013
E-mail: ksulliva@winonacotter.org

Crested Butte Academy
Karin Holmen, Director of Admission
P.O. Box 1180, 505 Whiterock Avenue
Crested Butte, CO 81224
Phone: 888-633-0222 Fax: 970-349-0997
E-mail: admissions@crestedbutteacademy.com

Cross Creek Programs
Jeni Salmi, Director of Admissions
150 North State Street
LaVerkin, UT 84745
Phone: 800-818-6228 Fax: 435-635-2331

Crossroads School
Herb Hillman, Director
4650 Southwest 61st Avenue
Fort Lauderdale, FLORIDA 33314
Phone: 954-584-1100 Fax: 954-998-3105

Crotched Mountain Rehabilitation Center School
Debra Flanders, Director of Admissions
1 Verney Drive
Greenfield, NH 03047
Phone: 603-547-3311 Ext. 235 Fax: 603-547-3232
E-mail: flanders@cmf.org

Darlington School
Mr. Casey Zimmer, Director of Admission
1014 Cave Spring Road
Rome, GA 30161
Phone: 706-236-0479 Fax: 706-232-3600
E-mail: czimmer@darlingtonschool.org

Deck House School
Mr. James R. Clarke, II, Headmaster
124 Deck House Road
Edgecomb, ME 04556
Phone: 207-882-7055 Fax: 207-882-8151
E-mail: bar@deckhouseschool.org

Deerfield Academy
Patricia L. Gimbel,
Dean of Admission and Financial Aid
Old Main Street
Deerfield, MA 01342
Phone: 413-774-1400 Fax: 413-772-1100
E-mail: admission@deerfield.edu

The Delphian School
Donetta Phelps, Director of Admissions
20950 Southwest Rock Creek Road
Sheridan, OR 97378
Phone: 800-626-6610 Fax: 503-843-4158
E-mail: info@delphian.org

The DeSisto School
Ann Schulman, Director of Admissions
Route 183, P.O. Box 369
Stockbridge, MA 01262
Phone: 413-298-3776 Ext. 112 Fax: 413-298-5175
E-mail: admns@vgernet.net

Detroit Country Day School
Jorge Dante Hernandez Prosperi, Director of Admission
22305 West Thirteen Mile Road
Beverly Hills, MI 48025-4435
Phone: 248-646-7717 Fax: 248-203-2184
E-mail: jprosperi@dcds.edu

Dirigo Day School
Mark Baxter, Program Director
98 Russell Street
Lewiston, ME 04240
Phone: 207-784-7144 Fax: 207-784-5919

Dublin Christian Academy
Mr. Kevin Moody, Principal
106 Page Road, Box 521
Dublin, NH 03444
Phone: 603-563-8505 Fax: 603-563-8008
E-mail: kmoody@dublinchristian.org

Dulwich International College
Mr. Graham P. Dewey, Registrar
59 Moo 2 Thepkrasattri Road, Koh Kaew
Phuket 83000 Thailand
Phone: 76-238 711 Ext. 1113 Fax: 76-238-750
E-mail: gdewey@dulwich.ac.th

Dunn School
Ann E. Greenough-Coats, Director of Admissions
P.O. Box 98, 2555 Highway 154 West
Los Olivos, CA 93441
Phone: 800-287-9197 Fax: 805-686-2078
E-mail: admissions@dunnschool.com

Eaglebrook School
Mr. Theodore J. Low, Director of Admission
Pine Nook Road
Deerfield, MA 01342
Phone: 413-774-9111 Fax: 413-774-9119
E-mail: tlow@eaglebrook.org

Eagle Hill School
Erin E. Wynne, Director of Admission
P.O. Box 116, 242 Old Petersham Road
Hardwick, MA 01037
Phone: 413-477-6000 Fax: 413-477-6837
E-mail: admission@ehs1.org

Eagle Hill School
Rayma-Joan Griffin, Director of Admissions and Placement
45 Glenville Road
Greenwich, CT 06831
Phone: 203-622-9240 Fax: 203-622-0914
E-mail: r.griffin@eaglehill.org

Eagle Rock School
Philbert Smith, Director of Admissions
P.O. Box 1770
Estes Park, CO 80517-1770
Phone: 970-586-0600 Fax: 970-586-4805
E-mail: sherlcks@psd.k12.co.us

Eckerd Youth Alternatives
Francene Hazel, Director of Admissions
100 North Starcrest Drive
Clearwater, FL 33765
Phone: 800-914-3937 Ext. 464 Fax: 727-442-5911
E-mail: fhazel@eckerd.org

Ecole d'Humanite
Kathleen Hennessy, Co-Director
Bernese Alps
CH 6085 Hasliberg-Goldern, Switzerland
Phone: 41-33-972-9272 Fax: 41-33-972-9272
E-mail: us.office@ecole.ch

The Edge
Ms. Carol Clark, Administrative Assistant
c/o Gables Academy, 811 Gordon Street
Stone Mountain, GA 30083
Phone: 770-465-7500 Fax: 770-465-7700
E-mail: gables@gablesacademy.com

Elan School
Ms. Deanna L. Valente, Admissions Director
No. 5 Road, P.O. Box 578
Poland, ME 04274
Phone: 207-998-4666 Fax: 207-998-4660
E-mail: info@elanschool.com

Emerson Honors High Schools
Mrs. Cathie Peterson, Administration
4100 East Walnut Street
Orange, CA 92869
Phone: 714-633-4774 Fax:
E-mail: majelix@socal.rr.com

Emma Willard School
Mr. Kent H. Jones, Director of Enrollment and Public Relations
285 Pawling Avenue
Troy, NY 12180
Phone: 518-883-1320 Fax: 518-883-1805
E-mail: admissions@emmawillard.org

Episcopal High School
Mr. Douglas C. Price, Director of Admission
1200 North Quaker Lane
Alexandria, VA 22302
Phone: 703-933-4062 Fax: 703-933-3016
E-mail: admissions@episcopalhighschool.org

The Ethel Walker School
Ms. Anne Rodriguez Frame, Dean of Enrollment Management
230 Bushy Hill Road
Simsbury, CT 06070
Phone: 860-408-4200 Fax: 860-408-4201
E-mail: anne_rodriguez@ethelwalker.org

The Family Foundation School
Mrs. Mary Musgrove, Director of Admissions
431 Chapel Hill Road
Hancock, NY 13783
Phone: 845-887-5213 Fax: 845-887-4939
E-mail: mmusgrove@thefamilyschool.com

Father Flanagan's Boys' Home
Director of Admissions
13727 Flanagan Boulevard
Boys Town, NE 68010
Phone: 402-498-1900 Fax:

Fay School
Suzanne E. Walker, Director of Admission
48 Main Street
Southborough, MA 01772-9106
Phone: 508-485-0100 Fax: 508-481-7872
E-mail: fayadmit@fayschool.org

The Fenster School of Southern Arizona
Don Saffer, Headmaster
8500 East Ocotillo Drive
Tucson, AZ 85750
Phone: 520-749-3340 Fax: 520-749-3349
E-mail: fenadm@mindspring.com

Flandreau Indian High School
Kathy R Renville, Registrar
1000 North Crescent
Flandreau, SD 57028-1292
Phone: 605-997-3773 Ext. 114 Fax: 605-997-5202
E-mail: katherinerenville@bia.gov

F. L. Chamberlain School
Lawrence H. Mutty, LCSW, Director of Admissions
1 Pleasant Street, Box 778
Middleborough, MA 02346
Phone: 508-947-7825 Ext. 3142 Fax: 508-946-9339
E-mail: admissions@chamberlainschool.org

Flintridge Sacred Heart Academy
Annemarie Noltner, Admissions Assistant
440 Saint Katherine Drive
La Canada Flintridge, CA 91011
Phone: 626-685-8333 Fax: 626-685-8520
E-mail: admissions@fsha.org

Florida Air Academy
Mrs. Deb Hill, Deputy Director of Admissions
1950 South Academy Drive
Melbourne, FL 32901
Phone: 321-723-3211 Ext. 30040 Fax: 321-676-0422
E-mail: dhill@flair.com

Forest Heights Lodge
Linda Clefisch, Executive Director
P.O. Box 789
Evergreen, CO 80437-0789
Phone: 303-674-6681 Fax: 303-674-6805

Forest Lake Academy
Mrs. Claudia Osorio, Admissions Officer
3909 East Semoran Boulevard
Apopka, FL 32707
Phone: 407-862-8411 Ext. 729 Fax: 407-862-7050
E-mail: osorioc@mail.forestlake.org

The Forman School
Beth A. Rainey, Director of Admissions
12 Norfolk Road, P.O. Box 80
Litchfield, CT 06759
Phone: 860-567-1803 Fax: 860-567-3501
E-mail: admissions@formanschool.org

Fountain Valley School of Colorado
Mr. Kilian J. Forgus, Director of Admission
6155 Fountain Valley School Road
Colorado Springs, CO 80911
Phone: 719-390-7035 Fax: 719-390-7762
E-mail: admis@fvs.edu

Foxcroft School
Rebecca B. Gilmore, Director of Admission
P.O. Box 5555
Middleburg, VA 20118
Phone: 800-858-2364 Fax: 540-687-3627
E-mail: admissions@foxcroft.org

Fox River Country Day School
Mrs. Linda M. Thomas, Director of Admissions
1600 Dundee Avenue
Elgin, IL 60120
Phone: 847-888-7910 Ext. 138 Fax: 847-888-7947
E-mail: admissions@frcds.org

Freeman Academy
Cindy Boese, Administrative Assistant
748 South Main Street
Freeman, SD 57029
Phone: 605-925-4237 Fax: 605-925-4271
E-mail: cboese@freemanacademy.pvt.k12.sd.us

Fryeburg Academy
Alan D. Whittemore, Director of Admission
152 Main Street
Fryeburg, ME 04037-1329
Phone: 207-935-2013 Fax: 207-935-4292
E-mail: admissions@fryeburgacademy.org

Gables Academy
Mrs. Carol Clark, Administrative Assistant
811 Gordon Street
Stone Mountain, GA 30083
Phone: 877-465-7500 Ext. 10 Fax: 770-465-7700
E-mail: admin@gablesacademy.com

Gables Albania
Ms. Carol Clark, Administrative Assistant
811 Gordon Street
Stone Mountain, GA 30083
Phone: 877-465-7500 Fax: 770-465-7700
E-mail: gables@gablesacademy.com

Garrison Forest School
A. Randol Benedict, Director of Admission and Financial Aid
300 Garrison Forest Road
Owings Mills, MD 21117
Phone: 410-363-1500 Fax: 410-363-8441
E-mail: gfs_info@gfs.org

Gem State Adventist Academy
Karen Davies, Registrar
16115 Montana Avenue
Caldwell, ID 83607
Phone: 208-459-1627 Fax: 208-454-9079
E-mail: registrar@gemstate.org

Georgetown Preparatory School
Mr. Michael J. Horsey, Dean of Admissions
10900 Rockville Pike
North Bethesda, MD 20852-3299
Phone: 301-214-1215 Fax: 301-493-6128
E-mail: admissions@gprep.org

Gilmour Academy
Mr. Devin K. Schlickmann, Dean of Admissions and Enrollment Management
34001 Cedar Road
Gates Mills, OH 44040-9356
Phone: 440-473-8050 Fax: 440-473-8010
E-mail: schlickd@gilmour.org

Girard College
Admission Receptionist
2101 South College Avenue, Admissions #121
Philadelphia, PA 19121-4897
Phone: 215-787-2620 Fax: 215-787-4402
E-mail: admissions@girardcollege.com

Glacier Mountain Academy
Dr. Larry Bauer, Director
301 North 1st Avenue
Sandpoint, ID 83864
Phone: 208-290-6745 Fax: 208-265-8712
E-mail: glacierm@micron.net

Glencairn Academy
Mr. Patrick Downey, Director of Studies
61 Talbot Road East
Cayuga, ON N0A 1E0 Canada
Phone: 905-772-6060 Fax: 905-772-6161
E-mail: aspire@glencairnacademy.com

The Glenholme School
Kathi Fitzherbert, Director of Admissions
81 Sabbaday Lane
Washington, CT 06793
Phone: 860-868-7377 Fax: 860-868-7413
E-mail: admissions@theglenholmeschool.org

Gould Academy
John A. Kerney, Director of Admission
P.O. Box 860
Bethel, ME 04217
Phone: 207-824-7777 Fax: 207-824-2926
E-mail: john.kerney@gouldacademy.org

Governor Dummer Academy
Peter T. Bidstrup, Director of Admission
1 Elm Street
Byfield, MA 01922
Phone: 978-499-3120 Fax: 978-462-1278
E-mail: admissions@gda.org

The Governor French Academy
Ms. Carol Wilson, Director of Admissions
219 West Main Street
Belleville, IL 62220-1537
Phone: 618-233-7542 Fax: 618-233-0541
E-mail: admiss@gfacademy.com

The Gow School
Mr. Robert Garcia, Director of Admission
P.O. Box 85
South Wales, NY 14139-9778
Phone: 716-652-3450 Fax: 716-687-2003
E-mail: admissions@gow.org

Great Lakes Christian College
Miss Scott L Mansfield, Director of Admissions
4875 King Street
Beamsville, ON L0R 1B0 Canada
Phone: 905-563-5374 Ext. 212 Fax: 905-563-0818
E-mail: study@admin.glcc.on.ca

Green Mountain Valley School
Cindy Gavett Mumford, Director of Admissions
Bragg Hill Road
Waitsfield, VT 05673
Phone: 802-496-2150 Ext. 106 Fax: 802-496-6819

The Greenwood School
Stewart Miller, Assistant Headmaster
14 Greenwood Lane
Putney, VT 05346
Phone: 802-387-4545 Fax: 802-387-5396
E-mail: smiller@greenwood.org

Grenville Christian College
Mrs. Barbara M. Gordon, Administrative Assistant, Admission Office
Box 610
Brockville, ON K6V 5V8 Canada
Phone: 613-345-5521 Ext. 351 Fax: 613-345-3826
E-mail: bgordon@grenvillecc.ca

The Grier School
Andrew M. Wilson, Assistant Head/Director of Admissions
Route 453
Tyrone, PA 16686-0308
Phone: 814-684-3000 Fax: 814-684-2177
E-mail: admissions@grier.org

Groton School
Mr. John M. Niles, Director of Admission
Box 991, Farmers Row
Groton, MA 01450
Phone: 978-448-7510 Fax: 978-448-9623
E-mail: jniles@groton.org

Grove School
Mr. Peter J. Chorney, Executive Director
175 Copse Road, P.O. Box 646
Madison, CT 06443
Phone: 203-245-2778 Fax: 203-245-6098

Gstaad International School
Alain Souperbiet, Headmaster/Director/Director of Admissions
3780 Gstaad
Gstaad 3780 Switzerland
Phone: 41-33-744-2373 Fax: 41-33-744-3578
E-mail: gis@gstaad.ch

The Gunnery
Thomas W. Adams, Director of Admissions
99 Green Hill Road, Route 47
Washington, CT 06793
Phone: 860-868-7334 Fax: 860-868-1614
E-mail: admissions@gunnery.org

Hackley School
Dianne Doty, Admissions Associate
293 Benedict Avenue
Tarrytown, NY 10591
Phone: 914-366-2642 Fax: 914-366-2636
E-mail: ddoty@hackleyschool.org

Hampshire Country School
William Dickerman, Headmaster
122 Hampshire Road
Rindge, NH 03461
Phone: 603-899-3325 Fax: 603-899-6521
E-mail: hampshirecountry@monad.net

Harding Academy
Mark Benton, High School Principal
Box 775 Harding University
Searcy, AR 72149-0001
Phone: 501-279-7200 Fax: 501-279-7213

Hargrave Military Academy
Cmdr. Frank Martin, Director of Admissions
200 Military Drive
Chatham, VA 24531
Phone: 800-432-2480 Fax: 434-432-3129
E-mail: admissions@hargrave.edu

Harmony Heights Residential and Day School
Ellen Benson, Principal
P.O. Box 569
Oyster Bay, NY 11771
Phone: 516-922-6688 Fax: 516-922-6126

Harrow School
Mrs. Margot McKay, Admissions Secretary
Harrow-on-the-Hill
Middlesex HA1 3HW United Kingdom
Phone: 44-0208-8728003 Fax: 44-020-8872-8012
E-mail: admissions@harrowschool.org.uk

The Harvey School
Mr. Ronald H. Romanowicz, Director of Admission
260 Jay Street
Katonah, NY 10536
Phone: 914-232-3161 Ext. 138 Fax: 914-232-6034
E-mail: romanowicz@harveyschool.org

Havergal College
Pamela Newson, Assistant to the Director of Admission
1451 Avenue Road
Toronto, ON M5N 2H9 Canada
Phone: 416-482-4724 Fax: 416-483-9644
E-mail: pam_newson@havergal.on.ca

Hawaiian Mission Academy
Mrs. Linn Madsen, Registrar
1438 Pensacola Street
Honolulu, HI 96822
Phone: 808-536-2207 Fax: 808-524-3294
E-mail: registrar@hawaii.rr.com

Hawaii Preparatory Academy
Mr. Brian K. Chatterley, Esq., Director of Admission
65-1692 Kohala Mountain Road
Kamuela, HI 96743-8476
Phone: 808-881-4074 Fax: 808-881-4003
E-mail: bchatterley@hpa.edu

The Hewlett School of East Islip
Ms. Janet Ovietor Torres, Administration Assistant to the President
74 Suffolk Lane
East Islip, NY 11730
Phone: 631-581-1035 Ext. 11 Fax: 631-581-9386
E-mail: hewlettschool@mail.com

Hidden Lake Academy
Mr. Brian D. Church, Director of Admissions
830 Hidden Lake Road
Dahlonega, GA 30533
Phone: 800-394-0640 Fax: 706-864-9109
E-mail: admissions@hiddenlakeacademy.com

High Mowing School
Sam Rosario, Director of Admissions
Abbot Hill Road, P.O. Box 850
Wilton, NH 03086
Phone: 603-654-2391 Ext. 103 Fax: 603-654-6588
E-mail: admissions@highmowing.org

Hillside School
Mr. Tom O'Dell, Director of Admissions
Robin Hill Road
Marlborough, MA 01752
Phone: 508-303-5731 Fax: 508-485-4420
E-mail: todell@hillsideschool.net

Hokkaido International School
Mr. Wayne D. Rutherford, Headmaster
1-55 5-jo 19-chome, Hiragishi, Toyohira-Ku
Sapporo 062-0935 Japan
Phone: 81-11-816-5000 Fax: 81-11-816-2500
E-mail: his@his.ac.jp

Holderness School
Peter B. Barnum, Director of Admissions
Chapel Lane, P.O. Box 1879
Plymouth, NH 03264-1879
Phone: 603-536-1747 Ext. 231 Fax: 603-536-2125
E-mail: admissions@holderness.org

Horizons School
Mr. Les Garber, Administrator
1900 DeKalb Avenue
Atlanta, GA 30307
Phone: 404-378-2219 Fax: 404-378-8946
E-mail: horizonsschool@mindspring.com

Houghton Academy
Ronald J. Bradbury, Director of Admissions
9790 Thayer Street
Houghton, NY 14744
Phone: 585-567-8115 Fax: 585-567-8048
E-mail: admissons@houghtonacademy.org

Howe Military School
Dr. Brent E. Smith, Director of Admission
5755 North State Road 9
Howe, IN 46746
Phone: 260-562-2131 Ext. 221 Fax: 260-562-3678
E-mail: admissions@howemilitary.com

The Hun School of Princeton
Mr. P. Terence Beach, Director of Admissions
176 Edgerstoune Road
Princeton, NJ 08540
Phone: 609-921-7600 Fax: 609-279-9398
E-mail: admiss@hunschool.org

Hyde School
Richard K. Truluck, Director of Admissions
616 High Street
Bath, ME 04530
Phone: 207-443-7155 Fax: 207-442-9346
E-mail: rtruluck@hyde.edu

Hyde School
Georgia G. MacMillan, Director of Admissions
150 Route 169
Woodstock, CT 06281
Phone: 860-963-4747 Fax: 860-928-0612
E-mail: gmacmillan@hyde.edu

Ideal Girls School of Maharishi Vedic City
Mary Catherine Lair, Director of Admissions
3555 Heavenly Mountain Drive, Suite 3
Boone, NC 28607
Phone: 828-264-1424 Fax: 828-264-5069
E-mail: igs@heavenly-mountain.com

Imperial College of Toronto
Ms. Regina Tan, Admission officer
20 Queen Elizabeth Boulevard
Etobicoke, ON M8Z 1L8 Canada
Phone: 416-251-4970 Fax: 416-251-0259
E-mail: info@imperialcollege.org

Incarnate Word High School
Louise Stevenson Martinez, Director of Enrollment
727 East Hildebrand Avenue
San Antonio, TX 78212-2598
Phone: 210-829-3100 Ext. 3123 Fax: 210-829-3101
E-mail: stevenso@universe.uiwtx.edu

Indian Mountain School
Mark E. Knapp, Director of Admission
211 Indian Mountain Road
Lakeville, CT 06039
Phone: 860-435-0871 Ext. 137 Fax: 860-435-0641
E-mail: mark_knapp@indianmountain.org

Indian Springs School
Shelby S. Hammer, Associate Director of Admissions and Financial Aid
190 Woodward Drive
Indian Springs, AL 35124
Phone: 205-988-3350 Fax: 205-988-3797
E-mail: shammer@indiansprings.org

Institut auf dem Rosenberg, Anglo-American Section
Mrs. M. Schmid, Admissions Director
Hoehenweg 60
CH-9000 St. Gallen, Switzerland
Phone: 41-71-277 7777 Fax: 41-71-277 9827
E-mail: info@instrosenberg.ch

International Academy of Minnesota
Mr. Alex Thomas, Director of Admissions
325 Dayton Avenue
St. Paul, MN 55102
Phone: 651-228-0599 Fax: 651-228-0680
E-mail: athomas@academymn.com

J Bar J Learning Center
Betsy Jacobson-Warren, Program Manager
Academy at Sisters Campus, P.O. Box 5986
Bend, OR 97708-5986
Phone: 541-389-2748 Fax: 541-389-2897

The John Dewey Academy
Dr. Thomas E. Bratter, President
Searles Castle, 389 Main Street
Great Barrington, MA 01230
Phone: 413-528-9800 Fax: 413-528-5662

John F. Kennedy Memorial High School
Mr. Michael Willis, Director of Admissions
140 South 140th Street
Burien, WA 98168-3496
Phone: 206-246-0500 Ext. 306 Fax: 206-242-0831
E-mail: willism@kennedyhs.org

The Judge Rotenberg Educational Center
Julie Gomes
240 Turnpike Street
Canton, MA 02021-2341
Phone: 781-828-2202 Fax:

Keio Academy of New York
Admissions Office
3 College Road
Purchase, NY 10577
Phone: 914-694-4825 Fax: 914-694-4830
E-mail: info@keio.edu

Kemper Military School
Ms. Janet M. Wirths, Coordinator of Admissions
701 Third Street
Boonville, MO 65233
Phone: 660-882-5623 Ext. 3122 Fax: 660-882-3332
E-mail: enroll@kemper.org

Kent School
Mr. Marc L. Cloutier, Director of Admissions / Dean of Faculty
P.O. Box 2006, 1 Skiff Mountain Road
Kent, CT 06757
Phone: 860-927-6111 Fax: 860-927-6109
E-mail: admissions@kent-school.edu

Kents Hill School
Ms. Loren B. Mitchell, Director of Admissions and Financial Aid
P.O. Box 257, 1614 Main Street, Route 17
Kents Hill, ME 04349-0257
Phone: 207-685-4914 Ext. 118 Fax: 207-685-9529
E-mail: lmitchell@kentshill.org

Kildonan School
Bonnie A. Wilson, Director of Admissions
425 Morse Hill Road
Amenia, NY 12501
Phone: 845-373-8111 Fax: 845-373-2004

Kimball Union Academy
Mr. Joseph P. Williams, Director of Admissions
Main Street
Meriden, NH 03770
Phone: 603-469-2102 Fax: 603-469-2041
E-mail: jwilliams@kua.org

King George School
Angie Holmes, Admissions Director
2684 King George Farm Road
Sutton, VT 05867
Phone: 800-218-5122 Ext. 107 Fax: 802-467-8630
E-mail: information@kinggeorgeschool.com

King Richard III College
James Berry, Head of School
Calle Oratorio, 4, Portals Nous
Mallorca 07015 Spain
Phone: 34-71-675-850 Fax: 34-71-676-820

The King's Academy
Janice Mink, Director of Admissions
202 Smothers Road
Seymour, TN 37865
Phone: 865-573-8321 Fax: 865-573-8323
E-mail: jmink@thekingsacademy.net

King's-Edgehill School
Reception Office
254 College Road
Windsor, NS B0N 2T0 Canada
Phone: 902-798-2278 Fax: 902-798-2105

Kingsway College
Mr. Walter Wasyliuk, Director of Public Relations and Development
1200 Leland Road
Oshawa, ON L1K 2H4 Canada
Phone: 905-433-1144 Ext. 212 Fax: 905-433-1156
E-mail: wasyliukw@kingswaycollege.on.ca

The Kiski School
Mr. Lawrence J. Jensen, Director of Admissions
1888 Brett Lane
Saltsburg, PA 15681
Phone: 877-547-5448 Fax: 724-639-8596
E-mail: admissions@kiski.org

The Knox School
Joanna Hulsey, Director of Admissions
541 Long Beach Road
St. James, NY 11780
Phone: 631-584-6562 Fax: 631-584-6566
E-mail: jhulsey@knoxschool.org

Kodaikanal International School
Mrs. Sara Ann Lockwood, Director of Admissions
P.O. Box 25
Kodaikanal 624 101 India
Phone: 91-4542-41105 Fax: 91-4542-41109
E-mail: admissions@kis.ernet.in

Lakefield College School
Mrs. Barbara M. Rutherford, Assistant Director of Admissions
4391 County Road #29
Lakefield, ON K0L 2H0 Canada
Phone: 705-652-3324 Ext. 345 Fax: 705-652-6320
E-mail: admissions@lakefieldcs.on.ca

Lake Forest Academy
Admissions Office
1500 West Kennedy Road
Lake Forest, IL 60045
Phone: 847-615-3267 Fax: 847-615-3202
E-mail: info@lfanet.org

La Lumiere School
John P. Imler, Director of Admission
6801 North Wilhelm Road
La Porte, IN 46350
Phone: 219-326-7450 Fax: 219-325-3185
E-mail: admiss@lalumiere.org

Lancaster Mennonite High School
Ms. Eliza J Ayers, Admissions Counselor
2176 Lincoln Highway, E
Lancaster, PA 17602
Phone: 717-299-0436 Ext. 312 Fax: 717-299-0823
E-mail: ayersej@lancastermennonite.org

Landmark East School
Janet Cooper, Administrative Assistant
708 Main Street
Wolfville, NS B4P 1G4 Canada
Phone: 902-542-2237 Fax: 902-542-4147
E-mail: admissions@landmarkeast.org

Landmark School
Jo Truslow, Administrative Assistant
P.O. Box 227, 429 Hale Street
Prides Crossing, MA 01965-0227
Phone: 978-236-3000 Ext. 3225 Fax: 978-927-7268
E-mail: jtruslow@landmarkschool.org

La Salle
James P. Abbatiello, Admissions Director
500 Montauk Highway
Oakdale, NY 11769-1796
Phone: 631-218-7704 Fax: 631-218-7768
E-mail: info@lasalle-oakdale.org

La Salle Institute
Mrs. Jane Fitzmaurice, Coordinator of Admissions
174 Williams Road
Troy, NY 12180
Phone: 518-283-2500 Fax: 518-283-6265
E-mail: jfitzmaurice@lasalleinstitute.org

Laurinburg Institute
Cynthia McDuffie, Director of Records Management
125 Mcgirts Bridge Road
Laurinburg, NC 28353
Phone: 910-276-0684 Fax: 910-276-2948

The Lawrenceville School
Gregg W. M. Maloberti, Dean of Admission
P.O. Box 6008, 2500 Main Street
Lawrenceville, NJ 08648
Phone: 800-735-2030 Fax: 609-895-2217
E-mail: admissions@lawrenceville.org

Lee Academy
Mr. Jeffrey Wright, Director of Admission
4 Winn Road
Lee, ME 04455
Phone: 207-738-2255 Fax: 207-738-3257
E-mail: admissions@leeacademy.lee.me.us

The Leelanau School
Mrs. Heather M. Sack, Director of Admission
One Old Homestead Road
Glen Arbor, MI 49636
Phone: 231-334-5800 Fax: 231-334-5898
E-mail: admissions@leelanau.org

Leysin American School in Switzerland
Paul Dyer, US Director of Admissions
Batiment Savoy
Leysin 1854 Switzerland
Phone: 603-431-7654 Fax: 603-431-1280
E-mail: usadmissions@las.ch

Lincoln American School
Mark D. Myers, Principal
#193 Chung Chin Road, Sec. 1, P.O. Box 27-111
Taichung, Taiwan
Phone: Fax: 886-4-568-0337
E-mail: lincoln@tc.globalnet.com.tw

Linden Hill School
Patricia K. Sanieski, Academic Dean
154 South Mountain Road
Northfield, MA 01360-9681
Phone: 413-498-2906 Fax: 413-498-2908
E-mail: pksanieski@lindenhs.org

The Linsly School
James Hawkins, Director of Admissions
60 Knox Lane
Wheeling, WV 26003-6489
Phone: 304-233-1436 Fax: 304-234-4614
E-mail: admit@linsly.org

Little Keswick School
Terry Columbus, Director
P.O. Box 24
Keswick, VA 22947
Phone: 434-295-0457 Ext. 14 Fax: 434-977-1892
E-mail: columbuslks@aol.com

Living Faith Christian School
Mr. Terry Burnett, Principal
P.O. Box 100
Caroline, AB T0M 0M0 Canada
Phone: 403-772-2225 Fax: 403-722-2459
E-mail: lfcs@telusplanet.net

Long Trail School
Patricia Midura, Assistant Director of Admissions
1045 Kirby Hollow Road
Dorset, VT 05251-9776
Phone: 802-867-5717 Ext. 190 Fax: 802-867-0147
E-mail: applylts@longtrailschool.org

The Loomis Chaffee School
Thomas D. Southworth, Director of Admission
4 Batchelder Road
Windsor, CT 06095
Phone: 860-687-6400 Fax: 860-298-8756
E-mail: tom_southworth@loomis.org

The Lowell Whiteman School
Mike Whitacre, Director of Admission
42605 RCR 36
Steamboat Springs, CO 80487
Phone: 970-879-1350 Ext. 15 Fax: 970-879-0506
E-mail: admissions@whiteman.edu

Lustre Christian High School
Al Leland, Supervising Teacher
Box 57
Lustre, MT 59225
Phone: 406-392-5735 Fax: 406-392-5765
E-mail: 2lchs@nemontel.net

Luther College High School
Mrs. Jan Schmidt, Registrar
1500 Royal Street
Regina, SK S4T 5A5 Canada
Phone: 306-791-9154 Fax: 306-359-6962
E-mail: lutherhs@luthercollege.edu

Lyman Ward Military Academy
Charles F. Livings, Director of Student Affairs
P.O. Box 550 P, 174 Ward Circle
Camp Hill, AL 36850-0550
Phone: 256-896-4127 Fax: 256-896-4661
E-mail: info@lwma.org

Lyndon Institute
Mary B. Thomas, Assistant Head for Admissions and Special Programs
P.O. Box 127
Lyndon Center, VT 05850-0127
Phone: 802-626-5232 Fax: 802-626-6138
E-mail: mthomas@lyndon.k12.vt.us

The MacDuffie School
Carol K. Murchie, Associate Director of Admissions
One Ames Hill Drive
Springfield, MA 01105
Phone: 413-734-4971 Ext. 140 Fax: 413-734-6693
E-mail: sclayton@macduffie.com

The Madeira School
Cheryl D. Plummer, Director of Admissions and Financial Aid
8328 Georgetown Pike
McLean, VA 22102-1200
Phone: 703-556-8273 Fax: 703-821-2845
E-mail: admissions@madeira.org

Maharishi School of the Age
Mr. Rod Falk, Director of Admissions
804 North Third Street
Fairfield, IA 52556-2200
Phone: 641-472-9400 Ext. 5064 Fax: 641-472-1211
E-mail: rfalk@msae.edu

Malaspina International High School
Mr. Tom Lewis, Principal
900 Fifth Street
Nanaimo, BC V9R 5S5 Canada
Phone: 604-740-6317 Fax: 604-740-6470
E-mail: lewist@mala.bc.ca

Manlius Pebble Hill School
Lynne E. Allard, Director of Admission
5300 Jamesville Road
DeWitt, NY 13214
Phone: 315-446-2452 Ext. 131 Fax: 315-446-2620
E-mail: lallard@mph.net

Maplebrook School
Jennifer L. Scully, Director of Admissions
5142 Route 22
Amenia, NY 12501
Phone: 845-373-8191 Ext. 224 Fax: 845-373-7029
E-mail: mbsecho@aol.com

Marianapolis Preparatory School
Mr. Daniel M. Harrop, Director of Admissions and Chief Immigration Officer
P.O. Box 304, 26 Chase Road
Thompson, CT 06277-0304
Phone: 860-923-9565 Ext. 233 Fax: 860-923-3730
E-mail: dharrop@marianapolis.org

Marine Military Academy
Ms. Jennifer Perez, Admissions Officer
320 Iwo Jima Boulevard
Harlingen, TX 78550
Phone: 956-423-6006 Ext. 251 Fax: 956-412-3848
E-mail: admissions@mma-tx.org

Marion Military Institute
Chief Robert D. Sumlin, Director of Admissions
1101 Washington Street
Marion, AL 36756
Phone: 800-664-1842 Ext. 305 Fax: 334-683-2383
E-mail: rsumlin@marionmilitary.edu

The Marvelwood School
Todd Holt, Director of Admissions
476 Skiff Mountain Road, P.O. Box 3001
Kent, CT 06757-3001
Phone: 860-927-0047 Ext. 26 Fax: 860-927-0021
E-mail: marvelwood.school@snet.net

Marymount International School
Mr. Cliff Canning, HM, Headmaster
George Road, Kingston upon Thames
Surrey KT2 7PE United Kingdom
Phone: 44-(0) 20 8949 0571 Fax: 44-020-8336-2485
E-mail: headmaster@marymountlondon.com

Massanutten Military Academy
Mr. Frank Thomas, Director of Admissions
614 South Main Street
Woodstock, VA 22664
Phone: 877-466-6222 Fax: 540-459-5421
E-mail: admissions@militaryschool.com

Maur Hill Prep School
Mr. Michael W. McGuire, Director of Admission
1000 Green Street
Atchison, KS 66002
Phone: 913-367-5482 Ext. 237 Fax: 913-367-5096
E-mail: admissions@mh-ma.com

Maxwell International Baha'i School
Sharon Jensen, Admissions Director
Bag 1000, 2371 East Shawnigan Lake Road
Shawnigan Lake, BC V0R 2W0 Canada
Phone: 250-743-7144 Ext. 112 Fax: 250-743-3522
E-mail: admit@maxwell.bc.ca

The McCallie School
Mr. David L. Hughes, Director of Boarding Admissions
500 Dodds Avenue, Missionary Ridge
Chattanooga, TN 37404
Phone: 423-624-8300 Fax: 423-493-5426
E-mail: admissions@mccallie.org

McDonogh School
Anita Hilson, Director of Admissions
P.O. Box 380
Owings Mills, MD 21117-0380
Phone: 410-581-4719 Fax: 410-998-3537
E-mail: ahilson@mcdonogh.org

The Meeting School
Christine Smith, Administrative Assistant
56 Thomas Road
Rindge, NH 03461
Phone: 603-899-3366 Fax: 603-899-6216
E-mail: office@meetingschool.org

Memorial Hall School
Kimberly Smith, Coordinator
3721 Dacoma
Houston, TX 77092
Phone: 713-688-5566 Fax: 713-956-9751
E-mail: memhallsch@aol.com

Mercersburg Academy
Mr. Christopher R. Tompkins, Director of Admission and Financial Aid
300 East Seminary Street
Mercersburg, PA 17236
Phone: 717-328-6173 Fax: 717-328-6319
E-mail: admission@mercersburg.edu

Merchiston Castle School
Mrs. Sara McGuckin, Admissions Secretary
294 Colinton Road, Colinton
Edinburgh EH13 0PU United Kingdom
Phone: 44-131-312-2201 Fax: 44-131-441-6060
E-mail: adsec@merchiston.co.uk

Middlesex School
Sibyl F. Cohane, Director of Admissions
1400 Lowell Road
Concord, MA 01742
Phone: 978-371-6524 Fax: 978-402-1400
E-mail: scohane@middlesex.edu

Midland School
Derek Svennungsen, Director of Admissions
5100 Figueroa Mountain Road
Los Olivos, CA 93441
Phone: 805-688-5114 Ext. 14 Fax: 805-686-2470
E-mail: dsvennungsen@midland-school.org

Mid-Pacific Institute
Dorothy L. Crowell, Director of Admissions
2445 Kaala Street
Honolulu, HI 96822-2299
Phone: 808-973-5004 Fax: 808-973-5099
E-mail: admisoff@midpac.edu

Milford Academy
Dr. Andrew Porto, Director of Admissions
150 Gulf Street, P.O. Box 5279
Milford, CT 06460
Phone: 203-878-5921 Fax: 203-882-5160

Millersburg Military Institute
Capt. Christopher M. Reid, Director of Admissions
Post Office Box 278
Millersburg, KY 40348
Phone: 859-484-3352 Fax: 859-484-3342
E-mail: admissions@mmiky.com

Miller School
Jay Reeves, Director of Admissions
Miller School Road, 1000 Samuel Miller Loop
Charlottesville, VA 22903-9328
Phone: 434-823-4805 Fax: 434-823-6617
E-mail: jay@millerschool.org

Milo Adventist Academy
Mr. Steve Rae,
Director of Marketing and Admissions
P.O. Box 278
Days Creek, OR 97429-0278
Phone: 541-825-3200 Ext. 3317 Fax: 541-825-3723
E-mail: steve.rae@miloacademy.org

Milton Academy
Mrs. Patricia Finn, Admission Assistant
170 Centre Street
Milton, MA 02186
Phone: 617-898-2227 Fax: 617-898-1701
E-mail: admissions@milton.edu

Milton Hershey School
Mr. Danny Warner, Senior Officer, Admissions
P.O. Box 830
Hershey, PA 17033-0830
Phone: 717-520-2100 Fax: 717-520-2117
E-mail: warnerd@mhs-pa.org

Missouri Military Academy
Director of Admissions
1000 Grand Avenue
Mexico, MO 65265-9918
Phone: 573-581-1776 Ext. 323 Fax: 573-581-0081

Montana Academy
Mrs. Rosemary Eileen McKinnon, Director of Admissions
9705 Lost Prairie
Marion, MT 59925
Phone: 406-755-3149 Fax: 406-755-3150
E-mail: rosemarym@montanaacademy.com

Montcalm School
Dean Norman Ostrum, Dean of Students
13725 Starr Commonwealth Road
Albion, MI 49224
Phone: 517-629-5591 Ext. 211 Fax: 517-629-4650
E-mail: ostrumn@starr.org

Montclair College Preparatory School
Director of Admissions
8071 Sepulveda Boulevard
Van Nuys, CA 91402-4420
Phone: 818-787-5290 Fax: 818-786-3382

Monterey Bay Academy
Ms. Donna J. Baerg, Vice Principal for Academic Affairs
783 San Andreas Road
La Selva Beach, CA 95076-1907
Phone: 831-728-1481 Fax: 831-728-1485
E-mail: academics@montereybayacademy.org

Montverde Academy
Mrs. Marie Szymanski, Dean of Admissions
17235 Seventh Street, Lake County Road 455
Montverde, FL 34756
Phone: 407-469-2561 Ext. 204 Fax: 407-469-3711
E-mail: mszymanski@montverde.org

Morrison Academy High School
Ralph E. Bressler, Principal
136-1 Shui Nan Road
Taichung 406 Taiwan
Phone: 886-4-292-1171 Fax: 886-4-295-6140
E-mail: bressler@mail.mca.tc.edu.tw

Mount Bachelor Academy
Admissions Department
33051 NE Ochoco Highway
Prineville, OR 97754
Phone: 800-462-3404 Fax: 541-462-3430
E-mail: mba@bendnet.com

Mount Michael Benedictine High School
Dr. Charles Collins, Director of Student Promotion
22520 Mount Michael Road
Elkhorn, NE 68022-3400
Phone: 402-289-2541 Ext. 1003 Fax: 402-289-4539
E-mail: ccollins@muntmichael.org

Mount St. Scholastica Academy
Faye E. Trotter, Director of Admissions
810 R Street
Atchison, KS 66002
Phone: 913-367-1334 Fax: 913-367-5108
E-mail: mssa@best.com

Nacel International School
Caitlin Weaver, Project Administrator
1536 Hewitt Avenue, Box 268
Saint Paul, MN 55104
Phone: 800-622-3553 Fax: 651-686-9601
E-mail: cweaver@nacelopendoor.org

Nakorn Payap International School
Mr. John Allen, Principal
114 M001 Super Highway Road, Tambon Nongpha-Krung
Chiangmai 50000 Thailand
Phone: 66-53-304 573 Fax: 66-53-304 577

National Sports Academy at Lake Placid
Gun Rand, Assoc. Director of Admissions
12 Lake Placid Club Drive
Lake Placid, NY 12946
Phone: 518-523-3460 Ext. 22 Fax: 518-523-3488
E-mail: grand@nationalsportsacademy.com

Native American Preparatory School
Rachel Nelson, Assistant to the Director
355 East Palace Avenue
Rowe, NM 87562
Phone: 505-474-6801 Fax: 505-474-6816
E-mail: admnaps2@aol.com

Navajo Preparatory School, Inc.
Mrs. Laura A. Tom, Director of Admissions
1220 West Apache Street
Farmington, NM 87401
Phone: 505-326-6571 Ext. 128 Fax: 505-564-8099
E-mail: ltom@opus.nps.bia.edu

NAWA Academy
Jason T. Hull, Admissions Director
17351 Trinity Mountain Road
French Gulch, CA 96033
Phone: 800-358-6292 Fax: 530-359-2229
E-mail: nawa@concentric.net

Nebraska Christian Schools
Mrs. Jo Moody, Director, International Programs
1847 Inskip Avenue
Central City, NE 68826
Phone: 308-946-3836 Fax: 308-946-3837
E-mail: ncschools@cconline.net

New Dominion School
Mrs. Tracy Lynn Smith, Director of Admissions
20700 Wagner Cutoff Road, P.O. Box 8
Oldtown, MD 21555
Phone: 301-478-5721 Ext. 18 Fax: 301-478-5723
E-mail: tsmith@threesprings.com

New Dominion School
Michael Forman, Director of Admissions
P.O. Box 540
Dillwyn, VA 23936
Phone: 434-983-2051 Fax: 434-983-2068
E-mail: mforman@ndsvirginia.com

New Hampton School
Mrs. Laurie Madan, Admissions Administrative Assistant
P.O. Box 579, 70 Main Street
New Hampton, NH 03256
Phone: 603-677-3407 Fax: 603-677-3481
E-mail: lmadan@newhampton.org

New Haven
Marsha Powell, Admissions Manager
P.O. Box 50238
Provo, UT 84605-0238
Phone: 801-794-1220 Fax: 801-794-1223
E-mail: marshap@newhavenrtc.com

New Horizon Youth Ministries
Kellie Blossom, Registrar
1002 South 350 East
Marion, IN 46953
Phone: 800-333-4009 Ext. 113 Fax: 765-662-1407
E-mail: admissions@nhym.org

New Mexico Military Institute
Lt. Col. Craig C. Collins, Director of Admissions
101 West College Boulevard
Roswell, NM 88201-5173
Phone: 505-624-8050 Fax: 505-624-8058
E-mail: craig@nmmi.edu

New York Military Academy
Ms. Maureen T. Kelly, Director of Admissions
78 Academy Avenue
Cornwall-on-Hudson, NY 12520
Phone: 845-534-3710 Ext. 4279 Fax: 845-534-7699
E-mail: mkelly@nyma.ouboces.org

Noble and Greenough School
Ms. Jennifer Hines, Director of Admission
10 Campus Drive
Dedham, MA 02026-4099
Phone: 781-326-3700 Fax: 781-320-1329
E-mail: admission@nobles.edu

The North Broward Preparatory Upper School
Director of Admissions
7600 Lyons Road
Coconut Creek, FL 33073
Phone: 954-247-0011 Ext. 303 Fax: 954-247-0012
E-mail: trentacostes@nbps.org

North Country School
Christine LeFevre, Director of Admissions
Cascade Road, Route 73
Lake Placid, NY 12946
Phone: 518-523-9329 Fax: 518-523-4858

Northwest Academy
Christy Slate
P.O. Box 230
Naples, ID 83847
Phone: 877-882-0980 Fax: 208-267-0703
E-mail: nwa@cedu.com

The Northwest School
Anne Smith, Director of Admissions
1415 Summit Avenue
Seattle, WA 98122
Phone: 206-682-7309 Fax: 206-467-7353
E-mail: anne.smith@northwestschool.org

Northwood School
Timothy Weaver, Director of Admissions
Northwood Road
Lake Placid, NY 12946
Phone: 518-523-3382 Fax: 518-523-3405
E-mail: weavert@northwoodschool.com

Oak Grove Lutheran School
Linda Olson, Director of Admissions
124 North Terrace
Fargo, ND 58102
Phone: 701-237-0212 Ext. 152 Fax: 701-237-4217
E-mail: linda.j.olson@sendit.nodak.edu

Oak Grove School
Joy Maguire Parsons, Admissions Associate
220 West Lomita Avenue
Ojai, CA 93023
Phone: 805-646-8236 Ext. 109 Fax: 805-646-6509
E-mail: enroll@oakgroveschool.com

Oak Hill Academy
Dr. Michael D. Groves, President
2635 Oak Hill Road
Mouth of Wilson, VA 24363
Phone: 276-579-2619 Fax: 276-579-4722
E-mail: info@oak-hill.net

Oakland School
Mrs. Carol Smieciuch, Director
Boyd Tavern
Keswick, VA 22947
Phone: 434-293-9059 Fax: 434-296-8930
E-mail: oaklandschool@earthlink.net

Oakley School
Mollie Mylar, Director of Admissions
251 West Weber Canyon Road
Oakley, UT 84055
Phone: 435-783-5001 Ext. 103 Fax: 435-783-5010
E-mail: molliemylar@oakley-school.com

Oak Ridge Military Academy
Capt. Gary E. Humphreys, Director of Admissions and Financial Aid
2309 Oak Ridge Road, P.O. Box 498
Oak Ridge, NC 27310
Phone: 336-643-4131 Ext. 196 Fax: 336-643-1797
E-mail: ghumphreys@oakridgemilitary.com

Oakwood Friends School
Robert J. Suphan, Director of Admissions
22 Spackenkill Road
Poughkeepsie, NY 12603
Phone: 845-462-4200 Fax: 845-462-4251
E-mail: bsuphan@oakwoodfriends.org

Olney Friends School
Sandra Skinner Sterrett, Director of Admissions
61830 Sandy Ridge Road
Barnesville, OH 43713
Phone: 740-425-3655 Fax: 740-425-3202
E-mail: admissions@olneyfriends.org

Oneida Baptist Institute
Admissions
11 Mulberry Street
Oneida, KY 40972
Phone: 606-847-4111 Ext. 233 Fax: 606-847-4496
E-mail: admissions@oneidaschool.org

Oregon Episcopal School
Miss Nancy Pickering,
Admissions Administrative Assistant
6300 Southwest Nicol Road
Portland, OR 97223-7566
Phone: 503-768-3115 Fax: 503-768-3140
E-mail: admit@oes.edu

The Oxford Academy
Ms. Michele L. Mildrum, Admissions Director
1393 Boston Post Road
Westbrook, CT 06498-0685
Phone: 860-399-6247 Ext. 100 Fax: 860-399-6805
E-mail: admissions@oxfordacademy.net

Palmer College Preparatory School
Mrs. Lucy Matuszewski, Registrar
14500 North 46th Street
Tampa, FL 33613
Phone: 813-977-0737 Fax: 813-971-1180

The Pathway School
Louise Robertson, Director of Admissions
162 Egypt Road
Norristown, PA 19403
Phone: 610-277-0660 Ext. 212 Fax: 610-539-1493
E-mail: louiser@pathwayschool.org

The Patterson School
Mr. John D. Hardy, Assistant Director of Admissions
P.O. Box 500
Patterson, NC 28661
Phone: 828-758-2374 Fax: 828-758-9179
E-mail: tps@twave.net

The Penikese Island School
Pam Brighton, Clinical Coordinator
Box 161
Woods Hole, MA 02543
Phone: 508-548-7276 Fax: 508-457-9580
E-mail: penikesei@capecod.net

The Phelps School
Mr. F. Christopher Chirieleison, Director of Admissions
583 Sugartown Road, P.O. Box 476
Malvern, PA 19355-0476
Phone: 610-644-1754 Fax: 610-644-6679
E-mail: admis@phelpsschool.org

Pickering College
Jayne Fillman, Director of Admissions
16945 Bayview Avenue
Newmarket, ON L3Y 4X2 Canada
Phone: 905-895-1700 Fax: 905-895-1306
E-mail: admissions@pickeringcollege.on.ca

Pine Forge Academy
Ms. Karen Y. Christmas, Administrative Assistant
Pine Forge Road
Pine Forge, PA 19548
Phone: 610-326-5800 Ext. 10 Fax: 610-326-4260
E-mail: kchristmas@pineforgeacademy.org

Pine Ridge Academy
Ms. Randie Riegler, Admission Director
P.O. Box 909
Draper, UT 84020
Phone: 801-572-6989 Fax: 801-572-6997
E-mail: rriegler@youthcare.com

Pine Ridge School
Joshua Doyle, Director of Admissions
9505 Williston Road
Williston, VT 05495
Phone: 802-434-6915 Fax: 802-434-5512
E-mail: jdoyle@pineridgeschool.com

Pinewood — The International School of Thessaloniki, Greece
Peter B. Baiter, Director
P.O. Box 21001, Pilea
Thessaloniki 55510 Greece
Phone: 30-31-301-221 Fax: 30-31-323-196
E-mail: pinewood@spark.net.gr

Platte Valley Academy
Mr. Larry Clements, Vice Principal for Finance
19338 West Campus Drive
Shelton, NE 68876
Phone: 308-647-5151 Fax: 308-647-5368
E-mail: lclements@plattevalley.org

Portland Lutheran School
Ms. Jana Lilja, Administrative Assistant
740 Southeast 182nd Avenue
Portland, OR 97233-4960
Phone: 503-667-3199 Ext. 301 Fax: 503-667-4520
E-mail: jlilja@portland-lutheran.org

Portsmouth Abbey School
Mrs. Ann Motta, Admissions Coordinator
285 Cory's Lane
Portsmouth, RI 02871
Phone: 401-683-2005 Fax: 401-683-6766
E-mail: admissions@portsmouthabbey.org

Presbyterian Pan American School
Irene Jimenez-Orta, Principal
P.O. Box 1578
Kingsville, TX 78364-1578
Phone: 512-592-4307 Fax: 512-592-6126

The Principia Upper School
Margery J. Savoye, Director of Admissions
13201 Clayton Road
St. Louis, MO 63131-1099
Phone: 314-434-2100 Fax: 314-275-3519
E-mail: ms@prin.edu

Proctor Academy
Charlie Durell, Admissions Coordinator
P.O. Box 500, 204 Main Street
Andover, NH 03216
Phone: 603-735-6312 Fax: 603-735-6284
E-mail: charlie_durell@proctornet.com

Provo Canyon School
Admissions Office
4501 North University Avenue
Provo, UT 84603
Phone: 800-848-9819 Fax: 801-223-7130
E-mail: pcsinfo@provocanyon.com

Purnell School
Ms. Lara Ellis, Associate Director of Admission
51 Pottersville Road
Pottersville, NJ 07979
Phone: 908-439-2154 Fax: 908-439-4088
E-mail: lellis@purnell.org

The Putney School
Ann McBroom, Admission Assistant
Elm Lea Farm
Putney, VT 05346-8675
Phone: 802-387-6219 Fax: 802-387-6278
E-mail: admission@putneyschool.org

Queen Margaret's School
Mrs. Rebecca McKay, Director of Admissions
660 Brownsey Avenue
Duncan, BC V9L 1C2 Canada
Phone: 250-746-4185 Fax: 250-746-4187
E-mail: admissions@qms.bc.ca

Queenswood
Mrs. Susan Barber, Assistant Registrar
Shepherd's Way, Brookmans Park
Hatfield, Hertfordshire AL9 6NS United Kingdom
Phone: 440-1707602500 Fax: 440-1707602561
E-mail: registry@queenswood.herts.sch.uk

The Rectory School
Stephen A. DiPaolo, Director of Admission
528 Pomfret Street, P.O. Box 68
Pomfret, CT 06258
Phone: 860-928-1328 Fax: 860-928-4961
E-mail: admissions@rectoryschool.org

Redemption Christian Academy
Laura Holmes, Vice Principal
192 Ninth Street, P.O. Box 753
Troy, NY 12181
Phone: 518-272-6679 Fax: 518-270-8039
E-mail: info@rcastudents.com

Remi Vista Ranch School
Mr. James E. Shidler, Admissions
P.O. Box 369
Corning, CA 96021
Phone: 888-268-5781 Fax: 530-824-1127
E-mail: rvrschool@snowcrest.net

Ridley College
Don Rickers, Director of Admission
2 Ridley Road, P.O. Box 3013
St. Catharines, ON L2R7C3 Canada
Phone: 905-684-1889 Ext. 2255 Fax: 905-684-8875
E-mail: admission@ridley.on.ca

Rio Lindo Adventist Academy
Mrs. Karen Nicola,
Recruiting and Marketing Coordinator
3200 Rio Lindo Avenue
Healdsburg, CA 95448
Phone: 707-431-5100 Ext. 132 Fax: 707-431-5115
E-mail: knicola@riolindo.org

Riverside Military Academy
Mr. James A. Davis, Director of Admissions
2001 Riverside Drive
Gainesville, GA 30501
Phone: 770-532-6251 Ext. 2183 Fax: 678-291-3364
E-mail: jdavis@cadet.com

Riverview School
Mrs. Jeanne M. Pacheco,
Director of Admission and Placement
551 Route 6A
East Sandwich, MA 02537
Phone: 508-888-0489 Fax: 508-888-1315
E-mail: admissions@riverviewschool.org

Robert Land Academy
Capt. William Bates, Admissions Officer
RR 3, 6726 South Chippawa Rd
Wellandport, ON L0R 2J0 Canada
Phone: 905-386-6203 Fax: 905-386-6607
E-mail: rla@niagara.com

Rocklyn Academy
Dale Stohn, Director
RR # 2 (Rocklyn)
Meaford, ON N4L 1W6 Canada
Phone: 519-538-2992 Fax: 519-538-1106
E-mail: rocklynacademy@bmts.com

Rock Point School
Hillary Kramer, Director of Admissions
1 Rock Point Road
Burlington, VT 05401
Phone: 802-863-1104 Ext. 12 Fax: 802-863-6628
E-mail: hkramer@rockpoint.org

Rockway Mennonite Collegiate
Mr. Tom Bileski, Director of Community Relations
110 Doon Road
Kitchener, ON N2G 3C8 Canada
Phone: 519-743-5209 Ext. 3029 Fax: 519-743-5935
E-mail: admin@rockway.on.ca

Rocky Mountain Academy
Claudia Peterson, Director of Admissions
Route 1, Box 511
Bonners Ferry, ID 83805
Phone: 877-457-6170 Fax: 208-267-7703
E-mail: rma@cedu.com

Rosseau Lake College
Ms. Kelly J. Haywood,
Associate Director of Admissions
1967 Bright Street
Rosseau, ON P0C 1J0 Canada
Phone: 705-732-4351 Ext. 21 Fax: 705-732-6319
E-mail: admissions@rlc.on.ca

Rothesay Netherwood School
Ms. Vera G. Turnbull, Director of Admission
40 College Hill Road
Rothesay, NB E2E 5H1 Canada
Phone: 506-847-8224 Fax: 506-848-0851
E-mail: admissions@rns.cc

Rumsey Hall School
Matthew S. Hoeniger, Assistant Headmaster
201 Romford Road
Washington Depot, CT 06794
Phone: 860-868-0535 Fax: 860-868-7907
E-mail: admiss@rumseyhall.org

Saddlebrook Preparatory School
Ms. Donna Claggett, Administrative Manager
5700 Saddlebrook Way
Wesley Chapel, FL 33543
Phone: 813-929-2177 Fax: 813-991-4713
E-mail: dclaggett@saddlebrookresort.com

Sagesse High School
Admissions Office
Ain Saadeh
Metn, Lebanon
Phone: 961-1-872145 Fax: 961-1-872149

St. Albans School
Mrs. Ann G. Selinger, Upper School Admissions
Mount Saint Alban
Washington, DC 20016
Phone: 202-537-6412 Fax: 202-537-5288
E-mail: aselinger@cathedral.org

St. Andrew's College
Mrs. Dolly Moffat-Lynch, Associate Director of Admission
15800 Yonge Street
Aurora, ON L4G 3H7 Canada
Phone: 905-727-3178 Ext. 224 Fax: 905-727-9032
E-mail: admission@sac.on.ca

St. Andrew's School
Louisa H. Zendt, Director of Admissions
350 Noxontown Road
Middletown, DE 19709
Phone: 302-285-4230 Fax: 302-378-7120
E-mail: lzendt@standrews-de.org

St. Andrew's School
Brenda Migliaccio, Admissions Assistant
63 Federal Road
Barrington, RI 02806
Phone: 401-246-1230 Ext. 3025 Fax: 401-246-0510
E-mail: admissions@standrews-ri.org

St. Andrew's—Sewanee School
Mr. Jim Tucker,
Director of Admission and Financial Aid
290 Quintard Road
Sewanee, TN 37375-3000
Phone: 931-598-5651 Ext. 3217 Fax: 931-598-0039
E-mail: admissions@sasweb.org

St. Anne's—Belfield School
Jean W. Craig, Director of Admissions
2132 Ivy Road
Charlottesville, VA 22903
Phone: 434-296-5106 Fax: 434-979-1486
E-mail: admission@stab.org

St. Anthony Catholic High School
Mr. Alejandro Calderon, Director of Enrollment
3200 McCullough Avenue
San Antonio, TX 78212-3099
Phone: 210-832-5600 Ext. 5632 Fax: 210-832-5633
E-mail: calderon@universe.uiwtx.edu

St. Bernard Preparatory School, Inc.
Mr. Daniel Hutchinson, Admissions Department
1600 Saint Bernard Drive, SE
Cullman, AL 35055
Phone: 800-722-0999 Ext. 128 Fax: 256-734-2925
E-mail: dhutchinson@stbernardprep.com

St. Catherine's Military School
Mrs. Lori Gutierrez, Director of Admissions
215 North Harbor Boulevard
Anaheim, CA 92805
Phone: 714-772-1363 Fax: 714-772-3004
E-mail: lgutierrez@stcatherinesmilitary.com

St. Clare's, Oxford
Mary Balkwill, Senior Registrar
139 Banbury Road
Oxford OX2 7AL United Kingdom
Phone: 44-1865 552 031 Fax: 44-1865-513-359
E-mail: ib.admissions@stclares.ac.uk

St. Croix Lutheran High School
Mrs. Beverly Leier, Assistant to President
1200 Oakdale Avenue
West St. Paul, MN 55118
Phone: 651-455-1521 Fax: 651-451-3968
E-mail: baleier@sclhs.org

St. George's School
James A. Hamilton, Director of Admission
372 Purgatory Road
Middletown, RI 02842-5984
Phone: 401-842-6600 Fax: 401-842-6696
E-mail: admissions_office@stgeorges.edu

St. George's School
Bill McCracken, Director of Admissions
4175 West 29th Avenue
Vancouver, BC V6S 1V6 Canada
Phone: 604-224-1304 Ext. 115 Fax: 604-221-3616
E-mail: info@stgeorges.bc.ca

St. George's School in Switzerland
Ms. V. Perbos-Parsons, Head of Admissions
Chemin de St. Georges 19
1815 Clarens/Montreux 1815 Switzerland
Phone: 41-21-9643411 Fax: 41-21-9644932
E-mail: office@st-georges.ch

Saint Gregory's Academy
Mrs. Sylvia Burnett, Registrar
RR 8 Box 8214
Moscow, PA 18444
Phone: 570-842-8112 Fax: 570-842-4513

Saint James School
Mr. William W. Ellis, Jr., Director of Admissions and Financial Aid
St. James, MD 21781-9999
Phone: 301-733-9330 Fax: 301-739-1310
E-mail: admissions@stjames.edu

St. John's Military School
Mrs. Judy C. Rutherford, Associate Director of Admissions
P.O. Box 827
Salina, KS 67402-0827
Phone: 785-823-7231 Ext. 7725 Fax: 785-823-7236
E-mail: judyr@sjms.org

St. John's Northwestern Military Academy
Maj. Charles E. Moore, Director of Enrollment Services
1101 North Genesee Street
Delafield, WI 53018-1498
Phone: 262-646-7199 Fax: 262-646-7128
E-mail: admissions@sjnma.org

St. John's-Ravenscourt School
Jane Baizley, Director of Admissions
400 South Drive
Winnipeg, MB R3T 3K5 Canada
Phone: 204-477-2400 Fax: 204-477-2429
E-mail: admissions@sjr.ca

Saint John's School of Alberta
Mrs. Deb McDonald, Admissions Contact
RR 5
Stony Plain, AB T7Z 1X5 Canada
Phone: 780-789-4826 Ext. 127 Fax: 780-848-2395
E-mail: dmcdonald@sjsa.ab.ca

St. Lawrence Seminary
Mr. Leon Dufoor, Admission Director
301 Church Street
Mt. Calvary, WI 53057
Phone: 920-753-7518 Fax: 920-753-7507
E-mail: ldufoor@stlawrence.edu

St. Luke's College
Olga Fedoruk, Principal
P.O. Box. 40, 4705-50 Street
Vegreville, AB T9C 1R1 Canada
Phone: 780-603-5853 Fax: 780-603-5854
E-mail: stlukecollege@aol.com

St. Margaret's School
Gayle Stewart-Loutit, Director of Admissions
1080 Lucas Avenue
Victoria, BC V8X 3P7 Canada
Phone: 250-479-7171 Fax: 250-479-8976
E-mail: gstewartloutit@stmarg.ca

St. Margaret's School
Kimberly McDowell, Assistant Head, External Affairs, Director of
Admission
444 Water Lane, P.O. Box 158
Tappahannock, VA 22560
Phone: 804-443-3357 Fax: 804-443-6781
E-mail: admit@sms.com

Saint Mark's School
Molly H. King, Director of Admission
25 Marlborough Road
Southborough, MA 01772
Phone: 508-786-6000 Fax: 508-786-6120
E-mail: mollyking@stmarksschool.org

Saint Mary's Academy
Ruth Griffiths, Admissions Director
105 Wells Street, P.O. Box 158
Nauvoo, IL 62354
Phone: 800-742-3997 Fax: 217-453-2316
E-mail: smal@darkstar.rsa.lib.il.us

St. Mary's Preparatory School
Kevin Kosco, Dean of Admissions
3535 Indian Trail
Orchard Lake, MI 48324
Phone: 248-683-0532 Fax: 248-683-1740
E-mail: kkosco@stmarysprep.com

Saint Mary's School
Mr. George Myers, Director of Admissions
900 Hillsborough Street
Raleigh, NC 27603-1689
Phone: 919-424-4100 Fax: 919-424-4122
E-mail: admiss@saint-marys.edu

St. Michael's College Preparatory High School of the Norbertine Fathers
Rev. Gabriel D. Stack, OPRAEM, Headmaster
19292 El Toro Road
Silverado, CA 92676-9710
Phone: 949-858-0222 Ext. 237 Fax: 949-858-7365
E-mail: st,michaelsprep@juno.com

St. Michaels University School
Ms. Tammy Fowler, Admissions Assistant
3400 Richmond Road
Victoria, BC V8P 4P5 Canada
Phone: 250-370-6170 Fax: 250-592-2812
E-mail: admit@smus.bc.ca

Saint Paul Lutheran High School
Gloria A. Burrow, Director of Admissions
205 South Main Street, P.O. Box 719
Concordia, MO 64020
Phone: 660-463-2238 Ext. 231 Fax: 660-463-7621
E-mail: gloriaburrow@yahoo.com

St. Paul's Preparatory Academy
Julie Vaughan, Director of Admission
P.O. Box 32650
Phoenix, AZ 85064
Phone: 602-956-9090 Ext. 206 Fax: 602-956-3018
E-mail: admissions@stpaulsacademy.com

St. Paul's School
Ms. Holly Foote, Office Coordinator
325 Pleasant Street
Concord, NH 03301-2591
Phone: 603-229-4700 Fax: 603-229-4771
E-mail: admissions@sps.edu

Saint Pius X High School
Dr. Edward Philip Carlin, Principal
1500 Northeast 42 Terrace
Kansas City, MO 64116

St. Stanislaus College Prep
Mrs. Dolores Richmond, Admissions Director
304 South Beach Boulevard
Bay St. Louis, MS 39520
Phone: 800-517-6257 Fax: 228-466-2972
E-mail: admissions@ststan.com

St. Stephen's Episcopal School
Lawrence Sampleton, Director of Admission
P.O. Box 1868
Austin, TX 78767-1868
Phone: 512-327-1213 Ext. 210 Fax: 512-327-6771
E-mail: admission@ststephens-texas.com

St. Stephen's School, Rome
Suzanne Fusi, Admissions Coordinator
Via Aventina 3
Rome 00153 Italy
Phone: 39-06-575-0605 Fax: 39-06-574-1941
E-mail: ststephens@mclink.it

St. Thomas Choir School
Ms. Margo E. Cantiello, Admissions Associate
202 West 58th Street
New York, NY 10019-1406
Phone: 212-247-3311 Ext. 303 Fax: 212-247-3393
E-mail: admissions@choirschool.org

Salem Academy
C. Lucia Uldrick, Director of Admissions
500 Salem Avenue
Winston-Salem, NC 27108-0578
Phone: 336-721-2643 Fax: 336-917-5340
E-mail: academy@salem.edu

San Domenico School
Ms. Abbi Smith, Associate Director of Admission
1500 Butterfield Road
San Anselmo, CA 94960
Phone: 415-258-1905 Ext. 1122 Fax: 415-258-1906
E-mail: asmith@sandomenico.org

San Marcos Baptist Academy
Bobby Dupree, Director of Admission
2801 Ranch Road Twelve
San Marcos, TX 78666-9406
Phone: 800-428-5120 Fax: 512-753-8031
E-mail: admissions@smba.org

Santa Catalina School
Susannah Rinker, Director of Enrollment and Financial Aid
1500 Mark Thomas Drive
Monterey, CA 93940-5291
Phone: 831-655-9356 Fax: 831-655-7535
E-mail: admissions@santacatalina.org

Scattergood Friends School
Ms. Erin Lane, Director of Admissions
1951 Delta Avenue
West Branch, IA 52358-8507
Phone: 319-643-7628 Fax: 319-643-7638
E-mail: admissions@scattergood.org

SCECGS Redlands
Mr. B. H. Robinson, Registrar
Blue Street
North Sydney 2060 Australia
Phone: 61-9232277 Fax: 61-99561124

Schiller International School
Dr. Renee Miller, PhD, Director of Studies
Royal Waterloo House, 51-55 Waterloo Rd
London SE1 8TX United Kingdom
Phone: 44-(0) 20 7928 1372 Fax: 44-20-7620-1226
E-mail: dr.miller@schiller-academy.org.uk

Schule Schloss Salem
Mrs. Margaret Tzanakakis, Director of Admissions
Salem D88682 Germany
Phone: 49-7553-919 Ext. 337 Fax: 49-7553-919-303
E-mail: margaret.tzanakakis@salem-net.de

Sedbergh
Douglas Wetherill, Director of Admission
810 Cote Azelie
Montebello, QC J0V 1L0 Canada
Phone: 819-423-5523 Fax: 819-423-5769
E-mail: info@sedbergh.com

Sequoyah High School
Ms. Gina Stanley, Director of Curriculum, Instruction, and Counseling
P.O. Box 520
Tahlequah, OK 74465
Phone: 918-456-0631 Ext. 225

Shady Side Academy
Ms. Katherine H. Mihm, Academy Director of Admission
423 Fox Chapel Road
Pittsburgh, PA 15238
Phone: 412-968-3179 Fax: 412-968-3213
E-mail: kmihm@shadysideacademy.org

Shattuck—St. Mary's School
Elizabeth M. Trister, Director of Admissions
1000 Shumway Avenue, P.O. Box 218
Faribault, MN 55021
Phone: 507-333-1616 Fax: 507-333-1661
E-mail: etrister@s-sm.org

Shawnigan Lake School
Mrs. Naz Sicherman, Admissions Officer
1975 Renfrew Road
Shawnigan Lake, BC V0R 2W0 Canada
Phone: 250-743-6207 Ext. 207 Fax: 250-743-6280
E-mail: nsicherman@sls.bc.ca

Shedd Academy
Judy Brindley, Director of Admissions
P.O. Box 493, 401 South 7th
Mayfield, KY 42066-0493
Phone: 270-247-8007 Fax: 270-247-0637
E-mail: thompsonp55@hotmail.com

Sheila Morrison School
Adm. Scott Morrison, Headmaster
8058 Concession 8
Utopia, ON L0M 1T0 Canada
Phone: 705-424-1110 Fax: 705-424-7068
E-mail: admissions@sheilamorrisonschool.com

Shenandoah Valley Academy
Sandie Wile, Registrar
234 West Lee Highway
New Market, VA 22844
Phone: 540-740-3161 Ext. 207 Fax: 540-740-3336
E-mail: wiles@sva-va.org

Sorenson's Ranch School
Mr. J. L. Moss, Director of Admissions
410 North 100 East Street, P.O. Box 440219
Koosharem, UT 84744
Phone: 435-638-7318 Ext. 125 Fax: 435-638-7582
E-mail: srs@color-country.net

South Kent School
Mr. William A. Darrin, Director of Admissions
40 Bull's Ridge Road
South Kent, CT 06785
Phone: 860-927-3539 Ext. 202 Fax: 860-927-0024
E-mail: darrinw@southkentschool.net

The Southport School
Ms. Gerry Northausen, Assistant Director of Admissions
Winchester Street
Southport, Queensland 4215 Australia
Phone: 617-55319978 Fax: 617-55912124
E-mail: gerry@tss.qld.edu.au

Southwestern Academy
Mr. Troy Ferguson, Co-Director of Admissions
Beaver Creek Ranch Campus
Rimrock, AZ 86335
Phone: 928-567-4472 Fax: 928-567-5036
E-mail: tferguson@southwesternacademy.edu

Spring Ridge Academy
Mary Hickey, Director of Admission
13690 South Burton Road
Spring Valley, AZ 86333
Phone: 928-632-4602 Ext. 103 Fax: 928-632-7661
E-mail: sraenrol@northlink.com

Squaw Valley Academy
Amye Cole, Office of Student Development
235 Squaw Valley Road
Olympic Valley, CA 96146
Phone: 530-583-1558 Ext. 21 Fax: 530-581-1111
E-mail: enroll@sva.org

Stevenson School
Mr. Thomas W. Sheppard, Director of Admission
3152 Forest Lake Road
Pebble Beach, CA 93953
Phone: 831-625-8309 Fax: 831-625-5208
E-mail: info@rlstevenson.org

Stone Mountain School
Paige Thomas, Admissions Coordinator
126 Camp Elliott Road
Black Mountain, NC 28711
Phone: 828-669-8639 Fax: 828-669-2521
E-mail: pthomas@stonemountainschool.com

The Stony Brook School
Jane A. Taylor, Director of Admissions
1 Chapman Parkway
Stony Brook, NY 11790
Phone: 631-751-1800 Ext. 1 Fax: 631-751-4211
E-mail: admissions@stonybrookschool.org

Storm King School
Mrs. Caroline Petro, Admissions Specialist
314 Mountain Road
Cornwall-on-Hudson, NY 12520-1899
Phone: 845-534-9860 Ext. 234 Fax: 845-534-4128
E-mail: clagrange@sks.org

Stratton Mountain School
Todd Ormiston, Director of Admissions
World Cup Circle
Stratton Mountain, VT 05155
Phone: 802-297-1886 Ext. 111 Fax: 802-297-0020
E-mail: tormiston@strattonmountainschool.org

Subiaco Academy
Mr. Jason A. Gaskell, Director of Admission
405 North Subiaco Avenue
Subiaco, AR 72865
Phone: 800-364-7824 Fax: 479-934-1033
E-mail: jgaskell@subi.org

Sunshine Bible Academy
Sarah Fiebelkorn, Principal
400 Sunshine Drive
Miller, SD 57362-6821
Phone: 605-853-3071 Fax: 605-853-3072

Sun Valley Indian
Mrs. Debra J. Robbins, Principal
P.O. Box 4013
Sun Valley, AZ 86029-4013
Phone: 928-524-6211 Fax: 928-524-3230
E-mail: debbie@indianschool.org

Sutton Park School
Gayle K. Nagle, Secretary to Headmaster
Saint Fintan's Road, Sutton
Dublin 13 Ireland
Phone: 353-1-832-2940 Fax: 353-1-832-5929
E-mail: suttonpk@iol.ie

Tabor Academy
Andrew L. McCain, Director of Admissions
Front Street
Marion, MA 02738
Phone: 508-748-2000 Ext. 2219 Fax: 508-748-0353
E-mail: admissions@taboracademy.org

Tallulah Falls School
Ms. Amanda Wilson, Director of Admission
P.O. Box 249
Tallulah Falls, GA 30573
Phone: 706-754-0400 Ext. 5149 Fax: 706-754-3595
E-mail: admissions@tallulahfalls.org

TASIS Hellenic International School
Ms. Betty Haniotakis, Director of Admissions
Xenias and Artemidos Streets, P.O. Box 51051
Kifissia - Athens GR-145 10 Greece
Phone: 30-210-623-3888 Ext. 113
Fax: 30-210-623-3160
E-mail: bhani@tasis.edu.gr

TASIS The American School in England
Ms. Bronwyn Thorburn, Director of Admissions
Coldharbour Lane
Thorpe, Surrey TW20 8TE United Kingdom
Phone: 44-1932-565252 Fax: 44-1932-564644
E-mail: ukadmissions@tasis.com

TASIS, The American School in Switzerland
William E. Eichner, Director of Admissions
CH-6926 Montagnola-Lugano, Switzerland
Phone: 91-960-5151 Fax: 91-993-2979
E-mail: admissions@tasis.ch

Texas Military Institute
Mrs. Megan Maturo, Director of Admission
20955 West Tejas Trail
San Antonio, TX 78257
Phone: 210-698-7171 Fax: 210-698-0715
E-mail: m.maturo@tmi-sa.org

Thomas Jefferson School
Ms. Marie De Jesus, Director of Admissions
4100 South Lindbergh Boulevard
St. Louis, MO 63127
Phone: 314-843-4151 Ext. 128 Fax: 314-843-3527
E-mail: admissions@tjs.org

Thomas More Prep-Marian School
Michelle Fairbank, Director of Admissions
1701 Hall Street
Hays, KS 67601-3199
Phone: 785-625-6577 Fax: 785-625-3912
E-mail: fairbankm@tmp-m.org

Three Springs
Raquel Barnes, Customer Relations
1131 Eagletree Lane
Huntsville, AL 35801
Phone: 888-758-4356 Fax: 256-880-7026
E-mail: rbarnes@threesprings.com

Thunderbird Adventist Academy
Karen Lewis, Administrative Secretary
7410 East Sutton Drive
Scottsdale, AZ 85260
Phone: 602-948-3300 Fax: 602-443-4548
E-mail: dldrbowers@aol.com

Tilton School
Jonathan C. Rand, Director of Admission
30 School Street
Tilton, NH 03276
Phone: 603-286-1733 Fax: 603-286-1705
E-mail: jrand@tiltonschool.org

Timber Ridge School
Mr. Philip E. Arlotta, Director of Admissions
1463 New Hope Road
Cross Junction, VA 22625
Phone: 877-877-3025 Ext. 123 Fax: 540-888-4511
E-mail: arlotta@trschool.org

Trafalgar Castle School
Irene Talent, Admissions Officer
401 Reynolds Street
Whitby, ON L1N 3W9 Canada
Phone: 905-668-3358 Ext. 227 Fax: 905-668-4136
E-mail: talenti@castle-ed.com

Trinity-Pawling School
Mr. MacGregor Robinson, Director of Admission
700 Route 22
Pawling, NY 12564
Phone: 845-855-4825 Fax: 845-855-3816
E-mail: grobinson@trinitypawling.org

Union Springs Academy
Mr. Robert W. Raney, Recruitment Director
40 Spring Street
Union Springs, NY 13160
Phone: 315-889-7314 Ext. 26 Fax: 315-889-7188
E-mail: unionsprings_info@yahoo.com

The United World College — USA
Greg Walsh,
Director of Admissions and University Advising
State Highway 65, P.O. Box 248
Montezuma, NM 87731
Phone: 505-454-4201 Fax: 505-454-4294
E-mail: greg.walsh@uwc.net

Upper Canada College
David Mumby, Director of Admission, Boarding
200 Lonsdale Road
Toronto, ON M4V 1W6 Canada
Phone: 416-488-1125 Ext. 4020 Fax: 416-484-8611
E-mail: dmumby@ucc.on.ca

Upper Columbia Academy
Nancy Davis, Registrar
3025 E Spangle-Waverly Road
Spangle, WA 99031-9799
Phone: 509-245-3627 Fax: 509-245-3643
E-mail: ndavis@ucaa.org

Valley Forge Military Academy and College
Lt. Col. Kelly M. DeShane, Dean of Admissions
1001 Eagle Road
Wayne, PA 19087-3695
Phone: 610-989-1300 Fax: 610-688-1545
E-mail: admissions@vfmac.edu

Valley Grande Academy
Mrs. Iona B. Hernandez, Registrar
1000 South Bridge Avenue
Weslaco, TX 78596
Phone: 956-968-0573 Ext. 103 Fax: 956-968-9814
E-mail: vgaone@yahoo.com

Valley View School
Dr. Philip G. Spiva, Director
91 Oakham Road, P.O. Box 338
North Brookfield, MA 01535
Phone: 508-867-6505 Fax: 508-867-3300
E-mail: valview@aol.com

The Vanguard School
Melanie Anderson, Director of Admissions
22000 Highway 27
Lake Wales, FL 33859-6858
Phone: 863-676-6091 Fax: 863-676-8297
E-mail: vanadmin@vanguardschool.org

Venta Preparatory School
Mrs. Tracey H. Quinn, Director of Public Relations and Enrollment
2013 Old Carp Road
Ottawa, ON K0A 1L0 Canada
Phone: 613-839-2175 Ext. 240 Fax: 613-839-1956
E-mail: info@ventapreparatoryschool.com

Verdala International School
Cheryl Buttigieg, Secretary
Fort Pembroke
Pembroke STJ 14 Malta
Phone: 356-375133 Fax: 356-372387
E-mail: vis@maltanet.net

Verde Valley School
Meg Casey, Admissions Assistant
3511 Verde Valley School Road
Sedona, AZ 86351
Phone: 800-552-1683 Ext. 128 Fax: 928-284-0432
E-mail: admission@verdevalleyschool.org

Villanova Preparatory School
Mr. Peter C. Gieseke, Director of Resident Student Admissions
12096 North Ventura Avenue
Ojai, CA 93023-3999
Phone: 805-646-1464 Ext. 139 Fax: 805-646-4430
E-mail: pgieseke@villanovaprep.org

Virginia Episcopal School
Mrs. Pamela D. Barile, Director of Admission
400 V.E.S. Road
Lynchburg, VA 24503
Phone: 434-385-3605 Fax: 434-385-3603
E-mail: pbarile@ves.org

Wasatch Academy
Mr. Dan Kemp, Director of Admissions
120 South 100 West
Mt. Pleasant, UT 84647
Phone: 800-634-4690 Ext. 121 Fax: 435-462-1450
E-mail: admissions@wacad.org

Washington College Academy
Office of Admissions
116 Doak Lane
Limestone, TN 37681
Phone: 423-257-5151 Fax: 423-257-5156
E-mail: wcastudent@chartertn.net

Wayland Academy
Mr. Eric S. Peters, Dean of Admission & College Counseling
101 North University
Beaver Dam, WI 53916-2253
Phone: 920-885-3373 Ext. 241 Fax: 920-887-3373
E-mail: epeters@wayland.org

The Webb School
Mr. Matt Radtke, Director of Admissions
Highway 82
Bell Buckle, TN 37020
Phone: 931-389-6003 Fax: 931-389-6657
E-mail: admissions@webbschool.com

The Webb Schools
Mr. Leo G. Marshall, Director of Admission and Financial Aid
1175 West Base Line Road
Claremont, CA 91711
Phone: 909-482-5214 Fax: 909-621-4582
E-mail: admission@webb.org

Wediko School Program
Marianne Hammond, Administrative Coordinator
11 Bobcat Boulevard
Windsor, NH 03244
Phone: 603-478-5236 Ext. 203 Fax: 603-478-2049
E-mail: mhammond@wediko-nh.org

Wellspring Foundation
Christa Pelletier, Admissions Coordinator
21 Arch Bridge Road, P.O. Box 370
Bethlehem, CT 06751
Phone: 203-266-8022 Fax: 203-266-8030
E-mail: christap@wellspring.org

Wentworth Military Academy and Junior College
Maj. Todd L. Kitchen, SR, Director of Admissions
1880 Washington Avenue
Lexington, MO 64067-1799
Phone: 660-259-2221 Ext. 211 Fax: 660-259-2677
E-mail: tkitchen@wma1880.org

Western Mennonite School
Mr. Paul Schultz, Director of Admissions
9045 Wallace Road NW
Salem, OR 97304-9716
Phone: 503-363-2000 Fax: 503-370-9455
E-mail: pschultz@westrnmennoniteschool.org

Westminster School
Jon C. Deveaux, Director of Admissions
995 Hopmeadow Street
Simsbury, CT 06070
Phone: 860-408-3060 Fax: 860-408-3042
E-mail: admit@westminster-school.org

West Nottingham Academy
Heidi K. L. Sprinkle, Director of Admission and Financial Aid
1079 Firetower Road
Colora, MD 21917-1599
Phone: 410-658-5556 Ext. 9224 Fax: 410-658-9264
E-mail: admissions@wna.org

Westover School
Ms. Sara Lynn Leavenworth, Director of Admission and Financial Aid
1237 Whittemore Road
Middlebury, CT 06762
Phone: 203-758-2423 Fax: 203-577-4588
E-mail: admission@westoverschool.org

Wilbraham & Monson Academy
Christopher Moore, Director of Admission and Financial Aid
423 Main Street
Wilbraham, MA 01095
Phone: 413-596-6811 Ext. 109 Fax: 413-599-1749
E-mail: cmoore@wmanet.org

The Williston Northampton School
Ann C. Pickrell, Director of Admission and Financial Aid
19 Payson Avenue
Easthampton, MA 01027
Phone: 413-529-3241 Fax: 413-527-9494
E-mail: admission@williston.com

Windermere St. Anne's School
Registrar
Browhead
Windermere LA23 1NW United Kingdom
Phone: 44-153-944-6164 Fax: 44-153-948-8414

Wisconsin Academy
Mrs. Holly Roy, Registrar
North 2355 Duborg Road
Columbus, WI 53925
Phone: 920-623-3300 Ext. 13 Fax: 920-623-3318
E-mail: wareg@wi.net

Woodberry Forest School
Mr. Joseph G. Coleman, Director of Admissions
10 Woodberry Station
Woodberry Forest, VA 22989
Phone: 540-672-6023 Fax: 540-672-6471
E-mail: joe_coleman@woodberry.org

The Woodhall School
Sally Campbell Woodhall, Head of School
58 Harrison Lane
Bethlehem, CT 06751
Phone: 203-266-7788 Fax: 203-266-5896
E-mail: woodhallschool@lycos.com

Woodlands Academy of the Sacred Heart
Kathleen Creed, Director of Admission and Financial Aid
760 East Westleigh Road
Lake Forest, IL 60045-3298
Phone: 847-234-4300 Ext. 213 Fax: 847-234-0865
E-mail: admissions@woodlands.lfc.edu

Woodside Priory School
Mr. Al D. Zappelli, Dean of Admissions
302 Portola Road, Admissions Office
Portola Valley, CA 94028-7897
Phone: 650-851-8223 Fax: 650-851-2839
E-mail: azappelli@woodsidepriory.com

Woodstock School
Ms. Cathy E. Holmes, Director of Admissions
Mussoorie
Uttaranchal 248 179 India
Phone: 91-135-2632547 Ext. 2424 Fax: 91-135-2630897
E-mail: admissions@woodstock.ac.in

Yeshiva High School
Mr. Sheldon Schaffel, Assistant Principal
7135 North Carpenter Road
Skokie, IL 60077
Phone: 847-982-2500 Ext. 124 Fax: 847-677-6381
E-mail: schaffel@htcnet.edu

GEOGRAPHICAL INDEX

United States

Arizona
Oak Creek Ranch School
The Orme School

California
Antelope Valley Christian School
The Athenian School
Happy Valley School
Idyllwild Arts Academy
Monte Vista Christian School
Ojai Valley School
Southwestern Academy
The Thacher School

Connecticut
Avon Old Farms School
The Hotchkiss School
Miss Porter's School
Pomfret School
Saint Thomas More School
Salisbury School
Suffield Academy
The Taft School

Florida
Admiral Farragut Academy
Saint Andrew's School

Georgia
Brenau Academy
Rabun Gap-Nacoochee School

Indiana
Culver Military Academy/
  Culver Girls Academy

Maine
Hebron Academy
Maine Central Institute
Washington Academy

Maryland
Oldfields School
Saint Timothy's School
Sandy Spring Friends School

Massachusetts
Brooks School
Buxton School
The Cambridge School of Weston
Cushing Academy
Dana Hall School
The Fessenden School
Lawrence Academy
Miss Hall's School
The Newman School
Northfield Mount Hermon School
Phillips Academy
Stoneleigh-Burnham School
Walnut Hill School
Winchendon School
Worcester Academy

Michigan
Cranbrook Schools
Interlochen Arts Academy

Minnesota
Saint John's Preparatory School

New Hampshire
Dublin School
Phillips Exeter Academy
The White Mountain School

New Jersey
The Peddie School
Pennington School

New York
Darrow School
Hoosac School
The Masters School
Millbrook School

North Carolina
Asheville School

Ohio
The Andrews School
The Grand River Academy
Western Reserve Academy

Pennsylvania
George School
The Hill School
Linden Hall School for Girls
Perkiomen School
Solebury School
Westtown School
Wyoming Seminary

Tennessee
Baylor School

Texas
The Hockaday School

Vermont
Saint Johnsbury Academy
Vermont Academy

Virginia
The Blue Ridge School
Fishburne Military School
Fork Union Military Academy
Randolph-Macon Academy
Saint Catherine's School
Stuart Hall

Canada

Ontario
The Bishop Strachan School
Trinity College School

Quebec
Bishop's College School
Stanstead College

142

Index

SECTION II

WORLDWIDE ENRICHMENT PROGRAMS

PROGRAMAS MUNDIALES DE ENRIQUECIMIENTO

PROGRAMMES DE PERFECTIONNEMENT INTERNATIONAUX

世界各地での強化プログラム

國際強化項目

INTRODUCTION

INTRODUCCIÓN   INTRODUCTION
はじめに   導言

Welcome to *Peterson's American and Canadian Boarding Schools and Worldwide Enrichment Programs*. In this section of the book you'll find in-depth descriptions of more than 30 summer programs located all over the world. The choices are endless—all kinds of exciting opportunities to learn, travel, and make new friends can be found on these pages. Most programs feature English as a second language (ESL) courses; all are dedicated to offering an enjoyable and stimulating summer experience to students from other countries. Expert advice guides you in deciding how to match your needs with the right program, and graphical icons designed especially for the guide help you quickly find the information you'll need to make your choice.

The editors at Peterson's hope the information presented here will help you choose a terrific summer program—one with just the right combination of learning, adventure, and fun. We look forward to hearing your comments, and we welcome suggestions for future editions.

Bienvenido al *Internados en los Estados Unidos y Canadá y Programas Mundiales de Enriquecimiento*. En este libro encontrará descripciones detalladas de más de 30 programas de verano en todo el mundo. La selección es infinita—en estas páginas encontrará todo tipo de oportunidades atractivas para aprender, viajar y hacer nuevos amigos. La mayoría de los programas ofrecen cursos de inglés como segundo idioma (ESL); todos están dedicados a ofrecer una experiencia veraniega grata y estimulante a los estudiantes de otros países. Los consejos expertos lo guían para decidir cómo combinar sus necesidades con el programa ideal, y los iconos gráficos, diseñados especialmente para el directorio, le ayudarán a encontrar rápidamente la información que necesitará para decidirse.

Los editores de Peterson esperan que la información presentada le ayude a elegir un programa de verano fantástico, aquel que tenga la combinación adecuada de aprendizaje, aventura y diversión. Esperamos recibir sus comentarios y sugerencias para futuras ediciones.

Voici le *Internats américains et canadiens, et Programmes de perfectionnement internationaux*. Il contient des descriptions détaillées d'environ 30 programmes estivaux offerts partout dans le monde. Ses pages contiennent des possibilités infinies: des occasions d'apprendre, de voyager et de se faire des amis. La majorité des programmes comprend les cours d'anglais en taut que langue étrangère (ESL) et tous sont conçus de manière à offrir une expérience estivale agréable et stimulante aux jeunes de tous les pays. Des conseils judicieux vous guident dans le choix du programme répondant le mieux à vos besoins et des icônes graphiques, conçues spécialement pour ce guide, vous aident à trouver rapidement l'information nécessaire à une prise de décision éclairée.

Les rédacteurs de Peterson's souhaitent sincèrement que l'information présentée ici vous aidera à choisir un programme estival sans pareil — un programme combinant la juste dose d'instruction, d'aventure et de plaisir. Nous espérous recevoir vos commentaires et apprécions toutes suggestions visant à améliorer les éditions futures.

「米国、カナダの全寮制学校および世界各地での強化プログラム」をご利用いただきありがとうございます。本書では世界各地の30以上の夏期プログラムをご紹介いたします。各ページには学習、旅行、新しい友達との交流など、多種多様な楽しい機会が満載されています。プログラムのほとんどがESL（外国人向英語）コースを特色とし、海外からの学生たちに楽しく刺激に満ちた夏の体験を提供しています。本書はまた、自分のニーズに合ったプログラムが選択できるよう専門家によるアドバイスを掲載している他、本書の特色とするグラフィック・アイコンで必要な情報を素早く見つけることができます。

ピーターソンの編集者一同、本書に掲載されている情報により皆様のご希望通りの学習、冒険、楽しい体験が組み合わされたすばらしい夏期プログラムの発見のお手伝いができますことを心から願っております。皆様のご意見・ご感想をお寄せください。また、今後の改訂版へのご提案をいただければ幸いです。

歡迎參閱美國與加拿大寄宿學校及國際強化項目。本書詳細説明世界各地30多項的夏令營活動。您可任意挑選您喜歡的夏令營，各種興奮的學習、旅遊和交友活動內容均可在本書內找到。大部分的夏令營都安排ESL課程，為來自其他國家的學生提供愉快的暑期學習經驗。這本書為您提供專家意見，指導您如何根據需要選擇合適的課程，另外，這本指南專門為您設計一些圖像標識，以協助您迅速查到您需要的訊息。

彼得森的編輯希望這本指南能協助您選出學習、歷險和娛樂搭配合宜的暑期課程。我們期望聽到您的意見，也歡迎您對我們的未來版本提出建議。

Worldwide Enrichment Programs—
HOW TO USE THIS SECTION

This section of the guide is divided into five main parts: introductory advice, one-page presentations of summer programs, an appendix of summer programs, a list of abbreviations, and program information request forms. To make the most of all the information found in *Peterson's American and Canadian Boarding Schools and Worldwide Enrichment Programs* follow the steps outlined below.

Step One

Before you begin to search for the perfect summer program, read "Family Guide to Summer Programs" by Diane Rapp, which begins on page 150. The article outlines your options—academic programs, wilderness, and travel programs—and provides invaluable information about program locations, facilities, duration, enrollment, and costs as well as a description of a typical day at camp and advice on what clothes to pack and what to expect meals to be like. Rules and safety at camp are discussed, as are application procedures and transportation arrangements. The article also offers advice on the important questions to ask of any program you're considering; be sure to write these questions down before you begin using the "One-Page Presentations"—most of the answers you'll need can be found there.

Step Two

Once you know the questions to ask to find out if a program's right for you, you're ready to use the One-Page Presentations to narrow your search. First consult the "Explanation of the One-Page Presentations" on the next page, which shows you where on each page you'll find the information you need to make a choice. Then turn to the "One-Page Presentations," which begin on page 169. More than 20 programs that completed Thomson Peterson's 2004 Questionnaire are highlighted in this section. Programs are divided into different sections: academic programs, English language programs, camps, travel programs, and wilderness/outdoor programs. Macro icons in the top outer corner of each page identify the program type. (See the next page for more macro icon information.) For each program, you'll find location and contact information as well as an expanded description written by the program director, a photograph of the program's facilities, and in-depth information about international participant enrollment, English as a second language course availability, English language proficiency necessary for enrollment, program dates and application deadlines, costs, housing, rules, and much more. To help you use the "One-Page Presentations," a "Key to the Graphical Icons" can be found on page 168 as well as inside the cover. A list of abbreviations used in the book can be found on page 229.

Step Three

This book also includes "Other Summer Programs," which begins on page 197. In this section you'll find names and contact information for more than 600 summer programs not highlighted in the "One-Page Presentations" section. Use the contact information found here to request additional information from the programs, who expressed an interest to Peterson's in enrolling international participants.

Step Four

When you've finished compiling a list of programs that have piqued your interest, use the "Information Request Form" to receive additional information or to request admission to an upcoming session. This form, which appears on page 231, can be faxed or mailed to program contacts; use the fax numbers and addresses found in the Contact section of the "One-Page Presentation" or in the "Other Summer Programs" section to ensure correct transmission of the form. (Remember to add your country's international dialing code to the beginning of fax numbers when dialing out of country!) Feel free to photocopy the form and use it as many times as you like to contact as many programs as you like. Once the programs are contacted, they will send you additional detailed information about their program's offerings.

EXPLANATION OF ONE-PAGE PRESENTATIONS

The "One-Page Presentations" beginning on page 169 provide in-depth information about summer programs offered around the world. This information was provided to Thomson Peterson's in the spring and summer of 2004 by the program directors, who completed a special questionnaire developed by Thomson Peterson's.

WHAT YOU'LL FIND IN THE ONE-PAGE PRESENTATIONS

1. Program type:
   a. Academic programs   b. English language programs   c. Camps   d. Travel programs
2. Name of program sponsor
3. Summer location (*if different from contact information*) OR Program name (*if different from program sponsor*)
4. Program logo or crest (if available)
5. Contact information (*Remember to add your country's international dialing code to the beginning of all phone and fax numbers when contacting programs!*)
6. Program photo
7. Expanded description of program offerings
8. Geographical location of program, or, for travel programs, point of departure for trips
9. Distance from nearest international airport and large city

Summer Program Icons
(You may also use the "Key to the Graphical Icons" found on page 174 and inside the back cover when reading One-Page Descriptions.)

10. Summer temperature range
11. Setting
12. Religious affiliation
13. Age of participants
14. Enrollment: number of boys, number of girls
15. Number and percentage of international participants
16. Countries most frequently represented
17. English language proficiency required
18. Availability of ESL instruction and cost
19. Housing information
20. Session dates
21. Staff-participant ratio
22. Application deadline
23. Off-site trip locations
24. Standard fees, additional fees, spending money
25. Evaluations by former international participants available
26. Availability of airport pick-up
27. On-site medical care

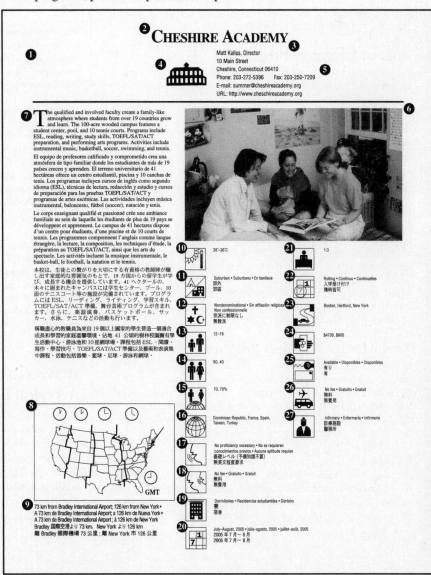

149

FAMILY GUIDE TO SUMMER PROGRAMS

ummer is a wonderful time for students to expand their horizons and build on skills and
talents learned during the regular school year. Programs located all over the world accommodate
students of all ages with all sorts of interests. Some participants live in comfortable, well-supervised housing
while studying a variety of subjects; participating in sports, arts, and crafts; and sight-seeing. Others take part in
wilderness and travel programs, where adventure and excitement in the great outdoors is found in many different
locations. Whatever program students choose to participate in, they return home from their summer experience with new
abilities and interests, new friends, and happy memories.

WHAT ARE MY OPTIONS?
Academic Programs

Summer academic programs are run by private secondary schools,
colleges, and universities. Students live in dormitories and
generally engage in classes in the morning, sports and activities in
the afternoon, and study hall at night. Weekends are spent traveling
and sight-seeing or participating in outdoor adventures. Most
participants study one or two subjects; international students
usually study English as a second language (ESL) and one other
subject. Academic programs offer an excellent opportunity for
students from overseas to improve their English speaking, reading,
and writing skills. A wide variety of courses is available on many
levels—language and literature, math, science, computers, social
sciences, and engineering, to name just a few.

English Language Programs

Programs that concentrate on improving the student's writing and
speaking skills are offered by language schools, private secondary
schools, colleges, and universities.

Traditional Camps

In traditional summer camps students live in a beautiful, safe
setting surrounded by woods, lakes, and mountains, away from the
noise and congestion of the city. They participate in many kinds of
sports, arts and crafts, and nature studies. Campers live in tents or
small cabins and spend most of the day outdoors. A summer
camping experience offers students an opportunity to make close
friends through shared living and activities. Counselors and other
professionals supervise all activities closely and help create a
warm, family-like atmosphere. Some spend many years at the
same camp, first as young campers, then as senior campers, and
finally as counselors. While enjoying the wonders of the natural
world, campers develop self-confidence and leadership skills. Most
camps do not provide English instruction, and many require
campers to understand basic English.

Travel and Wilderness Programs

Participants in travel programs may bicycle, hike, ski, or travel by
motorcoach as they explore hundreds of miles of terrain
throughout the world. As participants must often help each other
through rough terrain, communication within the group is
fundamental on these programs; because of this safety concern,
basic English ability is required for most of these programs.

For those who want adventure, wilderness programs offer an
opportunity to climb mountains, white-water raft down beautiful
rivers, and cook meals over a campfire. Accommodations for
campers on wilderness trips range from tents set up in different
areas each day to bunks on boats in the middle of the sea.

WHERE ARE PROGRAMS LOCATED?
WHAT ARE THE FACILITIES LIKE?

Academic programs listed in this guide are located at boarding
schools, colleges, and universities in North America and Europe.
The majority of traditional camps are located in the United States
and Canada. Travel and wilderness programs, located all over the
world, give students an opportunity to explore a wide geographical
area. Programs located in beautiful, spacious rural areas offer
students from cities the opportunity to run, play, hike, and enjoy a
summer outdoors, while programs located in metropolitan areas
provide endless opportunities for cultural and educational
activities.

Private schools and universities have excellent academic and
recreational facilities available for student use, and students
usually live in dormitories in single or double rooms. In camps,
participants may share a tent or cabin with 5 or 6 other campers
and a counselor.

HOW LONG ARE PROGRAMS?
WHO ELSE ENROLLS?

Summer sessions usually last anywhere from four to eight weeks,
beginning in late June and ending in August. Shorter and longer
programs are also available, and students with limited school
vacations can sometimes join a program later in the summer.
Families should contact program directors for specific dates and
for information about enrollment options.

Programs range in size from a few campers sharing a tent to
several hundred students at a summer boarding school. In all
programs, classes or activities are in small, closely supervised
groups. Most programs enroll students from many parts of the
United States and from several other countries. Surrounded by
native English speakers, international students have an unrivaled
opportunity to improve English speaking abilities.

HOW ARE PROGRAMS STRUCTURED?
A Typical Day at Camp

Days are full of learning, fun, and friendship. Students get up early
to start a day full of activities. Breakfast and room or tent clean-up
are followed by activity periods, lunch, and more activities.
Students in academic programs usually attend classes in the
morning and spend afternoons participating in sports, arts and
crafts, and music or drama or exploring local areas of interest.
There is free time before dinner and study hall or more activities
until bedtime. All activities are supervised by adults and older
students.

Food

Meals may be served in a school dining room or from a backpack on a mountain hike. Food is nutritious, with lots of fresh fruits and vegetables. All programs provide three meals per day as well as snacks throughout the day. International students who find it difficult to get used to "camp food" often bring their favorite snack food from home. Some programs will provide special meals for students who require a special diet.

Clothing

Dress at summer schools is informal. Few programs require uniforms; many allow campers to wear casual clothes—usually jeans and T-shirts. Summer evenings may be cool, so participants should be sure to bring sweaters or light jackets. Some programs advise students to bring one or more formal outfits for special events. Special clothing and equipment may be required for sports camps and wilderness and travel programs. All programs will provide a more detailed list of what to bring.

Rules and Policies

In order for a school or camp to run smoothly, it is important for all members of the summer community to cooperate and work together. Strict rules include prohibition of smoking, using or possessing alcohol and other illegal substances, leaving the grounds without permission, and cheating. Failure to obey these rules is serious and may result in expulsion from a program.

Health and Safety

All programs require participants to have a doctor's examination and basic immunizations before they arrive. Schools and camps have health centers staffed by trained nurses and other medical staff members, and doctors and hospital services are always available. Parents must give permission for emergency medical care. Some programs provide medical insurance; others require that students carry their own policies.

Programs are carefully supervised. Students must take responsibility for their own safety, however, when traveling and when leaving the campus or camp area. Parents should teach their children basic rules of safety before they leave for a summer program. Although drugs and alcohol are prohibited during all programs, your child should be warned that some students may possess them illegally and that such people should be avoided.

HOW DO I APPLY?

Admission to summer programs does not usually require special testing or ability; application procedures usually involve simply providing basic information. Some specialized art and music programs may ask for samples of a student's work, academic programs may require academic transcripts and recommendations, and some programs require a certain level of English ability. Most programs have limited enrollment, and many fill up early in the spring; it is always advisable to apply as early as possible. Programs normally require a deposit to secure a place; full payment is required before the program begins.

HOW MUCH WILL IT COST?
HOW DO I GET THERE?

The average cost for a program ranges from $2000 to $4000. Basic fees cover activities, housing, and meals. There may be extra fees for uniform and linen rental, transportation to and from the airport, and other activities such as horseback riding. Parents can wire money directly to a U.S. bank account for payment—be sure to ask the program director for specific information if you choose this payment option. Students should also carry a small amount of extra money for personal use.

Camps and schools will meet students coming from overseas at the closest airport; some programs charge a fee for this service. Some programs arrange participants' travel itineraries for them, while others require students to make their own arrangements.

Choosing a summer program can be fun, but you should also remember to ask a few important questions when deciding in which program you'd like to enroll. Find out what the program's English language requirements are—is total command of the English language necessary, or can participants be just minimally proficient? Explore your enrollment options—sometimes you can join a program at a later time or leave earlier if your schedule back home conflicts with program dates. Ask about program rules—if smoking is prohibited, for example, be sure to find out before you go. And inquire about payment options—if the program allows you to wire money to its bank electronically, make sure you know all the details necessary for this type of transaction.

Here's wishing you the best summer ever!

*Diane Rapp is President of Diane Rapp Associates
Educational Consultants
85 River Road, Scarborough, New York 10510
U.S.A.*

Programas Mundiales de Enriquecimiento—
CÓMO USAR ESTA SECCIÓN

Esta sección de guía se divide en cinco partes principales: consejos preliminares, presentación de una página de los programas de verano, apéndice de los programas de verano, lista de abreviaturas y formularios para solicitar Información sobre los programas. Para aprovechar al máximo toda la información del *Internados en los Estados Unidos y Canadá y Programas Mundiales de Enriquecimiento*, siga los pasos que se describen a continuación.

Primer paso

Antes de comenzar a buscar el programa de verano ideal en el libro, lea la "Guía familiar para programas de verano" escrita por Diane Rapp, que comienza en la página 154. El artículo describe las opciones —programas académicos, programas en reservas naturales y de viajes—y ofrece valiosa información sobre la ubicación, las instalaciones, la duración, la matriculación y el costo, y también una descripción de un día típico en el campamento y consejos acerca de qué ropa empacar y qué esperar de las comidas. Se discuten los reglamentos y la seguridad en el campamento, así como el procedimiento de solicitud y la organización del transporte. El artículo también ofrece consejos sobre las preguntas importantes que debe formular acerca de todo programa que esté considerando; asegúrese de escribirlas antes de comenzar a usar "las presentaciones de una página"—allí encontrará la mayoría de las respuestas que necesite.

Segundo paso

Una vez que haya formulado las preguntas necesarias para averiguar si el programa es adecuado para usted, estará listo para usar las presentaciones de una página, y así concentrar su búsqueda. Consulte primero la "explicación de las presentaciones de una página" en la página siguiente, la cual le indicará dónde encontrar la información que necesita para decidir en cada página. Continúe luego con las presentaciones de una página, en la página 169. En esta sección encontrará más de 20 programas que completaron los cuestionarios de Thomson Peterson's 2004. Los programas están divididos en secciones: programas académicos, programas de inglés, campamentos, programas de viajes y programas en reservas naturales/al aire libre. Los íconos de programas en la esquina superior exterior de cada página identifican el tipo de programa. (Consulte la página siguiente para obtener más información sobre los íconos de programas.) Para cada programa encontrará información sobre la ubicación y el contacto, y también una descripción extensa escrita por el (la) director(a) del programa, una fotografía de las instalaciones del programa e información detallada sobre matriculación de los participantes extranjeros, disponibilidad de cursos de inglés como segundo idioma, conocimientos del idioma inglés necesarios para matricularse, fechas de los programas y fecha límite para presentar la solicitud, costos, alojamiento, reglamento y mucho más. Para ayudarle a utilizar "las presentaciones de una página", encontrará las "Leyenda de íconos gráficos" en la página 168 y en la parte interior de la cubierta. Encontrará una lista de las abreviaturas usadas en el libro en la página 229.

Tercer paso

Este libro también incluye "Otros programas de verano", que comienza en la página 197. En este sección encontrará nombres e información sobre contactos para más de 600 programas de verano no descritos en la sección de "presentaciones de una página". Use la información de los contactos de esta sección para solicitar información adicional sobre los programas que expresaron a Peterson's interés en matricular participantes extranjeros.

Cuarto paso

Cuando termine de recopilar una lista de programas que hayan despertado su interés, use el "Formulario para solicitar información" para recibir información adicional o para solicitar la admisión para una futura sesión. Este formulario, a partir de la página 231, puede ser enviado por fax o correo a los contactos de los programas; consulte los números de fax y las direcciones en la sección de contactos de la presentación de una página o en la sección "Otros programas de verano" para asegurar la transmisión correcta del formulario. (¡Recuerde agregar el código telefónico internacional de su país antes del número de fax cuando llame desde el extranjero!) Puede fotocopiar el formulario y utilizarlo tantas veces como desee para ponerse en contacto con todos los programas que desee. Una vez que se ponga en contacto con los programas, le enviarán información adicional detallada sobre las actividades que ofrecen.

EXPLICACIÓN DE LAS PRESENTACIONES DE UNA PÁGINA

"Las presentaciones de una página" que comienzan en la página 169 ofrecen información detallada sobre los programas de verano ofrecidos en todo el mundo. Los directores de los programas, suministraron esta información a Thomson Peterson's durante la primavera yel verano de 2004 por medio de un cuestionario especial desarrollado por Thomson Peterson's.

LO QUE ENCONTRARÁ EN LAS PRESENTACIONES DE UNA PÁGINA

1. Tipo de programa:
   a. Programas académicos   b. Programas de idioma inglés   c. Campamentos   d. Programas de viajes
2. Nombre del patrocinador del programa
3. Localidad de verano *(si es diferente a la localidad en la información del contacto)*
   o Nombre del programa *(si es diferente al del patrocinador del programa)*
4. Logo o escudo del programa *(si lo hay)*
5. Información del contacto *(¡Recuerde agregar el código telefónico internacional de su país antes de marcar los números de teléfono o fax cuando se ponga en contacto con los programas!)*
6. Fotografía del programa
7. Descripción ampliada de los programas
8. Ubicación geográfica del programa, o una lista de los destinos en el caso de programas de viajes
9. La distancia al aeropuerto internacional y a la ciudad importante más cercanos

Iconos de los programas de verano

(También puede usar la "Leyenda de íconos gráficos" en la página 174 y en la parte interior de la cubierta posterior cuando lea las descripciones de una página.)

10. Temperatura durante el verano
11. Ubicación
12. Afiliación religiosa
13. Edad de los participantes
14. Matriculación: Número de niños/niñas
15. Número y porcentaje de participantes extranjeros
16. Países representados con mayor frecuencia
17. Nivel de idioma inglés requerido
18. Disponibilidad de cursos de inglés como segundo idioma (ESL) y costo
19. Información sobre alojamiento
20. Fechas de las sesiones
21. Número de miembros del personal por estudiantes
22. Plazo para presentar la solicitud
23. Excursiones fuera de las instalaciones
24. Cuotas estándar, cuotas adicionales, cantidad de dinero recomendada para gastos
25. Se dispone de evaluaciones realizadas por participantes extranjeros
26. Servicio para recoger a los estudiantes en el aeropuerto
27. Atención médica en las instalaciones

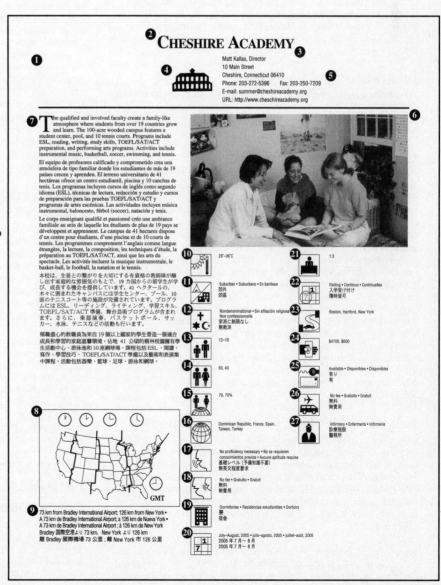

153

Guía familiar para programas de verano

El verano es una época maravillosa para que los estudiantes amplíen sus horizontes y desarrollen habilidades y talentos aprendidos durante el año escolar. Los programas en diversas partes del mundo reciben a estudiantes de todas las edades con todo tipo de intereses. Algunos participantes viven en edificios cómodos, bien supervisados, mientras estudian distintos temas, participan en actividades deportivas, artísticas, de trabajos manuales y excursiones. Otros participan en programas en reservas naturales y viajes, donde encuentran aventuras y la atracción al aire libre en diferentes localidades. Cualquiera que sea el programa que elijan los estudiantes, regresarán a su casa después de su experiencia veraniega con nuevas habilidades e intereses, nuevas amistades y recuerdos felices.

¿CUÁLES SON MIS OPCIONES?
Programas académicos

Los programas académicos de verano están organizados por escuelas secundarias privadas y de enseñanza superior. Los estudiantes viven en residencias estudiantiles y por lo general asisten a clases por la mañana, tienen deportes y actividades durante la tarde y estudian durante la noche. Los fines de semana viajan y tienen excursiones o participan en aventuras al aire libre. La mayoría de los participantes estudian una o dos materias; los estudiantes extranjeros generalmente estudian inglés como segundo idioma (ESL) y otra materia. Los programas académicos ofrecen una excelente oportunidad para que los estudiantes extranjeros mejoren sus conocimientos de expresión, de lectura y de redacción del idioma inglés. Se ofrece una amplia variedad de cursos en varios niveles—idioma y literatura, matemáticas, ciencias, computación, ciencias sociales e ingeniería, para nombrar sólo algunos.

Programas de idioma inglés

Programas que hacen énfasis en el mejoramiento de las habilidades orales y escritas de los estudiantes se ofrecen en escuelas de idiomas, colegios de secundaria privados, colegio universitarios y universidades.

Campamentos tradicionales

En los campamentos tradicionales, los estudiantes viven en un ambiente hermoso y seguro rodeados de bosques, lagos y montañas, lejos del ruido y del congestionamiento de la ciudad. Los acampantes participan en varios tipos de actividades deportivas, artísticas, realizan trabajos manuales y estudian la naturaleza. Los acampantes viven en carpas o cabañas pequeñas y pasan la mayor parte del día al aire libre. La experiencia del campamento de verano ofrece a los estudiantes la oportunidad de formar amistades a través de la convivencia y de las actividades compartidas. Los consejeros y otros profesionales supervisan de cerca todas las actividades y ayudan a crear un ambiente cálido, de tipo familiar. Algunos pasan años en el mismo campamento, primero como jóvenes acampantes, luego como acampantes veteranos y finalmente como consejeros. Mientras disfrutan de las maravillas del mundo natural, los acampantes desarrollan la confianza en sí mismos y habilidades de liderazgo. La mayoría de los campamentos no ofrecen enseñanza de inglés y muchos requieren que los acampantes tengan conocimientos básicos del idioma.

Programas de viajes y en reservas naturales

Los participantes de los programas de viajes pueden andar en bicicleta, caminar, esquiar o viajar en autobús mientras exploran cientos de kilómetros de terreno en todo el mundo. Puesto que los participantes deben ayudarse mutuamente a lo largo de los terrenos difíciles, la comunicación dentro del grupo es fundamental en estos programas; dada esta preocupación por la seguridad, se requieren conocimientos básicos del idioma inglés para la mayoría de estos programas.

Para quienes disfrutan de las aventuras, los programas en reservas naturales ofrecen la oportunidad de escalar montañas, navegar en balsa por aguas rápidas de ríos de gran belleza y cocinar alimentos en una fogata. Los alojamientos para los campistas que participan en viajes por reservas naturales varían desde tiendas de campaña colocadas en diferentes zonas todos los días hasta literas en embarcaciones en alta mar.

¿DÓNDE ESTÁN UBICADOS LOS PROGRAMAS? ¿CÓMO SON LAS INSTALACIONES?

Los programas académicos incluidos en esta guía están ubicados en internados, escuelas de enseñanza superior en América del Norte y Europa. La mayoría de los campamentos tradicionales están ubicados en los Estados Unidos y Canadá. Los programas de viajes y en reservas naturales ubicados en todo el mundo brindan a los estudiantes la oportunidad de explorar una amplia área geográfica. Los programas ubicados en hermosas y espaciosas zonas rurales ofrecen a los estudiantes de las ciudades la oportunidad de correr, jugar, recorrer y disfrutar del aire libre en el verano, mientras que los programas ubicados en las áreas metropolitanas ofrecen innumerables oportunidades para actividades culturales y educativas.

Las escuelas y universidades privadas ofrecen a los estudiantes excelentes instalaciones académicas y de recreación. Los estudiantes viven generalmente en residencias estudiantiles en habitaciones simples o dobles. En los campamentos, los participantes comparten a veces una carpa o cabaña con 5 ó 6 acampantes y un consejero.

¿CUÁNTO DURAN LOS PROGRAMAS? ¿QUIÉN MÁS SE MATRICULA?

Las sesiones de verano duran generalmente de cuatro a ocho semanas, comenzando a fines de junio y finalizando en agosto. También se ofrecen programas más cortos y más largos. Los estudiantes con vacaciones escolares limitadas pueden a veces incorporarse a un programa de verano más tarde. Las familias deben ponerse en contacto con los directores de los programas para obtener información sobre las fechas específicas y las opciones de matriculación.

Los programas varían en tamaño desde varios acampantes que comparten una carpa a varios cientos de estudiantes en un internado de verano. En todos los programas, las clases o actividades se llevan a cabo en grupos pequeños y supervisados de cerca. La mayoría de los programas matriculan estudiantes de muchas partes de los Estados Unidos y de algunos otros países. Al estar rodeados de jóvenes cuya lengua materna es el inglés, los estudiantes extranjeros tienen una oportunidad única de mejorar sus conocimientos de expresión oral del idioma inglés.

¿CÓMO ESTÁN ESTRUCTURADOS LOS PROGRAMAS?

Un día típico en el campamento

Los días están llenos de experiencias de aprendizaje, diversión y camaradería. Los estudiantes se levantan temprano para comenzar un día lleno de actividades. Después del desayuno y de la limpieza de la habitación o la carpa, siguen los períodos de actividades, almuerzo y más actividades. Los estudiantes de los programas académicos generalmente asisten a clases por la mañana y por la tarde participan en actividades deportivas, de arte y trabajos manuales, música o teatro o explorando puntos locales de interés. Hay tiempo libre antes de la cena y sala de estudios o más actividades antes de ir a dormir. Todas las actividades están supervisadas por adultos y estudiantes mayores.

Comidas

Las comidas se sirven en un comedor escolar o se incluyen en la mochila en caminatas por la montaña. Los alimentos son nutritivos, con muchas frutas frescas y verduras. Todos los programas ofrecen tres comidas diarias y bocadillos durante todo el día. Los estudiantes extranjeros a quienes les resulta difícil acostumbrarse a la "comida de campamento" a menudo traen sus bocadillos favoritos de casa. Algunos programas ofrecen comidas especiales para estudiantes que necesitan una dieta especial.

Ropa

La vestimenta en las escuelas de verano es informal. Pocos programas requieren uniforme. Muchas permiten que los acampantes vistan informalmente, generalmente jeans y camisetas. Durante el verano, puede refrescar por la noche, de modo que los participantes deberían traer suéteres o chaquetas livianas. Algunos programas aconsejan que los estudiantes traigan uno o más conjuntos formales para eventos especiales. Para los campamentos de deportes y los programas en reservas naturales y viajes podría necesitarse ropa y equipos especiales. Todos los programas ofrecerán una lista más detallada de lo que hay que traer.

Reglas y normas generales

Para que una escuela o campamento funcione sin problemas, es importante que todos los miembros de la comunidad veraniega cooperen y trabajen conjuntamente. Las reglas estrictas incluyen la prohibición de fumar, ingerir o poseer bebidas alcohólicas u otras sustancias ilegales, abandonar las instalaciones sin permiso y hacer trampa. El incumplimiento de las reglas es una falta grave que puede provocar la expulsión del programa.

Salud y seguridad

Todos los programas exigen que los participantes sean examinados por un médico y tengan la vacunación básica antes de llegar. Las escuelas y campamentos cuentan con instalaciones adecuadas, y personal médico y de enfermería para proporcionar atención médica. Siempre existen servicios médicos y hospitales disponibles. Los padres deben dar permiso para tratamiento médico de emergencia. Algunos programas ofrecen seguro médico, otros requieren que los estudiantes tengan sus propias pólizas.

Los programas son objeto de cuidadosa supervisión. Sin embargo, los estudiantes deben asumir responsabilidad por su propia seguridad al viajar y al retirarse del terreno o del área del campamento. Los padres deberían enseñar a sus hijos las reglas básicas de seguridad antes de partir hacia un programa de verano. Aunque las drogas y las bebidas alcohólicas están prohibidas en todos los programas, debe advertirle a su hijo/hija que algunos estudiantes podrían tener dichas sustancias en forma ilegal y que deben evitar tener contacto con estas personas.

¿CÓMO SOLICITO LA ADMISIÓN?

La admisión a los programas de verano generalmente no requiere pruebas o conocimientos especiales. El procedimiento de matriculación generalmente requiere información básica. Algunos programas especializados en arte y música podrían solicitar muestras del trabajo de un estudiante, los programas académicos podrían requerir certificados académicos y recomendaciones, y algunos programas exigen cierto nivel de conocimiento de inglés. La mayoría de los programas tienen una matriculación limitada, y muchos llenan el cupo a comienzos de la primavera. Es siempre aconsejable presentar la solicitud lo antes posible. Los programas generalmente requieren un depósito para asegurar el lugar y el pago completo será requerido antes del comienzo del programa.

¿CUÁNTO COSTARÁ? ¿CÓMO LLEGO ALLÁ?

El costo promedio de un programa oscila entre $2000 y $4000. Los honorarios básicos cubren las actividades, el alojamiento y las comidas. Puede haber honorarios adicionales para uniformes y alquiler de ropa de cama y toallas, el traslado desde y hacia el aeropuerto y otras actividades como equitación. Los padres pueden girar dinero directamente a una cuenta en los EE.UU. para el pago —asegúrese de preguntar al(a la) director(a) del programa la información específica si elige esta opción de pago. Los estudiantes también deben llevar una pequeña suma de dinero adicional para uso personal.

Los campamentos y las escuelas recibirán a estudiantes que lleguen del extranjero en el aeropuerto más cercano. En algunos casos se cobra una cuota por ese servicio. Algunos programas organizan los itinerarios de viaje para los participantes, mientras que otros requieren que los estudiantes hagan sus propios preparativos.

La elección de un programa de verano puede ser divertida, pero también debe recordar que es importante formular algunas preguntas importantes cuando decida en qué programa desea matricularse. Averigüe cuáles son los conocimientos del idioma inglés requeridos ¿es necesario tener un comando total del idioma, o los participantes pueden simplemente tener conocimientos mínimos? Explore las opciones de matriculación —a veces puede participar en un programa más tarde o partir antes si las fechas en su lugar de origen no concuerdan con las fechas del programa. Si, por ejemplo, está prohibido fumar, asegúrese de averiguarlo antes de emprender el viaje. Y solicite información acerca de las opciones de pago—si el programa permite que gire electrónicamente el dinero al banco con el que opera, asegúrese de enterarse de todos los detalles necesarios para realizar este tipo de transacción.

Deseamos que pase el mejor verano de su vida!

Diane Rapp es President de Diane Rapp Associates
Educational Consultants
85 River Road, Scarborough, New York 10510
U.S.A.

Programmes de perfectionnement internationaux—
COMMENT UTILISER CETTE SECTION

Cette partie du répertoire est divisé en cinq sections principales: les remarques préliminaires, les pages d'introduction aux programmes estivaux, un appendice de ces programmes, une liste des abréviations et des formulaires de demande de renseignements. Pour tirer plein avantage *Internats américains et canadiens, et Programmes de perfectionnement internationaux de Peterson's*, veuillez suivre les étapes cidessous.

Première étape

Avant de commencer à feuilleter le répertoire à la recherche du programme estival idéal, consultez la section « Guide familial des programmes estivaux » de Diane Rapp, commençant à la page 158. Cet article donne un bref aperçu des diverses options qui vous sont offertes—programmes académiques, et sauvages et touristiques, ainsi que les colonies—et fournit des renseignements indispensables sur la situation géographique, les installations, la durée, les modalités d'inscription et les frais des programmes. Vous y trouverez également une description d'une journée caractéristique à la colonie, des conseils concernant les vêtements à emporter et une idée des repas. Les règlements et la sécurité de la colonie y sont passés en revue, tout comme la procédure d'inscription et les modalités de transport. L'article traite enfin des questions importantes à poser sur tout programme envisagé; assurez-vous de noter ces questions en note avant de commencer la lecture des pages d'introduction puisque vous y trouverez la majorité des réponses.

Deuxième étape

Après avoir déterminé les questions pertinentes à la sélection du programme qui vous convient, vous pouvez passer à la lecture des pages d'introduction afin de restreindre le cadre de votre recherche. Consultez d'abord la partie « Explication des pages d'introduction » à la page suivante. Elle vous indique l'endroit sur la page où vous trouverez l'information nécessaire à votre prise de décision. Passez ensuite aux pages d'introduction commençant à la page 169. Cette section souligne les aspects importants de plus de 20 programmes, tirés des réponses au questionnaire de Thomson Peterson's, édition 2004. Les programmes sont divisés en sections différentes : les programmes académiques, les programmes des cours d'anglais, les colonies, les programmes touristiques et les programmes en régions sauvages/plein air. Les icônes de programmes, situées dans le coin extérieur supérieur de chaque page identifient le type de programme. (Consultez la page suivante pour plus d'information sur ces icônes de programmes.) Pour chaque programme, vous trouverez des renseignements relatifs à la situation géographique ainsi que les coordonnées, en plus d'une description détaillée fournie par le directeur du programme, une photographie des installations et des renseignements complets sur la façon d'inscrire les participants internationaux, la disponibilité des cours d'anglais comme langue étrangère, le niveau de compétence en anglais nécessaire pour l'inscription, les dates du programme, la date limite pour s'inscrire, le coût, l'hébergement, les règlements et d'autres renseignements. Pour faciliter la consultation des pages d'introduction, une « Légende des icônes graphiques » est fournie à la page 168 et à l'intérieur de la couverture. Une liste des abréviations utilisées dans le répertoire se trouve à la page 229.

Troisième étape

Ce livre contient également « D'autres programmes estivaux » commençant à la page 197. Vous y trouverez les noms et les coordonnés de plus de 600 programmes estivaux ne figurant pas dans la section des pages d'introduction. Servez-vous des coordonnés s'y trouvant pour demander des renseignements supplémentaires aux responsables des programmes ayant indiqué aux rédacteurs de *Peterson's* leur désir de recevoir des participants internationaux.

Quatrième étape

Une fois la liste des programmes vous intéressant complétée, servez-vous du « Formulaire de demande de renseignements » pour obtenir des renseignements supplémentaires ou pour effectuer une demande d'admission à une séance future. Ce formulaire, commençant à la page 231, peuvent être envoyés aux responsables par la poste ou par télécopie; servez-vous des numéros de télécopieurs et des adresses se trouvant dans la section des coordonnées des pages d'introduction ou dans l'appendice afin d'assurer qu'ils soient envoyés au bon endroit. (Prenez également soin d'ajouter l'indicatif de ce pays lorsque vous composez des numéros de télécopieur à l'extérieur du pays !) N'hésitez pas à photocopier le formulaire afin de vous en servir pour autant de programmes que vous désirez. Une fois en communication avec les responsables d'un programme, ces derniers se chargent de vous faire parvenir tous les détails.

EXPLICATION DES PRÉSENTATIONS D'UNE PAGE

« Les pages d'introduction », commençant à la page 169, fournissent des informations détaillées sur les programmes estivaux offerts partout dans le monde. Ces renseignements ont été transmis aux rédacteurs de Thomson Peterson's au cours du printemps et de l'été 2004 par les directeurs des programmes ayant pris soin de répondre au questionnaire spécialement conçu par le groupe Thomson Peterson's.

CE QUE VOUS TROUVEREZ DANS LES PAGES D'INTRODUCTION

1. Types de programmes :
   a. Programmes académiques   b. Programmes des cours d'anglais   c. Colonies
   d. Programmes touristiques
2. Le nom du parrain du programme
3. L'adresse pendant l'été (si elle est différente des coordonnées) OU le nom du programme (s'il est différent du nom du parrain)
4. Le logo ou l'emblème du programme (s'ils sont disponibles)
5. Les coordonnées (Souvenez-vous d'inscrire l'indicatif du pays avant les numéros de téléphone et de télécopieur lorsque vous communiquez avec les responsables des programmes !)
6. Une photographie
7. Une description détaillée des activités du programme
8. La situation géographique du programme ou, pour les programmes touristiques, une liste des destinations
9. La distance de l'aéroport international et de la ville importante les plus proches

Icônes des programmes estivaux

(Vous pouvez également vous servir de la « Légende des icônes graphiques » se trouvant à la page 174 et à l'intérieur de la couverture arrière lorsque vous lisez les pages d'introduction.)

10. Écarts de température en été
11. Cadre
12. Affiliation religieuse
13. Âge des participants
14. Inscription par séance : nombre de garçons, nombre de filles
15. Nombre et pourcentage des participants internationaux
16. Pays les plus représentés
17. Degré d'aptitude requis en langue anglaise
18. Disponibilité des cours d'anglais ESL et coût
19. Informations sur l'hébergement
20. Calendrier des séances
21. Rapport personnel/participants
22. Dates limites d'inscription
23. Lieux visités lors des excursions
24. Tarif, frais supplémentaires, argent de poche
25. Évaluations d'anciens participants disponibles
26. Transport depuis l'aéroport
27. Soins médicaux sur place

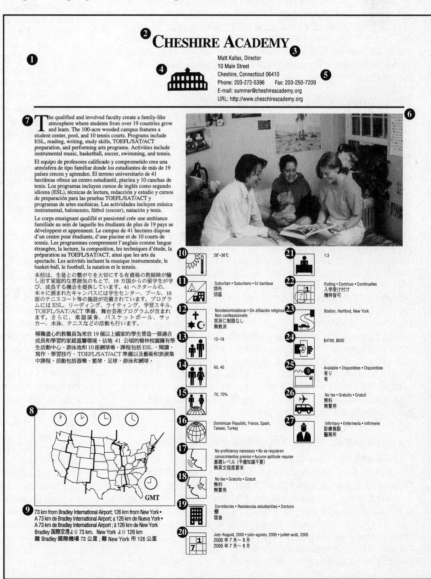

GUIDE FAMILIAL DES PROGRAMMES ESTIVAUX

L'été est la saison idéale pour permettre aux jeunes d'élargir leurs horizons et d'améliorer les techniques et les compétences acquises durant l'année scolaire. Des programmes situés partout à travers le monde sont disponibles aux jeunes de tous les âges et ayant les intérêts les plus divers. Certains participants choisissent de vivre dans des logements confortables et bien surveillés afin d'approfondir leurs connaissances de diverses matières : ils pratiquent certains sports, approfondissent leurs connaissances artistiques, apprennent des travaux manuels et visitent des attractions touristiques. D'autres choisissent des programmes en régions sauvages ou des programmes touristiques offrant des aventures et des amusements en plein air dans plusieurs endroits différents. Quel que soit le programme choisi, les jeunes participants reviennent de cette expérience estivale unique avec de nouvelles aptitudes, de nouveaux intérêts, de nouveaux amis et de bons souvenirs.

QUELLES SONT MES OPTIONS?
Programmes académiques

Les programmes académiques estivaux sont offerts par les lycées privés et les universités. Les jeunes sont logés dans des dortoirs et suivent généralement des cours le matin, pratiquent des sports et autres activités l'après-midi et étudient le soir. Les week-ends sont passés à voyager et à visiter les attractions touristiques ou à participer aux activités en plein air. La majorité des participants étudient une ou deux matières ; les jeunes provenant d'autres pays choisissent généralement l'anglais comme langue étrangère (ESL) et une autre matière. Les programmes académiques offrent une excellente occasion aux jeunes d'outre-mer d'améliorer leur anglais, que ce soit au niveau de la conversation, de la lecture ou de l'écriture. Une vaste sélection de cours est disponible pour les jeunes de tous les niveaux, notamment, les langues et la littérature, les mathématiques, les sciences, l'informatique, les sciences sociales et l'ingénierie.

Programmes des cours d'anglais

Les programmes visant à améliorer l'anglais écrit et parlé sont offerts par des écoles de langues, des écoles privées d'enseignement général, des établissements d'enseignement supérieur et des universités.

Colonies traditionnelles

Dans les colonies traditionnelles estivales, les jeunes vivent dans un milieu paisible et sécuritaire, entouré de bois, lacs et montagnes, loin du bruit et du surpeuplement des villes. Ils pratiquent divers sports, apprennent des techniques d'artisanat et participent à des études sur la nature. Les campeurs sont logés dans des tentes ou des cabanes et passent le gros de la journée à l'extérieur. Une expérience de camping estival offre aux jeunes une occasion de se faire de bons amis en vivant ensemble et en prenant part aux mêmes activités. Des moniteurs et autres professionels surveillent attentivement les activités et aident à créer une atmosphère chaleureuse et familiale. Il arrive souvent qu'un jeune passe plusieurs années dans une même colonie, d'abord en tant que jeune campeur, puis en tant que campeur aîné et, enfin, en tant que moniteur. Tout en apprenant à apprécier les mystères de la nature, les campeurs développent des techniques de direction et la confiance en soi. La majorité des colonies n'offre pas les cours d'anglais et nombre d'entre eux exigent des campeurs une connaissance de base de l'anglais.

Programmes touristiques et en régions sauvages

Les participants aux programmes touristiques, quant à eux, peuvent se retrouver à bicyclette, à faire de l'escalade, à skier ou à voyager par car pour découvrir des centaines de kilomètres de terres inconnues à travers le monde. Comme les participants doivent s'entraider dans les passages difficiles, la communication dans groupe est un aspect fondamental de ce genre de programme. La sécurité des participants étant en jeu, la majorité des programmes exige une connaissance de base de l'anglais.

Pour ceux qui aiment l'aventure, les programmes en régions sauvages offrent l'occasion d'escalader des montagnes, de descendre de magnifiques rivières en raft et de préparer des repas au-dessus d'un feu de camp. Lors des excursions en régions sauvages, les campeurs peuvent dormir aussi bien sous des tentes dressées dans différentes régions chaque jour, que sur des couchettes dans un bateau au milieu des mers.

OÙ SONT SITUÉS LES PROGRAMMES? COMMENT SONT LES INSTALLATIONS?

Les programmes académiques figurant dans ce guide sont offerts par les pensionnats et les universités de l'Amérique du Nord et de l'Europe. La majorité des colonies et traditionnelles sont situées aux États-Unis d'Amérique et au Canada. Les programmes touristiques et en régions sauvages sont situés partout à travers le monde et constituent une bonne occasion pour les jeunes d'explorer de grandes étendues géographiques. Les programmes situés dans les vastes et magnifiques milieux ruraux permettent aux jeunes citadins de courir, de jouer, de faire des randonnées et de profiter de l'été en plein air, alors que les programmes situés en milieux urbains offrent une infinité d'activités culturelles et éducatives.

Les institutions scolaires privées et les universités disposent d'excellentes installations académiques et récréatives à l'intention des jeunes qui sont généralement logés dans des dortoirs comprenant des chambres simples ou doubles. Dans les colonies, les participants partagent une tente ou une cabane avec 5 ou 6 autres campeurs et un moniteur.

QUELLE EST LA DURÉE DES PROGRAMMES? QUI S'Y INSCRIT?

Les séances d'été durent généralement de quatre à huit semaines, commençant à la fin juin et finissant au mois d'août. Des programmes plus longs et plus courts sont disponibles et les jeunes dont les vacances scolaires ne coïncident pas tout à fait avec ces dates peuvent se joindre à certains programmes plus tard au cours de l'été. Les familles intéressées peuvent communiquer avec les directeurs des programmes pour obtenir les dates spécifiques et les renseignements relatifs aux options d'inscription.

La taille des programmes varie de quelques campeurs partageant une tente à plusieurs centaines de jeunes en pensionnats d'été. Ils comprennent tous des cours et des activités offerts à des groupes de petite taille étroitement surveillés. La majorité de ces programmes reçoit les jeunes de divers endroits des États-Unis d'Amérique et de plusieurs autres pays. Entourés par des gens de langue maternelle anglaise, les jeunes ressortissants d'autres pays disposent d'une occasion unique d'amélieorer leurs aptitudes à parler l'anglais.

COMMENT LES PROGRAMMES SONT-ILS STRUCTURES?

Une journée caractéristique en colonie

Les journées sont passées à apprendre, à se détendre et à se faire des amis. Les jeunes se lèvent tôt pour entreprendre une journée chargée d'activités. Après le petit déjeuner et le nettoyage de la chambre ou de la tente s'amorce la première période d'activité, suivie du déjeuner et d'une seconde période d'activité. Les jeunes qui participent aux programmes académiques sont généralement en salle de classe le matin et prennent part, l'après-midi, aux activités sportives, artisanales, musicales ou théâtrales, ou ils explorent les sites d'intérêt locaux. Une période d'activité libre est prévue avant le dîner et la soirée est passée à étudier ou à participer à d'autres activités jusqu'au coucher. Toutes les activités sont dirigées par des adultes ou des participants plus âgés.

La nourriture

Les repas peuvent être servis dans la salle à manger de l'institution scolaire ou peuvent avoir été apportés dans un sac à dos lors d'une randonnée en montagne. On sert une nourriture saine, comportant fruits et légumes frais. Tous les programmes comprennent trois repas par jour, en plus des collations durant la journée. Les jeunes d'autres pays qui éprouvent de la difficulté à s'accoutumer à la « nourriture de colonie » peuvent généralement apporter leurs propres collations de la maison. Certains programmes offrent des repas spéciaux aux jeunes suivant une diète particulière.

La tenue vestimentaire

En été, la tenue vestimentaire est informelle dans les institutions scolaires. Rares sont les programmes exigeant le port de l'uniforme et nombre d'entre eux permettent aux campeurs de porter des vêtements sports—généralement blue-jeans et t-shirts. Comme les soirées d'été peuvent être fraîches, les participants devraient apporter des tricots et des vestes légères. Certains programmes recommandent aux jeunes d'apporter quelques tenues de soirée pour les occasions particulières. Des vêtements et des équipements spéciaux sont requis pour certains colonies sportives et programmes touristiques et en régions sauvages. Une liste détaillée des articles à apporter est fournie par tous les programmes.

Les règlements et les principes

Afin que tout se déroule sans incident dans les institutions scolaires et les colonies, il est important que tous les membres de la communauté estivale coopèrent et s'entraident. Les règlements à respecter comprennent la défense de fumer, de consommer ou d'être en possession de boissons alcoolisées et autres produits défendus par la loi, de quitter les lieux sans permission et de tricher. Désobéir à ces règlements est très grave et peut mener à l'expulsion du programme.

La santé et la sécurité

Tous les programmes exigent que les participants subissent un examen médical et reçoivent les immunisations de base avant leur arrivée. Les institutions scolaires et les colonies disposent de centres de santé avec infirmier ou infirmière qualifiés et autre personnel médical et les services hospitaliers et de médecins sont toujours disponibles. Les parents doivent autoriser les soins médicaux d'urgence. Certains programmes fournissent l'assurance médicale ; d'autres exigent que les jeunes souscrivent à leurs propres polices d'assurance.

Les programmes sont étroitement surveillés. Les jeunes sont cependant responsables de leur propre sécurité lorsqu'ils voyagent et lorsqu'ils quittent le campus ou la colonie. Les parents doivent apprendre à leurs enfants les règles de sécurité de base avant de les envoyer dans les programmes estivaux. Bien que les drogues et les boissons alcoolisées soient interdites dans tous les programmes, votre enfant doit être averti de la possibilité que certains jeunes en possèdent illégalement et qu'ils doivent éviter ces derniers.

COMMENT S'INSCRIRE?

L'admission aux programmes estivaux ne requiert généralement aucun essais ou aptitudes particuliers, les modalités d'inscription se limitant le plus souvent à fournir des informations de base. Certains programmes spécialisés en art ou en musique demandent parfois des échantillons du travail du jeune; les programmes académiques peuvent demander des copies du dossier académique et des lettres de recommandations, et certains autres programmes exigent un certain niveau de compétence en anglais. La majorité d'entre eux acceptent un nombre limité d'inscriptions et certains sont complets tôt au printemps. Il est donc conseillé de s'inscrire dès que possible. Un dépôt est généralement requis pour réserver une place et le paiement complet doit être versé avant le début du programme.

QUEL EST LE COÛT?
COMMENT S'Y RENDRE?

Le coût moyen des programmes se situe entre 2000 et 4000 dollars américains. Les frais de base couvrent les activités, le logement et les repas. Des frais supplémentaires peuvent être exigés pour la location d'un uniforme et du linge de maison, le transport aller-retour de l'aéroport et d'autres activités telles que les randonnées à cheval. Les parents peuvent télégraphier les sommes nécessaires au paiement directement à un compte bancaire américain—s'assurer, dans ce cas, de demander tous les détails au directeur du programme. Les jeunes devraient également disposer d'une petite somme d'argent pour leur usage personnel.

Les responsables des colonies et des institutions scolaires rencontrent les jeunes arrivant d'outre-mer à l'aéroport le plus près; certains programmes exigent cependant des frais pour ce service. L'itinéraire de voyage des jeunes est parfois organisé pour ces derniers, alors qu'en d'autres occasions, on exige qu'ils s'organisent eux-mêmes.

Il peut s'avérer très amusant de sélectionner un programmestival mais assurez-vous de poser les questions importantes lorsque vous décidez du programme dans lequel vous voulez vous inscrire. Déterminez le niveau de maîtrise de l'anglais qui est exigé : les participants doivent-ils parler couramment ou une connaissance de base est-elle suffisante? Considérez toutes les options d'inscription : il est parfois possible de se joindre à un programme plus tard ou de quitter en avance si votre calendrier ne coïncide pas avec celui du programme. Informez-vous des règlements du programme : s'il est défendu de fumer, par exemple, il est bon de le savoir avant de partir. Et demandez quelles sont les modalités de paiement : si le programme permet de transférer électroniquement des fonds à sa banque, obtenez les détails nécessaires pour ce genre de transaction.

Et la soussignée vous souhaite le meilleur été de votre vie !

Diane Rapp est Présidente de Diane Rapp Associates,
Consultants en éducation,
85 River Road, Scarborough, New York 10510
U.S.A.

世界各地での強化プログラム—
このセクションの使い方

このセクションは導入的アドバイス、夏期プログラムの「1 ページ案内」、夏期プログラム付録、略語一覧、プログラム情報請求用紙の 5 つの主なパートに分かれています。米国 カナダの全寮制学校および世界各地での強化プログラムに掲載されている情報を最大限に活用するためには、以下に概説するステップに従ってください。

ステップ1

本書を開いて最適の夏期プログラムを探し始める前に、Diane Rapp 著「夏期プログラムに関するご家族へのご案内」(ページ162)をお読みください。この欄は学科プログラム、野外体験・旅行プログラム、各種オプションを概説し、プログラムの所在地、施設、期間、参加受付、費用、ならびにキャンプでの典型的な 1 日の描写、またどんな服を用意してくるか、食事はどんなものが出されるかなど貴重な情報を提供するものです。キャンプでの規則と安全にも触れ、参加申込手続きや交通手段もわかります。この欄ではまた、皆さんが参加したいプログラムで考えられそうな重要な質問もアドバイスしています。これらの質問をまず書き取ってから、「1 ページ案内」を読み始めてください。質問に対する答えのほとんどはそこで得られると思います。

ステップ 2

プログラムが自分に適しているかどうかの質問が用意できたら、「1 ページ案内」を使って更に的を絞ってください。まず、次ページの「1 ページ案内について」をご覧ください。各ページのどこに必要な情報が掲載されているかが分かります。それから 169 ページ以降にある「1 ページ案内」を開いてください。このセクションでは、トムソンピーターソンの 2004 年版アンケートに回答した 20 以上のプログラムの説明に重点が置かれています。全プログラムは学科プログラム、英語プログラム、キャンプ、旅行プログラム、野生探検／野外プログラムといった様々なセクションに分かれています。各ページの上端隅の大きなアイコンが各プログラムの種類を表しています。(大きなアイコンの詳しい説明は次ページをご覧ください。)各プログラムにつき、所在地、連絡先、プログラム・ディレクターによる詳しい説明、施設の写真、海外からの参加者受付についての詳しい情報 外国人向英語 (ESL)コースの有無、参加に必要な英会話力、プログラムの日程と参加申込締切日、費用、宿泊施設、規則、その他いろいろな情報が掲載されています。「1 ページ案内」を読むための手助けとして「グラフィック・アイコンの説明」が表表紙内側と168 ページに掲載され、本書で使用される略語の一覧は 229 ページにあります。

ステップ3

本書にはまた、197 ページから始まる「その他の夏期プログラム」もあります。このセクションには、「1 ページ案内」には含まれない 600 以上の夏期プログラムの名称と連絡先が掲載されています。これらのプログラムは海外からの学生受付についてピーターソンに関心を伝えたものばかりなので、詳しい情報については本書に掲示されているプログラム連絡先までお問い合わせください。

ステップ4

興味あるプログラムをすべて書き出した後、「プログラム情報請求用紙」に記入して更に情報を請求するか、あるいはこれから開始するセッションへの参加を申請してください。231 ページ以降にある用紙はプログラム連絡先まで FAX または郵便にて送付してください。「1 ページ案内」または「その他の夏期プログラム」にある連絡先、FAX 番号、住所を使って正確に申込書を送ってください。(国外の FAX 番号にダイヤルする時は、番号の前に自国の国際電話コードをダイヤルする事をお忘れなく!)申込用紙は自由にコピーして、希望のプログラムとの連絡にご使用ください。連絡を受け次第、各プログラムから内容についての更に詳しい情報が送られます。

「1ページ案内」について

169ページから始まる「1ページ案内」は世界各国の夏期プログラムを広く情報を提供します。この情報はトムソンピーターソンによって作られたアンケートに回答したプログラムディレクターによって、2004年春と夏にトムソンピーターソンに提供されました。

1ページ案内で何がわかるか

1. プログラム
   a.学科　　　　b.英語プログラム　　　　c.キャンプ場　　　　d.旅行プログラム
2. プログラム・スポンサー名
3. 夏期プログラム所在地(問い合わせ情報と異なる場合)もしくはプログラム名(プログラム・スポンサーと異なる場合)
4. プログラムロゴもしくは記号(ある場合)
5. 問い合わせ先(プログラム問い合わせの場合、電話番号やファックス番号の前に、自国の国番号を加えることをお忘れなく!)
6. プログラムの写真
7. プログラムについての詳しい説明
8. プログラムの所在地、または旅行プログラムの場合は旅行先
9. 最寄りの国際空港と大都市からの距離

夏期プログラムアイコン

(1ページ案内を読む際、174ページと裏表紙内側にあるグラフィック・アイコンの説明もお使いになれます。)

10. 夏の最高・最低気温
11. 立地
12. 所属宗教団体
13. 参加者の年齢構成
14. 参加男子・女子数
15. 海外からの参加者数、パーセント
16. 参加者の多い国々
17. プログラムに参加するために必要な英会話力
18. 外国人向英語(ESL)コースの有無と費用
19. 宿泊施設
20. クラスの日程
21. スタッフ数と参加者数の比率
22. 参加申込締切日
23. 敷地外の旅行先
24. 基本費用、追加費用、小遣金額
25. 過去の海外参加者の意見
26. 空港への送迎の有無
27. 敷地内での医療施設

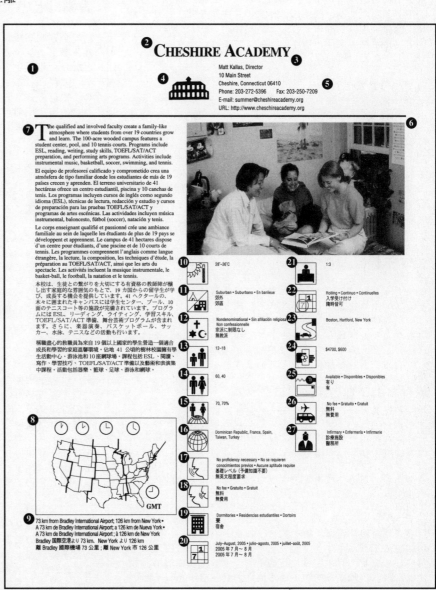

161

夏期プログラムに関するご家族へのご案内

夏は生徒にとって、日頃学校で学んだ技術や才能をもっと伸ばし視野を広めることのできる、すばらしい時です。プログラムは世界各地で行われ、生徒の全ての年齢や興味に合わせてあります。各種の教科を学び、スポーツや芸術、手工芸、観光に参加しながら、快適でよく管理された宿舎で生活する人もいるでしょう。他に、様々な地域ですばらしい野外の冒険や興奮を味わえる野外体験・旅行プログラムに参加する人もいるでしょう。どのプログラムを選ぼうと、生徒は、夏の体験から、新しい能力、興味、友達、幸せな思い出を得て、家庭に戻って行くことでしょう。

どれを選ぶか？
学科プログラム
夏期学科プログラムは私立の中学・高校、カレッジ、大学で運営されます。生徒は寮で生活し、一般に午前中は授業に出席し、午後はスポーツやその他の活動をし、夜はホールで自習します。週末は旅行や観光、野外冒険などに参加して過ごします。ほとんどの参加者は、1〜2科目を学習します。海外からの生徒はESL（外国人向英語）コースともう1科目を学習します。学科プログラムは、海外からの生徒が英語の会話、読解力、作文力スキルを向上させる絶好の機会です。各種のレベルで広範囲のコースが提供されます。言語学・文学、数学、科学、コンピューター、社会学、工学などはほんの一例です。

英語プログラム
学生の作文力と会話力の向上に重点を置いたプログラムが、語学学校、私立高等学校、短大、大学より提供されています。

伝統的キャンプ
伝統的キャンプでは、生徒は、都市の騒音や混雑から遠くはなれた森や湖、山に囲まれた美しく安全な環境で生活します。生徒は多種のスポーツ、芸術、手工芸、野外体験に参加します。キャンプ参加者はテントや小さなキャビンで生活し、1日のほとんどを野外で過ごします。生活や活動を共にすることにより、夏期キャンプの経験は親友を作るよい機会となるでしょう。キャンプ指導員や他のプロの指導員が活動を注意深く監督し、暖かく家庭的な雰囲気作りを手助けします。初めは年少キャンプ参加者として、次に年長キャンプ参加者として、最後には指導員として同じキャンプで長年を過ごしている人もいます。キャンプ参加者は自然界の不思議にひたり、自信とリーダーシップ術を向上させます。ほとんどのキャンプでは英語学習はしません。そして、多くのキャンプでは参加者が基礎的な英語力を持っていることを参加条件としています。

旅行および野生探検プログラム
旅行プログラム参加者は、サイクリング、ハイキング、スキーをしたり、何百キロにも広がる世界中の地域をバスで旅行します。参加者はたびたびお互いに荒野など過酷な環境で助けあわなければならないので、これらのプログラムではグループ内でのコミュニケーションは必須となります。安全確保のため、ほとんどのプログラムでは基礎的英語力が要求されます。

冒険を望む参加者は、野生探検プログラムで登山、美しい川の急流下り、キャンプ・ファイアーを使っての料理などが楽しめます。野生探検旅行のキャンプ参加者の宿泊施設には、毎日移動するテントから海洋の真っ直中を行く船の寝台まで色々あります。また旅行プログラムでは参加者は、世界中の地域で何百マイルもの距離を自転車、ハイキング、スキー、長距離バスなどで移動します。このプログラムでは、お互いに助け合いながら険しい地形を乗り越えて行くため、グループ内でのコミュニケーションが基本的に重要になります。そのため安全性の面でも、ほとんどのプログラムにおいて基礎的な英語力が必要になります。

どこでおこなわれるか？
設備はどのようなものか？
このガイドブックにある学科プログラムは北米とヨーロッパの全寮制高校、カレッジ、大学で行われます。旅行・野外体験プログラムは、生徒に地理的視野を広めるよい機会となり、世界中で行われます。美しく、ゆったりとしたいなかで行われるプログラムは、都会の生徒が、遊んだり、ハイキングしたり、夏の野外生活が楽しめるようになっており、また反対に、都市で行われるプログラムは文化と教育の機会を果てしなく与えるものです。

私立学校や大学は、生徒が使える優れた学習・レクリエーション用施設を提供します。生徒は普通、寮の1人部屋または2人部屋で暮らします。キャンプでは、参加者は、1つのテントまたはキャビンに参加者5〜6人と指導員1人が共に暮らすことでしょう。

プログラムの期間は？他に誰が参加するか？
夏期セッションは普通、6月下旬から8月までの4〜6週間続きます。これよりも長いプログラムや短いプログラムもあります。学校の休みが短い生徒は、時に夏の後半になってからプログラムに参加できる場合もありますので、生徒の家族は、具体的な日程や参加のしかたについてのオプションがあるか、プログラムのディレクターにお問い合わせください。

プログラムは数人のキャンプ参加者が1つのテントで暮らすだけの小規模なものから、数百人もの生徒が夏期全寮制学校で暮らすものまで、さまざまな規模のものがあります。どのプログラムも、授業やその他の活動を、数人数のよく監督の行き届いたグループで行います。大半のプログラムでは、アメリカの様々な地域出身の生徒と外国からの生徒を参加させています。海外からの生徒は、英語を母国語とする生徒に囲まれて、英語の会話能力を向上させるまたとない機会を得ます。

プログラムの構成は？
キャンプでの典型的な1日
毎日学習、娯楽、友達との交流に満ちています。生徒は朝早く起きて、活動いっぱいの1日を始めます。朝食と、部屋またはテントの掃除に続いて各種活動の時間、昼食、さ

らに多くの活動が続きます。学科プログラムの生徒は普通、午前に授業を受け、午後はスポーツや美術、手工芸、音楽、または演劇に参加し、あるいは地元付近を探索します。夕食前には自由時間があり、その後、就寝までホールで自習するか他の活動を行います。全ての活動は成人または年長生徒の監督下で行われます。

食事
食事は、学校の食堂で食べるか、山のハイキングの際はリュックサックに入れて行きます。食事は栄養豊富で、新鮮な果物や野菜がたっぷりあります。全てのプログラムでは、1日3回の食事と、1日中おやつが出されます。「キャンプの食事」に慣れない海外からの生徒は、故国から好きなおやつを持ってくることがよくあります。プログラムによっては、特別食を必要とする生徒にそれを提供するところもあります。

服装
夏期学校の服装はカジュアルです。制服を義務づけるプログラムはわずかで、多くのプログラムでは、普通、ジーンズとTシャツといったカジュアルウェアです。ただし、夏の夜は涼しい場合があるので、参加者はセーターか軽い上着を必ず持って行きましょう。プログラムによっては、特別な行事のために、フォーマルな服を1～2着、持ってくるよう勧めているところもあります。スポーツ・キャンプや野外学習・旅行プログラムでは、特別な服装や道具が必要な場合があります。全てのプログラムは、持ってくるべきものの詳細なリストを配布します。

規則・方針
学校またはキャンプを円滑に運営するためには、夏期学校またはキャンプの構成員全員が協力し、力を合わせることが大切です。厳しい規則の中には、禁煙、アルコール飲料やその他の不法薬物の使用や所持の禁止、許可なく敷地から出ることの禁止、カンニングやその他の不正の禁止が含まれます。こうした規則違反は深刻に受け止められ、プログラムから追放されてることもあります。

健康と安全
全てのプログラムで、参加者は、現地到着前に医師の健康診断と基本的な予防接種を受けていることが義務づけられています。学校やキャンプでは、訓練を受けた看護婦やその他の医療従事者を配置した保健室などを設置するほか、医師や病院の医療が常に受けられる状態にあります。親は、子供が救急医療を受ける許可を事前に出しておかねばなりません。また、独自の医療保険を提供するプログラムもありますが、そうでないものは、生徒が自分の加入している保険の保険証を持参することを義務づけています。

プログラムは注意深い監督を受けていますが、旅行中やその他でキャンパスやキャンプの場所を離れた場合、生徒は自分自身の安全には責任をとらなければなりません。親は、子供が夏期プログラムに出発する前に、安全の基本ルールを教えておくべきです。全てのプログラムでその期間中、麻薬やアルコール飲料が禁じられていますが、親は、生徒の中にはそれらを不法に所持している者もいるかもしれないので、そうした者と親しくならないように警告しておく必要があります。

申込方法は？
夏期プログラムへの参加は普通、特別なテストや能力を要求しておらず、申込手続きでは普通、単に基本的情報を求めているだけです。ただし、専門的な美術や音楽のプログ

ラムでは、生徒の過去の作品の見本提出を求めたり、学科プログラムでは成績表や推薦状を求めるものがあるほか、特定の水準の英語力を要求するプログラムもあります。大半のプログラムには定員があり、多くのプログラムが春に満員になりますので、なるべく早く申し込んだ方がよいでしょう。プログラムは普通、申込を保証するために保証金を求め、残額はプログラム開始前に支払うよう義務づけられています。

費用は？ 交通手段は？
プログラムの平均参加費用は2000ドル～4000ドルです。基本料金には各種活動、宿泊、食事の費用が含まれます。制服、ベッドシーツのレンタル料、空港と学校・キャンプ間の交通費、その他、乗馬などの活動に追加料金をとられることがあります。親が、料金を米国の銀行口座へ直接送金することも可能ですが、この支払い手段を選ぶ場合は、必ずプログラムのディレクターに具体的な手続等を尋ねてください。また生徒は、小額の小遣いを持っていくとよいでしょう。

キャンプや学校では、海外から参加する生徒には最寄りの空港に出迎えの人を出してくれます。プログラムによっては、この送迎サービスを有料としているところもあります。まvた参加者の旅行を手配してくれるプログラムもあれば、自分で手配することを要求しているプログラムもあります。

夏期プログラムを選ぶのは楽しみですが、どのプログラムに申し込むかを決める時には、いくつかの重要な質問を忘れずにしてください。プログラムが要求する英語力はどの程度か？つまり英語の総合力が必要か、または参加者は最低限の英語力があればよいのか？また、参加期間に融通がきくのか？つまり、自国での予定がプログラムの日程とかち合う場合、プログラムに途中から参加したり、早く抜けてもよい場合があります。またプログラムのルールについても、質問をしてください。たとえば禁煙jkなら、参加する前にそれを知っておいてください。そして、費用の支払い方法についても質問をしてください。プログラムが銀行への電信送金を許している場合、この種の取り引きに必要な詳細を全て確実に知っておいてください。

それでは、最高の夏になることを祈っております。

Diane Rapp は、教育コンサルタント会社である
Diane Rapp Associates
85 River Road, Scarborough, New York 10510 U.S.A. の
社長です。

國際強化項目—
如何使用本章

本指南分為五大部分：序言、夏令營單頁介紹、夏令營附錄、縮略語一覽表以及夏令營資料索取表格。為能迅速有效地使用 *彼得森美國與加拿大寄宿學校及國際強化項目*，請遵循下列步驟。

第一步

在查找本書中最適合您的夏令營之前，請先閱讀第166頁由Diane Rapp撰寫的〝夏令營家庭指導〞一文。這篇文章概述所有的夏令營選擇（學術課程、野外與旅遊活動），並提供有關夏令營地點、設施、日期、註冊、學費以及研習營的一天生活、帶甚麼衣服、膳食等寶貴資訊。文中也討論到夏令營的規則和安全、申請手續以及交通安排等事項。這篇文章還建議您在考慮選擇任何夏令營時該提出哪些重要的問題；切記在使用夏令營單頁介紹前先將這些問題寫下來—大部分問題的答案都可在單頁說明內找到。

第二步

一旦您知道要問哪些問題來判斷哪個夏令營適合您的需要，您可以開始使用夏令營單頁介紹來進行挑選。首先請參閱下一頁的〝夏令營單頁介紹解釋〞，它會告訴您在每一頁的哪個部分可以找到您需要的資訊，然後翻到從第169頁開始的夏令營單頁介紹。完成2004年兒童和青少年夏令營國際指南問卷調查的20多個暑期課程活動均在此部分列出。夏令營分為幾個不同的類別：學術、英語學習、研習營、旅遊以及野外/戶外活動。每一頁上端角落的圖像標識是說明夏令營的種類。（請參看下一頁的圖像標識說明。）每一頁的夏令營介紹均列有上課地點、聯絡資訊、由夏令營指導主任撰寫的課程說明、學校設施的圖片、以及有關國際學生入學的詳細資訊、是否提供英語為第二語言的課程、英文程度要求、課程日期、申請截止日期、學費、住宿、規定等等。第168頁彼得森和背面封面內的〝圖像標識說明〞能協助您使用夏令營單頁介紹。本書第229頁也列有縮略語一覽表。

第三步

本指南第197頁開始的〝其他夏令營活動附錄〞提供未列入夏令營單頁介紹部份的其他600多項夏令營的名稱和聯絡資訊。您可使用此部分的聯絡訊息索取詳細資料。

第四步

在您列出所有您有興趣的夏令營後，您可以使用〝資料索取表格〞取得詳細資料或申請參加下一期課程。這些表格從第231頁開始，您可以傳真或郵寄的方式聯絡各夏令營；為確保表格傳送到正確的地址，請使用列在夏令營單頁介紹聯絡資訊部份內或者附錄內的傳真號碼和郵寄地址。（記得在撥外國號碼時，要在傳真號碼前加上您國家的對外國際碼！）您可以影印這些表格，聯絡所有您有興趣的暑期學校。暑期學校收到您的表格後，會寄給您有關它們暑期課程的詳細資料。

夏令營單頁介紹解釋

自第169頁開始的夏令營單頁介紹，旨在提供有關世界各地夏令營的詳細資料。這些資料是由每個夏令營的指導主任藉由填寫彼得森設計的特別問卷調查，於2004年的春季和夏季期間提供給彼得森的。

夏令營單頁介紹內有那些內容

1. 夏令營種類：
   a. 學術課程　　b. 英語學習課程　c. 研習營　　d. 旅遊活動
2. 夏令營贊助人的姓名
3. 夏令營地點（如與聯絡訊息不同）或夏令營名稱（如與夏令營贊助人不同）
4. 夏令營標誌或飾章（如有的話）
5. 聯絡資料（記得以電話和傳真聯絡校方時，要加上您國家打至國外的國際碼。）
6. 夏令營照片
7. 夏令營內容介紹
8. 夏令營的授課地點，或如為旅遊活動，則為出發地點
9. 離最近的國際機場和大城市的距離

夏令營標識說明

（你在閱讀夏令營單頁介紹時也可使用第174頁和背頁內面的"圖像標識說明"）

10. 夏季氣溫範圍
11. 環境
12. 宗教派別
13. 學員年齡
14. 註冊：男生人數，女生人數
15. 國際學員的人數和比例
16. 學生最常來自的國家
17. 要求的英文程度
18. 有無 ESL 課程及費用
19. 住宿資訊
20. 課程日期
21. 教職員與學員的比例
22. 申請截止日期
23. 授課地點外的郊遊地點
24. 標準學費、雜項費用、個人花費
25. 有無過去的國際學員提供的評估報告
26. 有無機場接機
27. 校園內有無醫療保健

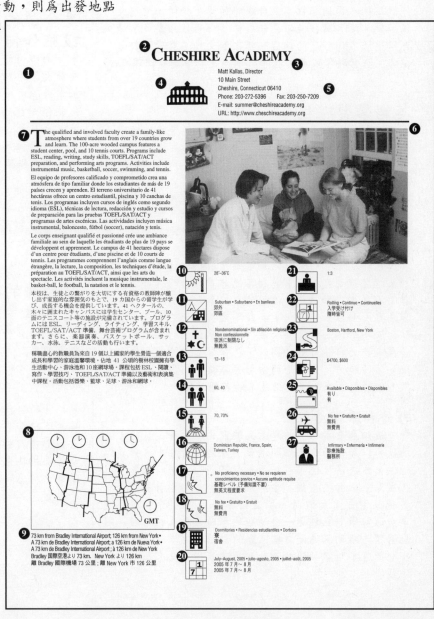

夏令營家庭指導

暑假是學生擴展視野和加強學年期間學習的技藝和才能的最佳時間。不論年紀大小、興趣所在，學生都可在世界各地找到合適的夏令營。有些學生住在舒適、管理嚴格的宿舍，並修習不同學科、參加體育、藝術和手工藝製作、以及觀光等活動。有些學員則參加野外郊遊活動，到各地體驗充滿冒險和刺激的戶外生活。不論學生參加的是甚麼活動，當他們收拾行囊回家時，都會滿載而歸，帶回新的技能、嗜好、朋友以及快樂美好的回憶。

我有哪些選擇？

學術課程

暑期的學術課程是由私立中學、學院和大學舉辦。參加的學生住在宿舍，一般是上午上課，下午參加體育和其他活動，晚上則溫習功課。週末安排郊遊和觀光或戶外探險活動。大部分的學生修習一或兩門課程；國際學生通常修習英語(ESL)作為第二語言的課程以及其他另外一門課程。學術課程為來自海外的學生提供了增進英文聽、說、讀、寫技能的最佳機會。課程種類繁多，學生可以選修不同程度的課程—語言和文學、數學、科學、電腦、社會科學以及工程學只不過是其中的幾門課程。

英語學習課程

由語言學校、私立中學、學院和大學提供著重增進學生說、寫能力的課程。

傳統的研習營

傳統的研習營中，學生住宿在遠離都市塵囂，周圍環繞樹林、湖泊以及高山的幽美、安全環境裡。學生參加不同的體育、藝術、手工藝活動以及學習認識大自然。夏令營的學員住在帳篷或小木屋裡，白天大部份的時間是參加戶外活動。研習營活動讓學生有機會通過共宿和活動來結交新朋友。指導員和其他專業人士均嚴密監管所有的活動並為學員營造溫馨的家庭氣氛。有一些指導員和專業人士參加同一研習營數年之久，他們先是在童年和青少年時參加研習營，最後便成為該處的指導員。學員在享受大自然奇妙的同時，也學習如何建立自信心和培養領導能力。大部分的研習營不提供英文課程，而且很多研習營要求學員具備基本的英語技能。

野外和旅遊活動

野外活動為喜歡探險的學生提供爬山、順著美麗的河流放筏、以及用營火烹飪的機會。在野外行程中，營員們的住宿方式多樣化，包括每天在不同地點架設帳篷，以及在海上船艙內搭鋪。參加旅遊夏令營的學員可在世界各地探索自然景觀時，騎自行車、健行、滑雪或搭汽車。通常學員在經過一些崎嶇地形時需要互相幫助，因此團體之間的溝通是這些活動的最基本要求。出于這點安全顧慮，這類性質的活動大多要求學員具有基本的英語技能。

旅遊夏令營

參加旅遊夏令營的學員可在世界各地探索自然景觀時，騎車、健行、滑雪或搭汽車。通常學員在經過一些崎嶇地形時需要互相幫助，因此團體之間的溝通是這些活動的最基本要求。由於這點安全顧慮，這類性質的活動大多要求學員具有基本的英語技能。

夏令營的地點在哪兒？
設施如何？

本指南所列的夏令營均在北美洲和歐洲的寄宿學校、學院和大學內開辦。大部分的傳統的研習營是設於美國和加拿大境內。旅遊和野外探險夏令營則遍佈世界各地，以提供學生有機會探索不同的地理區域。位於鄉村遼闊、幽美景色的夏令營，使來自都市的學生有機會享受跑步、遊玩、健行等夏季戶外活動；而位於大都會的夏令營則提供學員接觸文化和教育活動的大量機會。

私立學校和大學擁有一流的教學和娛樂設施供學生使用。學生通常住在單人房或雙人房的宿舍內。若為夏令營區，學生則可能和其他五、六個學員以及指導員共住一間帳篷或小木屋。

夏令營的時間多長？
還有誰參加？

夏令營通常為期四到八星期，一般是從六月下旬開始到八月結束。另外也有時間較短或較長的夏令營，而且如果學生的暑假有限，有時也可稍後再加入。學生的父母應聯絡夏令營的指導主任，查詢開課日期和註冊事宜。

夏令營的規模各異，從幾個人共用一個帳篷到幾百個人一起住宿在暑期寄宿學校。所有暑期課程安排的上課或活動都是人數不多的小組制並受嚴密的監管。大多數夏令營都招收來自美國各地以及世界其他國家的學生。國際學生在此一英語環境中，有極好的增進英語口語技能的機會。

夏令營活動如何安排？
夏令營典型的一天
白天的課程活動包括上課、娛樂活動以及結交朋友。學員早起以後，接下來就是一連串的活動。早餐、整理房間或清理帳篷之後，便開始上課；午餐之後，還有更多的活動。參加學術課程的學生通常是上午上課，下午參加體育、藝術和手工藝、音樂或戲劇、或參觀當地的名勝古蹟。晚餐和晚間溫習之前屬於學生的自由時間或者在就寢之前也會安排其他的晚間活動。所有的活動均由成人和年紀較長的學生監管。

飲食
餐飲是由學校的餐廳供應，如為爬山健行，則隨身攜帶食物。學校供應大量新鮮蔬果，食物營養充分。所有的暑期課程每天都供應三餐和點心。不習慣"夏令營食物"的國際學生通常都會從他們國家帶來一些自己喜愛的零食。有些暑期課程也會為一些需要特定餐飲的學生供應特別食物。

衣著
暑期課程對學生的衣著並無要求。只有極少數的暑期學校要求學生穿制服；大部分的地方都要求學生穿著以簡單輕便為主—通常是牛仔褲和T恤。夏季夜晚的天氣可能會較涼，學生應攜帶毛衣或輕便夾克。有些暑期課程會要求學員帶一、兩件正式場合用的正式衣服。參加體育、野外和旅遊活動研習營的學生可能需要帶一些特別的衣服和設備。所有的暑期課程都會提供學生有關攜帶物品的詳細清單。

規定和政策
為了使學校或夏令營舉辦順利，所有參加暑期活動的學員必須互相幫忙、合作。學生也要遵守一些嚴屬的規定，包括禁止抽煙、禁止使用或持有酒類和其他非法物質、未經允許不得擅自離開營地以及不得說謊。學生不遵守這些規定，嚴重時有可能會遭退學。

健康和安全
所有的課程活動均要求學員在到達之前，接受身體健康檢查和必需的預防注射。學校和營區皆設有保健中心，由受過專門訓練的護士和其他的醫務人員為學生提供服務；如有必要，學校也提供醫生和醫院的服務。急診治療須取得學生父母的同意。有些課程活動提供醫療保險；其他的則要求學生自行投保醫療保險。所有的暑期課程均受嚴密監管，但學生在旅遊、離開校園或營區時，須自行負責自身安全。學員在離家之前，父母應教導一些基本的安全原則。雖然暑期課程禁止學生使用毒品和酒類，但父母應告知孩子，有些學生可能還是會攜帶這些違禁品，應避免和這類的學生交往。

如何申請？
申請參加暑期課程的學生一般不需要通過特定的測試或能力鑑定；申請程序通常是要求學生提供一些基本的資料。有些特殊的藝術和音樂研習營可能會要求學生提供作品樣本、有些學術課程可能會要求學生提交學業成績單和推薦信函、而有些課程則要求學生具有特定的英文程度。大部分的夏令營招收的學生人數有限，有很多在春天就已額滿，因此最好儘早申請。夏令營一般都會要求學生繳交訂金確保名額；課程活動開始前，所有的學費應全數繳清。

夏令營的費用是多少？
如何抵達？
夏令營的費用平均在 2000 到 4000 美元之間。基本的收費包括活動、住宿以及餐飲。其他可能的費用包括制服和床具租用、機場的交通往返以及其他活動費，如騎馬。學生父母可以直接電匯美國銀行帳戶的方式繳付學費—如果您選擇電匯，請事先向夏令營的指導主任要求有關資訊。學生也應隨身攜帶一些個人零用錢。

夏令營和學校會派人到最近的機場接送海外學員；有些學校會收取接送費。有些夏令營也會為學員安排旅遊行程，有些則要求學生自行安排。

選擇夏令營雖然很有意思，但您須記住，在決定要參加的課程之前須先問一些重要的問題。暑期課程的英文程度要求為何—須完全掌握英文、或者具備初級英文程度即可？您有甚麼樣的註冊選擇—有時候您可稍後再加入課程活動或者如您安排的回程日期與課程撞期，您也可提早離開。您在離家之前，詢問一下有關夏令營的規定—例如是否禁止吸菸。另外，您也須詢問一下是否可以電匯方式繳付學費，如可以，切記取得所有必要的資訊。

祝您有個愉快的暑假！

DianeRapp 是 DianeRapp 聯合教育諮詢
顧問公司的總裁，該公司的地址是
85 RiverRoad, Scarborough,
NewYork 10510 U.S.A

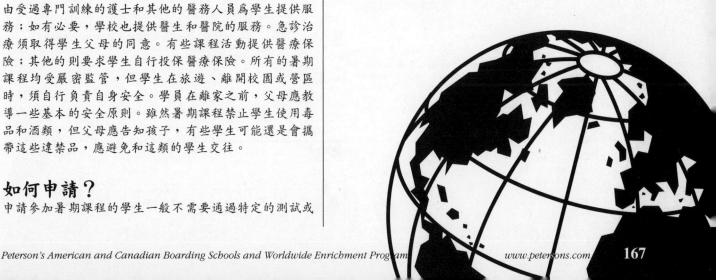

Summer temperature range
Temperatura durante el verano
Écarts de température d'été
夏期の最高・最低気温
夏季的氣溫變化

Setting
Ubicación
Cadre
立地
場地

Religious affiliation
Afiliación religiosa
Affiliation
所属宗教団体
宗教信仰

Age range of participants
Edad de los participantes
Barème d'âge des participants
参加者の年齢構成
參加者的年齡組成

Number of boys per session, number of girls per session
Número de niños por sesión, número de niñas por sesión
Nombre de garçons par session, nombre de filles par session
1セッションにおける男子数、1セッションにおける女子数
每期男生人數、女生人數

Number of international participants per session, percentage of international participants
Número de participantes extranjeros por sesión, porcentaje de participantes internacionales
Nombre de participants internationaux par session, pourcentage de participants internationaux
1セッションにおける海外からの参加者数、海外からの参加者の割合
每期國際學生人數、國際學生比例

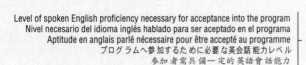

Countries most frequently represented
Países representados con mayor frecuencia
Pays représentés le plus souvent
参加者の多い国々
最常參加課程的學生國籍

Level of spoken English proficiency necessary for acceptance into the program
Nivel necesario del idioma inglés hablado para ser aceptado en el programa
Aptitude en anglais parlé nécessaire pour être accepté au programme
プログラムへ参加するために必要な英会話能力レベル
參加者需具備一定的英語會話能力

Availability of English as a second language (ESL) courses, and cost of ESL courses
Disponibilidad de cursos de inglés como segundo idioma (ESL) y el costo de los mismos
Disponibilité de cours d'anglais comme langue étrangère (ESL), coût des cours ESL
外国人向英語（ESL）コースの有無、ESLコースの費用
提供ESL課程、ESL課程費用

Housing information
Información sobre alojamiento
Renseignements relatifs à l'hébergement
宿泊施設
宿舍資料

Session dates
Fechas de las sesiones
Dates des sessions
セッションの日程
課程日期

Staff-participant ratio
Proporción de personal y participantes
Rapport personnel-participants
スタッフ数と参加者数の割合
教職員與學生比例

Application deadline
Fecha límite para presentar la solicitud
Date(s) limite(s) des demandes d'admission
参加申込締切日
申請截止日期

Off-site trip locations
Excursiones fuera de las instalaciones
Lieux visités lors des excursions
敷地外の旅行先
當地以外的旅遊點

Standard fees, additional fees, recommended spending money
Cuotas estándar, cuotas adicionales, cantidad de dinero recomendada para gastos
Tarifs normaux, tarifs supplémentaires, argent de poche recommandé
基本費用、追加費用、適切な小遣金額
基本費用、額外費用、適當的零用花費

Evaluations by former international participants available
Se dispone de evaluaciones realizadas por ex-participantes extranjeros
Possibilité d'évaluations par les anciens participants internationaux
海外からの参加者紹介の有無
提供從前國際學生對課程的評估

Availability of airport pickup
Servicio para recoger a los estudiantes en el aeropuerto
Disponibilité d'accueil/transport de l'aéroport
空港への送迎の有無
提供機場接送

On-site medical care
Atención médica en las instalaciones
Soins médicaux sur place
敷地内での医療施設
當地的醫療設施

ONE-PAGE PRESENTATIONS

LAS PRESENTACIONES DE UNA PÁGINA
1ページ案内

LES PAGES D'INTRODUCTION
單頁學校簡介

Summer programs in this section supplied additional information about themselves and supported the distribution of this directory to help international families understand the value of summer programs and the spectrum of camps, schools, and travel programs serving international students.

Los programas de verano en esta sección brindaron información individual adicional y respaldaron la distribución de este directorio para ayudar a que las familias extranjeras aprecien el valor de los programas de verano y la variedad de campamentos, escuelas y programas de viajes dedicados a los estudiantes extranjeros.

Les responsables des programmes estivaux apparaissant dans cette section ont fourni des informations supplémentaires concernant les activités de leurs programmes respectifs et ont contribué à la distribution du présent répertoire afin d'aider les familles de divers pays à comprendre l'importance des programmes estivaux et la variété des colonies, écoles et programmes touristiques offerts aux participants internationaux.

このセクションの夏期プログラムは夏期プログラム自体の追加情報を提供します。また、海外の参加希望者の家族が夏期プログラムの価値や海外の生徒向けのキャンプ・学校・旅行のプログラムの範囲について理解できるよう、このディレクトリーを援助するものです。

此部分的各個夏令營提供的各自的詳細資料並支持本書的發行以協助各國家長了解夏令營的重要性及為國際學生服務的各種研習營、學校和旅遊活動。

ACADEMIC STUDY ASSOCIATES—ASA PROGRAMS
AT UMASS-AMHERST, UC-BERKELEY, AND OXFORD UNIVERSITY

Marcia E. Evans, Academic Study Associates
10 New King Street
White Plains, New York 10604, USA
Phone: 914-686-7730 Fax: 914-686-7740
E-mail: summer@asaprograms.com
URL: http://www.asaprograms.com

Each of ASA's sessions is designed to give students the opportunity to experience life in a university setting while participating in a full range of academic, social, recreational, and excursion programs. Courses/ activities include chemistry, drawing, English, English for overseas students, ESL, TOEFL, film, art history, history, photography, political science, SAT preparation, soccer, theater, writing, and Tennis Programs. ASA also provides college admission workshops and advice.

Cada una de las sesiones de ASA está diseñada para ofrecer a los estudiantes la oportunidad de experimentar la vida en un ambiente universitario mientras participan en una completa variedad de programas académicos, sociales, recreativos y de excursiones. Los cursos y las actividades incluyen química, dibujo, inglés, inglés para estudiantes extranjeros, cursos de inglés como segundo idioma, preparación para el examen de inglés como segundo idioma, TOEFL, cinematografía, historia del arte, historia, fotografía, ciencias políticas, preparación para la prueba SAT, fútbol, teatro, redacción y los programas de tenis. ASA también ofrece consejos y talleres de admisión a la universidad.

Chacune des sessions de l'ASA est conçue pour donner aux étudiants la possibilité de vivre dans un cadre universitaire tout en participant à une gamme complète de programmes académiques, sociaux, récréatifs, et d'excursions. Parmi les cours/activités, on compte la chimie, le dessin, l'anglais, l'anglais pour les étudiants étrangers, l'anglais comme langue étrangère, la préparation au TOEFL, le cinéma, l'histoire de l'art, l'histoire, la photographie, les sciences politiques, la préparation pour l'examen SAT, le football, le théâtre, la composition et les Programmes de Tennis. ASA fournit aussi des ateliers d'orientation et des conseils pour l'admission dans les universités.

各 ASA のクラスは、生徒が学科、社交、娯楽、旅行の広範なプログラムに参加しながら、大学のキャンパス生活が体験できるようにつくられたものです。科学、素描、英語、海外からの学生のための英語、ESL、TOEFL、映画、美術史、敵視、写真、政治経済、SAT 準備、サッカー、演劇、作文、テニスなどの各種コースや活動を行います。また ASA では、大学進学のためのワーク・ショップとアドバイスを提供しています。

ASA 為學生設計的每一期課程，均提供學生在參加學術、社會、娛樂和戶外郊游等各種活動時，也有機會體驗大學環境的生活。課程／活動包括化學、繪圖、英文、外國學生英語課、ESL、TOEFL、電影、藝術史、歷史、攝影、政治學、SAT 輔導、足球、戲劇、寫作以及網球等項目。ASA 還提供大學錄取咨詢和教導服務。

| Program • Programa • Programme |
| プログラム　　　　　科系課程 |

University of Massachussetts (Amherst, MA)

University of California - Berkeley (Berkeley, CA)

Oxford University (Oxford, England)

 16°–30° C

 1:10

 Academic • Académica • Académique
大学
學術

 Rolling • Continuo • Continuelles
随時入学受付
隨時皆可

 Nondenominational • Sin afiliación religiosa • Non confessionnelle
宗教上の制限無し
無教派

 London, Boston, Los Angeles, San Francisco, Cape Cod

 12–18

 $3995–$6695, $65–$550, $75

 100, 120

 Available • Disponibles • Disponibles
有り
有

 10%

 No fee • Gratuito • Gratuit
無料
無費用

 Brazil, Ecuador, England, France, Germany, Hong Kong, Italy, Japan, Korea, Spain, Taiwan, Turkey

 Nurse • Enfermero(a) • Infirmier(ère)
看護婦
護士

 Moderate proficiency necessary • Se requieren conocimientos moderados • Aptitude modérée requise
中級レベル
中級英文程度

 No fee • Gratuito • Gratuit
無料
無費用

 Dormitories • Residencias estudiantiles • Dortoirs
寮
宿舍

 Late June–Mid August • Fines de junio–mediados de agosto • Fin juin–mi-août
6月末から8月中旬
6月下旬 –8月中

ASHEVILLE SCHOOL
SUMMER ACADEMIC ADVENTURES

E. Versen, Director
360 Asheville School Road
Asheville, North Carolina 28806
Phone: 828-254-6345 Fax: 828-252-8666
E-mail: saa@ashevilleschool.org
URL: http://www.ashevilleschool.org

Set on 300 acres in the cool, picturesque mountains, Asheville School's Summer Academic Adventures is a program designed for talented, high-achieving students. Students choose from among exciting enrichment courses in mathematics, Intermediate ESL, creative writing, acting, experimental science, visual arts, and literary studies, among other subjects. In the afternoons, students participate in outdoor challenge, as well as a wide range of intramural athletics-tennis, basketball, swimming, soccer, Frisbee, and more. Weekend excursions include whitewater rafting, as well as trips to cultural and recreational destinations.

El programa "Aventuras Académicas de Verano" de Asheville School, que se lleva a cabo en un pintoresco paraje montañoso de clima fresco, está diseñado para estudiantes talentosos que desarrollan al máximo su potencial. Los estudiantes pueden elegir cursos en matemáticas, actuación, ciencias experimentales, artes visuales, literatura y otros, todos igualmente estimulantes y enriquecedores. En las horas de la tarde, los estudiantes participan en actividades al aire libre, así como en una amplia gama de deportes dentro del colegio: tenis, baloncesto, natación, fútbol (soccer), Frisbee y otros. Las excursiones de fin de semana incluyen navegación en balsa en aguas rápidas, así como visitas a sitios culturales y recreativos.

Asheville School, situé sur 121 hectares au coeur de montagnes pittoresques, offre les « Summer Academic Adventures », un programme conçu pour les très bons élèves. Des cours d'enrichissement intéressants sont proposés aux étudiants dans différents sujets, tels que les mathématiques, l'anglais comme langue étrangère (ESL) niveau intermédiaire, la création littéraire, l'interprétation, les sciences expérimentales, les arts visuels et la littérature. L'après-midi est consacré aux activités de plein air et aux différents sports offerts sur le campus, comme par exemple l'athlétisme, le tennis, le basket-ball, la natation, le football et le frisbee. Le week-end, les excursions comprennent le rafting en eau vive ainsi que des sorties vers des destinations culturelles et récréatives.

Asheville School は、気候の良い、絵のように美しい山あいの120 ヘクタールの地に位置しています。夏期アカデミック・アドベンチャーは、才能豊かで学力の優れた学生のために設計されたプログラムです。学生達は数学や中級 ESL、クリエイティブ ライティング、演劇、ビジュアルアート、文学などのエキサイティングな強化コースから科目を選択することができます。午後にはテニスやバスケットボール、水泳、サッカー、フリスビーなど広範囲な学内競技に参加する他、アウトドアにも挑戦します。週末の小旅行は文化的またレクリエーショナルな場所の他、急流ラフティングも含まれています。

Asheville School 座落於幽美涼爽的山間，校園面積 121 公頃。本校 "暑期學術探索" 項目專為天資聰穎、成績優秀的學生設計。學生可選修極富趣味的強化課程，包括數學、中級 ESL、創造性寫作、表演、實驗科學、觀賞藝術、文學及其他科目。下午，學生們參加互外競賽活動，以及各種各樣的校內體育運動，包括網球、籃球、游泳、飛碟等等。週末外出活動包括急流放筏以及文化和娛樂旅行。

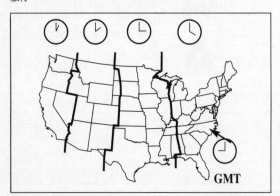

300 km from Atlanta Airport; 200 km from Charlotte, NC •
A 300 km del Aeropuerto de Atlanta; a 200 km de Charlotte, NC •
À 300 km de l'aéroport d'Atlanta ; à 200 km de Charlotte, Caroline du Nord
Atlanta 空港から 300 km ； North Carolina 州 Charlotte から 200 km
離 Atlanta 機場 300 公里；離 Charlotte, NC 200 公里

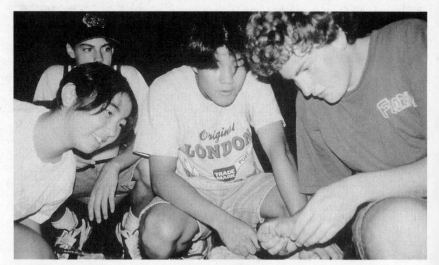

 15°–30° C

 1:5

 Boarding school • Internado • Internat
ボーディング・スクール
寄宿學校

 Rolling/May 1 • Continuo/1 de mayo •
Continuelles/1 mai
随時入学受付／5 月 1 日
隨時皆可，5 月 1 日

 Nondenominational • Sin afiliación religiosa •
Non confessionnelle
特定宗教に無関係
無教派

 Biltmore Estate, white-water rafting

 12–16

 $2550, $30

 37, 45

 Available • Disponibles • Disponibles
有り
有

 9, 10%

 No fee • Gratuito • Gratuit
無料
無費用

 Germany, Japan, Korea, Thailand

 On-site, hospital • En las instalaciones,
hospital • Sur place, hôpital
キャンパス内での医療施設、病院
實地、醫院

 Moderate proficiency necessary • Se requieren
conocimientos moderados • Aptitude modérée requise
中級レベル
中級英文程度

 No fee • Gratuito • Gratuit
無料
無費用

 Dormitories • Residencias estudiantiles • Dortoirs
寮
宿舍

 June 19–July 9, July 10–July 30 • 19 de junio–9 de julio, 10 de julio–30 de julio •
19 juin–9 juillet, 10 juillet–30 juillet
6 月 19 日～7 月 9 日, 7 月 10 日～7 月 30 日
6 月 19 日～7 月 9 日, 7 月 10 日～7 月 30 日

BISHOP'S COLLEGE SCHOOL
SUMMER PROGRAMME

Denise Addona
c/o BCS, P.O. Box 5001
Lennoxville, Quebec, J1M 1Z8
Phone: 819-566-0227 Fax: 819-822-8917
E-mail: summer@bishopscollegeschool.com

Participants enjoy summer as they learn English or French as a second language. Every day includes language instruction and sports or activities. During the month, many trips to places of interest are offered. Bishop's College School, set in beautiful Quebec, has extensive facilities and a caring staff. Courses/activities include English, French, football, golf, horseback riding, soccer, swimming, tennis, volleyball, and water sports.

Los participantes disfrutan del verano mientras aprenden inglés o francés como segundo idioma. El programa diario incluye clases de idioma así como deportes y otras actividades. Durante el transcurso del mes se realizan visitas a sitios de interés. Bishop's College School, ubicado en el hermoso Quebec, cuenta con extensas instalaciones y personal atento. Los cursos y actividades incluyen inglés, francés, fútbol americano, golf, equitación, fútbol, natación, tenis, volibol y deportes acuáticos.

Les participants profitent de l'été tout en apprenant l'anglais ou le français comme langue étrangère. Des cours de langue et des sports ou autres activités remplissent chaque journée. Pendant le mois, nous offrons de nombreux voyages vers des sites intéressants. Bishop's College School, située dans la magnifique province de Québec, propose des installations complètes et un personnel attentif. Parmi les cours/activités on compte l'anglais, l'équitation, le français, le football et le football américain, le golf, la natation, le tennis, les sports aquatiques ainsi que le volley-ball.

参加者は、英語またはフランス語を第二言語として習得しながら楽しい夏を過ごすことができます。毎日、語学の授業とスポーツまたはその他の各種活動が行われます。コース期間中、興味深い場所への数多くの旅行が実施されます。Bishop's College School は美しいケベック州にあり、大規模な施設が完備され、気配りの行き届いたスタッフによって運営されています。英語、フランス語、フットボール、ゴルフ、乗馬、サッカー、水泳、テニス、バレーボール及び水上スポーツ等のコース・活動が行われます。

學員在享受夏日生活的同時，並修習第二語言為英語或法語的課程。日常生活包括語言學習和運動或活動。此外，學校也多次安排學生參觀、郊遊不同的地方。 Bishop's College School 位於風景優美的魁北克，擁有廣泛的設施和專注的教職員。課程／活動包括英文、法文、美式足球、高爾夫球、騎馬、足球、游泳、網球、排球以及水上活動。

 26°–32° C

 1:4

 Rural • Rural • Rurale
郡部
鄉村

 Montreal, Quebec City, Ottawa

 Nondenominational • Sin afiliación religiosa • Non confessionnelle
宗派に制限なし
無教派

 11–16

 $2600 (Canadian: all inclusive)

 80, 90

 Available • Disponibles • Disponibles
有り
有

 55, 30%

 Can$55

 Asia, Bermuda, Canada, France, Korea, Mexico, Saudi Arabia, Spain, U.S.A.

 No proficiency necessary • No se requieren conocimientos previos • Aucune aptitude requise
基礎レベル（予備知識不要）
無英文程度要求

 No fee • Gratuito • Gratuit
無料
無費用

 2 per room in various residences • 2 por habitación en varias residencias • 2 par chambre dans de nombreuses résidences
2 人 1 部屋
居住不同住處、每兩個人一間

June 26–July 23 • 26 de Junio–23 de Julio • 26 Juin–23 Juillet
6月26日～7月23日
6月26日～7月23日

60 km from Montreal's Mirabel or Dorval Airport •
160 km del aeropuerto Mirabel o Dorval de Montreal •
160 km de l'aéroport Mirabel ou Dorval de Montréal
Montreal の Mirabel または Dorval Airport から 160 km
離 Montreal's Mirabel 和 Dorval 機場 160 公里

CHESHIRE ACADEMY

Matt Kallas, Director
10 Main Street
Cheshire, Connecticut 06410
Phone: 203-272-5396   Fax: 203-250-7209
E-mail: summer@cheshireacademy.org
URL: http://www.cheshireacademy.org

The qualified and involved faculty create a family-like atmosphere where students from over 19 countries grow and learn. The 100-acre wooded campus features a student center, pool, and 10 tennis courts. Programs include ESL, reading, writing, study skills, TOEFL/SAT/ACT preparation, and performing arts programs. Activities include instrumental music, basketball, soccer, swimming, and tennis.

El equipo de profesores calificado y comprometido crea una atmósfera de tipo familiar donde los estudiantes de más de 19 países crecen y aprenden. El terreno universitario de 41 hectáreas ofrece un centro estudiantil, piscina y 10 canchas de tenis. Los programas incluyen cursos de inglés como segundo idioma (ESL), técnicas de lectura, redacción y estudio y cursos de preparación para las pruebas TOEFL/SAT/ACT y programas de artes escénicas. Las actividades incluyen música instrumental, baloncesto, fútbol (soccer), natación y tenis.

Le corps enseignant qualifié et passionné crée une ambiance familiale au sein de laquelle les étudiants de plus de 19 pays se développent et apprennent. Le campus de 41 hectares dispose d'un centre pour étudiants, d'une piscine et de 10 courts de tennis. Les programmes comprennent l'anglais comme langue étrangère, la lecture, la composition, les techniques d'étude, la préparation au TOEFL/SAT/ACT, ainsi que les arts du spectacle. Les activités incluent la musique instrumentale, le basket-ball, le football, la natation et le tennis.

本校は、生徒との繋がりを大切にする有資格の教師陣が醸し出す家庭的な雰囲気のもとで、19カ国からの留学生が学び、成長する機会を提供しています。41ヘクタールの、木々に囲まれたキャンパスには学生センター、プール、10面のテニスコート等の施設が完備されています。プログラムにはESL、リーディング、ライティング、学習スキル、TOEFL/SAT/ACT準備、舞台芸術プログラムが含まれます。さらに、楽器演奏、バスケットボール、サッカー、水泳、テニスなどの活動も行います。

稱職盡心的教職員為來自19個以上國家的學生營造一個適合成長和學習的家庭溫馨環境。佔地41公頃的樹林校園擁有學生活動中心、游泳池和10座網球場。課程包括ESL、閱讀、寫作、學習技巧、TOEFL/SAT/ACT準備以及藝術和表演集中課程。活動包括器樂、籃球、足球、游泳和網球。

 28°–36°C

 1:3

 Suburban • Suburbano • En banlieue
郊外
郊區

 Rolling • Continuo • Continuelles
入学受け付け
隨時皆可

 Nondenominational • Sin afiliación religiosa • Non confessionnelle
宗派に制限なし
無教派

 Boston, Hartford, New York

 12-18

 $4700, $600

 60, 40

 Available • Disponibles • Disponibles
有り
有

 70, 70%

 No fee • Gratuito • Gratuit
無料
無費用

 Dominican Republic, France, Spain, Taiwan, Turkey

 Infirmary • Enfermería • Infirmerie
診療施設
醫務所

 No proficiency necessary • No se requieren conocimientos previos • Aucune aptitude requise
基礎レベル（予備知識不要）
無英文程度要求

 No fee • Gratuito • Gratuit
無料
無費用

 Dormitories • Residencias estudiantiles • Dortoirs
寮
宿舎

 July–August, 2005 • julio–agosto, 2005 • juillet–août, 2005
2005年7月〜8月
2005年7月〜8月

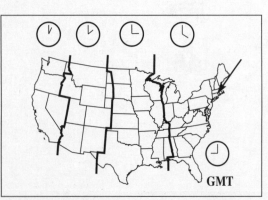

73 km from Bradley International Airport; 126 km from New York •
A 73 km de Bradley International Airport; a 126 km de Nueva York •
A 73 km de Bradley International Airport; à 126 km de New York
Bradley 国際空港より 73 km、New York より 126 km
離 Bradley 國際機場 73 公里; 離 New York 市 126 公里

CORNELL UNIVERSITY SUMMER COLLEGE
SUMMER PROGRAM

Janna Bugliosi, Assistant to the Director
B20 Day Hall
Ithaca, New York 14853
Phone: 607-255-6203 Fax: 607-255-6665
E-mail: summer_college@cornell.edu
URL: http://www.summercollege.cornell.edu

Cornell University Summer College is a six-week academic program for high school juniors and seniors. The program provides students with the opportunity to earn an average of 6 college credits, participate in one of eleven academic and career exploration seminars, and attend workshops in math, writing, study skills, and college admissions.

Cornell University Summer College es un programa académico de seis semanas para estudiantes de primero y segundo año de secundaria. El programa proporciona a los estudiantes la oportunidad de acumular un promedio de 6 créditos para la universidad, participar en uno de once seminarios de exploración académica y profesional y asistir a talleres de matemática, redacción, técnicas de aprendizaje y admisión en la universidad.

Cornell University Summer College est un programme académique de six semaines pour les élèves de la seconde à la terminale. Le programme offre aux étudiants la possibilité d'obtenir une moyenne de 6 unités de valeur universitaires, de participer à l'un des onze séminaires d'étude et d'exploration de carrières, et d'assister à des ateliers consacrés aux mathématiques, à la rédaction, aux techniques d'études et à l'admission dans les universités.

コーネル大学サマー・カレッジは、高校2、3年生のための6週間にわたるアカデミック・プログラムです。当プログラムでは、学生が大学課程の単位を平均6単位取得し、11種類の学習・キャリア発掘セミナーの1つに参加でき、数学、英作文、学習法、大学進学のワークショップに参加できます。

Cornell University Summer College 是為期六周的初中高中生學期校制。該項目為學生提供機會，平均獲取六個大學學分，參加十一種之一的學術與事業探索研討班，并可參加數學、寫作、研讀技巧以及大學入學等各種講習班。

 15°–27° C

 1:20

 Boarding school • Internado • Internat
ボーディング・スクール
寄宿學校

 Rolling/May 3 • Continuo/3 de mayo •
Continuelles/3 mai
随時入学受付／5月3日
隋時皆可，5月3日

 Nondenominational • Sin afiliación religiosa •
Non confessionnelle
特定宗教に無関係
無教派

 Parks, theater

 15–18

 $4150–$6960, $150–$200

 263, 308

 100, 18%

 $80–$100

 Canada, Colombia, Hong Kong, Korea, Turkey,

 On-site, hospital • En las instalaciones,
hospital • Sur place, hôpital
キャンパス内での医療施設、病院
實地、醫院

 Moderate proficiency necessary • Se requieren
conocimientos moderados • Aptitude modérée requise
中級レベル
中級英文程度

 No fee • Gratuito • Gratuit
無料
無費用

 Dormitories • Residencias estudiantiles • Dortoirs
寮
宿舍

 June 26–August 10 • 26 de junio–10 de agosto • 26 juin–10 août
6月26日～8月10日
6月26日～8月10日

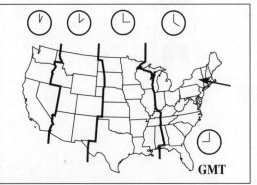

20 km from Syracuse International Airport •
120 kilómetros del Aeropuerto Internacional de Syracuse •
120 km de l'aéroport international de Syracuse
yracuse 国際空港から120 km
Syracuse 國際機場120 公里

CUSHING ACADEMY

G. Daniel Frank, Director of Summer Session
P.O. Box 8000, 39 School Street
Ashburnham, Massachusetts 01430
Phone: 978-827-7700 Fax: 978-827-6927
E-mail: summersession@cushing.org
URL: http://www.cushing.org

Cushing Academy combines challenging academic programs with interesting artistic and athletic electives in a structured and supportive New England boarding school environment. It provides a summer of learning, fun, and exciting excursions. Activities include basketball, computer design, dance, English, history, mathematics, painting, study skills, SAT preparation, science, soccer, tennis, and jewelry design.

Cushing Academy combina programas que estimulan a los participantes con clases opcionales de arte y atletismo en un ambiente estructurado y complementario de un internado de New England. Se ofrece un verano de aprendizaje, diversión y atractivas excursiones. Las actividades incluyen baloncesto, diseño de computadora, baile, inglés, historia, matemáticas, pintura, técnicas de estudio, preparación para el exámen SAT, ciencias, fútbol, tenis y diseño de joyería.

Cushing Academy combine des programmes académiques excitants avec des cours facultatifs athlétiques et artistiques dans une ambiance structurée et renforçante d'internat de New England. Elle fournit des possibilités d'apprendre, de s'amuser et de faire des excursions passionnantes pendant l'été. Parmi les activités on compte le basket-ball, la création informatique, la danse, l'anglais, l'histoire, les mathématiques, le techniques d'études, la préparation pour l'examen SAT, les sciences, le football, le tennis et la création de bijoux.

Cushing Academy は、やりがいのある学科プログラムと興味深い芸術が一体になった、組織的で充実したニューイングランドの全寮制学校です。教育的で楽しい小旅行等も実施されます。バスケットボール、コンピューターデザイン、ダンス、英語、歴史、数学、絵画、学習スキル、SAT準備、科学、サッカー、テニス、貴金属デザインのクラス・諸活動があります。

Cushing Academy 提供學生在設施完善和相互扶持的新英格蘭寄宿學校環境裡，修習高難度的學術課程以及有趣的藝術和體育選修課程。學生在學習、娛樂和郊游中度過暑假。活動包括籃球、電腦設計、舞蹈、英文、歷史、數學、繪畫、研讀技巧、SAT輔導、科學、足球、網球以及首飾設計。

 16°–29° C

 1:8

 Small town • Pueblo pequeño • Petite ville
小都市
小鎮

 Rolling • Continuo • Continuelles
随時入学受付
隨時皆可

 Nondenominational • Sin afiliación religiosa • Non confessionnelle
宗教上の制限無し
無教派

 Boston

 12–18

 $5450, $50, $500

 170, 130

 Available • Disponibles • Disponibles
有り
有

 200, 66%

 No fee • Gratuito • Gratuit
無料
無費用

 Brazil, Germany, Hong Kong, Japan, Saudi Arabia, Venezuela

 Nurse, infirmary • Enfermero(a), enfermería • Infirmier(ère), infirmerie
看護婦、キャンプ内の診療所
護士、醫務所

 No proficiency necessary • No se requieren conocimientos previos • Aucune aptitude requise
基礎レベル（予備知識不要）
無英文程度要求

 No fee • Gratuito • Gratuit
無料
無費用

 Dormitories • Residencias estudiantiles • Dortoirs
寮
宿舍

 July 5–August 14 • 5 de julio–14 de agosto • 5 juillet–14 août
7月5日～8月14日
7月5日～8月14日

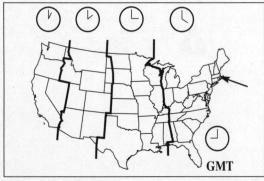

96 km from Logan International Airport and Boston •
A 96 km del aeropuerto internacional de Logan y de Boston •
A 96 km de l'aéroport international Logan et de Boston
Logan 国際空港および Boston より 96 km
離 Logan 國際機場和 Boston 市 96 公里

EDUCATION UNLIMITED SUMMER PROGRAMS

Matt Fraser, Director
1700 Shattuck Avenue, #305
Berkeley, CA 94709
Phone: 510-548-6612 Fax: 510-548-0212
E-mail: camps@educationunlimited.com
URL: http://www.educationunlimited.com

Education Unlimited conducts summer academic programs at universities in the United States. The sessions are safe and well supervised, and are designed to be both fun and educational. Programs include public speaking, computers, debate, acting, summer college classes, a tour of east coast colleges, and comprehensive college admission preparation. All programs include housing and meals. Come join us!

Education Unlimited realiza programas académicos de verano en universidades en los Estados Unidos. Las sesiones son seguras y muy bien supervisadas y están diseñadas para ser divertidas y educativas. Los programas incluyen hablar en público, computadoras, debate, actuación, clases universitarias de verano, un tour de universidades en el este y una preparación completa de admisión universitaria. Todos los programas incluyen alojamiento y comidas. ¡Venga con nosotros!

Education Unlimited organise des programmes d'études pour l'été dans des universités de tous les États-Unis. Les cours offrent toute sécurité et sont encadrés avec soin pour combiner savoir et plaisir d'apprendre. Les programmes présentent des cours d'expression orale, d'informatique, de débat, de théatre et d'enseignement secondaire d'été. Ils prévoient aussi une visite des établissements de la côte est et une préparation complète aux tests d'admission d'entrée dans le secondaire. Tous nos programmes s'entendent logement et repas compris. Alors inscrivez-vous avec nous !

Education Unlimited は、 夏期学習プログラムをアメリカ中の大学に於いて運営しています。授業は安全で整った指導下にあり、楽しみながら学べるように作られています。プログラムには公共の場での話術、コンピュータ、討論、演技、夏期大学クラス、東海岸の大学への旅行、広範囲に渡る大学進学準備が含まれます。全てのプログラムには、宿泊と食事が含まれています。どうぞお越し下さい！

Education Unlimited 在美國大學中開設暑期學術活動。活動安全，有良好的組織系統，使學生們既享受娛樂又受教育。課程包括演講，計算機應用，辯論，表演，暑期大學課程，參觀東海岸大學，了解如何做好大學入學準備。所有安排均包括食宿。歡迎您加入！設

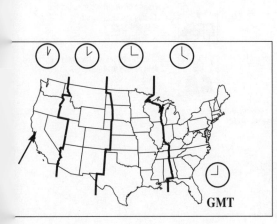

 18°–28° C

 1:8

 Urban / Suburban • Urbano / Suburbano • Ville / En banlieue
都市部／郊外
市區／郊區

 Rolling • Continuo • Continuelles
隨時入學受付
隨時皆可

 Nondenominational • Sin afiliación religiosa • Non confessionnelle
特定宗教に無関係
無教派

 Beaches, Amusement parks, Baseball games

 10–18

 $800–$4700, $0, $75–$450

 Available • Disponibles • Disponibles
有り
有

 5%

 $45

 Europe, Hong Kong, Latin America, Singapore, Taiwan

 Local hospital • Hospital de la localidad • Hôpital local
地元の病院
地方醫院

 Moderate proficiency necessary • Se requieren conocimientos moderados • Aptitude modérée requise
中級レベル
中級英文程度

 Dormitories • Residencias estudiantiles • Dortoirs
寮
宿舍

 June–August • junio–agosto • juin–août
6 月〜 8 月
6 月〜 8 月

HARVARD SECONDARY SCHOOL PROGRAM

Harvard Summer School
51 Brattle Street, Department S763
Cambridge, Massachusetts 02138-3722
Phone: 617-495-3192 Fax: 617-496-4525
URL: http://www.ssp.harvard.edu

Students who apply to the program must have completed one, two, or three years of secondary school (before university) and must be fluent in English. They take Summer School courses for undergraduate credit; they have access to Harvard's museums, libraries, and laboratories and may join in many athletic and social activities. Courses include computer science, economics, English, history, mathematics, psychology, science, writing, and foreign languages.

Los estudiantes que deseen participar en el programa deben haber finalizado uno, dos o tres años de educación secundaria (antes de la universidad) y hablar inglés con fluidez. Los estudiantes toman clases de verano reconocidas a nivel universitario; gozan de acceso a los museos, las bibliotecas y los laboratorios de Harvard y pueden participar en muchas actividades atléticas y sociales. Los cursos incluyen computación, economía, inglés, historia, matemáticas, psicología, ciencias, redacción e idiomas extranjeros.

Les étudiants qui désirent participer au programme doivent avoir un, deux ou trois ans de lycée et doivent parler couramment l'anglais. Les étudiants suivront des cours d'été certifiés en faculté. Les étudiants auront la possibilité de visiter les musées, les bibliothèques et les laboratoires de Harvard et de participer à diverses activités sportives et sociales. Parmi les cours on compte l'informatique, l'économie, l'histoire, les mathématiques, l'anglais, la psychologie, les sciences, la composition et les langues étrangères.

高校の 1 年、2 年、3 年の過程を 終了していること、英語に堪能であることが、本プログラム参加のための応募資格です。参加者は大学の正規単位を習得するためにこのコースを受け、同時にハーバード大学の美術館、図書館、実験室や他のスポーツ、社交活動に参加できます。コンピューター、経済学、数学、心理学、科学やライティング、外国語、英語、歴史等のコースがあります。

申請研習的學生必須已修完進入大學前一年，二年，或三年的高中課程，而且英文必須流利。學生在暑期班研習的課程學分可計入大學的學分。學生可使用哈佛的博物館、圖書館以及實驗室，並且也可參加很多體育和社交活動。課程包括電腦、經濟學、英文、歷史、數學、心理學、科學、寫作以及外語。

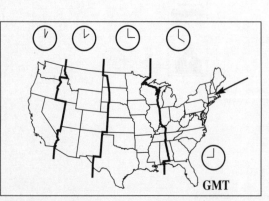

10 km from Logan International Airport; 8 km from Boston •
A 10 km del aeropuerto internacional de Logan; a 8 km de Boston •
A 10 km de l'aéroport international Logan ; à 8 km de Boston
Logan 国際空港より 10 キロ、Boston より 8 キロ
離 Logan 國際機場 10 公里 ；離 Boston 市 8 公里

 16°–33° C

 Urban • Urbano • Ville
都市部
市區

 Nondenominational • Sin afiliación religiosa •
Non confessionnelle
宗教上の制限無し
無教派

 15–19

 500, 500

 100, 10%

 Brazil, Japan, Korea, Mexico, Taiwan

 Must have total command of English • Se requiere dominio
total del idioma inglés • Aptitude parfaite de l'anglais
英語総合能力が必要
須能完全掌握英文

 Available, $6685 • Disponibles • Disponibles
有り
有

 Dormitories • Residencias estudiantiles • Dortoirs
寮
宿舍

 June 27–August 20 • 27 de junio–20 de agosto • 27 juin–20 août
6 月 27 日～8 月 20 日
6 月 27 日～8 月 20 日

 Varies • Varía • Variable
様々
不同

 Rolling • Continuo • Continuelles
随時入学受付
隨時皆可

 Cape Cod, Boston-area colleges • Cape Cod, Colegios del área
de Boston • Cape Cod, Universités de la région de Boston
その他の大学
科德角、 以及波士頓地區的大學

 $7435, $40–$400, $1000

 Not available • No disponibles • Pas
disponibles
無し
無

 Mass transit • Transporte público •
Transports en commun
公共輸送機間
大衆運輸工具

 On-site • En las instalaciones • Sur place
敷地内医療施設
實地

MUSIKER TOURS/SUMMER DISCOVERY
LOS ANGELES, CALIFORNIA

Jennifer Krava
International Admissions Director
1326 Old Northern Boulevard
Roslyn, New York 11576

Phone: 516-621-3939
Fax: 516-625-3438
E-mail: discovery@summerfun.com
URL: http://www.summerfun.com

Summer Discovery at UCLA, UC Santa Barbara, UC San Diego, the University of Michigan, Georgetown University, University of Vermont, University of Sydney, Australia, and Cambridge University, England, offers pre-college enrichment programs. Courses and activities include ESL, TOEFL and SAT preparation, career exploration, introduction to college, reading, study skills, writing, computers, economics, science, and basketball. There are also exciting trips and excursions.

Summer Discovery at UCLA, UC Santa Barbara, UC San Diego, la Universidad de Michigan, la Universidad de Georgetown, la Universidad de Vermont, la Universidad de Sydney Australia y la Universidad de Cambridge, Inglaterra, ofrecen programas de enriquecimiento preuniversitario. Los cursos y las actividades incluyen preparación para los exámenes ESL, TOEFL y SAT, orientación vocacional, introducción a la universidad, lectura, técnicas de estudio, redacción, computadoras, economía, ciencias y baloncesto. También hay emocionantes viajes y excursiones.

Summer Discovery á UCLA, UC Santa Barbara, UC San Diego, à University of Michigan, à Georgetown University, à University of Vermont, á Université de Sydney en Australie, et à Cambridge University en Angleterre, offre des programmes d'enrichissement avant l'entrée à l'université. Les cours et les activités comprennent l'anglais comme langue étrangère, la préparation au TOEFL et à l'examen du SAT, la prospection de carrière, l'introduction à l'université, la lecture, les techniques d'étude, la rédaction, l'informatique, l'économie, les sciences et le basket-ball. Des excursions et voyages passionnants sont également disponibles.

UCLA、UC Santa Barbara、UC San Diego、University of Michigan、Georgetown University、University of Vermont、University of Sydney Australia そして英国の Cambridge University で行われる Summer Discovery では、来る大学生活を充実させるためのプログラムを提供しています。授業及び諸活動には、ESL/TOEFL/SAT 準備講座、キャリアの探索、大学入門講座、読書、学習法、ライティング、コンピュータ、経済、科学、バスケットボールが含まれます。楽しい小旅行や遠足もあります。

洛杉磯加州大學，聖塔巴巴拉加州大學，聖地亞哥加州大學，密西根大學，喬治敦大學，威蒙大學，澳大利亞悉尼大學，以及英國劍橋大學都有"夏令探趣"活動，它提供一系列的大學學前補習課程和文體活動，包括 ESL，托福，SAT 輔導，職業探討，大學介紹，閱讀，學習技巧，寫作，電腦，經濟，科學，籃球。同時也安排了激動人心的旅行和探險。

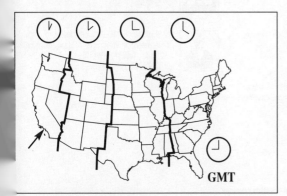

 13°–30° C

 1:10

 Suburban • Suburbano • En banlieue
郊外
郊區

 Rolling • Continuo • Continuelles
随時入学受付
隨時皆可

 Nondenominational • Sin afiliación religiosa • Non confessionnelle
宗教上の制限無し
無教派

 College visits, major cities, overnight camping

 15–18

 $3100–$5900, $125–$500, $300

 45%, 55%

 Available • Disponibles • Disponibles
有り
有

 15-20%

 Fee varies • Honorario variado • Les tarifs varient
費用は場合によって異なる
費用不同

 France, Hong Kong, Japan, Kuwait, Turkey

 Minimal proficiency necessary • se requieren conocimientos mínimos • Aptitude minimum requise
初級レベル
初級英文程度

 No fee • Gratuito • Gratuit
無料
無費用

 Dormitories • Residencias estudiantiles • Dortoirs
寮
宿舍

6 km from Los Angeles International Airport • A 16 km de Los Angeles International Airport • A 16 km de Los Angeles International Airport
ロサンゼルス国際空港から 16 キロ
離 Los Angeles 國際機場 16 公里

June 25–August 5, August 1–August 21 • 25 de junio-5 de agosto o 1 de agosto-21 de agosto • Du 25 juin au 5 août ou du1 août au 21 août •
6 月 25 日～8 月 5 日、8 月 1 日～8 月 21 日
6 月 25 日～8 月 5 日，8 月 1 日～8 月 21 日

Peterson's American and Canadian Boarding Schools and Worldwide Enrichment Programs
www.petersons.com
179

NORTHFIELD MOUNT HERMON

Northfield Mount Hermon Summer Session
206 Main Street
Northfield, Massachusetts 01360-1089
Phone: 413-498-3290 Fax: 413-498-3112

NMH, one of the nation's leading prep schools, offers summer academic programs and welcomes students from many countries and cultures. The campus includes 10 dormitories, 5 classroom buildings, a 40,000-volume library, gym, and student center on 300 acres. Courses include, English, history, mathematics, SAT preparation, science, and writing.

NMH, uno de los principales colegios secundarios privados del país, ofrece programas académicos durante el verano y acoge a estudiantes de muchos países y culturas. Las instalaciones incluyen 10 residencias estudiantiles, 5 edificios con aulas, una biblioteca con 40.000 volúmenes, gimnasio y un centro estudiantil de 122 hectáreas. Los cursos incluyen, historia, matemáticas, preparación para los exámenes SAT, ciencias, inglés y redacción.

NMH, l'un des lycées privés les plus renommés du pays, propose des programmes scolaires d'été et accueille des étudiants d'un grand nombre de pays et de cultures différentes. Sur le campus de 122 hectares, il y a 10 dortoirs, 5 bâtiments de classes, une bibliothèque comptant 40,000 livres, un gymnase, et un centre estudiantin. Parmi les cours on compte, l'histoire, les mathématiques, la préparation pour les examens SAT, les sciences, l'anglais et la rédaction.

Northfield Mount Hermon は全国有数の大学進学予備校で、夏期プログラムに海外や異文化圏から多くの学生を歓迎しています。122 ヘクタールのキャンパスには、10 棟の寮、5 棟の教室用のビル、蔵書 4 万冊の図書館、体育館、学生センター等が完備されています。英語、歴史学、数学、SAT 準備、科学、等のコースがあります。

Northfield Mount Hermon 是全美最好的預備學校之一。本校提供夏季學習計劃，歡迎來自許多國家和文化的學生參加。佔地 300 英畝的校園擁有 10 棟宿舍、5 棟教室大樓、具有 40,000 冊藏書的圖書館、體育館以及學生活動中心。課程包括英文、歷史、數學、SAT 輔導、科學、以及寫作。

 15°–37° C

 1:4

 Rural • Rural • Rurale
郡部
郷村

 Rolling • Continuo • Continuelles
随時入学受付
隨時皆可

 Nondenominational • Sin afiliación religiosa • Non confessionnelle
宗教上の制限無し
無教派

 Boston, Boston Symphony at Tanglewood, Six Flags Amusement Park

 12–19

 $4700, $250–$750, $300

 200, 200

 Available • Disponibles • Disponibles
有り
有

 200, 45–50%

 No fee • Gratuito • Gratuit
無料
無費用

 Germany, Japan, Korea, Spain, Taiwan, Thailand, Turkey

 Physician, nurse, infirmary • Médico, enfermero(a), enfermería • Médecin, infirmier(ère)
医師、看護婦、保健室
醫生、護士、醫務所

 Minimal proficiency necessary • Se requieren conocimientos mínimos • Aptitude minimale requise
初級レベル
初級英文程度

 No fee • Gratuito • Gratuit
無料
無費用

 Dormitories • Residencias estudiantiles • Dortoirs
寮
宿舍

 July 3–August 7 • 3 de julio–7 de agosto • 3 juillet–7 août
7 月 3 日～8 月 7 日
7 月 3 日～8 月 7 日

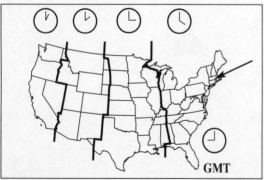

GMT

160 km from Logan International Airport; 80 km from Springfield, MA •
A 160 km del aeropuerto internacional de Logan; a 80 km de Springfield, MA •
A 160 km de l'aéroport international Logan ; à 80 km de Springfield, MA
Logan 国際空港より 160 キロ、Springfield より 80 キロ
離 Logan 國際機場 160 公里；離 Springfield 市 80 公里

OAK CREEK RANCH SCHOOL

Jay Wick, Headmaster
P.O. Box 4329
West Sedona, Arizona 86340
Phone: 928-634-5571 Fax: 928-634-4915
E-mail: admissions@ocrs.com
URL: http://www.ocrs.com

Students are instructed by experienced, certified teachers in all educational fields. Summer school is both academic and adventurous. Small classes and high technology help students excel in a structured and safe environment. Academics include ESL, TOEFL prep, computer science, math, science, and study skills. Activities include swimming, horseback riding, paintball games, Grand Canyon trips, and water parks. Sessions are 4 weeks.

Los estudiantes reciben instrucción de maestros certificados con experiencia en todos los campos de la educación. El colegio de verano incluye programas académicos y actividades al aire libre. Clases con pocos alumnos y dispositivos de alta tecnología ayudan a los estudiantes a destacarse en un ambiente estructurado y seguro. Los cursos académicos incluyen inglés como segundo idioma (ESL), preparación para el TOEFL, ciencias de computación, matemáticas, ciencias y técnicas de estudio. Las actividades incluyen natación, equitación, juegos de paintball, excursiones al Grand Canyon y parques acuáticos. Las sesiones duran 4 semanas.

Les étudiants reçoivent un enseignement dispensé par des professeurs certifiés et expérimentés dans tous les domaines éducatifs. Le programme d'été est aussi bien académique que récréatif. Grâce à des classes restreintes et à un excellent support technologique, les étudiants se réalisent pleinement dans un environnement sécuritaire et structuré. Le programme académique comprend l'anglais comme langue étrangère, la préparation au TOEFL, l'informatique, les mathématiques, les sciences et les techniques d'étude. Les activités comprennent la natation, l'équitation, des jeux de "paintball", des voyages au Grand Canyon et des journées dans des parcs d'attractions nautiques. Les cours sont de 4 semaines.

全ての教育分野において、経験豊かで有資格の先生が教授します。サマースクールはアカデミックでもあり、冒険でもあります。少人数のクラスと高度なテクノロジーで、生徒は組織立てられた安全な環境で一層効果を上げることができます。アカデミックな授業には、ESL、TOEFL準備講座、コンピューター・サイエンス、数学、科学、学習法があります。活動には、水泳、乗馬、ペイントボール・ゲーム、グランド・キャニオンへの旅行、ウォーター・パークが含まれます。授業の期間は4週間です。

學生由有經驗、有證書的教師講授所有教育課程。夏季學校既具有學術性又具有刺激性。小課堂和高科技幫助學生在有秩序且安全的環境中勤奮好學。學習課包括 ESL、TOEFL 培訓、電腦課、數學、科學及學習技巧。各項活動包括游泳、騎馬、彩球遊戲、大峽谷旅遊及水上公園游。各課程為期四周。

 29°–35° C

 1:8

Rural • Rural • Rurale
郡部
郷村

Rolling • Continuo • Continuelles
随時入学受付
隨時皆可

Nondenominational • Sin afiliación religiosa • Non confessionnelle
宗教上の制限無し
無教派

Grand Canyon, Phoenix, Flagstaff, Sedono, Cottonwood, AZ

12–19

$3950, $500, $500

20, 10

Available • Disponibles • Disponibles
有り
有

6–8, 15%

No fee • Gratuito • Gratuit
無料
無費用

Hong Kong, Japan, Korea, Thailand

Local hospital, On-site medical personnel•
Hospital de la localidad, personal médico en las instalaciones• Hôpital local, personnel médical sur place
地元の病院、キャンパス内での医療専門人員
地方醫院、實地醫務人員

No proficiency necessary • No se requieren conocimientos previos • Aucune aptitude requise
基礎レベル（予備知識不要）
無英文程度要求

No fee • Gratuito • Gratuit
無料
無費用

Dormitories • Residencias estudiantiles • Dortoirs
寮
宿舎

Sessions begin June 10, June 24, July 8 • Las sesiones comienzan el 10 de junio, el 24 de junio y el 8 de julio • Les cours commencent le 10 juin, le 24 juin et le 8 juillet
始業日は6月10日、6月24日、7月8日
各課程於6月10日、6月24日、7月8日開始

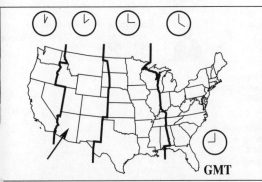

161 km from Phoenix International Airport; 72 km from Flagstaff, AZ • A 161 km del aeropuerto internacional de Phoenix; a 72 km de Flagstaff, AZ • A 161 km de l'aéroport international de Phoenix ; à 72 km de Flagstaff, AZ
Phoenix 国際空港より 161 キロ、Flagstaff, AZ より 72 キロ
離 Phoenix 國際機場 161 公里；離 Flagstaff, AZ 80 公里

SOUTHWESTERN ACADEMY
SOUTHWESTERN INTERNATIONAL SUMMER SCHOOL

Jane Whitmire, Director of Admission
2800 Monterey Road
San Marino, California 91108
Phone: 626-799-5010 Fax: 626-799-0407
E-mail: admissions@southwesternacademy.edu
URL: http://www.southwesternacademy.edu

Southwestern Academy's International Summer School program is offered at our San Marino, California campus. Full-semester, half-semester, and shorter sessions are available. Summer is an excellent time to start or finish your ESL requirements. We have a beautiful and safe campus with friendly and helpful faculty.

El programa internacional de la escuela de verano de Southwestern Academy se ofrece en nuestro recinto de California, en San Marino. Se encuentran disponibles sesiones de semestre completo, medio semestre y sesiones más cortas. El verano es un tiempo excelente para completar los requisitos de inglés como segundo idioma (ESL). Contamos con un recinto seguro y hermoso y con un profesorado amigable y que ofrece ayuda.

Été de l'école internationale Southwestern Academy est offert sur notre campus californien de San Marino. Les sessions sont proposées par semestre, demi-semestre ou sur une période encore plus courte. L'été est un moment excellent pour terminer la préparation a l'examen d'Anglais comme langue étrangère. Nous sommes situés dans un environnement sur et agréable avec un corps enseignant aimable et dévoué.

Southwestern Academy の国際夏期プログラムは、カルフォルニア州サン・マリノ市のキャンパスにて行われます。1学期、半学期、または短期受講の中から期間選択が可能です。夏はESLプログラム修得には、とても良い機会です。親切で親しみやすく、美しく安全なキャンパスを提供します。

Southwestern Academy 國際夏日課程設於加州的 San Marino，提供全學期，半學期和短期課程。夏季對不同成度的學生來說都是學習 ESL 的最佳季節。該學院的校園美麗而安全，充滿友好互助的氣氛。

 24°-35° C

 1:7

 Suburban • Suburbano • En banlieue
郊外
郊區

 Rolling • Continuo • Continuelles
随時入学受付
随時皆可

 Nondenominational • Sin afiliación religiosa • Non confessionnelle
宗教上の制限無し
無教派

 Disneyland, Knotts Berry Farm, Magic Mountain, Southern California beaches, Getty Museum, Huntington Library

 12-18

 $5000-$16,500, $500-$1000

 50, 40

 80, 90%

 $50

 China, Japan, Korea, Russia, Taiwan

Local hospital • Hospital de la localidad • Hôpital local
地元の病院
地方醫院

 No proficiency necessary • No se requieren conocimientos previos • Aucune aptitude requise
基礎レベル（予備知識不要）
無英文程度要求

 Three levels of ESL; No extra fee • Tres niveles de ESL; sin costo adicional
Trois niveaux d'Anglais comme langue étrangère; Pas de frais supplémentaire.
3段階の ESL レベル；追加料金なし
三個級別的 ESL 課程。不加額外費用。

 Dormitories • Residencias estudiantiles • Dortoirs
寮
宿舍

 Mid June–Mid September • Mediados de junio–mediados de septiembre • Mi juin–mi septembre
6月中旬～9月中旬
6月中旬～9月中旬

GMT

48 km from Los Angeles International Airport; 3 km from Pasadena, CA • A 48 km del Aeropuerto Internacional de Los Angeles; a 3 km de Pasadena, CA • À 48 km de l'aéroport international de Los Angeles; à 3 km de Pasadena, CA
Los Angeles 国際空港より 48 km、Pasadena , CA より 3 km
離 Los Angeles 國際機場 48 公里；離 Pasadena , CA 3 公里

STANFORD SUMMER COLLEGE
FOR HIGH SCHOOL STUDENTS

Stanford Summer Session
Building 590, Room 103
Stanford, California 94305-3005
Phone: 650-723-3109 Fax: 650-725-6080
Email: summersession@stanford.edu
URL: http://summersession.stanford.edu

Located on a stunning 8,100-acre campus in Northern California, Stanford University is renowned for its dedication to scholarly pursuits. The Summer College for high school students offers exceptional juniors and seniors an opportunity to explore the academic and personal challenges of university life. Courses include anthropology, art and art history, biological science, chemistry, computer science, economics, engineering, English literature, mathematics, political science, psychology, religious studies, and writing. Special three-week topical courses are also available to sophomores and juniors.

Ubicado en un impresionante campus de 8.100 acres en el norte de California, Stanford University es famosa por su dedicación a los logros académicos. El Summer College para estudiantes secundarios ofrece a estudiantes sobresalientes del penúltimo e último año una oportunidad para explorar los retos académicos y personales y la vida universitaria. Los cursos incluyen antropología, arte e historia del arte, ciencias biológicas, química, informática, economía, ingeniería, literatura inglesa, matemáticas ciencias políticas, psicología, estudios de religión y redacción. También se ofrecen cursos temáticos de tres semanas para estudiantes secundarios de primer y segundo año.

Située sur un magnifique campus de plus de 3 000 hectares en Californie du Nord, Stanford University est renommée pour stimuler la recherche sous tous ses aspects. Le Collège d'été pour les étudiants du secondaire donne aux élèves entrant en première et en terminale l'occasion d'explorer les défis académiques et personnels de la vie universitaire. Parmi les cours offerts, on peut citer l'anthropologie, l'art, l'histoire de l'art, les sciences biologiques, la chimie, l'informatique, l'économie, l'ingénierie, la littérature anglaise, les mathématiques, les sciences politiques, la psychologie, les études religieuses et la rédaction. Des cours de trois semaines sur une matière spécifique sont également disponibles aux élèves de seconde et de première.

北カリフォルニアの美しい 3,278 ヘクタールのキャンパスに位置する、Stanford University は、学術探究に対し尽力してきたことで名高い大学です。高校生のための夏季大学では、特に優秀な高校 3 年生と 4 年生に、大学生活のにおける学業的また個人的チャレンジを体験していただく機会を提供しています。開設コースは、人類学、芸術および／芸術史、生物学、化学、コンピュータ科学、経済学、工学、英文学、数学、政治学、心理学、宗教学、そして作文です。3 週間の特別専門コースが、2 年生と 3 年生に開設されます。

坐落於加州北部的斯坦福大學以其竭誠的學術追求著稱於世。校園佔地 3278 公頃，令人嘆為觀止。為高中學生開辦的暑期大學使十一、十二年級的優秀學生有機會探索大學生活中的學業及個人挑戰。課程包括人類學，藝術與藝術史，生物科學，化學，電腦科學，經濟學，工程，英語文學，數學，政治學，心理學，宗教研究以及寫作。還為十、十一年級學生開設為期三週的特別專題課程。

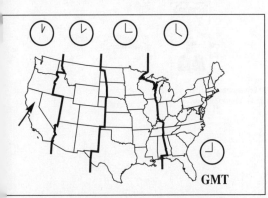
GMT

15°–32° C	1:15
Suburban • Suburbano • En banlieue 郊外 郊區	Rolling, Feb. 15, April 15 • Continuo/15 de febrero, 15 de abril • Continuelles/15 février , 15 avril 隨時入學受付、2 月 15 日、4 月 15 日 隨時皆可，2 月 15 日，4 月 15 日
Nondenominational • Sin afiliación religiosa • Non confessionnelle 特定宗教に無関係 無教派	San Francisco, Yosemite, Monterey, Pacific coast beaches
15–18	$7600–$10,000, $757, $500
175, 175	Available • Disponibles • Disponibles 有り 有
100, 33%	$25
Africa, the Americas, Asia, Europe	On-site, hospital • En las instalaciones, hospital • Sur place, hôpital キャンパス内での医療施設、病院 實地、醫院
Total command of English • Se requiere pleno dominio del inglés • Maîtrise parfaite de l'anglais 上級レベル 須能完全掌握英文	
Not available • No está disponible • Non disponible 無し 無	
Dormitories • Residencias estudiantiles • Dortoirs 寮 宿舍	
8 weeks, June–August • 8 semanas: junio–agosto • 8 semaines : juin–août 8 週間: 6 月～8 月 8 周: 6 月～8 月	

48 km from San Francisco International Airport; 64 km from San Francisco • A 48 km del Aeropuerto Internacional de San Francisco; a 64 km de San Francisco • À 48 km de l'aéroport international de San Francisco; à 64 km de San Francisco • San Francisco 国際空港から 48km、San Francisco から 64km • 離 San Francisco 國際機場 48 公里；離 San Francisco 市 64 公里

SUMMER STUDY AT PENN STATE
UNIVERSITY PARK, PENNSYLVANIA

Mr. Bill Cooperman, Executive Director
900 Walt Whitman Road
Melville, New York 11747

Phone: 631-424-1000 Fax: 631-424-0567
E-mail: info@summerstudy.com
URL: http// www.summerstudy.com

This total pre-collegiate program combines a strong academic program at a "Big Ten" university with sports and recreation facilities. Program fee includes athletics, exciting supervised evening activities, and 3 trips to 8 universities in NY, PA, and MD. Activities and courses include art, chemistry, computers, English, golf, introduction to college programs, law, math, photography, SAT/ACT preparation, science, soccer, and tennis. Six-week college credit and 3 1/2-week enrichment programs are offered.

Este programa completo preuniversitario combina un intenso programa académico en una de las diez universidades más grandes en atletismo con deportes e instalaciones para recreación. El costo del programa incluye atletismo, emocionantes actividades vespertinas supervisadas y tres viajes a ocho universidades en Nueva York, Pennsylvania y Maryland. Las actividades y cursos incluyen arte, química, computación, inglés, golf, introducción a programas universitarios, derecho, matemáticas, fotografía, preparación para los exámenes SAT/ACT, ciencias, fútbol y tenis. Se ofrece un programa de seis semanas con crédito universitario y un programa de enriquecimiento de 3 semanas y media.

Ce programme complet pré-universitaire réunit un programme académique important dans une des dix plus prestigieuses universités disposant d'installations de sports et de loisirs. Sont compris dans le tarif un programme d'athlétisme, de passionnantes activités surveillées le soir, et 3 excursions vers 8 universités des états de New York, de Pennsylvanie, et du Maryland. Parmi les activités et les cours, on compte la chimie, l'informatique, l'anglais, le golf, l'introduction au programmes universitaires, le droit, les mathématiques, la photographie, la préparation pour les examens SAT/ACT, les sciences, le football et le tennis. Sont offerts un programme universitaire de six semaines avec unités de valeur et un programme d'enrichissement de 3 1/2 semaines.

この大学準備プログラムでは、十大大学の一つでの強力な学科プログラム指導が行われます。現代的なスポーツやレクリエーションの施設が活動が組み合わされています。授業料には体育、監督下での楽しい夜の活動、ニューヨーク州、ペンシルベニア州、メリーランド州にある8大学への3回の旅行が含まれています。美術、化学、コンピューター、英語、ゴルフ、大学プログラムの紹介、法律、数学、写真、SAT/ACT準備、科学、サッカー、テニス等の各種活動およびコースがあります。大学単位が取れる6週間プログラムと3週間半の強化プログラムがあります。

此一大學預備班課程提供學生"十大"大學的紮實學科課程、運動和娛樂設施。暑期班的費用包括體育、精彩的監管下的夜間活動以及參觀位於紐約、賓州和馬里蘭州八所大學的三次活動。活動和課程包括藝術、化學、電腦、英文、高爾夫球、大學科系介紹、法律、數學、攝影、SAT/ACT輔導、科學、足球以及網球。提供六週大學學分課程和三週半強化課程。

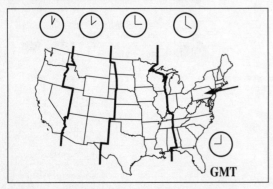

250 km from Philadelphia; 0.1 km from State College, PA •
A 250 km de Filadelfia; a 0,1km de State College, PA •
A 250 km de Philadelphie ; à 0,1 km de State College, PA
Philadelphia より 250 km, State College, PA より 0.1 km
離 Philadelphia 市 250 公里；離 State College, PA 0.1 公里

 21°–29° C

 1:15

 Rural • Rural • Rurale
郡部
郷村

 Rolling • Continuo • Continuelles
随時入学受付
随時皆可

 Nondenominational • Sin afiliación religiosa • Non confessionnelle
宗教上の制限無し
無教派

 Cornell University, Ithaca, George Washington University, Johns Hopkins University, University of Maryland, Franklin and Marshall College

 15–18

 $5995–6 1/2 weeks, $65–$695, $100-$300, $3795–3 1/2 weeks
$5995–6 1/2 semanas, $65–$695, $100-$300, $3795–3 1/2 semanas
$5995–6 1/2 semaines, $65–$695, $100-$300, $3795–3 1/2 semaines
$5995–6 1/2 週間、 $65–$695, $100-$300、 $3795–3 週間半
$5995–6 1/2 週、 $65–$695, $100-$300、 $3795–3 個半月

 250, 250

 Available • Disponibles • Disponibles
有り
有

 50, 10%

 No fee • Gratuito • Gratuit
無料
無費用

 England, Japan, Korea, Puerto Rico, Switzerland

 On-site • En las instalaciones • Sur place
敷地内医療施設
實地

 Moderate proficiency necessary • Se requieren conocimientos moderados • Aptitude modérée requise
中級レベル
中級英文程度

 No fee • Gratuito • Gratuit
無料
無費用

 Dormitories • Residencias estudiantiles • Dortoirs
寮
宿舎

 Late June–early August (6 weeks); Early July–late July (3 1/2 weeks) •
Finales de junio–principios de agosto (6 semanas); principios de julio–finales de julio (3 1/2 semanas) •
fin juin–début août (6 semaines); début juillet–fin juillet (3 1/2 semaines)
6 月下旬～ 8 月初旬(6 週間); 7 月初旬～ 7 月下旬(3 週間半)
6 月下旬－ 8 月初旬(6 週); 7 月初旬 －7 月下旬(3 個半周)

SUMMER STUDY AT THE UNIVERSITY OF COLORADO AT BOULDER
SUMMER PROGRAM AT BOULDER, COLORADO

Mr. Bill Cooperman, Executive Director
900 Walt Whitman Road
Melville, New York 11747
Phone: 631-424-1000 Fax: 631-424-0567
E-mail: info@summerstudy.com
URL: http://www.summerstudy.com

This total pre-collegiate, college credit program combines a strong academic program at a western university with sports, recreation, and outdoor activities. Program fee includes outstanding daytime athletics and recreational activities, and weekend excursions to Vail, Denver, Pike's Peak, etc., all amidst the great Rocky Mountains. Activities include whitewater rafting, horseback riding, mountain biking, rock climing, hiking, and more. Courses include art, chemistry, computers, English, environmental studies, law, math, photography, SAT/ACT preparation, science, soccer, and tennis.

Este programa completo pre-universitario, que concede créditos que serán reconocidos en la universidad, combina un exigente programa académico en una universidad del Oeste, con deportes, y con actividades recreativas y al aire libre. El precio del programa incluye extraordinarias actividades deportivas y recreativas, que se realizan durante el día y excursiones durante los fines de semana en Vail, Denver, Pike's Peak, etc todo esto en medio de impresionantes paisajes de la Montañas Rocallosas. Las actividades incluyen piragüismo en aguas rápidas, montar a caballo, ciclismo en montaña, escalada en roca, excursionismo y más. Los cursos incluyen: arte, química, computadoras, inglés, estudios ecológicos, leyes, matemáticas, fotografía, preparación para los exámenes SAT/ACT, ciencias, fútbol (soccer) y tenis.

Dispensé dans une université, l'ensemble de ce programme, qui s'adresse aux étudiants du secondaire et permet d'obtenir des unités de valeur universitaires, combine un solide cursus scolaire, des activités sportives, des loisirs et des activités de plein air. Sont compris dans le prix du programme l'accès à d'excellentes activités sportives et récréatives dans la journée ainsi que des excursions le week-end à Vail, Denver, Pike's Peak, etc, le tout au sein des magnifiques Rocky Mountains. Les activités comprennent le rafting, l'équitation, le VTT, la varappe, des randonnées et bien d'autres. Les cours comprennent l'art, la chimie, l'informatique, l'anglais, l'étude de l'environnement, le droit, les mathématiques, la photographie, la préparation au SAT/ACT, les sciences, le football et le tennis.

この総合大学準備、大学単位取得プログラムは某西部大学での強固な学科プログラムとスポーツ、レクリエーション、アウトドア活動が統合されています。プログラム料金には、ロッキー山脈での傑出した日中のスポーツやレクリエーション活動、週末のVail、デンバー、パイク山頂等への小旅行の代金が含まれています。野外活動は、ホワイトウォーター川下り、乗馬、マウンテン・バイク、ロック・クライミング、ハイキングなど盛り沢山です。コースには、芸術、化学、コンピュータ、英語、環境学、法律、数学、写真、SAT/ACT準備、科学、サッカー、テニスがあります。

全部為大學預科及大學學分課程,將一所西部大學的實力雄厚的學術課程與體育、娛樂和戶外活動結合為一體。學費中包括水平出色的白天體育和娛樂活動以及周末外出活動,這些活動全部在 Vail 和丹佛等景色壯麗的落基山脈地點中進行。活動包括淡水行舟、馬術、山間登腳踏車、攀岩、登山等等。課程包括藝術、化學、電腦、英語、環境研究、法律、數學、攝影、SAT/ACT 備考、科學、足球和網球。

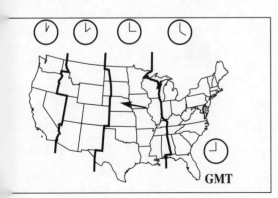

 18°–28° C

 1:15

 Rural • Rural • Rurale
郡部
郷村

 Rolling • Continuo • Continuelles
随時入学受付
隨時皆可

 Nondenominational • Sin afiliación religiosa • Non confessionnelle
特定宗教に無関係
無教派

 Outdoor excursions • Excursiones al aire libre • Excursions en plein air
アウトドア探検の旅
外出活動

 15–18

 $5795 - 5 weeks, $65–$295, $200
$3495 - 3 weeks

 100, 100

 Available • Disponibles • Disponibles
有り
有

 20, 10%

 $35

 England, Japan, Puerto Rico, Switzerland

 Available • Disponibles • Disponibles
有り
有

 Moderate proficiency necessary • Se requieren conocimientos moderados • Aptitude modérée requise
中級レベル
中級英文程度

 No fee • Gratuito • Gratuit
無料
無費用

 Dormitories • Residencias estudiantiles • Dortoirs
寮
宿舎

 Early July–Late July (3 weeks) • Principios de julio–fines de julio (3 semanas) • Debut juillet–fin juillet (3 semaines)
7 月初旬〜 7 月下旬 （3 週間）
7 月初旬〜 7 月下旬 （3 週）

SUMMER STUDY IN PARIS
AT THE AMERICAN UNIVERSITY OF PARIS
PARIS, FRANCE

Bill Cooperman, Executive Director
900 Walt Whitman Road
Melville, New York 11747

Phone: 631-424-1000 Fax: 631-424-0567
E-mail: info@summerstudy.com
URL: http://www.summerstudy.com

Centered in the most exciting city in the world, Paris, this total pre-collegiate experience immerses students in the language and culture of France. The strong college credit academic program includes visits to world-famous sights and museums, sports and recreation, supervised evening activities, SAT/ACT preparation, and weekend excursions throughout France and London. Activities and courses include art, art history, computers, drawing, English, fashion and design, French, introduction to college programs, music, painting, photography, SAT/ACT preparation, theater, swimming, and tennis. All courses except French language are taught in English. French language immersion prepares interested students to increase their fluency. Five-week college credit and three-week enrichment programs are offered.

Ubicada en la ciudad más emocionante del mundo, París, esta experiencia preuniversitaria total sumerge a los estudiantes en el idioma y la cultura francesa. El programa académico válido a nivel universitario incluye visitas a lugares y museos famosos en todo el mundo, deportes y actividades recreativas, actividades nocturnas supervisadas, preparación para los exámenes SAT/ACT, y excursiones de fin de semana por Francia y Londrés. Las actividades y cursos incluyen arte, historia del arte, computadoras, dibujo, inglés, moda y diseño, francés, introducción a los programas universitarios, música, pintura, fotografía, preparación para los exámenes SAT/ACT, teatro, natación y tenis. Todas las clases son impartidas en inglés, con excepción de la clase del idioma francés. La inmersión en el idioma francés prepara a los estudiantes interesados para hablarlo con más soltura. Se ofrece un programa de cinco semanas con crédito universitario y un programa de enriquecimiento de tres semanas.

Cette expérience complète pré-universitaire dans l'une des villes les plus passionnantes au monde, Paris, plonge les étudiants et étudiantes dans la langue et la culture française. Le programme académique de niveau universitaire très poussé aboutissant à des unités de valeur comprend des visites de musées et de sites de renommée mondiale, des activités sportives et récréatives, des activités de groupe en soirée, la préparation pour les examens SAT/ACT et des excursions de week-end à travers la France et Londres. Les activités et les cours sont les suivants : art, histoire de l'art, informatique, dessin, anglais, mode et stylisme, français, introduction aux programmes de niveau universitaire, musique, peinture, photographie, préparation pour les examens SAT/ACT, théâtre, natation et tennis. Tous les cours à l'exception du français sont enseignés en anglais. La possibilité d'être plongé dans la langue française permet d'accroître les capacités linguistiques des étudiants intéressés. Sont offerts un programme universitaire de cinq semaines avec unités de valeur et un programme d'enrichissement de trois semaines.

世界で最も刺激的な街、パリでのこのプログラムでは、大学進学前の学生にフランスの言語と文化に浸る総合的な経験をご提供します。このアカデミックなプログラムでは、フランスからロンドンに至る有名な観光地やミュージアム、スポーツやレクレーション、監視下での夜の活動、SAT/ACTの準備、週末の遠足などが含まれており、大学の単位取得も可能です。開設される活動およびコースには、美術、美術史、コンピュータ、デッサン、英語、ファッションとデザイン、フランス語、大学過程への入門、音楽、絵画、写真、SAT/ACT準備、演劇、水泳、テニスなどが含まれます。フランス語以外の授業はすべて英語で行われます。フランス語に浸ることで学生は流暢なフランス語が得られます。大学単位が取れる5週間プログラムと3週間の強化プログラムがあります。

進修地點位於巴黎這個世界上最令人興奮的城市，讓學生在進大學前完全浸淫在法國語言和文化里。該學院提供的多樣化學術課程包括參觀世界聞名的名勝和博物館、體育和娛樂、受監管的晚間活動、以及在全法國內和倫敦地區的週末旅遊。活動及課程包括藝術、藝術史、電腦、素描、英文、時裝與設計、法文、大學科系介紹、音樂、繪畫、攝影、SAT/ACT輔導、戲劇、游泳以及網球。所有課程，除法文以外，均用英文授課。法語密集訓練幫助有興趣的學員提高流利程度。提供五週大學學分課程和三週強化課程。

---

32 km from Charles DeGaulle Airport •
A 32 km del aeropuerto Charles DeGaulle •
A 32 km de l'aéroport Charles DeGaulle
Charles DeGaulle 空港より 32 km
離 Charles DeGaulle 機場 32 公里

 21°–29° C

 1:15

Urban • Urbano • Ville
都市部
市區

Rolling • Continuo • Continuelles
随時入学受付
隨時皆可

Nondenominational • Sin afiliación religiosa •
Non confessionnelle
宗教上の制限無し
無教派

Loire Valley Chateau Country, Disney Paris, Palace of Versailles

 15–18

$4595–3-week program; $6495–5-week program; $30–$395, $300 • $4595–Programa de 3 semanas; $6495–Programa de 5 semanas • $4595–Programme de 3 semaines; $6495–Programme de 3 semaines • $4595–3 週間プログラム; $6495–5 週間プログラム • $4595– 三週課程; $6495– 五週課程

125, 175 (5 weeks)
75, 125 (3 weeks)

Available • Disponibles • Disponibles
有り
有

 50, 20%

 $27.50

Canada, England, Japan, Korea, Kuwait
Puerto Rico, United States

Moderate proficiency necessary • Se requieren conocimientos moderados • Aptitude modérée requise
中級レベル
中級英文程度

Available • Disponibles • Disponibles
有り
有

All suites hotel • Hotel de suites únicamente • Hôtel avec suites
スイート・ホテル
旅店套間

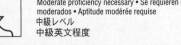
Early July–Early August (5 weeks), Early July–Late July (3 weeks) • Principios de julio–principios de agosto (5 semanas), Principios de julio–fines de julio (3 semanas) • Debut juillet–debut août (5 semaines), Debut juillet–fin juillet (3 semaines)
7 月初旬～ 8 月初旬 (5 週間)、 7 月初旬～ 7 月下旬 (3 週間)
7 月初旬～ 8 月初旬 (5 週)、 7 月初旬～ 7 月下旬 (3 週)

THE WINCHENDON SCHOOL

J. William LaBelle, Headmaster
172 Ash Street
Winchendon, Massachusetts 01475
Phone: 978-297-1223 Fax: 978-297-0911
URL: http://www.winchendon.org

Winchendon offers a strong ESL program for students at various levels of proficiency. Located in a safe and scenic mountain and lake region, Winchendon is close to Boston and its recreational and cultural opportunities. Activities include basketball, golf, soccer, swimming, tennis, volleyball, weight training, horseback riding, English, TOEFL, SAT/ACT prep, and study skills.

Winchendon ofrece un programa de ESL (inglés como segundo idioma) bien estructurado para estudiantes de varios niveles de conocimiento. Ubicado en una región segura con paisajes de montañas y lagos, Winchendon está cerca de Boston y sus oportunidades recreativas y culturales. Las actividades incluyen baloncesto, golf, fútbol (soccer), natación, tenis, volibol, entrenamiento con pesas, equitación, inglés, preparación para los exámenes TOEFL, SAT/ACT y técnicas de estudio.

Winchendon offre aux étudiants un excellent programme d'anglais comme langue étrangère à plusieurs niveaux. Située dans une région tranquille et magnifique, dans les montagnes et près d'un lac, l'école est à proximité de Boston et de ses activités culturelles et de loisir. Les activités comprennent le basket-ball, le golf, le football, la natation, le tennis, le volley-ball, la musculation, l'équitation, l'anglais, la préparation aux TOEFL, SAT/ACT et les techniques d'étude.

当校は様々な英語力の学生に、効果的な ESL プログラムを提供しています。山々と湖に囲まれた安全で美しい地域に位置し、ボストン近郊でもあり、レクレーションと文化的な機会にも恵まれています。バスケットボール、ゴルフ、サッカー、水泳、テニス、バレーボール、ウェイト・トレーニング、乗馬、英語、TOEFL、SAT/ACT 準備などの各種活動も含まれています。

威成頓學校為不同程度的學生提供行之有效的 ESL 課程。學校倚山傍水，風景優美，區域安全，靠近波士頓及其各種娛樂和文化設施。它提供的活動包括藍球，高爾夫，足球，游泳，網球，排球，舉重訓練，騎馬，英語，TOEFL，SAT/ACT 輔導以及學習技巧。

 18°–29° C

 1:6

 Rural • Rural • Rurale
郡部
郷村

 Rolling • Continuo • Continuelles
随時入学受付
随時皆可

 Nondenominational • Sin afiliación religiosa • Non confessionnelle
宗教上の制限無し
無教派

 Boston, Seashore

 13–19

 $5600, $0, $120

 35, 25

 Available • Disponibles • Disponibles
有り
有

 30, 40%

 No fee • Gratuito • Gratuit
無料
無費用

 Croatia, Germany, Japan, Korea, Poland, Taiwan

 Nurse, infirmary • Enfermero(a), enfermería • Infirmier(ère), infirmerie
看護婦、キャンプ内の診療所
護士、醫務所

 No proficiency necessary • No se requieren conocimientos previos • Aucune aptitude requise
基礎レベル（予備知識不要）
無英文程度要求

 No fee • Gratuito • Gratuit
無料
無費用

 Dormitories; students can request English-speaking roommates • Residencias estudiantiles; los esudiantes pueden solicitar compañeros de habitación de habla inglesa • Dortoirs ; les étudiants peuvent demander des camarades de chambre anglophones
寮、英語が話せるルームメイトをリクエストできる
宿舍、學生可要求母国語為英語的屋友

 June 27–August 7 • 27 de junio–7 de agosto • 27 juin–7 août
6 月 27 日～8 月 7 日
6 月 27 日～8 月 7 日

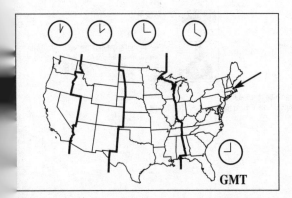

104 km from Logan International Airport; 65 km from Worchester, MA • A 104 km del aeropuerto internacional de Logan; a 65 km de Worchester, MA • A 104 km de l'aéroport Logan International ; à 65 km de Worchester, MA
Logan 国際空港より 104 km、Worchester, MA より 65 km
離 Logan 國際機場 104 公里 ; 離 Worchester, MA 65 公里

WYOMING SEMINARY
SEM SUMMER 2004

John R. Eidam
201 North Sprague Avenue
Kingston, Pennsylvania 18704
Phone: 570-270-2186 Fax: 570-270-2198
E-mail: summeratsem@wyomingseminary.org
URL: http://www.wyomingseminary.org

Nine weeks of ESL summer at Wyoming Seminary combine 8 weeks of intensive language study with one week in Maine. Along the Atlantic Coast, students continue to study ESL and, at the same time, develop important life skills. Because there is no better way to learn a language, students work together to conquer outdoor challenges and experience the beautiful New England countryside. During the 8 weeks at Wyoming Seminary, students may take classes like English, Introduction to Web Design, Desktop Publishing, Introduction to College Programs, Mathematics, Pottery, SAT Preparation, Speech, Study Skills, and Writing.

Nueve semanas de inglés como segundo idioma (ESL) durante el verano en el seminario Wyoming combina 8 semanas de estudio intensivo del idioma con una semana en Maine. Junto a la costa del atlántico, los estudiantes continúan estudiando inglés como segundo idioma (ESL), y a su vez, desarrollan importantes destrezas para la vida. Debido a que no hay mejor forma para aprender, los estudiantes trabajan juntos para superar retos y disfrutar de los campos de Nueva Inglaterra. Durante las 8 semanas del seminario Wyoming, los estudiantes podrán tomar clases como Inglés, Introducción al diseño del sitio Web, Edición Electrónica, Introducción a programas universitarios, Matemáticas, Cerámica, Preparación para los exámenes SAT, Oratoria, Programa de Estudio y Redacción.

Le programme d'été ESL (anglais deuxième langue) de 9 semaines proposé par Wyoming Seminary comprend 8 semaines de cours de langue intensifs et une semaine dans le Maine. Le long de la côte Atlantique, les étudiants peuvent ainsi conjuguer développement personnel et cours ESL. Parce qu'il n'y a pas de meilleur moyen pour apprendre une langue, les étudiants travaillent en groupe à la conquête de challenges exterieurs et jouissent du magnifique paysage de la Nouvelle Angleterre. Pendant les huit semaines du séminaire du Wyoming, les étudiants peuvent prendre des cours tel que l'Anglais, Introduction à la creation d'un site internet, Programmation Assistée par Ordinateur, Introduction aux Programmes Universitaires, Poterie, Préparation pour l'examen SAT, Cours de Prononciation et d'Ecriture.

Wyoming Seminary での9週間の夏期 ESL プログラムは、8週間の集中語学学習とメイン州に於ける1週間の滞在を合わせたものです。生徒達は大平洋岸における生活で、美しいニュー・イングランドの田舎と野外での様々な経験を共に分かち合いながら、ESL を学び、且つ、大切な社会性を身につけて行きます。8週間の期間中、英語、初歩のウェブ・デザイン、デスクトップパブリッシング、大学のプログラムの紹介、数学、陶器造作、SAT の準備、演説、学習方法、作文のクラスを受講します。

Wyoming 學院的 ESL 暑期課程為期九周。學生們將在八周的嚴密的語言訓練以外在大西洋海岸的 Maine 度過一周，在繼續 ESL 課程的同時培養重要的生活技能。學生們一起克服戶外活動中的挑戰，陶醉在新英格蘭美麗的鄉村景色中，這種環境最有利於對語言能力的提高。在 Wyoming Seminary 的八周中，學生可選修英語、初級網路設計、平面排版、大學課程簡介、數學、陶器藝術、SAT 預備課程、寫作課程。

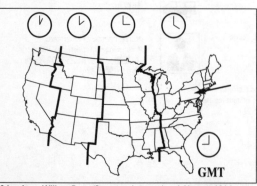

16 km from Wilkes-Barre/Scranton International Airport; 161 km from Philadelphia • A 16 km del aeropuerto internacional Wilkes-Barre/ Scranton; a 161 km de Filadelfia • A 16 km de l'aéroport international Wilkes-Barre/Scranton ; à 161 km de Philadelphie
Wilkes-Barre/Scranton 国際空港より 16 km, Philadelphia より 161 km
離 Wilkes-Barre/Scranton 國際機場 16 公里；離 Philadelphia 市 161 公里

21°–32° C	1:15
Small town • Pueblo pequeño • Petite ville 小都市 小鎮	Rolling • Continuo • Continuelles 随時入学受付 隨時皆可
Methodist • Metodista • Méthodiste メソディスト 衛理公會	Philadelphia, New York City, Baltimore, Washington, D.C.
13–18	$3400–$8600
20, 25	Available • Disponibles • Disponibles' 有り 有
45, 30%	No fee • Gratuito • Gratuit 無料 無費用
Japan, Korea, Taiwan, Thailand	Nurse, infirmary • Enfermero(a), enfermería • Infirmier(ère), infirmerie 看護婦、キャンプ内の診療所 護士、醫務所
Minimal proficiency necessary • Se requieren conocimientos mínimos • Aptitude minimale requise 初級レベル 初級英文程度	
No fee • Gratuito • Gratuit 無料 無費用	
Dormitories • Residencias estudiantiles • Dortoirs 寮 宿舍	
June 27–July 24, July 25–August 27 • 27 de junio–24 de julio, 25 de julio–27 de agosto • 27 juin–24 juillet, 25 juillet–27 août • 6月27日〜7月24日、7月25日〜8月27日 6月27日〜7月24日、7月25日〜8月27日	

COLLÈGE DU LÉMAN

Francis A. Clivaz
74, Route de Sauverny
CH-1290 Versoix-Genève, Switzerland
Phone: (4122) 775 55 55   Fax: (4122) 775 55 59
E-mail: info@cdl.ch   URL: http://www.cdl.ch

During Summer students are offered the opportunity to take language courses (French, English, German) or revise and be awarded credit in academic subjects. Collège du Léman, accredited by both CIS (Council of International Schools) and NEASC (New England Association of Schools and Colleges), allows credits to be transferred from one institution to another and to become part of the official school report. The afternoons are devoted to sports activities and cultural trips. Activities include basketball, bicycling, horseback riding, soccer, swimming, tennis, and water sports.

En el verano se ofrece a los estudiantes la oportunidad de tomar cursos de idiomas (alemán, francés, e inglés) o repasar y obtener crédito en materias académicas. La universidad de Leman, acreditado tanto por el Consejo de Escuelas Internacionales (Council of International Schools, CIS) y la Asociación de Nueva Inglaterra de Escuelas y Universidades (New England Association of Schools and Colleges, NEASC), permite que los créditos se transfieran de una institución a otra y que formen parte del informe escolar oficial. Las tardes se dedican a actividades de deportes y viajes culturales. Las actividades incluyen, baloncesto, ciclismo, correr a caballo, fútbol, natación, tenis, y deportes acuáticos.

Durant l'été nous offrons aux étudiants la possibilité de suivre des cours de langues (français, anglais, allemand) ou de réviser et d'acquérir des crédits dans les matières académiques. Le Collège du Léman, institution accredité à la fois par le CIS (Council of International Schools) et la NEAC (New England Association of Schools and Colleges), permet aux crédits d'être transférés d'une institution à l'autre et de faire partie intégrante du bulletin scolaire officiel. L'après-midi est consacré aux activités sportives et aux excursions culturelles. Parmi les activités, on compte le basket-ball, le cyclisme, l'équitation, le football, la natation, le tennis et les sports nautiques.

夏の間学生は語学コース（フランス語、英語、ドイツ語）を受講、または復習でき、学科の履修単位を授与されます。当校は CIS と NEASC の公認校であり、学校間の転校を許可また評価に加え、公の学業成績評価の一部に加えます。午後はスポーツ（バスケットボール、自転車、乗馬、サッカー、水泳、テニス、水上スポーツ）や文化的な小旅行に当てられます。

整個夏季中學生們有機會選修語言課程（如法語，英語，德語）或選修有學分的課程。College du Leman 在 CIS（國際學生協會）和 NEASC（新英格蘭學院協會）的准許下，學生可將學分從一個學院轉到另一個學院，併入正式的總體學分報告。下午時間多用來做體育運動和文化遊覽。活動項目包括籃球，自行車，馬術，足球，游泳，網球，以及水上運動。

 25°–30° C

 1:10

 Small town • Pueblo pequeño • Petite ville
小都市
小鎮

 Rolling • Continuo • Continuelles
随時入学受付
隨時皆可

 Nondenominational • Sin afiliación religiosa • Non confessionnelle
宗教上の制限無し
無教派

 Crans-Montana, Lake Geneva, cities in Switzerland, Zermatt

 8–18

 CHF 4500 (3-week language program)
CHF 5400 (3-week academic program)

 100, 100

 Available • Disponibles • Disponibles
有り
有

 200, 95%

 No fee • Gratuito • Gratuit
無料
無費用

 Germany, Italy, Spain, Switzerland, United States

 Nurse, infirmary • Enfermero(a), enfermería • Infirmier(ère), infirmerie
看護婦、キャンプ内の診療所
護士、醫務所

 No proficiency necessary • No se requieren conocimientos previos • Aucune aptitude requise
基礎レベル（予備知識不要）
無英文程度要求

 No fee • Gratuito • Gratuit
無料
無費用

 Dormitories • Residencias estudiantiles • Dortoirs
寮
宿舍

 June 27–July 17, July 18–August 7 • 27 de junio–17 de julio, 18 de julio–7 de agosto • 27 juin–17 juillet, 18 juillet–7 août
6 月 27 日～7 月 17 日、7 月 18 日～8 月 7 日
6 月 27 日～7 月 17 日，7 月 18 日～8 月 7 日

10 km from Geneva International Airport and downtown Geneva • A 10 km del aeropuerto internacional Ginebra y del centro de la ciudad • A 10 km de l'aéroport international de Genève et du centre de Genève.
Geneva 国際空港および Geneva 都心より 10 キロ
離 Geneva 國際機場和 Geneva 市中心 10 公里

EXPLORATION SUMMER PROGRAMS

![ESL]

EXPLORATION®
SUMMER PROGRAMS

Barbara Targum
P.O. Box 368, 470 Washington Street
Norwood, Massachusetts 02062
Phone: 781-762-7400 Fax: 781-762-7425
URL: http://www.explo.org

Students enjoy the educational and recreational facilities of Yale University, Wellesley College, and St. Mark's School. The campuses are near the cultural resources of New York City and Boston, making them ideal settings for learning and recreation. Options include business, science, theater, soccer, swimming, tennis, and ESL preparation.

Los estudiantes disfrutan de las instalaciones educativas y recreativas de Yale University, Wellesley College y St. Mark's School. Las instalaciones se encuentran cerca de los recursos culturales de las ciudades de Nueva York y Boston, lo cual las convierten en el lugar ideal para aprender y divertirse. Entre las opciones se hallan las actividades comerciales, ciencias, teatro, fútbol, natación, tenis y preparación para el examen ESL.

Les étudiants profitent des installations éducatives et récréatives de Yale University, Wellesley College et St. Mark's School. Les campus, proches des ressources culturelles de New York et de Boston, sont situés de façon idéale pour apprendre aussi bien que pour se détendre. Parmi les choix on compte le business, les sciences, le football, la natation, le tennis, le théâtre et la préparation pour l'examen ESL.

学生はイェール大学、ウェレズリー大学、セント・マークス高校の教育、レクリエーション施設を利用できます。キャンパスはニューヨークとボストンの文化施設に近く、学習とレクリエーションに最適の環境です。ビジネス、科学、演劇、サッカー、水泳、テニス、ライティング、ESL 準備講座等のコースがあります。

參加的學生都喜歡 Yale University、Wellesley College 和 St. Mark's School 的教育和娛樂設施。由於校園離紐約市和波士頓這兩個文化中心較近，因此是學習和娛樂的理想場所。選修課程包括商業、科學、戲劇、足球、游泳、網球、以及 ELS 輔導。

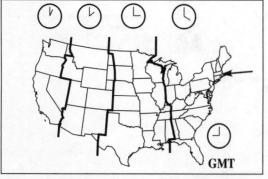
GMT

30 km from Logan International Airport; 25 km from Boston •
A 30 km del aeropuerto internacional de Logan; a 25 km de Boston •
A 30 km de l'aéroport international Logan ; à 25 km de Boston
Logan 国際空港より 30 km, Boston より 25 km
離 Logan 國際機場 30 公里 ; 離 Boston 市 25 公里

21°–32° C

1:7

Small town and small city • Pueblo y ciudad pequeño • Petite ville et petite agglomération
小さな町や市
小鎮和小城市

Nondenominational • Sin afiliación religiosa • Non confessionnelle
宗教上の制限無し
無教派

Rolling • Continuo • Continuelles
随時入学受付
隨時皆可

Boston, throughout New England, New York City

9–17

$3550, $6795, $195, $295, $250

200–300, 200–300

Available • Disponibles • Disponibles
有り
有

120–140, 20%

No fee • Gratuito • Gratuit
無料
無費用

China, England, France, India, Israel, Italy, Japan, Korea, Philippines, Poland, Russia, Spain, Switzerland, Taiwan, Turkey

On-site • En las instalaciones • Sur place
敷地内医療施設
實地

Moderate proficiency necessary • Se requieren conocimientos moderados • Aptitude modérée requise
中級レベル
中級英文程度

$195

Dormitories • Residencias estudiantiles • Dortoirs
寮
宿舎

June 26–July 16, July 17–August 6 • 26 de junio–16 de julio, 17 de julio–6 de agosto •
26 julio–16 juillet, 17 juillet–6 août •
6 月 26 日～7 月 16 日、7 月 17 日～8 月 6 日
6 月 26 日～7 月 16 日，7 月 17 日～8 月 6 日

FLS INTERNATIONAL
YEAR-ROUND PROGRAMS

Brian Henry, VP for Academic Affairs
101 East Green Street, #14
Pasadena, California 91105
Phone: 626-795-2912 Fax: 626-795-5564
E-mail: fls@fls.net
URL: http://www.fls.net

ESL

FLS International's year-round programs offer students the exciting combination of popular destinations, stimulating English programs, and varied excursions, all set on thriving college campuses. Experienced instructors and an extensive curriculum provide strong academic content. Options include business, computers, English, hiking, introduction to college, reading, study skills, swimming, volleyball, and writing. Each program includes a variety of guided excursions.

Los programas de año completo de FLS International ofrecen a los estudiantes la emocionante combinación de destinos populares, programas de inglés estimulantes y diferentes tipos de excursiones, todo en recintos universitarios florecientes. Instructores con experiencia y planes de estudio extensos brindan una sólida preparación académica. Las opciones incluyen negocios, computación, inglés, excursionismo, introducción a la universidad, lectura, técnicas de estudio, natación, voleibol y redacción. Cada programa incluye una variedad de excursiones guiadas.

Les programmes à l'année des FLS International offrent aux étudiants une combinaison parfaite : des destinations très appréciées, des programmes d'anglais stimulants et des excursions variées, le tout sur de magnifiques campus universitaires. La grande expérience des professeurs et l'ampleur du cursus scolaire offrent un programme académique solide. Les options comprennent le commerce, l'informatique, l'anglais, la randonnée, l'introduction à l'université, la lecture, les techniques d'études, la natation, le volley-ball et la composition. Chaque programme comprend une variété d'excursions guidées.

FLS International の通年プログラムは、人気のあるロケーション、活気のある英語プログラム、様々な遠足を組み合わせており、すべてが活気に溢れた大学のキャンパスで行われます。経験豊富な教師陣と広範囲なカリキュラムで強固な学習内容を提供します。オプションには、ビジネス、コンピューター、英語、ハイキング、大学入門講座、読解力、学習法、水泳、バレーボール、英作文があります。各プログラムには様々なガイド付き小旅行が含まれています。

FLS International 全年開辦的項目為學員提供有趣的熱門景點綜合游，富有促進性的英文課程，以及各種遠足活動；所有這些都在各大學生機勃勃的校園中進行。我們的教師經驗豐富、課程範圍廣，可以提供極佳的學習內容。選課包括工商、學習技能、游泳、排球和寫作。每個計劃都包括種類不同的有引導的遊覽。

Program • Programa • Programme
プログラム　　　　　科系課程

Las Vegas, Nevada	Oxnard, California
Glendora, California	Lock Haven, Pennsylvania
Oceanside, California	Franklin, Massachusetts

 Varies • Varía • Varie
様々
不同

 Varies • Varía • Varie
様々
不同

 Nondenominational • Sin afiliación religiosa • Non confessionnelle
特定宗教に無関係
無教派

 14–24

 50%, 50%

 Las Vegas: 75; Glendora: 111; Oxnard: 93; Lock Haven: 60; Franklin: 75; Oceanside: 75

 Brazil, Chile, Colombia, France, Hong Kong, Indonesia, Italy, Japan, Peru, Russia, South Korea, Spain, Taiwan, Turkey, Venezuela

 No proficiency necessary • No se requieren conocimientos previos • Aucune aptitude requise
基礎レベル（予備知識不要）
無英文程度要求

 No fee • Gratuito • Gratuit
無料
無費用

 Dormitories and homestays with American families, student apartments • Residencias estudiantiles y casas privadas con familias estadounidenses, apartamentos para estudiantes • Dortoirs et séjours avec une famille américaine, appartements pour étudiants
寮またはアメリカ家庭でのホームステイ、学生アパート
宿舍，當地家庭，學生部

 2-4 weeks sessions available starting: Any Monday • Sesiones de 2-4 semanas disponibles a partir del cualquier lunes • Des séances de 2 à 4 semaines sont disponibles à partir du : Tout lundi
2-4 週間の授業はそれぞれ以下の日付から始まります: 月曜日
提供為期兩周的課程，開課時間分別為：任何一個星期一

 1:8

 Rolling • Continuo • Continuelles
随時入学受付
随時皆可

 Las Vegas and Utah: Grand Canyon, Zion National Park; California: Disneyland, Universal Studios; Lock Haven; New York City; Amish Community; Franklin, Massachusetts; Rhode Island; Boston

 $1295-$2595, $0, $150/week

 Available • Disponibles • Disponibles
有り
有

 No fee • Gratuito • Gratuit
無料
無費用

 Hospital • Hospital • Hôpital
病院
醫院

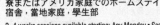

THE PUTNEY SCHOOL SUMMER PROGRAMS
PROGRAM FOR INTERNATIONAL EDUCATION

Thomas D. Howe, Director
The Putney School, Putney, Vermont 05346
Phone: 802-387-6297 Fax: 802-387-6216
E-mail: summer@putney.org
URL: http://www.putneyschool.org/summer

The Program for International Education instructs students in using English as a living language, guides them in acculturation to the United States, and integrates them into the residential, recreational, social, and artistic activities with students from the United States in a beautiful New England setting. In addition to English language instruction, activities include field trips, sports, canoeing, computers, visual and performing arts, hiking, and writing.

El Program for International Education instruye a los estudiantes en el uso del inglés como idioma vivo, los ayuda a adaptarse a la vida en los EE.UU. e integra una serie de actividades residenciales, recreativas, sociales y artísticas con estudiantes de los Estados Unidos en un hermoso lugar en Nueva Inglaterra. Además de las clases de inglés, las actividades incluyen excursiones de estudio, deportes, canotaje, computación, artes visuales y escénicas, excursionismo y redacción.

Le Program for International Education instruit les étudiants sur l'usage de l'anglais comme langue vivante, les guide dans leur adaptation à la culture américaine et les integre dans des activités résidentielles, récréatives, sociales et artistiques avec des étudiants américains dans une magnifique ambiance de Nouvelle Angleterre. En plus des cours d'anglais, d'autres activités vous sont proposées: sorties, sports, canoë, informatique, arts visuelles, arts du spectacle, randonnée et composition.

美しいアメリカ、ニューイングランドで開講される国際教育のための本プログラムは日常生活言語として英語が使われ、現地での実生活に融合させ、レクリエーション、社交及び文化活動を通じて生徒がアメリカ文化に適応するための指導を行います。英語の授業に加えて、実地見学、スポーツ、カヌー、コンピューター、映像と舞台芸術、ハイキング、ライティングなどの活動があります。

國際教育課程在新英格蘭幽美的環境裡教導學生如何在日常生活中使用英文,指導學生適應美國文化,幫助外籍學生融入美國學生,共享寄宿性、娛樂性、社交性以及藝術性的活動。除英語語言指導外,還設有各種活動,包括外出實習、體育、划獨木舟、電腦、觀賞及表演藝術、健行以及寫作。

 20°–30° C

 1:3

 Rural • Rural • Rurale
郡部
郷村

 Rolling, June 1, 2005 • Continuo, 1 de junio • Continuelles, 1ᵉʳ juin
随時入学受付、6月1日
随時皆可 2005 年 6 月 1 日

 Nondenominational • Sin afiliación religiosa • Non confessionnelle
宗教上の制限無し
無教派

 Boston, Northampton, Massachusetts, Burlington, Vermont

 14–17

 $3000--$5600

 10, 10

 Available • Disponibles • Disponibles
有り
有

 20–25, 20%

 Fee varies • Honorario variado • Les tarifs varient
費用は場合によって異なる
費用不同

 Bulgaria, France, Japan, Korea, Mexico, Russia, Venezuela

 On-site • En las instalaciones • Sur place
敷地内医療施設
實地

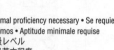 Minimal proficiency necessary • Se requieren conocimientos mínimos • Aptitude minimale requise
初級レベル
初級英文程度

 No fee • Gratuito • Gratuit
無料
無費用

 Dormitories • Residencias estudiantiles • Dortoirs
寮
宿舎

 June 26–July 15, July 17–August 5 • 26 de junio–15 de julio, 17 de julio–5 de agosto • 26 juin–15 juillet, 17 juillet–5 août
6 月 26 日～7 月 15 日、7 月 17 日～8 月 5 日
6 月 26 日～7 月 15 日，7 月 17 日～8 月 5 日

GMT

150 km from Bradley International Airport ; 185 km from Boston, MA • A 150 km del aeropuerto internacional de Bradley; a 185 km de Boston, MA • A 150 km de l'aéroport international Bradley ; à 185 km de Boston, MA
Bradley 国際空港より 150 キロ、Boston, MA より 185 キロ
離 Bradley 國際機場 150 公里 ；離 Boston, MA 185 公里

CAMP REGIS–APPLEJACK
PAUL SMITHS, NEW YORK

Michael P. Humes
60 Lafayette Road West
Princeton, New Jersey 08540
Phone: 609-688-0368 Fax: 609-688-0369
E-mail: campregis@aol.com
URL: http://www.campregis-applejack.com

Family owned since 1946, Camp Regis-Applejack is best known for its friendly atmosphere. Located in one of the most spectacular areas of the United States, its many lakes and mountains greatly enhance the camping experience. Activities include hiking, overnight trips, mountain biking, white-water rafting, horseback riding, sailing, windsurfing, waterskiing, tennis, soccer, art, pottery, music, theater, dance, English, and travel in Canada and the United States.

El campamento Regis-Applejack, operado por una familia desde el 1946, es mejor conocido por su ambiente amistoso. Localizado en una de las áreas más espectaculares de los Estados Unidos, la experiencia de campamento es realzada por sus varios lagos y montañas. Las actividades incluyen, caminatas, excursiones de una noche, ciclismo de montaña, paseos en aguas rápidas, paseos ecuestres, vela, esquí acuático, "windsurfing", tenis, sóccer, arte, cerámica, música, teatro, baile, inglés, y viajes en Canadá y los Estados Unidos.

Camp Regis-Applejack est une propriété familiale depuis 1946 et son atmosphère accueillante a fait sa réputation. Sa situation exceptionnelle, dans l'une des régions les plus belles des États-Unis, au cœur de nombreux lacs et montagnes, fait du camping une expérience inoubliable. Les activités comprennent randonnée, excursions avec bivouac, rafting en eau vive, équitation, voile, planche à voile, ski nautique, tennis, football, arts, poterie, musique, théâtre, danse, cours d'Anglais et voyages au Canada et à travers les Etats-Unis.

1946 年以来の親族経営による Camp Regis Applejack は、親しみやすい雰囲気で知られています。 米国内で最も壮大な地域に位置し、多くの湖と山々でのキャンプは素晴らしい体験となります。ハイキング、一泊旅行、マウンテン・バイク、いかだ下り、乗馬、帆走、ウィンドサーフィン、水上スキー、テニス、サッカー、美術、陶芸、音楽、舞台芸術、ダンス、英語、カナダと米国内の旅行が活動に含まれます。

為私家擁有的 Camp Regis-Applejack 建于 1946 年，為其友好的校園氣氛而著稱。位處于美國最美好的景點之一，諸多的湖泊和山脈為學生提供難忘的野宿記憶。活動包括爬山，過夜旅行，山間腳踏車，激流泛舟，騎馬，航行，滑浪風帆，滑水，網球，足球，美術，陶藝，音樂，戲劇，舞蹈，英文，以及去加拿大及美國內地旅遊。

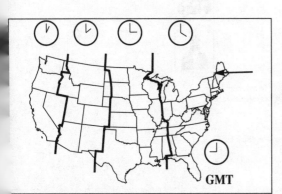

GMT

90 km from Montreal International Airport •
A 90 km del Aeropuerto Internacional de Montreal •
À 90 km de l'aéroport international de Montreal •
Montreal 国際空港より 90 km
離 Montreal 國際機場 90 公里

 20°-32° C

 1:3

 Rural • Rural • Rurale
郡部
郷村

 Rolling • Continuo • Continuelles
随時入学受付
隨時皆可

 Nondenominational • Sin afiliación religiosa •
Non confessionnelle
特定宗教に無関係
無教派

 Montreal, Lake Placid, Lake George, Quebec City, Vermont, New York City

 Regis: 6-12; Applejack: 13-16

 $2800-$5100, $0, $0

 130, 130

 Available • Disponibles • Disponibles
有り
有

 10%

 No fee • Gratuito • Gratuit
無料
無費用

 France, Germany, Italy, Japan, Mexico, Venezuela

 Nurse, infirmary • Enfermero(a), enfermería •
Infirmier(ère), infirmerie
看護婦、キャンプ内の診療所
護士、醫務所

 No proficiency necessary • No se requieren conocimientos previos • Aucune aptitude requise
基礎レベル（予備知識不要）
無英文程度要求

 $10/hour • (añadido a la matrícula) • (inclus dans les frais de scolarité)
1 時間 10 ドル
每小時 10 美元

 Cabins • Cabañas • Cabanes
キャビン
木屋

 Late June through August; one 8-week session, two 4-week sessions • A finales de junio hasta agosto; una sesión de 8 semanas, dos sesiones de 4 semanas • De fin juin à fin août ; un programme de 8 semaines ou deux programmes de 4 semaines
6月末から8月；8週間セッション1回、4週間セッション2回
在 6 月至 8 月間設有一個為期八周課程和兩個為期四周的課程。

SEACAMP

Grace Upshaw,
Camp Director
1300 Big Pine Avenue
Big Pine Key, Florida 33043

Phone: 305-872-2331
Fax: 305-872-2555
E-mail: snorkelingfun@seacamp.org
URL: http://www.seacamp.org

Seacamp's tropical location offers teenagers an opportunity to explore the Florida Keys waters. Marine science/scuba courses are taught by experienced, academically trained science and scuba instructors who provide campers with a safe environment in which to live and learn. Activities include marine science, scuba diving, drawing, environmental science, journalism, photography, pottery, sailing, and water sports.

La ubicación tropical de Seacamp ofrece a los adolescentes una oportunidad para explorar las aguas de los cayos de Florida. Los cursos de ciencias marinas y buceo están a cargo de instructores experimentados y con acreditación académica, lo cual proporciona a los participantes un ambiente seguro de aprendizaje. Las actividades incluyen ciencias marinas, buceo, dibujo, ciencias ambientales, periodismo, fotografía, cerámica, velerismo y deportes acuáticos.

Le site tropical de Seacamp offre aux adolescents et adolescentes l'occasion d'explorer les eaux de la région des Keys de Floride. Des instructeurs chevronnés et qualifiés de plongée/ sciences marines offrent aux campeurs un milieu sûr où vivre et apprendre. Les activités comprennent les sciences de la mer, la plongée sous-marine, le dessin, les sciences de l'environnement, le journalisme, la photographie, la poterie, la voile et les sports nautiques.

シーキャンプは熱帯地域にあり、ティーンエージャーがフロリダ諸島周辺の海を探索する機会を提供しています。海洋科学、スキューバダイビングの各コースは、経験豊かで、正式なトレーニングを受けた教官が、安全な生活・学習環境の中で指導に当たっています。海洋科学、スキューバダイビング、美術（描画）、環境科学、ジャーナリズム、写真技術、陶芸、セーリング、及び水上スポーツ等のクラス・諸活動があります。

位於熱帶地區的 Seacamp 提供青少年探尋佛羅里達州 Keys 水域的机會。海洋科學／潛水課程是由經驗豐富、受過專業科學和潛水訓練的指導老師授課，學員在安全的環境中生活与學習。活動包括海洋科學、潛水、素描、環境科學、新聞學、攝影、陶器製作、風帆和水上活動。

 26°–33° C

 1:3

 Rural • Rural • Rurale
郡部
郷村

 Rolling • Continuo • Continuelles
随時入学受付
隨時皆可

 Nondenominational • Sin afiliación religiosa • Non confessionnelle
宗教上の制限無し
無教派

 Key West

 12–17

 $2650, $375, $75

 90, 70

 Available • Disponibles • Disponibles
有り
有

 10, 7%

 $75

 Belgium, Canada, England, Germany, Greece, Italy, Japan, Poland, Russia, Spain, Venezuela

 Minimal proficiency necessary • Se requieren conocimientos mínimos • Aptitude minimale requise
初級レベル
初級英文程度

 Not available • No disponibles • Pas disponibles
無し
無

 Dormitories • Residencias estudiantiles • Dortoirs
寮
宿舎

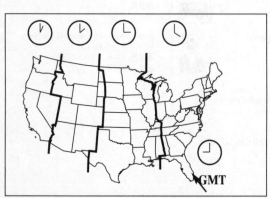

242 km from Miami International Airport and Miami •
A 242 km de Miami International Airport y de Miami •
A 242 km de Miami International Airport et de Miami
マイアミ国際空港から 242 km
離 Miami 國際機場和 Miami 市 242 公里

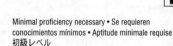 June 24–July 11, July 14–July 31, August 3–August 20 • 24 de junio–11 de julio, 14 de julio–31 de julio, 3 de agosto–20 de agosto • 24 juin–11 juillet, 14 juillet–31 juillet, 3 août–20 août
6 月 24 日～7 月 11 日、7 月 14 日～7 月 31 日、8 月 3 日～8 月 20 日
6 月 24 ～7 月 11 日、7 月 14 日～7 月 31 日、8 月 3 日～8 月 20 日

ACTIONQUEST

James Stoll, Director
P.O. Box 5517
Sarasota, Florida 34277
Phone: 941-924-6789 Fax: 941-924-6075
E-mail: info@actionquest.com
URL: http://www.actionquest.com

Teens live aboard 50-ft sailing yachts while earning sailing and scuba certifications in the British Virgin Islands, Galapagos, Mediterranean, Tahiti, Australia, and Leeward Islands. No previous experience is needed. Programs center on goal-oriented achievement in a noncompetitive atmosphere. Activities include sailing, water skiing, wakeboarding, windsurfing, scuba diving, environmental and marine sciences, and leadership training.

Los adolescentes viven a bordo de yates de 15 m mientras obtienen sus certificados en velerismo y buceo en las Islas Vírgenes Británicas, las islas Galápagos, el Mediterráneo, Tahití, Australia y las Islas Leeward. No se requiere experiencia previa en velerismo. Los programas se concentran en el logro de objetivos en un ambiente no competitivo. Entre las actividades se cuentan, la vela, el esquí acuático, el esquí acuático sobre una tabla (wakeboarding) el surfing a vela, el buceo, ciencias ecológicas y marinas y capacitación en liderazgo.

Les jeunes vivent à bord de voiliers de 15 m et obtiennent un diplôme de navigation à voile et de plongée sous-marine dans les îles Vierges, les Galapagos, la Méditerranée, Tahiti, l'Australie et les îles Sous-le-Vent. Aucune expérience précédente n'est requise. Les programmes sont axés sur la réalisation des buts personnels dans un cadre non concurrentiel. Les activités comprennent la voile, le ski nautique, le wakeboard, la planche à voile, la plongée sous-marine, les sciences de la mer et de l'environnement, et la formation au leadership.

十代の若者が英領バージン島、ガラパゴス、地中海、タヒチ、オーストラリアそしてリワード諸島で長さ15メートルのヨットで生活しながら、ヨットとスキューバ・ダイビング認定を取得します。ヨットの経験は問いません。プログラムは協調的な雰囲気の中で、目標達成を重視して作られています。活動にはヨット、水上スキー、ウェイクボーディング、ウィンドサーフィン、スキューバダイビング、環境・海洋科学、リーダーシップトレーニングが含まれます。

青少年居住在16公尺長的風帆快艇上，在英屬維京群島、加拉帕戈斯、地中海、斐濟、塔希提、圣布拉斯群島、博耐爾和背風群島等地，修習風帆和潛水證書。參加學員無需入學前風帆經驗。課程強調學員在輕松的環境裡達到目標成就。活動包括航海、滑水、滑水板、沖浪、蛙人潛水、環境和海洋科學，以及領導能力訓練。

Program • Programa • Programme プログラム	科系課程
British Virgin Islands	Galapagos
Leeward Islands	Tahiti
Mediterranean Sea	Australia

 25°–30 °C

 1:4

 Caribbean, Mediterranean, Galapagos, Tahiti, Australia

 Rolling • Continuo • Continuelles 随時入学受付 隨時皆可

 Nondenominational • Sin afiliación religiosa • Non confessionnelle 宗教上の制限無し 無教派

 Tortola, Nice, Monte Carlo, Rome, St. Martin, St. Kitts and Nevis, Galapagos, Tahiti, Australia, Amazon Delta,

 13–19

 $3470–$4470, $0, $150

 50, 50

 Available • Disponibles • Disponibles 有り 有

 20, 10%

 No fee • Gratuito • Gratuit 無料 無費用

 Including: all over Europe (England, France, Germany), the Far East, South America, USA

 Infirmary • Enfermería • Infirmerie 診療施設 醫務所

 Minimal proficiency necessary • Se requieren conocimientos mínimos • Aptitude minimale requise 初級レベル 初級英文程度

 Not available • No disponibles • Pas disponible 無し 無

 Sailing yachts, hostels, host family homes • Yates, residencias estudiantiles, casas de familia • Voiliers, auberges de jeunesse, résidences familiales ヨット、ホステル、ホストファミリー 風帆快艇，旅店，住家

 June 16–July 6, July 8–July 28, July 29–August 16 • 16 de junio–6 de julio , 8–28 de julio, 29 de julio–16 de agosto • 16 juin–6 juillet, 8–28 juillet, 29juillet–16 août
6月16日〜7月6日、7月8日〜7月28日、7月29日〜8月16日
6月16日〜7月6日，7月8日〜7月28日，7月29日〜8月16日

OTHER SUMMER PROGRAMS

OTROS PROGRAMAS DE VERANO   AUTRES PROGRAMMES ESTIVAUX

夏期夏期プログラム   其他夏令營活動

Programs listed in this section have indicated by survey response that they welcome international students in their summer camp programs. The addresses and telephone and fax numbers provided are those of their winter (off-season) offices. Families who need to contact programs from June through August can use the off-season phone and fax numbers; they will usually be referred to the summer numbers.

Las respuestas de las encuestas realizadas indican que los programas incluidos en esta sección acogen a estudiantes extranjeros en sus campamentos y programas de verano. La dirección, números de teléfono y de fax suministrados son los de sus oficinas de invierno (temporada baja). Las familias que necesiten ponerse en contacto con los programas de junio a agosto pueden llamar a los números de teléfono y de fax de invierno, donde generalmente obtendrán información del contacto durante el verano.

Les participants internationaux sont acceptés aux colonies et programmes estivaux apparaissant dans cette section, tel qu'indiqué par les résponses des responsables respectifs aux questionnaires. Les adresses, numéros de téléphone et de télécopieur qui sont fournis servent à rejoindre les bureaux d'hiver (hors saison). Les familles désirant communiquer avec les responsables des programmes des mois de juin à août peuvent utiliser ces numéros et adresses d'hiver.

このセクションにあるプログラムは、夏期プログラムに留学生を受け入れるとアンケートに答えた学校を掲載しています。学校の住所、電話番号、ファックス番号は各校の冬期プログラム（オフシーズン）のものです。しかし、6月から8月の間に連絡をとる必要がある場合にも、まずこれらのオフシーズンの電話番号やファックス番号にアクセスし、夏期プログラムの連絡先を確認して下さい。

此部份所列夏令營課程乃經過問卷調查，歡迎國際學生參加其暑期班課程及活動。在此所列的地址、電話和傳真號碼皆屬寒假（淡季）聯絡通訊之用。如慾聯絡有關六月到八月的課程，可使用此寒假電話和傳真號碼；聯絡單位通常會提供暑期課程的電話號碼。

AAC-Aloha Adventure Camps
Kate Stanley, Camp Coordinator
P.O. Box 12229, Lahaina, Hawaii 96761-7229
Phone: 877-755-2267 Fax: 808-665-0707
E-mail: info@hawaiicamps.com

AAVE-America's Adventure Ventures Everywhere
Abbott Wallis, Owner
2245 Stonecrop Way, Golden, Colorado 80401
Phone: 800-222-3595 Fax: 303-526-0885
E-mail: info@aave.com

Abbey Road Overseas Programs
Arthur Kian, Managing Director
8904 Rangely Avenue,
West Hollywood, California 90048
Phone: 888-462-2239 Fax: 866-488-4642
E-mail: info@goabbeyroad.com

Abilene Christian University Leadership Camps
Jan Meyer, Director of Leadership Camps
ACU Box 29004, 129 McKinzie Hall,
Abilene, Texas 79699-9004
Phone: 325-674-2033 Fax: 325-674-6475
E-mail: leadership.camps@campuslife.acu.edu

Academic Camps at Gettysburg College
Doug Murphy, Director
101 Murray Street, Suite 427,
New York, New York 10007
Phone: 800-289-7029 Fax: 212-815-9256
E-mail: academiccamps@gettysburg.edu

L' Académie de Paris
Oxbridge Academic Programs
Andrea Mardon, Executive Director,
Oxbridge Academic Programs
601 West 110th Street, Suite 7R
New York, New York 10025-2186
Phone: 800-828-8349 Fax: 212-663-8169
E-mail: info@oxbridgeprograms.com

Academy by the Sea
The Academy by the Sea/Camp Pacific
Lori Adlfinger, Associate Director
P.O. Box 3000, Carlsbad, California 92018-3000
Phone: 760-434-7564 Fax: 760-729-1574
E-mail: info@abts.com

Acadia Institute of Oceanography
Sheryl Gilmore, Director
P.O. Box 285, Seal Harbor, Maine 04675
Phone: 207-276-9825 Fax: 207-276-9825
E-mail: info@acadiainstitute.com

Access to Careers in the Sciences (ACES) Camps
Texas Woman's University
DeAnna Taylor, Project Coordinator
Science and Math Center, P.O. Box 425846, Denton, Texas 76204-5846
Phone: 800-860-2237 Fax: 940-898-2767
E-mail: dtaylor@twu.edu

Acteen
Rita Litton, Acteen Director
35 West 45th Street, New York, New York 10036
Phone: 212-391-5915 Fax: 212-768-8918
E-mail: rita@acteen.com

Acting Academy at Pali Overnight Adventures
Pali Overnight Adventures
Andy Wexler, Owner/Founder
P.O. Box 2237, Running Springs, California 92382
Phone: 909-867-5743 Fax: 909-867-7643
E-mail: info@paliadventures.com

Adirondack Camp
Matt Basinet, Director
P.O. Box 97, Putnam Station, New York 12861
Phone: 518-547-8261 Fax: 518-547-8973
E-mail: matt@adirondackcamp.com

Adventure Camps
Ligonier Camp and Conference Center
Registrar, LCCC
Phone: 724-238-6428 Fax: 724-238-6971
E-mail: ligcamp@ligoniercamp.org

Adventure Ireland
Niamh Hamill, Director
Donegal Adventure Centre, Bundoran, Co.
Donegal, Ireland
Phone: 353-7198-42418 Fax: 353-7198-42429
E-mail: info@adventure-ireland.com

Adventure Links
Elena Gonzalez, Summer Camp Director
21498 Blue Ridge Mountain Road,
Paris, Virginia 20130
Phone: 540-592-3682 Fax: 540-592-3316
E-mail: elena@adventurelinks.net

!Adventures-Afloat/Odyssey Expeditions
Jason Buchheim, Director
650 Southeast Paradise Point Road, #100,
Crystal River, Florida 34429
Phone: 800-929-7749 Fax: 801-340-5000
E-mail: odyssey@usa.net

Adventures Cross-Country
Scott von Eschen, Director
242 Redwood Highway,
Mill Valley, California 94941
Phone: 415-332-5075 Fax: 415-332-2130
E-mail: arcc@adventurescrosscountry.com

Adventures in Science and Arts
Western Washington University
Debbie Young Gibbons, Program Manager
Extended Education and Summer Programs, Mail Stop 5293, 516 High Street,
Bellingham, Washington 98225
Phone: 360-650-6820 Fax: 360-650-6858
E-mail: adventures@wwu.edu

Adventures in Veterinary Medicine
Tufts University School of Veterinary Medicine
Kasey Kobs, Director
Office of Special Programs, Tufts University School of Veterinary Medicine,
North Grafton, Massachusetts 01536
Phone: 508-839-7962 Fax: 508-839-7952
E-mail: avm@tufts.edu

Adventure Treks, Inc.
John Dockendorf, Director
P.O. Box 1321, Flat Rock, North Carolina 28731
Phone: 888-954-5555 Fax: 828-696-1663
E-mail: info@advtreks.com

Aerospace Camp Experience
The Museum of Flight
Erik Oost, Ace Coordinator
The Museum of Flight,
Phone: 206-768-7141 Fax: 206-764-5707
E-mail: ace@museumofflight.org

AFS-USA
Manager, AFS Info Center
506 Southwest 6th Avenue, 2nd Floor, Portland, Oregon 97204
Phone: 800-AFS-INFO Fax: 503-248-4076
E-mail: afsinfo@afs.org

Alabama Museum of Natural History Summer Expedition
The University of Alabama
Randy Mecredy, Education Programs Coordinator / Expedition Leader
Alabama Museum of Natural History, Box 870340, Tuscaloosa, Alabama 35487-0340
Phone: 205-348-2136 Fax: 205-348-9292
E-mail: museum.expedition@ua.edu

Alexander Muss High School in Israel
Judy Dunner, National Director of Admissions
12550 Biscayne Boulevard, Suite 604, North Miami, Florida 33181
Phone: 800-327-5980 Fax: 305-891-8806
E-mail: amhsi1@aol.com

Alex Brown and Dustin Lyman Football Camp/Sports International
Sports International, Inc.
Customer Service
8924 McGaw Court, Columbia, Maryland 21045
Phone: 800-555-0801 Fax: 410-309-9962
E-mail: info@footballcamps.com

All Arts and Sciences Camp
Kisha Carmichael, Camp Director
P.O. Box 26170, Greensboro, North Carolina 27402-6170
Phone: 336-334-5414 Fax: 336-334-4733
E-mail: allarts@uncg.edu

Aloha Camp
Aloha Foundation, Inc.
Nancy Pennell, Director
2039 Lake Morey Road, Fairlee, Vermont 05045
Phone: 802-333-3410 Fax: 802-333-3404
E-mail: nancy_pennell@alohafoundation.org

Alpengirl, Inc.
Alissa Farley, Camp Owner
P.O. Box 1138, Manhattan, Montana 59741
Phone: 800-585-7476 Fax: 406-284-9036
E-mail: alissa@alpengirl.com

American Academy of Dramatic Arts Summer Program at Hollywood, California
Dan Justin, Director of Admissions
1336 North LaBrea Avenue, Hollywood, California 90028
Phone: 800-222-2867

American Academy of Dramatic Arts Summer Program at New York
Karen Higginbotham, Director of Admissions
120 Madison Avenue, New York, New York 10016
Phone: 800-463-8990 Fax: 212-685-8093
E-mail: admissions-ny@aada.org

American Collegiate Adventures
Jason Lubar, Director of Summer Programs
1811 W. North Avenue, Suite 201, Chicago, Illinois 60622
Phone: 800-509-SUMR Fax: 773-342-0246
E-mail: info@acasummer.com

American Youth Foundation-Camp Merrowvista
American Youth Foundation
Lisa Boucher, Merrowvista Registrar
147 Canaan Road, Center Tuftonboro, New Hampshire 03816
Phone: 603-539-6607 Fax: 603-539-7504
E-mail: merrowvista@ayf.com

American Youth Foundation-Camp Miniwanca
American Youth Foundation
Lori Greene, Registrar
8845 West Garfield Road, Shelby, Michigan 49455
Phone: 231-861-4313 Fax: 231-861-5244
E-mail: miniwancacamps@ayf.com

Anderson Western Colorado Camps, Ltd.
Christopher Porter, Director
7177 Colorado River Road, Gypsum, Colorado 81637
Phone: 970-524-7766 Fax: 970-524-7107
E-mail: andecamp@andersoncamps.com

Andy McCollum Football Camp
Sports International, Inc.
Customer Service
8924 McGaw Court, Columbia, Maryland 21045
Phone: 800-555-0801 Fax: 410-309-9962
E-mail: info@footballcamps.com

Antwaan Randle Football Camp/Sports International
Sports International, Inc.
Customer Service
8924 McGaw Court, Columbia, Maryland 21045
Phone: 800-555-0801 Fax: 410-309-9962
E-mail: info@footballcamps.com

Apogee Outdoor Adventures
Kevin Cashman, Director
40 Bowker Street, Brunswick, Maine 04011
Phone: 207-725-7025 Fax: 509-693-8868
E-mail: info@apogeeadventures.com

Appel Farm Summer Arts Camp
Appel Farm Arts and Music Center
Matt Sisson, Director
P.O. Box 888, Elmer, New Jersey 08318-0888
Phone: 856-358-2472 Fax: 856-358-6513
E-mail: appelcamp@aol.com

Appleby College Summer Academy
Yigin Wu, Director, Summer Academy
540 Lakeshore Road West, Oakville, Ontario L6K 3P1, Canada
Phone: 905-845-4681 Fax: 905-845-9828
E-mail: ywu@appleby.on.ca

Applejack Teen Camp
Camp Regis, Inc.
Michael Humes, Director
P.O. Box 245, Paul Smiths, New York 12970
Phone: 518-327-3117 Fax: 518-327-3193
E-mail: campregis@aol.com

Art Center College of Design Art Center for Kids
Alegria Castro, Program Coordinator
1700 Lida Street, Pasadena, California 91103
Phone: 626-396-2319 Fax: 626-796-9564
E-mail: kids@artcenter.edu

The Art Institute of Seattle-Studio 101
Chris Galbraith, High School Admissions Information Specialist
2323 Elliott Avenue, Seattle, Washington 98121
Phone: 800-275-2471 Fax: 206-269-0275
E-mail: cgalbraith@aii.edu

Art Monk Football Camp/Sports International
Sports International, Inc.
Customer Service
8924 McGaw Court, Columbia, Maryland 21045
Phone: 800-555-0801 Fax: 410-309-9962
E-mail: info@footballcamps.com

The Arts! at Maryland
University of Maryland, Office of Continuing and Extended Education
Terrie Hruzd, Program Manager, Summer and Special Programs
2103 Reckord Armory, College Park, Maryland 20742
Phone: 301-405-8588 Fax: 301-314-9572
E-mail: hruzd@umd.edu

Arts on the Lake
St. Stephen's Episcopal School
Elizabeth Moon, Director
2900 Bunny Run, Austin, Texas 78746
Phone: 512-327-1213 Fax: 512-327-1311
E-mail: emoon@sstx.org

Atelier des Arts
Bruce Smith, Director
55 Bethune Street, B645, New York, New York 10014
Phone: 212-727-1756 Fax: 212-691-0631
E-mail: info@atelierdesarts.org

Atlanta College of Art-Pre-College Program
Director of Pre-College Program
1280 Peachtree Street, NE, Atlanta, Georgia 30309
Phone: 404-733-5202 Fax: 404-733-5007

American Trails West
Director
92 Middle Neck Road, Great Neck, New York 11021
Phone: 800-645-6260 Fax: 516-487-2855
E-mail: info@americantrailswest.com

Audubon Journeys
Audubon Vermont
Ryan Young, Director
255 Sherman Hollow Road, Huntington, Vermont 05462
Phone: 802-434-3068 Fax: 802-434-4686
E-mail: ryoung@audubon.org

Audubon Vermont Youth Camp
Audubon Vermont
Ryan Young, Director
255 Sherman Hollow Road, Huntington, Vermont 05462
Phone: 802-434-3068 Fax: 802-434-4686
E-mail: ryoung@audubon.org

Ball State University Summer Journalism Workshops
Mark Herron, Director
Ball State University, AJ 304, Muncie, Indiana 47306
Phone: 765-285-8900 Fax: 765-285-7997
E-mail: bsuworkshops@bsu.edu

Barat Foundation Summer Program in Provence and Paris
Chandri Barat, Executive Director
P.O. Box 609, Montville, New Jersey 07045
Phone: 973-263-1013 Fax: 973-263-2287
E-mail: info@baratfoundation.org

Bark Lake Leadership Through Recreation Camp
Brent Gordon, Camp Director
1033 Main Street West, Hamilton, Ontario L8S 1B7, Canada
Phone: 905-577-0705 Fax: 905-577-0704
E-mail: info@barklake.com

Barnard's Summer in New York City: One-Week Mini-Course
Barnard College/Columbia University
Bari Meltzer, Director of Pre-College Programs
New York, New York 10027
Phone: 212-854-8866 Fax: 212-854-8867
E-mail: pcp@barnard.edu

Barton Adventure Camp
The Barton Center for Diabetes Education, Inc.
Gaylen McCann, Resident Camps Director
P.O. Box 356, 30 Ennis Road, North Oxford, Massachusetts 01537
Phone: 508-987-3856 Fax: 508-987-2002
E-mail: gaylen.mccann@bartoncenter.org

Barton Day Camp
The Barton Center for Diabetes Education, Inc.
Kerry Packard, Program Coordinator
P.O. Box 356, 30 Ennis Road, North Oxford, Massachusetts 01537
Phone: 508-987-3856 Fax: 508-987-2002
E-mail: kerry.packard@bartoncenter.org

Bay Area Shakespeare Camp
The San Francisco Shakespeare Festival
John Western, Marketing Director
P.O. Box 460937, San Francisco, California 94146
Phone: 415-422-2222 Fax: 415-626-1138
E-mail: sfshakes@sfshakes.org

Belvoir Terrace
Nancy Goldberg, Director
80 Cliffwood Street, Lenox, Massachusetts 01240
Phone: 413-637-0555 Fax: 413-637-4651
E-mail: belvoirt@aol.com

Berklee College of Music
Office of Special Programs
1140 Boylston Street, MS-155, Boston, Massachusetts 02215
Phone: 617-747-2245 Fax: 617-262-5419
E-mail: summer@berklee.edu

Bicycle Africa Tours
International Bicycle Fund
David Mozer, Director
4887 Columbia Drive South, Seattle, Washington 98108-1919
Phone: 206-767-0848 Fax: 206-767-0848
E-mail: ibike@ibike.org

BICYCLE TRAVEL ADVENTURES-Student Hosteling Program
Ted Lefkowitz, Director
1356 Ashfield Road, P.O. Box 419, Conway, Massachusetts 01341
Phone: 800-343-6132 Fax: 413-369-4257
E-mail: shpbike@aol.com

Birch Trail Camp for Girls
Gabriel Chernov, Director
P.O. Box 527, Minong, Wisconsin 54859
Phone: 715-466-2216 Fax: 715-466-2217
E-mail: gabe@birchtrail.com

Birmingham-Southern College Student Leaders in Service Program
Birmingham-Southern College
John Hawkins, Assistant Director of Admission
BSC Box 549008, Birmingham, Alabama 35254
Phone: 800-523-5793 Fax: 205-226-3074
E-mail: jhawkins@bsc.edu

Birmingham-Southern College Summer Scholar Program
Birmingham-Southern College
David Driskill, Director
BSC Box 549008, Birmingham, Alabama 35254
Phone: 205-226-4684 Fax: 205-226-3074
E-mail: ddriskil@bsc.edu

Blue Lake Fine Arts Camp
Admissions
300 East Crystal Lake Road, Twin Lake, Michigan 49457
Phone: 800-221-3796 Fax: 231-893-5120
E-mail: international@bluelake.org

Blue Ridge School—Adventure Camps
The Blue Ridge School
Tony Brown, Director of Outdoor Programs
Highway 627, St. George, Virginia 22935
Phone: 434-985-2811 Fax: 434-985-7215
E-mail: tbrown@blueridgeschool.com

Blue Star Camps
Rodger Popkin, Co-Director/Owner
P.O. Box 1029, Crab Creek Road, Hendersonville, North Carolina 28793
Phone: 828-692-3591 Fax: 828-692-7030
E-mail: info@bluestarcamps.com

Blyth Education
9 Sultan Street, Suite 300, Toronto, Ontario M5S 1L6, Canada
Phone: 416-960-3552 Fax: 416-960-9506
E-mail: info@blytheducation.com

Bonnie Castle Riding Camp
Stoneleigh-Burnham School
Mina Cooper, Director of Riding Program
574 Bernardston Road, Greenfield, Massachusetts 01301
Phone: 413-774-2711 Fax: 413-772-2602
E-mail: summerprograms@sbschool.org

The Boston Conservatory
Toby Hanchett, Summer Programs Coordinator
Dance Division, 8 The Fenway, Boston, Massachusetts 02215
Phone: 617-912-9166 Fax: 617-247-3159
E-mail: thanchett@bostonconservatory.edu

Boston University High School Honors Program
Boston University Summer Term
Scott Alessandro, Director, High School Honors Program
755 Commonwealth Avenue, Room 105, Boston, Massachusetts 02215
Phone: 617-353-1378 Fax: 617-353-5532
E-mail: salessan@bu.edu

Boston University Promys Program
Bridget Walsh, Program Coordinator
111 Cummington Street, #142, Boston, Massachusetts 02215
Phone: 617-353-2563 Fax: 617-353-8100
E-mail: promys@math.bu.edu

Boston University Summer Challenge Program
Boston University Summer Term
Scott Alessandro, Director, Summer Challenge Program
Boston University Summer Term, 755 Commonwealth Avenue, Room 105, Boston, Massachusetts 02215
Phone: 617-353-1378 Fax: 617-353-5532
E-mail: salessan@bu.edu

Boston University Summer Theatre Institute
Paolo DiFabio, Assistant Director
855 Commonwealth Avenue, #470, Boston, Massachusetts 02215
Phone: 617-353-3390 Fax: 617-353-4363

Boston University Tanglewood Institute
Chung-Un Seo, Administrative Director
855 Commonwealth Avenue, Boston, Massachusetts 02215
Phone: 800-643-4796 Fax: 617-353-7455
E-mail: tanglewd@bu.edu

Brad Hoover and Will Witherspoon Football Camp/Sports International
Sports International, Inc.
Customer Service
8924 McGaw Court, Columbia, Maryland 21045
Phone: 800-555-0801 Fax: 401-309-9962
E-mail: info@footballcamps.com

Brant Lake Camp
Kirstin Been Spielman, Director
7586 State Route 8, Brant Lake, New York 12815
Phone: 518-494-2406 Fax: 518-494-7372
E-mail: brantlakec@aol.com

Brevard Music Center
Dorothy Knowles, Admissions Coordinator and Registrar
P.O. Box 312, Brevard, North Carolina 28712
Phone: 828-862-2140 Fax: 828-884-2036
E-mail: bmcadmission@brevardmusic.org

Brewster Academy Summer Session
Christine Brown, Summer Programs Manager
80 Academy Drive, Wolfeboro, New Hampshire 03894
Phone: 603-569-7155 Fax: 603-569-7050
E-mail: summer@brewsteracademy.org

Brighton College Admissions Prep at Tufts University
David Allen, Executive Director
101 East Green Street, Suite 14, Pasadena, California 91105
Phone: 626-795-2985 Fax: 626-795-5564
E-mail: info@brightonedge.org

BROADREACH Academic Treks
Carlton Goldthwaite, Director
P.O. Box 27076, Raleigh, North Carolina 27611
Phone: 888-833-1907 Fax: 919-833-2129
E-mail: info@gobroadreach.com or info@academictreks.com

Brown Ledge Camp
Co-Director
25 Wilson Street, Burlington, Vermont 05401
Phone: 802-862-2442 Fax: 802-658-1614
E-mail: blc@brownledge.org

Brown University Summer Programs-Pre-College Program
Karen Sibley, Dean of Summer Studies
133 Waterman Street, Box T, Providence, Rhode Island 02912-9120
Phone: 401-863-7900 Fax: 401-863-7908
E-mail: summer@brown.edu

Bryn Mawr College-Writing for College
Ann Brown, Coordinator
101 North Merion Avenue, Bryn Mawr, Pennsylvania 19010-2899
Phone: 610-526-5376 Fax: 610-526-7471
E-mail: writingforcollege@brynmawr.edu

Buckswood Summer Programs
Katie Bleck, Buckswood Summer Programmes
Belle Vue House, 259 Greenwich High Road,
London, SE10 8NB, United Kingdom
Phone: 44-(0)208-269-0044 Fax: 44-(0)208-293-1199
E-mail: info@buckswood.com

Burgundy Center for Wildlife Studies Summer Camp
Burgundy Farm School
Lavinia Schoene, Director
HC 83, Box 38DD, Capon Bridge, West Virginia 26711
Phone: 304-856-3758 Fax: 304-856-3758
E-mail: bcws2@earthlink.net

Burklyn Ballet Theatre, Inc.
Joanne Whitehill, Artistic Director
P.O. Box 302, Johnson, Vermont 05656-0302
Phone: 802-635-1390

California Campus Tours
Nichelle Rodriguez, Director
305 North 2nd Avenue, #118, Upland, California 91786
Phone: 909-982-8059 Fax: 909-982-5328
E-mail: educationsvc@msn.com

California College of the Arts Pre-College Program
Kate Wees, Director of Undergraduate Admissions
1111 Eighth Street, San Francisco, California 94107
Phone: 415-703-9523 Fax: 415-703-9539
E-mail: enroll@cca.edu

California Cruzin' Overnight Camp
KidsMakeADifference.org
Andy Mars, Director
P.O. Box 24922, West Los Angeles, California 90024-0922
Phone: 818-344-7838

California State Summer School for the Arts/Inner Spark
Cynthia Bextine, Office Technician
1010 Hurley, Suite 185, Sacramento, California 95825
Phone: 916-227-9320
Fax: 916-227-9455
E-mail: cynthia@cssa.org

Cal Poly State University Young Scholars Prepare for the PSAT & SAT I
California Polytechnic State University, San Luis Obispo
Carroll Busselen, Director
807 Skyline Drive, San Luis Obispo, California 93405
Phone: 805-544-6777

The Cambridge Tradition
Oxbridge Academic Programs
Andrea Mardon, Executive Director, Oxbridge Academic Programs
601 West 110th Street, Suite 7R, New York, New York 10025-2186
Phone: 800-828-8349 Fax: 212-663-8169
E-mail: info@oxbridgeprograms.com

Camden Military Academy Summer Session/Camp
Casey Robinson, Director of Admissions
520 Highway 1, North, Camden, South Carolina 29020
Phone: 803-432-6001 Fax: 803-425-1020
E-mail: admissions@camdenmilitary.com

Camp AK-O-MAK
Pat Kennedy, Director
General Delivery, 240 AK-O-MAK Road, Ahmic Harbour,
Ontario P0A 1A0, Canada
Phone: 705-387-3810 Fax: 705-387-4838
E-mail: akomak@aol.com

Camp Allen
Manchester, NH Lions and Boston, MA Kiwanis Clubs
Mary Constance, Executive Director
56 Camp Allen Road, Bedford, New Hampshire 03110
Phone: 603-622-8471 Fax: 603-626-4295
E-mail: campallennh@aol.com or campallenmary@aol.com

Camp All-Star
Craig Rosen, Owner/Director
P.O. Box 217, Kents Hill, Maine 04349
Phone: 207-685-7242 Fax: 207-685-4169
E-mail: info@campallstar.com

Camp Aloha Hive
Aloha Foundation, Inc.
Helen Butler, Director
846 Vermont Route 244, Fairlee, Vermont 05045
Phone: 802-333-3420 Fax: 802-333-3404
E-mail: helen_rankinbutler@alohafoundation.org

Camp Arowhon-Boys and Girls Camp
Camp Arowhon, Ltd.
Joanne Kates, Director
72 Lyndhurst Avenue, Toronto, Ontario M5R 2Z7, Canada
Phone: 416-975-9060 Fax: 416-975-0130
E-mail: info@camparowhon.com

Camp Atwater-Boys Session
Urban League of Springfield, Inc.
Camp Office
765 State Street, Springfield, Massachusetts 01109
Phone: 413-732-7211 Fax: 413-732-9364

Camp Atwater-Girls Session
Urban League of Springfield, Inc.
Camp Office
765 State Street, Springfield, Massachusetts 01109
Phone: 413-739-7211 Fax: 413-732-9364
E-mail: sulcamp@ulspringfield.org

Camp Awosting
Ebner Camps, Inc.
Buzz Ebner, Director
1 Torrington Office Plaza, Suite 308, Torrington, Connecticut 06790
Phone: 860-567-9678 Fax: 860-485-1681
E-mail: info@awosting.com

Camp Barney Medintz
Jim Mittenthal, Director
4165 Highway 129 North, Cleveland, Georgia 30528-2309
Phone: 706-865-2715 Fax: 706-865-1495
E-mail: summer@campbarney.org

Camp Berachah Ministries Christian Camps and Conferences
Steve Altick, Executive Director
19830 South East 328th Place, Auburn, Washington 98092-2212
Phone: 800-859-CAMP Fax: 253-833-7027
E-mail: staff@campberachah.org

Camp Betsey Cox
Camp Betsey Cox/Camp Sangamon for Boys, Inc.
Lorrie Byrom, Director
140 Betsey Cox Lane, Pittsford, Vermont 05763
Phone: 802-483-6611
E-mail: betcoxvt@aol.com

Camp Birch Trails
Girl Scouts of the Fox River Area, Inc.
Carrie Schroyer, Program/Resident Camp Director
4693 North Lynndale Drive, Appleton, Wisconsin 54913-9614
Phone: 920-734-4559 Fax: 920-734-1304
E-mail: cschroyer@girlscoutsfoxriverarea.org

Camp Bon Coeur
Susannah Craig, Executive Director
P.O. Box 53765, Lafayette, Louisiana 70505
Phone: 318-233-8437 Fax: 318-233-4160
E-mail: info@heartcamp.com

Camp Buckskin
Tom Bauer, Director
P.O. Box 389, Ely, Minnesota 55731
Phone: 218-365-2121 Fax: 218-365-2880
E-mail: buckskin@spacestar.net

Camp Burgess
South Shore YMCA Camps
Lloyd Ewart, Camp Director
75 Stowe Road, Sandwich, Massachusetts 02563
Phone: 508-428-2571 Fax: 508-420-3545
E-mail: camp@ssymca.org

Camp Butterworth
Girl Scouts-Great Rivers Council, Inc.
Kellee Echeverria, Program Services Manager
4930 Cornell Road, Cincinnati, Ohio 45242
Phone: 513-489-1025 Fax: 513-489-1417
E-mail: kecheverria@grgsc.org

Camp Canonicus
Canonicus Camp and Conference Center
Mark Bates, Director of Camping and Conferencing
P.O. Box 330, Exeter, Rhode Island 02822-0330
Phone: 800-294-6318 Fax: 401-294-7780
E-mail: mark@canonicus.org

Camp Carysbrook
Camp Carysbrook
Sarah Baughman, Owner/Director
3500 Camp Carysbrook Road, Riner, Virginia 24149
Phone: 540-382-1670
E-mail: sarah@campcarysbrook.com

Camp Carysbrook Equestrian
Camp Carysbrook
Rachel Baughman, Owner/Director
3500 Camp Carysbrook Road, Riner, Virginia 24149
Phone: 540-382-1670
E-mail: sarah@campcarysbrook.com

Camp Cayuga
Brian Buynak, Camp Director
Pocono Mountains, Niles Pond Road, Suite Petg, Honesdale, Pennsylvania 18431
Phone: 570-253-3133 Fax: 570-253-3194
E-mail: info@campcayuga.com

Camp Chateaugay
Hal Lyons, Owner/Director
233 Gadway Road, Merrill, New York 12955
Phone: 518-425-6888 Fax: 518-425-3487

Camp Chatuga
Kelly Moxley, Director/Personnel
291 Camp Chatuga Road, Mountain Rest, South Carolina 29664
Phone: 864-638-3728 Fax: 864-638-0898
E-mail: mail@campchatuga.com

Camp Cheerio YMCA
YMCA of Greater High Point, North Carolina, Inc.
Michaux Crocker, Director
1430 Camp Cheerio Road, Glade Valley, North Carolina 28627-9731
Phone: 336-363-2604 Fax: 336-363-3671
E-mail: director@campcheerio.org

Camp Chen-A-Wanda
Morey Baldwin, Director
RR #1, Box 32, Thompson, Pennsylvania 18465
Phone: 570-756-2016 Fax: 570-756-2086
E-mail: carlyma@aol.com

Camp Chewonki
Chewonki Foundation, Inc.
Dick Thomas, Camp Director
485 Chewonki Neck Road, Wiscasset, Maine 04578
Phone: 207-882-7323 Fax: 207-882-4074
E-mail: camp@chewonki.org

Camp Chi
Camp Chi/Jewish Community Center of Chicago
Ron Levin, Director
P.O. Box 104, Lake Delton, Wisconsin 53940
Phone: 608-253-1681 Fax: 608-253-4302
E-mail: info@campchi.com

Camp Chikopi for Boys
Camp Chikopi
Bob Duenkel, Director
1 Chikopi Road, Ahmic Harbour, Ontario P0A 1A0, Canada
Phone: 705-387-3811 Fax: 705-387-4747
E-mail: campchikopi@aol.com

Camp Chinqueka
Ebner Camps, Inc.
Kristin Martin, Director
1 Torrington Office Plaza, Suite 308, Torrington, Connecticut 06790
Phone: 860-567-9678 Fax: 860-626-8301
E-mail: info@chinqueka.com

Camp Chosatonga for Boys
Camps Kahdalea for Girls and Chosatonga for Boys
David Trufant, President
2500 Morgan Mill Road, Brevard, North Carolina 28712
Phone: 828-884-6834 Fax: 828-884-6834
E-mail: office@kahdalea.com

Camp Courageous of Iowa
Jeanne Muellerleile, Camp Director
12007 190th Street, P.O. Box 418, Monticello, Iowa 52310
Phone: 319-465-5916 Fax: 319-465-5919
E-mail: jmuellerleile@campcourageous.org

Camp Craig
Angela Robinson, Owner
Box 265, Ailsa Craig, Ontario N0M 1A0, Canada
Phone: 519-293-3484
E-mail: angelaandbob@msn.com

Camp Crestridge for Girls
Lifeway Christian Resources
Ron Springs, Director
P.O. Box 279, Ridgecrest, North Carolina 28770
Phone: 800-968-1630 Fax: 828-669-5512
E-mail: uncron@aol.com

Camp Curtain Call
Eddie Armbrister, Director
849 River Road, Dugspur, Virginia 24325
Phone: 276-730-0233 Fax: 276-730-0233
E-mail: info@campcurtaincall.com

Camp Discovery-Teaneck
Fairleigh Dickinson University
Karen Nelson, Senior Program Director
1000 River Road, HDHI-02, Teaneck, New Jersey 07666
Phone: 201-692-6500 Fax: 201-692-6505

Camp Dudley
Andy Bisselle, Director
126 Dudley Road, Westport, New York 12993-9711
Phone: 518-962-4720 Fax: 518-962-4320
E-mail: andy@campdudley.org

Camp Echo in Coleman High Country
Coleman Family Camps
Jessica Pearson, Assistant Director
210 Echo Road, P.O. Box 105, Burlingham, New York 12722
Phone: 516-620-4301 Fax: 516-620-4330
E-mail: jessica@campecho.com

Camp Echoing Hills
Shaker Samuel, Camp Administrator
36272 County Road 79, Warsaw, Ohio 43844
Phone: 740-327-2311 Fax: 740-327-6371

Camp Encore-Coda for a Great Summer of Music, Sports, and Friends
James Saltman, Director
50 Encore/Coda Lane, Sweden, Maine 04040
Phone: 207-647-3947 Fax: 207-647-3259
E-mail: jamie@encore-coda.com

Camp Exploration Travel Day Camp
KidsMakeADifference.org
Andy Mars, Director
P.O. Box 24922, West Los Angeles, California 90024-0922
Phone: 818-344-7838

Camp Friendship
Ray Ackenbom, Co-Director
P.O. Box 145, Palmyra, Virginia 22963
Phone: 800-873-3223 Fax: 434-589-5880
E-mail: info@campfriendship.com

Camp Friendship Challenge Program
Ray Ackenbom, Co-Director
P.O. Box 145, Palmyra, Virginia 22963
Phone: 434-589-8950 Fax: 434-589-5880
E-mail: info@campfriendship.com

Camp Ganadaoweh
M. Hipkin, Director
Ayr, Ontario N0B 1E0, Canada
Phone: 519-632-7559 Fax: 519-632-9607
E-mail: camp@ganadaoweh.ca

Camp Glen Arden for Girls
Casey Thurman, Director/Owner
P.O. Box 7, Tuxedo, North Carolina 28784
Phone: 828-692-8362 Fax: 828-692-6259
E-mail: tajarden@aol.com

Camp Glen Brook
James Madsen, Director
35 Glenbrook Road, Marlborough, New Hampshire 03455-2207
Phone: 603-876-3342 Fax: 603-876-3763
E-mail: glenbrook@glenbrook.org

Camp Greenbrier for Boys
Will Harvie, Director
Route 2, Box 5A, Alderson, West Virginia 24910
Phone: 304-445-7168 Fax: 304-445-7168
E-mail: woofus@juno.com

Camp Greenkill
YMCA Camping Services of Greater New York
Chris Scheuer, Director of Camping
P.O. Box B, 300 Big Pond Road, Huguenot, New York 12746
Phone: 845-858-2200 Fax: 845-858-7823
E-mail: camps@ymcanyc.org

Camp Greylock for Boys
Michael Marcus, Director
P.O. Box 278, Becket, Massachusetts 01223
Phone: 413-623-8921 Fax: 413-623-5049
E-mail: info@campgreylock.com

Camp Hayward
South Shore YMCA Camps
Sacha Johnston, Camp Hayward Director
75 Stowe Road, Sandwich, Massachusetts 02563
Phone: 508-428-2571 Fax: 508-420-3545
E-mail: camp@ssymca.org

Camp Henry
Westminster Presbyterian Church of Grand Rapids, MI/Camp Henry
Jeff Jacobs, Summer Camp Director
47 Jefferson, SE, Grand Rapids, Michigan 49503
Phone: 231-652-6472 Fax: 231-652-9460
E-mail: jake@camphenry.org

Camp Hillside
Hillside School
Office of Admissions for Summer Program
404 Robin Hill Road, Marlborough, Massachusetts 01752
Phone: 508-485-2824 Fax: 508-485-4420
E-mail: admissions@hillsideschool.net

Camp Hilltop
Bill Young, Owner/Director
7825 County Highway 67, Hancock, New York 13783
Phone: 607-637-5201 Fax: 607-637-2389
E-mail: hilltop@hancock.net

Camp Holiday Trails
Holiday Trails, Inc.
Tina La Roche, Executive Director
400 Holiday Trails Lane, Charlottesville, Virginia 22903
Phone: 434-977-3781 Fax: 434-977-8814
E-mail: tina.laroche.cht@nexet.net

Camp Horizons
John Hall, Director/Owner
3586 Horizons Way, Harrisonburg, Virginia 22802
Phone: 800-729-9230 Fax: 540-896-5455
E-mail: camp@horizonsva.com

Camp Horseshoe
Jordan Shiner, Director
P.O. Box 458, Rhinelander, Wisconsin 54501
Phone: 715-362-2000 Fax: 715-362-2001
E-mail: fun@camphorseshoe.com

Camp Illahee for Girls
Laurie Strayhorn, Director
500 Illahee Road, Brevard, North Carolina 28712-0272
Phone: 828-883-2181 Fax: 828-883-8738
E-mail: info@campillahee.com

Camp JCA Shalom
Brandy Ivener, Business Director
34342 Mulholland Highway, Malibu, California 90265
Phone: 818-889-5500 Fax: 818-889-5132
E-mail: shalom_institute@jcc-gla.org

Camps Kahdalea for Girls and Chosatonga for Boys
David Trufant, President
2500 Morgan Mill Road, Brevard, North Carolina 28712
Phone: 828-884-6834 Fax: 828-884-6834
E-mail: office@kahdalea.com

Camp Kawanhee for Boys
Mark Nelson, Director
58 Kawanhee Lane, Weld, Maine 04285
Phone: 207-585-2210 Fax: 207-585-2620
E-mail: lizmark5@aol.com

Camp Kingsmont
Marc Manoli, Owner/On-Site Director
Hampshire College, 893 West Street, Amherst, Massachusetts 01002
Phone: 800-854-1377 Fax: 413-528-8104
E-mail: info@campkingsmont.com

Camp Kiniya
Marnie Williams, Associate Director
1281 Camp Kiniya Road, Colchester, Vermont 05446
Phone: 802-893-7849 Fax: 802-893-7849
E-mail: marnieatkiniya@aol.com

Camp Kirkwold
Girl Scouts of Kennebec Council
Anne Johnson, Director of Programs
P.O. Box 9421, South Portland, Maine 04116-9421
Phone: 207-772-1177 Fax: 207-874-2646
E-mail: annej@gskc.org

Camp Kodiak
David Stoch, Director
General Delivery, McKellar, Ontario P0G 1C0, Canada
Phone: 705-389-1910 Fax: 705-389-1911
E-mail: dave@campkodiak.com

Camp Kostopulos
Kostopulos Dream Foundation
Amy Stoeger, Program Director
2500 Emigration Canyon, Salt Lake City, Utah 84108
Phone: 801-582-0700 Fax: 801-583-5176
E-mail: astoeger@campk.org

Camp La Junta
Blake Smith, Camp Director
P.O. Box 136, Hunt, Texas 78024
Phone: 830-238-4621 Fax: 830-238-4888
E-mail: lajunta@ktc.com

Camp Lanakila
Aloha Foundation, Inc.
D. Boffey, Director
2899 Lake Morey Road, Fairlee, Vermont 05045
Phone: 802-333-3430 Fax: 802-333-3404
E-mail: barnes_boffey@alohafoundation.org

Camp Laney for Boys
Rob Hammond, Director
P.O. Box 289, Mentone, Alabama 35984
Phone: 800-648-2919 Fax: 256-634-4098
E-mail: info@camplaney.com

Camp Laurel South
Roger Christian, Camp Director
48 Laurel Road, Casco, Maine 04015
Phone: 207-627-4334 Fax: 207-627-4255
E-mail: fun@camplaurelsouth.com

Camp Lee Mar
Ariel Segal, Executive Director
450 Route 590, Lackawaxen, Pennsylvania 18435
Phone: 570-685-7188
E-mail: gtour400@aol.com

Camp Lincoln/Camp Lake Hubert
Sam Cote, Director
Box 1308, Lake Hubert, Minnesota 56459
Phone: 218-963-2339 Fax: 218-963-2447
E-mail: home@lincoln-lakehubert.com

Camp Lindenmere
Enid Marcus, Co-Director
RR #1, Box 1765, Henryville, Pennsylvania 18332
Phone: 570-629-0240 Fax: 208-723-3288
E-mail: admin@camplindenmere.com

Camp Lohikan in the Pocono Mountains
Mark Buynak, Director
24 Wallerville Road, P.O. Box 217, Lake Como, Pennsylvania 18473
Phone: 908-798-2707 Fax: 908-470-9319
E-mail: info@lohikan.com

Camp Lookout
Crystalaire Camp, Inc.
Katherine Houston, Director
2768 South Shore Road East, Frankfort, Michigan 49635
Phone: 231-352-7589 Fax: 231-352-6609
E-mail: camp_info@crystalairecamp.com

Camp Louemma, Inc.
Hal Pugach, Director
214-45 42nd Avenue, Bayside, New York 11361
Phone: 973-316-0362 Fax: 973-316-0980
E-mail: camplouemma@aol.com

Camp Maplehurst
Laurence Cohn, Director
1455 Quarton Road, Birmingham, Michigan 48009
Phone: 231-264-9675 Fax: 231-264-5041
E-mail: info@campmaplehurst.com

Camp Maromac
Joseph Marovitch, Director/Owner
4999 Rue Ste. Catherine Ouest, Suite 232, Montreal,
Quebec H3Z 1T3, Canada
Phone: 800-884-2267 Fax: 514-485-1124
E-mail: info@maromac.com

Camp Matoaka for Girls
Michael Nathanson, Director
1 Great Place, Smithfield, Maine 04978-1288
Phone: 207-362-2500 Fax: 207-362-2525
E-mail: matoaka@matoaka.com

Camp McAlister
YMCA Camping Services of Greater New York
Chris Scheuer, Director of Camping
P.O. Box B, 300 Big Pond Road, Huguenot, New York 12746
Phone: 845-858-2200 Fax: 845-858-7823
E-mail: camps@ymcanyc.org

Camp Menominee
Steve Kanefsky, Owner/Director
4985 County Road D, Eagle River, Wisconsin 54521
Phone: 715-479-2267 Fax: 715-479-5512
E-mail: fun@campmenominee.com

Camp Mi-A-Kon-Da
Pam Lamont, Director
RR #2, Dunchurch, Ontario P0A 1G0, Canada
Phone: 705-389-1462

Camp Mishawaka for Boys
New Camps, Inc.
Steve Purdum, Executive Director
P.O. Box 368, Grand Rapids, Minnesota 55744
Phone: 218-326-5011 Fax: 218-326-9228
E-mail: info@campmishawaka.com

Camp Modin
Howard Salzberg, Director
Modin Way, Belgrade, Maine 04917
Phone: 207-465-4444 Fax: 207-465-4447
E-mail: modin@modin.com

Camps Mondamin and Green Cove
Frank Bell, Director
P.O. Box 8, Tuxedo, North Carolina 28784
Phone: 828-693-7446 Fax: 828-696-8895
E-mail: mondamin@mondamin.com

Camp Mowglis, School of the Open
K. Bengtson, Director
P.O. Box 9, Hebron, New Hampshire 03241
Phone: 603-744-8095 Fax: 603-744-9350
E-mail: campoffice@mowglis.org

Camp Nakanawa
Pepe Perron, Owner/Director
1084 Camp Nakanawa Road, Crossville, Tennessee 38571-2146
Phone: 931-277-3711 Fax: 931-277-5552
E-mail: campnak@tnaccess.com

Camp Namanu
Camp Fire USA Portland Metro Council
Brian Hayes, Camp Director
619 Southwest 11th Avenue, Suite 200, Portland, Oregon 97205
Phone: 503-224-7800 Fax: 503-223-3916
E-mail: info@portlandcampfire.org

Camp Nawaka
Camp Fire USA Eastern Massachusetts Council
Christopher Egan, Camp Director
56 Roland Street, Suite 305, Boston, Massachusetts 02129
Phone: 617-591-0300 Fax: 617-591-0310
E-mail: egan@nawaka.org

Camp Nominingue
Grant McKenna, Executive Director
1889 Chemin des Mésanges, Nominingue, Quebec J0W 1R0, Canada
Phone: 819-278-3383 Fax: 819-278-1307
E-mail: camp@axess.com

Camp North Star for Boys
Robert Lebby, Director
10970 West Boys Camp Road, Hayward, Wisconsin 54843
Phone: 715-462-3254 Fax: 715-462-9278
E-mail: leb@northstarcamp.com

Camp Nor'wester
Paul Henriksen, Director
P.O. Box 4395, Roche Harbor, Washington 98250
Phone: 360-468-2225 Fax: 360-468-2472
E-mail: norwester@rockisland.com

Camp O-AT-KA
Keith Reinhardt, Executive Director
593 Sebago Road, Sebago, Maine 04029
Phone: 800-818-8455 Fax: 207-787-3930
E-mail: director@campoatka.com

Camp Onaway
Onaway Camp Trust
Anne Conolly, Director
27 Camp Onaway Road, Hebron, New Hampshire 03241
Phone: 603-744-2180 Fax: 603-744-2180

Camp Pacific's Recreational Camp
The Academy by the Sea/Camp Pacific
Lori Adlfinger, Associate Director
P.O. Box 3000, Carlsbad, California 92018
Phone: 760-434-7564 Fax: 760-729-1574
E-mail: info@abts.com

Camp Pacific's Surf and Bodyboard Camp
The Academy by the Sea/Camp Pacific
Lori Adlfinger, Associate Director
P.O. Box 3000, Carlsbad, California 92018
Phone: 760-434-7564 Fax: 760-729-1574
E-mail: info@abts.com

Camp Pasquaney
Vincent Broderick, Director
19 Pasquaney Lane, Hebron, New Hampshire 03241
Phone: 603-744-8043 E-mail: office@pasquaney.org

Camp Pinehurst
John Curtis, Director
23 Curtis Road, Raymond, Maine 04071
Phone: 207-627-4670 Fax: 207-627-4793
E-mail: director@camppinehurst.com

Camp Pocono Ridge
Shellie Visinski, Director
1 Pine Grove Road, South Sterling, Pennsylvania 18460
Phone: 570-676-3478 Fax: 570-676-9823
E-mail: poconoridge@aol.com

Camp Pok-O-MacCready
Chris Durlacher, Director of Admissions
P.O. Box 397, Willsboro, New York 12996
Phone: 518-963-8366 Fax: 518-963-1128
E-mail: pokomac@aol.com

Camp Pondicherry
Girl Scouts of Kennebec Council
Anne Johnson, Director of Program
P.O. Box 9421, South Portland, Maine 04116-9421
Phone: 207-772-1177 Fax: 207-874-2646
E-mail: annej@gskc.org

Camp Quinebarge
David Hurley, Director
P.O. Box 608, Center Harbor, New Hampshire 03226
Phone: 603-253-6029 Fax: 603-253-6027

Camp Redwood
Irma Estis, Co-Director
576 Rock Cut Road, Walden, New York 12586
Phone: 888-600-6655 Fax: 845-564-1128
E-mail: info@camp-redwood.com

Camp Ridgecrest for Boys
Lifeway Christian Resources
Ron Springs, Director
P.O. Box 279, Ridgecrest, North Carolina 28770
Phone: 800-968-1630 Fax: 828-669-5512
E-mail: uncron@aol.com

Camp Rim Rock
Deborah Matheson, Director
P.O. Box 69, Yellow Spring, West Virginia 26865
Phone: 800-662-4650 Fax: 304-856-3201
E-mail: office@camprimrock.com

Camp Rio Vista for Boys
Vista Camps
Freddie Hawkins, Owner/Director of Vista Camps
175 Rio Vista Road, Ingram, Texas 78025
Phone: 830-367-5353 Fax: 830-367-4044
E-mail: riovista@ktc.com

Camp Robin Hood for Boys and Girls
Jamie Cole, Owner/Director
65 Robin Hood Lane, Freedom, New Hampshire 03836
Phone: 603-539-4500 Fax: 603-539-4599
E-mail: dc@camprobinhood.com

Camp Roger
Jim Wingerden, Executive Director
8356 Belding Road, Rockford, Michigan 49341
Phone: 616-874-7286 Fax: 616-874-5734
E-mail: jimvwg@juno.com

Camp Runoia
Pamela Cobb, Director
P.O. Box 450, Belgrade Lakes, Maine 04918
Phone: 207-495-2228 Fax: 207-495-2287
E-mail: info@runoia.com

Camp Saginaw
Jay Petkov, Director
740 Saginaw Road, Oxford, Pennsylvania 19363-2167
Phone: 610-932-8467 Fax: 610-932-3313
E-mail: campsaginaw@comcast.net

Camp St. John's Northwestern
St. John's Northwestern Military Academy
Director of Camp Enrollment
1101 North Genesee Street, Delafield, Wisconsin 53018
Phone: 800-SJ-CADET Fax: 262-646-7128
E-mail: admissions@sjnma.org

Camp Sandy Cove
Morning Cheer, Inc.
Tim Nielsen, Director
Rt. 1, Box 471, High View, West Virginia 26801
Phone: 304-856-2959 Fax: 304-856-1683
E-mail: chieftimn@aol.com

Camp Sangamon for Boys
Camp Betsey Cox/Camp Sangamon for Boys, Inc.
Mike Byrom, Executive Director
382 Camp Lane, Pittsford, Vermont 05763
Phone: 802-483-2862
E-mail: sangamonvt@aol.com

Camp Scatico
David Fleischner, Director
1558 Route 19, P.O. Box 6, Elizaville, New York 12523
Phone: 845-756-4040 Fax: 845-756-2298
E-mail: info@scatico.com

Camp Seagull
Bill Schulman, Director
301 Mercer Boulevard, Charleviox, Michigan 49720
Phone: 231-547-6556
E-mail: seagull@freeway.net

Camp Shohola
Duncan Barger, Director
105 Weber Road, Greeley, Pennsylvania 18425
Phone: 570-685-7186 Fax: 570-685-4563
E-mail: duncan@shohola.com

Camp Sierra Vista for Girls
Vista Camps
Debbie Griffin, Camp Director
175 Rio Vista Road, Ingram, Texas 78025
Phone: 830-367-5353 Fax: 830-367-4044
E-mail: dgriffin@vistacamps.com

Camp Skylemar
Arleen Shepherd, Director
457 Sebago Road, Naples, Maine 04055
Phone: 207-693-6414 Fax: 207-693-3865
E-mail: info@campskylemar.com

Camp Skyline
Sally Johnson, Director
P.O. Box 287, Mentone, Alabama 35984
Phone: 800-448-9279 Fax: 256-634-3018
E-mail: info@campskyline.com

Camp Skyline
Sally Johnson, Director
P.O. Box 287, Mentone, Alabama 35984
Phone: 800-448-9279 Fax: 256-634-3018
E-mail: info@campskyline.com

Camp Stanislaus
Michael Reso, Camp Director
304 South Beach Boulevard, Bay St. Louis, Mississippi 39520
Phone: 228-467-9057 Fax: 228-466-2972
E-mail: mreso@ststan.com

Camp Streamside
Streamside Foundation, Inc./BCM International
Dale Schoenwald, Director
RR #3, Box 3307, Possinger Drive, Stroudsburg, Pennsylvania 18360
Phone: 570-629-1902 Fax: 570-629-9650
E-mail: summercamp@streamside.org

Camp Susquehannock, Inc.
Dave Williams, Executive Director
Box 1375, RR #1, Brackney, Pennsylvania 18812
Phone: 570-967-2323 Fax: 570-967-2631
E-mail: info@susquehannock.com

Camp Talcott
YMCA Camping Services of Greater New York
Chris Scheuer, Director of Camping
P.O. Box B, 300 Big Pond Road, Huguenot, New York 12746
Phone: 845-858-2200 Fax: 845-858-7823
E-mail: camps@ymcanyc.org

Camp Tall Timbers
Glenn Smith, Director
Route 1, Box 472, High View, West Virginia 26808
Phone: 304-856-3722 Fax: 304-856-3765
E-mail: funcamp@aol.com

Camp Tapawingo
Jane Lichtman, Director
166 Tapawingo Road, Sweden, Maine 04040
Phone: 207-647-3351 Fax: 207-647-2232
E-mail: camptap@aol.com

Camp Tawonga (Tawonga Jewish Community Corp.)
Nina Kaufman, Director of Teen Service Learning
131 Steuart Street, Suite 460, San Francisco, California 94105
Phone: 415-543-2267 Fax: 415-543-5417
E-mail: nina@taworga.org

Timber-lee Science Camp
Camp Timber-lee
Tom Parsons, Director, Human Resources
N8705 Scout Road, East Troy, Wisconsin 53120
Phone: 262-642-7345 Fax: 262-642-7517
E-mail: tomp@timber-lee.com

Camp Tioga
Ron Kuznetz, Director/Owner
RD 1, Box 54, Thompson, Pennsylvania 18465
Phone: 570-756-2660 Fax: 516-938-3184
E-mail: info@camptioga.com

Camp Tohkomeupog
Andrew Mahoney, Director
1251 Eaton Road, Madison, New Hampshire 03849
Phone: 603-367-8362 Fax: 603-367-8664
E-mail: tohko@tohko.com

Camp Towanda
Mitch Reiter, Director
Camp Towanda Road, RR #1, Box 1585, Honesdale,
Pennsylvania 18431-9798
Phone: 570-253-3266 Fax: 570-253-6334
E-mail: staff@camptowanda.com

Camp Treetops
North Country School
Karen Culpepper, Director
P.O. Box 187, Lake Placid, New York 12946
Phone: 518-523-9329 Fax: 518-523-4858
E-mail: ctt@nct.org

Camp Walden
Renee Pitt, Owner/Director
429 Trout Lake Road, Diamond Point, New York 12824
Phone: 518-644-9441 Fax: 518-644-2929
E-mail: waldenmail@yahoo.com

Camp Watitoh
William Hoch, Director
Center Lake, Becket, Massachusetts 01223
Phone: 413-623-8951 Fax: 413-623-8955
E-mail: info@campwatitoh.com

Camp Watonka
Donald Wacker, Director
P.O. Box 127, Hawley, Pennsylvania 18428
Phone: 570-857-1401 E-mail: donwackr@voicenet.com

Camp Wawenock
June Gray, Director/Owner
33 Camp Wawenock Road, Raymond, Maine 04071-6824
Phone: 207-655-4657

Camp Wayne
Peter Corpuel, Director
HC 60, Box 30, Preston Park, Pennsylvania 18455
Phone: 570-798-2511 Fax: 570-798-2193
E-mail: info@campwayne.com

Camp Waziyatah
Dawn Broussard, Director
530 Mill Hill Road, Waterford, Maine 04088
Phone: 207-583-6781 Fax: 207-583-6755
E-mail: info@wazi.com

Camp Westmont
Jack Pinsky, Camp Director
P.O. Box 15, Poyntelle, Pennsylvania 18454
Phone: 570-448-2500 Fax: 570-448-2063
E-mail: westmont4u@aol.com

Camp Wicosuta
Cole Kelly, Co-Director
21 Wicosuta Drive, Hebron, New Hampshire 03241
Phone: 603-744-3301 Fax: 603-744-5570
E-mail: campwicosuta@campwicosuta.com

Camp Wilvaken
Maya Willis, Co-Director
241 Chemin Willis, Magog, Quebec J1X 3W2, Canada
Phone: 819-843-5353 Fax: 819-843-3024
E-mail: wilvaken@wilvaken.com

Camp Winding Gap
Ann Hertzberg, Director
Route 1, Box 56, Lake Toxaway, North Carolina 28747
Phone: 888-CWG-CAMP Fax: 828-883-8720
E-mail: campwgap@citcom.net

Camp Wingate Kirkland
Will Rubenstein, Director
79 White Rock Road, Yarmouth Port, Massachusetts 02675
Phone: 508-362-3798 Fax: 508-362-1614
E-mail: office@campwk.com

Camp Winnebago
Andy Lilienthal, Director
19 Echo Lake Road, Fayette, Maine 04349
Phone: 207-685-4918 Fax: 207-685-9190
E-mail: unkandycw@aol.com

Canadian Rockies Adventurer Camp
Howling Wolf Adventures
Todd Hebert, Camp Director
411 13th Avenue South, Cranbrook, British Columbia V1C 2W3, Canada
Phone: 250-426-7989 Fax: 250-426-3933
E-mail: info@howlingwolfadventures.com

Canadian Rockies Outdoor Leader Camp
Howling Wolf Adventures
Todd Herbert, Camp Director
411 13th Avenue South, Cranbrook, British Columbia V1C 2W3, Canada
Phone: 250-426-7989 Fax: 250-426-3933
E-mail: info@howlingwolfadventures.com

Cape Cod Sea Camps-Monomoy/Wono
David Peterson, Director
Box 1880, Brewster, Massachusetts 02631
Phone: 508-896-3451 Fax: 508-896-8272
E-mail: info@capecodseacamps.com

The Cardigan Mountain School Summer Session
Thomas Pastore, Director of the Summer Session
62 Alumni Drive, Cardigan Mountain School,
Canaan, New Hampshire 03741-9307
Phone: 603-523-3528 Fax: 603-523-3565
E-mail: tpastore@cardigan.org

Career Explorations
Josh Flowerman, Director
119 Headquarters Plaza, Morristown, New Jersey 07960
Phone: 973-984-8808 Fax: 973-984-5666
E-mail: jflowerman@ceinternships.com

Carmel Valley Tennis Camp
Susan Reeder, Owner/Director
20805 Cachagua Road, Carmel Valley, California 93924
Phone: 831-659-2615 Fax: 831-659-2840
E-mail: cvtcl@aol.com

Carnegie Mellon University Pre-College Program in the Fine Arts
Joel Ripka, Office of Admission, Pre-College Programs
5000 Forbes Avenue, Pittsburgh, Pennsylvania 15213-3890
Phone: 412-268-2082 Fax: 412-268-7838
E-mail: precollege@andrew.cmu.edu

Carolina Master Scholars Adventure Series
University of South Carolina Continuing Education
Continuing Education
Summer Academic Programs
1600 Hampton Street Annex, Suite 203, Columbia, South Carolina 29208
Phone: 803-777-9444 Fax: 803-777-2663
E-mail: confs@gwm.sc.edu

Carroll Center for the Blind
Margaret Cleary, Director of Admissions
770 Centre Street, Newton, Massachusetts 02458
Phone: 617-969-6200 Fax: 617-969-6204
E-mail: mecleary@carroll.org

Carson-Newman College-EXCEL Program
Sheryl Gray, Director of Admissions
C-N Box 72025, Jefferson City, Tennessee 37760
Phone: 865-471-3223 Fax: 865-471-3502
E-mail: sgray@cn.edu

Catholic University The Catholic University of America
Jessica Madrigal, Director of Summer Sessions
330 Pangborn Hall, 620 Michigan Avenue, NE, Washington, District of Columbia 20064
Phone: 202-319-5257 Fax: 202-319-6725
E-mail: cua-summers@cua.edu

Catholic University Eye on Engineering
The Catholic University of America
School of Engineering, 102 Pangborn Hall, Washington,
District of Columbia 20064
Phone: 202-319-5160 E-mail: coxe@cua.edu

Catholic Youth Camp
Maggie Braun, Co-Director
19590 520th Lane, McGregor, Minnesota 55760
Phone: 218-426-3383 Fax: 218-426-4675
E-mail: camp@cycamp.org

Cazadero Music Camp
Cazadero Performing Arts Camp
Jim Mazzaferro, Camp Director
9068 Shetland Court, Elk Grove, California 95624
Phone: 916-685-3867 Fax: 916-681-7505
E-mail: jim@cazadero.org

Cedar Lodge
Amy Edwards, Program Director
P.O. Box 218, Lawrence, Michigan 49064
Phone: 269-674-8071 Fax: 269-674-3143
E-mail: info@cedarlodge.com

Celtic Learning and Travel Services
Mark Burke, Program Director
17 Carysfort Road, Dalkey County, Dublin, Ireland
E-mail: info@celticsummer.com

Centauri Summer Arts Camp
Julie Hartley, Director
c/o Robert Land Academy, RR #3, Wellandport, Ontario L0R 2J0, Canada
Phone: 416-766-7124 Fax: 416-766-7655
E-mail: directors@centauri.on.ca

Center for American Archeology
Mary Pirkl, Director of Education
P.O. Box 366, Kampsville, Illinois 62053
Phone: 618-653-4316 Fax: 618-653-4232
E-mail: caa@caa-archeology.org

Center for Creative Youth
Capitol Region Education Council
Nancy Wolfe, Director
Wesleyan University, 350 High Street, Middletown, Connecticut 06459
Phone: 860-685-3307 Fax: 860-685-3311
E-mail: ccy@wesleyan.edu

Center for Talent Development Summer Academic Program
Northwestern University's Center for Talent Development
Susie Hoffmann, Summer Program Coordinator
617 Dartmouth Place, Evanston, Illinois 60208
Phone: 847-491-3782 Fax: 847-467-4283
E-mail: ctd@northwestern.edu

Center Summer Academy
Boston Architectural Center
Michael Daniels, Coordinator
320 Newbury Street, Boston, Massachusetts 02115
Phone: 617-585-0101 Fax: 617-585-0121
E-mail: michael.daniels@the-bac.edu

Cheerio Adventures
YMCA of Greater High Point, North Carolina, Inc.
Keith Russell, Director
1430 Camp Cheerio Road, Glade Valley, North Carolina 28627
Phone: 336-363-2604 Fax: 336-363-3671
E-mail: krussell@campcheerio.org

Cheley Colorado Camps
Enrollment Manager
P.O. Box 1170, Estes Park, Colorado 80517
Phone: 970-586-4244 Fax: 970-586-3020
E-mail: office@cheley.com

Children's Creative and Performing Arts Academy of San Diego
Janet Cherif, Principal
4431 Mt. Herbert Avenue, San Diego, California 92117
Phone: 858-279-4744 Fax: 858-279-1243
E-mail: jmcherif@yahoo.com

China Summer Learning Adventures
Xi'an Jiao Tong University Campus/Xi'an Winning Training Center
David Schoon, USA Representative / China Link Company, LLC
2150 44th Street, SE, Suite 309, Grand Rapids, Michigan 49508
Phone: 616-281-0000 Fax: 616-281-2118
E-mail: dbschoon@chinalinkcompanyllc.com

Choate Rosemary Hall English Language Institute
Mariann Arnold, Director of Admission
333 Christian Street, Wallingford, Connecticut 06492
Phone: 203-697-2365 Fax: 203-697-2519
E-mail: marnold@choate.edu

Choate Rosemary Hall Summer Arts Conservatory
Randi Brandt, Admissions Director
Paul Mellon Arts Center, 333 Christian Street, Wallingford, Connecticut 06492
Phone: 203-697-2423 Fax: 203-697-2396
E-mail: rbrandt@choate.edu

Choate Rosemary Hall Summer in China
Choate Rosemary Hall
Carol Chen-Lin, Director Summer in China
333 Christian Street, Wallingford, Connecticut 06492
Phone: 203-697-2080 Fax: 203-697-2519
E-mail: cchen@choate.edu

Chop Point Camp
David Wilkinson, Director
420 Chop Point Road, Woolwich, Maine 04579
Phone: 207-443-5860 Fax: 207-443-6760
E-mail: wilk@choppoint.org

Circle Pines Center Summer Camp
Kyle Hodnett, Summer Camp Director
8650 Mullen Road, Delton, Michigan 49046
Phone: 269-623-5555 Fax: 269-623-9054
E-mail: circle@net-link.net

Clara Barton Family Camp
The Barton Center for Diabetes Education, Inc.
Gaylen McCann, Resident Camps Director
30 Ennis Road, P.O. Box 356, North Oxford, Massachusetts 01537
Phone: 508-987-3856 Fax: 508-987-2002
E-mail: gaylen.mccann@bartoncenter.org

Clearwater Camp for Girls
Sunny Moore, Executive Director
7490 Clearwater Road, Minocqua, Wisconsin 54548
Phone: 715-356-5030 Fax: 715-356-3124
E-mail: clearwatercamp@newnorth.net

Cloverleaf Ranch Summer Camp
Chris Rhodes, Camp Manager
3892 Old Redwood Highway, Santa Rosa, California 95403
Phone: 707-545-5906 Fax: 707-545-5908
E-mail: cloverleafranch@netdex.com

College Impressions
Arthur Mullaney, President
64 Shore Drive, Kingston, Massachusetts 02364
Phone: 781-585-4070 Fax: 781-585-4070
E-mail: collegeimp@cape.com

College Quest
Western Washington University
Debbie Gibbons, Program Manager
Extended Education and Summer Programs, Mail Stop 5293, 516 High Street, Bellingham, Washington 98225
Phone: 360-650-6820 Fax: 360-650-6858
E-mail: adventures@wwu.edu

Collegiate Summer Program for High School Students
Thomas More College of Liberal Arts
Joanne Geiger, Director of Admissions
6 Manchester Street, Merrimack, New Hampshire 03054
Phone: 800-880-8308 Fax: 603-880-9280
E-mail: admissions@thomasmorecollege.edu

Colorado Academy Summer Programs
Lyn Hills, Registrar
3800 South Pierce Street, Denver, Colorado 80235
Phone: 303-914-2531 Fax: 303-914-2532
E-mail: lyhills@mail.coloacad.org

Columbia University Summer Program for High School Students
Columbia University Continuing Education
Darlene Giraitis, Director of Secondary School Programs
Columbia Univ., 2970 Broadway, Mail Code 4110, New York, New York 10027
Phone: 212-854-3771 Fax: 212-854-5861
E-mail: hsp@columbia.edu

Community Sailing of Colorado, Ltd.
Steven Frank, Director
Box 102613, Denver, Colorado 80250
Phone: 303-757-7718 Fax: 303-692-9024
E-mail: stevefrank@communitysaiing.org

Concordia Language Villages
Concordia College
Alex Loehrer, Assistant Director, Public Relations
901 South Eighth Street, Moorhead, Minnesota 56562
Phone: 218-299-4544 Fax: 218-299-3807
E-mail: clv@cord.edu

The Congressional Seminar
Washington Workshops Foundation
Aaron Corbett, Director
3222 N Street NW, Suite 340, Washington, District of Columbia 20007
Phone: 800-368-5688 Fax: 202-965-1018
E-mail: info@workshops.org

Corcoran College of Art and Design
Director of Continuing Education
500 17th Street, NW, Washington, District of Columbia 20007
Phone: 202-298-2542 Fax: 202-298-2543

Cordova 4-H
Linda Brown, 4H Community Coordinator
Box 1053, Cordova, Alaska 99574
Phone: 907-424-3943 Fax: 907-424-3943
E-mail: cordovabluegrass@hotmail.com

Costa Rica Rainforest Outward Bound School
Student Administrator
Box 1817-2050, San Pedro-San Jose, Costa Rica
Phone: 011-506-278-6058 Fax: 011-506-278-6059
E-mail: info@crrobs.org

Cottonwood Gulch Family Trek
Cottonwood Gulch Foundation
Jeff Zemsky, Executive Director
P.O. Box 969, Thoreau, New Mexico 87323
Phone: 505-862-7503 Fax: 505-862-7503
E-mail: jeff@cottonwoodgulch.org

Craftsbury Camps
535 Lost Nation Road, Craftsbury Common, Vermont 05827
Phone: 802-586-7767 Fax: 802-586-7768
E-mail: stay@craftsbury.com

Cross Keys
Richard Bernstein, Managing Director
48 Fitzalan Road, Finchley, London, N3 3PE, United Kingdom
Phone: 020-8371-9686 Fax: 020-8343-0625
E-mail: richard@xkeys.co.uk

Crow Canyon Archaeological Center
Theresa Titone, School Programs Marketing Manager
23390 Road K, Cortez, Colorado 81321
Phone: 800-422-8975 Fax: 970-565-4859
E-mail: ttitone@crowcanyon.org

Crystalaire Camp
David Reid, Director
2768 South Shore Road East, Frankfort, Michigan 49635
Phone: 231-352-7589 Fax: 231-352-6609
E-mail: camp_info@crystalairecamp.com

Cuernavaca Summer Program for Teens
AuLangue Idiomas & Culturas
Eugenio Palomares-Gonzalez, Director and General Coordinator
Allende #106, Colonia El Empleado, Cuernavaca, Morelos, 62520, Mexico
E-mail: aulangue@yahoo.com.mx

Culver Summer Camps
Anthony Mayfield, Director
1300 Academy Road, #138, Culver, Indiana 46511
Phone: 800-221-2020 Fax: 574-842-8462
E-mail: summer@culver.org

Cybercamps
Cybercamps Information Office
2401 4th Avenue, Suite 1110, Seattle, Washington 98121
Phone: 206-442-4500 Fax: 206-442-4501
E-mail: info@cybercamps.com

Catholic Youth Organization
Caroline Krucker, Director of Parish Services and Camps
305 Michigan Avenue, Detroit, Michigan 48226
Phone: 313-963-7172 Fax: 313-963-7179
E-mail: ckrucker@cyodetroit.org

Damon Huard and Matt Light Football Camp/Sports International
Sports International, Inc.
Customer Service
8924 McGaw Court, Columbia, Maryland 21045
Phone: 800-555-0801 Fax: 401-309-9962
E-mail: info@footballcamps.com

Darlington School Summer Camps
Ballard Betz, Assistant Director of Summer Programs and Admissions
1014 Cave Spring Road, Rome, Georgia 30161-4700
Phone: 706-235-6051 Fax: 706-232-3600
E-mail: bbetz@darlingtonschool.org

Darrow Wilderness Trips
Darrow Foundation
John Houghton, Director
P.O. Box 9, Grand Lake Stream, Maine 04637
Phone: 207-592-5827 E-mail: darrow@gwi.net

Davidson College July Experience
Davidson College
Evelyn Gerdes, Director, July Experience
Box 7151, Davidson, North Carolina 28035-7151
Phone: 704-894-2508 Fax: 704-894-2645
E-mail: julyexp@davidson.edu

The Deep River Science Academy
Mary MacCafferty, National Registrar
Box 600, 20 Forest Avenue, Deep River, Ontario K0J 1P0, Canada
Phone: 613-584-4541 Fax: 613-584-9597
E-mail: info@drsa.ca

Deer Hill Expeditions
Beverly Capelin, Founder and Owner
P.O. Box 180, Mancos, Colorado 81328
Phone: 800-533-7221 Fax: 970-533-7221
E-mail: info@deerhillexpeditions.com

Dhani Jones Football Camp/Sports International
Sports International, Inc.
Customer Service
8924 McGaw Court, Columbia, Maryland 21045
Phone: 800-555-0801 Fax: 410-309-9962
E-mail: info@footballcamps.com

Dickinson College Summer Programs
Jennifer Howland, Office of Summer Programs
P.O. Box 1773, Carlisle, Pennsylvania 17013
Phone: 717-254-8782 Fax: 717-245-1972
E-mail: summer@dickinson.edu

DigiPen Institute of Technology
Gina Corpening, Admissions and Outreach Coordinator
5001 150th Avenue, NE, Redmond, Washington 98052
Phone: 425-558-0299 Fax: 425-558-0378
E-mail: gcorpeni@digipen.edu

Diplomacy and Global Affairs Seminar
Washington Workshops Foundation
Aaron Corbett, Director
3222 N Street NW, Suite 340, Washington, District of Columbia 20007
Phone: 800-368-5688 Fax: 202-965-1018
E-mail: info@workshops.org

Discovery Camp
Keystone Science School
Steve Remer, Director
1628 Sts. John Road, Keystone, Colorado 80435
Phone: 970-468-2098 Fax: 970-468-7769
E-mail: amcintyre@keystone.org

Discovery Works New England Community Service Experience
Double "H" Hole in the Woods Ranch Summer Camp
Peter Carner, Camp Director
97 Hidden Valley Road, Lake Luzerne, New York 12846
Phone: 518-696-5676 Fax: 518-696-4528
E-mail: petecarner@doublehranch.org

Drama Kids International Summer FUN Camp
Liz Starn, Director
4730 Warm Springs Road, Houston, Texas 77035
Phone: 713-721-5200 Fax: 713-721-5202
E-mail: dramakidshouston@aol.com

Dunnabeck at Kildonan
Kildonan School
Ronald Wilson, Headmaster
425 Morse Hill Road, Amenia, New York 12501
Phone: 845-373-8111 Fax: 845-373-9793
E-mail: bsattler@kildonan.org

Dwight-Englewood Summer Academic Session
Mark Shultz, Summer School Principal
315 East Palisade Avenue, Englewood, New Jersey 07631
Phone: 201-569-9500 Fax: 201-568-5018
E-mail: shultm@d-e.org

Eagle Hill School Summer Session
Erin Wynne, Director of Admission
P.O. Box 116, 242 Old Petersham Road, Hardwick, Massachusetts 01037
Phone: 413-477-6000 Fax: 413-477-6837
E-mail: admission@ehs1.org

Eagle Lake Camp
The Navigators
Office Manager
P.O. Box 6000, Colorado Springs, Colorado 80934
Phone: 719-472-1260 Fax: 719-623-0148
E-mail: registrar_el@navigators.org

Eagle's Nest Camp
Eagle's Nest Foundation
R. Emmylou Ferris, Assistant Camp Director
43 Hart Road, Pisgah Forest, North Carolina 28768
Phone: 828-877-4349 Fax: 828-884-2788
E-mail: promotions@enf.org

Earthwatch Institute
General Information Desk
P.O. Box 75, Maynard, Massachusetts 01754
Phone: 800-776-0188 Fax: 978-461-2332
E-mail: info@earthwatch.org

Eastern U.S. Music Camp, Inc.
Colgate University
Thomas Brown, Director
Dana Arts Center, Hamilton, New York 13346-1398
Phone: 315-228-7041 Fax: 315-228-7557
E-mail: eusmc@hotmail.com

ECOES: Exploring Career Options in Engineering and Science
Stevens Institute of Technology
Rae Talerico, Director, Pre-College Programs
Lore-El Center, Castle Point on Hudson, Hoboken, New Jersey 07030
Phone: 201-216-5245 Fax: 201-216-5175
E-mail: ataleric@stevens.edu

EDUCO Summer Adventure Programs
Kimberly Dazey, Administrator
619 South College Avenue, Suite 16, Fort Collins, Colorado 80524
Phone: 800-332-7340 Fax: 970-494-0753
E-mail: info@educocolorado.org

EKOCAMP International
Louis Gibeau, President
4433 Rive, Val-Morin, Quebec J0T 2R0, Canada
Phone: 819-322-7051 Fax: 819-322-2872
E-mail: info@ekocamp.com

Elite Educational Institute
Julian Chou, Program Director
19735 Colima Road, # 2, Rowland Heights, California 91748
Phone: 909-444-0876 Fax: 909-444-0877

Emagination Computer Camps
Kathi Rigg, Director
110 Winn Street, Suite 207, Woburn, Massachusetts 01801
Phone: 888-226-6733 Fax: 781-933-0749
E-mail: camp@computercamps.com

Embry-Riddle Aeronautical University-Aerospace Summer Camp
Pamela Peer, Program Manager
600 South Clyde Morris Boulevard, Daytona Beach, Florida 32114
Phone: 800-359-4550 Fax: 386-226-7630
E-mail: summer@erau.edu

Enforex-General Spanish
Enforex Spanish in the Spanish World
Spanish Department
Alberto Aguilera 26, Madrid, 28015, Spain
Phone: 34-91-594-3776 Fax: 34-91-594-5159
E-mail: registration@enforex.es

Ensemble Theatre Community School
Seth Orbach, Associate Director
P.O. Box 188, Eagles Mere, Pennsylvania 17731
Phone: 570-525-3043 Fax: 570-525-3548
E-mail: info@etcschool.org

Environmental Studies and Solutions
Scandinavian Seminar
Leslie Evans, Program Coordinator
24 Dickinson Street, Amherst, Massachusetts 01002
Phone: 413-253-9736 Fax: 413-253-5282
E-mail: study@scandinavianseminar.org

Environmental Studies Summer Youth Institute
Hobart and William Smith Colleges
Brooks McKinney, Director, ESSYI
Geneva, New York 14456-3397
Phone: 315-781-4401 Fax: 315-781-4400
E-mail: essyi@hws.edu

Excalibur
Langskib Wilderness Programs
Clay Stephens, Program Director
P.O. Box 358, Temagami, Ontario P0H 2H0, Canada
Phone: 518-962-4869 Fax: 518-962-8768
E-mail: canoe@langskib.com

Excel
Putney Student Travel
Tim Weed, Director
345 Hickory Ridge Road, Putney, Vermont 05346
Phone: 802-387-5000 Fax: 802-387-4276
E-mail: excel@goputney.com

The Experiment in International Living
Annie Thompson, Enrollment Director
Summer Abroad, Kipling Road, P.O. Box 676, Brattleboro, Vermont 05302-0676
Phone: 800-345-2929 Fax: 802-258-3428
E-mail: eil@worldlearning.org

Exploration Intermediate Program at Wellesley College
Exploration School, Inc.
Mary-Ann Sullivan, Head of Program
Wellesley College, 106 Central Street, Wellesley, Massachusetts 02481
Phone: 781-283-3781

Exploration Junior Program at St. Mark's School
Exploration School, Inc.
David Torcoletti, Head of Program
Exploration, St. Mark's School, 25 Marlborough Road, Southborough, Massachusetts 01772
Phone: 508-786-1350 Fax: 508-786-1360

Exploration of Architecture
University of Southern California, School of Architecture
Jennifer Park, Director of Undergraduate Admission
USC School of Architecture, Watt Hall 204, Los Angeles, California 90089-0291
Phone: 213-740-2420 Fax: 213-740-8884
E-mail: jenpark@usc.edu

Exploration Senior Program at Yale University
Exploration School, Inc.
Bill Clough, Head of Program
Exploration Senior Program, P.O. Box 205187, New Haven, Connecticut 06520-5187
Phone: 203-432-1777 Fax: 203-432-2134
E-mail: summer@explo.org

Explore-A-College
Earlham College
Dee Johnson, Director of Summer Studies
Drawer 188, Richmond, Indiana 47374-4095
Phone: 800-EARLHAM Fax: 765-983-1560
E-mail: ballde@earlham.edu

Explore Nor'wester
Camp Nor'wester
Paul Henriksen, Director
P.O. Box 4395, Roche Harbor, Washington 98250
Phone: 360-468-2225 Fax: 360-468-2472
E-mail: norwester@rockisland.com

Falcon Horse Lover Camp
Emily Devey, Director
4251 Delta Road, SW, Carrollton, Ohio 44615
Phone: 800-837-CAMP Fax: 330-627-2220
E-mail: falconhorsecamp@aol.com

Falling Creek Camp
Donnie Bain, Director
Box 98, Tuxedo, North Carolina 28784
Phone: 828-692-0262 Fax: 828-696-1616
E-mail: mail@fallingcreek.com

Farm and Wilderness Camps
Linda Berryhill, Registrar
263 Farm and Wilderness Road, Plymouth, Vermont 05056
Phone: 802-422-3761 Fax: 802-422-8660
E-mail: fandw@fandw.org

Fay Summer School
Fay School
George Noble, Director of Athletics and Special Programs
P.O. Box 9106, Southborough, Massachusetts 01772
Phone: 508-485-0100 Fax: 508-481-7872
E-mail: gnoble@fayschool.org

The Fessenden School Summer ESL Program
The Fessenden School
Mark Hansen, Director
250 Waltham Street, West Newton, Massachusetts 02465
Phone: 617-630-2300 Fax: 617-928-8888
E-mail: esl@fessenden.org

Film Institute at Pali Overnight Adventures
Pali Overnight Adventures
Andy Wexler, Owner/Founder
P.O. Box 2237, Running Springs, California 92382
Phone: 909-867-5743 Fax: 909-867-7643
E-mail: info@paliadventures.com

Fishburne Summer Session

Fishburne Military School
Carl Lambert, Director of Admissions
P.O. Box 988E, Waynesboro, Virginia 22980
Phone: 800-946-7773 Fax: 540-946-7738
E-mail: lambert@fishburne.org

Fleur de Lis Camp
Liz Young, Director
120 Howeville Road, Fitzwilliam, New Hampshire 03447-3465
Phone: 603-585-7751 Fax: 603-585-7751
E-mail: fdlcamp@aol.com

Flint Hill School-"Summer on the Hill"
Peggy Laurent, Director of Special and Summer Programs
3320 Jermantown Road, Oakton, Virginia 22124
Phone: 703-584-2315 Fax: 703-242-0718
E-mail: plaurent@flinthill.org

Flying Moose Lodge
Christopher Price, Director
Craig Pond Trail, East Orland, Maine 04431
Phone: 207-941-9202
E-mail: prices@flyingmooselodge.com

Forest Ridge Summer Program
Forest Ridge School of the Sacred Heart
Melissa Miller, Summer Program Director
4800 139th Avenue, SE, Bellevue, Washington 98006
Phone: 425-641-0700 Fax: 425-643-3881
E-mail: mmiller@forestridge.org

Forrestel Farm Riding and Sports Camp
Mary Herbert, Owner/Director
4536 South Gravel Road, Medina, New York 14103
Phone: 585-798-2222 Fax: 585-798-0941
E-mail: summer@ffridingsportscamp.com

Fort Union Civil War Camp
Historical Experiences
Arn Kind, Camp Director
20150 589th Avenue, Mankato, Minnesota 56001
Phone: 507-625-8011
E-mail: akind1@mail.isd77.k12.mn.us

Foster Guitar Camp
Eastern Kentucky University Department of Music
Joe Allison, Camps Director
521 Lancaster Avenue, Richmond, Kentucky 40475-3102
Phone: 859-622-3161 Fax: 859-622-1333

Foster Middle School Band Camp
Eastern Kentucky University Department of Music
Joe Allison, Camps Director
521 Lancaster Avenue, Richmond, Kentucky 40475-3102
Phone: 859-622-3161 Fax: 859-622-1333
E-mail: fostercamp@eku.edu

Four Corners School of Outdoor Education: Southwest Ed-Venture
Prescott College
David Bragg, SW Ed-Ventures Program Manager
P.O. Box 1029, Monticello, Utah 84535
Phone: 435-587-2156 Fax: 435-587-2193
E-mail: dbragg@fourcornersschool.org

4 Star Academics Junior Camp at the University of Virginia
4 Star Summer Camps at the University of Virginia
Marietta Naramore, Admissions Director
P.O. Box 3387, Falls Church, Virginia 22043-0387
Phone: 800-334-7827 Fax: 703-866-7775
E-mail: info@4starcamps.com

Four Winds * Westward Ho
Four Winds, Inc.
Michael Douglas, Interim Director
P.O. Box 140, Deer Harbor, Washington 98243
Phone: 360-376-2277
E-mail: info@fourwindscamp.org

French Woods Festival of the Performing Arts
Ronald Schaefer, Director
P.O. Box 609, Hancock, New York 13783
Phone: 845-887-5600
E-mail: admin@frenchwoods.com

Friends Camp
Nat Shed, Director
729 Lakeview Drive, South China, Maine 04358
Phone: 207-445-2361 Fax: 207-445-5451
E-mail: director@friendscamp.org

From the Forest to the Sea
Prince William Sound Science Center
Kate Alexander, Education Specialist
Box 705, Cordova, Alaska 99574
Phone: 907-424-5800 Fax: 907-424-5820
E-mail: kate@pwssc.gen.ak.us

Frontiers Program
Worcester Polytechnic Institute
Julie Chapman, Frontiers Program/Assistant Director of Admissions
Student Affairs Office, 100 Institute Road, Worcester, Massachusetts 01609-2280
Phone: 508-831-5286 Fax: 508-831-5875
E-mail: frontiers@wpi.edu

FUN-damental Basketball Camp, Inc.
Stu Maloff, Owner/Director
P.O. Box 970446, Boca Raton, Florida 33497-0446
Phone: 877-545-8423 Fax: 561-218-0536
E-mail: basketballcamp@aol.com

Future Astronaut Training Program
Kansas Cosmosphere and Space Center
Laurie Givan, Camp Registrar
1100 North Plum, Hutchinson, Kansas 67501
Phone: 800-397-0330 Fax: 620-662-3693
E-mail: laurieg@cosmo.org

Genesis at Brandeis University
Bradley Solmsen, Director
Genesis at Brandeis University, P.O. Box 549110, MS 085, Waltham, Massachusetts 02454-9110
Phone: 781-736-8416 Fax: 781-736-8122
E-mail: genesis@brandeis.edu

Georgetown Prep School Summer English Program
Georgetown Preparatory School
10900 Rockville Pike, Rockville, Maryland 20852
Phone: 301-214-1250 Fax: 301-214-8600
E-mail: rwhitman@gprep.org

Georgetown University Programs for High School Students
Emma Harrington, Special Programs Director
School for Summer and Continuing Education, P.O. Box 571010, Washington, District of Columbia 20057-1010
Phone: 202-687-5719 Fax: 202-687-8954
E-mail: harringe@georgetown.edu

George Washington University Summer Scholars Pre-college Program
Margaret Myers, Program Assistant
2100 Foxhall Road, Mount Vernon Campus, Washington, District of Columbia 20007
Phone: 202-242-6802
E-mail: memyers@gwu.edu

Geronimo Program
Betsy Leslie, Program Coordinator
P.O. Box 1910, Newport, Rhode Island 02840-0190
Phone: 401-842-6702 Fax: 401-842-6696
E-mail: betsy_leslie@stgeorges.edu

GIC Arg-Cultural Exchange Group of Argentina
Marcos Salusso, Director
Lavalle 397-1-1, Buenos Aires, C1047AAG, Argentina
E-mail: info@gicarg.org

Girl Scouts of Genesee Valley Day Camp
Mary McDowell, Director of Outdoor Program
1020 John Street, West Henrietta, New York 14586
Phone: 585-239-7915 Fax: 585-292-1086
E-mail: marym@gsgv.org

GirlSummer at Emma Willard School
Doug Murphy, Director
285 Pawling Avenue, Troy, New York 12180
Phone: 866-EWS-CAMP Fax: 212-815-9256
E-mail: girlsummer@emmawillard.org

The Glen at Lake of the Woods
Lake of the Woods Camp for Girls and Greenwoods Camp for Boys
Dayna Hardin, Director
84600 47 1/2 Street, Decatur, Michigan 49045
Phone: 269-423-3091 Fax: 269-423-8889
E-mail: lwcgwc@aol.com

Global Teen
Language Liaison
Nancy Forman, Director
P.O. Box 1772, Pacific Palisades, California 90272
Phone: 800-284-4448 Fax: 310-454-1706
E-mail: learn@languageliaison.com

GLOBAL WORKS
Erik Werner, Director
1113 South Allen Street, State College, Pennsylvania 16801
Phone: 814-867-7000 Fax: 814-867-2717
E-mail: info@globalworksinc.com

GLS German Language School Berlin
Barbara Jaeschke, Managing Director
Kolonnenstrasse 26, Berlin, 10829, Germany
Phone: 49-30-780089-24 Fax: 49-30-787-4192
E-mail: barbara.jaeschke@gls-berlin.com

Gold Arrow Camp
Steven Monke, Director
P.O. Box 155, Lakeshore, California 93634
Phone: 559-893-6641 Fax: 559-893-6201
E-mail: mail@goldarrowcamp.com

Gordon Kent's New England Tennis Camp
Gordon Kent, Director/Owner
P.O. Box 840, Pawling, New York 12564
Phone: 800-528-2752 Fax: 845-855-9661
E-mail: netennis@aol.com

The Governor's Program for Gifted Children
George Middleton, Director
Box 91490, Lake Charles, Louisiana 70609
Phone: 800-291-7840 Fax: 337-475-5447
E-mail: office@gpgc.org

Grandparents' and Grandchildren's Camp
Sagamore Institute of the Adirondacks
M. Wilson, Associate Director
P.O. Box 40, Raquette Lake, New York 13436-0040
Phone: 315-354-5311 Fax: 315-354-5851
E-mail: sagamore@telenet.net

The Grand River Summer Academy
Sam Corabi, Director of Admission
3042 College Street, Austinburg, Ohio 44010
Phone: 440-275-2811 Fax: 440-275-1825
E-mail: academy@grandriver.org

Great Escapes (Adventure Trips for Teens)
South Shore YMCA Camps
Joe O'Keefe, Great Escapes Director
75 Stowe Road, Sandwich, Massachusetts 02563
Phone: 508-428-2571 Fax: 508-420-3545
E-mail: joeokeefe@ssymca.org

Greek Summer
American Farm School
Hilary Goldstein, Program Coordinator
1133 Broadway, Suite 1625, New York, New York 10010
Phone: 212-463-8434 Fax: 212-463-8208
E-mail: info@greeksummer.org

Greenbrier River Outdoor Adventures,
Tom Bryant, Camp Director
HC77, Box 117, Bartow, West Virginia 24920
Phone: 304-456-5191 Fax: 304-456-5572
E-mail: groa@groa.com

Green River Preserve
Missi Schenck, Founder/Director
301 Green River Road, Cedar Mountain, North Carolina 28718
Phone: 828-698-8828 Fax: 828-698-9201
E-mail: grpreserve@citcom.net

Greenwoods Camp for Boys
Lake of the Woods Camp for Girls and Greenwoods Camp for Boys
Dayna Hardin, Director
84600 47 1/2 Street, Decatur, Michigan 49045
Phone: 269-423-3091 Fax: 269-423-8889
E-mail: lwcgwc@aol.com

Grinnell Summer Institute
Grinnell College
Jim Sumner, Dean of Admissions/Financial Aid
Office of Admissions, 1103 Park Street, Grinnell, Iowa 50112-0810
Phone: 800-247-0113 Fax: 641-269-4800
E-mail: sumnerj@grinnell.edu

The Grove at Greenwoods
Lake of the Woods Camp for Girls and Greenwoods Camp for Boys
Dayna Hardin, Director
84600 47 1/2 Street, Decatur, Michigan 49045
Phone: 269-423-3091 Fax: 269-423-8889
E-mail: lwcgwc@aol.com

Guitar Workshop Plus
Brian Murray, Director
P.O. Box 21207, Meadowvale Postal Outlet, Mississauga, Ontario L5N 6A2, Canada
Phone: 905-785-7087 Fax: 905-785-2831
E-mail: info@guitarworkshopplus.com

Hamilton Learning Centre Summer Fun in the Sun Camp
Maureen Pangan, Director
1603 Main Street West, Hamilton, Ontario L8S 1E6, Canada
Phone: 905-521-1333 Fax: 905-521-1106
E-mail: info@hamiltonlearningcentre.com

Hancock Field Station
Oregon Museum of Science and Industry
Travis Neumeyer, Programming Coordinator
1945 Southeast Water Avenue, Portland, Oregon 97214
Phone: 503-239-7824 Fax: 503-239-7838
E-mail: tneumeyer@omsi.edu

Hante School
Eagle's Nest Foundation
John Carrico, Hante Director
43 Hart Road, Pisgah Forest, North Carolina 28768
Phone: 828-877-4349 Fax: 828-884-2788
E-mail: hante@enf.org

Harand Camp of the Theatre Arts
Sulie Harand, Director
Carthage on the Lake, 2001 Alford Park Drive, Kenosha, Wisconsin 53140-1994
Phone: 920-885-4517 Fax: 920-885-4521
E-mail: harandcamp@aol.com

Hargrave Summer Program
Hargrave Military Academy
Frank Martin, Director of Admissions
Chatham, Virginia 24531
Phone: 800-432-2480 Fax: 434-432-3129

Harker Summer English Language Institute
The Harker School
Joe Rosenthal, Executive Director
500 Saratoga Avenue, San Jose, California 95129
Phone: 408-345-9264 Fax: 408-984-2395
E-mail: joer@harker.org

Harmon's Pine View Camp
Lee Harmon, Director
P.O. Box 644, Candlewood Lake, Galion, Ohio 44833
Phone: 419-947-3197

Hawaii Extreme Adventure Scuba Camp
Sophie Miladinovich, Director of Hawaii Extreme Adventure Scuba Camp
Oahu, Hawaii
Phone: 925-708-0855 Fax: 925-831-1432
E-mail: scubaforlife@aol.com

Hawaii Preparatory Academy Summer Session
Special Programs Office
65-1692 Kohala Mountain Road, Kamuela, Hawaii 96743
Phone: 808-881-4088 Fax: 808-881-4071
E-mail: summer@hpa.edu

Hidden Valley Camp
Meg Kassen, Co-Owner/Director
161 Hidden Valley Road, Freedom, Maine 04941
Phone: 207-342-5177 Fax: 207-342-5685
E-mail: summer@hiddenvalleycamp.com

Hidden Villa Summer Camp
Jill Kilty-Newburn, Director, Family and Youth Programs
26870 Moody Road, Los Altos Hills, California 94022
Phone: 650-949-8641 Fax: 650-948-1916
E-mail: camp@hiddenvilla.org

High Cascade Snowboard Camp
Meagan Stein, Camp Administrator
P.O. Box 368, Government Camp, Oregon 97028
Phone: 800-334-4272 Fax: 503-272-3637
E-mail: highcascade@highcascade.com

Hiker's Heaven Overnight Camp
KidsMakeADifference.org
Andy Mars, Director
P.O. Box 24922, West Los Angeles, California 90024-0922
Phone: 818-344-7838

Hill Top Summer Programs
The Hill Top Preparatory School
Natan Gottesman, Director, Hill Top Summer Programs
737 South Ithan Avenue, Rosemont, Pennsylvania 19010
Phone: 610-527-3230 Fax: 610-527-7683
E-mail: natangottesman@hilltopprep.org

The Hockaday School Summer Session
Nancy Gale, Director of Summer Session
11600 Welch Road, Dallas, Texas 75229
Phone: 214-360-6586 Fax: 214-739-8867
E-mail: ngale@mail.hockaday.org

Hockey Opportunity Camp
Lance Barrs, Director
Box 448, Sundridge, Ontario P0A 1Z0, Canada
Phone: 888-576-2752 Fax: 705-386-0179
E-mail: lance@learnhockey.com

Hollinsummer
Hollins University
Julie Aavatsmark, Sr. Assistant Director of Admissions
P.O. Box 9707, Roanoke, Virginia 24020
Phone: 800-456-4595 Fax: 540-362-6218
E-mail: jaavatsmark@hollins.edu

The Hollows Camp
Janet Fine, Director
RR #3, 3309 13th Line, Cookstown, Ontario L0L 1L0, Canada
Phone: 905-775-2694 Fax: 905-775-2694
E-mail: fine@hollowscamp.com

Houghton Academy Summer ESL
Ron Bradbury, Director of Admissions
9790 Thayer Street, Houghton, New York 14744
Phone: 716-567-8115 Fax: 716-567-8048
E-mail: admissions@houghtonacademy.org

Hulbert Voyageurs Youth Wilderness Trips
Aloha Foundation, Inc.
Greg Auch, Director, Hulbert Voyageurs
2968 Lake Morey Road, Fairlee, Vermont 05045-9400
Phone: 802-333-3405 Fax: 802-333-3404
E-mail: greg_auch@alohafoundation.org

Humanities Spring in Assisi
Jane Oliensis, Director
Santa Maria di Lignano, 2, Assisi, 06081, Italy
Phone: 39-075-802400 Fax: 39-075-802400
E-mail: info@humanitiesspring.com

The Hun School of Princeton-Summer Academic Session
LeRhonda Greats, Summer Academic Director
176 Edgerstoune Road, Princeton, New Jersey 08540
Phone: 609-921-7600 Fax: 609-683-4410
E-mail: summer@hunschool.org

Hyde School Summer Challenge Program-Bath, ME
Richard Truluck, Director of Admission
616 High Street, Bath, Maine 04530-5002
Phone: 207-443-7101 Fax: 207-442-9346
E-mail: rtruluck@hyde.edu

Hyde School Summer Challenge Program-Woodstock, CT
Hyde School
Gigi MacMillan, Director of Admissions
P.O. Box 237, Woodstock, Connecticut 06281-0237
Phone: 860-963-9096 Fax: 860-928-0612
E-mail: gmacmillan@hyde.edu

Ibike Cultural Tours
International Bicycle Fund
David Mozer, Director
4887 Columbia Drive South, Seattle, Washington 98108-1919
Phone: 206-767-0848 Fax: 206-767-0848
E-mail: ibike@ibike.org

iD Tech Camps-Cal Lutheran University, Thousand Oaks, CA
Client Service Representatives
1885 Winchester Boulevard, Suite 201, Campbell, California 95008
Phone: 888-709-TECH Fax: 408-871-2228
E-mail: requests@internaldrive.com

iD Tech Camps
Client Service Representatives
1885 Winchester Boulevard, Suite 201, Campbell, California 95008
Phone: 888-709-TECH Fax: 408-871-2228
E-mail: requests@internaldrive.com

Idyllwild Arts Summer Program
Idyllwild Arts Foundati on
Diane Dennis, Summer Program Registrar
P.O. Box 38, Idyllwild, California 92549
Phone: 909-659-2171 Fax: 909-659-5463
E-mail: summer@idyllwildarts.org

Institute for Mathematics & Computer Science (IMACS)
Terry Kaufman, President
7435 Northwest 4th Street, Plantation, Florida 33317
Phone: 954-791-2333 Fax: 954-791-0260
E-mail: info@imacs.org

Indiana University School of Music Office of Special Programs
Helena Walsh, Registration Coordinator
Office of Special Programs, Indiana University School of Music,
Bloomington, Indiana 47405-7006
Phone: 812-855-6025 Fax: 812-855-9847
E-mail: musicsp@indiana.edu

Indian Head Camp
Joel Rutkowski, Assistant Director
P.O. Box 2005, Honesdale, Pennsylvania 18431
Phone: 570-224-4111 Fax: 570-224-4067
E-mail: joel@indianhead.com

Instituto de Idiomas Geos-Costa Rica
Instituto de Idiomas Geos
Tetsuko Motte, Admissions
Centro Commercial Boulevard, Local 2, Escazu, San José, Costa Rica
Phone: 506-288-8576
E-mail: geoscr@racsa.co.cr

Instituto de Idiomas Geos-Granada, Spain
Instituto de Idiomas Geos
Erika Hjelm, Admissions
Calle Puentezuelas, 3, 2B, Granada, 18002, Spain
Phone: 34-958-523100 Fax: 34-958-866337
E-mail: granada@geos-spain.com

Interlochen Arts Camp
Interlochen Center for the Arts
Tom Bewley, Director of Admissions
P.O. Box 199, Interlochen, Michigan 49643
Phone: 231-276-7472 Fax: 231-276-7464
E-mail: admissions@interlochen.org

International Junior Golf Academy
Golf Academy of Hilton Head Island
Thomas Layer, Program Director
P.O. Box 5580, Hilton Head, South Carolina 29938
Phone: 843-785-4540 Fax: 843-785-5116
E-mail: tom@ijga.com

International Music Camp
Joseph T. Alme, Director
RR #1, Box 116 A, Dunseith, North Dakota 58329
Phone: 701-263-4211 Fax: 701-263-4212

International Summer Camp Montana, Switzerland
Philippe Studer, Director
La Moubra, CH-3963, Crans-Montana 1, Switzerland
Phone: 412-7481-5663 Fax: 412-7481-5631
E-mail: info@campmontana.ch

International Summer Centre
32 Rempart de L'Est, Angouleme, 16022, France
Phone: 335-45974190 Fax: 335-45942063
E-mail: nathalie.d@silc.fr

Iroquois Springs
Mark Newfield, Owner/Director
P.O. Box 487, Bowers Road, Rock Hill, New York 12775
Phone: 845-434-6500 Fax: 845-434-6508
E-mail: summers@iroquoissprings.com

ISB Chinese Language Camp
International School of Beijing-Shunyi
Theresa Chao, Chinese Program Principal
10 An Hua Road, Shunyi, Beijing, 101300, China
E-mail: tchao@isb.bj.edu.cn

Israel Discovery
Young Judea
Benji Lovitt, Assistant Director, Short-term Israel Programs
50 West 58th Street, New York, New York 10019
Phone: 212-303-4577 Fax: 212-303-7411
E-mail: blovitt@youngjudea.org

Jayhawk Debate Institute
University of Kansas
Jacob Thompson, Associate Debate Institute Director
Department of Communication Studies, 1440 Jayhawk Boulevard - SB 103
Bailey Hall, Lawrence, Kansas 66045
Phone: 785-864-9893 Fax: 785-864-5203
E-mail: coms3@raven.cc.ukans.edu

Jay Novacek Football Camp/Sports International
Sports International, Inc.
Customer Service
8924 McGaw Court, Columbia, Maryland 21045
Phone: 800-555-0801 Fax: 410-309-9962
E-mail: info@footballcamps.com

Jewish Community Center Day Camp
Jewish Community Center of Greater Monmouth
Jeff Weisenberg, Camp Director
100 Grant Avenue, Deal Park, New Jersey 07723
Phone: 732-531-9100 Fax: 732-531-4718
E-mail: jweisenberg@msn.com

Joe Krivak Quarterback Camp
Sports International, Inc.
Customer Service
8924 McGaw Court, Columbia, Maryland 21045
Phone: 800-555-0801 Fax: 410-309-9962
E-mail: info@footballcamps.com

Joel Ross Tennis & Sports Camp
Joel Ross, Director
Kent School, Kent, Connecticut 06757
Phone: 860-927-5773 Fax: 860-927-6340
E-mail: rosstennis@aol.com

Joe Machnik's No. 1 Camps
Joseph Machnik, Director
P.O. Box 389, 916 Palm Boulevard, Isle of Palms, South Carolina 29451
Phone: 800-622-4645 Fax: 843-886-0885
E-mail: info@no1soccercamps.com

The Johns Hopkins University Zanvyl Krieger School of Arts and Sciences Summer Programs
The Johns Hopkins University
Erin Warhurst, Admissions Assistant
3400 North Charles Street, Suite G1/Wyman Park Building, Baltimore, Maryland 21218
Phone: 800-548-0548 Fax: 410-516-5585
E-mail: summer@jhu.edu

Julian Krinsky Camps and Programs
Julian Krinsky, Owner
P.O. Box 333, Haverford, Pennsylvania 19041-0333
Phone: 800-TRY-JKST
E-mail: info@jkcp.com

Junior Institute
American Cultural Exchange
Chris Gilman, Junior Institute Coordinator
200 West Mercer Street #504, Seattle, Washington 98119
Phone: 206-217-9644 Fax: 206-812-2257
E-mail: cgilman@cultural.org

Junior Statesmen Summer School
Junior Statesmen Foundation
Matthew Randazzo, National Summer School Director
400 South El Camino Real, Suite 300, San Mateo, California 94402
Phone: 650-347-1600 Fax: 650-347-7200
E-mail: jsa@jsa.org

Kamp Kohut
Lisa Tripler, Owner / Director
151 Kohut Road, Oxford, Maine 04270
Phone: 207-539-0966 Fax: 207-539-4701
E-mail: lisa@kampkohut.com

Kampus Kampers
Lynn University
Sue Merrill, Camp Director
3601 North Military Trail, Boca Raton, Florida 33431
Phone: 561-237-7316 Fax: 561-237-7962
E-mail: smerrill@lynn.edu

Kansas Journalism Institute
University of Kansas
John Hudnall, Director
200 Stauffer-Flint Hall, 1435 Jayhawk Boulevard, Lawrence, Kansas 66045
Phone: 785-864-0605 Fax: 785-864-5945
E-mail: kspa@ku.edu

Kayak Adventures Unlimited
Wilderness Experiences Unlimited, Inc.
Taylor Cook, Executive Director
499 Loomis Street, Westfield, Massachusetts 01085
Phone: 413-562-7431 Fax: 413-562-7431
E-mail: adventures@weu.com

Keenan McCardell and Jimmy Smith Football Camp/Sports International
Sports International, Inc.
Customer Service
8924 McGaw Court, Columbia, Maryland 21045
Phone: 800-555-0801 Fax: 410-309-9962
E-mail: info@footballcamps.com

Keewaydin Camps
Doug Mosle, Director
10 Keewaydin Road, Salisbury, Vermont 05769
Phone: 802-352-4709 Fax: 802-352-4772
E-mail: doug@keewaydin.org

Kendall College Culinary Camp
Office of Admissions
900 N. North Branch Street, Chicago, Illinois 60622
Phone: 877-588-8860 Fax: 312-752-2021
E-mail: culinarycamp@kendall.edu

Kent School Summer Writers Camp
Kent School
Amy Van Sickle, Summer Camp Admissions Director
P.O. Box 2006, Kent, Connecticut 06757
Phone: 860-927-6114 Fax: 860-927-6109
E-mail: vansicklea@kent-school.edu

Kenyon Review Young Writers
Kenyon College/The Kenyon Review
Walton House, Gambier, Ohio 43022
Phone: 740-427-5208 Fax: 740-427-5417
E-mail: kenyonreview@kenyon.edu

Keystone Science School
Steve Remer, Summer Programs Director
1628 Sts. John Road, Keystone, Colorado 80435
Phone: 970-468-2098 Fax: 970-468-7769
E-mail: camp@keystone.org

KidzZone Summer Camp
Church In The Now
Melissa Camp-King, Camp Director
1873 Iris Drive, Conyers, Georgia 30013
Phone: 678-607-3100 Fax: 678-607-3122
E-mail: mcamp@churchinthenow.org

Killooleet
Kate Seeger, Director
P.O. Box 70, Hancock, Vermont 05748
Phone: 802-767-3152

Kingsley Pines Camp
Alan Kissack, Director
51 Coughlan Cove Road, Raymond, Maine 04071
Phone: 207-655-7181 Fax: 207-655-4121
E-mail: staff@kingsleypines.com

Kinhaven Music School
Nancy Bidlack, Admissions Director
P.O. Box 68, Weston, Vermont 05161
Phone: 802-824-4332 Fax: 802-824-4332

Kiski Summer Camp
The Kiski School
David Melgard, Director
1888 Brett Lane, Saltsburg, Pennsylvania 15681
Phone: 724-639-3586 Fax: 724-639-8596
E-mail: david.melgard@kiski.org

Knowledge Exchange Institute
Kei Program Manager
111 John Street, Suite 800, New York, New York 10038
Phone: 800-831-5095 E-mail: info@knowledgeexchange.org

Kooch-I-Ching
Camping and Education Foundation
David Plain, Executive Director
Box 271, International Falls, Minnesota 56649
Phone: 218-286-3141 Fax: 218-286-3255
E-mail: office@koochiching.org

Kroka Expeditions of Vermont
Misha Golfman, Executive Director
659 West Hill Road, Putney, Vermont 05346
Phone: 802-387-5397 Fax: 802-387-4536
E-mail: kroka@sover.net

KU Jazz Workshop
University of Kansas
James Hudson, Director
452 Murphy Hall, 1530 Naismith Drive, #452, Lawrence, Kansas 66045-3120
Phone: 785-864-4730 Fax: 785-864-5023
E-mail: musicamp@ku.edu

Kutsher's Sports Academy
Marc White, Executive Director
Anawana Lake Road, Monticello, New York 12701
Phone: 845-794-5400

Lady Wildcat Basketball Camp
Louisiana College
Tonya McIntosh, Head Coach, Women's Basketball
P.O. Box 543, Pineville, Louisiana 71359
Phone: 318-487-7350

Lake of the Woods Camp for Girls and Greenwoods Camp for Boys
Dayna Hardin, Director
84600 47 1/2 Street, Decatur, Michigan 49045
Phone: 269-423-3091 Fax: 269-423-8889
E-mail: lwcgwc@aol.com

Landmark School Summer Academic Program
Director of Admission
P.O. Box 227, Prides Crossing, Massachusetts 01965-0227
Phone: 978-236-3000 Fax: 978-927-7268
E-mail: jtruslow@landmarkschool.org

Landmark Volunteers, Inc.
Ann Barrett, Executive Director
P.O. Box 455, Sheffield, Massachusetts 01257
Phone: 413-229-0255 Fax: 413-229-2050
E-mail: landmark@volunteers.com

Langskib Wilderness Programs
Clay Stephens, Program Director
P.O. Box 358, Temagami, Ontario P0H 2H0, Canada
Phone: 518-962-4869 Fax: 518-962-8768
E-mail: canoe@langskib.com

Leadership Adventure in Boston
Pine Manor College
Whitney Retallic, Program Director
Center for Inclusive Leadership and Social Responsibility, 400 Heath Street, Chestnut Hill, Massachusetts 02467
Phone: 617-731-7620 Fax: 617-731-7185

Leadership Training at Pali Overnight Adventures
Pali Overnight Adventures
Andy Wexler, Owner/Founder
P.O. Box 2237, Running Springs, California 92382
Phone: 909-867-5743 Fax: 909-867-7643
E-mail: info@paliadventures.com

Learn English and Discover Canada
Columbia International College of Canada
Ping Tse, Liaison Director
1003 Main Street West, Hamilton, Ontario L8S 4P3, Canada
Phone: 905-572-7883 Fax: 905-572-9332
E-mail: liaison01@cic-totalcare.com

Les Elfes International Summer/Winter Camp
Philippe Stettler, Director
P.O. Box 174, 1936 Verbier, Switzerland
Phone: 41-27-775-35-90 Fax: 41-27-775-35-99
E-mail: leselfes@axiom.ch

LIFEWORKS International
James Stoll, Director
P.O. Box 5517, Sarasota, Florida 34277
Phone: 800-808-2115 Fax: 941-924-6075
E-mail: info@lifeworks-international.com

Ligonier Camp
Ligonier Camp and Conference Center
Sal Hanna, Summer Camp Director
188 Macartney Lane, Ligonier, Pennsylvania 15658
Phone: 724-238-6428 Fax: 724-238-6971
E-mail: shanna@ligoniercamp.org

Linden Hill Summer Program
James McDaniel, Headmaster and Summer Program Director
154 South Mountain Road, Northfield, Massachusetts 01360-9681
Phone: 413-498-2906 Fax: 413-498-2908
E-mail: admissions@lindenhs.org

Lions Camp Merrick Diabetes Program
Lions Club Organization
Robert Rainey, Camp Administrator
P.O. Box 56, 3650 Rick Hamilton Place, Nanjemoy, Maryland 20662
Phone: 301-870-5858 Fax: 301-246-9108
E-mail: campmerrick@aol.com

Litchfield Jazz Festival Summer Music School Program
Litchfield Performing Arts
Lindsey Muir, Program Director
P.O. Box 69, Litchfield, Connecticut 06759
Phone: 860-567-4162 Fax: 860-567-3592
E-mail: lindseymuir@litchfieldjazzfest.com

Longacre Expeditions
Meredith Schuler, Director
4030 Middle Ridge Road, Newport, Pennsylvania 17074
Phone: 717-567-6790 Fax: 717-567-3955
E-mail: longacre@longacreexpeditions.com

Longacre Leadership Program
Longacre Farm
Susan Smith, Director
4028 Middle Ridge Road, Newport, Pennsylvania 17074
Phone: 717-567-3349 Fax: 717-567-3955
E-mail: connect@longacre.com

Longhorn Music Camp
The University of Texas at Austin, School of Music
Lynne Lange, Program Coordinator
1 University Station E3100, Austin, Texas 78712-0435
Phone: 512-232-2080 Fax: 512-232-3907
E-mail: lmc@www.utexas.edu

The Loomis Chaffee School
Curtis Robison, Director, Summer Programs Abroad
The Loomis Chaffee School, 4 Batchelder Road, Windsor, Connecticut 06095
Phone: 860-687-6341 Fax: 860-687-6181
E-mail: curt_robison@loomis.org

Loras All-Sports Camp
Loras College
Robert Tucker, Director
1450 Alta Vista Street, Dubuque, Iowa 52004
Phone: 563-588-7196 Fax: 563-588-4975
E-mail: sportscamp@loras.edu

Louisiana College Summer Superior Program
Director of Admissions
P.O. Box 560, Pineville, Louisiana 71359
Phone: 318-487-7439 Fax: 318-487-7550
E-mail: admissions@lacollege.edu

Language Studies Abroad, Inc.
Director
1801 Highway 50 East, Suite I, Carson City, Nevada 89701
Phone: 800-424-5522 Fax: 775-883-2266
E-mail: info@languagestudiesabroad.com

Maine College of Art Early College Program
Cheslye Ventimiglia, Director of Continuing Studies
97 Spring Street, Portland, Maine 04101
Phone: 207-775-3052 Fax: 207-879-5748
E-mail: earlycollege@meca.edu

Maine Conservation School Summer Camps
Conservation Education Foundation of Maine
Scott Olsen, Operations Director
P.O. Box 188, Bryant Pond, Maine 04219
Phone: 207-665-2068 Fax: 207-665-2768
E-mail: mcsops@megalink.net

Maine Golf and Tennis Academy
Joel Lavenson, Director
35 Golf Academy Drive, Belgrade, Maine 04917
Phone: 800-465-3226 Fax: 207-465-3226
E-mail: fun@golfcamp.com

Maine Teen Camp
Monique Rafuse-Pines, Associate Director
481 Brownfield Road, Porter, Maine 04068
Phone: 207-625-8581 Fax: 207-625-8738
E-mail: mtc@teencamp.com

Maplebrook School's Summer Program
Maplebrook School
Jennifer Scully, Director of Admissions
5142 Route 22, Amenia, New York 12501
Phone: 845-373-8191 Fax: 845-373-7029
E-mail: mbsecho@aol.com

Marine and Environmental Science Program
Ocean Educations, Ltd.
Ian Mitchell, Director
341 Price Road, Salt Spring Island, British Columbia V8K 2E9, Canada
Phone: 250-537-8464 Fax: 250-537-8465
E-mail: ian@oceaned.com

Marine Military Academy
Jay Perez, Admissions
320 Iwo Jima Boulevard, Harlingen, Texas 78550
Phone: 956-423-6006 Fax: 956-412-3848
E-mail: admissions@mma-tx.org

Marrowstone Music Festival
Seattle Youth Symphony Orchestras
Mary Jensen, Marrowstone Music Festival Coordinator
11065 5th Avenue, NE, Suite A, Seattle, Washington 98125
Phone: 206-362-2300 Fax: 206-361-9254
E-mail: marrowstone@syso.org

The Marsh
Morning Cheer, Inc.
Jenny Welte, Director
60 Sandy Cove Road, North East, Maryland 21901
Phone: 410-287-5433 Fax: 410-287-3196
E-mail: themarsh@sandycove.org

Massachusetts College of Art/Creative Vacation
Nell Agayan, Program Administrative Assistant
621 Huntington Avenue, Boston, Massachusetts 02115
Phone: 617-879-7170 Fax: 617-879-7171
E-mail: nagayan@massart.edu

Massanutten Military Academy
Frank Thomas, Director of Admissions
614 South Main Street, Woodstock, Virginia 22664
Phone: 877-466-6222 Fax: 540-459-5421
E-mail: admissions@militaryschool.com

Maui Surfer Girls
Dustin Tester, Director/Founder
P.O. Box 1158, Puunene, Hawaii 96784
Phone: 808-280-8165 Fax: 808-242-4125
E-mail: dustin@mauisurfergirls.com

McCallie Lacrosse Camp
The McCallie School
Troy Kemp, Lacrosse Head Coach
Missionary Ridge, 500 Dodds Avenue, Chattanooga, Tennessee 37404
Phone: 800-MSC-CAMP
E-mail: tkemp@mccallie.org

Meadowood Springs Speech and Hearing Camp
The Institute for Rehabilitation, Research, and Recreation, Inc.
Rhonda Hack, Executive Administrator
P.O. Box 1025, Pendleton, Oregon 97801-0030
Phone: 541-276-2752 Fax: 541-276-7227
E-mail: meadowood@oregontrail.net

Medeba Summer Camp
Medeba
Glenda Dunning, Registrar
General Delivery, West Guilford, Ontario K0M 2S0, Canada
Phone: 705-754-2444 Fax: 705-754-1530
E-mail: glenda@medeba.com

Med-O-Lark Camp
Jay Stager, Director
82 Medolark Road, Washington, Maine 04574
Phone: 800-292-7757 Fax: 207-845-2332
E-mail: medolark@acadia.net

Mercersburg Academy Summer and Extended Programs
Rick Hendrickson, Director of Summer and Extended Programs
300 East Seminary Street, Mercersburg, Pennsylvania 17236
Phone: 717-328-6225 Fax: 717-328-9072
E-mail: summerprograms@mercersburg.edu

MexArt
Carly Cross, Director/Owner
413 Inter America, BC-2323, Laredo, Texas 78045
E-mail: carly@gomexart.com

Miami University Junior Scholars Program
Robert Smith, Director
301 South Patterson Avenue, Room 202, Oxford, Ohio 45056-3414
Phone: 513-529-5825 Fax: 513-529-1498
E-mail: juniorscholars@muohio.edu

Michigan State University High School Engineering Institute
Jonathan Lembright, Director, High School Engineering Institute
1410 Engineering Building, East Lansing, Michigan 48824
Phone: 517-355-6616 Fax: 517-432-1350
E-mail: lembrigh@egr.msu.edu

Michigan Technological University Explorations in Engineering Workshop
John Lehman, Youth Programs Coordinator
1400 Townsend Drive, Houghton, Michigan 49931-1295
Phone: 906-487-2219 Fax: 906-487-3101
E-mail: yp@mtu.edu

Midsummer in London
British American Drama Academy (BADA)
Frances Mayhew, Program Coordinator
14 Gloucester Gate, London, NW1 4HG, United Kingdom
Phone: 44-207-487-0730 Fax: 44-207-487-0731
E-mail: info@badaonline.com

MidSummer Macon
Wesleyan College
Jo Ann Green, Executive Director MidSummer Macon
4760 Forsyth Road, Macon, Georgia 31210-4462
Phone: 478-757-5174 Fax: 478-757-3990
E-mail: jogreen@wesleyancollege.edu

Millennium Entrepreneurs "Training Tomorrow's Business Leaders Today"
Millennium Entrepreneurs
Tonja McCoy, President/Camp Director
P.O. Box 14, Malibu, California 90265
Phone: 301-582-0235 E-mail: teensceo@yahoo.com

Milwaukee School of Engineering (MSOE)-Discover the Possibilities
Linda Levandowski, Special Events Coordinator MSOE
1025 North Broadway, Milwaukee, Wisconsin 53202
Phone: 800-332-6763 Fax: 414-277-7475
E-mail: levandow@msoe.edu

MIMC-Intensive Music Camp
Carl Urquhart, Senior Director
500 Place d'Armes, Suite 1600, Montreal, Quebec H2Y 2W2, Canada
Phone: 514-875-1116 Fax: 514-875-0660
E-mail: curquhart@unitam.com

Mini-Camp in the Pocono Mountains

Camp Lohikan in the Pocono Mountains
Mark Buynak, Director
24 Wallerville Road, P.O. Box 217, Dept PETG,
Lake Como, Pennsylvania 18437
Phone: 908-798-2707 Fax: 908-470-9319
E-mail: info@lohikan.com

Mini Minors
Cross Keys
Richard Bernstein, Managing Director
48 Fitzalan Road, Finchley, London, N3 3PE, United Kingdom
Phone: 020-8371-9686 Fax: 020-8343-0625
E-mail: richard@xkeys.co.uk

Miss Porter's School Summer Challenge
John Barrengos, Director of Summer Programs
60 Main Street, Farmington, Connecticut 06032
Phone: 860-409-3692 Fax: 860-409-3515
E-mail: summer_programs@missporters.org

The Monarch School Summer Course
Debra Hall, Program Director, Summer Camp
1231 Wirt Road, Houston, Texas 77055
Phone: 713-479-0800 Fax: 713-464-7900
E-mail: dhall@monarchschool.org

Montclair State University Summer Camp for Academically Gifted and Talented Youth
Richard Taubald, Director, Academically Gifted/Talented Youth Programs
876 Valley Road, Upper Montclair, New Jersey 07043
Phone: 973-655-4104 Fax: 973-655-7895
E-mail: taubaldr@mail.montclair.edu

Monte Vista ESL Intensive Language Institute
Susan Bernal, Director of Resident Admissions
Two School Way, Watsonville, California 95076
Phone: 831-722-8178 Fax: 831-722-6003
E-mail: susanbernal@mvcs.org

Montverde Academy Summer School
Marie Szymanski, Dean of Admissions
17235 Seventh Street, Montverde, Florida 34756
Phone: 407-469-2561 Fax: 407-469-3711
E-mail: mszymanski@montverde.org

Mountain Adventure Guides
Richard Dulworth, Director
13490 US Highway 25/70, Marshall, North Carolina 28753
Phone: 866-813-5210 Fax: 828-649-0561
E-mail: guide@mtwadventure.guides.com

Mountain Camp
Don Whipple, Director
3717 Buchanan Street, Suite 300, San Francisco, California 94123
Phone: 415-351-2267 Fax: 415-351-3939
E-mail: info@mountaincamp.com

Mountain Meadow Ranch
Jack "Chip" Ellena, Owner/Director
P.O. Box 610, Susanville, California 96130
Phone: 530-257-4419 Fax: 530-257-7155
E-mail: info@mountainmeadow.com

Mountain Retreat Overnight Camp
KidsMakeADifference.org
Andy Mars, Director
P.O. Box 24922, Los Angeles, California 90024-0922
Phone: 818-344-7838

Mount Holyoke College SEARCH
James Morrow, Director, SEARCH
50 College Street, South Hadley, Massachusetts 01075-1441
Phone: 413-538-2608 Fax: 413-538-2002
E-mail: search@mtholyoke.edu

Music and Dance Summer Workshops
Cottey College
Denise Carrick, Coordinator of P.E.O. Relations
1000 West Austin, Nevada, Missouri 64772
Phone: 417-667-8181 Fax: 417-667-8103
E-mail: peorelations@cottey.edu

Nantahala Outdoor Center-Kids Adventure Sports Camp
NOC Guest Relations Office
13077 Highway 19 West, Bryson City, North Carolina 28713
Phone: 800-232-7238 Fax: 828-488-0301
E-mail: programs@noc.com

National Guitar Workshop
Emily Flower, Registrar
P.O. Box 222, Lakeside, Connecticut 06758
Phone: 860-567-3736 Fax: 860-567-0374
E-mail: emily@guitarworkshop.com

National Student Leadership Conference
Mike Sims, Executive Director
111 West Jackson Boulevard, 7th Floor, Chicago, Illinois 60604
Phone: 312-322-9999 Fax: 312-765-0081
E-mail: information@nslcleaders.org

NAWA Academy
Jason Hull, Director of Admissions and Summer Programs
17351 Trinity Mountain Road, French Gulch, California 96033
Phone: 800-358-6292 Fax: 530-359-2229
E-mail: nawa@concentric.net

Nelson/Feller Tennis Camp
Bob Feller, Co-Director
3925 Seneca Lane, Manitowoc, Wisconsin 54220
Phone: 920-684-0830 Fax: 920-684-3641
E-mail: nftc@lsol.net

The Nepal Cultural Immersion Experience
International Cultural Adventures
David Pruskin, Program Director
35 Suprenant Circle, Brunswick, Maine 04011-7142
Phone: 888-339-0460 Fax: 208-728-7338
E-mail: info@ICAdventures.com

New Jersey YMHA-YWHA Camps
Jeff Braverman, Director
HCR 60, Box 5000, Lake Como, Pennsylvania 18437
Phone: 570-798-2373 Fax: 570-798-2663
E-mail: nesher@njycamps.org

New Jersey YMHA-YWHA Camps
Sheira Director-Nowack, Assistant Director
21 Plymouth Street, Fairfield, New Jersey 07004
Phone: 570-798-2551 Fax: 570-798-2784
E-mail: rlc@njycamps.org

The New York Film Academy
Admissions
100 East 17th Street, New York, New York 10003
Phone: 212-674-4300 Fax: 212-477-1414
E-mail: film@nyfa.com

Next Level Camp
Ligonier Camp and Conference Center
Sal Hanna, Summer Camp Director
188 Macartney Lane, Ligonier, Pennsylvania 15658
Phone: 724-238-6428 Fax: 724-238-6971
E-mail: shanna@ligoniercamp.org

92nd Street YM-YWHA
Alan Saltz, Director of Camp Programs
1395 Lexington Avenue, New York, New York 10128
Phone: 212-415-5600 Fax: 212-415-5637
E-mail: camps@92y.org

North Carolina Outward Bound/Outward Bound, USA
Student Services Representative
2582 Riceville Road, Asheville, North Carolina 28805
Phone: 877-776-2627 Fax: 828-299-3928
E-mail: challenge@ncobs.org

North Carolina School of the Arts Summer Session
North Carolina School of the Arts
Sheeler Lawson, Assistant Director of Admissions for Summer Session
1533 South Main Street, Winston-Salem, North Carolina 27127
Phone: 336-770-3290 Fax: 336-770-3370
E-mail: admissions@ncarts.edu

North Country Camps
Nancy Birdsall, Director
395 Frontage Road, Keeseville, New York 12944
Phone: 518-834-5152 Fax: 518-834-5527
E-mail: nancy@nccamps.com

Northern Lights
Northwaters Wilderness Programs
C. Stephens, Program Director
P.O. Box 358, Temagami, Ontario P0H 2H0, Canada
Phone: 518-962-4869 Fax: 518-962-8768
E-mail: canoe@northwaters.com

Northfield Mount Hermon Summer Session
Debra Frank, Dean of Admission, NMH Summer Session
206 Main Street, Northfield, Massachusetts 01360-1089
Phone: 413-498-3290 Fax: 413-498-3112
E-mail: summer_school@nmhschool.org

Northwestern University's College Preparation Program
Stephanie Teterycz, Associate Director of Summer Sessions
405 Church Street, Evanston, Illinois 60208
Phone: 847-491-4358 Fax: 847-491-3660
E-mail: s_teterycz@northwestern.edu

Northwestern University's National High School Institute
Northwestern University
Nick Kanel, Department Assistant
617 Noyes Street, Evanston, Illinois 60208
Phone: 800-662-NHSI Fax: 847-467-1057
E-mail: nhsi@northwestern.edu

The Northwest School Summer Program
Susan Mueller, Summer Program Director
1415 Summit Avenue, Seattle, Washington 98122
Phone: 206-682-7309 Fax: 206-467-7353

North Woods Camp for Boys
YMCA of Greater Boston-Camping Services Branch
Amy Goodman, Registrar
P.O. Box 230, Mirror Lake, New Hampshire 03853
Phone: 603-569-2725 Fax: 603-569-5869
E-mail: agoodman@ymcaboston.org

Oak Hill Academy Summer Program
Michael Groves, Director of Admissions
2635 Oak Hill Road, Mouth of Wilson, Virginia 24363
Phone: 276-579-2619 Fax: 276-579-4722
E-mail: info@oak-hill.net

Oak Ridge Summer Leadership Camp
Oak Ridge Military Academy
Dan Carpinetti, Vice President of Admissions
P.O. Box 498, Oak Ridge, North Carolina 27310
Phone: 336-643-4131 Fax: 336-643-1797
E-mail: dcarpinetti@ormila.com

!Adventures-Afloat/Odyssey Expeditions
Jason Buchheim, Director
650 Southeast Paradise Point Road, #100, Crystal River, Florida 34429
Phone: 800-929-7749 Fax: 801-340-5000
E-mail: odyssey@usa.net

OES-Challenge Workshops
Oregon Episcopal School
Joan Lowe, Program Director
6300 SW Nicol Road, Portland, Oregon 97223
Phone: 503-768-3145 Fax: 503-416-9801
E-mail: lowej@oes.edu

Offense-Defense Golf Camp, Massasachusetts
Mike Meshken, Director
P.O. Box 6, Easton, Connecticut 06612
Phone: 203-256-9844 Fax: 203-255-5666
E-mail: golfcamp@localnet.com

Offense-Defense Tennis Camp
Mehdi Belhassan, Director
P.O. Box 48018, Tampa, Florida 33647
Phone: 813-972-0101 Fax: 813-972-0128
E-mail: mbtennis@aol.com

Ojai Valley School Summer Programs
John Williamson, Director of Admission
723 El Paseo Road, Ojai, California 93023
Phone: 805-646-1423 Fax: 805-646-0362
E-mail: admission@ovs.org

OMNI Camp
Betsy Roper, Co-Director
200 Verrill Road, Poland Spring, Maine 04274
Phone: 207-998-4777 Fax: 207-998-4722
E-mail: info@omnicamp.com

On the Wing
Rocky Mountain Bird Observatory
Jennie Rectenwald, Camp Director
1510 South College Avenue, Fort Collins, Colorado 80524
Phone: 970-482-1707 Fax: 303-654-0791
E-mail: jennie.rectenwald@rmbo.org

Operafestival di Roma
Louisa Panou, Artistic Director
1445 Willow Lake Drive, Charlottesville, Virginia 22902
Phone: 434-984-4945 Fax: 434-984-5220
E-mail: operafest@aol.com

Organic Farm Camp
Wilderness Education Institute
Kevin Snyder, Executive Director
2260 Baseline Road, Suite 205, Boulder, Colorado 80302
Phone: 877-628-9692
E-mail: information@weiprograms.org

Outdoor Adventure
Western Washington University
Debbie Gibbons, Program Manager
Extended Education and Summer Programs, Mail Stop 5293, 516 High Street, Bellingham, Washington 98225
Phone: 360-650-6820 Fax: 360-650-6858
E-mail: adventures@wwu.edu

Outpost Wilderness Adventure
Quentin Keith, Director
20859 County Road 77, Lake George, Colorado 80827
Phone: 719-748-3080 Fax: 719-748-3046
E-mail: q@owa.com

Outward Bound
Thompson Island Outward Bound/Outward Bound, USA
Jon Hislop, Director of Admissions
Thompson Island, P.O. Box 127, Boston, Massachusetts 02127-0002
Phone: 617-328-3900 Fax: 617-328-3710
E-mail: admissions@thompsonisland.org

Outward Bound West
Outward Bound West/Outward Bound, USA
Admissions Advisor
910 Jackson Street, Golden, Colorado 80401
Phone: 866-746-9777 Fax: 720-497-2421
E-mail: info@obwest.org

Overland Travel, Inc.
Brooks Follansbee, Director
P.O. Box 31, Williamstown, Massachusetts 01267
Phone: 800-458-0588 Fax: 413-458-5208
E-mail: overland@adelphia.net

The Oxford Academy Summer Program
Michele Deane, Director of Admissions
1393 Boston Post Road, Westbrook, Connecticut 06498
Phone: 860-399-6247 Fax: 860-399-6805
E-mail: admissions@oxfordacademy.net

Oxford Advanced Seminars Programme
Albion International Study Centre, Oxford
Carolyn Llewelyn, Principal
Bocardo House, St. Michael's Street, Oxford, OX1 2EB, United Kingdom
Phone: 44-1865244470 Fax: 44-1865244112
E-mail: info@albionschools.co.uk

Oxford Advanced Studies Program
Oxford Tutorial College
Joan Ives, Program Registrar
P.O. Box 2043, Darien, Connecticut 06820
Phone: 203-966-2886 Fax: 203-972-3083
E-mail: oxedge@aol.com

The Oxford Experience
Academic Study Associates, Inc. (ASA)
Marcia Evans, President
10 New King Street, White Plains, New York 10604
Phone: 914-686-7730 Fax: 914-686-7740
E-mail: summer@asaprograms.com

Oxford Media School
Desmond Smith, Director
110 Pricefield Road, Toronto, Ontario M4W 1Z9, Canada
Phone: 416-964-0746 Fax: 416-929-4230
E-mail: newsco@sympatico.ca

The Oxford Prep Experience
Oxbridge Academic Programs
Andrea Mardon, Executive Director, Oxbridge Academic Programs
601 West 110th Street, Suite 7R, New York, New York 10025-2186
Phone: 800-828-8349 Fax: 212-663-8169
E-mail: info@oxbridgeprograms.com

Oxford School Summer Camp
Michelle Cheng, Coordinator
18760 East Colima Road, Rowland Heights, California 91748
Phone: 626-964-9588 Fax: 626-913-3919
E-mail: michelle_c@oxfordschool.org

Pacific Marine Science Camp
Oregon Museum of Science and Industry
Travis Neumeyer, Programming Coordinator
1945 Southeast Water Avenue, Portland, Oregon 97214
Phone: 503-239-7824 Fax: 503-239-7838
E-mail: tneumeyer@omsi.edu

Parsons Summer Intensive Studies-New York
Parsons School of Design
Charlotte Rice, Director, Pre-Enrollment Programs
66 Fifth Avenue, New York, New York 10011
Phone: 212-229-8925 Fax: 212-229-8975
E-mail: summer@newschool.edu

Parsons Summer Intensive Studies-Paris
Parsons School of Design
Roland Schneider, Program Coordinator
Paris, France
Phone: 212-229-8925 Fax: 212-229-8975
E-mail: summer@newschool.edu

Pathways at Marywood University
Marywood University
Meg Cullen-Brown, Program Director, Pathways
2300 Adams Avenue, Scranton, Pennsylvania 18509
Phone: 800-724-0399 Fax: 570-961-4776
E-mail: brownm@ac.marywood.edu

Paul Hogan Sports Camps
Paul Hogan, Director
P.O. Box 1136, Concord, New Hampshire 03302
Phone: 603-340-1719 Fax: 603-271-6431
E-mail: paul@hogancamps.com

Performance PLUS-Positive Learning Using the Stage+Studio+Screen
Performance PLUS
Lori Murphy, Producing Director
Performance PLUS at New Hampton School, P.O. Box 579, New Hampton, New Hampshire 03256
Phone: 603-677-3403 Fax: 603-677-3481
E-mail: lmurphy@performanceplus.org

Perry-Mansfield Performing Arts School and Camp
June Lindenmayer, Executive Director
40755 Routt County Road 36, Steamboat Springs, Colorado 80487
Phone: 800-430-2787 Fax: 970-879-5823
E-mail: p-m@perry-mansfield.org

The Peru Cultural Immersion Experience
International Cultural Adventures
David Pruskin, Program Director
35 Suprenant Circle, Brunswick, Maine 04011-7142
Phone: 888-339-0460 Fax: 208-728-7338
E-mail: info@ICAdventures.com

Phillips Academy Summer Session
Maxine Grogan, Dean of Admission
Phillips Academy Summer Session, 180 Main Street, Andover, Massachusetts 01810
Phone: 978-749-4400 Fax: 978-749-4414
E-mail: summersession@andover.edu

Phillips Exeter Academy
20 Main Street, Exeter, New Hampshire 03833-2460
Phone: 603-777-3409 Fax: 603-777-4396
Phillips Exeter Academy Taiwan and Beijing Summer Study Tour
Ming Fontaine, Program Director
20 Main Street, Exeter, New Hampshire 03833
Phone: 603-772-7708 Fax: 603-777-4384
E-mail: mfontaine@exeter.edu

Pine Tree Camps at Lynn University
Diane DiCerbo, Director
3601 North Military Trail, Boca Raton, Florida 33431
Phone: 561-237-7310 Fax: 561-237-7962
E-mail: ddicerbo@lynn.edu

Pingry Academic Camps
The Pingry School
Norman LaValette, Program Director/ Chair, Foreign Language Department
Emanuel Tramontana, Camp Director/Chair, Mathematics Department
Mike Webster, Program Director - Lacrosse
Carolyn Gibson, Assistant Director - Lower School
The Pingry School, Box 366, Martinsville, New Jersey 08836
Phone: 908-647-5555 Fax: 908-647-3037
E-mail: info@pingry.org

Plato College-English/French Intensive Courses
Chris Kavathas, Vice President
4521 Park Avenue, Montreal, Quebec H2V 4E4, Canada
Phone: 514-281-1016 Fax: 514-281-6275
E-mail: info@collegeplaton.com

Pleasant Valley Camp for Girls
YMCA of Greater Boston-Camping Services Branch
Amy Goodman, Registrar
P.O. Box 230, Mirror Lake, New Hampshire 03853
Phone: 617-569-2725 Fax: 603-569-5869
E-mail: agoodman@ymcaboston.org

Point CounterPoint Chamber Music Camp
Paul Roby, Director
1361 Hooker Road, Brandon, Vermont 05733
Phone: 802-247-8467 Fax: 802-247-8467
E-mail: pointcp@aol.com

Point O' Pines Camp for Girls
Sue Himoff, Director
7201 State Route 8, Brant Lake, New York 12815-2236
Phone: 518-494-3213 Fax: 518-494-3489
E-mail: sue@pointopines.com

Portsmouth Abbey Summer School
Robert Sahms, Director of Summer School
Portsmouth Abbey School, Portsmouth, Rhode Island 02871
Phone: 401-683-2000 Fax: 401-683-5888
E-mail: summer@portsmouthabbey.org

Poulter Colorado Camps
Jay Poulter, Director
P.O. Box 772947, Steamboat Springs, Colorado 80477
Phone: 888-879-4816 Fax: 800-860-3587
E-mail: poulter@poultercamps.com

Power Chord Academy
7336 Santa Monica Boulevard, #107, Los Angeles, California 90046
Phone: 800-897-6677 Fax: 775-306-7923
E-mail: bryan@powerchordacademy.com

Pre-College Summer Institute, The University of the Arts
The University of the Arts
Erin Elman, Director, Pre-College Programs
320 South Broad Street, Philadelphia, Pennsylvania 19102
Phone: 215-717-6430 Fax: 215-717-6433
E-mail: precollege@uarts.edu

Preparatory Academics for Vanderbilt Engineers (PAVE)
Vanderbilt University
John Veillette, Director/Associate Dean
Pre-College Division, Box 351736, Station B, Nashville, Tennessee 37235-1736
Phone: 615-322-7827 Fax: 615-322-3297
E-mail: pave-req@vuse.vanderbilt.edu

Presbyterian Clearwater Forest
David Jeremiason, Director
16595 Crooked Lake Road, Deerwood, Minnesota 56444-8173
Phone: 218-678-2325 Fax: 218-678-3196
E-mail: dj@clearwaterforest.org

Pripstein's Camp
Ronnie Braverman, Director
5702 Cote Saint Luc Road, Suite 202, Montreal, Quebec H3X 2E7, Canada
Phone: 866-481-1875 Fax: 514-481-7863
E-mail: ronnie@pripsteinscamp.com

Professional Sports Camps
Vincent Carlesi, Camp Director
P.O. Box 15, Sparta, New Jersey 07871
Phone: 973-691-0070 Fax: 973-347-5832
E-mail: sportscamp@aol.com

Program of Audubon Research for Teens (Take P.A.R.T.)
Audubon Vermont
Ryan Young, Director
255 Sherman Hollow Road, Huntington, Vermont 05462
Phone: 802-434-3068 Fax: 802-434-4686
E-mail: ryoung@audubon.org

Programs Abroad Travel Alternatives
Heather Kenley, Director of Operations
6200 Adel Cove, Austin, Texas 78749
Phone: 888-777-PATA Fax: 512-282-7076
E-mail: immerse@gopata.com

Project SUCCEED
Shodor Education Foundation, Inc.
Matthew Lathrop, Project SUCCEED Director
923 Broad Street, Suite 100, Durham, North Carolina 27705
Phone: 919-286-1911 Fax: 919-286-7876
E-mail: mlathrop@shodor.org

ProShot Basketball Camp
John Szela, Director
142 Buck River Road, Thornhurst, Pennsylvania 18424
Phone: 570-842-7044 Fax: 570-842-7044
E-mail: info@proshot.us

Ramey Summer Tennis Camps
Ramey Tennis and Equestrian Schools
Joan Ramey, Director/Owner
2354 S 200W, Rockport, Indiana 47635
Phone: 812-649-2668
E-mail: jramey66@yahoo.com

The Ranch-Lake Placid Academy
Marleen Goodman, Admissions
4 Yankee Glen, Madison, Connecticut 06443
Phone: 518-891-5684 Fax: 518-891-6350
E-mail: marleengoodman@hotmail.com

Randolph-Macon Academy Summer Programs
Frank Gardner, Recruiter
200 Academy Drive, Front Royal, Virginia 22630
Phone: 800-272-1172 Fax: 540-636-5419
E-mail: admissions@rma.edu

Rassias Programs
Bill Miles, Director
P.O. Box 5456, Hanover, New Hampshire 03755
Phone: 603-643-3007 Fax: 603-643-4249
E-mail: rassias@sover.net

Rawhide Ranch
Paul Tate, Program Director
P.O. Box 216, Bonsall, California 92003
Phone: 760-758-0083 Fax: 760-758-0440
E-mail: paul@rawhideranch.com

Rectory School Summer Session
The Rectory School
Stephen DiPaolo, Director of Admissions
P.O. Box 68, 528 Pomfret Street, Pomfret, Connecticut 06258
Phone: 860-928-1328 Fax: 860-928-4961
E-mail: admissions@rectoryschool.org

Red Pine Camp for Girls
Sarah Rolley, Director
P.O. Box 69, Minocqua, Wisconsin 54548
Phone: 715-356-6231 Fax: 715-356-1077
E-mail: redpinec@newnorth.net

Rein Teen Tours
Norman Rein, President
30 Galesi Drive, Wayne, New Jersey 07470
Phone: 800-831-1313 Fax: 973-785-4268
E-mail: summer@reinteentours.com

Rhode Island School of Design Pre-College Program
Marc Torick, Continuing Education Office/Summer Programs
2 College Street, Providence, Rhode Island 02903-2787
Phone: 401-454-6200 Fax: 401-454-6218
E-mail: cemail@risd.edu

Rhodes Summer Writing Institute
Rhodes College
Rebecca Finlayson, Director, Rhodes College Summer Writing Institute
Department of English, 2000 North Parkway, Memphis, Tennessee 38112
Phone: 901-843-3293 Fax: 901-843-3728
E-mail: finlayson@rhodes.edu

Ringling School of Art and Design Pre-College Perspective
Nancee Clark, Director of Continuing Studies and Special Programs
2700 North Tamiami Trail, Sarasota, Florida 34234
Phone: 941-955-8866 Fax: 941-955-8801
E-mail: cpe@ringling.edu

Riverside Military Academy Summer Programs
Donna Davis, Admissions Director
2001 Riverside Drive, Gainesville, Georgia 30501
Phone: 800-GO-CADET Fax: 678-291-3364
E-mail: admissions@cadet.com

River Way Ranch Camp
Nancy Oken Nighbert, Director
6450 Elwood Road, Sanger, California 93657
Phone: 800-821-2801 Fax: 559-787-3851
E-mail: rwrcamp@aol.com

Road's End Farm Horsemanship Camp
Thomas Woodman, Owner/Director
Jackson Hill Road, Chesterfield, New Hampshire 03443-0197
Phone: 603-363-4900 Fax: 603-363-4949

Roaring Brook Camp for Boys
J. Raines, Director/Owner
480 Roaring Brook Road, Bradford, Vermont 05033
Phone: 802-222-5702

Robotics Camp
School of Engineering and Technology/Lake Superior State University
Jeanne Shibley, Special Assistant to the Provost
650 West Easterday Avenue, Sault Ste. Marie, Michigan 49783
Phone: 906-635-2597 Fax: 906-635-6663
E-mail: jmshibly@lssu.edu

Rockbrook Camp
Brenda Ivers, Office Manager
P.O. Box 792, Brevard, North Carolina 28712
Phone: 828-884-6151 Fax: 828-884-6459
E-mail: office@rockbrookcamp.com

Rocky Mountain Village
Easter Seals Colorado
Roman Krafczyk, Director
P.O. Box 115, Empire, Colorado 80438
Phone: 303-569-2333 Fax: 303-569-3857
E-mail: campinfo@eastersealscolorado.org

Rumsey Hall School Summer Session
201 Romford Road, Washington Depot, Connecticut 06794
Phone: 860-868-0535 Fax: 860-868-7907
E-mail: admiss@rumseyhall.org

Rust College Study Abroad in Africa
A. J. Stovall, Director, International Studies
150 Rust Avenue, Holly Springs, Mississippi 38635
Phone: 662-252-8000 Fax: 662-252-6107
E-mail: astovall@rustcollege.edu

Rustic Pathways
Chris Stakich, Business Development Director
4121 Erie Street, Willoughby, Ohio 44094
Phone: 440-975-9691 Fax: 440-975-9694
E-mail: chris@rusticpathways.com

Sail Caribbean
Michael Liese, Director
79 Church Street, Northport, New York 11768
Phone: 800-321-0994 Fax: 631-754-3362
E-mail: info@sailcaribbean.com

St. Andrew's Summer Programs
St. Andrew's Episcopal School
Amanda Macomber, Director of Summer Programs
8804 Postoak Road, Potomac, Maryland 20854
Phone: 301-983-5200 Fax: 301-983-4710
E-mail: summerprograms@saes.org

St. George's Summer Session
St. George's School
Anthony Jaccaci, Director of Summer Session
P.O. Box 1910, Newport, Rhode Island 02840-0190
Phone: 401-842-6712 Fax: 401-842-6763
E-mail: tony_jaccaci@stgeorges.edu

St. John's Northwestern Military Academy
Director of Camp Enrollment
1101 North Genesee Street, Delafield, Wisconsin 53018
Phone: 800-SJ-CADET Fax: 262-646-7128
E-mail: admissions@sjnma.org

St. Margaret's School International Summer ESL Programme
ESL Summer Programme Director
St. Margaret's School, 1080 Lucas Avenue, Victoria,
British Columbia V8X 3P7, Canada
Phone: 250-479-7171 Fax: 250-479-8976
E-mail: stmarg@stmarg.ca

Saint Thomas More School-Summer Academic Camp
Timothy Riordan, Director of Admissions
45 Cottage Road, Oakdale, Connecticut 06370
Phone: 860-823-3861 Fax: 860-823-3863
E-mail: stmadmit@stthomasmoreschool.com

Saint Vincent College Challenge Program
Joanne Krynicky, Challenge Director-Saint Vincent College
300 Fraser Purchase Road, Latrobe, Pennsylvania 15650
Phone: 724-532-5093

Salisbury Summer School of Reading and English
Director of Admissions
251 Canaan Road, Salisbury, Connecticut 06068
Phone: 860-435-5700 Fax: 860-435-5750
E-mail: sss@salisburyschool.org

Salmon Camp Research Team for Native Americans
Oregon Museum of Science and Industry
Travis Neumeyer, Programming Coordinator
1945 Southeast Water Avenue, Portland, Oregon 97214
Phone: 503-239-7824 Fax: 503-239-7838
E-mail: sciencecamps@omsi.edu

Sanborn Western Camps: Big Spring Ranch for Boys
Sanborn Western Camps
Mike McDonald, Director
P.O. Box 167, Florissant, Colorado 80816
Phone: 719-748-3341 Fax: 719-748-3259
E-mail: info@sanbornwesterncamps.com

Sandy Island Camp for Families
YMCA of Greater Boston-Camping Services Branch
Jill Gary, Associate Executive Director
316 Huntington Avenue, Boston, Massachusetts 02115-5019
Phone: 617-927-8220 Fax: 617-927-8156
E-mail: jgary@ymcaboston.org

San Juan Island Camps
Oregon Museum of Science and Industry
Travis Neumeyer, Programming Coordinator
1945 Southeast Water Avenue, Portland, Oregon 97214
Phone: 503-239-7824 Fax: 503-239-7838
E-mail: teumeyer@omsi.edu

Sargent Center Adventure Camp
Marijean Parry, Director, Adventure Camp
36 Sargent Camp Road, Hancock, New Hampshire 03449
Phone: 603-525-3311 Fax: 603-525-4151
E-mail: mj@busc.mv.com

Saturday High at Art Center College of Design
Art Center College of Design
Alegria Castro, Program Coordinator
1700 Lida Street, Pasadena, California 91103
Phone: 626-396-2319 Fax: 626-796-9564
E-mail: saturdayhigh@artcenter.edu

Sciencescape
Cottey College
Denise Carrick, Coordinator of P.E.O. Relations
1000 West Austin, Nevada, Missouri 64772
Phone: 417-667-8181 Fax: 417-667-8103
E-mail: dcarrick@cottey.edu

Scuba Adventures at Pali Overnight Adventures
Pali Overnight Adventures
Andy Wexler, Owner/Founder
P.O. Box 2237, Running Springs, California 92382
Phone: 909-867-5743 Fax: 909-867-7643
E-mail: info@paliadventures.com

Sea Camp
Texas A&M University at Galveston
Daisy Duerson, Administrative Assistant
P.O. Box 1675, Galveston, Texas 77553
Phone: 409-740-4525 Fax: 409-740-4894
E-mail: seacamp@tamug.tamu.edu

SEACAMP San Diego
Phil Zerofski, Director
1380 Garnet Avenue, PMB E6, San Diego, California 92109
Phone: 800-SEACAMP Fax: 619-268-0229
E-mail: seacamp@seacamp.com

SeaWorld/Busch Gardens Tampa Bay Adventure Camp
SeaWorld Adventure Park
Education Reservations
P.O. Box 9157, Tampa, Florida 33674
Phone: 877-248-2267 Fax: 813-987-5878
E-mail: education@buschgardens.org

SeaWorld Orlando Adventure Camp
Education Reservations
7007 Sea Harbor Drive, Orlando, Florida 32801
Phone: 866-479-2267 Fax: 407-363-2399
E-mail: education@seaworld.com

SeaWorld San Antonio Adventure Camp
SeaWorld Adventure Park
Ann Quinn, Director of Education
10500 SeaWorld Drive, San Antonio, Texas 78251-3002
Phone: 210-523-3608 Fax: 210-523-3898
E-mail: ann.quinn@seaworld.com

Secret Agent Camp at Pali Overnight Adventures
Pali Overnight Adventures
Andy Wexler, Owner/Founder
P.O. Box 2237, Running Springs, California 92382-2237
Phone: 909-867-5743 Fax: 909-867-7643
E-mail: info@paliadventures.com

Service-Learning in Paris
International Seminar Series
John Nissen, Director
P.O. Box 1212, Manchester, Vermont 05254-1212
Phone: 802-362-5855 Fax: 802-362-5855
E-mail: iss@study-serve.org

76ers Basketball Camp
Sonny Elia, Director
RD #1, Box 1454, Stroudsburg, Pennsylvania 18360
Phone: 610-668-7676 Fax: 610-668-7799
E-mail: sonny@sixerscamps.com

Shaffer's High Sierra Camp
Scott Shaffer, Co-Director
Tahoe National Forest, 38782 State Highway 49, Sattley, California 96124
Phone: 800-516-3513 Fax: 415-897-0316
E-mail: info@highsierracamp.com

Shane (Trim-Down) Camp
David Ettenberg, Certified Camp Director
302 Harris Road, Ferndale, New York 12734
Phone: 845-292-4644 Fax: 845-292-8636
E-mail: office@campshane.com

Shattuck-St. Mary's Summer Discovery and English Language Institute
Shattuck-St. Mary's School
Mike Frankenfield, Director of Summer Programs
Box 218, Faribault, Minnesota 55021
Phone: 507-333-1674 Fax: 507-333-1591
E-mail: mfrankenfield@s-sm.org

Shippensburg University Academic Camps
Randal Hammond, Director of Conferences
1871 Old Main Drive, Shippensburg, Pennsylvania 17257-2299
Phone: 717-477-1256 Fax: 717-477-4014

Sidwell Friends Bethesda Day Camp
Sidwell Friends School
Summer Programs Office
3825 Wisconsin Avenue, NW, Washington, District of Columbia 20016
Phone: 202-537-8133 Fax: 202-537-2483
E-mail: sidwellsummer@yahoo.com

The Sikkim Cultural Immersion Experience
International Cultural Adventures
David Pruskin, Program Director
35 Suprenant Circle, Brunswick, Maine 04011-7142
Phone: 888-339-0460 E-mail: info@ICAdventures.com

Simon's Rock College of Bard Young Writers Workshop
Jamie Hutchinson, Program Director
84 Alford Road, Great Barrington, Massachusetts 01230
Phone: 413-528-7231 Fax: 413-528-7365
E-mail: jamieh@simons-rock.edu

Skidmore College
James Chansky, Director of Summer Special Programs
815 North Broadway, Saratoga Springs, New York 12866
Phone: 518-580-5590 Fax: 518-580-5548
E-mail: jchansky@skidmore.edu

Skylake Yosemite Camp
Jeff Portnoy, Director
37976 Road 222, Wishon, California 93669
Phone: 559-642-3720 Fax: 559-642-3395
E-mail: jpskylake@aol.com

Smith College Summer Science and Engineering Program
Gail Scordilis, Director of Educational Outreach
Clark Hall, Northampton, Massachusetts 01063
Phone: 413-585-3060 Fax: 413-585-3068
E-mail: gscordil@smith.edu

Snow Farm: The New England Craft Program
Mary Colwell, Director
5 Clary Road, Williamsburg, Massachusetts 01096
Phone: 413-268-3101 Fax: 413-268-3163
E-mail: info@snowfarm-art.org

Snowy Owl Camp for Girls
Burt Jordan, Director
74 South Merrill Road, Harmony, Maine 04942
Phone: 866-632-4718
E-mail: info@snowyowlcamp.com

Southern Methodist University-College Experience
Marilyn Swanson, Assistant Director of Pre-College Programs
P.O. Box 750383, Dallas, Texas 75275
Phone: 214-768-0123 Fax: 214-768-3147
E-mail: gifted@smu.edu

South Shore YMCA Camps
Sacha Johnston, Camp Director
75 Stowe Road, Sandwich, Massachusetts 02563
Phone: 508-428-2571 Fax: 508-420-3545
E-mail: camp@ssymca.org

Space Camp Turkey 6-Day International Program
Space Camp Turkey
Beth Mitchell, Program Advisor
ESBAS-Aegean Free Zone, Gaziemir, Izmir, 35410, Turkey
Phone: 90-232-252-3500 Fax: 90-232-252-3600
E-mail: beth@spacecampturkey.com

Spanish Through Leadership
Nicaragua/Costa Rica High School Summer Exchange
Ilba Prego, Director
1650 Monroe Street, Madison, Wisconsin 53711
Phone: 608-255-1426
E-mail: nica@terracom.net

Spoleto Study Abroad
Jill Muti, Director
P.O. Box 99147, Raleigh, North Carolina 27624-9147
Phone: 919-384-0031
E-mail: spoleto@mindspring.com

Sports and Arts Center at Island Lake
Beverly Stoltz, Co-Director
Island Lake Road, Starrucca, Pennsylvania 18462
Phone: 570-798-2550 Fax: 570-798-2346
E-mail: info@islandlake.com

Stagedoor Manor Performing Arts Training Center/Theatre and Dance Camp
Barbara Martin, Director
116 Karmel Road, Loch Sheldrake, New York 12759-5308
Phone: 888-STAGE 88 Fax: 888-STAGE 88

Jim Nadel, Executive Director
P.O. Box 20454, Stanford, California 94309
Phone: 650-736-0324 Fax: 650-856-4155
E-mail: info@stanfordjazz.org

Stanford University Summer Session
Patricia Brandt, Associate Dean and Director
Building 590, Room 103, Stanford, California 94305-3005
Phone: 650-723-3109 Fax: 650-725-6080
E-mail: summersession@stanford.edu

Stanstead College-French as a Second Language
Louise Retchless, Summer School Director
450 Dufferin Street, Stanstead, Quebec J0B 3E0, Canada
Phone: 819-876-7891 Fax: 819-876-5891
E-mail: lretchless@stansteadcollege.com

Stevenson School Summer Camp
Stevenson School
Rosemary Tintle, Administrative Secretary
3152 Forest Lake Road, Pebble Beach, California 93953
Phone: 831-625-8315 Fax: 831-625-5208

Stoneleigh-Burnham School Summer Dance Camp
Ann Sorvino, Director
574 Bernardston Road, Greenfield, Massachusetts 01301
Phone: 413-774-2711 Fax: 413-772-7602
E-mail: asorvino@sbschool.org

Stony Brook Summer Music Festival
Stony Brook University, State University of New York
Linda Sinanian, Director
Stony Brook Summer Music Festival, Department of Music, Stony Brook,
New York 11794-5475
Phone: 631-220-0911 Fax: 631-632-7404
E-mail: lsinanian@notes1.cc.sunysb.edu

Streamside Camp and Conference Center
Streamside Foundation, Inc./BCM International
Dale Schoenwald, Director
RR #3, Box 3307, Stroudsburg, Pennsylvania 18360
Phone: 570-629-1902 Fax: 570-629-9650
E-mail: retreats@streamside.org

Streamside Family Camp
Streamside Foundation, Inc./BCM International
Dale Schoenwald, Director
RR #3, Box 3307, Stroudsburg, Pennsylvania 18360
Phone: 570-629-1902 Fax: 570-629-9650
E-mail: summercamp@streamside.org

Student Conservation Association (SCA)
Recruitment Office
P.O. Box 550, Charlestown, New Hampshire 03603
Phone: 603-543-1700 Fax: 603-543-1828
E-mail: getreal@thesca.org

Student Conservation Association (SCA)
Eve Cowen, Regional Program Manager
655 13th Street, Suite 100, Oakland, California 94612
Phone: 510-832-1966 Fax: 510-832-4726
E-mail: ecowen@thesca.org

Study Tours in the USA
FLS International
Veronica Perez, Director of Admissions
101 East Green Street #14, Pasadena, California 91105
Phone: 626-795-2912 Fax: 626-795-5564
E-mail: veronica@fls.net

Success Oriented Achievement Realized (SOAR)
Ed Parker, Admissions Director
P.O. Box 388, Balsam, North Carolina 28707
Phone: 828-456-3435 Fax: 828-456-3449
E-mail: ed@soarnc.org

The Summer Academy at Suffield
Suffield Academy
Bryson Tillinghast, Director, Summer Academy Admissions
185 North Main Street, Suffield, Connecticut 06078
Phone: 860-386-4475 Fax: 860-386-4476
E-mail: summer@suffieldacademy.org

Summer Dance '05
Summer Delegation to León, Nicaragua
New Haven/León Sister City Project
Program Director
608 Whitney Avenue, New Haven, Connecticut 06511
Phone: 203-562-1607 Fax: 203-624-1683
E-mail: nh@newhavenleon.org

Summer Focus at Berkeley
Summer Institute for the Gifted
Stephen Gessner, Director
River Plaza, 9 West Broad Street, Stamford, Connecticut 06902-3788
Phone: 866-303-4744 Fax: 203-399-5598
E-mail: sig.info@aifs.com

Summer in the City
The School for Film and Television
Steven Chinni, Director of Admission
39 West 19th Street, 12th Floor, New York, New York 10011
Phone: 888-645-0030 Fax: 212-624-0117
E-mail: schinni@sft.edu

Summer Leadership Education and Training
Massanutten Military Academy
Frank Thomas, Director of Admissions
614 South Main Street, Woodstock, Virginia 22664
Phone: 540-459-2167 Fax: 540-459-5421
E-mail: admissions@militaryschool.com

Summer Music at The Hollows
The Hollows Camp, Ltd.
Janet Fine, Director
RR #3, 3309 13th Line, Cookstown, Ontario L0L 1L0, Canada
Phone: 905-775-2694 Fax: 905-775-2694
E-mail: fine@hollowscamp.com

Summer Music Clinic
University of Wisconsin-Madison
Anne Aley, Program Manager
5554 Humanities, 455 North Park Street, Madison, Wisconsin 53706
Phone: 608-263-2242 Fax: 608-265-0452
E-mail: maaley@facstaff.wisc.edu

Summer Programs on the River
Christchurch School
Admissions at Christchurch School
49 Seahorse Lane, Christchurch, Virginia 23031
Phone: 800-296-2306 Fax: 804-758-0721
E-mail: admission@christchurchschool.org

Summer School at New York Military Academy
New York Military Academy
Maureen Kelly, Director of Admissions
78 Academy Avenue, Cornwall-on-Hudson, New York 12520
Phone: 845-534-3710 Fax: 845-534-7699
E-mail: admissions@nyma.ouboces.org

Summer Science Program at the South Carolina Governor's School for Science and Math
South Carolina Governor's School for Science and Math
Clyde Smith, SSP Director, GSSM
401 Railroad Avenue, Hartsville, South Carolina 29550
Phone: 843-383-3937 Fax: 843-383-3903
E-mail: smith@gssm.k12.sc.us

The Summer Science Program
Summer Science Program, Inc.
Richard Bowdon, Executive Director
108 Whiteberry Drive, Cary, North Carolina 27519
Phone: 866-728-0999 Fax: 419-735-2251
E-mail: info@summerscience.org

SummerSkills at Albany Academy for Girls
Albany Academy for Girls
Donna Keegan, Program Director
140 Academy Road, Albany, New York 12208
Phone: 518-463-2201 Fax: 518-463-5096
E-mail: keegand@albanyacademyforgirls.org

Summer Summit on Leadership
Pine Manor College
Whitney Retallic, Director of Youth and Student Programs
Center for Inclusive Leadership and Social Responsibility, 400 Heath Street, Chestnut Hill, Massachusetts 02467
Phone: 617-731-7620 Fax: 617-731-7185
E-mail: retalliw@pmc.edu

Summer Theatre Institute-2005
Youth Theatre of New Jersey's Teen Program in Residence at Columbia University, NYC
Allyn Sitjar, Artistic Director
23 Tomahawk Trail, Sparta, New Jersey 07871
Phone: 201-415-5329 Fax: 973-729-3654
E-mail: youththeatreallyn@yahoo.com

SummerWorks
Rowland Hall-St. Mark's School
Rich Weeks, Director
720 South Guardsman Way, Salt Lake City, Utah 84108
Phone: 801-355-7485 Fax: 801-355-0388
E-mail: richweeks@rowland-hall.org

Summit Travel Program
Summit Camp
Mayer Stiskin, Director
18 East 41st Street, # 402, NY, New York 10017
Phone: 800-323-9908 Fax: 212-689-4347
E-mail: summitcamp@aol.com

SuperCamp
Enrollments Department
1725 South Coast Highway, Oceanside, California 92054
Phone: 800-285-3276 Fax: 760-722-3507
E-mail: info@supercamp.com

Surf Quest
Camp Timberline-Kama'aina Kids, Inc.
Tiffany Sirmans, Program Director
P.O. Box 700308, Kapolei, Hawaii 96709
Phone: 877-672-4386
E-mail: campprograms@kamaainakids.com

Surprise Lake Camp
Sylvie Erlich, Executive Assistant/Registrar
Lake Surprise Road, Cold Spring, New York 10516
Phone: 845-265-3616 Fax: 845-265-3646
E-mail: info@surpriselake.org

Swift Nature Camp
Jeff Lorenz, Director
W7471 Ernie Swift Road, Minong, Wisconsin 54859
Phone: 715-466-5666 Fax: 715-466-5666
E-mail: swiftcamp@aol.com

Swiss Challenge
Eric Rohr, Director, Recruiting and Marketing
Wheeler Professional Park, Suite 10B, 1 Oak Ridge Road, West Lebanon,
New Hampshire 03784
Phone: 800-762-0023 Fax: 603-643-1927
E-mail: swisschallenge@hotmail.com

Syracuse University Summer College
Jack Carr, Interm Director
111 Waverly Avenue, Suite 240, Syracuse, New York 13244-1270
Phone: 315-443-5297 Fax: 315-443-3976
E-mail: sumcoll@syr.edu

Taft Summer School
The Taft School
Stephen McCabe, Director
110 Woodbury Road, Watertown, Connecticut 06795
Phone: 860-945-7961 Fax: 860-945-7859
E-mail: summerschool@taftschool.org

Talisman Summer Programs
Linda Tatsapaugh, Director
126 Camp Elliott Road, Black Mountain, North Carolina 28711
Phone: 828-692-3568 Fax: 828-669-2521
E-mail: summer@stonemountainschool.com

Tanager Lodge
Tad Welch, Director
85 Youngs Road, Merrill, New York 12955
Phone: 518-425-3386 TASC for Teens
Paul Oesterreicher, Director
5439 Countryside Circle, Jeffersonton, Virginia 22724
Phone: 800-296-8272 Fax: 540-937-8272
E-mail: tasc@peoplepc.com

TASIS The American School in England
W. Fleming, US Director
1640 Wisconsin Avenue NW, Washington, District of Columbia 20007
Phone: 202-965-5800 Fax: 202-965-5816
E-mail: usadmissions@tasis.com

Technology Encounters-Video Encounter/Computer Encounter
Ducks in a Row Foundation, Inc./Technology Encounters
Jane Sandlar, Director
8 Wemrock Drive, Ocean, New Jersey 07712
Phone: 732-695-0827 Fax: 732-493-4282
E-mail: jane@technologyencounters.com

Teen Tours of America
Ira Solomon, Director
318 Indian Trace #336, Weston, Florida 33326
Phone: 888-868-7882 Fax: 954-888-9781
E-mail: tourtta@teentoursofamerica.com

Teen Tour USA and Canada
New England Vacation Tours Inc.
William Buswell, President and CEO
P.O. Box 560, West Dover, Vermont 05356-0560
Phone: 802-464-2076 Fax: 802-464-2629
E-mail: nevt@sover.net

TENNIS: EUROPE
Martin Vinokur, Co-Director
73 Rockridge Lane, Stamford, Connecticut 06905
Phone: 800-253-7486 Fax: 203-322-0089
E-mail: tenniseuro@aol.com

Teton Valley Ranch Camp Education Foundation
Jim Walter, Director
P.O. Box 3968, Jackson, Wyoming 83001
Phone: 307-733-2958 Fax: 307-733-0258
E-mail: mailbag@tvrcamp.org

Thunderbird Ranch
Bruce Johnson, Director
9455 Highway 128, Healdsburg, California 95448
Phone: 707-433-3729 Fax: 707-433-2960
E-mail: alexvalley@aol.com

Tice Brothers Football Camp
Sports International, Inc.
Customer Service
8924 McGaw Court, Columbia, Maryland 21045
Phone: 800-555-0801 Fax: 410-309-9962
E-mail: info@footballcamps.com

Camp Timber-lee
Tom Parsons, Director, Human Resources
N8705 Scout Road, East Troy, Wisconsin 53120
Phone: 262-642-7348 Fax: 262-642-7517
E-mail: timber-lee@timber-lee.com

Tisch School of the Arts
New York University
Josh Murray, Assistant Director of Recruitment
Special Programs, 721 Broadway, 12th Floor, New York, New York 10003
Phone: 212-998-1500 Fax: 212-995-4610
E-mail: tisch.special.info@nyu.edu

Towering Pines Camp
John Jordan, Director
5586 County D, Eagle River, Wisconsin 54521
Phone: 715-479-4540 Fax: 715-466-7710

Trailmark Outdoor Adventures
Rusty Pedersen, Director
16 Schuyler Road, Nyack, New York 10960
Phone: 845-358-0262 Fax: 845-348-0437
E-mail: info@trailmark.com

Trailridge Mountain Camp
David Broshar, Director
198 Holland Drive, Black Mountain, North Carolina 28711
Phone: 828-669-5636
E-mail: broshar@aol.com

Tufts Summit
Tufts University
Christine Woodman, Office Coordinator
108 Packard Avenue, Tufts European Center, Medford, Massachusetts 02155
Phone: 617-627-3290 Fax: 617-627-3457
E-mail: france@tufts.edu

Tuskegee University Vet Step II
Tuskegee University College of Veterinary Medicine
Phillip Mitchell, Vet-Step Coordinator
Office of Veterinary Admissions, Tuskegee University,
Tuskegee, Alabama 36088
Phone: 334-727-8309 Fax: 334-727-8177
E-mail: pmitchell@tuskegee.edu

UCAELI Summer Camp
University of Connecticut American English Language Institute
Kristi Newgarden, Director
Storrs, Connecticut 06269
Phone: 860-486-2127 Fax: 860-486-3834
E-mail: kristi.newgarden@uconn.edu

United Soccer Academy, Inc.
Camps Information
50 Tannery Road, Unit 8, Branchburg, New Jersey 08876
Phone: 908-823-0130 Fax: 908-823-0466
E-mail: info@unitedsocceracademy.com

University of Chicago-Insight
Valerie Huston, Secretary, Summer Session Office
The Graham School of General Studies, Summer Sessions Office, 1427 East
60th Street, Chicago, Illinois 60637
Phone: 773-702-6033 Fax: 773-702-6814
E-mail: uc-summer@uchicago.edu

University of Connecticut College of Continuing Studies-Community School of the Arts
Community School of the Arts
3 Witryol Place, Unit 5195, Storrs, Connecticut 06269-5195
Phone: 860-486-1073 Fax: 860-486-4981
E-mail: csa@uconn.edu

University of Delaware Summer College
F. Charles Shermeyer, Coordinator
207 Elliott Hall, Newark, Delaware 19716-1256
Phone: 302-831-6560 Fax: 302-831-4339
E-mail: summercollege@udel.edu

University of Kansas-Midwestern Music Camp-Junior and Senior Divisions
James Hudson, Director
452 Murphy Hall, 1530 Naismith Drive, #452, Lawrence, Kansas 66045-3120
Phone: 785-864-4730 Fax: 785-864-5023
E-mail: musicamp@ku.edu

University of Maryland Young Scholars Program
University of Maryland, Office of Continuing and Extended Education
Terrie Hruzd, Program Manager, Summer and Special Programs
2103 Reckord Armory, College Park, Maryland 20742
Phone: 301-405-8588 Fax: 301-314-9572
E-mail: hruzd@umd.edu

University of Miami Summer Scholar Programs
Brian Blythe, Director of High School Programs
111 Allen Hall, P.O. Box 248005, Coral Gables, Florida 33124-1610
Phone: 305-284-6107 Fax: 305-284-2620
E-mail: ssp.cstudies@miami.edu

University of St. Andrews Summer Programs
M. Ian Hunter, Director
66 North Street, St. Andrews, Fife, KY16 9AH, United Kingdom
Phone: 44-1334-462238 Fax: 44-1334-462208
E-mail: mish@st-and.ac.uk

University of San Diego Sports Camps
Lila Chan, USD Sports Camps
5998 Alcala Park, San Diego, California 92110-2492
Phone: 800-991-1873 Fax: 619-260-4185
E-mail: sportscamps@sandiego.edu

University of Vermont Summer Institute for High School Students Discovering Engineering, Computers, and Mathematics
University of Vermont, College of Engineering and Mathematics
Dawn Densmore, Director
College of Engineering and Mathematics, 109 Votey Building, Burlington, Vermont 05405
Phone: 802-656-8748 Fax: 802-656-8802

University of Wisconsin-Green Bay, SummerPrograms
Mona Christensen, Director of Youth Opportunities
2420 Nicolet Drive, Green Bay, Wisconsin 54311
Phone: 920-465-CAMP (2267) Fax: 920-465-2552
E-mail: summercamps@uwgb.edu

University of Wisconsin-Superior Youthsummer 2005
Gregory Burke, Director
Rothwell Student Center, Room 50, P.O. Box 2000, Superior, Wisconsin 54880
Phone: 715-394-8173 Fax: 715-394-8445
E-mail: gburke@uwsuper.edu

Valley Forge Military Academy and College
Jeffrey Bond, Director of Summer Camps
1001 Eagle Road, Wayne, Pennsylvania 19087-3695
Phone: 610-989-1253 Fax: 610-688-1260
E-mail: summercamp@vfmac.edu

Vans Skateboard Camp
High Cascade Snowboard Camp
Meagan Stein, Camp Administrator
P.O. Box 368, Government Camp, Oregon 97028
Phone: 800-334-4272 Fax: 503-272-3637
E-mail: highcascade@highcascade.com

Ventures Travel Service-Arizona
Friendship Ventures
Georgann Rumsey, President/CEO
10509 108th Street, NW, Annandale, Minnesota 55302
Phone: 952-852-0101 Fax: 952-852-0123
E-mail: fv@friendshipventures.org

Vermont Arts Institute at Lyndon Institute
Mary Thomas, Director of Admissions
Lyndon Institute, P.O. Box 127, College Road, Lyndon Center, Vermont 05850

Phone: 802-626-5232 Fax: 802-626-6138
E-mail: mthomas@lyndon.k12.vt.us

Village Camps
Roger Ratner, Director
14 Rue de la Morâche, Nyon, CH-1260, Switzerland
Phone: 41-22-990-9400 Fax: 41-22-990-9494
E-mail: camps@villagecamps.ch

Visions
Joanne Pinaire, Director
P.O. Box 220, Newport, Pennsylvania 17074
Phone: 717-567-7313 Fax: 717-567-7853
E-mail: info@visionsserviceadventures.com

Volunteers for Peace International Work Camps
Peter Coldwell, Director
1034 Tiffany Road, Belmont, Vermont 05730
Phone: 802-259-2759 Fax: 802-259-2922
E-mail: vfp@vfp.org

Washington and Lee University Summer Scholars
Mimi Milner Elrod, Director
Hill House, Lexington, Virginia 24450
Phone: 540-458-8727 Fax: 540-458-8113
E-mail: summerscholars@wlu.edu

Washington International School Passport to Summer
Washington International School
Michelle Broadie, Auxiliary Programs Director
1690 36th Street, N.W., Washington, District of Columbia 20007
Phone: 202-243-1727 Fax: 202-243-1797
E-mail: broadie@wis.edu

Washington Internship Experience
Washington Workshops Foundation
Sharon Sievers, Director
3222 N Street NW, Suite 340, Washington, District of Columbia 20007
Phone: 800-368-5688 Fax: 202-965-1018
E-mail: info@workshops.org

Washington University High School Summer Scholars Program
Washington University in St. Louis
Marsha Hussung, Director, High School Summer Scholars Program
Campus Box 1145, 1 Brookings Drive, St. Louis, Missouri 63130
Phone: 314-935-6834 Fax: 314-935-4847
E-mail: mhussung@wustl.edu

WEI Leadership Training
Wilderness Education Institute
Kevin Snyder, Executive Director
2260 Baseline Road, Suite 205, Boulder, Colorado 80302
Phone: 877-628-9692
E-mail: information@weiprograms.org

Weissman Teen Tours
Ronee Weissman, Owner/Director
517 Almena Avenue, Ardsley, New York 10502
Phone: 800-942-8005 Fax: 914-693-4807
E-mail: wtt@cloud9.net

Wentworth Military Academy Pathfinder Adventure Camp
Wentworth Military Academy and Junior College
Todd Kitchen, Director of Admissions
1880 Washington Avenue, Lexington, Missouri 64067
Phone: 800-962-7682 Fax: 660-259-2677
E-mail: admissions@wma1880.org

Wesleyan Summer Gifted Program
West Virginia Wesleyan College
Joseph Wiest, Founder
Box 89, Buckhannon, West Virginia 26201
Phone: 304-473-8072
E-mail: sgp@wvwc.edu

Westcoast Connection
Mark Segal, Director
154 East Boston Post Road, Mamaroneck, New York 10543
Phone: 800-767-0227 Fax: 914-835-0798
E-mail: usa@westcoastconnection.com

Westminster Choir College of Rider University
Scott Hoerl, Director of Continuing Education
101 Walnut Lane, Princeton, New Jersey 08540-3899
Phone: 609-924-7416 Fax: 609-921-6187
E-mail: woce@rider.edu

West River United Methodist Center
Andrew Thornton, Manager
P.O. Box 429, Churchton, Maryland 20733
Phone: 410-867-0991 Fax: 410-867-3741
E-mail: westriver.center@verizon.net

Where There Be Dragons
Chris Yager, Director
P.O. Box 4651, Boulder, Colorado 80306
Phone: 800-982-9203 Fax: 303-413-0857
E-mail: info@wheretherebedragons.com

Wildcat Basketball Camp
Louisiana College
Gene Rushing, Head Coach, Men's Basketball
P.O. Box 541, Pineville, Louisiana 71359
Phone: 318-487-7503

Wilderness Adventure
Wilderness Education Institute
Kevin Snyder, Executive Director
2260 Baseline Road, Suite 205, Boulder, Colorado 80302
Phone: 877-628-9692 Fax: 877-628-9692
E-mail: information@weiprograms.org

Wilderness Adventure at Eagle Landing
Dave Cohan, Director of Administration
P.O. Box 760, New Castle, Virginia 24127
Phone: 800-782-0779 Fax: 540-864-6800
E-mail: info@wilderness-adventure.com

Wilderness Experiences Unlimited-Leaders In Training Camp
Taylor Cook, Executive Director
499 Loomis Street, Westfield, Massachusetts 01085
Phone: 413-562-7431 Fax: 413-569-6445
E-mail: adventures@weu.com

Wilderness Ventures
Mike Cottingham, Director
P.O. Box 2768, Jackson Hole, Wyoming 83001
Phone: 800-533-2281 Fax: 307-739-1934
E-mail: info@wildernessventures.com

Wildlife Camp
Wilderness Education Institute
Kevin Snyder, Executive Director
2260 Baseline Road, Suite 205, Boulder, Colorado 80302
Phone: 877-628-9692 Fax: 877-628-9692
E-mail: information@weiprograms.org

Williwaw Adventures
Mike Dawson, Director
P.O. Box 166, Kingston, Massachusetts 02364
Phone: 781-585-3459 Fax: 801-720-4378
E-mail: info@williwawadventures.com

Willow Hill Farm Camp
Gerald Edwards, Owner/Director
75 Cassidy Road, Keeseville, New York 12944
Phone: 518-834-9746 Fax: 518-834-9476
E-mail: edwardsj@westelcom.com

Windridge Tennis Camps
Charles Witherell, Director
P.O. Box 27, Craftsbury Common, Vermont 05827
Phone: 802-586-9646 Fax: 802-586-8033
E-mail: wcampsmichelle@pshift.com

Windsor Mountain:
Interlocken at Windsor Mountain
Richard Herman, Director
19 Interlocken Way, Windsor, New Hampshire 03244
Phone: 800-862-7760 Fax: 603-478-5260
E-mail: mail@windsormountain.org

Wohelo-Luther Gulick Camps
Quincy Van Winkle, Director
P.O. Box 39, South Casco, Maine 04077
Phone: 207-655-4739 Fax: 207-655-2292
E-mail: quincy@wohelo.com

Wolfeboro: The Summer Boarding School
Edward Cooper, Assistant Head of School
93 Camp School Road, Wolfeboro, New Hampshire 03894
Phone: 603-569-3451 Fax: 603-569-4080
E-mail: wolfe@wolfeboro.org

Women in Engineering Summer Camp
University of Dayton
Annette Packard, Program Coordinator
300 College Park, Kettering Labs, Dayton, Ohio 45469-0228
Phone: 937-229-3296 Fax: 937-229-2756
E-mail: wie@udayton.edu

Women in Science & Engineering Camp
The Pennsylvania State University-WISE
Katie Rung, Assistant Director
111G Kern Building, University Park, Pennsylvania 16802
Phone: 814-865-3342 Fax: 814-863-0085
E-mail: cxg1@psu.edu

Women in Technology
School of Engineering and Technology/Lake Superior State University
Jeanne Shibley, Special Assistant to the Provost
650 West Easterday Avenue, Sault Ste. Marie, Michigan 49783
Phone: 906-635-2597 Fax: 906-635-6663
E-mail: jmshibly@lssu.edu

Woodberry Forest Junior Adventure
Woodberry Forest School
W. McRae, Director
Woodberry Forest Summer Experience, Woodberry Forest, Virginia 22989
Phone: 540-672-6047 Fax: 540-672-9076
E-mail: wfs_summer@woodberry.org

Woodland
Towering Pines Camp
Anne Jordan, Director
5513 Highway D, Eagle River, Wisconsin 54521
Phone: 715-479-4540 Fax: 715-466-7710

World Affairs Seminar
Wisconsin World Affairs Council, Inc.
Frederick Luedke, General Manager
800 West Main Street, University of Wisconsin-Whitewater, Whitewater, Wisconsin 53190
Phone: 888-404-4049 Fax: 262-472-5210
E-mail: was@uww.edu

World Horizons International
Stuart Rabinowitz, Executive Director
P.O. Box 662, Bethlehem, Connecticut 06751
Phone: 800-262-5874 Fax: 203-266-6227
E-mail: worldhorizons@att.net

Wright State University Residential Camps and Institutes
Chris Hoffman, Assistant Director, Pre-College Programs
120 Millet Hall, Wright State University, Dayton, Ohio 45435-0001
Phone: 937-775-3135 Fax: 937-775-4883
E-mail: precollege@wright.edu

XUK
Cross Keys
Richard Bernstein, Managing Director
Riddlesworth Hall, Norfolk, United Kingdom
Phone: 020-8371-9686 Fax: 020-8343-0625
E-mail: richard@xkeys.co.uk

Greater Burlington YMCA
Jon Kuypers, Camp Director
1252 Abnaki Road, North Hero, Vermont 05474
Phone: 802-372-8275
E-mail: jkuypers@gbymca.org

YMCA Camp Bernie
Ridgewood YMCA
David Shelanskey, Summer Camp Director
327 Turkey Top Road, Port Murray, New Jersey 07865
Phone: 908-832-5315 Fax: 908-832-9078
E-mail: dshelanskey@campbernieymca.org

YMCA Camp Fitch
William Lyder, Executive Camp Director
17 N. Champion Street, Youngstown, Ohio 44501-1287
Phone: 330-744-8411 Fax: 330-744-8416
E-mail: campfitch@hotmail.com

YMCA Camp Icaghowan
YMCA of Metropolitan Minneapolis
Peter Wieczorek, Camp Director
4 West Rustic Lodge, Minneapolis, Minnesota 55409
Phone: 612-821-2904 Fax: 612-823-2482
E-mail: info@campicaghowan.org

YMCA Camp Ihduhapi
YMCA of Metropolitan Minneapolis
Brian Burns, Summer Camp Director
Box 37, Loretto, Minnesota 55357
Phone: 763-479-1146 Fax: 763-479-1333
E-mail: info@campihduhapi.org

YMCA Camp Matollionequay
YMCA Camp Ockanickon, Inc.
Tom Rapine, Associate Executive Director
1303 Stokes Road, Medford, New Jersey 08055
Phone: 609-654-8225 Fax: 609-654-8895
E-mail: info@ycamp.org

YMCA of Greater Long Beach
Marc Wilson, YMCA Camping Services
P.O. Box 90995, Long Beach, California 90809-0995
Phone: 562-496-2756 Fax: 562-425-5451
E-mail: camp@lbymca.org

YMCA Camp Oakes Teen Leadership
YMCA of Greater Long Beach
Marc Wilson, YMCA Camping Services
P.O. Box 90995, Long Beach, California 90809-0995
Phone: 562-496-2756 Fax: 562-425-5451
E-mail: camp@lbymca.org

YMCA Camp Ockanickon
Tom Rapine, Associate Executive Director
1303 Stokes Road, Medford, New Jersey 08055
Phone: 609-654-8225 Fax: 609-654-8895
E-mail: info@ycamp.org

YMCA Camp Pendalouan
Darryl Powell, Summer Camp Director
1243 East Fruitvale Road, Montague, Michigan 49437
Phone: 231-894-4538 Fax: 231-894-4448
E-mail: summer@pendalouan.org

YMCA Camp Seymour Summer Camp
Magill Lange, Camping Director
9725 Cramer Road KPN, Gig Harbor, Washington 98329
Phone: 253-884-3392 Fax: 253-460-8897
E-mail: campseymour@ymcatocoma.org

YMCA Camp Shand
Lancaster Family YMCA
Brenda Barrett, Camp Director
572 North Queen Street, Lancaster, Pennsylvania 17603
Phone: 717-397-7474 Fax: 717-397-7815
E-mail: ymcacampshand@dejazzd.com

YMCA Camp Tippecanoe-Adventure Camp
YMCA of Central Stark County
Patrick Dunlop, Program Director
81300 YMCA Road, Tippecanoe, Ohio 44699
Phone: 800-922-0679 Fax: 740-922-1152
E-mail: ycamptippe@aol.com

YMCA Camp U-Nah-Li-Ya
Greater Green Bay YMCA
Kathleen McKee, Program Director
13654 South Shore Drive, Suring, Wisconsin 54174
Phone: 715-276-7116 Fax: 715-276-1701
E-mail: mckeeka@greenbayymca.org

YMCA Camp Warren for Boys
YMCA of Metropolitan Minneapolis
Cheri Keepers, Camp Director
4 West Rustic Lodge, Minneapolis, Minnesota 55409
Phone: 612-821-2903 Fax: 612-823-2482
E-mail: info@campwarren.org

YMCA Camp Widjiwagan
Alissa Johnson, Program Director
2125 East Hennepin Avenue, Minneapolis, Minnesota 55413
Phone: 612-465-0489 Fax: 651-646-5521
E-mail: info@widji.org

YMCA Lake Stockwell
YMCA Camp Ockanickon, Inc.
Tom Rapine, Associate Executive Director
1303 Stokes Road, Medford, New Jersey 08055
Phone: 609-654-8225 Fax: 609-654-8895
E-mail: info@ycamp.org

YMCA Wanakita Summer Family Camp
YMCA of Hamilton/Burlington
Steve Heming, General Manager
YMCA Wanakita, RR #2, Koshlong Lake, Haliburton, Ontario K0M 1S0, Canada
Phone: 705-457-2132 Fax: 705-457-1597
E-mail: info@ymca-wanakita.on.ca

YMCA Wanakita Summer Resident and Day Camp
YMCA of Hamilton/Burlington
Steve Heming, General Manager
YMCA Wanakita, RR #2, Koshlong Lake Road, Haliburton, Ontario K0M 1S0, Canada
Phone: 705-457-2132 Fax: 705-457-1597
E-mail: info@ymca-wanakita.on.ca

YMCA Wilderness Camp Menogyn
YMCA of Metropolitan Minneapolis
Paul Danicic, Camp Director
4 West Rustic Lodge, Minneapolis, Minnesota 55409
Phone: 612-821-2905 Fax: 612-823-2482
E-mail: info@campmenogyn.org

Yosemite Backpacking Adventures
Yosemite Institute
Peggy Lovegreen, Administrative Assistant
P.O. Box 487, Yosemite, California 95389
Phone: 209-379-9511 Fax: 209-379-9510
E-mail: yi@yni.org

Young Musicians & Artists
Brian Biggs, Executive Director
P.O. Box 13277, Portland, Oregon 97213
Phone: 503-281-9528
E-mail: brian@ymainc.org

Youth Program in Spain
Don Quijote
Manne Arranz, Area Manager
Plaza San Marcos 7, Salamanca, 37002, Spain
Phone: 34-923-26-88-60 Fax: 34-923-26-88-15
E-mail: manuel.arranz@donquijote.org

Index

ABBREVIATIONS

ABREVIATURAS • ABRÉVIATIONS • 略語一覧 • 縮略語一覧表

ACA American Camping Association
Asociación Americana de Camping
Association américaine du camping
米国キャンプ協会
美國夏令營協會

EFL English as a foreign language
Inglés como idioma extranjero
L'anglais comme langue étrangère
外国人向英語
英語作為外國語

ESL English as a second language
Inglés como segundo idioma
L'anglais comme langue seconde
外国人向英語
英語作為第二外國語

FAA Federal Aviation Administration
Administración Federal de Aviación
Administration fédérale de l'aviation
米連邦航空局
美國聯邦航空局

TOEFL Test of English as a Foreign Language
Prueba de inglés como lengua extranjera
Épreuve de l'anglais comme langue étrangère
外語人のための英語試験
托福考試

WAIC Western Association of Independent Camps
Asociación Occidental de Campamentos
    Independientes
Association occidentale de camps independents
西部独立キャンプ場協会
西部獨立夏令營協會

GEOGRAPHICAL ABBREVIATIONS

ABREVIATURAS GEOGRÁFICAS • ABRÉVIATIONS GÉOGRAPHIQUES • 地名略語 • 地名縮寫

AL	Alabama	**ME**	Maine	**PA**	Pennsylvania
AK	Alaska	**MD**	Maryland	**RI**	Rhode Island
AZ	Arizona	**MA**	Massachusetts	**SC**	South Carolina
AR	Arkansas	**MI**	Michigan	**SD**	South Dakota
CA	California	**MN**	Minnesota	**TN**	Tennessee
CO	Colorado	**MS**	Mississippi	**TX**	Texas
CT	Connecticut	**MO**	Montana	**UT**	Utah
DE	Delaware	**NE**	Nebraska	**VT**	Vermont
D.C.	District of Columbia	**NV**	Nevada	**VA**	Virginia
FL	Florida	**NH**	New Hampshire	**WA**	Washington
HI	Hawaii	**NJ**	New Jersey	**WV**	West Virginia
ID	Idaho	**NM**	New Mexico	**WI**	Wisconsin
IL	Illinois	**NY**	New York	**WY**	Wyoming
IN	Indiana	**NC**	North Carolina		
IA	Iowa	**ND**	North Dakota	**ON**	Ontario
KS	Kansas	**OH**	Ohio	**PQ**	Quebec
KY	Kentucky	**OK**	Oklahoma		
LA	Louisiana	**OR**	Oregon		

Please **photocopy** this page and fax it to the schools in this Directory that best meet your needs. Check the schools' listings for their fax numbers.

Para obtener más información sobre las escuelas que le interesan, sírvase **fotocopiar** esta página y enviarla por fax al colegio respectivo. Ud. encontrara el numero de fax de las escuelas en la página correspondiente.

Veuillez **photocopier** cette page et la renvoyer par télécopie aux établissements de cet annuaire correspondant le mieux à vos besoins. Vous trouverez le numéro de fax des établissements à la page les concernant.

このページをコピーし、本書の中であなたの希望に最も適した学校にファックスして下さい。ファックス番号は学校索引ページを参照して下さい。

請影印此頁並將它傳真到最符合您需要的學校。請由學校目錄中查詢該校的傳真號碼。

Thomson Peterson's
American and Canadian Boarding Schools, 2005 Edition
Internados en los Estados Unidos y Canadá, Edíción 2005
Internats américains et canadiens, édition 2005
米国とカナダの全寮制学校 − 2005 年度版
美國與加拿大寄宿學校 − 2005 年版

School Information Request Form

Formulario de solicitud de información sobre colegios / Formulaire de demande d'information des écoles / 学校案内請求用紙／學校資料索取表格

Student Name / Nombre del alumno / Nom de l'élève / 学生氏名／學生姓名

Home Address / Dirección del domicilio / Adresse / 住所／番地／住家地址

City / Ciudad / Ville / 市町村／城市　　　**Postal Code** / Código postal / Code postal / 郵便番号／郵遞區號

Country / País / Pays / 国名／國家 _____

Gender / Sexo / Sexe / 性別／性別　**M** / 男／男 ❏　**F** / 女／女 ❏　**Age** / Edad / Age / 年齢／年齢 _____

Current Grade / Grado que cursa actualmente / Actuellement en classe de / 現在の学年／現就讀年級 _____

Applying for Grade / Grado al que desea ingresar / Candidat(e) pour la classe de / 入学希望学年／申請就讀年級 _____

Parent Name / Nombre del padre o la madre / Nom des parents / 保護者氏名／家長姓名

Telephone / Teléfono / Numéro de téléphone / 電話番号／電話　　　**Telefax** / Facsimile / Télécopie / ファックス番号／傳真

This is an information request form only. Completing it does not imply acceptance at any school. Schools will contact you with additional information about their institutions, which will usually be in English. Included in this information packet will be an application form and an outline of the steps required for admission.

Schools may require an application fee of up to $200. This fee covers the expenses of the preadmission process and does not guarantee admission.

Este formulario es para fines de solicitud solamente. El llenarlo no implica la acepta-ción en ningún colegio. Los colegios se comunicarán con usted, generalmente en inglés, para suministrarle información adicional sobre sus instituciones. En este paquete informativo encontrará un formulario de solicitud y un esquema de los pasos necesarios para la admisión.

Los colegios podrían requerir una cuota de hasta $200 por cada solicitud de admisión. Esta cuota cubre los gastos del proceso de preadmisión y no garantiza que el alumno sea aceptado.

Ce fomulaire ne constitue qu'une demande de ren-seignements. Le fait de la remplir ne veut en aucun cas dire que l'élève sera admis par l'établissement. Sur demande, les établissements adresseront des informations complémentaires, générale-ment rédigées en anglais. Le dossier de renseignements comprendra un formulaire de demande d'inscription et expliquera le processus d'admission.

Certains établissements exi-gent le paiement de frais de dossier pouvant aller jusqu'à 200 dollars. Cette somme couvre les frais d'examen du dossier et son versement ne garantit pas l'inscription.

この用紙は学校案内資料の請求用紙であり、この用紙への記入が学校への入学を意味するものではありません。学校に関するより詳しい資料が送られてきますが、それらは通常英語で書かれています。その中には願書、入学までに必要な手続きの概要なども含まれています。

学校によっては、最高200ドルの出願料を必要とするところがありますが、この費用は入学審査過程に充当するものであり、入学を保証するものではありません。

本表格僅供資料索取之用，填寫本表格並不保證進入某校就讀。學校方面將與您聯繫，並提供您該校的相關資料，校方的聯繫工作通常以英語進行。學校提供的資料中包括一份申請表格以及申請入學的概要步驟。

學校可能要求付上最多200美元的申請費，這項費用將用來辦理申請前的手續，並不保證入學。

Please **photocopy** this page and fax it to the programs in this Directory that best meet your needs. Check listings for fax numbers.

Por favor, haga **fotocopisa** de esta página y envíelas por fax a los programmas de este Directorio que mejor correspondan a sus necesidades. Verifique los números de fax en el listado.

Veuillez **photocopier** cette page et la transmettre par télécopieur aux reponsables des programmes de ce répertoire répondant le mieux à vos attentes. Consultez la section des coordonnées pour obtenir les numéros de télécopieur.

このページをコピーして、希望のプログラムへファックスしてください。ファックスの番号のリストをよくお確かめください。

請影印此頁並將它傳真到資料中最符合您需要的夏令營。請由學校目錄中查詢該校的傳真號碼。

 THOMSON PETERSON'S WORLDWIDE ENRICHMENT PROGRAMS, 2005 EDITION

THOMSON PETERSON'S – PROGRAMAS MUNDIALES DE ENRIQUECIMIENTO, EDÍCIÓN 2005
THOMSON PETERSON'S – PROGRAMMES DE PERFECTIONNEMENT INTERNATIONAUX, ÉDITION 2005
トムソンピーターソンの世界各地での強化プログラム－2005 年度版
THOMSON PETERSON'S 兒童和青少年夏令營國際指南－2005 年版

ENRICHMENT PROGRAM INFORMATION REQUEST FORM

FORMULARIO PARA SOLICITAR INFORMACIÓN DE LOS PROGRAMAS • FORMULAIRE DE DEMANDE D'INFORMATION CONCERNANT LES PROGRAMMES
資料請求用紙 • 資料索取表格

Participant Name / Nombre del participante / Nom du participant / 参加者名 / 參加者姓名

Home Address / Dirección / Adresse / 住所／番地 / 住家地址

City / Ciudad / Ville / 市町村 / 城市   **State, Province** / Estado, Provincia / État ou province / 都道府県 / 州，省

Country / País / Pays / 国名 / 國家   **Postal Code** / Código Postal / Code postal / 郵便番号 / 郵遞區號

Gender / Sexo / Sexe / 性別 / 性別   **Age** / Edad / Age / 年齢 / 年齡

Current Grade / Grado que cursa actualmente / Année scolaire courante / 現在の学年 / 現就讀年級

Parent Name / Nombre de uno de los padres / Nom du parent / 保護者名 / 家長姓名

Telephone / Teléfono / Numéro de téléphone / 電話番号 / 電話

THOMSON PETERSON'S AMERICAN AND CANADIAN BOARDING SCHOOLS AND WORLDWIDE ENRICHMENT PROGRAMS

THOMSON PETERSON'S – INTERNADOS EN LOS ESTADOS UNIDOS Y CANADÁ Y PROGRAMAS MUNDIALES DE ENRIQUECIMIENTO

THOMSON PETERSON'S – INTERNATS AMÉRICAINS ET CANADIENS, ET PROGRAMMES DE PERFECTIONNEMENT INTERNATIONAUX

トムソンピーターソンの米国、カナダの全寮制学校および世界各地での強化プログラム

THOMSON PETERSON'S – 美國與加拿大寄宿學校及國際強化項目

ORDER FORM

If you would like to order additional copies of this book, please call Customer Service at 1-800-338-3282 ext. 5660 or 1-609-896-1800 ext. 5660 (Monday through Friday, 8:30 A.M. until 4:30 P.M., U.S. Eastern Standard Time) or fax this completed form to 1-609-896-4531. Fax lines are available 24 hours a day, seven days a week. You can also reach customer service by e-mail: custsvc@petersons.com.

Formulario de pedido—Si desea adquirir copias adicionales de este libro, por favor llame a Servicios para clientes al 1-800-338-3282 ext. 5660 o 1-609-896-1800 ext. 5660 (de lunes a viernes de 8:30 de la mañana a las 4:30 de la tarde, horario del este) o envíe este formulario completado por fax al 1-609-896-4531. Las líneas de fax funcionan las 24 horas del día, siete días a la semana. Usted también puede comunicarse con servicio al cliente por correo electrónico: custsvc@petersons.com.

Formulaire de commande—Si vous désirez commander des exemplaires supplémentaires de ce répertoire, veuillez téléphoner au Service clientèle au 1-800-338-3282 poste 5660 ou 1-609-896-1800 post 5660 (du lundi au vendredi, entre 8h30 et 16h30, heure normale de l'Est des États-Unis) ou transmettez ce formulaire dûment complété par télécopie au 1-609-896-4531. Les télécopieurs reçoivent vos commandes 24 heures sur 24, sept jours sur sept. Vous pouvez également contacter notre service clientèle par e-mail : custsvc@petersons.com.

注文書
本書の追加注文を希望される場合はカスタマーサービス800-338-3282 内線5660 または 609-896-1800 内線5660 （アメリカ東部標準時間、月－金、午前8:30-午後4:30 まで）にお電話下さるか、この注文書をご記入のうえ、609-896-4531 までファックスして下さい。ファックスは毎日24時間受け付けています。またはカスタマーサービスまでe-メール: custsvc@petersons.com にてお問い合わせ下さい。

訂購表格
如欲加訂本手冊，請耳聯絡客戶服務部門1.800.338.3282 轉5660 或1.609.896.1800 轉5660 （週一至週五，美國東部標準時間上午8:30到下午4:30）或將此表格填妥並傳真至1.609.896.4531，一星期七天，一天二十四小時，隨時皆可傳真；也可以透過電子郵件custsvc@petersons.com 與客戶服務部聯絡 。

Name / Nombre / Nom / 氏名 / 姓名

Exact Street Address / Dirección completa / Adresse / 番地（正確に記入のこと）/ 正確地址

City / Ciudad / Ville / 市町村 / 城市   **State; Province** / Estado, Provincia / État ou province / 都道府県 / 州，省

Country / País / Pays / 国 / 國家   **Postal Code** / Código postal / Code postal / 郵便番号 / 郵遞區號

Telephone / Teléfono / Numéro de téléphone / 電話番号 / 電話   **Fax** / Fax / Numéro de télécopieur / ファックス / 傳真

❑ **MasterCard** / マスターカード / 萬事達   ❑ **Visa** / ビザ / 威士   ❑ **American Express** / アメリカンエキスプレス / 美國通進用

Card Number / Número de la tarjeta / Numéro de carte / カード番号 / 信用卡號碼   **Expiration Date** / Fecha de vencimiento / Date d'expiration / カードの有効期限 / 有效期限

Signature / Firma / Signature / 署名 / 簽名   **Date** / Fecha / Date / 日付 / 日期

Price / Precio / Prix / 価格 / 價格   **$17.95 U.S. / $26.95 CAN**

Quantity / Cantidad / Quantité / 数量 / 數量 _____   ISBN 0-7689-1548-1

Shipping (based on weight and distance) and handling will be added to your order.
Se agregarán gastos de envío (basados en el peso y la distancia) y de procesamiento de su pedido.
Les frais d'expédition (selon le poids et la distance) et de manutention seront ajoutés à la commande.

郵送料（重量と距離による）と取扱手数料が別途加算されます。

運費和包裝費外加

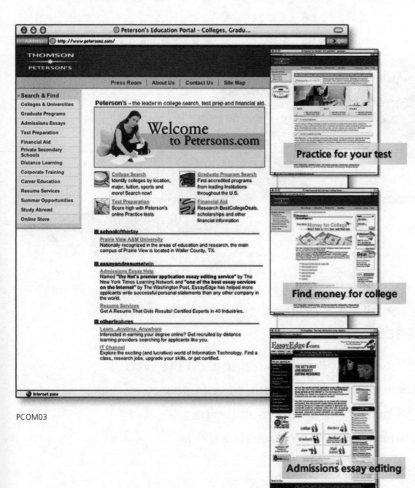